...бца̃ъ. тлъковани
...х҃ъіюбовосъхъ·
...тъвила· нѣвѣнѥ
...ръ̃ і ѣцѣсълаже
...їнаго̃ттр̃лѣтъ
...ѣтꙑнищ̃стого·
...т̃ъ вꙑлꙋдꙗ҃
...ъкоу̃ ;—

A Textbook

General Editor Academician
Dmitry Likhachev

Translated by
K. M. Cook-Horujy

of

A HISTORY RUSSIAN LITERATURE

11th-17th Centuries

RADUGA PUBLISHERS MOSCOW

Translation from the Russian

Contributors:
  Lev Dmitriev, Dmitry Likhachev,
  Yakov Lurie, Alexander Panchenko,
  Oleg Tvorogov
Bibliography compiled by
  Nadezhda Droblenkova,
  Milena Rozhdestvenskaya,
  Tatiana Bulanina
Illustrations selected by
  Olga Belobrova
Designed by
  Eduard Zaryansky

ISBN 5-05-001715-7

CONTENTS

CHAPTER 7

CHAPTER 8

The Significance of Old Russian Literature of the Eleventh to Seventeenth Centuries. Old Russian literature con-

INTRODUCTION

tains works that the Russian people rightly cherish irrespective of the extent to which they influenced the subsequent development of Russian literature. Such works, which are of great value, include, first and foremost, *The Tale of Bygone Years*—the first Russian chronicle, the *Instruction* of Vladimir Monomachos, *The Lay of Igor's Host, The Lay of the Ruin of the Russian Land, The Tale of Batu's Capture of Ryazan, The Trans-Doniad, The Tale of Peter and Febronia of Murom, Afanasy Nikitin's Voyage Beyond Three Seas*, the *Life* of Archpriest Avvakum and *The Tale of Woe-Misfortune*. This is by no means an exhaustive list of all the fine works that Russian literature produced in the first seven centuries of its existence.

The significance of Old Russian literature lies in the fact that it helps us to understand the achievements of Russian literature of the nineteenth and twentieth centuries. Old Russian literature is the source of the civic spirit and ideological content found in Russian literature of the modern period. Old Russian literature passed on to Russian literature of the modern and most recent period its noble ideals, vast experience, and rich flexible language and imagery.

The Peculiar Nature of the Form in Which Old Russian Literature Existed. Russian literature of the eleventh to seventeenth centuries developed in somewhat exceptional circumstances. It was entirely handwritten. Book printing, which appeared in Moscow in the mid-sixteenth century, did little to change the character and means of distribution of literary works. Even in the seventeenth century literary works continued for the most part to be copied out by hand. In the process of copying the scribes inserted their own corrections, changes and abridgements, or developed and expanded the text. As a result Old Russian literary works did not have a fixed text. New redactions and new types of works appeared in response to new practical requirements, or under the influence of changes in literary tastes.

Some Old Russian literary works were read and copied over several centuries. Others disappeared quickly, but those parts to which the scribes took a liking were included in other works, since the sense of authorship was not yet sufficiently developed to protect an author's text against amendments or insertions from other works. In this respect there is a certain similarity between the works of Old Russian literature and folklore.

Literary Convention. There is something else that Old Russian literature has in common with folklore. As in folklore, recurrent themes occupy a special place in Old Russian literature. A literary work of Old Russia seeks not to impress the reader by its novelty, but rather to charm him with its familiarity. In composing his literary work the author is, as it were, performing a kind of rite, taking part in a ritual. He narrates everything in ceremonial forms appropriate to the subject. He praises or blames that which it is accepted to praise or blame, and the form of his eulogy or censure befits the occasion. Consequently the text of literary works generally lacks any artistic "surprises". Surprises are as undesirable here as they would be in any ceremony or rite.

In studying the devices of artistic abstraction and convention in Old Russian literature we must bear in mind, however, that in almost every work there are numerous breaches of convention, "undesirable surprises", in which the author expresses his own attitude to the subject of his work. To some extent elements typical of mediaeval naturalism find their way into works under the influence of public indignation at the princely misdeeds, hatred of foreign invaders, compassion for the hapless, love or grief.

Under the influence of these elements the literary method of artistic representation gradually changes; a personal element begins to appear in literature and representational devices become richer.

Tradition in Literature. The author of a literary work "robes" it in an appropriate "literary attire". This not only brings literature closer to folklore, but, as in folklore too, introduces a special element of improvisation into Old Russian literary creation, giving it a collective, traditional nature. The more strictly the author follows the traditions of literary convention, the easier it is for him to create new works within the framework of a given tradition. As a result Old Russian literary works are not separated from one another by strict divisions, their text is not fixed by precise ideas about literary ownership. The collective, choral element is strong in Old Russian literature, the same choral element that is so characteristic of Russian music as well. To a certain extent the works repeat familiar forms and therefore possess a certain "fluidity", instability of text which in the overall literary process not only "blurs" the chronological limits, but also creates the illusion of the literary process being slowed down. We say the illusion, because in fact Old Russian literature developed fairly quickly. Its development was no slower than in the modern period, but it is more difficult to grasp and harder to define.

There are also certain aspects of the development of Russian literature, however, that facilitate our observation of it, above all, its close link with the historical process, in other words, the distinctive, very clearly expressed mediaeval historicism of Old Russian literature.

The Mediaeval Historicism of Old Russian Literature. What exactly is this mediaeval historicism? In Old Russia artistic generalisation is based for the most part on a single concrete historical fact. New works in Old Russian literature are always connected with a concrete historical event, a concrete historical figure. They are tales about battles (victories and defeats), princely misdeeds, pilgrimages to the Holy Land, and sometimes real people, but more often saints and warrior princes. There are stories about icons and the building of churches, about miracles that people believed in and visitations that are supposed to have taken place. But there are no new works on purely imaginary subjects. From the mediaeval point of view, literary invention is tantamount to lying, and lies are not permissible. Even preachers avoid allegories and fables. Invention creeps in from folklore or is encountered in translated works, but on Russian soil invented subjects (for example, those of parables) gradually take on an historical hue and are linked with this or that historical figure. Literature accompanies Russian life, Russian history, like a mighty

Russian Scribe at Work. From a 17th-century hagiographical miscellany. Institute of Russian Literature, Leningrad

stream, following on its heels. The gap between an event and the first literary work about it is rarely a large one. Subsequent works change and revise earlier ones, but rarely create a completely new view of the events. In their fear of falsehood, writers base their works on documents, which for them mean all that has been written earlier.

Civic Fervour and Patriotism in Old Russian Literature. The mediaeval historicism of Russian literature from the eleventh to seventeenth centuries is connected with another important feature that has been preserved and developed in Russian literature right up to the present day: its civic fervour and patriotism.

Called upon to examine reality, to investigate and assess it, the Old Russian writer already by the eleventh century regarded his vocation as that of serving his native land. Old Russian literature was always distinguished by a special seriousness. It sought to answer the fundamental questions of life, urged the transformation of that life, and had various, invariably high ideals. Russian literature was always highly edifying and instructive.

The deep patriotism of Old Russian literature derives not only from the authors' pride in their native land, but also from their sorrow at the defeats and suffering inflicted on it, their attempts to make the princes and boyars see reason, and sometimes even to censure them and incite the reader's wrath against the worst of them.

All Russian writers, in their own way, hold the writer's vocation in great esteem. Each of them is to some extent a prophet and denouncer, and some are teachers, disseminators of knowledge, interpreters of reality and participants in the civic life of their country. During the period of feudal disunity, when the state did not exist as a single entity, literature helped to keep alive the awareness of the unity of the Russian land and of its people. It showed a high degree of civic responsibility.

This sense of the noble calling of the writer was also handed down to the literature of the modern period. Russian literature was influenced by its creators' strong sense of civic responsibility. This has been a constant feature of Russian literature throughout its development.

Periods in the History of Old Russian Literature. The literature of Old Russia bears testimony to Russian life. This is why history itself to a considerable extent dictates the periods of literature. Literary changes coincide mainly with historical ones. What periods can we distinguish in the history of Russian literature from the eleventh to seventeenth centuries?

The first period in the history of Old Russian literature is that of the relative unity of literature, when literature developed mainly in two centres (connected by cultural links): Kiev in the south and Novgorod in the north. It lasted for one century, the eleventh, and included the beginning of the twelfth. This was the period of the formation of the monumental-historical style in literature, in which monumental forms were combined with important content, when it was felt that every event and every personage was connected with world history and with the whole of mankind. It was the period of the first Russian *vitae*, the Lives of SS Boris and Gleb and the monks of the Kiev Crypt Monastery, and the first Russian chronicle to have survived — *The Tale of Bygone Years*. It was the period of the united Old Russian Kievan-Novgorodian state.

The second period, from the mid-twelfth to the first third of the thirteenth century, saw the emergence of new literary centres in Vladimir-Zalessky and Suzdal, Rostov and Smolensk, Galich and Vladimir-Volynsky. During this period local features and themes appeared, the genres became more varied, and a strong topical and publicistic stream emerged in literature. This period marks the beginning of feudal disunity.

A number of features common to these two periods enable us to examine them together (particularly bearing in mind the difficulty of dating certain translated and original works). These first two periods are both characterised by a prevalence of the monumental-historical style.

Then comes the comparatively short period of the terrible Mongol invasion, followed by many long years of Mongol overlordship. This short period saw the creation of tales about the invasion of Russia by the Mongols, the battle on the Kalka, the capture of Vladimir-Zalessky, *The Lay of the Ruin of the Russian Land* and *The Life of Alexander Nevsky*. Literature concentrates on a single theme, but this theme manifests itself with unusual intensity, and the monumental-historical style acquires a tragic imprint and the lyrical fervour of deep patriotic feeling. This brief, but vivid period should be examined separately. It is easily distinguished.

The following period, from the end of the fourteenth to the middle of the fifteenth century, is the age of the Pre-Renaissance, which coincides with the economic and cultural rebirth of the Russian land in the period immediately preceding and following the Battle of Kulikovo in 1380. It is a period of the expressive, emotional style and profound patriotism in literature, a period of the rebirth of chronicle-writing, the historical tale and panegyric hagiography.

In the second half of the fifteenth century new phenomena appeared in Russian literature: translations of secular tales (fiction) began to circulate and original works of the same type, such as *The Tale of Dracula* and *The Tale of Basarga*, appeared. These phenomena were linked with the reformationist and humanist movements at the end of the fifteenth century. However, the insufficient development of the towns (which were centres of the Renaissance in Western Europe), the subjection of the Novgorod and Pskov republics, and the suppression of heretical movements impeded the advance towards the Renaissance. The conquest of Byzantium by the Turks (Constantinople fell in 1453), with which Russia had close cultural ties, left Russia isolated within its own cultural borders. The Florence-Ferrara Union of the Greek and Catholic churches, which was flatly rejected in Russia, created mistrust of the West and its culture. The organisation of a united Russian centralised state absorbed most of the people's spiritual energy. Literature became increasingly publicistic: the domestic policy of the state and the transformation of society increasingly occupied the attention of writers and readers.

From the middle of the sixteenth century an official current becomes increasingly evident in literature. The period of "second monumentalism" arrived, which saw the production of impressive chronicles, lengthy chronographs, and a huge compilation of all the works read in Russia, known as *The Great Menology*. Traditional forms of literature dominated, suppressing the personal element that had begun to emerge in the age of the Russian Pre-Renaissance. The events of the second half of the sixteenth century produced by the despotic rule of Ivan the Terrible impeded the development of secular literature.

The seventeenth century is the century of the transition to the literature of the modern age. It is the century of the development of the personal element in everything: in the actual type of writer and in his work; the century of the development of personal tastes and styles, of literary professionalism and the sense of authorship, of individual, personal protest connected with tragic events in a writer's biography. The personal element promoted the emergence of syllabic poetry and drama. It is from the seventeenth century that most Russian historians and Lenin date the beginning of the modern period in Russian history.[1]

The Names of Peoples. In this book we speak of Russia and the Russians of the tenth to thirteenth centuries, although during this period the three Eastern Slavic peoples, the Ukrainians, Byelorussians and Russians, had not yet formed and were still a single ethnic unit—the Eastern Slavs, the "Rus" or "russkiye", as they called themselves in the chronicles and all other works, including *The Lay of Igor's Host*. The reader should bear in mind that the Russia of the tenth to thirteenth centuries was not yet modern Russia, and the Russians of the same period were the Eastern Slavs as a whole, the ancestors of the modern Russians, Ukrainians and Byelorussians, three fraternal peoples.

Likewise we should bear in mind that the Mongols or Tartars of Old Russian literary works and folklore are not a single ethnic concept. This is the name by which works refer to the conquerors and oppressors of Russia who were united under the rule of Genghis Khan, Batu and later the Golden Horde. They were unions of various tribes, primarily nomadic and semi-nomadic.

The Range of Works to Be Examined. We shall discuss primarily those works that continue to interest us today, that have become part of the literary heritage, and that are the best known and most easily understood and accessible. Such a selection obviously results in a certain simplification of perspective, a simplification that is both permissible and inevitable.

The large compilations of Old Russian works have not yet been sufficiently studied: the different types of *paleyas* ("interpretive", "historical"—special works expounding the Old Testament), *The Great Menology* (a compilation of the works read in Old Russia), the *Prologues* (short collections of *vitae* arranged according to months and days), miscellanies with a fixed content (such as, for example, the *Chrysostom, The Emerald* and others) have been so little studied that it is difficult to discuss them in a history of literature. Yet many of them were read more often and survived in a larger number of manuscripts than works which we know and without which no history of literature could be of general educative value for the modern reader. Thus, for example, the miscellany of homilies entitled *The Emerald* was undoubtedly read more often and was of greater importance in the sixteenth and seventeenth centuries than the *Household Management* better known in the nineteenth and twentieth centuries (a collection of rules concerning the running of the household and the family) which, incidentally, itself depended on *The Emerald*. Nevertheless we include the *Household Management* in a history of Russian literature and omit *The Emerald*. And we do so advisedly: for the *Household Management* is not only better known in the history of Russian culture than *The Emerald*, but is also more indicative of the historico-literary process. The *Household Management* bears the imprint of the sixteenth century. As for *The Emerald* (fourteenth century) the traces of its age (the Russian Pre-Renaissance) have yet to be revealed by research.

Although some highly distinguished scholars have studied Old Russian literature, it has for the most part been insufficiently researched.

Some manuscript collections of Old Russian works have not

been studied at all or have been described with insufficient accuracy and detail.

Collections of Old Russian Manuscripts of Literary Content. The main collections of Old Russian manuscripts containing Old Russian literary works are in Moscow, Leningrad and Kiev. There are also fairly large collections in Novosibirsk, Pskov, Yaroslavl, Vladimir, Rostov, Kostroma and some other towns. Small numbers of Old Russian manuscripts are scattered about in various museums of local lore, university libraries and archives, and are also in the private possession of book collectors, Old Believers and their descendants, and others.

In Moscow the main, very rich collections are in the Lenin State Library of the USSR, the State History Museum, the Central State Archives of Old Documents, and the library of Moscow State University. In Leningrad the main collections are in the Saltykov-Shchedrin State Public Library, the Library of the Academy of Sciences of the USSR, the Central State Historical Archives of the USSR, the Leningrad Department of the Institute of History of the Academy of Sciences of the USSR, and the Malyshev Archives of the Institute of Russian Literature of the Academy of Sciences of the USSR. In Novosibirsk there are manuscripts in the Scientific Library and in Pskov in the Archives of the Pskov Museum of Art and Architecture. There are also a relatively small number of Old Russian manuscripts abroad: in Bulgaria, Yugoslavia, Mount Athos, the British Museum in London, the Bibliothèque Nationale in Paris, the Vatican Library, Oslo, etc.

In each of the main repositories mentioned the manuscripts form part of collections that belonged to monasteries, scholars, book collectors, etc. Thus, for example, the Saltykov-Shchedrin State Public Library has the collection of the historian Mikhail Pogodin who purchased Pavel Stroyev's vast collection and also collected manuscripts independently; there are also manuscript collections from the libraries of the Solovetsky Monastery, the White Lake Monastery of St Cyril, and so on. The Malyshev Archives manuscripts are arranged according to the collectors from whom they were acquired or who donated them, and also according to the places where they were found by special archaeographic expeditions. There is the Karelian collection (manuscripts found in the Karelian ASSR), the Ust-Tsilma collection and others. The State History Museum has the collection of Alexei Uvarov. Uvarov not only collected manuscripts himself, but also acquired a large collection from the merchant Tsarsky. Both collections have separate printed scientific descriptions. This should be borne in mind, for information about manuscripts printed in one scientific description may be repeated and

Illumination from the Gospel written for the Yuriev Monastery (Novgorod). C. 1120. History Museum, Moscow

amplified in another. There is an extensive literature of scientific descriptions of collections in the major manuscript repositories. These scientific descriptions have been compiled and published at different times. The manuscripts mentioned in them have suffered different fates. Anyone making a study of Old Russian manuscripts must at least be familiar with the history of the major collections of these manuscripts. The major manuscript archives usually have an information section where scientific descriptions can be consulted. Scientific descriptions help the researcher to find literary works of interest to him. Apart from printed scientific descriptions there are handwritten descriptions or card indexes of varying degrees of comprehensiveness and accuracy. There are also guides to manuscript collections in the archives in question and a brief description of their contents. The researcher should be proficient at consulting these descriptions and guides and have a clear idea of their merits and defects.

The Nature and Types of Old Russian Manuscripts. What exactly are Old Russian manuscripts? The most widespread type of manuscript with literary materials is the miscellany. The scribe copied various works onto quires which were then bound by the scribe himself or a binder.

It also happened that the binder took quires written at different times by different scribes and bound them all together simply because they were similar in size or content, etc. These collections of manuscripts copied by different scribes at different times are usually called convolutes.

Miscellanies written by one scribe are divided into those with a definite, i.e., traditional, content, such as *The Stream of Gold, The Emerald,* and the *Festal Sermons,* and collections with an indefinite content that reflected the personal tastes and interests of the scribe who wrote them, selecting the material for himself or the person who commissioned them.

Large works could be copied and bound into separate volumes: some chronicle compilations, works on world history, paterica, liturgical writings, prologues, and so on. But works such as the *Supplication* of Daniel the Exile or *The Lay of the Ruin of the Russian Land,* were too small to constitute a whole book.

Manuscripts that have survived in unbound form are mainly later ones, of the seventeenth and eighteenth centuries, with Old Russian materials. But they are few in number and in poor condition, evidently because they were not valued and carefully preserved.

The Main Types of Script. Texts were copied by scribes either across the whole sheet or in two columns (particularly if the sheets were large). It is customary to divide the script into three

2*

types—uncial, which had large, rounded letters that were not joined; various forms of semi-uncial, which was faster and less strict, occasionally sloping, but still retained the clarity and separate writing of each letter (this type appeared at the end of the fourteenth century); and, finally, cursive, in which the letters were joined, enabling the scribe to write more quickly.

Apart from these main types there were many intermediate ones: the semi-uncial verging on the cursive; the calligraphic semi-uncial in which, incidentally, the volumes of the sixteenth-century *Illustrated Chronicle* are written, the interesting cursive script of the birch-bark documents found in Novgorod and other Old Russian towns, and so on.

The Writing Material. Manuscripts were originally written on specially treated animal skin. In Old Russia this leather had several names: it was called *kozha* (skin), *telyatina* (calf skin), and later *khartia* (this material was usually prepared from calf skins). The accepted term for this material is *pergamen* (parchment), named after the town of Pergamum, where its preparation is said to have been perfected in the second century B.C. It was replaced by paper later. The borderline between the use of parchment and paper lies roughly at the end of the fourteenth century and the beginning of the fifteenth, but it is not a clear one. Paper was imported into Old Russia. There is evidence that under Ivan the Terrible and in the seventeenth century paper was also produced in Russia. Paper usually had watermarks which can be seen when the sheet is held up against the light. During the fabrication of paper from old rags the pulp was drained on a wire mesh. The finished sheets of paper retained the marks from the mesh. Paper manufacturers put the watermark of their factory on the mesh. When the mesh wore out it was replaced and the watermarks themselves were changed. From these watermarks one can establish the date when the paper was manufactured and roughly when the manuscript was copied on the sheet. There are many albums and guides to help one identify a watermark and from it the period to which it and, consequently, the manuscript written on paper with this watermark belong.

Methods of Studying Manuscript Texts of Literary Works. Texts of literary works discovered in manuscripts are studied, first of all, from the point of view of whether or not they have been published. If the work is already known, it is essential to ascertain whether the text that has been found corresponds to the known texts, whether it has any special features and to which of the published texts it bears most resemblance.

If the researcher wishes to study all the texts of a certain work, he must first try to locate these texts from existing scientific

Birch-bark letter by the boy Onfim. Novgorod. 13th century. History Museum, Moscow

16th-century semi-uncial—a page from *The Tsar's Book* showing a fire in Moscow in 1547. History Museum, Moscow

descriptions, printed and handwritten, by examining manuscripts not yet described in which there may be new texts. He then divides all the texts he has found into groups. If there is a deliberate effort in one group of manuscripts to give a special text for certain ideological, stylistic or other considerations, this group of texts is called a *redaction* of the work. If another group does not show any deliberate effort to change the text, but is merely a version of the text formed as a result of errors in the process of copying it and the more or less successful correction of these errors, such a group of texts is called a *type* or *version* of the text. If a group of manuscripts contains local features of language or dialect, united by the general process of copying the text in a given country or locality, such a group is called a *recension*. There may, for example, be a Novgorodian, Ukrainian, Byelorussian, Bulgarian, Serbian, or Moldavo-Wallachian recension. Sometimes a recension coincides with a redaction (the scribe introduces not only special linguistic features, but also deliberate changes). Occasionally a text that has been copied in different places and countries has mixed recensions: Ukrainian-Serbian or Bulgaro-Russian, for example. This means that the text was copied first in one country, then in another, and that it bears the imprint not of one language, but two or even three. In the Middle Ages manuscripts written in a literary language that could be understood in several Slav countries were often transferred from one, country to another, donated, sold, and so on. It might happen that a Russian scribe was working in Bulgaria, on Mount Athos or in Constantinople, or that a South Slav scribe came to Russia where he not only copied books, but also wrote himself (for example, the Bulgarian Metropolitan Cyprian, Pachomius the Serb and others, see below).

The study of the handwriting of manuscripts, the material on which they were written, and the texts of literary works is made by special disciplines, such as palaeography and textology.[2]

The Main Studies of Old Russian Literature. From the fifteenth, sixteenth and seventeenth centuries there are several extant inventories, tables of contents and library catalogues, which suggests that already in Old Russia there was a need for systematised information about books: the table of contents for the twelve-volume *Menology* of Metropolitan Macarius (sixteenth century) compiled by the redactor Euthymius, the inventory of books of the Volokolamsk Monastery of St Joseph, the inventory of books of Patriarch Philaret (the father of Tsar Michael) and many others.

Among these inventories and catalogues the most detailed and accurate is the description of the manuscripts of the White Lake Monastery of St Cyril compiled in the late fifteenth century by an unknown monk from the monastery. It gives details of the size, composition, contents, number of sheets and (wherever possible) the date of the book. The author of this description quotes the titles of individual items, reproduces the opening words of individual works, and indicates the number of sheets in each item and their order in the book. Since most of the manuscript books described have been preserved in the collection of the Leningrad State Public Library, we can verify the scrupulous accuracy of this description.

Another excellent work is *A List of Contents of Books and Their Compilers* drawn up in the seventeenth century. Here too printed and manuscript books are described in great detail, item by item, giving the titles of the individual items and the opening words of each, indicating the existence of forewords and afterwords and, where possible, giving information about the authors. It is interesting that the author of the *List* makes use of conventional abbreviations and signs, which enable him to present the information in highly systematic form.

Peter the Great was extremely interested in Old Russian literature. In 1722 he issued a decree on the collection from monasteries and eparchies of manuscripts "of bygone days" on parchment and paper, with special reference to chronicles, books of degrees and chronographs.

On Peter the Great's personal orders a copy was made (very carefully for those days) of *The Radziwill Chronicle* and brought from Königsberg to St Petersburg in 1716. Nor was *The Radziwill Chronicle* forgotten subsequently: in 1758 on the instructions of the president of the Academy of Sciences the chronicle itself was brought from Königsberg to the library of the Academy of Sciences. The text of the chronicle was published in 1767.

The publication of *The Radziwill Chronicle* in 1767 was followed by that of *The Russian Chronicle* from the Nikon manuscript (which began to come out in 1767), *The Tsar's Book* (1769), *The Tsar's Chronicle* (1772), *The Ancient Chronicle* (1774-1775), *The Russian Chronicle from the Manuscript of St Sophia of Novgorod the Great* (Part 1 — 1795), *The Book of Degrees of the Tsar's Genealogy* (1775), and many others.

One of Peter's close associates, the famous Russian historian Vasily Tatishchev, was most active in collecting old manuscripts, particularly chronicles. In his extensive *History of Russia* Tatishchev attempts to give precise information on Russian chronicles and other Old Russian writings.

In the 1720s the Academy of Sciences was founded in St Petersburg[3]. Academicians Gerhardt Friedrich Miller and August Ludwig Schlözer did a great deal for the collection and study of old manuscripts on Russian history. Although Miller interpreted the early period of Russian history tendentiously from the viewpoint of Normanism, which argues that the Varangians (Normans) played a decisive role in the formation of the early Russian state, he performed the important service of collecting some very rare manuscript material and publishing many literary works, including *The Book of Degrees* (in two parts, Moscow, 1775). August Schlözer devoted forty years to the careful study of Russian chronicles and published an extensive work in German and Russian on *The Nestor Chronicle* (German edition in five volumes, 1802-1809, Russian edition in three volumes, 1809-1819).

A great deal was done for the study of Old Russian literature by the famous eighteenth-century educator Nikolai Novikov. In 1772 he published his *Historical Dictionary of Russian Writers,* which contains information on more than 300 writers from the early period of Russian literature up to and including the eighteenth century. In 1773-1774 he published the *Old Russian Library.* The first edition consisted of ten volumes. In 1788-1791 it was enlarged with new material and came out in thirty volumes, containing many Old Russian literary works.

The collection and publication of manuscripts gained even more momentum in the early nineteenth century. The publication in 1800 of *The Lay of Igor's Host* produced a new upsurge of interest in Old Russian literary works. This interest became even more widespread after the War of 1812 against Napoleon which played an important part in the development of national consciousness and interest in Russian history.

The activity of the collector Count Nikolai Rumyantsev (1754-1826) was of particular importance. He collected old manuscripts and financed expeditions to old monasteries. In 1861 the Rumyantsev collection was moved from St Petersburg to Moscow and formed the nucleus of the book collection of the Rumyantsev Museum, now the Lenin State Library of the USSR.

The eminent Russian philologist Alexander Vostokov (1781-1864) produced a detailed scientific description of Count Rumyantsev's manuscripts. His *Description of Russian and Slavonic Manuscripts of the Rumyantsev Museum,* which contains a description of each item based on laborious research, came out in 1842. This description retains its scholarly importance to this day and can in many respects be called exemplary.

Of Nikolai Rumyantsev's other colleagues mention must be made of Metropolitan Evgeny Bolkhovitinov (1767-1837), who collected and studied manuscripts in all the old Russian towns where he was sent. He is the author of two bibliographical works:

A Historical Dictionary of Writers in Holy Orders in Russia (two editions in two volumes, 1818 and 1827) and the posthumously published *Dictionary of Russian Secular Writers, Native and Foreign, Writing in Russia* (Volume 1, 1838, and both volumes together in 1845).

Another colleague of Rumyantsev's was Konstantin Kalaidovich (1792-1832) who died at an early age. He published many Old Russian works for the first time in his *Monuments of Russian Literature of the Twelfth Century* (1821) and a study of the tenth-century Bulgarian writer popular in Old Russia, *John, the Bulgarian Exarch* (1824).

Finally, Rumyantsev's colleagues included Pavel Stroyev (1796-1876). From 1829 to 1834 Stroyev made a systematic study (as head of an archaeographic expedition organised by him) of the manuscript collections of all the old monasteries and assembled a vast number of extremely rare items. In order to categorise these manuscripts the Archaeographical Commission was set up in 1834. The Commission worked independently at first and later, from 1921, as part of the Academy of Sciences of the USSR until the 1930s when together with its archives it was put under the Leningrad Department of the Institute of History of the Academy of Sciences of the USSR. After categorising the manuscripts collected by the archaeographic expedition, the Commission soon turned to the independent study of Old Russian manuscripts. It published a large number of works. Of particular importance was the publication, beginning in 1841, of the *Complete Collection of Russian Chronicles* which is still in process (Volume 37 was the last to come out).

As we can see, in the eighteenth and the early nineteenth century, Old Russian literary and historical works were collected, and studied mainly from the bibliographical and bibliological point of view.

The very concept of "literature" in the modern sense of *fiction* hardly appeared in Russia until Karamzin[4] at the beginning of the nineteenth century. Up till then Old Russian writings, both literary and historical, were collected, studied and published by the same scholars and the aims of their studies hardly varied. The first attempts to produce a history of literature were not made until relatively late.

Various brief surveys of the history of Old Russian literature began to appear in the 1820s. The most interesting is *A History of Old Russian Literature* by the Kievan scholar Mikhail Maximovich (republished in Volume III of his collected works, Kiev, 1880). Maximovich (1804-1873) was extremely interested in *The Lay of Igor's Host* and was the first to make a detailed comparison of the literary features of the *Lay* with folk poetry. His *History* also shows a preoccupation with the artistic aspect of Old Russian literary works to some extent. At the beginning of his book he was the first to divide Old Russian literature into periods, linking it with the general course of Russian history, but he made a concrete study of works up to the thirteenth century only.

In its day Stepan Shevyryov's *History of Russian Literature, Predominantly Old Russian,* first published in 1846 and republished in 1887, was well known. It was written from the romantic standpoint and idealised Old Russian spiritual and ecclesiastical life. It linked and to some extent subordinated the history of literature to that of the church.

The second half of the nineteenth century produced four of the most eminent historians of Russian literature: Fyodor Buslayev (1818-1897), Alexander Pypin (1833-1904), Nikolai Tikhonravov (1832-1893) and Alexander Veselovsky (1838-1906).

At the beginning of his activity Fyodor Buslayev belonged to the Mythological School created primarily by the German scholar Jakob Grimm. The mythologists believed that literary subjects and folkloric motifs and themes originated in the dim and distant past, the time when the Indo-European peoples lived in their hypothetical common homeland. Works deriving from this distant past were thought to reflect the mythological views of the remote ancestors of these peoples.

The views of the Mythological School influenced Fyodor Buslayev primarily in his studies on Russian language. However in his case the extremes and fantasies of the Mythological School were mitigated to a large extent by the historico-comparative approach. Alexander Afanasyev, Orest Miller and many other students of Russian mythology and folklore did not avoid these extremes, as we know.

The many lines of interest and research that Fyodor Buslayev pursued were very fertile for the study of Old Russian literature: his interest in apocryphal literature, oral religious verse *(dukhovniye stikhi)* with their unorthodox, purely popular views, and Old Russian art vis-à-vis works of literature.

The last of Fyodor Buslayev's major works, *The Russian Illustrated Apocalypse* (St Petersburg, 1884), was an outstanding study for its day and emphasised the importance of popular views.

For all his great love of Old Russian literature and art Buslayev was not a narrow-minded nationalist. The importance of his Mythological School for the study of Old Russian literature lay in the fact that this school compared Old Russian literary works with works of other lands and with the development of folklore in general. It was a forceful and effective rejection of the view that

Old Russian literature was imitative, weak, and divorced from the development of world literature as a whole.

The Mythological School was superseded (even in some of Buslayev's works) by the theory of literary borrowing, first expounded by the German scholar Theodor Benfey. This was a return to the historical method and to the concrete study of different subjects and motifs. The historical role of the theory of borrowing was that it made scholars concentrate not so much on prehistoric phenomena as the concrete period of the Middle Ages, and stressed even more strongly than the Mythological School the importance of international contacts, in particular, contacts with Byzantium and the Orient, the relationship of folklore and literature, and the importance of subjects and motifs being handed down through merchants and Crusaders, pilgrims and artisans.

Following Fyodor Buslayev the theory of borrowing was upheld by Academician Vatroslav Jagić, a Croatian by birth, and also Academician Alexander Veselovsky, Academician Ivan Zhdanov, and others.

The supporters of the theory of borrowing studied primarily the influence of Oriental poetic culture on the West. They attributed a special role in this influence to the Arabs and Buddhism, but above all to Byzantium, as the country of Oriental subjects and motifs. This enhanced the importance not only of Byzantine but also of Old Russian literature in world literary exchange. The traditionally disparaging attitude to Byzantium gradually disappeared, and with it disparagement of Old Russian literature, at least among philologists. The importance of Byzantium as a repository of the antique classical literary heritage was also enhanced.

Unlike Fyodor Buslayev and Alexander Veselovsky, Nikolai Tikhonravov was the first historian of Russian literature to set the discipline new tasks. He maintained that a history of literature should not be "a collection of aesthetic analyses" of selected writers and should not serve "empty marvelling" at "literary geniuses". A history of literature should explain the "historical course of literature" in relation to the intellectual and moral state of the society to which the literature belongs.

Tikhonravov made an important contribution in two spheres. He based the study of literature on a study of history. For all its shortcomings the culturo-historical school led by him sought to interpret literary works on the basis of historical data. Moreover in his views on Russian history Tikhonravov diverged from official viewpoints and took a special interest in works proscribed by the church. His second important contribution was that he published a large number of works very accurately and efficiently for his day. The level of the publication of Old Russian texts, which was high by the latter half of the nineteenth century, also helped Tikhonravov to publish texts by modern Russian writers, such as Nikolai Gogol, the correspondence of Nikolai Novikov, and folklore.

The writings on Old Russian literature of Academician Alexander Pypin are also of interest. In his youth Pypin was strongly influenced by his cousin, Nikolai Chernyshevsky, but later he joined the West European historico-cultural school which was close to the bourgeois democratic enlightenment. He was interested mainly in the socio-ideological aspect of literature and stressed the connection of literature with popular life. Consequently he studied ethnography and folklore, concentrating mainly on genres which expressed popular views (apocryphas, folk tales, polemics), but were of little interest to "aesthetic" criticism. He wrote more than 1,200 scholarly works. One of his first major works, *A Literary History of Old Russian Tales and Stories* (St Petersburg, 1857), is still of importance to scholars today.

The research of the fourth giant of the history of Russian literature, Alexander Veselovsky, was influenced by many features characteristic of the scientific premises of his great predecessors: Fyodor Buslayev and Nikolai Tikhonravov.

Alexander Veselovsky contributed an extraordinary breadth of knowledge to the study of Old Russian literature. He brought the Russian, Byzantine and West European Middle Ages closer together by establishing common features not only in individual subjects and motifs, but also in aesthetic principles and laws of development, which was most important. In this respect Veselovsky was far more realistic than the founder of the comparative historical method, Theodor Benfey. He looked not only for common features between literatures, but also for a concrete historical explanation of these features. Moreover, and this is particularly important, Veselovsky was interested in the literatures not only of advanced peoples, but also of peoples at a relatively low level of cultural development. For him all peoples were equal in literary interchange. For him there was no literary elite: he was interested in the interchange of all literatures, strong and weak, in the works of "mediocre" writers, in mass phenomena. And he did not regard this interchange as the sole source of literary subjects and motifs.

Like Nikolai Tikhonravov, Alexander Veselovsky took a special interest in works of Old Russian literature with an unorthodox, popular view of the world: religious verse, apocryphas, legends and *vitae* (of all the genres of religious literature the Lives of the saints contain the strongest deviations from official, canonical views).

The high level of Russian philological studies was maintained by the excellent organisation of academic publishing.

In the 1850s two outstanding philological journals began publication under the editorship of Izmail Sreznevsky: *The Proceedings of the Department of Russian Language and Literature of the Academy of Sciences* (1852-1863) and *The Transactions of the Second Department of the Academy of Sciences* (1854-1863), subsequently continued as the *Collections of the Department of Russian Language and Literature* (about ninety volumes have come out since 1867). Resumed in 1896 on the initiative of Academician Alexei Shakhmatov, *The Proceedings of the Department of Russian Language and Literature of the Academy of Sciences* became one of the leading philological journals in the world. It printed many studies of Old Russian literature that bear witness to the high level of Russian research in the late nineteenth and early twentieth centuries. The *Proceedings* are still of value today.

In the late nineteenth and the first quarter of the present century the scientific principles of Russian classical textology were based on the vast experience gained in publishing Old Russian works and a critical review of the principles of West European formalistic textology.

By the end of the nineteenth century the Academy of Sciences in St Petersburg had become the centre of textological research well ahead of West European centres in its methods.

Independently of each other Alexei Shakhmatov (1864-1920) in St Petersburg and Vladimir Peretts (1870-1935) in Kiev (the latter was elected to the Academy of Sciences in 1914 and moved to Petrograd) created their own, but in some respects similar, schools of textological study of Old Russian (the latter also of Old Ukrainian) literature. Unlike the textological school that prevailed in the West, whose supporters attached prime importance in the study of texts to a formal classification of variant readings without analysis of their causes, Shakhmatov and Peretts sought to present the "literary history" of the work in all its redactions, types and recensions. For both scholars the most important element in this history was the person who had created the text, the author, and after him the unknown editors and copyists who had been guided in their work by certain ideas and aims, sometimes also literary tastes.

Shakhmatov, and Peretts after him, based their textological studies on the historical method, the principle of studying a text through its history and changes.

In assessing today the new textological ideas contributed by these two academicians, we can also discern considerable differences between them. Shakhmatov developed his textological practice on more complex material, the chronicles, where it is hard to establish not only different redactions, but even the works themselves, and where textological connections can be found between all works of the chronicle genre. Consequently his textology developed more subtle devices of textual interpretation.

Vladimir Peretts was primarily an historian of literature and he was most successful at the literary-historical interpretation of changes in a text and its different redactions. Of major importance also were his observations on concrete folklore-literary connections, on the shifting of individual works from one literature to another, from one environment to another, from literature to folklore and vice versa.

The historical principle in the study of texts was no accident: the development not only of textology, but of the study of Old Russian monuments as a whole in the nineteenth and twentieth centuries was based increasingly firmly on the historical method. The gradual mastering of the historical approach is characteristic of all the most eminent scholars who studied Old Russian literature.

The Soviet study of literature inherited the fine achievements of the preceding period and grew up on a broad base of research literature and systematic archaeographic (collection, description and publication) activity. The Soviet study of Old Russian literature has developed the finest traditions of pre-revolutionary scholarship, gradually discarding its limitations and general methodological shortcomings.

Archaeographic expeditions ceased for a while in the 1920s in connection with the general difficulties of the period. The work of producing a systematic description of manuscripts continued, however, largely because manuscript collections became concentrated in a few major central book repositories at that time.

Mention must be made of the activity in the 1920s and 1930s of the Commission on the Publication of Works of Old Russian Literature, the work of a team of qualified specialists to produce something that had become essential for all students of Old Russian literature, namely the card index of Academician Nikolai Nikolsky (1863-1936) which combined information on the various manuscripts of individual works in different institutions, making it possible to locate quickly the necessary manuscript material for a given work. This card index is kept in the Manuscript Department of the Library of the USSR Academy of Sciences in Leningrad.

Of similar importance was the card index produced in the 1930s by the Sector of Old Russian Literature of the Institute of

Russian Literature of the USSR Academy of Sciences in Leningrad, which gave information about manuscripts, publications and studies of individual works. The work on this card index stopped in the late 1930s however.

In spite of their incompleteness, the card indexes of Nikolsky and the Sector of Old Russian Literature are still indispensable for all students of Old Russian literature.

In the middle of the 1930s, on the initiative of Vladimir Malyshev (1910-1976) the archaeographic expeditions were resumed. This work saved a large number of manuscripts which for a variety of reasons had ceased to be valued by their owners. At the present time the search for manuscrips is being carried on by the Institute of Russian Literature (the Pushkin House) of the USSR Academy of Sciences, the manuscript departments of the Lenin State Library, the State Public Library in Leningrad, the libraries of the USSR Academy of Sciences in Leningrad, Moscow and Leningrad universities, the Siberian Section of the USSR Academy of Sciences, and others.

As a result of the concentration after the October 1917 Revolution of most manuscript collections in a few central repositories and the formation of card indexes on manuscripts the study of Old Russian manuscripts became more scientific. Already in pre-revolutionary research Academician Alexei Shakhmatov and Academician Vladimir Peretts had stressed the need to study the literary history of works with reference to all the extant manuscripts, all the surviving copies. This requirements could now be fulfilled if the publication of monuments continued. But it was not only the concentration of manuscripts that helped to turn principles long advocated by scholars into practice. This was promoted also by concentrating the researchers themselves in a few centres for the study of Old Russian literature, of which the two main ones were the Sector of Old Russian Literature of the Institute of Russian Literature of the USSR Academy of Sciences, organised in 1934, and the Group for the Study of Old Russian Literature that functioned intermittently at the Institute of World Literature of the USSR Academy of Sciences. These centres set up in the 1930s began collective research, putting out serial publications and generalising works. Collective efforts also became possible in organising archaeographic expeditions, and compiling bibliographies and descriptions. New works and whole sections of literature were discovered and systematically studied.

Undoubtedly one of the most important spheres of Russian literature of the seventeenth century is that of democratic satire. A few works of democratic satire were known in the nineteenth century, but they were usually ranked with the lowest type of literature and no special significance was attached to them. Consequently these works were not studied and were rarely published. The credit for establishing the historico-literary importance of seventeenth-century democratic satire and for publishing a complete collection of these works must go to Varvara Adrianova-Peretts.[5] She demonstrated that satirical literature was of great importance as the expression of the ideas of the exploited strata of the people. In seventeenth-century satirical literature we find a whole layer of urban literature, the literature of the artisans, small tradesmen, peasants and lower ranks of the oppositionally-minded clergy that had links with the people.

In the sphere of chronicle study Soviet researchers continued the work of Alexei Shakhmatov and produced a general history of Russian chronicle-writing. It was presented to us for the first time in the works of Mikhail Priselkov (1881-1941) and Arseny Nasonov (1898-1965) in its complex development from the eleventh to the sixteenth century as a history closely connected with the political thought of Old Russia. The clear chronological landmarks in Russian chronicle-writing made it possible to date other works of Old Russian literature in relation to them. Thus, for example, the dating of individual chronicle compilations enabled scholars to date many works connected with them, such as historical tales, Lives of the saints, accounts of pilgrimages and epistles. Chronicle-writing provided the framework that made it possible to put works of Old Russian literature, most of them being anonymous and therefore difficult to place chronologically, into historical perspective. The history of chronicle-writing provided a basis for the history of literature. In this connection chronicle-writing itself began to be studied from the historico-literary point of view: its history, as the history of a literary genre, the fictional and artistic elements of chronicle-writing and its link with folklore. A literary interpretation of the history of Russian chronicle-writing is given in Dmitry Likhachev's book *Russian Chronicles* (Moscow and Leningrad, 1947). Whereas earlier students of folklore had searched in the chronicles for traces of the historical events on which the subjects of the heroic poems *(bylinas)* were based, after the October Revolution researchers began to look for the reverse as well: the reflection of folkloric subjects in the chronicle.[6] The works of Boris Rybakov are of great importance for determining the relationship between the *bylinas* and the chronicles.[7]

Thus the study of the history of Russian literature began to include whole categories of works whose aesthetic value had previously been ignored. Historians of literature included in their subject chronicles, chronographs, some so-called counterfeit documents, and so on. The writings of Joseph of Volokolamsk, first evaluated by Igor Eremin,[8] began to be studied from the historico-literary viewpoint. A whole volume of *Newly-Found and Unpublished Works of Old Russian Literature* was published.[9]

Among the newly-found works we would mention *The Tale of Sukhan* discovered, studied and published by Vladimir Malyshev, the writings of Ermolai-Erasmus discovered and studied by Vyacheslav Rzhiga, the works of Andrei Belobotsky, discovered and studied by Alexander Gorfunkel, individual written songs found and published by Alexander Pozdneyev, the works of the redactor Savvaty, studied by Leonid Sheptayev, and so on. Of special importance is Oleg Tvorogov's book *The Old Russian Chronographs* (Leningrad, 1975), which examines a great deal of chronicle material in manuscripts.

Due to the vast increase in the copies of individual works published and studied, new redactions and new types came to light. Newly discovered redactions made it possible to gain a fuller idea of the literary history of individual works and, consequently, to have a more complete picture of the historico-literary process.

The Institute of Russian Literature of the USSR Academy of Sciences is publishing a series of monographs on works of Old Russian literature. Bearing in mind that many Old Russian works had not been published at all, that some had been published without account being taken of all the extant manuscripts and that others had been published a long time ago and in an unsatisfactory form, the editors of this series set themselves the task of making a thorough examination of all surviving manuscripts of important works and publishing them afresh.

The following publications in this series deserve special mention: *The Tale of the Princes of Vladimir,*[10] *The "Tale" of Abraham Palitsyn,*[11] *The Tale of Sukhan,*[12] *The Comedy of Artaxerxes,*[13] *Tales of the Life of Michael of Klopsk,*[14] the works of Vassian Patrikeyev,[15] *The Deeds of Digenes,*[16] *The New Tale of the Most Glorious Russian Tsardom,*[17] *The Tale of Dracula,*[18] *The Tale of the Founding of Moscow,*[19] *Tales of the Dispute of Life and Death,*[20] *The Lay of the Ruin of the Russian Land,*[21] and *The Tale of Peter and Febronia.*[22] Thirty volumes in this series have been published to date.

A number of Old Russian works have been published in the *Literary Monuments* series. This series aims at publishing works of different ages and peoples, and it has brought out a considerable number of Old Russian works, namely: *The Tale of Bygone Years,*[23] *The Lay of Igor's Host,*[24] *The Military Tales of Old Russia,*[25] *Afanasy Nikitin's Voyage Beyond Three Seas,*[26] *The Epistles of Ivan the Terrible,*[27] the official reports of Russian ambassadors from

Andrei Rublev (?). An illuminated letter from the Khitrovo Gospel. Late 14th-early 15th century. State Lenin Library, Moscow

17th-century cursive—an inscription in a book donated to the Solovetsky Monastery. State Public Library, Leningrad

abroad,[28] the works of Simeon of Polotsk,[29] *The "Annals" of Ivan Timofeyev,*[30] *Russian Democratic Satire of the Seventeenth Century,*[31] *Tales of the Battle of Kulikovo,*[32] and the *Alexandreid*[33]. Finally, some works were also published independently of any series, such as *The Tale of the Campaign of Stephen Bathory Against Pskov,*[34] *The Lives of Avvakum and Epiphanius,*[35] and *Russian Syllabic Poetry of the 17th-18th Centuries.*[36] Each of these editions contained all the extant versions of the work in order to show how it had moved and changed in different social environments at different times. They were extremely important for studying the history of literature because they made it possible to trace changes of ideas, literary styles and demands made on the work by readers and copyists. These publications were historico-literary ones in the true sense of the word, and have contributed greatly to the task of constructing a history of Old Russian literature.

From 1932 onwards the most important studies of Old Russian literature have been published in the almost annual *Transactions of the Department of Old Russian Literature (TODRL)* of the Institute of Russian Literature of the USSR Academy of Sciences. The most recent (fortieth) volume came out in 1985. In Moscow the Group for the Study of Old Russian Literature attached to the Gorky Institute of World Literature of the USSR Academy of Sciences issues *Studies and Materials on Old Russian Literature* of which four volumes have appeared (1961, 1967, 1971 and 1976).

Let us now turn to general courses and textbooks on the history of Old Russian literature that retain their importance today.

In the latter half of the nineteenth century and early twentieth many important works were published on *The Lay of Igor's Host* by Elpidifor Barsov,[37] Nikolai Tikhonravov,[38] Alexander Potebnya,[39] Vladimir Peretts[40] and many others.

In 1938 Nikolai Gudzii's textbook entitled *Old Russian Literature* was published. It was the first textbook on the subject that was free of vulgar sociologism. This textbook has been republished many times. It gives a clear idea of the works, expounds the material well and to some extent narrates the contents of works.

A little earlier a course of lectures was published by Academician Alexander Orlov entitled *Old Russian Literature of the Eleventh to Sixteenth Centuries* (Moscow and Leningrad, 1937). This course is noteworthy because it attempts to analyse primarily the literary aspect of individual works. The account of sixteenth-century literature is of indisputable value. In 1939 the course was republished under the title *A Course of Lectures on the History of Old Russian Literature,* and in 1946 it came out again with the addition of a short account of seventeenth-century literary works.

Orlov's course was followed by three collective academic histories of Old Russian literature. Shortly before the Great Patriotic War (1941-1945) the Institute of Russian Literature of the USSR Academy of Sciences published the first volume, dealing with the early period, of a three-volume *History of Russian Literature*,[41] which was unfortunately not completed. Immediately before and during the war two volumes (the second in two parts) of a ten-volume *History of Russian Literature*[42] of the Institute of Russian Literature were published. This is the largest history of Old Russian literature ever published. It is not only the most voluminous, but also the most complete in terms of the number of works examined. It analyses many works previously not included in the history of literature. Only literary works were selected, but the criterion for including works in this category was very broad. The authors sought to extend the secular sections of literature, including chronicles, chronographs, numerous historical tales, seventeenth-century satirical works, folklore recordings, etc. Historico-literary phenomena were viewed against a broad historical background together with general cultural changes and the history of Russian art. This history of Old Russian literature was written not only by all the eminent literary specialists of the day, but also with the help of the distinguished art historians Dmitry Ainalov and Nikolai Voronin and the historian Mikhail Priselkov. A major shortcoming of this work, however, is the almost total absence of a bibliography and name indices (of authors and works) and the inadequate headings.

Among the academic histories of Old Russian literature mention must be made of volume one of *A History of Russian Literature*[43] in three volumes published jointly by two academic institutions: the Institute of Russian Literature (Pushkin House) of the USSR Academy of Sciences and the Institute of World Literature of the USSR Academy of Sciences. The first volume contains a concise account of the development of Old Russian literature with a revised division into periods and attempts to describe works in the light of new research on them since the publication of the first two volumes of the ten-volume *History of Russian Literature*.

A History of Old Russian Literature by Professor Vladimir Kuskov of Moscow University (fourth edition, revised and enlarged, Moscow, 1972) is a good concise textbook.[44]

The study of Old Russian literature outside Russia by foreign specialists has been almost contemporaneous with its study at home. The first works to attract the attention of foreign scholars were the chronicles and *The Lay of Igor's Host*. The Russian *Primary Chronicle* was studied by August Schlözer, who published his huge five-volume study *Nestor* in 1802-1809 which appeared shortly afterwards in Nikolai Yazykov's translation in three volumes.[45]

The Lay of Igor's Host[46] attracted the attention of Czech scholars but more than a century passed before translations and studies of the *Lay* in foreign languages became widespread.

From the second quarter of the twentieth century one finds a heightened interest abroad in Russian literature, and in Russian culture in general. This interest has led to the publication of a large number of separate studies and monographs, and also of general courses of Old Russian literature.

These studies and courses cannot be examined as we have examined Russian ones, for they are related to the specific features of the country in question and the development of its research. We shall therefore only list the most comprehensive surveys of Old Russian literature and periodicals. Individual studies and monographs published abroad will be mentioned in the appropriate places as will those in Russian.

The course of Old Russian literature by Riccardo Picchio, published in Italian, English and Spanish, conforms most closely to modern requirements.[47] This course takes into account all the basic works of literature and expresses the most well-founded points of view. A shorter course of Old Russian literature and Russian literature of the eighteenth century is that by the Oxford specialists John Fennell and Antony Stokes.[48]

The course of Old Russian literature by Dmitry Tschiževskij,[49] which enjoys great authority abroad, contains many arbitrary assessments of works and their researchers and has some lacunae in its historiographical outlines and information. Adolf Stender-Petersen's[50] and Wilhelm Lettenbauer's[51] courses of Old Russian literature are out-of-date from the bibliographical point of view. A course of Old Russian literature published recently in Bulgaria has the original aim of showing the relationship between Russian and Bulgarian literature.[52]

Special studies and publications of Old Russian texts have been appearing for many decades now in the excellent Czechoslovak Slavistics journal *Slavia* which first came out in 1922. The *Revue des Etudes Slaves* published in Paris is of special interest because of its full bibliographical data. The collections entitled *Russia Mediaevalis* and edited by Rudolph Müller, Andrzej Poppe and John Fennell are published in the Federal German Republic. They contain both profound studies and full bibliographical data. Four have come out to date, all comparatively recently.

REFERENCES

[1] Lenin, V. I., *Collected Works*, Vol. I, Progress Publishers, Moscow, 1972, p. 155.

[2] Щепкин В. Н. *Русская палеография.* Moscow, 1967 (first edition published in 1918-1920); Черепнин Л. В. *Русская палеография.* Moscow, 1956; Лихачев Д. С. *Текстология на материале русской литературы X-XVII вв.* Second edition. Leningrad, 1983; Лихачев Д. С. *Текстология. Краткий очерк.* Moscow and Leningrad, 1964.

[3] The Academy of Sciences in St Petersburg must not be confused with the Russian Academy, a scholarly centre for the study of Russian language and literature. The Russian Academy existed from 1783 to 1841, and its first president was Countess Ekaterina Dashkova. Its most important achievement was the compilation and publication of a dictionary of the Russian language (the first edition was published in six volumes in 1789-1794 and the second, considerably enlarged, in 1806-1822).

[4] On this point see: Сухомлинов М. И. "О трудах по истории русской литературы". *Журнал Министерства народного просвещения.* St Petersburg, August 1871, p. 148.

[5] On this point see: *Русская демократическая сатира XVII века.* Preparation of texts, article and commentaries by V. P. Adrianova-Peretts. Moscow and Leningrad, 1954 (second edition, 1977).

[6] For a full list of studies on chronicle-writing up to 1960 see: *Библиография русского летописания.* Compiled by R. P. Dmitrieva. Moscow and Leningrad, 1962.

[7] Рыбаков Б. А. *Древняя Русь, сказания, былины, летописи.* Moscow, 1963.

[8] Еремин И. П. *Литература Древней Руси. Этюды и характеристики.* Moscow and Leningrad, 1966.

[9] *Труды отдела древнерусской литературы (ТОДРЛ),* Vol. XXI, 1965.

[10] Дмитриева Р. П. *Сказание о князьях владимирских.* Moscow and Leningrad, 1955.

[11] *Сказание Авраамия Палицына.* Preparation of texts and commentaries by O. A. Derzhavina and E. V. Kolosova. Moscow and Leningrad, 1955.

[12] Малышев В. И. *"Повесть о Сухане". Из истории русской повести XVII века.* Moscow and Leningrad, 1956.

[13] *"Артаксерксово действо". Первая пьеса русского театра XVII в.* Preparation of text, article and commentaries by I. M. Kudryavtsev. Moscow and Leningrad, 1957.

[14] *Повести о житии Михаила Клопского.* Preparation of texts and article by L. A. Dmitriev. Moscow and Leningrad, 1958.

[15] Казакова Н. А. *Вассиан Патрикеев и его сочинения.* Moscow and Leningrad, 1960.

[16] Кузьмина В. Д. *Девгениево деяние. (Деяние прежних времен храбрых человек).* Moscow, 1962.

[17] Дробленкова Н. Ф. *"Новая повесть о преславном Российском царстве" и современная ей агитационная патриотическая письменность.* Moscow and Leningrad, 1960.

[18] *Повесть о Дракуле.* Study and preparation of texts by Y. S. Lurie. Moscow and Leningrad, 1964.

[19] *Повести о начале Москвы.* Study and preparation of texts by M. A. Salmina. Moscow and Leningrad, 1964.

[20] *Повести о споре жизни и смерти.* Study and preparation of texts by R. P. Dmitrieva. Moscow and Leningrad, 1964.

[21] Бегунов Ю. К. *Памятник русской литературы XIII века "Слово о погибели Русской земли".* Moscow and Leningrad, 1965.

[22] *Повесть о Петре и Февронии.* Preparation of texts and study by R. P. Dmitrieva. Leningrad, 1979.

[23] *Повесть временных лет.* Part I. Text and translation. Part II. Appendix. Edited by V. P. Adrianova-Peretts. Moscow and Leningrad, 1950.

[24] *Слово о полку Игореве.* Edited by V. P. Adrianova-Peretts. Moscow and Leningrad, 1950.

[25] *Воинские повести Древней Руси.* Introductory article by L. A. Dmitriev. Leningrad, 1985.

[26] *Хожение за три моря Афанасия Никитина.* (Серия "Литературные памятники"), Second edition, revised and enlarged. Leningrad, 1986.

[27] *Послания Ивана Грозного.* Edited by V. P. Adrianova-Peretts. Moscow and Leningrad, 1951.

[28] *Путешествия русских послов XVI-XVII вв. Статейные списки.* Moscow and Leningrad, 1954.

[29] Полоцкий Симеон. *Избранные сочинения.* Preparation of text, article and commentaries by I. P. Eremin. Moscow and Leningrad, 1953.

[30] *"Временник" Ивана Тимофеева.* Edited by V. P. Adrianova-Peretts. Moscow and Leningrad, 1951.

[31] *Русская демократическая сатира XVII века.* Preparation of texts, article and commentaries by V. P. Adrianova-Peretts. Moscow and Leningrad, 1954 (second edition, 1977).

[32] *Повести о Куликовской битве.* Prepared by M. N. Tikhomirov, V. F. Rzhiga and L. A. Dmitriev. Moscow, 1959; *Сказания и повести о Куликовской битве.* Prepared by L. A. Dmitriev and O. P. Likhacheva. Leningrad, 1982.

[33] *"Александрия". Роман об Александре Македонском по русской рукописи XV в.* Prepared by M. N. Botvinnik, Y. S. Lurie and O. V. Tvorogov. Moscow and Leningrad, 1965.

[34] *Повесть о прихожении Стефана Батория на град Псков.* Preparation of text and article by V. I. Malyshev. Moscow and Leningrad, 1952.

[35] Робинсон А. Н. *Жизнеописания Аввакума и Епифания.* Studies and texts. Moscow, 1963.

[36] *Русская силлабическая поэзия XVII-XVIII вв.* Introductory article, preparation of text and notes by A. M. Panchenko. Second edition, Leningrad, 1970.

[37] Барсов Е. В. *"Слово о полку Игореве" как художественный памятник Киевской дружинной Руси.* Vol. I, Moscow, 1887; Vol. II, 1888; Vol. III, 1889.

[38] Тихонравов Н. С. *Слово о полку Игореве.* Moscow, 1866 (second edition, 1868).

[39] Потебня А. А. *Слово о полку Игореве.* Text and notes. Second edition, Kharkov, 1914.

[40] *"Слово о полку Ігоревім". Пам'ятка феодальної України-Руси XII віку.* Kiev, 1926 (a summary of Peretts' studies in Ukrainian).

[41] *История русской литературы.* Edited by V. A. Desnitsky, Vol. I, parts 1-2, Moscow, 1941.

[42] *История русской литературы.* Vol. I (Литература XI-начала XIII века). Moscow and Leningrad, 1941; Vol. II, Part I (Литература 1220-1580-х гг.). Moscow and Leningrad, 1945; Vol. II, Part 2 (Литература 1590-1690-х гг.). Moscow and Leningrad, 1948.

[43] *История русской литературы.* In three volumes. Edited by D. D. Blagoy. Vol. I, Moscow and Leningrad, 1958 (Volume I was translated into Bulgarian and published in Sofia in 1960).

[44] N. V. Vodovozov's textbook *История древней русской литературы* (third edition, Moscow, 1972) is easily obtainable. Many works are not included in it, however, and others are described and dated in a somewhat subjective fashion.

[45] Before August Schlözer the Russian chronicles had aroused the interest of Sigismund von Herberstein in the sixteenth century, Herbini and Berg in the seventeenth century, and Leibnitz in the early eighteenth century. But not one of these authors left us any substantial comments on them.

[46] Wollman, S., "Dobrovský a *Slovo a pluku Igorově.*" *Slavia,* Praha, 1955, ročnik XXIV, číslo 2-3, s. 269-282; Г. Н. Моисеева. "*Задонщина и Слово о полку Игореве* в восприятии Й. Добровского." *Slavia,* Praha, 1979, ročnik XLVIII, číslo 2-3, s. 168-173.

[47] Picchio, Riccardo, *Storia della litteratura russa antica.* Milano, 1959.

[48] Fennell, John, and Stokes, Antony, *Early Russian Literature.* London, 1974.

[49] Tschiževskij, D., *Altrussische Literaturgeschichte im 11, 12 und 13 Jahrhundert. Kiever Epoche.* Frankfurt am Main, 1948.

[50] Stender-Petersen, Adolf, *Geschichte des russischen Literatur,* Band I. München, 1957; Zweite Aufgabe München, 1974.

[51] Lettenbauer, Wilhelm, *Russische Literaturgeschichte.* Frankfurt am Main. Humboldt, 1955.

[52] Михайлов М. Н. *Староруска литература (X-XVII вв.).* Велико-Търново, 1979.

CHAPTER 1

1. The Emergence of Old Russian Literature

During the ninth and tenth centuries Old Russia turned from an unstable alliance of tribes into a united feudal

THE LITERATURE OF KIEVAN RUSSIA
(Eleventh to Early Thirteenth Centuries)

state. Close diplomatic, trading and cultural ties with its southern and western neighbours brought the country into the sphere of European politics. The acceptance of Christianity marked a most important stage in the history of Kievan Russia.

There were Christians in Russia long before its official conversion. Olga (died 969), the wife of Prince Igor of Kiev, was a Christian, there was a Christian Church of St Elijah in Kiev, and some of the boyars and retainers were Christians, although Christianity did not become the official religion until the reign of Vladimir, in 988, according to the chronicle. The acceptance of Christianity conformed to the urgent requirements of princely power and feudal society. In religious-ethical terms it brought

Russia even closer to the other Slav states which had already accepted Christianity by that time (Bulgaria, Bohemia and Poland) and also the largest and culturally most important state in South-Eastern Europe — Byzantium.

The consequences of the acceptance of Christianity were also considerable for Russian culture. Together with Christianity, writing and literature became widespread in Russia. This was a fundamentally new cultural phenomenon. There were people who could read and write in Russia before the acceptance of Christianity, and those who had embraced the new religion probably possessed books. But when Christianity was adopted as the state religion, there was an urgent need to acquire or copy a large number of books essential for performing divine service and preaching the Christian faith. What is more, the Christianisation of Russia required a radical changing of world outlook: pagan ideas of the origin and structure of the universe, the history of the human race and the ancestry of the Slavs were now rejected, and Russian scholars needed works to expound the new, Christian views of world history and provide a new, Christian interpretation of the world and the phenomena of nature.

Although the young Christian state's need for books was very great, the possibilities of satisfying it were very limited at first: there were still few experienced scribes in Russia, the actual process of copying was very lengthy, and books were extremely expensive. The earliest manuscripts were written in uncials, large, geometrically strict letters that were not joined, so that books were drawn, rather than written. Joined letters did not appear until the sixteenth century. Books were written on parchment, which in both Western Europe and Russia was not replaced by paper until the fourteenth or fifteenth century. Consequently books were commissioned either by the rich, the princes and boyars, or the Church.[1]

Nevertheless book copying assumed considerable proportions in Kievan Russia. The oldest Russian chronicle, *The Tale of Bygone Years*, says under the year 1037 that Prince Yaroslav the Wise of Kiev (1019-1054), who was well-read, assembled scribes who translated and copied many books. This is borne out by the fact that a large number of Christian churches were functioning at that time, whose services could not have been performed without liturgical books, and also that eleventh-century Russian authors quote Byzantine works (chronicles, homiletic literature, *vitae*, etc.), which must have been available to them in Slavonic translation. Of course most of the books that were copied and translated were liturgical texts or works that expounded Christian philosophy and Christian morals. But scribes also brought from Bulgaria translated or copied works of different genres: chronicles, historical and popular tales, scholarly writings, and collections of sayings.

Out of more than 130 manuscript books of the eleventh and twelfth centuries now in Soviet archives and libraries about 80 are liturgical ones.[2] This is explained not only by the fact that they comprised the main body of texts reproduced (which was dictated by the needs of the Church) but also because these books were kept in stone churches and therefore less likely to be destroyed in the frequent fires to which wooden buildings, including the palaces of the princes and boyars, were particularly vulnerable. So precisely which books or works and how many copies were circulating in Russia in the eleventh and twelfth centuries we can only surmise from indirect evidence, for the manuscripts that have survived represent only an insignificant proportion of them.

Nevertheless it can be said that the literature of Kievan Russia dealt mainly with philosophical questions. Its system of genres reflected the philosophy typical of many Christian states in the early Middle Ages. The characteristic features of the literature belonging to the earliest period of Russian history were summed up by Dmitry Likhachev as follows: "Old Russian literature can be seen as a literature with a single theme and a single subject. The subject is world history, and the theme is the meaning of human life."[3]

2. Translated Literature of the Eleventh to Early Thirteenth Centuries

We shall begin our examination of Old Russian literature of the early period with a survey of translated literature. And not without good reason. In the eleventh and twelfth centuries translations often preceded the creation of original works in a given genre. Generally speaking Russians read foreign works before writing their own. This should not be interpreted as a sign of the cultural "inferiority" of the Eastern Slavs. All European mediaeval states learned from the countries that inherited the culture of Ancient Greece and Rome. For Russia a most important role in this respect was played by Bulgaria and Byzantium. We would also emphasise that in the case of the Eastern Slavs the absorbing of this foreign culture with its long traditions was an active, creative process in keeping with the internal requirements of the Old Russian state, and that it stimulated the emergence of an original literature.

Byzantine and Bulgarian Books in Old Russia. The Transplantation Phenomenon. Before considering which works and genres of translated literature became known in Old Russia in the two centuries following the creation of the written language, let us first examine the activity of the Old Russian translators.

Many of the books, particularly liturgical ones, were brought from Bulgaria in the tenth and eleventh centuries. The Old Slavonic (Old Bulgarian) and Old Russian languages were so close that Russia was able to make use of the Old Slavonic Cyrillic alphabet created by the great Bulgarian enlighteners Cyril and Methodius [4] in the ninth century, and Bulgarian books, although formally in a foreign tongue, did not actually need to be translated. Some features of the Bulgarian morphological system and some of the vocabulary (the so-called Old Slavonicisms) were absorbed into the Old Russian literary language.

At the same time translations were made directly from the Greek, and the Old Russian translators not only produced accurate renderings of the original, but also preserved its style and rhythm. Translation from other languages was rarer. [5]

The interaction of the Old Slavonic literatures and their relations with the literature of Byzantium have sometimes been interpreted as the process of one literature influencing another. In this interpretation Old Russian literature, which was young compared with the literature of Bulgaria and even more so with that of Byzantium, appears as the passive object of such influence. It would be more correct, however, to speak not of influence but of the transplantation of the literature of one country into another. Before the adoption of Christianity there was no literature in Old Russia and, consequently, there was nothing for Byzantine literature to influence. Therefore, in the early years after the adoption of Christianity, Byzantine literature was transplanted, as it were, to Russia either directly or through Bulgarian literature. [6] It was not a mechanical transplantation, however. Works were not only translated or copied. They continued their literary history on new soil. This means that new redactions were made of works, their subject matter was changed, the original text of the translation became russified in the subsequent copyings or redactions, and new compilative works were created on the basis of translated works. [7] This applied, in particular, to secular and historical works; liturgical writings, patristics and the works of the Holy Scriptures retained their canonical text to a greater extent.

Consequently, the division of Old Russian literature into original and translated is significant only if we are referring to the origin of a work and not to its place in Old Russian literature.

The transplantation phenomenon was extremely progressive:

in a relatively short time Russia obtained a literature with a ramified system of genres, a literature represented by scores, even hundreds of works. Only a few decades after the beginning of this process original works began to appear in Russia modelled on translations: *vitae*, rhetorical and homiletic discourses, tales, etc.

Literature as an Intermediary. There is yet another specific feature characteristic of mediaeval literatures—the existence of literatures which acted as intermediaries or "go-betweens". For the Southern and Eastern Slavs the intermediary was Old Bulgarian literature. It included both works of early Christian literature (translations from the Greek) and works created in Bulgaria, Moravia and Bohemia, and later in Russia and Serbia.

This intermediary literature united the literatures of the Slavonic peoples (particularly of Bulgaria, Serbia and Russia) for a very long time, almost up to the modern period, although naturally the relative importance of original works grew increasingly in each of the individual national literatures.[8]

Genres of Translated Literature. The Holy Scriptures. Let us now consider the main genres of translated literature in the eleventh to thirteenth centuries. This broad time span is a necessary convention, because for the most part the works of this period have survived only in later copies, and we can establish the time of their translation or appearance in the literature of Old Russia from indirect evidence only.

The foundation of the Christian faith and philosophy were the books of the Holy Scriptures, and also the writings of the Church Fathers, Byzantine and Slav theologians and preachers.

The Bible was not fully translated in Russia until the fifteenth century, but Bulgarian and Russian translations of individual books were already known in Kievan Russia. The most widespread at that time were the books of the New Testament and the Psalter. It is probable that some of the Old Testament books were also known (the Pentateuch and the books of Joshua, Judges, Kings, Prophets and Ruth). It is hard to say when they appeared in Russia because the oldest surviving manuscripts belong to the fourteenth century. Yet indirect evidence enables us to conclude, for example, that the whole of the Pentateuch, the books of Joshua, Judges, and Kings and fragments from some other Old Testament books were included in a chronograph compilation of the mid-thirteenth century.[9]

Russian readers could become acquainted with the content of the Old Testament books also through Greek chronicles (in particular the *Chronicle* of Georgios Hamartolos) and through the *paleya* which expounded and interpreted the text of the Old Testament.

The Scriptures, the *paleya,* the chronicles and writings of the
Church Fathers were intended for independent reading by
believers. In church, however, other books, specially intended for
church services, were used.

These included, first and foremost, the Aprakos Gospels and
Aprakos Apostles (from the Greek *apraktos* meaning "festive") —
selected readings from the Gospels and the Acts and Epistles of
the Apostles arranged in the order in which they were read in
church services (certain readings for certain days of the week or
church feasts). The *Paroemia* was read (a selection of passages
from the Holy Scriptures prescribed for certain church services),
liturgical menologies (books containing encomiums to the saints
arranged in the order of their feasts days), collections of anthems,
canons, etc.[10]

Apart from their purely instructive and liturgical functions, the
books of the Holy Scriptures and liturgical works were also of
considerable aesthetic importance. The Bible contained vivid
stories, the books of the Prophets were full of strong emotion,
striking imagery and impassioned denunciations of vices and social
injustice, the Psalter and the menologies were fine examples of
religious poetry, although their Slavonic translations were in prose.

Patristics. In Old Russian, as in any other mediaeval Christian literature, great
authority was attached to patristics, the writings of Roman and Byzantine
theologians of the third to eleventh centuries who were revered as "Church
Fathers" (Greek *patros* and Latin *pater* mean "father", hence the name given to
their writings—patristics).

The writings of the Church Fathers substantiated and commented upon the
basic precepts of the Christian religion, carried on polemics with heretics, and
expounded principles of Christian morality or rules of monastic life in the form of
instructions and exhortations.

In Old Russia the writings of St John Chrysostom (c. 350-407), the eminent
Byzantine preacher, were widely read. In his discourses and sermons John
exhorted believers to practise the Christian virtues, passionately denounced sins
and occasionally condemned social injustice. In Bulgaria during the reign of King
Simeon a collection of his works entitled *The Stream of Gold* was compiled, the
oldest Russian copy of which belongs to the twelfth century; individual sermons of
St John Chrysostom are included in Russian miscellanies of the twelfth and
thirteenth centuries. In the fifteenth and sixteenth centuries miscellanies were
compiled in Russia with a fixed set of items. They were the *Chrysostom* and the
Festal Sermons which also include a large number of the Byzantine theologian's
writings. In addition, passages from St John Chrysostom's writings were widely
used in the homilies compiled by unknown Russian scribes, but also frequently
signed with his name.

The works of the following writers also enjoyed great authority in Old Russia:
the Byzantine preacher St Gregory of Nazianzus (Gregory the Theologian)
(329-390), St Basil the Great (c. 330-379), the author of polemical and dogmatic
works and the *Hexaëmeron* (a cycle of sermons on the Bible story of the Creation
that enjoyed great popularity in the Middle Ages), St Ephraem of Syria (died 373),
St Athanasius, the author of the *Pareneses* (a collection of exhortations for
newly-converted Christians), St John Climacus (died 649), the author of the *Ladder*

Prince Svyatoslav of Kiev with His Wife and Sons. Illumination from the *Svyatoslav Miscellany* of 1073. History Museum, Moscow

to *Paradise* (on the attainment of moral perfection), and St Athanasius of Alexandria (c. 295-373), who championed orthodox dogmas against the various heresies of the early Christian period. Patristic literature played an important role in forming the ethical ideals of the new religion and in strengthening the foundations of Christian dogma. At the same time the works of the Byzantine theologians, most of whom were brilliant rhetoricians who had mastered the finest traditions of classical rhetoric, helped to improve the oratorical skills of Russian religious writers.

Kievan Russia was also familiar with miscellanies which, as well as the works of the Church Fathers, contained other writings of varied content. The oldest extant specimens of these are the two miscellanies of the 1070s. One of them, the *Svyatoslav Miscellany* of 1073, is a copy of a Bulgarian work compiled at the beginning of the tenth century for King Simeon of Bulgaria. The *Miscellany* was copied in Russia for Prince Izyaslav of Kiev, but the prince's name was later erased and replaced by that of Svyatoslav, who seized the throne in 1073. The *Miscellany* is a folio of large dimensions executed with sumptuous artistry. The frontispiece (the left-hand side of the first sheet) bears a picture of Svyatoslav surrounded by his family. The items in the *Miscellany* include a handbook on rhetoric written by Georgios Choiroboskos entitled "Concerning Figures of Speech", in which he explains the meaning of the various tropes (allegory, metaphor, hyperbole, etc.) illustrating them with examples taken, inter alia, from the *Iliad* and the *Odyssey*. Many copies were subsequently made of the *Svyatoslav Miscellany*. To date 27 copies of its Russian redaction made between the fifteenth and seventeenth centuries have come to light.[11]

The other work, the *Miscellany* of 1076, is simpler and smaller and was compiled, as the manuscript tells us, "in the year 6584 (1076) ... in the reign of Svyatoslav, Prince of the Russian land." Among the works in this *Miscellany* is an encomium on the reading of books and also a collection of sayings by Patriarch Gennadius of Constantinople (died 471).[12]

Collections of aphorisms appeared in Russia at a later period also. They included the very popular miscellanies *The Wisdom of Menander the Wise*, the sayings of Hesychius and Barnabas, and particularly *Melissa (The Bee)*, a collection of aphorisms by ancient philosophers, quotations from the Bible and writings of the Church Fathers. A definitive study of the miscellanies of sayings and aphorisms has been made by Mikhail Speransky.[13]

Vitae. The collections of sayings and aphorisms had an openly didactic aim. Addressing themselves directly to readers and listeners, the preachers and theologians extolled virtues and condemned vices, promising the righteous eternal bliss after death and threatening the remiss and the sinners with Divine retribution.

The Christian virtues were also preached and extolled by works of another genre—the *vitae*, i.e., stories about the life, sufferings or pious acts of people canonised by the Church, that is, officially recognised as saints whom it was permissible to worship.[14] This type of literature is also called *hagiography* (from the Greek *hagios*—sacred, and *grapho*—I write). In the *vitae* we frequently find plenty of action, since their authors readily made use of the plots and narrative devices of Greek tales of adventure. The hagiographers usually wrote about miracles performed by the saints (which was supposed to demonstrate their saintliness); these miracles, the intervention of celestial forces—angels or devils—

were described with a wealth of vivid detail. The authors of the *vitae* strove to give even most fantastic episodes the illusion of authenticity.

Many Byzantine Lives of saints were translated even in Kievan Russia. We have copies of or references by Russian scribes to *The Life of Alexis, the Man of God,* the Lives of Basil the New, Sabas the Blessed, Irene, Anthony the Great, Theodore and others.

An example of the hagiographic romance (a term coined by the specialist on Byzantine hagiography Pavel Bezobrasov) [15] is *The Life of St Eustace.*

Eustace is a *stratilates* (general), famed for his military prowess and just deeds. But he is a pagan. One day out hunting he meets a stag who speaks to him in a human voice and tells him to be baptised. Straightway Eustace hears another voice that tells him he will have to prove the sincerity of his faith by his deeds and endure all the sufferings that fall to his lot. And, indeed, shortly afterwards Eustace loses all his riches and, ashamed of his poverty, leaves his native town. He is separated from his wife, and his children are carried away by a wolf and a lion. Their father thinks they have perished. For fifteen years Eustace lives in a strange place and keeps watch over the crops, with no news of his family. Then Rome is threatened, and the Emperor sends for his once renowned general. The messengers find Eustace and take him to Rome, where he leads a victorious campaign.

In the meantime Eustace's sons quite by chance meet and recognise each other in the house of their mother, whom they do not recognise (and who does not recognise them). Then Eustace himself finds his wife and children. The *vita* does not end on this happy note, however: following the canon of the life of a martyr, the hagiographer tells how, after the death of the Emperor Trajan who loved Eustace, Trajan's successor demands that Eustace make a sacrifice in the temple of Apollo. Eustace refuses and perishes together with his wife and children after terrible torments.

Another type of *vita* is found in *The Life of Alexis, the Man of God.* Alexis, a pious and virtuous youth, voluntarily renounces riches, honour and love. He leaves the house of his father, a rich Roman patrician, and the beautiful bride he has just married, distributes money taken from his home to the poor and for seventeen years lives by begging in the narthex of the Church of Our Lady in Edessa. When the news of his saintliness has spread all over the land, Alexis leaves Edessa and returns to Rome after many wanderings. Unrecognised by anyone he lives in his father's house, eating at the same table with the other beggars to which the pious patrician gives alms each day, and patiently suffering the jibes and blows of his father's servants. Another seventeen years pass. Alexis is on his death-bed and only then do his parents and widow learn that their lost son and husband was living in their midst.[16]

Paterica. Paterica, collections of short stories usually about monks famed for their piety or asceticism, were well known in Kievan Russia.

The *Sinai Patericon*, translated in Russia in the eleventh century, contains a story, for example, about a stylite* who was so self-abnegating that he even left alms for beggars on the steps of his abode and did not hand them over himself, saying that it was the Virgin, not he, who gave to the needy. There is also a story about a young nun who puts her eyes out when she learns that their beauty has aroused desire in a young man. A righteous monk is accused of committing adultery, but in reply to his prayer a twelve-day-old infant answers the question "Who is his father?" by pointing to his real father. One hot day in response to the prayers of a devout sea-captain rain pours down onto the deck, quenching the thirst of the suffering travellers. A lion meets a monk on a narrow mountain path and stands on its hind legs to let him pass, etc.

Whereas the righteous are accompanied by divine help, what awaits the sinners in patericon legends is terrible and immediate retribution, characteristically in this life, not in the next. The thief who defiles graves has his eyes put out by a corpse that comes to life; a ship will not move until a woman child-killer has been taken off in a boat, and the boat with the sinful woman is immediately swallowed up by the waves; a servant who is planning to kill and rob his mistress is rooted to the spot and stabs himself to death.

The paterica depict a fantastic world in which the forces of good and evil are constantly struggling for people's souls, in which the righteous are not merely pious, but pious to the point of frenzy and exaltation, in which miracles sometimes happen in the most prosaic settings.

The subject matter of translated paterica influenced the work of Old Russian writers: in the Russian paterica and *vitae* we occasionally find similar episodes and descriptions borrowed from Byzantine patericon legends.[17]

Patericon legends were used by nineteenth-century Russian writers, such as Lev Tolstoy, Nikolai Leskov and Vsevolod Garshin.

Apocryphal Literature (Greek *apokrythos*—hidden). As well as the legends that formed part of the canonical books of the Bible, i.e., the Old and New Testaments, mediaeval literature abounded with apocryphas, legends about Biblical personages, which differed from those contained in the canonical books of the Bible. Sometimes the apocryphas adopted a different philosophical viewpoint in examining the origin of the world, its structure and the question of the "end of the world" of such great concern to mediaeval minds.[18] Finally, apocryphal motifs were sometimes included in works of traditional genres, for example, *vitae*.[19]

Originally there was a distinction between apocryphas intended for readers well versed in theological matters, who could interpret the apocryphal versions in line with the traditional ones, and the "proscribed books" containing heretical views which were clearly hostile to orthodox beliefs. But the borderline between apocryphal and proscribed books was not a strict one, different writers took

---

* A stylite was the name given to a recluse who lived in a cell built on the top of a pillar (Greek "στῦλος") or in a small pillar-shaped cell.

different views of them, and therefore both groups of writing are usually considered within the framework of apocryphal literature as a whole. It is sometimes hard to distinguish the apocryphas from the "true" (the term used by Old Russian writers) books. There was no unanimity of opinion on this question in mediaeval literature. Apocryphal subjects are found in chronicles, annals, and paleyas, and the apocryphas themselves in miscellanies alongside authoritative and revered works. The lists of proscribed books, or "indexes", compiled in Byzantium and by the Slavs, did not always correspond to one another, and in practice their recommendations were often ignored.[20]

Apocryphas were known already in the literature of Kievan Russia. Manuscripts copied before the thirteenth century contain apocryphal stories about the prohet Jeremiah, *The Journey of St Agapetus to Paradise, The Tale of Aphroditian, The Descent of the Virgin to Purgatory* and a number of others.[21] We also find apocryphal legends in the *Primary Chronicle*: there are, for example, apocryphal details in the story about the childhood of the Prophet Moses (how he knocked the crown off the head of the Egyptian Pharaoh when he was playing), and the reply of the leaders of the uprising in the Rostov lands to *voevoda* Jan Vyshatich quoted in the chronicle (under the year 1071) contains some Bogomil ideas about the Creation: "the Devil created man, and God put a soul into him". In a description of his pilgrimage to Palestine at the beginning of the twelfth century Abbot Daniel also mentions some apocryphal legends.

Apocryphas are characterised by an abundance of miracles, fantastic and exotic happenings. For example, *The Paralipomenon of Jeremiah* tells how the youth Abimelech, returning to town with a basket of figs, sat down in the shade of a tree and fell asleep. He woke up sixty-six years later, but miraculously the figs were still so fresh that the juice was dripping from them.

Another apocryphal tale tells how the pious Abbot Agapetus went off in search of paradise. Paradise is described as a beautiful garden, bathed in light that is seven times brighter than the sun. The bread that Agapetus receives in paradise is wonder-working bread: it can sate starving mariners, bring back to life a young youth who died two weeks before, and one crust of it keeps Agapetus himself alive for forty years.[22]

At the same time the apocryphas satisfied not only literary, but also theological interests. They raised problems of special concern to religious people: about the causes of the imperfections in the world which, as the church taught, had been created and ruled by an almighty and just divinity, about the future of the world, man's fate after death, etc. The popular *Descent of the Virgin to Purgatory*, for example, deals with the latter theme.

It tells how the Virgin accompanied by the Archangel Michael and the angels descends into purgatory. She sees the various torments of sinners there: some dwell constantly "in great darkness" because they did not believe in God, others are engulfed in a river of fire, because they were cursed by their parents or broke an oath sworn on the cross. Scandalmongers, sluggards who rose too late for matins, slanderers and debauchers, drunkards and money-grubbers are also suffering terrible torments. The Virgin sheds tears at the sight of this terrible retribution, and decides to ask God to have mercy on the sinners. But God the Father refuses to take pity on them. He cannot forgive men for crucifying Christ. And only after a new supplication, in which the Virgin is joined by the Prophets, Evangelists, Apostles and all the angels, does God the Father send Christ to descend into purgatory, where after severely reprimanding the sinners for not following the Divine behests, he grants them freedom from torment for two months each year.

Unlike the apocryphal tale of Jeremiah and Abimelech, which contains all the elements of an entertaining story about miracles, that of the Virgin raises the question of Divine justice and casts doubt on God's "ineffable love of mankind": for the Virgin, the angels and saints are forced to plead insistently for the alleviation of sinners' terrible torments, and for a long time God remains implacable. It was perhaps this idea that put the *Descent* among the apocryphal works, although the need to threaten people with Divine retribution for their sins would seem to be fully in keeping with ecclesiastical teaching and behests.

Apocryphal tales are found throughout Old Russian literature, and we shall return to those apocryphal subjects that became widespread at a later period.

Chronicles. Among the first translations and first books brought to Russia from Bulgaria were the Byzantine chronicles. The chronicle or chronograph was the name given to historiographical works recording world history. A particularly important role in the development of original Russian chronicle-writing and chronography was played by the *Chronicle* of Georgios Hamartolos. It was compiled by a Byzantine monk, Georgios the "Sinful", a traditional self-abasing epithet used by monks.

The *Chronicle* of Georgios Hamartolos begins with the story of the Creation; it then recounts Biblical history, the history of the Babylonian and Persian kings, and the Roman emperors of Byzantium, from Constantine the Great to Michael III. Originally the *Chronicle* went up to the middle of the ninth century, but later, still on Greek soil, an extract from the *Chronicle* of Simon Logothetes was added, and the narrative was continued up to the middle of the tenth century.

The chronicler is interested primarily in church history. He constantly quotes lengthy theological discourses and gives detailed accounts of church councils, heresies and the struggle of conflicting trends within the Byzantine Church. Purely historical events are mentioned very briefly, and only in the final part of the work (which belongs to the pen of Hamartolos' successor, Simon Logothetes) is the reader introduced to the complex political life of Byzantium in the ninth and tenth centuries.

The Old Russian scribe, however, was interested in history as such: the fates of the great powers of antiquity, information about their mighty rulers, and fascinating stories about the lives of famous kings, emperors and wise men. For example mediaeval scribes were particularly fond of the story of the twin brothers Romulus and Remus, who were suckled by a she-wolf and later became the founders of Rome, and the deeds of Alexander the Great who conquered nearly the whole of the ancient world. As early as the eleventh century Russian scribes compiled an abridged chronicle based on extracts from the *Chronicle* of Georgios Hamartolos, which appears to have been called *The Great Narrative Chronicle*. It contained brief information about the kings and emperors of the Orient, Rome and Byzantium, several interesting historical legends and stories about miracles and heavenly signs, and the decisions of church councils. *The Great Narrative Chronicle* was used in the compilation of Russian chronicles.

The *Chronicle* of Georgios Hamartolos existed as a single manuscript, and was also included almost in full in the lengthy chronographical collection of the thirteenth and fourteenth centuries entitled *The Hellenic and Roman Chronicle.** The Old Russian translation of the *Chronicle* of Georgios Hamartolos has been studied and published by Vasily Istrin.[23]

The *Chronicle* of John Malalas. The *Chronicle* of John Malalas, who lived in the town of Antioch in the Byzantine province of Syria in the sixth century, also became known in Russia not later than the eleventh century. Unlike Georgios Hamartolos, John Malalas wrote in simple, plain language, intending his work not for learned monks but for the broad mass of readers, and sought to make his narrative exciting. The *Chronicle* consists of 18 books. Four of them (Books One, Two, Four and Five) contain classical myths and the history of the Trojan War. Then follows an account of the Oriental rulers, the history of Rome and, finally, the history of Byzantium right up to the reign of the Emperor Justinian (sixth century).

The *Chronicle* of John Malalas was valuable for Old Russian historiographers and writers primarily because it provided an important addition to the *Chronicle* of Georgios Hamartolos. It is Malalas who provides detailed and fascinating stories about the Persian kings, a fuller account of the story of Romulus and Remus, the early Roman emperors, and the reigns of some Byzantine emperors. Therefore in Old Russian chronographical compilations, Malalas' text was used not only to complement but also in part to replace the somewhat dry account of the *Chronicle* of Georgios Hamartolos.

Moreover, as already mentioned, the *Chronicle* of John Malalas retold (albeit very briefly) some of the ancient myths. These accounts were used by Russian annalists and chroniclers. The *Chronicle* was first used in the compilation of *The Great Narrative Chronicle* in the eleventh century.

The full text of the Slavonic translation of the *Chronicle* of John Malalas has not survived. We can reconstruct it only from extracts in Russian chronographical compilations. The Slavonic translation of Malalas is of great importance for reconstructing the Greek text of which all that survives is one defective manuscript and a few fragments.[24]

The *History of the Jewish War* by Josephus Flavius. This exceptionally popular work in European mediaeval literature was translated in Russia not later than the beginning of the twelfth century. The *History* was written between 75-79 A.D. by Josephus, the son of Mattathias, who took part in the rebellion in Judaea against Rome, and later went over to the side of the Romans and was granted the right to assume the name of Flavius, the family name of Emperor Vespasian.

The *History* consists of seven books. The first two contain a history of Judaea from 175 B.C. to 66 A.D., the period of the rebellion against Roman dominion, the next four describe the crushing of the rebellion by Vespasian, and later by his son Titus, and the siege, capture and destruction of Jerusalem; the final, seventh, book tells of the triumphal return of Vespasian and Titus to Rome.

---

* The title reflects the main sections of the chronicle. It sets out Hellenic (Ancient Greek, pagan) history and Roman (Byzantine, Christian) history. Byzantines called themselves *rhomaioi,* which means Romans.

Assumption Miscellany. 12th-13th centuries. Page of manuscript. History Museum, Moscow

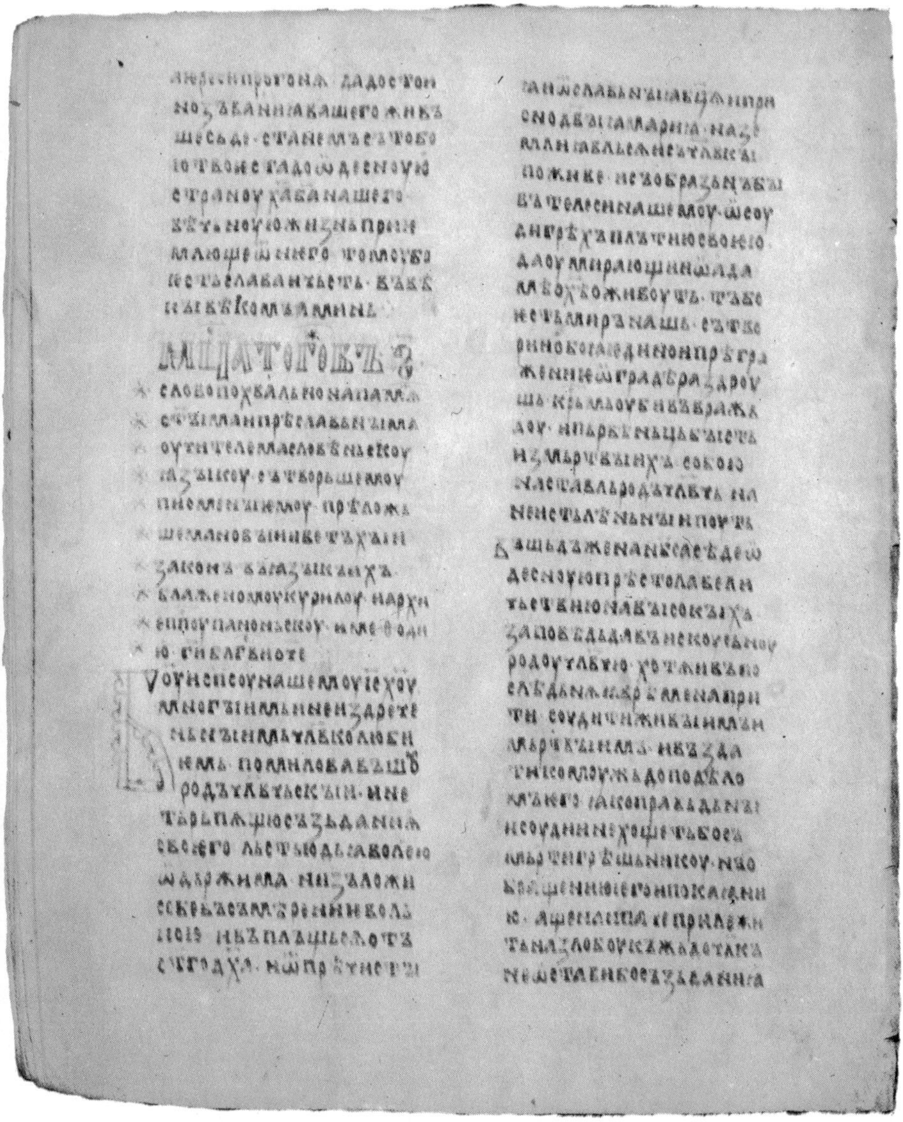

Flavius' *History* is by no means a dry historical account, but rather a literary, publicistic work. The author is tendentious. He does not hide his admiration for the mighty Roman emperors and his displeasure with his political opponents, the ordinary people of Judaea. Yet nor can he conceal his admiration for the courage of the rebels and his compassion for the sufferings that were their lot. The publicistic spirit of the work can be seen, in particular, in the speeches of Vespasian, Titus and Josephus himself (the author refers to himself in the third person). The main purpose of these speeches, which are constructed in full accordance with the rules of classical oratory, is to discredit the intentions of the rebels and extol the nobility and valour of the Romans. The stylistic art of Josephus Flavius is seen not only in the monologues and dialogues, but also in the descriptions, whether they are of the countryside of Judaea or its towns, battles or the terrible scenes of starvation in besieged Jerusalem; the rhythmic style, the vivid similes and metaphors, the apt epithets, and the concern for euphony (which is clearly evident in the original)—all this shows that the author attached great importance to the literary aspect of his work.

The Old Russian translator succeeded in preserving the literary merits of the original, its rich vocabulary, emotional speeches and lively descriptions. The translation also preserved the rhythmic segmentation of the sentences and parallelism of the syntactical constructions in the original. What is more, the translator independently expands the descriptions and makes them more concrete, replaces the indirect speech of the original by direct speech, adds new similes, metaphors and figures of speech that are traditional for Russian original works.[25] Thus, the translation of the *History* testifies to the skill of Old Russian writers in the eleventh and twelfth centuries.

The *History* was extremely popular. And not only because it described one of the most important events in world history. Full of military episodes, it was of great interest to Russian readers who had many times experienced the trials of war and hostile invasion. No wonder the chronicle writers of the twelfth and thirteenth centuries made use of favourite images or turns of phrase from the battle scenes of the *History.*

More than thirty manuscripts of the Old Russian translation of the *History* have survived. The oldest of these are to be found in the *Archive* and *Vilna* chronographs (late fifteenth and sixteenth centuries) which date back to a chronographical collection of the mid-thirteenth century.[26]

The Chronographical Alexandreid. Not later than the twelfth century a lengthy romance about the life and deeds of Alexander the Great, the so-called Pseudo-Callisthenes' *Alexandreid* (which was mistakenly attributed to Callisthenes, the historian who accompanied Alexander on his campaigns),was translated from the Greek. The original historico-biographical background of the story about Alexander in the *Alexandreid* can barely be traced. It is a typical adventure story of the Hellenic age, in which the life of the

Emperor of Macedonia is embellished with numerous legendary and fantastic details, and the main theme would appear to be the description of the strange lands that Alexander was supposed to have visited during his campaigns.[27]

One of the redactions of the *Alexandreid* was translated in Russia. This translation is found primarily in chronographical compilations, which is why it is called *The Chronographical Alexandreid* to distinguish it from *The Serbian Alexandreid* which came to Russia via the southern Slavs in the fifteenth century.

As already mentioned, the *Alexandreid* is not so much an historical romance or literary biography, as an adventure story, and Alexander himself also acquires some purely legendary features. For example, he is declared to be the son not of King Philip of Macedonia, but of the Egyptian King Nectanebes who appeared to Philip's wife Olympias in the form of the god Amon. The birth of Alexander is accompanied by magical signs: the earth quakes and there are peals of thunder. Contrary to history, the *Alexandreid* speaks of Alexander's campaign to Sicily and his conquest of Rome. This is no accident. The Macedonian general appears in the romance not only as the victor of the great power of Persia, but also as a hero who has conquered the whole world. The interpretation of Darius' death, for example, is typical. Mortally wounded by his satraps, King Darius himself gives Alexander the throne of Persia and with it his daughter Roxana to be his wife. In fact Roxana, one of Alexander's wives, was the daughter of a Bactrian satrap, not of Darius.

There are many exciting clashes in the romance. Thus, Alexander sets off to visit Darius dressed up as his own envoy and barely manages to escape recognition and captivity. Another time he pretends to be his friend and ally Antigones and comes to the Ethiopian Queen Candace whose son is thirsting to take vengeance on Alexander for killing his father-in-law, the Indian prince Porus. Candace recognises Alexander, and he manages to escape only because she conceals her guest's secret in gratitude for his saving her other son.

Alexander's death is also shrouded in mystery. A miraculous sign shows that his end is near: when he is dying, the sky darkens and a bright star comes out and gradually sinks into the sea.

The *Alexandreid* was included in Russian chronographical compilations and therefore regarded as an historical account of the famous hero of ancient times. But in fact Old Russian writers had made the acquaintance of a subject which was extremely popular in mediaeval European literature, and which formed the basis of numerous prose romances and poems written from the tenth to twelfth centuries in Italy, Germany, France and other countries.

In the second redaction of the *Alexandreid* (included in the second redaction of *The Hellenic and Roman Chronicle*) the element of entertainment was even stronger: the stories about Alexander's campaigns to strange lands inhabited by wondrous creatures were embellished with new details, episodes were added in which the hero goes up to heaven or descends to the bottom of the sea, etc. The *Alexandreid* in various redactions was an essential component of all Russian chronographical compilations and chronicles right up to the seventeenth century.[28]

The Deeds of Digenes. In the eleventh to twelfth centuries a translation was made of the Byzantine epic about the adventures of Digenes Akritas. The Greek original is not extant. Only some fourteenth- to sixteenth-century copies have survived of a Greek poem about Digenes which evidently reflects an earlier version of the work.[29]

The Old Russian translation of the tale of Digenes, usually called *The Deeds of Digenes,* recounts how Tsar Amir of Arabia carries off a beautiful young Greek girl. Her three brothers set off in pursuit and overpower him. He decides to become a Christian and settle in Greece with his beloved. The marriage of Tsar Amir and the Greek girl produces the child Digenes. Even in childhood he astounds everyone with his strength and courage: out hunting he strangles a bear with his bare hands and cleaves a lion in two. Later it tells of Digenes' victory over Philipapa[30] and the giant maiden Maximiana. Maximiana tells him that he will live sixteen years if he marries her and thirty-six if he marries Stratigovna. This makes Digenes seek the hand of Stratigovna. There is a detailed description of his wedding. In the Greek poem his betrothed has the name of Eudoxia, but in the Old Russian version she is called Stratigovna after her father Stratig (*strategus* is Greek for "general", and in the Russian version the title of a military rank is turned into a proper name). Digenes arrives on a splendid horse at the town where the girl lives, and parades under her window, singing "sweet songs". The young people meet, and Digenes begs Stratigovna to elope with him. She agrees, but Digenes believes that he will disgrace himself if he takes the girl away in the absence of her father and brothers, who are out hunting. So the young man waits for his beloved's relatives to return and takes her away openly almost before her father's eyes. Stratig is warned by his servants, but refuses to believe such a bold abduction possible. Digenes waits by the town walls for Stratig and his sons to come in pursuit of him, and overcomes them in battle. Stratig agrees to his daughter marrying Digenes. The families of the bride and bridegroom exchange gifts and a magnificent wedding is held. The final section of *The Deeds of Digenes* tells of his victory over Emperor Basil.

The Deeds of Digenes has all the features of the heroic epic. The hero is not only a handsome and valiant warrior, but his strength (like that of his mother's three brothers too) acquires totally fantastic features: he kills several thousand warriors at one go. For all its lack of authenticity the scene of the abduction of Stratigovna is most effective: Digenes rampages in her father's courtyard for three hours, challenging him to a duel and rending the gates with his spear, but Stratig insists stubbornly that not even a bird would dare to fly into his courtyard! The strength of Digenes' enemies is also greatly exaggerated. Thus, the *kmeti* (warriors) of Tsar Amir are capable of taking on a thousand singly and hordes in pairs.[31]

The Tale of Akir the Wise. A translation of *The Tale of Akir the Wise* was also known in Kievan Russia. This tale originated in Assyro-Babylon in the seventh century B.C.[32]

The *Tale* tells of how Akir, counsellor to King Sennacherib of Assyria and Nineveh, receives Divine instructions to adopt his nephew Anadan. He brings him up, teaches him all manner of wisdom (there is a list of Akir's exhortations to Anadan), and finally, presents him to the king as his pupil and successor. But Anadan starts misbehaving in Akir's house, and when his uncle tries to restrain him, he thinks up a cunning trick. Forging Akir's handwriting, Anadan writes some letters to make Sennacherib think that Akir is plotting treason. The king is dumbfounded by what appears to be his counsellor's treachery. Akir is too surprised to plead his innocence and merely begs that the death sentence demanded by Anadan be carried out by an old friend. Akir succeeds in persuading his friend of his innocence, and the friend executes a criminal instead of Akir, while Akir hides away.

Hearing of Akir's execution, the Egyptian pharaoh sends envoys to Sennacherib demanding that one of his counsellors should build a house between earth and heaven. Sennacherib is in despair: Anadan, on whom he had been relying, refuses to help, saying that only a god could perform such a task. Then Akir's friend tells the king that his disgraced counsellor is still alive. The king sends Akir to Egypt, where he answers all the riddles that the pharaoh puts to him. Then Akir makes the pharaoh take back his demand about building a house. Female eagles trained by Akir carry a boy up into the air who asks the Egyptians to hand him stones and mortar, which they cannot, of course. After receiving tribute for three years, Akir returns to Sennacherib, chains Anadan to the porch of his house and chastises him for the evil he has wrought. In vain Anadan begs for forgiveness. Unable to bear Akir's biting reproaches, he swells up "like a jug" and bursts with anger.

The tale's interest lies in its exciting plot: the evil cunning of Anadan who wrongfully accuses his foster-father, and the wisdom of Akir who finds a clever solution to all the difficult tasks that the pharaoh sets him produce many exciting situations in the work. Almost a quarter of the tale is taken up with Akir's exhortations to

Anadan; here we find maxims on friendship, justice, generosity, rules of conduct and denunciation of "evil women". Mediaeval writers were fond of wise sayings and aphorisms. In the various redactions and manuscripts of *The Tale of Akir* the list of maxims changes, but they always form part of its text.[33]

Natural History. Byzantine scholarship of the early mediaeval period was very closely bound up with theology. The world of nature, about which Byzantine scholars could obtain information both from their own observations and from the writings of the classical philosophers and naturalists, was seen primarily as living testimony to the wisdom of God who created the world, or as a kind of living allegory: natural phenomena, the behaviour of living creatures and the mineral world were regarded as the embodiment in living, material form of eternal truths, concepts or moral admonitions.

Byzantine scholarly writings of the early Middle Ages were known in Old Russia also. Although we cannot say precisely when certain translations appeared in Russia, it is possible that they were known there even before the Mongol invasion.

The Hexaëmeron. The hexaëmeron was extremely popular in mediaeval Christian literatures. It was a treatise on the Bible story of how God created the sky, the stars, the heavenly bodies, the earth, living creatures, plants and man in six days (hence the name of the book). This treatise turned into a compilation of all the information about animate and inanimate nature that Byzantine scholarship possessed. Of the many hexaëmerons that existed in Byzantine literature, for example, those of John, the Bulgarian Exarch, Severian of Gabala, and later Georgios Pisides were known in Old Russia.

The *Hexaëmeron* of John, the Bulgarian Exarch, is a compilative work based on the hexaëmerons of Basil the Great and Severian of Cabala, but the author also made use of a large number of other sources and added his own reflections. It consists of a prologue and six sections. They tell of the heavenly bodies and the earth, atmospheric phenomena, animals, plants and the nature of man himself. All this information, which sometimes reflects naturalist ideas of the day, and is sometimes obviously fantastic, is imbued with the same idea: admiration for the wisdom of God who has created such a fine, diverse and well ordered world. This idea from the *Hexaëmeron* attracted the attention of Vladimir Monomachos who quotes the work in his *Instruction* and marvels at "how the sky is made, the sun and the moon ... and the earth is placed on the waters", and how diverse are the birds and beasts.

The *Hexaëmeron* of John, the Bulgarian Exarch, was the most widespread in Russian literature. The oldest of the manuscripts in Soviet libraries is a Serbian one of 1263. Russian manuscripts belong to the fifteenth century and later, but the mention of the

Hexaëmeron by Vladimir Monomachos and the existence of fragments from it in a chronographical compilation of the thirteenth century indicate that a translation of the work existed in Russia much earlier.[34]

The Physiologos. Whereas the hexaëmeron was about nature as a whole, from heavenly bodies to plants and animals, another work, *The Physiologos*, dealt primarily with living creatures, both real (the lion, eagle, ant, whale, elephant, etc.) and imaginary (the phoenix, the siren, the centaur), and a few plants or precious stones (diamonds, flints, magnets and others).

Each account listed the properties of the creature or object, and then gave a symbolical interpretation of these properties. As a rule, however, the descriptions of animals, and particularly of plants or stones, are quite fantastic in *The Physiologos*, because the main aim was to find an analogy between the properties of the creature or object and some theological concept.[35]

Thus, for example, it says that when pelicans are born they begin to peck their parents until the latter are driven to killing them. After mourning their children for three days, the mother pierces her rib and her blood drips onto the young bringing them to life again. The behaviour of the pelican, *The Physiologos* declares, symbolises the fate of mankind which fell into sin, but was saved by Christ's blood shed for it. In the same way the fantastic story about lions (that the lioness gives birth to dead cubs, and the father brings them to life after three days by breathing on them) is also connected with the incarnation, death and resurrection of Christ.

Nevertheless these stories about animals are, as a rule, extremely entertaining: thus, it also says that the lion sleeps with its eyes open; the crocodile weeps as it devours its prey; the phoenix sets fire to itself on the altar, and a worm emerges from the ashes that turns into a fledgeling on the second day and a fully-grown bird on the third.

It also describes the behaviour of the fox: it pretends to be dead, and as soon as the birds alight and begin to peck it, it jumps up and catches them. The salamander, according to *The Physiologos*, puts out fire by entering it. Some redactions of the work say that after the death of its mate the lonely turtle-dove sits on a withered tree "lamenting its friend".[36]

We do not know of any manuscripts of *The Physiologos* before the beginning of the fifteenth century, but we can assume that there was a translation of it in Kievan Russia. It is interesting that in a letter from Prince Vladimir Monomachos of Kiev (who died in 1125) we find the same image of a turtle-dove weeping on a withered tree used to describe his dead son's widow.

The Christian Topography. The *Christian Topography* of Cosmas Indicopleustes was also known in Old Russia. Cosmas was a merchant who travelled to Egypt, Ethiopia and Arabia around the year 530. In spite of his nickname "Indicopleustes" ("sailor to India"), Cosmas appears not to have visited India itself and his information about this country is drawn from other people's accounts.

Illumination from **The Physiologos.** 15th century. **A Lion Breathing Life Into a New-Born Cub.** State Public Library, Leningrad

Cardinal Points. Illumination from *The Christian Topography* of Cosmas Indicopleustes. 17th century. Central State Archive of Ancient Documents

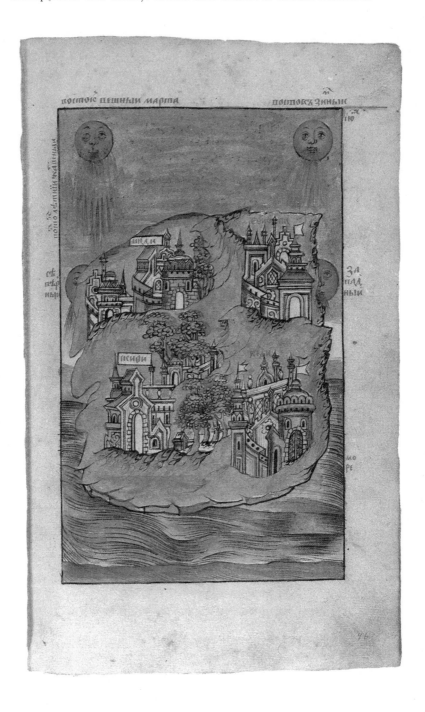

The work consists of twelve chapters which contain reflections on the structure of the universe. In particular, Cosmas states that the earth is flat, likening it and the sky above to a room with a vaulted ceiling. The sky that we see consists of water, but above it is another sky invisible to us. The movement of the heavenly bodies and atmospheric phenomena are guided by angels specially appointed for that purpose. The information about the animal and plant world of the countries Cosmas discusses is equally fantastic.

Fragments from the *Christian Topography* are found already in thirteenth-century manuscripts, although full copies of the work have survived only from a later period.[37]

3. The Earliest Chronicle-Writing

Let us now consider the original literature of Kievan Russia, i.e., that created by Russian writers. We already know that within a comparatively short time Russian writers became acquainted with a rich and varied translated literature. A whole system of genres was transplanted to new soil: chronicles, historical tales, *vitae*, paterica, apocryphal stories, sermons and homilies. These translated works enriched Russian writers with information about history and the natural world, and introduced them to the ancient myths and epics, to different types of subject matter, styles, and narrative.

But it would be quite wrong to assume that this was the only literary school for Old Russian translators and writers. They were greatly influenced by the rich traditions of folklore, above all by the traditions of the Slavonic epos.

As we shall see later, epic folk legends are an exceptionally vivid literary phenomenon without analogy in the works of translated literature known to us. The Old Russian writers made use of the rich traditions of public oratory: the short speeches in which the princes urged on their warriors before battle, the speeches of witnesses and judges at trials, the speeches uttered at meetings of the *veche,** the speeches with which princes dispatched their envoys to other princes or foreign rulers, and so on. Agreements, legal documents and decrees also played a part in the formation of the Russian literary language.[38]

Turning to an analysis of the first original literary works of Kievan Russia, we shall also see that this literature is distinctive not only in its language, not only in its system of imagery and subject

---

* Popular assembly in mediaeval Russian towns.

matter, but also in respect to its genres: the Russian chronicles, *The Lay of Igor's Host,* the *Instruction* of Vladimir Monomachos, the *Supplication* of Daniel the Exile and certain other works have no analogy among the genres of Byzantine and Bulgarian literatures.

One of the first and most important genres to emerge in Russian literature was that of chronicle-writing.

The historical memory of the Eastern Slav peoples stretched back several centuries: stories and legends were handed down from generation to generation about the settling of the Slavonic tribes, the clash of the Slavs with the Avars, the founding of Kiev, and the splendid deeds of the early princes of Kiev.

The emergence of a written language made it possible to record oral historical legends and to write down all the most important events of the day. This was the beginning of chronicle-writing. And chronicle-writing was for many centuries, right up to the seventeenth century, not a simple year-by-year account of events, but a leading literary genre, within which the Russian fictional narrative developed.

Byzantine and Russian Chronicles. Scholars of the nineteenth century and the beginning of the present one believed that Russian chronicle-writing emerged as an imitation of Byzantine chronography. Yet the Byzantine chronicles were not used by Russian writers in the early stage of the development of Russian chronicle-writing. Moreover, most Russian chronicles are based on a different principle. In the Byzantine chronicles (for example, the *Chronicle* of Georgios Hamartolos or that of John Malalas) the country's history is presented as a series of short biographies of the rulers, without any mention of the date of their accession to the throne, removal or death, but only the length of their reign. The structure of the Russian chronicle was fundamentally different: the very name of the genre ("chronicle" in Russian— *letopis*—from *leto*—year and *pisat*—to write) tells us that we are dealing with annals, yearly records. Each item begins with the words "in the year ...", followed by the date from the Creation and a list of events that took place in this particular year in Russia and sometimes in neighbouring states also. Together with reports of the births and deaths of princes, their marriages, diplomatic and military acts, the chronicles contain information about the building and consecration of churches, natural disasters, rare atmospherical or astronomical phenomena—in brief, all events which the chronicler considers worthy of attention and of being preserved for posterity. Consequently, the chronicle is not only a literary work, but also an historical document, first and foremost, thanks to its attempt to record and interpret all historical events of

importance. True, sometimes the chronicle narrative ignores the year-by-year principle of exposition: when political clashes extend over several years, the chronicler is compelled to depart from a strict chronology and narrate the event from beginning to end. This type of exposition is characteristic of chronicle tales, but it is not they that determined the structure of the chronicle as a whole.

Both chronicles and chronographs were compilations. The chronicler could not describe all the events from his own impressions and observations, albeit for the fact that he sought to begin his exposition from the "very beginning" (i.e., from the Creation, the formation of this or that state, etc.). Consequently, the chronicler was forced to draw on existing sources for an account of more ancient times. On the other hand, the chronicler could not simply continue the work of his predecessor. Firstly, because each chronicler usually tried to pursue his own political line and altered his predecessor's text accordingly, not only omitting material that he considered of little importance or politically unacceptable, but also inserting extracts from new sources, thereby creating his own version of the chronicle narrative different from that of his predecessors. Secondly, to prevent the work with the new information it had acquired in the latest redaction from becoming too large (many chronicles are made up of large folios with several hundred sheets in each), the chronicler had to sacrifice something, and therefore omitted the material that he considered least significant.

All this makes it very hard to study chronicle compilations, establish their sources and characterise the work of each chronicler. It has proved particularly difficult to reconstruct the history of the earliest Russian chronicle-writing, since the only extant manuscripts belong to a much later period (*The Novgorod Chronicle* of the thirteenth and fourteenth centuries, *The Laurentian Chronicle* of 1377, and *The Hypatian Chronicle* of the early fifteenth century), and do not reflect the earliest chronicle compilations, only later redactions of them.

Therefore the history of the earliest chronicle-writing is to some extent hypothetical. The most acceptable and authoritative hypothetical reconstruction is that of Academician Alexei Shakhmatov, which literary specialists and historians use in their study of most monuments of Kievan Russia.[39] It is based on careful examination and comparison of all the main chronicle compilations up to the sixteenth century in which the early chronicle-writing has been preserved to some extent or other. Therefore Shakhmatov's works are of value not only for their conclusions, but also for the method that he elaborated of studying chronicle texts. This method has been adopted by his followers, in particular, Mikhail Priselkov, Arseny Nasonov, and Dmitry Likhachev as well as many others. Shakhmatov's hypotheses have been expanded and amplified by his followers.[40]

The Early Chronicle-Writing. The earliest extant chronicle compilation is *The Tale of Bygone Years* which is dated at about 1113. However, as Shakhmatov has proved, the *Tale* was preceded by other chronicle compilations.

Among the facts which led Shakhmatov to the conclusion that marked the beginning of many years of enquiry in the field of early Russian chronicle-writing was the following: *The Tale of Bygone Years*, which has been preserved in the *Laurentian, Hypatian* and other chronicles, differs considerably in its treatment of many events from another chronicle that deals with the same early period of Russian history, *The Novgorod First Chronicle* of the younger recension. *The Novgorod Chronicle* does not contain the texts of treaties with the Greeks, Prince Oleg is called a *voevoda* serving the young Prince Igor, the campaigns against Constantinople are described differently, etc.

Shakhmatov concluded that the first part of *The Novgorod First Chronicle* was based on a different chronicle compilation that had preceded *The Tale of Bygone Years.*

At the present time the history of the earliest chronicle-writing is reconstructed as follows.

Oral historical legends existed long before chronicle-writing; with the emergence of a written language records of historical events began to appear, but chronicle-writing as a genre did not emerge until the reign of Yaroslav the Wise (1019-1054). During this time Russia which had adopted Christianity began to find the tutelage of the Byzantine Church irksome and sought to establish its right to ecclesiastical independence, for Byzantium was inclined to regard the states in whose conversion it had played a part as the spiritual flock of the Constantinople Patriarchate and also sought to turn them into its vassals politically.

It was precisely this that Yaroslav was opposing when .he appointed a Russian, Hilarion, as Metropolitan of Kiev and sought the canonisation of the first Russian saints, princes Boris and Gleb. These actions were intended to strengthen Russia's ecclesiastical and political independence of Byzantium and enhance the authority of the young Slavonic state.

Kievan scribes argued that the history of Old Russia was like the history of other Christian states. Here too there had been early converts who had sought by their personal example to encourage the people to accept the new religion: Princess Olga was christened in Constantinople and urged her son Svyatoslav to become a Christian too. There were martyrs in Old Russia as well, for example, the Varangian and his son who were torn to pieces by the pagan crowd for refusing to sacrifice to pagan gods. And there were saints—the princes Boris and Gleb who were murdered on the orders of their brother Svyatopolk, but did not violate the Christian precepts of brotherly love and obedience to the senior in succession. Russia even had its Prince Vladimir, who christened his people, thereby likening himself to Constantine the Great, the emperor who established Christianity as the official religion of Byzantium.

It was to support this idea, Dmitry Likhachev assumes,[41] that a collection of legends on the emergence of Christianity in Russia was compiled. It included stories about the christening and the death of Princess Olga, about the Varangian Christians, the Christianisation of Russia, the princes Boris and Gleb and, finally, a lengthy eulogy of Yaroslav the Wise (which is reflected in *The Tale of Bygone Years* under the year 1037). All these six legends, in Likhachev's opinion, show "that they belong to the same hand ... and are very closely interrelated: compositionally, stylistically and ideologically".[42]

This collection of legends (which Dmitry Likhachev tentatively calls *The Tale of the Spread of Christianity in Russia*) may have been compiled in the early 1040s by scribes in the chancellery of the Metropolitan of Kiev.

The next stage in the development of Russian chronicle-writing is the 1060s and 1070s. Alexei Shakhmatov links it with the activity of Nikon, a monk in the Kiev Crypt Monastery. He bases his argument on the following observation. After a quarrel with Prince Izyaslav, Nikon left the Crypt Monastery, fled to remote Tmutorokan (a principality on the eastern shore of the Black Sea on the Taman Peninsula), and did not return to Kiev until 1074. Shakhmatov draws attention to the fact that Nikon always seems to be "accompanied" by precise dates in the chronicle; the entries for the 1060s contain no precise dates for the events that took place in Kievan Russia, but there is detailed information (which even mentions the day on which an event took place) about what happened in Tmutorokan: how Prince Gleb was driven out by Rostislav Vladimirovich, and how Rostislav himself was poisoned by a certain *kotopan* (Greek priest).

It is possible that in this chronicle compilation the stories about the first Russian princes, Oleg, Igor and Olga, were added to the stories about the spread of Christianity in Russia. Finally, Nikon (if he really did compile this collection) probably added the legend that the dynasty of Russian princes holding the throne of the Grand Prince of Kiev was descended not from Igor, but from the Varangian prince Rurik, who was summoned by the Novgorodians. In addition Rurik is said to be the father of Igor, and the Kievan prince Oleg is presented by the chronicler as a *voevoda* serving first Rurik, and after his death, Igor.[43]

This legend was of considerable political and ideological significance. Firstly, in the Middle Ages the founder of the ruling dynasty was often declared to be a foreigner: this (the creators of such legends hoped) did away with the question of seniority and priority among the local dynasties. Secondly, recognition of the fact that the princes of Kiev were descended from a prince invited by the Slavs to bring "order" to Russia, was bound to give great authority to the reigning princes of Kiev. Thirdly, the legend turned all the Russian princes into "brothers" and proclaimed the legality of one princely family only—the line of Rurik.

In feudal times none of the chronicler's hopes were destined to work out, but the legend of the "summoning of the Varangians" became one of the basic ideas of Russian mediaeval historiography. Many centuries later it was resurrected and raised aloft on the shield of the Normanists, the school of thought that argued the foreign origin of the Russian state system.[44]

Scholars also assume that it was in the 1060s that the chronicle account took on the characteristic form of yearly entries (annals) which, as already mentioned, is a fundamental distinction between Russian and Byzantine chronicles.

The Primary Chronicle. Around 1095 a new chronicle was compiled, which Alexei Shakhmatov suggests calling *The Primary Chronicle.* He argues convincingly that *The Primary Chronicle* was preserved in *The Novgorod First Chronicle,* although in somewhat revised form. Thus, with a high degree of probability we can pick out from the extant text of *The Tale of Bygone Years* (the chronicle created on the basis of *The Primary Chronicle*) the material which originally belonged to this *Primary Chronicle.*

The compiler of *The Primary Chronicle* continued Nikon's work, extending the account of events from 1073 to 1095 and giving his narrative in this new section a distinctly publicistic tone, reproaching the princes for their internecine wars and complaining that they showed no concern for the defence of Russian land and did not heed the counsel of wise men.[45] Apart from Russian sources, the chronicler also drew on the oldest Russian chronographic compilation, *The Great Narrative Chronicle,* from which he inserted several fragments in his chronicle account: the story of the campaign by Höskuld and Dyri against Constantinople (found in *The Tale of Bygone Years* under the year 866), the story of Igor's campaign against Constantinople (under 941) and the story of the miraculous signs that occurred during the reigns of King Antiochus of Syria, the Roman Emperor Nero and the Byzantine emperors Justinian, Mauritius and Constantine (under 1065).

The Tale of Bygone Years. At the beginning of the 12th century (around 1113 it is assumed) *The Primary Chronicle* was again revised, this time by the monk Nestor of the Kiev Crypt Monastery. Nestor's work became known among specialists as *The Tale of Bygone Years* from the opening words of its lengthy title: "*Se povesti vremyanykh let...*" (that is, "This tale of bygone years, of the origins of the Russian land, the first to rule in Kiev and how the Russian land came to be.").[46]

Nestor was a scribe of great historical vision and literary skill: before his work on *The Tale of Bygone Years,* he wrote a *Life of SS Boris and Gleb* and a *Life of St Theodosius of the Caves.* Nestor set himself the impressive task of not only adding to *The Primary Chronicle* a description of the events of the late eleventh and early twelfth centuries, which were within his lifetime, but also of radically revising the account of the early period of Russian history.

Nestor brings the history of Russia into the mainstream of world history. He begins his chronicle with an account of the Bible story about the division of the earth between the sons of Noah. Quoting a long list of the peoples of the world (which he borrowed from the *Chronicle* of Georgios Hamartolos), Nestor inserts a reference to the Slavs; in another passage the Slavs are identified with the "Noricans", the inhabitants of a province of the Roman Empire on the banks of the Danube. Nestor gives a detailed account of the Ancient Slavs and the territory occupied by the different Slavonic tribes, with special detail about the tribes that inhabited the territory of Rus (Old Russia), in particular, about the "gentle and mild disposition" of the Polyane, on whose lands the town of Kiev was built. Nestor amplifies and develops Nikon's Varangian story: the Varangian princes Höskuld and Dyri mentioned in *The Primary Chronicle* are now declared to be boyars of Rurik's (and not even "of his tribe") and the campaign against Byzantium in the reign of Emperor Michael is ascribed to them. Having established from official documents (the texts of treaties with the Greeks) that Oleg was not Igor's *voevoda* but was a prince in his own right, Nestor proffers a version according to which Oleg was a relative of Rurik's and acted as regent during Igor's minority.[47]

At the same time Nestor includes some new (by comparison with *The Primary Chronicle*) historical folk legends, such as the story of Olga's fourth revenge on the Drevlyane and the tales of the combat of the young tanner with the giant Pecheneg and the siege of Belgorod by the Pechenegs.

So it is to Nestor that *The Tale of Bygone Years* owes its historical breadth of vision, the insertion of information about world history against the background of which the history of the Slavs, and subsequently of Old Russia, is developed. It is Nestor who elaborates and polishes the story about descent of the Russian princely dynasty from a "summoned" Norman prince. Nestor actively supported the ideal state organisation of Russia proclaimed by Yaroslav the Wise, namely, that all the princes were brothers and that they should all submit to the most senior brother who held the throne of the Grand Prince of Kiev.

Thanks to Nestor's statesmanlike views, breadth of vision and literary talent *The Tale of Bygone Years* was "not merely a collection of facts about Russian history, nor an historico-publicistic work concerning the pressing, though transient tasks of Russian life, but a complete history of Russia expounded in literary form".[48]

It is assumed that the first redaction of *The Tale of Bygone Years* is not extant. What has survived is the second redaction compiled in 1117 by Abbot Sylvester of the Vydubitsky Monastery outside Kiev and the third redaction compiled in 1118 on the orders of Prince Mstislav Vladimirovich. In the second redaction only the final section of the *Tale* was revised; it is this redaction that has survived in *The Laurentian Chronicle* of 1377 and other later chronicles. The third redaction is to be found in *The Hypatian Chronicle*, the oldest copy of which, the Hypatian MS, dates back to the first quarter of the fifteenth century.

This redaction contains some interesting references to sources on world history. Under the year 1110 the chronicler quotes an extract from the *Josippon*, a mediaeval chronicle of Jewish history (which is known to have been translated from Hebrew to Russian),[49] the story of how an angel forbade Alexander the Great to wage war on Jerusalem. Under the year 1114 in northern legends which say that newborn reindeer fall from clouds onto the earth, the chronicler quotes an extract from a chronicle (presumably *The Great Narrative Chronicle*) about wheat, bits of silver and even pincers falling from the sky, after which people learned to forge metal. Further on is a story about Egyptian women that comes from the *Chronicle of John Malalas*.[50]

The Composition of *The Tale of Bygone Years*. Let us now examine the composition of *The Tale of Bygone Years* as we find it in the *Laurentian* and *Radziwill* chronicles.

The introductory part contains the Bible story of the division of the earth between Noah's three sons, Shem, Ham and Japhet, and the story about the Tower of Babel that led to the branching of a "single stem" into seventy-two peoples, each with their own language. Having established that the "Slavonic people" is from the tribe of Japhet, the chronicle goes on to talk about the Slavs, the lands inhabited by them, and the history and customs of the Slavonic tribes. The chronicle gradually narrows down the subject of its narrative, concentrating on the history of the Polyane, and gives an account of the founding of Kiev. Speaking of ancient times when the Kievan Polyane paid tribute to the Khazars, *The Tale of Bygone Years* notes proudly that now, as had been long foreordained, the Khazars render tribute to the Kievan princes.

Precise references to the year begin with 852 in the *Tale*, because it was from that date, the chronicler says, that Russia is mentioned in "Greek chronicle-writing". This was the year when the Kievan princes Höskuld and Dyri attacked Constantinople. This is immediately followed by a chronological list of the number of years that passed between one important event and the next. The list finishes with the number of years "from the death of

Yaroslav to the death of Svyatopolk" (i.e., from 1054 to 1113). Hence it follows that *The Tale of Bygone Years* could not have been compiled before the beginning of the second decade of the twelfth century.

The chronicle goes on to recount the major events of the ninth century, the "summoning of the Varangians", the campaign against Byzantium of Höskuld and Dyri, and the taking of Kiev by Oleg. The story of the origin of the Slavonic written language in the chronicle finishes with the statement, which is important for the general purpose of *The Tale of Bygone Years*, that the Slavonic and Russian languages are identical, yet another reference to the place of the Polyane among the Slavonic peoples and of the Slavs among the peoples of the world.

Then follows an account of the reign of Oleg. The chronicle quotes the texts of his treaties with Byzantium and the popular legends about the prince: the story of his campaign against Constantinople with vivid episodes of an undoubted folkloric character—Oleg arrives at the city walls in boats that have sailed over dry land and hangs his shield on the gates of Constantinople as a sign of victory. This is followed by the legend of Oleg's death: a magician predicts that he will be killed by his favourite horse. The prince decides never to mount it again and tries not to set eyes on it. A few years later he learns that his horse is dead and laughs at the false prophesy. He wants to see the dead horse's bones. The prince is taken to the spot where the remains of his favourite lie. He stamps on the horse's skull, and at that moment a snake slithers out of the skull and bites the prince. Oleg immediately falls ill and dies. This chronicle story was used by Alexander Pushkin as the subject of his ballad "The Song of Oleg the Seer".

The chronicle story of Oleg's death is accompanied by a lengthy extract from the *Chronicle* of Georgios Hamartolos; the reference to the Byzantine chronicle was intended to stress that prophesies by pagan wise men sometimes come true, and that therefore it was not reprehensible for a Christian chronicler to include the story of Oleg's death predicted by a magician.

Oleg's successor to the throne of Kiev was Igor, whom the chronicler considers to be one of Rurik's sons. There is an account of Igor's two campaigns against Byzantium and the text of the treaty which he concluded in 945 with the Byzantine emperors and co-rulers, Romanus, Constantine and Stephanus. Igor's death was unexpected and ignominious: on the advice of his bodyguard he went to the land of the Drevlyane to collect tribute (this tribute was usually collected by his military deputy Sveinald). On the return journey the prince suddenly turned and said to his

The Tale of Bygone Years. The Byzantine Emperor with His Courtiers. Byzantine Envoys Bring a Sword to Prince Svyatoslav of Kiev. Illumination from *The Radziwill Chronicle.* 15th century. Academy of Sciences Library, Leningrad

warriors: "You return home with the tribute we have collected, but I shall go round their lands once again." Hearing that Igor wished to collect tribute a second time, the Drevlyane grew angry: "When a wolf takes to visiting a flock of sheep, he will destroy the lot of them, if he is not killed. And so it is with this one: he will destroy the lot of us, if we do not kill him." And Igor was killed by the Drevlyane.

The chronicle then recounts the popular legends of how Igor's widow, Olga, avenged herself three times on the Drevlyane for the murder of her husband.

After they had killed the prince, the Drevlyane sent messengers to Olga in Kiev inviting her to marry their prince Mal. Olga pretended to be flattered by the proposal and ordered the messengers to appear the next day, not on horseback, nor on foot, but in a very unusual way: the princess ordered the Kievans to bring the Drevlyane to the royal palace in a boat. She also had a deep pit dug by her chambers. When the triumphant Drevlyane messengers (who were sitting in a boat "putting on airs", the chronicler stresses) were borne into the palace courtyard, Olga ordered them to be cast together with the boat into the pit. Walking up to the edge, the princess called down mockingly: "Have you been rendered fine homage?" "We fare worse than Igor in his hour of death," the Drevlyane replied. And Olga had them buried alive in the pit.

The second delegation, which consisted of high-ranking Drevlyane, Olga had burnt in the bath-house whence they had been invited to "wash themselves". Finally, the princess gave orders for a retinue of Drevlyane sent to meet her and escort her to Mal with all honours to be murdered during the funeral repast by Igor's grave.

Careful examination of the legends of how Olga revenged herself thrice on the Drevlyane reveals the symbolic significance underlying the story. Each act of revenge corresponds to an element in the pagan funeral rite. According to the customs of that time high-born dead were buried after being lain in a boat; a bath was prepared for the dead man, and then his body was burnt. On the day of the burial a repast accompanied by military games was held.[51]

This story of Olga's three acts of revenge was included in *The Primary Chronicle.* Another story, about the princess' fourth act of revenge, was inserted in *The Tale of Bygone Years.*

After murdering the Drevlyane retinue, Olga failed to capture their capital, the town of Iskorosten. So she thought up another stratagem. She addressed the besieged inhabitants, saying that she did not intend to impose a heavy tribute on them, as Igor had, but asking for three sparrows and three doves from each household. The unsuspecting Drevlyane willingly sent her what she asked. Then Olga ordered her warriors to tie burning tinder to the birds' legs and let them go. The birds flew off to their nests, and soon the whole town was on fire. Those who sought to flee from the fire were taken captive by Olga's men. Thus, according to the legend, Princess Olga avenged her husband's death.

Then follows an account of Olga's visit to Constantinople. Olga did visit Constantinople in 957 and was received by the Emperor Constantine Porphyrogenitus. The story of how she outwitted him is sheer fantasy, however. According to it, Olga was christened in Constantinople, and Constantine was her godfather. When the emperor suggested that she should marry him, however, Olga said: "How can you want to make me your wife, when you yourself have christened me and called me daughter?"

The chronicler gives an admiring description of Igor's son, Svyatoslav, his military prowess and chivalry (he is said to have warned his enemies in advance: "I am coming to get you"), and his modest daily needs. The chronicle tells of his campaigns against Byzantium: how he almost reached Constantinople and planned to conquer the Balkan countries and move his capital to the Danube, for there, to quote his own words, "is the centre of the earth" where all riches abound—precious metals, precious fabrics, wine, horses and slaves. But this was not to be: Svyatoslav was ambushed and killed by the Pechenegs at the Dnieper rapids.

After Svyatoslav's death fighting broke out between his sons, Oleg, Yaropolk and Vladimir. Vladimir emerged the victor and became the sole ruler of Russia in 980.

In the section of *The Tale of Bygone Years* that deals with Vladimir's reign, considerable space is devoted to the conversion of Russia. The chronicle quotes the so-called *Philosopher's Discourse*, which a Greek missionary is said to have addressed to Vladimir to persuade him to accept Christianity. This discourse was highly edifying for the Old Russian reader, primarily because it set out, in concise but sufficiently detailed form, the Bible story about the Creation, the fall of Adam and Eve, the Flood, the lives of the patriarchs Abraham, Isaac and Moses, Joshua and the judges and kings of Israel. Then follows a number of sayings by the prophets predicting the birth, crucifixion and resurrection of Christ, and an account of the main events in the New Testament story from the Annunciation to Christ's appearance to his disciples after his resurrection. *The Philosopher's Discourse* is followed by an item in which the chronicler polemises with the "Latins", i.e., Catholics. This item could only have appeared in the chronicle text in the second half of the eleventh century, when the breach between the churches occurred and the differences of opinion between Orthodoxy and Catholicism became acute.

Many popular legends grew up around Vladimir's name. They too are reflected in the chronicle, in the stories about the prince's generosity, his huge banquets to which almost all his men were invited, the feats of the nameless heroes who lived during his reign—about the victory of the young tanner over the giant Pecheneg or the old man whose wisdom rescued the town of Belgorod from a siege by the Pechenegs.

After Vladimir's death in 1015, strife broke out between his sons. Svyatopolk, the son of Yaropolk and a captive nun whom Vladimir made his wife after killing his brother, murdered his two

Cathedral of St Sophia in Kiev. 11th century. Present appearance

step-brothers Boris and Gleb. The chronicle contains a short account of the fate of the martyr princes and the struggle between Yaroslav, son of Vladimir, and Svyatopolk, which ended in the military defeat of the latter and terrible Divine retribution. When Svyatopolk sought to flee after his defeat in battle, an "evil spirit descended" upon him. His "bones grew weak" and he could not sit in the saddle, so his retainers had to carry him on a stretcher. Svyatopolk felt that something was pursuing him, and he urged on his men. "Pursued by Divine wrath", Svyatopolk died in the "wilderness" (a wild, uninhabited spot) between Poland and Bohemia, and from his grave, the chronicle tells us, "comes ... a vile stench". The chronicler takes this opportunity to stress that Svyatopolk's terrible death should serve as a warning to the Russian princes not to resume their fratricidal quarrels. This idea will echo many a time from the pages of the chronicle: in the account of the death of Yaroslav, in the description of the discord between his sons in the 1070s, and in the story of the blinding of Prince Vasilko of Terebovl by his blood brothers David and Svyatopolk.

Under the year 1037 we find an account of the building in Yaroslav's reign (in particular, the founding of the famous Cathedral of St Sophia in Kiev and the city walls with the Golden Gate, etc.) and a reference to his love of books. The prince not only read books constantly himself, but also ordered many Greek books to be translated into Russian. Of great importance is Yaroslav's dying behest to his sons under the year 1054 to live in peace, cherish the land of their fathers and grandfathers which they had acquired "by their great labour" and obey the senior among them—the Prince of Kiev.

Annual entries in *The Tale of Bygone Years* alternate with stories and accounts sometimes only indirectly connected with the political history of Russia which, in fact, should be the main concern of a chronicle. Thus, under the year 1051 we find a lengthy account of the founding of the Kiev Crypt Monastery. This subject is continued later on in *The Tale of Bygone Years*: the entry for 1074 tells of the death of the monastery's abbot, Theodosius, and describes episodes from the saintly lives of Theodosius and other monks in the monastery; the entry for 1091 describes the transfer of Theodosius' relics and contains a eulogy to the saint. In connection with the Polovtsians' incursions into Russia the chronicler reflects in the entry for 1068 on the causes of the misfortunes suffered by the Russian land and explains the "presence of other tribes" as Divine punishments for sins. In the entry for 1071 we find an account of an uprising in the Rostov lands led by magicians; the chronicler reflects on the wiles of evil

spirits and quotes two more stories connected with the preceding one: about an inhabitant of Novgorod who had his fortune told by a sorcerer and about the appearance of a magician in Novgorod.

In 1093 the Russian princes were defeated by the Polovtsians. This event provided the chronicler with an occasion to reflect once more on why God "punishes the Russian land", why "the streets are filled with lamentation". There is a dramatic description of Russian captives being driven to foreign lands, "tormented, grief-stricken, exhausted, suffering from cold, hunger, thirst and hardships", saying tearfully to one another: "I was from that town" or "I was from that village". As mentioned above, it is possible that this item was the last in *The Primary Chronicle.*

The last decade of the eleventh century was full of turbulent events. After the internecine wars, the instigator and invariable participant of which was Oleg Svyatoslavich (*The Lay of Igor's Host* calls him Oleg Gorislavich meaning the Wretched), the princes assembled in 1097 at a conference in Lyubech* at which it was decided to live henceforth in peace and friendship, to hold their patrimony and not to encroach upon other principalities. Immediately after the conference, however, another foul deed was committed: Prince David of Volhynia persuaded Prince Svyatopolk of Kiev that Prince Vasilko of Terebovl was plotting against him. Svyatopolk and David lured Vasilko to Kiev, captured him, imprisoned him and put out his eyes. This event horrified all the other princes: Vladimir Monomachos, the chronicler writes, lamented that never before had such an evil deed been committed in Russia "not in our grandfathers' time, nor our fathers'". In the entry for 1097 we find a detailed account of the dramatic fate of Vasilko of Terebovl. It was probably written specially for the chronicle and is included in full.

Types of Chronicle Narrative. This account of the composition of *The Tale of Bygone Years* confirms the complexity of its content and the variety of its components in terms of both origin and genre. Apart from the brief annual entries there are texts of documents, popular legends, stories and extracts from translations.[52] We find both a theological treatise, *The Philosopher's Discourse,* a hagiographical type of story about Boris and Gleb, the patericon legends about the monks of the Crypt Monastery, a religious eulogy of St Theodosius of the Caves, and a simple story about an inhabitant of Novgorod who set off to have his fortune told by a sorcerer.

The genre of the chronicle is a very complex one: the chronicle is one of the "unifying genres" that subordinate the

---

* A town on the Dnieper to the west of Chernigov.

Virgin Orans. Mosaic in the apse of the Cathedral of St Sophia in Kiev. 11th century

Cathedral of St Sophia in Kiev. 11th century. Reconstruction

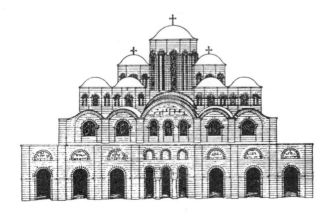

Bear Hunting. Fresco in the north section of the Cathedral of St Sophia in Kiev. 11th century

Two Mummers Fighting. Fresco in the north section of the Cathedral of St Sophia in Kiev. 11th century

genres of their component parts—the historical tale, the *vitae,* the homily, the eulogy and so on.[53] Nevertheless the chronicle is an integral work, which can be studied both as a work of a single genre and as a literary work.[54]

In *The Tale of Bygone Years,* as in any other chronicle, one can distinguish two types of narrative—the actual annual records and the chronicle stories. The annual records contain *reports* of events, while the chronicle stories offer *descriptions* of them. In the chronicle story the author strives to depict the event, to provide this or that concrete detail, to reproduce the dialogue of the personages, in brief, to help the reader to experience what is taking place, to arouse his emotions.

Thus, the story of the youth who flees from Kiev when it is besieged by the Pechenegs in order to deliver a request from Princess Olga to her commander Pretich, not only mentions the actual fact of the message being delivered, but also *recounts* how the boy runs through the Pecheneg camp with a bridle in his hand asking about his horse which has disappeared (and does not omit the important detail that the boy could speak the language of the Pechenegs), how he reaches the banks of the Dnieper, pulls off his clothes and dives into the water, and how Pretich's men sail out to meet him in a boat; the dialogue between Pretich and the Pecheneg prince is also reported. This is a story, not a brief annual entry like, for example, "Svyatoslav conquered the Vyatichi and lay them under tribute"; "Vladimir founded the [cathedral of] Saint Sophia in Novgorod", or "Vyacheslav, son of Yaroslav, died in Smolensk, and Igor was brought from Vladimir and enthroned in Smolensk", etc.

At the same time the chronicle stories themselves can also be divided into two types, largely determined by their origin. Some describe events that occurred in the chronicler's lifetime, others events that happened long before the chronicle was compiled. The latter are oral epic legends that were inserted in the chronicle later.

These epic legends are as a rule very entertaining: the events which they describe are exciting or impressive and the heroes are very strong, wise or cunning. They almost invariably contain an element of surprise.

The story of the young tanner (under the entry for 992) is based on the element of surprise. A Pecheneg prince who is fighting against Russia asks Vladimir to choose a warrior from his men who will try his strength against a huge Pecheneg. No one accepts the challenge. Vladimir is despondent, but then an old man comes to him and offers to send for his youngest son, who, the old man says, has been so strong since childhood that no one can get the better of him. One day, the father recalls, the son got angry with him and tore with his bare hands the piece of leather they were working (the old man is also a tanner). The youth is brought to Vladimir and demonstrates his strength to the prince by catching hold of a bull that is driven past him and pulling out a handful of its flesh. But the youth is short, and the giant Pecheneg who is "fearsome and great of stature" laughs at his opponent when he comes out to do combat with him. Here (as in the story of Olga's revenge) a surprise awaits the evil character; the reader already knows about the youth's strength and rejoices when the tanner strangles the huge Pecheneg with his bare hands.*

In another story it is not strength, but cunning that wins the day. Under the entry for 997 we read how the Pechenegs besieged the town of Belgorod (south of Kiev) and were sure that the inhabitants would surrender very soon, for there was "great hunger" in the town. And indeed the townsmen decided at a meeting of the *veche* to open the gates to the enemy. "They will kill some, but others will be spared," the people said. Otherwise everyone would starve to death. But a certain old man suggested a different solution. On his advice they dug two wells, in which they put tubs of *tsezh* (the mixture from which they made jelly) and *syta* (honey diluted with water). Then they invited the Pecheneg envoys into the town and said to them:

"Why destroy yourselves? Surely you don't think you can overcome us? What harm can you do us, even if you stay for ten years? We can get food out of the ground." The envoys marvelled at the "magic wells" and persuaded their princes to lift the siege.

The Epic Style in the Chronicle. These chronicle stories are united by a special, epic style of depicting reality. This concept reflects, first and foremost, the attitude of the narrator towards the object he is depicting, his own standpoint, and not only the purely linguistic features of the exposition.[55]

These stories are characterised by an exciting plot, anonymous heroes (a young tanner, an old man from Belgorod, a Kievan who informs the commander Pretich of Olga's decision—in the story about the siege of Kiev under the entry for 968), and short but lively dialogues; against the overall laconic description one or two details important for the development of the plot are singled out (the bridle in the youth's hand, the detailed account of how the "magic wells" were dug in the story about the siege of Belgorod).

---

* The popular character of the story is evident in the fact that the tanner's professionally strong hands, which have to tan leather, help him to conquer the giant Pecheneg.

The Tale of Bygone Years. **The Blinding of Vasilko of Terebovl.** Illumination from *The Radziwill Chronicle.* 15th century. Academy of Sciences Library, Leningrad

91

At the centre of each of these stories is a single event, a single episode, and it is this episode that characterises the hero, picks out his salient feature. In the story about the campaign against Constantinople· Oleg is, first and foremost, the wise and brave warrior. The hero of the story about the siege of Belgorod is an unknown old man, but his wisdom, which at the last moment saves the besieged town, is the characteristic feature which wins him immortality in the popular memory.[56] Epic stories are found primarily in *The Tale of Bygone Years* which is linked with the folk epic more closely than all the other chronicles. In later chronicle-writing they occur far less frequently.

The other group of stories is compiled by the chronicler himself or his contemporaries. It has a different style of narrative, in which we do not find a rounded plot or generalised epic characters. These stories may be more psychological, realistic and literary, since the chronicler is striving not simply to make the event known, but to relate it in such a manner as to produce a certain impression on the reader, to make him react in a certain way to the characters in the story. Among the stories of this kind in *The Tale of Bygone Years* the blinding of Vasilko of Terebovl stands out in particular (under the entry for 1097).

In order to show exactly how the chronicler achieves the required literary and emotional effect on the reader, let us examine two episodes from the story.

Prince Svyatopolk of Kiev is persuaded by Prince David of Volhynia to invite Vasilko in order to imprison and blind him. Unaware of what awaits him, Vasilko arrives at the prince's court. David and Svyatopolk take their guest inside. Svyatopolk persuades Vasilko to stay for a while. David, who is present during this conversation seems to be struck dumb. It was he who thought up the evil plot and now it is he who fears it. When Svyatopolk goes out, Vasilko starts talking to David, but David has lost his speech and hearing—he seems not to hear what is said to him and cannot reply. This is a very rare example in Old Russian writing of the early period, when the author seeks to convey a character's inner state by such untraditional means. Then David too goes out, and the princes' servants rush in. The chronicler describes the ensuing struggle in detail: in order to overcome Vasilko, who is strong and resists desperately, they knock him down and place a board taken from the stove on top of him. The men then sit on the board so heavily that Vasilko's chest "cracks". The blinding is described in similar detail. It is entrusted to the shepherd thus suggesting to the reader the comparison of Vasilko with a helpless lamb led to the slaughter.

All these details help the reader to picture the terrible scene and to persuade him that Vladimir Monomachos was right in taking up arms against Svyatopolk and David.

Specialists often quote another, equally expressive scene in the same story. The wounded and blinded Vasilko is being carried along in a cart. He is senseless. The men accompanying him (evidently David's "lads") take off his blood-stained shirt and give it to be washed to the wife of the priest in the village where they have stopped to dine. The priest's wife washes the shirt, then comes up to Vasilko and begins to mourn him, thinking that he is dead. Hearing her laments, Vasilko asks, "Where am I?" "In Zwizhden town," is the reply. Then he asks for water, and they

въ · Ꙅ · дн҃ь · прииде жекдⷧъ
ꙁвѣрь · оуловⷯи · и посⷣаиш
и пристависⷽа · л · моу · стеⷬ

мъ . акннѣ какін

. въдворѣвакнеык .

ч . нѣ ѿрока . оула

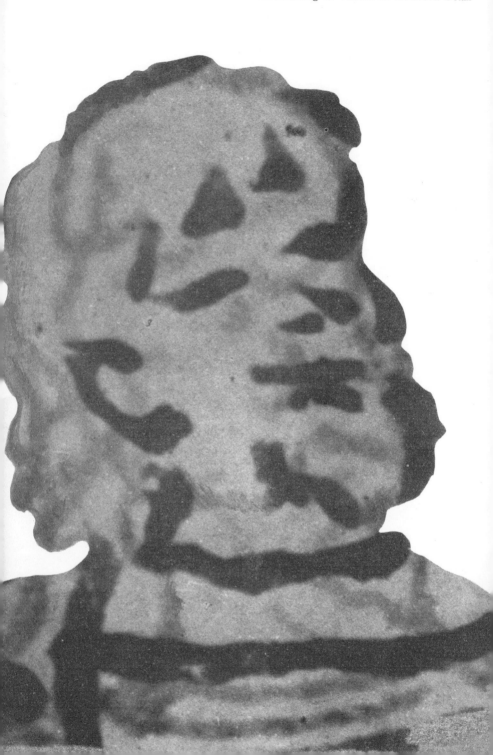

The Blinding of Vasilko of Terebovl. Detail.

give it to him, and he comes to, feels his shirt and says, "Why did they take it off me? It were better I had received death in that blood-stained shirt and gone before my Maker."

This episode is narrated so carefully, with such concrete details, that it revives the memory of the prince's terrible fate and arouses pity for him. The desire expressed by him to go before his Maker "in that blood-stained shirt" seems to serve as a reminder of inevitable retribution, to justify the "earthly" actions of the princes who waged war on David to restore Vasilko's rights to the appanage that had been taken from him.

Thus, together with the chronicle narrative we find the emergence of a special genre, subject to the chronicle, the genre of the tale about princely crimes.[57] The socio-political importance of these stories was so great that the authors obviously tried hard to perfect their literary form in order to make the narrative as moving as possible and justify the attitude of the side that denounces the crime in such stories.

The Monumental Historical Style in the Chronicle. Whereas the chronicle stories that derived from folk legends had a special epic style, the prevailing and all-embracing style in chronicle-writing of the eleventh and twelfth centuries, and in the literature of this period in general, was the monumental historical style.

This style reflects the striving of Old Russian scribes to assess everything from the viewpoint of the purpose and aim of human life. Therefore the writers in the eleventh to thirteenth centuries seek to depict only the major, most important things. The monumental historical style is characterised, first and foremost, by the striving to view the object portrayed at a considerable distance: spatially, temporally and hierarchically. It is a style within which all that is most significant and beautiful appears monumental and majestic, perceived from a great height, as it were.

The chroniclers (as well as the writers of *vitae*, eulogies and homilies) seem to be viewing the world from a great distance. This is a period of panoramic vision, of endeavours to combine in a single narrative different geographical points a long way from one another. The action in the chronicles suddenly switches from one place to another right on the other side of the Russian land. An account of events in Novgorod is followed by one about events in Vladimir or Kiev, then references to happenings in Smolensk or Galich, etc. This feature of the chronicle narrative is not only explained by the fact that the chronicle usually combines different sources written in different parts of the Russian land. It is also in keeping with the spirit of the narrative of that period. It is characteristic not only of the chronicle, but also of Vladimir Monomachos' *Instruction*, the *Patericon* of the Kiev Crypt Monastery, the Life of SS Boris and Gleb, and the sermons or homilies.

At the same time the monumentalism of the eleventh to

thirteenth centuries has one specific feature that distinguishes it from our modern view of the monumental as something inert, heavy and static. The monumentalism in Old Russian literature was linked with precisely the opposite qualities, in particular, with rapid movement over large geographical distances. The heroes are constantly on the move, travelling with their bodyguards from one town to another, from one principality to the next.

The historical aspect of the monumental style is expressed in the special predilection for historical themes. Old Russian writers sought to write not about imaginary things, but about historical facts, and even when they described something fantastic (miracles, for example), they themselves for the most part believed in it and tried to impress upon the reader that this or that event really did take place. The literature of that period did not have (or to be more precise, thought it did not have) any imaginary personages or imaginary events.

In addition scribes sought to link historical events and characters with other equally historical events or characters, to remind the reader of a prince's ancestors, his "fathers" and "forefathers", to compare a personage or an event with similar personages or events that they knew from the Byzantine chronicles or the Bible, to look for and find analogies for everything that took place in this vast world which was all governed by the same laws.[58]

Literary Convention in the Chronicle. At the same time the literature of this period was distinguished by a ceremonial quality. This is seen quite clearly in the phenomenon which Dmitry Likhachev calls literary convention.

Literary convention, as it were, defines the tasks of literature, its themes, the principles of constructing the plot and, finally, the representational means themselves, singling out a range of the most desirable expressions, similes and metaphors.

The concept of literary convention is based on the idea of a stable, orderly world in which there is a special code of behaviour for each person. Literature should sanction and portray this static, normative world. This means that its main subject should be the portrayal of normative situations. If a chronicle is being written, attention should be focused on descriptions of the prince's accession to the throne, battles, diplomatic acts, and the death and burial of the prince. In the latter case there is a kind of summing up of his life in generalised necrological form. Likewise in the lives of the saints there must be an account of their childhood, their path to sainthood, their traditional virtues (these, in particular, were almost compulsory for every saint), the miracles performed by them during their lifetime and after their death, etc.

Each of the above-mentioned situations, in which the hero of the chronicle or *vita* appears most clearly in his official capacity of prince or saint, must be portrayed in traditional expressions: the saint's parents must be described as pious, the child who later becomes a saint must be said to shun games with other children, and battles are described in traditional phrases of the type: "and a fierce battle ensued", "some were slain, others taken prisoner", "they fought hard, grappling with one another, and the blood flowed in rivulets", etc.[59]

The chronicle narrative is full of convention, especially the passages that are written in the monumental historical style. Here the chronicler selects for his narrative only the most important events and deeds of national significance. Of course, if we demand of a style that it should strictly observe certain linguistic features (i.e., stylistic devices proper), we see that by no means every line in the chronicle illustrates the monumental historical style.

Firstly, because the varied phenomena of real life, and the chronicle had to correspond to real life, would not fit into a prearranged scheme of conventional situations, and therefore we find the most vivid manifestation of this style in the description of these situations: in the portrayal of the prince's accession to the throne or his departure on a campaign, the descriptions of battles, obituaries, etc.

Secondly, because alongside the entries compiled by the chronicler in monumental historical style, we also find annual records, popular legends for which a different style is characteristic, namely, the epic style examined above, and stories of everyday life.

The monumental historical style is used, for example, for describing the events of the time of Yaroslav the Wise and his son Vsevolod. Suffice it to mention the description of the Battle on the Alta which brought Yaroslav victory over Svyatopolk the Accursed, the murderer of Boris and Gleb (under the year 1019 in *The Tale of Bygone Years*). Svyatopolk comes to the field of battle "with a vast host". Yaroslav also assembles a large hand of warriors and marches out to engage him on the River Alta. Before the battle Yaroslav prays to God and his murdered brothers, asking for their help in the battle against this "murderer and arrogant man". Then the two armies advance against each other "and the two great hosts did cover the Alta field". At dawn "a fierce battle ensued the like of which there had ne'er before been in Russia, and they fought hard, grappling with one another, and came together three times, so that the blood flowed in rivulets". Towards evening Yaroslav emerged victorious and Svyatopolk was put to flight. Yaroslav mounted the throne of Kiev, and "he and

Royal **barma.** Detail. Gold, filigree. 12th-13th centuries. Moscow Kremlin Museums

his men did wipe the sweat off their brows after their victory and great military feat".

Everything in this story is intended to stress the historical importance of the battle: the reference to the large numbers of warriors, the details about the fierceness of the battle, and the impressive ending with Yaroslav victoriously mounting the Kievan throne which he won in battle for a "just cause". But it is not so much an eyewitness account of a concrete battle, as a skilful interweaving of traditional subject matter and stock phrases in which other battles in *The Tale of Bygone Years* and later chronicles were described. The expression *secha zla* ("fierce battle") is traditional, as is the ending which tells us who won and who fled. The reference to the large number of warriors and the phrases depicting the fury of the battle are also common in the chronicles.

The details about the princes in their obituaries are written with special care in *The Tale of Bygone Years*. For example, in the words of the chronicler (see the year 1093), Prince Vsevolod was "from childhood god-loving, and just, cared for the poor and needy, revered bishops and priests but above all loved monks and gave them all they needed". This type of chronicle obituary was to be used many a time by the chroniclers of the twelfth and following centuries.[60]

The use of the formulas prescribed by literary convention gave the chronicle text a special flavour: not the effect of surprise, but, quite the reverse, the expectation of encountering something familiar, well known, expressed in a form polished and hallowed by tradition. The same device is well known in folklore as well—let us recall the traditional subjects of the *bylina* (heroic poem), the three-fold repetition of situations, the set epithets and similar devices of literary convention. Thus, the monumental historical style and its literary conventions do not signify a restriction of literary possibilities, but, quite the reverse, show a profound understanding of the role of the poetic word. At the same time, of course, this style did limit the freedom of the story-telling since it strove to standardise, to express different situations in set linguistic formulas and subject motifs.

This combination of the monumental historical and epic styles in *The Tale of Bygone Years* created its unique literary quality, and its stylistic influence was clearly felt for several centuries. Chroniclers began to use or adapt literary formulas first employed by the compilers of the *Tale*, to imitate the descriptions in it, and sometimes even to quote it, inserting passages from the *Tale* into their own text.[61] The *Tale* has preserved its aesthetic charm right up to the present day, bearing eloquent witness to the literary skill of the Old Russian chroniclers.

South Russian Chronicle-Writing of the Twelfth Century. *The Tale of Bygone Years* carried the account up to the first decade of the twelfth century. Throughout this century chronicle-writing continued in various Russian principalities. These chronicles have not survived, however, and we know about them only from later chronicles in which they were wholly or partially included.

We can learn of South Russian chronicle-writing, for example, from the so-called *Kievan Chronicle*. This is the conventional name given by specialists to those entries in *The Hypatian Chronicle* which record events from the year 1117 to the end of the twelfth century.[62]

This part of the chronicle, which is assumed to have been redacted at the end of the twelfth century by Abbot Moses of the Vydubitsky Monastery (near Kiev), is a compilation that made use of the chronicles of the Kievan grand princes, *The Chronicle of Pereyaslavl-Russky*, and the family chronicle of the Rostislaviches, the descendants of Prince Rostislav, grandson of Vladimir Monomachos.[63]

Whereas the chroniclers of the eleventh century sought to view the events of their age against the background of the earlier history of Old Russia, the South Russian chroniclers of the twelfth century concentrated solely on describing the turbulent life of their principalities and appanages. In *The Kievan Chronicle* we find not tales and epic legends, but annual records, sometimes brief, sometimes very detailed, but nevertheless lacking the compositional unity without which the chronicle tale is inconceivable.

The Kievan Chronicle, particularly the entries for the 1140s, shows the chroniclers' predilection for external, stylistic devices characteristic of the monumental historical style. Here one constantly finds traditional descriptions of battles, stereotype accounts of princes' burials and obituaries.[64]

The Chronicle-Writing of Vladimir-Suzdalian Russia in the Twelfth Century. From the middle of the twelfth century the role of the Vladimir-Suzdalian principality grew increasingly important for Russia as a whole. The growing military and political importance of this principality, until recently one of the "borderlands", was bound to lead to increased ideological activity as well. The brief records, which, we assume, were kept from the beginning of the twelfth century in Rostov and Vladimir, were replaced by chronicles.

These chronicles have not survived, but are reflected in later chronicles. Comparison of the latter has made it possible to establish that *The Vladimir Chronicle* of the late twelfth century was preserved in *The Laurentian Chronicle*, and a compilation of

the early thirteenth century in the *Radziwill* and *Moscow-Academic* chronicles, and also in *The Chronicle of Pereyaslavl-Suzdalsky*.[65]

Vladimir chronicle-writing sought to establish the authority of the principality and substantiate its claims to political and ecclesiastical hegemony in Old Russia. For this reason the Vladimir chronicle-writers did not limit themselves to describing local events, but presented a broad picture of the history of the whole Russian land. South Russian events were recounted mainly according to the chronicles of Pereyaslavl-Russky * with which the princes of Vladimir had strong political ties.

The Radziwill Chronicle, which dates back to *The Vladimir Chronicle* of the early thirteenth century, contains more than 600 miniatures illustrating *The Tale of Bygone Years* and *The Vladimir Chronicle* of the twelfth century.[66] It is possible that the thirteenth-century chronicle was also illustrated and that the miniatures in *The Radziwill Chronicle* are copies of its miniatures.

Novgorodian Chronicle-Writing of the Twelfth Century. Novgorodian chronicle-writing is of a completely different nature. Firstly, it is emphatically local: the Novgorodian chroniclers rarely make references to national Russian events or events in other Russian lands. The Novgorodian chronicle also lacks the religious rhetoric that was characteristic, as already mentioned, of the chronicle of Vladimir-Suzdalian Russia.

The Novgorodian chronicle is distinguished by its simple style (the conventional formulas of the monumental historical style so typical of South-Russian chronicle-writing are hardly found here at all), and its democratic language, which retains many dialect words and reflects the special features of the local Novgorodian spoken language.

The earliest Novgorodian chronicles are reflected in the two redactions (recensions) of the so-called *Novgorod First Chronicle*. The oldest recension is the Synod manuscript of the thirteenth and fourteenth centuries (which, unfortunately, lacks the beginning). This is the earliest extant manuscript of a chronicle text. The oldest manuscripts of the later recension of *The Novgorod First Chronicle* belong to the middle of the fifteenth century.[67]

For a long time Novgorodian chronicle-writing was isolated from that of the other Russian lands, until the Novgorodian chronicles were used in the fifteenth century as one of the sources for a new chronicle of the whole of Russia.

It is *The Novgorod First Chronicle*, however, that has preserved a most interesting literary work (possibly of Kievan origin), the

---

* Town to the south-east of Kiev.

Cathedral of St Sophia in Novgorod. 1045. General view

Cathedral of St Sophia in Novgorod. Plan

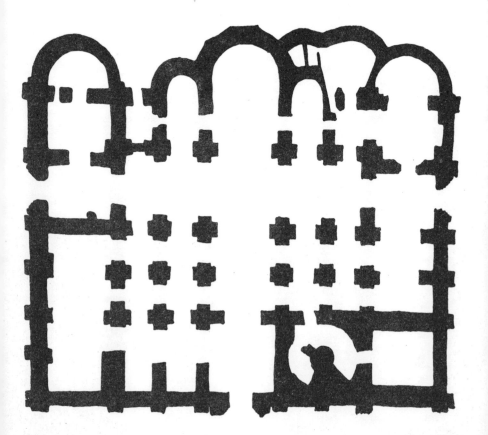

account of the capture of Constantinople by the Crusaders in 1204 during the Fourth Crusade. Compiled by an eyewitness (or from an eyewitness account), this description is a most valuable historical source, not only for its description of how this event was received in Russia, but also for the study of Byzantine history as such: the narrator is well versed in the political background to the events and describes the siege, capture and looting of Constantinople in great detail.[68]

4. Ceremonial and Homiletic Rhetoric

A place of honour among the genres of Byzantine literature was held by the writings of the Church Fathers, theologians and preachers. These sermons and homilies by Byzantine authors were widely known in Old Russia, and original works by Russian writers had appeared by the eleventh century: *The Sermon on Law and Grace* of Metropolitan Hilarion and the sermons of Bishop Luke Zhidyata of Novgorod and Abbot Theodosius of the Kiev Crypt Monastery.[69] In the twelfth century Old Russian literature was enriched by such masterpieces of rhetorical oratory as the sermons of Cyril of Turov.

The Sermon on Law and Grace. *The Sermon on Law and Grace*, written by the Kievan priest Hilarion (later Metropolitan of Kiev) was, Nikolai Rozov assumes, first delivered by him in 1049 in honour of the completion of the fortress wall around Kiev.[70]

However, the importance of the *Sermon* extends far beyond the framework of the genre of the ceremonial festive sermons delivered to the faithful in church. Hilarion's *Sermon* is a kind of ecclesiastical-political treatise extolling the Russian land and its princes.

The *Sermon* begins with a lengthy theological discourse. Hilarion contrasts the Old and New Testaments, pursuing the idea that the Old Testament is law established for the Jewish people alone, whereas the New Testament is grace that extends to all peoples without exception who have adopted Christianity. Hilarion returns several times to this idea which is of great importance to him; in order to substantiate it he analyses the symbolism of Biblical imagery, quotes sayings of the Church Fathers, and uses all sorts of arguments to support his thesis of the superiority of Christianity to Judaism which was intended for one people alone, and the high calling of the Christian peoples.

The first, dogmatic part of the *Sermon* leads up to the central idea of the work: Prince Vladimir of his own accord (not on the advice or insistence of the Greek clergy) performed a "great and wondrous" act—the baptising of Russia. Vladimir is the "teacher and mentor" of the Russian land, thanks to whom the "grace-giving faith" has "reached our Russian people". The role of Vladimir as the baptiser of Russia grows to universal proportions: Vladimir is as "wise" and as "pious" as Constantine the Great himself, the emperor of the "two Romes", the East and the West, who, according to ecclesiastical tradition proclaimed Christianity the official religion in Byzantium and was greatly revered in the empire. Similar deeds and merits confer the right to similar respect. Thus Hilarion introduces his audience to the idea of the need to recognise Vladimir as a saint. He puts him on a level with the Apostles John, Thomas and Mark, who performed the service of converting different countries and lands to Christianity.

Hilarion seeks to extol the power of the Russian land and stress its authority. The phraseology of the church sermon is sometimes replaced by that of the chronicle eulogy: Vladimir's forefathers, Igor and Svyatoslav, were renowned throughout the world for their courage and bravery, their "victories and valour", and they ruled not in an "unknown land", but in Russia, which "is known and heard by the four corners of the earth". Vladimir himself is not only a faithful Christian, but a mighty "autocrat of his land" who has subjugated neighbouring countries, "some by peace, but the unruly by the sword".

The third and final part of the *Sermon* is dedicated to Yaroslav the Wise. Hilarion depicts him not only as the continuer of the spiritual behests of Vladimir, not only as the zealous builder of new churches, but as a worthy "deputy ... of the dominion" of his father. Even in prayer Hilarion does not forget about Russia's wordly, political needs: he prays God to "drive away" enemies, establish peace, "subdue" neighbouring countries, make the boyars see reason, fortify towns... This civic element in a church sermon is easily explained by the situation in the 1030s and 1040s, when Yaroslav was doing his utmost to gain the independence of the Russian Church and Russian state policy and when the idea of the equality (and not subordination) of Russia in its relations with Byzantium was assuming most acute forms, influencing even church building. For example, churches in Old Russia were given the names of the famous cathedrals in Constantinople: the cathedrals of St Sophia in Kiev and Novgorod, the churches of St Irene and St George in Kiev, the Golden Gate in Kiev, and so on. Politicians and architects saw Kiev as a kind of rival to Constantinople.

There is a well-founded theory that Hilarion was also the author of the first work on Russian history, the cycle of tales on the conversion of Russia to Christianity, which may have marked the beginning of Russian chronicle-writing. This theory is, supported by numerous textual parallels in the two works.[71]

Clement of Smolensk. Hilarion's *Sermon* was by no means the only work of oratorial prose. In the middle of the twelfth century the writings of Metropolitan Clement of Smolensk [72] enjoyed great authority, of whom the chronicle said that he was "a writer and philosopher", the like of which had never been known before in the Russian land.[73] We know very little of Clement, however. He was born in Smolensk and was a monk in the Zarubsky Monastery near Kiev. In 1146 Grand Prince Izyaslav of Kiev decided to appoint him metropolitan. This attempt to appoint a Russian metropolitan without the blessing of the Patriarch of Constantinople encountered resistance from some of the Greek hierarchs in the Russian church, however. Clement's position was insecure, and after Izyaslav's death in 1154 he was forced to leave the office.

We also know little about Clement's writing. The only work that can be indisputably ascribed to him is the beginning of an *Epistle to Presbyter Thomas.* The events that led to its writing are as follows. In his correspondence with Prince Rostislav of Smolensk, Clement offended Presbyter Thomas in some way. The latter accused the metropolitan of vanity, of seeking to present himself as a "philosopher" and said that Clement borrowed "from Homer, from Aristotle, and from Plato", instead of basing himself on ecclesiastical authorities. Clement read his opponent's epistle publicly before the prince and addressed a reply to Thomas which has survived. In it Clement defends the right to interpret the Holy Scriptures with the help of parables.

This dispute, about which we can judge only from the scant information in Clement's *Epistle,* nevertheless testifies to the erudition of Clement who is reproached for quoting the Greek philosophers and Homer, and to the intensity of Russia's cultural and literary life in the mid-twelfth century, if disputes on ceremonial rhetoric and the quoting of Greek writers in sermons or epistles could acquire such importance and provoke such a reaction in that period. Unfortunately we know of very few monuments of twelfth-century ceremonial and homiletic rhetoric. The writings of the eminent twelfth-century preacher Cyril of Turov are a fortunate exception.

Cyril of Turov. A late *Life of St Cyril* says that he took vows early, became a hermit and during the period of his reclusion "expounded much of the Holy Scriptures". Later the prince and townspeople "begged" Cyril to become bishop of Turov (in the north-west of the principality of Kiev). Cyril died not later than 1182.

Cyril's writings enjoyed exceptional authority not only in Russia, but also among the Southern Slavs. Moreover his fame did not fade with time: thus, in widely read miscellanies of ceremonial and homiletic writings that began to circulate at the end of the fifteenth century, the *Chrysostom* and the *Festal Sermons,* Cyril's sermons gradually occupied more and more space, sometimes even ousting those of St John Chrysostom.

The authorship of a number of works bearing Cyril of Turov's name is doubtful, but there are sufficient grounds for considering that of the extant writings bearing his name the following were written by him: *The Parable of the Soul and the Body, The Tale of the White and Black Monkhood, The Tale of the Black Monkhood,* eight sermons for church feasts, thirty prayers and two canons (a cycle of hymns in honour of a saint).[74] In addition several sermons often bearing Cyril's name in a number of manuscript miscellanies are included in a thirteenth-century miscellany (in the State Public Library in Leningrad) which consists almost entirely of writings by the author. It is possible that they too (as Mikhail Sukhomlinov also considers) belong to the Turov bishop.

The Parable of the Soul and the Body, which Igor Eremin dates between 1160-1169, is a denunciatory pamphlet against Bishop Theodore of Rostov.[75] The parable is based on the story of a blind man and a lame man. Briefly it is as follows. The owner of a vineyard hires two men to guard it—a blind man and a lame man. He thinks that the lame man will not be able to walk into the vineyard, and the blind man will get lost if he goes in. But a lame man can see a thief and a blind man can hear one. The watchmen decide to outwit their master: the lame man climbs onto the blind man's back and tells him where to go. In this way they manage to rob the vineyard, but they pay for it dearly. In the parable the blind man is the allegory for the soul, and the lame man for the body. So it is the soul (the blind man) that tempts the body (the lame man) to commit evil. In his interpretation of the *Parable,* Cyril of Turov made it clear to the reader that the blind man was meant to represent Bishop Theodore, and the lame man Prince Andrew Bogolyubsky. The reason for writing the parable was Prince Andrew's attempt to set up a bishopric in Vladimir that would be independent of the Metropolitan of Kiev, to which end Theodore went to Constantinople to be consecrated by the Patriarch, and tricked the latter by pretending that Kiev had no metropolitan because he had died. The deception was subsequently revealed, the Metropolitan of Kiev excommunicated Theodore, and Andrew's attempt to achieve ecclesiastical independence of Kiev was condemned.

It is Cyril's sermons for church feasts that were best known. In them he amplifies and develops the New Testament stories on which they are based with new details and composes dialogues for the characters, thus fashioning a new subject which gives him more scope for an allegorical interpretation of the importance of this or that feast.

The main stylistic device in Cyril's sermons is rhetorical amplification. "With him this or that theme," writes Igor Eremin, "is always modified and enlarged until its content is completely exhausted." Each theme was presented in the form of a rhetorical tirade of alternating sentences synonymous in meaning and identical in syntactical structure.[76]

Let us examine one of Cyril of Turov's sermons, *The Sermon for Easter Sunday.*[77]

The *Sermon* begins with a kind of introduction explaining why it has been written: "The Church has need of a great mentor and wise interpreter to adorn this feast", but we are "poor in words" and "short of mind", Cyril continues, "we can say but little of the feast".

The author goes on to extol the feast of Easter, when everything changes: the earth is cleansed of the filth of evil spirits and becomes the heavens, people are renewed, for they have turned from pagans to Christians... Easter Week is a time of renewal for those who have embraced the Christian faith. Cyril of Turov paints a picture of the spring awakening of nature: freed from dark clouds, the sun rises up high and warms the earth, gentle breezes blow, the earth gives birth to green grass, lambs and calves frisk about, delighting in the spring, the flowers blossom and the leaves come out on the trees... For each element of this description Cyril of Turov immediately quotes a parallel, and it becomes clear that this vivid picture is a series of metaphors and similes designed to extol and, most important, explain to believers some tenets of the Christian faith. Spring is faith in Christ, the lambs are "the meek", the calves the "idol-worshippers" of pagan countries that have been or are being converted to Christianity, etc.

Each of Cyril's sermons is a striking example of festive, ceremonial oratory. The author is a past master of the art of rhetoric: he first addresses the congregation, then turns to a story from the New Testament or some complex theological concept with the aid of allegories, as shown above, or poses a question and immediately answers it himself, disputing and arguing with himself.

Students of the writings of Cyril of Turov established long ago that in the allegories, the devices for interpreting them and the rhetorical figures themselves, the author is by no means always original: he makes use of Byzantine models, quoting or retelling extracts from the sermons of the great Byzantine preachers. But all in all Cyril of Turov's works are not simply compilations of other writers' images and quotations—they are a free reinterpretation of traditional material which results in a new, formally perfect work that helps the hearer to appreciate the spoken word and enchants him with the harmony of its rhythmically constructed vocal periods.

The syntactical parallelism of forms, the extensive use of morphological rhymes (the use of a succession of similar grammatical forms) in Cyril of Turov's sermons compensated, as it were, for the lack of bookish poetry, preparing the Russian reader for the ornamental style ("braiding of words") of the fourteenth to sixteenth centuries. Let us quote but one example. In the tirade "<Christ> leads the souls of the Holy Prophets to the Kingdom of Heaven, confers abodes on his saints in the celestial city, opens up paradise to the righteous, crowns the martyrs who have suffered for his sake..." each of the three parts of the syntactical construction (predicate, direct and indirect object) are parallel. Then the rhythmic pattern becomes even more complex, for the direct object, which is expressed by a single word in the constructions of the extract quoted above, now turns into a phrase each of the components of which also has parallel constructions: "pardons all those who do his will and follow his behests, sends our loyal princes health for their bodies and salvation for their souls and victory over the enemy ... blesses all Christians, great and small, rich and poor, freemen and slaves, young and old, wives and maids..."

The writing of Cyril of Turov shows that twelfth-century Old Russian writers attained the heights of literary perfection and freely mastered all the devices of Greek rhetoric and the classical rhetorical oratory of Byzantium. Cyril of Turov embodied in his work the principles of "parabolic interpretation" that were championed by Clement of Smolensk and followed him also in the widespread use of rhetorical amplification.

5. The Works of Vladimir Monomachos

In the process of transplanting Byzantine and Old Bulgarian literature the Russian scribes acquired works representing the most varied genres of early Christian mediaeval literature.

The unique quality of Old Russian literature, however, revealed itself, in particular, in the fact that already in the early period of original literature Old Russian works were created that stand outside this traditional genre system. One such work is the famous *Instruction* of Vladimir Monomachos.[78]

Until recently this title covered four independent works, three of which really do belong to Vladimir Monomachos: these are the *Instruction* proper, an autobiography and a *Letter to Oleg Svyatoslavich*. The concluding fragment in this set of texts, a prayer, has now been established as not belonging to Monomachos. It was accidentally copied together with Monomachos' writings.[79]

All of the above-mentioned four works are found in one manuscript only: they are inserted in the text of *The Tale of Bygone Years* in *The Laurentian Chronicle*, in the middle of the entry for the year 1096.[80]

Vladimir Monomachos (Grand Prince of Kiev from 1113 to 1125) was the son of Vsevolod and the daughter of the Byzantine Emperor Constantine Monomachos (hence the prince's nickname). An energetic politician and diplomat and a consistent champion of feudal vassalage, Vladimir Monomachos sought both by his personal example and his *Instruction* to strengthen these principles and persuade others to follow them. Thus, in 1094 he voluntarily gave up the throne of Chernigov to Oleg Svyatoslavich. In 1097 Monomachos was one of the active participants in the conference at Lyubech at which the princes tried to settle disputes concerning the inheritance of appanages. He firmly condemned the blinding of Prince Vasilko of Terebovl, recalling the main idea of the Lyubech conference—that if the internecine strife did not end "and brother begins to kill brother", "the Russian land will perish, and our enemies, the Polovtsians, will come and seize the Russian land". At the conference at Dolobsk in 1103 Monomachos called for a joint campaign against the Polovtsians, stressing that this was in the interests of the common people, the peasants, who suffered most of all from Polovtsian incursions.

The *Instruction* appears to have been written by Monomachos in 1117.[81] The aged prince had a long and difficult life behind him, many military campaigns and battles, considerable experience as a diplomat and a ruler of the various principalities where the principle of accession by seniority, which he himself had defended, had taken him, and, finally, the honour and glory of his great reign in Kiev itself. In his declining years the prince had much to tell his younger contemporaries and progeny and much to teach them. And his *Instruction* is such a political and moral testament. Behind the instructions to observe the rules of Christian morality: to be meek, to heed one's elders and obey them, to befriend one's equals and inferiors, and not to offend orphans and widows, we can detect the outlines of a definite political programme. The main idea of the *Instruction* is that a prince should submit unquestioningly to his senior, live in peace with the other princes and not oppress the lesser princes or boyars; a prince should avoid unnecessary bloodshed, be a cordial host, not indulge in laziness, not be carried away by power, not rely on officials in the management of his household nor on *voevodas* in campaigns, but be conversant with everything himself...

Monomachos did not limit himself to practical advice and discourses of a moral or political nature, however. Continuing the tradition of his grandfather, Yaroslav the Wise, and father, Vsevolod, who "stayed at home yet knew five languages", Monomachos shows himself to have been a highly educated, scholarly man. The *Instruction* contains many quotations from the Psalms, the *Instruction* of St Basil the Great, the Book of Isaiah, the Triodion, and the Epistles of the Apostles. Monomachos reveals not only that he read widely, but also that he possessed breadth of mind, inserting alongside the didactic exhortations in the *Instruction* a description of the perfect world order and quotes, in slightly revised form, the *Hexaëmeron* of John, the Bulgarian Exarch.

In support of his admonitions and homilies, Monomachos quotes a long list of the campaigns and hunts in which he took part from the age of thirteen. In conclusion he stresses that throughout his life he has followed the same rules: he has tried to do everything himself, "giving himself no peace", not relying on his fellow warriors and servants, and not offending the "poor peasant and the wretched widow". The *Instruction* ends with an exhortation not to fear death either in battle or hunting, in the valorous performance of one's manly duties.

Another work by Monomachos is the *Letter to Oleg Svyatoslavich.* It was written in connection with a quarrel during which Oleg killed Monomachos' son, Izyaslav. True to his principles of justice and brotherly love, Monomachos finds the moral strength to act not as an enemy and revenger, but, quite the reverse, to urge Oleg to be sensible and make peace. He does not seek to justify his dead son, but merely says that he should not have heeded the *parobki* (probably his young warriors) and tried to take what was not his. Monomachos wants an end to their enmity and hopes that Oleg will reply to him, after due reflection, gain his appanage by peaceful means and then they will be even more friendly than before.

The letter is striking not only because of the prince's magnanimity and political wisdom, but also because of the lyrical quality, particularly in the passage where Monomachos asks Oleg to let Izyaslav's widow return, so that he might embrace his daughter-in-law and "mourn her husband". "And having wept with her," Monomachos goes on, "take her in, and she will sit grieving like a turtle-dove on a withered tree." *

Vladimir Monomachos' *Instruction* is the only known specimen in Old Russian literature of a political and moral exhortation written not by a churchman, but by a statesman. Scholars have quoted analogies in other mediaeval literatures: the *Instruction* has been compared with the *Testament* of the French King St Louis, the apocryphal instructions of the Anglo-Saxon King Alfred or the *Faeder Larcwidas* of which there was a copy in the library of the last of the Anglo-Saxon kings, Harold II, Monomachos' father-in-law (Monomachos was married to the king's daughter, Githa).[82] But these parallels are only of a typological nature: Monomachos' work is completely original, it fits in perfectly, first and foremost, with the political activity of Monomachos who sought to strengthen the principle of "brotherly love" in Russia and fought for strict observance of feudal duties and rights. Like *The Lay of Igor's Host* later, the *Instruction* did not so much follow the tradition of this or that literary genre, as respond to the political requirements of the day. It is typical, for example, that guided primarily by ideological considerations Monomachos inserted an autobiography in the *Instruction*. As a literary genre the autobiography did not appear in Russia until many centuries later, in the writings of Avvakum and Epiphanius.

Monomachos' works show that the author had mastered various styles of the literary language and applied them skilfully according to the genre and theme of the work. This is particularly evident if we compare the section of the *Instruction* in which Monomachos discourses on moral and ethical behaviour (it is written in lofty language, in keeping with the passages from the Bible and the Church Fathers quoted in it), and the autobiographical section in which his language is very close to the colloquial, extremely simple and expressive.[83]

6. Hagiography

The Russian Church was striving to achieve legal and ideological independence of the Byzantine Church. Ever since a Russian, Yaroslav the Wise's confessor, Hilarion, was appointed Metropolitan in 1051, the authority of the Russian monasteries, in particular the Kiev Crypt Monastery, had been growing.

It was extremely important for the Russian Church to achieve

---

* The turtle-dove grieving the death of her mate on a withered tree is mentioned in some versions of *The Physiologos*.

the canonisation of its own, Russian saints. An essential prerequisite, as mentioned above, was the existence of a written *vita*. These were the non-literary reasons for the emergence of original *vita* in Russia. But literary and aesthetic reasons undoubtedly also played a large part: familiarity with the translations of Byzantine hagiographies and patericon legends could not fail to arouse in Russian scribes the urge to try their hand at this genre.

The oldest Russian *vita* would appear to be *The Life of St Anthony of the Caves*, the monk who was the first to settle in a cave and thereby by his personal example prompted the founding of the crypt, which later became the famous Kiev Crypt Monastery. However *The Life of St Anthony of the Caves* has not survived.

In the latter half of the eleventh century *The Life of St Theodosius of the Caves* and two Lives of the murdered princes Boris and Gleb were written. They established two groups of hagiographical subjects: some *vitae* were "entirely devoted to the theme of the ideal Christian hero renouncing the 'earthly' life in order to win 'eternal' life by his feats, while the heroes of the other group of *vitae* sought to advocate by their conduct not only the general Christian, but also the feudal ideal." [84]

The Life of St Theodosius of the Caves. An example of the first group of subjects is *The Life of St Theodosius of the Caves*.[85] It was written by Nestor, a monk in the Kiev Crypt Monastery, whom we mentioned earlier as the compiler of *The Tale of Bygone Years*. There is some difference of opinion as to when it was written. Alexei Shakhmatov and Igor Eremin believe that it was written before 1088, Sergei Bugoslavsky places it at the beginning of the twelfth century. Nestor was well acquainted with Byzantine hagiography. Parallels with some episodes in the Life can be found in the Lives of Byzantine saints, such as St Sabas, St Anthony, St Euthymius the Great and St Benedict.[86] In his work he also paid tribute to the traditional composition of the Life: the future saint is born of pious parents, from early childhood "he strives with all his heart to love God", shuns games with other boys of his age, and goes to church every day. After taking monastic vows, Theodosius amazes all around by his asceticism and humility: thus, even when he is abbot, he dresses so simply that people who do not know him take him for a beggar or for one of the monastery cooks. Many ignorant people on meeting Theodosius scoff openly at his poor attire. To mortify the "flesh", Theodosius sleeps sitting up and does not wash (he has only been seen washing his hands). As behoves a saint, the abbot successfully overcomes "many legions of invisible demons", works miracles, and knows in advance the day of his demise. He accepts death with calm dignity, and even has time to make a farewell speech to the fraternity and appoint a new abbot. At the moment of Theodosius' death a pillar of fire rises up over the monastery. It is seen by Prince Svyatoslav who happens to be nearby. Theodosius' relics do not perish, and those who pray to him receive the saint's help: one is healed, another learns the name of the thief who robbed him from Theodosius who appears to him in a dream, a third, a disgraced boyar, is restored to his prince's favour.

Nevertheless this is by no means a traditional Life constructed in strict accordance with the Byzantine hagiographical canon.[87] *The Life of St Theodosius* contains many features not in keeping with this canon. This does not mean that the author was inexperienced and could not weave the facts and legends about the saint into the traditional scheme of a *vita*. On the contrary, it testifies to Nestor's boldness and independence as a writer.

The character of Theodosius' mother is particularly unusual for the traditional Life. Strong and masculine, with a rough voice, absorbed in wordly cares about villages and slaves, strong-willed, even cruel, she loves her son passionately, and cannot reconcile herself to the idea that the boy shuns all earthly things and has renounced the world. Although the author speaks of the piety of Theodosius' mother at the beginning of the *vita*, she does her utmost to thwart her son's pious intentions. She is irritated by Theodosius' religious fervour and finds it degrading that he stubbornly refuses to wear "fine raiment", preferring rags instead; the chains discovered on the young man's body send her into a frenzy. Probably these were features of Theodosius' real mother, and Nestor did not think it possible to change them to suit hagiographical tradition, particularly because the woman's grim determination highlights even more vividly the resolution of the boy Theodosius to "give himself to God".

But the charm of Nestor's literary manner lies not only in his striving to depict characters with lifelike features, but also in his ability to create the illusion of authenticity even in his descriptions of the fantastic episodes in which the Life abounds.

For example, this is how he describes one of the miracles performed by Theodosius. The steward tells Abbot Theodosius that there is no honey left in the monastery's larder, and says that he even "tipped the barrel on its side". These words are intended to convince Theodosius (and the reader also) that there was not a drop of honey left. This makes the miracle wrought by Theodosius all the more amazing: at the abbot's request the steward goes back and sees to his surprise that the empty barrel overturned by him is now standing upright and is full of honey.

On another occasion an empty flour bin is filled with flour

after a prayer from Theodosius so full that some of the flour spills over the edge onto the ground. This detail makes the picture more vivid, and the reader, encouraged by his powers of imagination, believes in the miracle described.

The Lives of SS Boris and Gleb. Examples of the second type of *vita*, the martyria (the story of a martyred saint), are the Lives written about the death of Boris and Gleb at the hand of their brother Svyatopolk. One of them (*The Reading Concerning the Life and Murder of SS Boris and Gleb*), like *The Life of St Theodosius of the Caves*, was written by Nestor.[88] The author of the other Life, entitled *The Tale and the Passion and the Encomium of the Holy Martyrs Boris and Gleb*, is not known. Specialists are divided as to when the *Tale* was written—in the middle of the eleventh century or the beginning of the twelfth—and, consequently, as to whether it came before or after *The Reading Concerning the Life and Murder* written by Nestor.[89]

The creation of the religious cult of Boris and Gleb had two aims. On the one hand, the canonisation of the first Russian saints enhanced the ecclesiastical authority of Russia and testified to the fact that Russia was "favoured before God" and had been blessed with its own saints. On the other hand, the cult of Boris and Gleb was of great political importance: it "sanctified" and affirmed the frequently proclaimed political idea that all the Russian princes were brothers, and also stressed the need for the younger princes to submit to the senior ones.[90] This is precisely what Boris and Gleb did: they obeyed their elder brother Svyatopolk unquestioningly, respecting him like a father, and he abused their brotherly obedience.

Let us now examine in more detail the events reflected in the *Tale* concerning Boris and Gleb. According to the chronicle version (in *The Tale of Bygone Years* under the entry for 1015), after Vladimir's death one of his sons, Prince Svyatopolk of Pinsk (some sources give Turov), seized the throne of the grand prince and decided to kill his brothers so as to "hold Russian power" alone.

Svyatopolk's first victim was Prince Boris of Rostov. Shortly before his death Vladimir had sent him off with his band of warriors to fight the Pechenegs. When Boris received the news of his father's death, Vladimir's warriors were ready to take the throne for the young prince by force, but Boris refused, for he did not wish to raise his hand against his elder brother, and declared his readiness to respect him like a father. The warrior band left Boris with nothing but a handful of his own "youths" (young warriors) and he was murdered on Svyatopolk's orders.

Then Svyatopolk sent a messenger to Prince Gleb of Murom,

The Tale of the Holy Martyrs Boris and Gleb. **The Murder of Boris.** Illumination from the *Sylvester Miscellany.* 14th century. Central State Archive of Ancient Documents, Moscow

asking him to make haste to his ailing father. Not suspecting anything, Gleb set off for Kiev. In Smolensk he was overtaken by a messenger from his brother Yaroslav with the terrible news: "Do not go, your father is dead, and your brother murdered by Svyatopolk." Gleb mourned his father and brother bitterly. And it was here, by Smolensk, that the murderers sent by Svyatopolk found him. On their orders the prince's cook stabbed him to death.

Yaroslav Vladimirovich entered the struggle against the murderer and did battle with Svyatopolk on the banks of the Dnieper. In the early morning Yaroslav's men crossed the river and "pushed away their boats from the shore", so as to fight for victory or death, then fell upon Svyatopolk's host. In the ensuing battle Svyatopolk was defeated. With the help of King Bolesław of Poland he managed to drive Yaroslav out of Kiev for a while, but in 1019 Svyatopolk's men were defeated once more, and he fled the country and died in a remote spot between Poland and Bohemia. The *Tale* appears to recount the same events, but greatly enhances the hagiographical element. It is characterised by heightened emotions and deliberate conventionality.

Feudal strife was a fairly common phenomenon in the Russia of this period, and the participants in these conflicts usually acted in accordance with self-interest, ambition, military prowess or diplomatic skill; they invariably fought hard in defence of their rights and life. Against this background the meekness of Boris and Gleb, as portrayed by the chronicle account, is unusual, but in the *Tale* it becomes quite excessive. Thus, having learnt of the attempt about to be made on his life, Boris not only does not think of trying to escape, but, quite the reverse, waits quietly for his fate and prays to God to forgive Svyatopolk the sin of fratricide, thus, as it were, predicting death for himself and for Svyatopolk the successful execution of his foul plan.

No less unexpected is the behaviour of Gleb. When the murderers leap into his boat with drawn swords and the prince's time has all but come, he manages to deliver three soliloquies and pray. All this time the murderers wait patiently, with drawn swords poised motionlessly over their victim.

Igor Eremin has drawn attention to another contradiction in the narrative. Boris is encamped by Kiev, but in the *Tale* it is said three times that he is "on his way" to his brother. Eremin believes that the logic of the narrative led the author to make this discrepancy. True to his duty as a vassal Boris should have gone to Kiev, but he would have seemed to be following the advice of the warrior band, "Go unto Kiev and take your father's throne", which did not fit in with his character. So Boris "goes" and stays

The Tale of the Holy Martyrs Boris and Gleb. Gleb's Body Between Two Boards.
Illumination from the *Sylvester Miscellany.* 14th century. Central State Archive of
Ancient Documents, Moscow

in the same place at the same time.[91] Boris is killed three times.
First they strike him with spears through the tent, then they urge
one another to "finish what has been ordered" (i.e., murder
Boris), when he rushes out of the tent and, finally, we learn that
the wounded but still alive Boris is killed by the swords of
pursuing Varangians sent by Svyatopolk.

Another characteristic detail. Scholars have drawn attention to
the lyrical portrayal of Gleb as "young and defenceless", who begs
his murderers for mercy "like a child" saying, "Let me alone... Let
me alone!"[92] This is a purely literary device. In fact, if we accept
the chronicle story about Vladimir, at the time of his death his
youngest son was at least twenty-seven. Boris and Gleb are thought
to be his sons from a Bulgarian wife, i.e., they were born when
Vladimir was still a pagan. Twenty-seven years elapsed between
Vladimir's conversion and marriage to the Byzantine princess
Anna and his death in 1015. Therefore both Boris and Gleb were
mature warriors, not youths.

Eremin quotes another example of "involuntary tribute to the
genre": Boris is portrayed in the *Tale* as a martyr for the faith,
although Svyatopolk was not threatening his faith, of course.[93]

Svyatopolk, on the other hand, personifies the evil that must
be present in a *vita* as the force against which the saint fights
successfully or not. Svyatopolk is cruel and cunning and does not
try to justify this evil even to himself. On the contrary, he
expresses his readiness to "add one unlawful act to another". He
succeeds in killing Boris, Gleb and Svyatoslav, and for a while, in
defeating Yaroslav. But Divine retribution is inescapable, and
Svyatopolk the Accursed (he bears this name throughout Old
Russian literature in which he is invariably the villain) was
defeated in a decisive battle and fled, terrified and sick ("his bones
grew weak" the chronicler tells us), to die in a remote spot. A vile
stench comes from his grave.

In spite of the indisputable tribute to the hagiographical genre,
the *Tale* could not be regarded as a model *vita* in its depiction of
events and particularly its portrayal of the characters. It was too
documentary and historical. This, according to Igor Eremin,
explains why Nestor decided to write another Life, more in
keeping with the strict requirements of a classical canon of this
genre.[94]

Nestor's *Reading* does indeed contain all the essential elements
of a canonical Life: it begins with a lengthy introduction
explaining why the author decided to undertake the writing of this
Life and a brief account of the history of the world from Adam to
the conversion of Russia. In the actual hagiographical part Nestor,
as the genre requires, describes the childhood of Boris and Gleb

and the piety which they showed all through their early years. In the account of their death the hagiographical element is strengthened even more: whereas in the *Tale* Boris and Gleb shed tears and pray for mercy, in the *Reading* they accept death joyfully and prepare to meet it as the noble suffering for which they have been preordained since birth. The *Reading*, also in keeping with the requirements of the genre, contains an account of the saints' posthumous miracles, the miraculous "discovery" of their relics, and the healing of the sick by their grave.

If we compare *The Life of St Theodosius of the Caves,* on the one hand, and the *Tale,* and particularly the *Reading* concerning Boris and Gleb, on the other, we can see different tendencies in them. Whereas in *The Life of St Theodosius of the Caves* realistic details broke through the hagiographical canons, in the Lives of Boris and Gleb the canon prevails and in some cases distorts the authenticity of the situations described and the characters. Nevertheless the *Tale,* more than the *Reading,* shows a lyrical quality which is most evident in the death scene soliloquies of Boris and particularly of Gleb who grieves for his father and brothers and fears his imminent death.

Abstractness in Hagiographical Literature. There is another feature that is characteristic of hagiographical literature. It is seen most clearly in later hagiographical works of the fourteenth and fifteenth centuries, but can already be found in the *vitae* of the eleventh and twelfth centuries. This feature is abstractness. The author deliberately avoids being definite, precise, omitting all details that would indicate the particular, individual nature of the situations described. This is not fortuitous, but a deliberate attempt to see the saint's Life, as it were, outside time and space as a set of ethical rules, eternal and universal. Thus, for example, *The Life of St Theodosius of the Caves* contains an account of the internecine strife in 1073 (when princes Vsevolod and Svyatoslav drove Grand Prince Izyaslav out of Kiev) which reads as follows: "Incited by the cunning foe (i.e., the Devil) discord broke out among the three princes, blood brothers: two of them waged war upon the third, their elder brother, the Christ-loving and truly God-loving Izyaslav. And he was driven out of his capital city, and they came to this city and sent for our blessed father Theodosius..." No mention is made of the names of the princes who oppose Izyaslav or of Kiev (it is merely referred to as the "capital"), and the feudal strife is depicted as the result solely of the Devil's work. It is typical of the abstracting tendency that proper names are omitted and people are referred to by their social position ("a certain boyar", "that man" or "a certain general"; in the latter case the Greek term *strategus* is used instead of the usual Russian term *voevoda*), geographical names, exact dates, etc., are also omitted. This tendency had just begun to appear in the hagiographical literature of Kievan Russia. It found fullest expression later, as already mentioned, in the fourteenth and fifteenth centuries.[95]

7. The Kiev Crypt Patericon

A patericon is a collection of stories about the life of monks in a particular area or monastery. The oldest Russian patericon is that of the Kiev Crypt Monastery. The monastery was founded in the middle of the eleventh century, and already in *The Tale of Bygone Years* there is an account of its founding under the year 1051 and of some of its monks under 1074. The *Patericon* was created much later, however, and was based on a correspondence at the beginning of the thirteenth century between Bishop Simon of Vladimir and Polycarp, a monk of the Crypt Monastery, although they, in turn, appear to have made use of records kept in the monastery itself.

Simon and Polycarp had both taken vows in the Kiev Crypt Monastery and were both educated and talented scribes. But their fates were different: Simon first became abbot of a monastery in Vladimir, then in 1214 was made bishop of Vladimir and Suzdal. Polycarp stayed in the monastery. The ambitious monk would not reconcile himself to his position which he felt was not in keeping with his knowledge and abilities, and with the help of influential patrons, Princess Verkhuslava-Anastasia, the daughter of Prince Vsevolod the Big Nest, and her brother Yuri, he began to connive for a bishopric. But Simon, to whom the princess turned for support, did not approve of Polycarp's ambitious strivings and wrote him a letter denouncing his love of high office and exhorting him to take pride in being a member of such a famous monastery. Simon accompanied this letter with some stories about other monks belonging to the monastery, in the hope that these stories would remind Polycarp of the monastery's fine traditions and calm his restless spirit. Simon's letter and the nine stories about monks of the Kiev Crypt Monastery that followed it were one of the main sources of the future *Patericon*.

Another important section of the work was Polycarp's letter to Abbot Akindin, in which Polycarp wrote that he had finally resolved to realise a plan conceived long ago of writing an account of the Life and "miracles of the Crypt saints". The letter was followed by eleven stories about famous monks.

Evidently at some point in the middle of the thirteenth century the letters of Simon and Polycarp (together with the stories that accompanied them) were assembled and added to from other writings about the monastery: *The Life of St Theodosius of the Caves* and the eulogy to him, the *Sermon on the Founding of the Crypt Church* written by Simon, etc.

Thus gradually the literary work was assembled which later became known as the *Kiev Crypt Patericon*. What we have is the Arsenius redaction of the *Patericon* made at the beginning of the fifteenth century on the initiative of Bishop Arsenius of Tver, the Theodosius redaction, possibly mid-fifteenth century, and two Cassian redactions compiled in the 1460s in the monastery itself.[96]

The literary and ideological importance of the *Patericon* was extremely great. It not only summed up the development of Russian hagiography over the eleventh and twelfth centuries, but also by recounting the famous monastery's glorious past aroused patriotic sentiments and in the terrible years of the Mongol overlordship recalled the former flowering and might of Kievan Russia.

The tales in the *Kiev Crypt Patericon* contain many traditional patericon motifs: righteous monks perform miracles, successfully resist worldly wiles and temptations, overcome demons and expose their cunning snares. All these fantastic collisions, however, take place against the background of real monastery life and the real political events in Kievan Russia in the eleventh and twelfth centuries. Alongside the idealised portraits of the monastery's ascetics appear real characters of cruel princes, greedy merchants and iniquitous judges. Nor are the monks themselves always beyond reproach: they are prey to envy and greed and frequently reproach and quarrel with one another.

Thus, the legend of Prochorus the Orach-Carrier tells how Prochorus supplied the starving Kievans with bread that had been baked from orach, but tasted as sweet as if it were made "with honey". If anyone stole the bread from Prochorus it tasted as bitter as wormwood. Then Prochorus collected ash from the cells and turned it into salt, which he also distributed to the needy. This angered the merchants who had put up the prices of their provisions. They complained to Prince Svyatopolk[97] about Prochorus. After conferring with his boyars the prince took Prochorus' magic salt away from him, hoping to get rich, but the salt turned back into ashes. On the third day the prince ordered the ashes to be thrown away, and they again turned into salt which was joyfully taken by the needy townspeople. It is easy to see how unfavourably the prince and his counsellors and the greedy merchants of Kiev appear in this story.

Another legend tells of the monk Gregory. Some thieves come

to rob him but he sends them into a deep sleep that lasts for five days. He makes other thieves stand rooted to the spot for two days, weighed down by the fruit and vegetables they have stolen. At first the monks cannot see the thieves, but when they finally notice them they cannot move them. Then it tells how the same Gregory on the banks of the Dnieper meets Prince Rostislav Vsevolodovich, who is on his way to the monastery to receive a blessing before his campaign against the Polovtsians. The prince's men laugh at the monk and "utter shameful words". Gregory reproaches them and predicts death by water. Angered by the monk's words, the prince exclaims proudly: "Is it to me, who can swim, that you predict death by water", and orders Gregory to be bound and drowned in the Dnieper. The monks seek in vain for Gregory for two days, and only on the third does his dead body—with a stone round the neck and in wet robes—appear miraculously in his locked cell. And Prince Rostislav, who had killed Gregory, did indeed drown while crossing the river at Trepolie.[98]

The story about the monk Theodore is also interesting. He suffers greatly from the wiles of demons who appear to him in the form of his friend, the monk Basil, and cause the friends to quarrel. At last he manages to overcome the demons and even make them serve him: in one night they grind five cartloads of grain at his command, then they carry up the hill heavy logs that have been floated down the Dnieper to rebuild a church and cells damaged by fire and pile them in the right places: for the floor, the roof and the walls. But this fantastic world of miracles is closely intertwined with the world of real people and human relationships. Firstly, the demons incite the carriers hired to transport the logs to the monastery to slander Theodore and, after bribing the judge, demand that he pay for the work done by the demons. Secondly, a demon appears to one of the Prince of Kiev's boyars in the guise of Basil and tells him of some rich treasure hidden in a place that is known to Theodore. The boyar takes the demon-Basil to Prince Mstislav. The prince decides to hunt for the treasure, sets off "as if to capture some strong warrior" with a large host of men, captures Theodore and tortures him to find out where the treasure is hidden. Theodore's friend, the real Basil, is also tortured. Both monks die after being tortured. True, the prince receives Divine retribution—he is killed by the same arrow with which he put Basil to death.[99] The interesting point, however, is that the princes and boyars of Kiev, according to the *Patericon,* do not even stop at murdering monks in their pride or love of money. The aura of respect which, as the *Patericon* declares, surrounded the Kiev Crypt Monastery and the aura of Christian piety round the princes of Kiev fade completely. The point is not whether the story is true or not, of course, but the nature of the relations between the monastery and the secular figures who are depicted in one way or another by the patericon legends.

The subjects of the stories about the Kiev Crypt monks are very engaging. Alexander Pushkin drew attention to this in a letter to Pyotr Pletnyov, speaking of the "charm of simplicity and invention" in the legends about the Kiev miracle-workers.[100] They combine purely hagiographical devices with the devices of the chronicle narrative; in spite of hagiographical conventions realistic details and lifelike character traits slip in from time to time. The *Kiev Crypt Patericon* thus represents an important stage in the development of the fictional narrative in Old Russian literature.[101]

8. *The Pilgrimage* of Abbot Daniel

The word pilgrimage (*khozhdenie*) in Old Russian literature was used for works describing pilgrimages to the holy places in the Near East and Byzantium. The earliest specimen of this genre is *The Pilgrimage* of Abbot Daniel.[102]

Very little is known about Daniel himself. He was the abbot of a Russian monastery which, it is believed, was situated in the Chernigov lands. Daniel made his pilgrimage at the beginning of the twelfth century. From certain historical facts mentioned by him we can assume that he visited the holy places in the Kingdom of Jerusalem that existed on territory taken from the Arabs by the Crusaders in 1106-1108.

On the way Daniel visited Constantinople, Ephesus and Cyprus. He spent sixteen months in the holy places. He lived in the monastery of St Sabas near Jerusalem, journeying to different parts of the kingdom, the towns of Jericho and Bethlehem, and the Sea of Galilee. He was accompanied by a monk "old in years and most well-read". As a pilgrim Daniel was naturally interested most of all in the holy places and monuments which ecclesiastical tradition linked with the name of Jesus or characters from the Bible. He describes the pool where Christ healed the cripple, the mount of the Crucifixion, the cave in which Christ's body was lain after the Crucifixion, etc. Daniel not only lists the things he has seen, but gives a short account of the Old and New Testament stories linked with them, showing his knowledge not only of the canonical books of the Bible, but also of apocryphal tales.

In his descriptions Daniel tries to be accurate, writing a kind of guide for future pilgrims. He indicates the direction which one should take to reach a certain spot and gives some highly graphic

заоутрѫже · бывшюсвѣтоу иприпѣвшюдкошєни
ю хлѣба · ипридеантонии пособычаю · исокончю· блго
словию̈ чєнбакий · ипєбыглапи послоушании · имногѥда
антонии · ипєбыпичтоже · ӥрєсоуꙗжєрєставилъ · ипо
главмонастырь по фєндосиипобрꙗю · ипꙁопавшетꙑжₐ̈тъ
бⷺꙁаꙃраꙁжємоуспгик · ипришєⷣшєꙁашашимꙗщєн мртⷡ̈а ·
ивынꙋсоши иположишӥпⷣрⷮпєщєрою · иоуꙃрѣшꙗкоꙁнⷣив̈
єстъ · ирⷷимъигоумєнъфєⷣоси · ꙗкосєӥматⷬєбыти
ⷴⷵєⷮсовꙇⷵкꙑагодѣтⷥєⷩⷮства · иположишиинӓлⷣрⷦ̈ · исⷧоужꙗ́
шаⷥйꙇоⷧⷴєⷢ̈о антонии · всиꙁжєⷥрⷴⷱⷰⷰⷩⷺⷪⷮⷷприключиса · иꙁаꙃⷧⷰⷰ
пⷪⷭⷴоⷲⷹⷰ́ꙁлⷮⷵⷲⷳⷰⷰⷰⷩⷣⷷⷷⷠⷦⷸⷮⷹⷩⷳⷰⷱⷮⷻ

information about distances: "And from that rock as far as a good archer can shot", or "And the distance from the town wall is as far as a person can throw a small piece of rock." He describes architectural buildings and their decor in detail. "That church," he writes of the Church of the Resurrection, "is circular ... in form; inside it has twelve round solid columns and six square ones; it is beautifully paved with marble; it has six doors; and there are sixteen columns in the choir gallery"; and there are many similar descriptions.

However, while reverently viewing "that longed-for land and the holy places" where Christ "suffered for us, sinners", Daniel does not remain indifferent to the countryside. He admires the fertility of the soil which yields rich harvests of barley and wheat and describes the groves of figs and olives. There is an interesting description of the River Jordan which Daniel compares with the River Snov in his native Chernigov land: one bank of the Jordan is steep, the other gently sloping, the current is fast and the water turbid, but pleasant to the taste; "in all things the Jordan is like unto the River Snov: in width, and depth and its winding course and swift-flowing current it is like unto the River Snov".

Daniel's descriptions of his life and the daily life of the Kingdom of Jerusalem are scant. He merely mentions in passing the mountain paths on which travellers are beset by Saracen robbers and notes that he only managed to reach the town of Tiberias by attaching himself to a band of warriors belonging to King Baldwin I. Only one episode is described in any detail. During a church service the king honours Daniel by leading him through the crowd of pilgrims ("the people were pushed back by force to make way for us ... and thanks to this we could pass through the crowd"). Daniel ascribes this honour not to himself, but to respect for Russia which he represented. Daniel stresses that when he was abroad he felt himself to be the envoy of the whole Russian land and expresses his concern for it, in the traditional way for the pilgrim, of course, by lighting an icon-lamp for it in the churches and "in all the holy places" and asking for prayers to be said "for the Russian princes and princesses, and their children, for the bishops and the abbots, the boyars, their spiritual children, and for all the Christians of Russia."

Valentin Yanin has drawn attention to the following fact. In mentioning memorial services for Russian princes, princesses and boyars—he held ninety such services for them in all—Daniel names only a few princes. Yanin has reconstructed the original form of this list of princes and established that the actual choice of names and even the order in which they were put was of a special significance for Daniel. He names the nine princes who formed "the supreme coalition which decided national affairs and guided the political development of the state". "Daniel," Yanin concludes, "was a Russian abbot in the highest meaning of the word and, remembering the princes, held liturgies for the system of relationships that had been drawn up at the princely conferences in the late eleventh and early twelfth centuries, seeing this as a means of preventing internecine strife, the destruction of the Russian land and fratricidal wars." [103]

Nevertheless it is still unclear under what circumstances Daniel's pilgrimage took place: the reference to the many people accompanying him, his liberal means and, finally, the indisputable marks of respect shown to him by King Baldwin, all suggest that Daniel was to some degree or other an official representative of the Russian land and was visiting the holy places with some diplomatic or ecclesiastical credentials, or, at least, was not an ordinary pilgrim. [104]

Abbot Daniel's *Pilgrimage* was extremely popular in Old Russian literature, as can be seen from the fact that about a hundred manuscripts of the work have survived.

9. *The Lay of Igor's Host*

The Lay of Igor's Host was discovered by the well-known collector of Old Russian manuscripts, Count Alexei Musin-Pushkin, at the end of the eighteenth century. The intensive study of this outstanding monument of Old Russian literature dates from that period. Today the list of books and articles about *The Lay of Igor's Host* published in Russian, Ukrainian, Byelorussian and other languages of the peoples of the Soviet Union and also in other countries numbers hundreds of titles. [105]

Scholars have analysed the text of the *Lay*, its literary merits and language, they have examined the ideological conception of the work and the historical range of its author, and they have sought to explain the circumstances in which the manuscript of the *Lay* was discovered and the principles of its publication. Most of these questions have now been studied fully.

The Story of the Discovery and Publication of the Lay. The first published references to the *Lay* are by Mikhail Kheraskov, the poet and dramatist, and the historian and writer Nikolai Karamzin. In 1797 Kheraskov stated in a note on the text of his poem *Vladimir*: "A manuscript, entitled *The Song of Igor's Host*, written by an unknown author has been discovered recently. Written many centuries before our day, it would seem, for it mentions the Russian bard, Boyan." The same year in a journal published in Hamburg by French emigres, the *Spectateur du Nord*, Karamzin published a note that read, inter alia, as follows: "Two years ago in our archives a fragment was discovered from a poem entitled *The Song to Igor's Host*, which may be compared with the finest Ossianic verse and which was written in the twelfth century by an unknown author."

The *Lay* became known to Musin-Pushkin somewhat earlier than in 1794-1795 however. Pavel Berkov expressed the well-founded view that in the article "On the Innate Character of the Russian People" published in the February issue of the *Zritel* (Spectator) journal for 1792, the publisher Pyotr Plavilshchikov had the *Lay* in mind when he stated that "even in the days of Yaroslav, son of Vladimir, there were verse poems in honour of him and his children"[106] and said that, in spite of the devastation after the "barbarous Tartar invasion", "these precious remains still exist to this day in the libraries of lovers of rare Russian antiquities and, perhaps, Russia will soon see them".[107] The following fact also points to these years as the time when the *Lay* was discovered. Musin-Pushkin made a copy of the Old Russian text of the *Lay* for Empress Catherine the Great who was interested at that time in Russian history. The text of the *Lay* was accompanied by a translation and notes. In these notes he made use of historical essays by Catherine herself, which were published in 1793. Since the notes contain no reference to a printed edition, it is likely that Catherine's copy was made before 1793.[108]

How did the manuscript find its way into Count Musin-Pushkin's collection? The count himself said that he had acquired it together with a number of other books from Archimandrite Joel of the Monastery of Our Saviour in Yaroslavl. It has recently been established that the miscellany containing the *Lay* did belong to this monastery and was included in an inventory of its manuscript books, but not later than 1788 it was "sent away" presumably for binding, according to an inventory (in the inventory for the following year the manuscript is already listed as "destroyed due to poor condition"). It was evidently sent away, directly or through Joel, to Musin-Pushkin.[109]

At the very end of the eighteenth century Alexei Musin-Pushkin together with the archivists Alexei Malinovsky and Nikolai Bantysh-Kamensky prepared the *Lay* for publication. It was published in 1800.[110] Twelve years later, however, the whole of the count's valuable collection of Old Russian manuscripts, including the miscellany with the *Lay*, perished in the fire in Moscow during the Napoleonic invasion. Part of the first edition of the *Lay* was also destroyed then: today there are about sixty copies of it in public libraries and private possession.[111]

The destruction of the only manuscript of the *Lay* made study of the work extremely difficult. The contents of the miscellany were not sufficiently clear, its date had not been established, and it transpired that the publishers had not reproduced the original text of the *Lay* altogether accurately. In several cases they had been unable to read certain passages correctly and had not noticed obvious errors in copying. It required considerable efforts from several generations of Russian and Soviet researchers to solve these problems.

The Contents of the Musin-Pushkin Miscellany. Mention is made of the contents of the miscellany in the introductory note to the edition of 1800. This gives only the titles of the works before and after the *Lay*, however, and they have been established by indirect evidence, in particular, with the help of extracts from tales included in the miscellany and quoted by Nikolai Karamzin in his *History of the Russian State*. It has now been established with a sufficient degree of probability that the miscellany began with a *Chronograph* of the Extended Redaction of 1617,[112] followed by *The Novgorod First Chronicle* of the younger recension,[113] the first redaction of *The Tale of the Indian Empire*,[114] the earliest redaction of *The Tale of Akir the Wise, The Lay of Igor's Host*, and the first redaction of *The Deeds of Digenes*. The composition of the miscellany is extremely interesting. The *Lay* is found together with works or redactions that are very rare in Russian literature. Thus, we have no other manuscript of the first redaction of *The Tale of the Indian Empire*, and only one more complete manuscript (fifteenth century) and two incomplete ones (fifteenth and seventeenth centuries) of the first redaction of *The Tale of Akir the Wise. The Deeds of Digenes* is known only from three manuscripts of the seventeenth and eighteenth centuries, although it was translated not later than the thirteenth century.

Information about the date of the miscellany was conflicting. The publishers merely announced that the manuscript "was a very old one, judging by the script". The orthography of the text of the *Lay* and the fragments of *The Tale of Akir the Wise* that we know because Nikolai Karamzin copied them out suggest that the manuscript was transcribed not later than the late sixteenth century. But the presence in the miscellany of the seventeenth-century chronograph suggests that the miscellany was a convolute, i.e., a manuscript consisting of two parts, one of which contained the chronograph of the seventeenth century and the other the chronicle and tales of an earlier period.[115]

It was most important to attempt to establish how accurately the Old Russian text of the *Lay* had been reproduced by the publishers. Pyotr Pekarsky's discovery of the Catherine copy in

1864 made it possible to compare the text of this copy with that of the published version. It transpired that there were a large number of discrepancies between them. A study of the Catherine copy, the passages from the *Lay* copied out by Alexei Malinovsky and Nikolai Karamzin[116] and an analysis of eighteenth-century publishing principles[117] made it possible to conclude that in striving to reproduce the *words* (the sense units of the text) the publishers, in keeping with the spirit of their age, had deviated considerably from the actual script, i.e., the orthography of the Old Russian manuscript.

Moreover the publishers had not been able to read and reproduce the text accurately at times and had not always understood the meaning of individual words. This explains why in the first edition of the *Lay* there were several obscure passages, which students of the *Lay* have been trying to decypher for more than a century and a half now. It proved relatively easy to correct the publishers' errors,[118] but the manuscript of the *Lay*, like all Old Russian manuscripts, undoubtedly had some obscure passages of its own, resulting from the scribe's errors or damage to the text in the manuscripts that preceded Musin-Pushkin's. There are not many such obscure passages, but it will probably not be possible to clarify them until another manuscript of the work is found.

That we know the *Lay* from one manuscript only should not be surprising. We have only one manuscript of Vladimir Monomachos' *Instruction* and two of *The Lay of the Ruin of the Russian Land*. A number of works, particularly those written before the Mongol invasion, are known only from indirect evidence, as not a single copy of them has survived (for example, the *Life of St Anthony of the Caves*). Many works of this period have survived in rare and very late manuscripts, such as *The Deeds of Digenes*.

The Question of When the *Lay* Was Written. The question of the authenticity of the *Lay* and the date when it was written occupies an important place in research literature on the work.

Doubt as to the authenticity of the *Lay* arose after the manuscript was destroyed in the Moscow fire of 1812. At that time there were many reasons for the emergence of a sceptical attitude to the *Lay* having been written in the twelfth century. Firstly, at the beginning of the nineteenth century scholars still knew very little about Old Russian literature, and therefore the *Lay* seemed to them unnaturally advanced for the level of literary culture in the late twelfth century.[119] Secondly, they were troubled by the obscure passages in the *Lay*, the abundance of incomprehensible words, which they sought to explain at first by reference to other

Slavonic languages, and this gave grounds for assuming that the author of the work was not an Old Russian writer, but, for example, a Western Slav. Thirdly, one reason for the emergence of doubts as to the authenticity of the *Lay* was the sceptical trend in Russian historiography during that period. The casting of doubt on the authenticity of the *Lay* was just one individual episode. Representatives of the sceptical school also challenged the age of the Russian chronicles, the collection of Old Russian laws entitled *Russian Law,* the works of Cyril of Turov, etc.[120]

In the middle of the nineteenth century *The Trans-Doniad* was discovered, the tale of the Battle of Kulikovo (1380) between the Russians and the Tartars of crucial importance for the Russian state. The language and imagery of this work were found to contain vivid parallels with *The Lay of Igor's Host.* Since the oldest of the known manuscripts of *The Trans-Doniad* belongs to the late fifteenth century, doubts as to the authenticity of the *Lay* were quietened. However, in the 1890s the French scholar Louis Léger advanced the thesis that it was not the author of *The Trans-Doniad* who had imitated the *Lay,* but vice versa, the *Lay* was an imitation of *The Trans-Doniad.*[121] This hypothesis was later developed in the writings of the French Academician A. Mazon,[122] and subsequently became one of the main arguments of the Soviet specialist Alexander Zimin. Zimin believed that the *Lay* had been written on the basis of *The Trans-Doniad* in the eighteenth century by the Yaroslavl Archimandrite Joel from whom Musin-Pushkin acquired the miscellany with the *Lay.*

Alexander Zimin's hypothesis was the most well-founded of the attempts to challenge the traditional view of the *Lay* as a literary work of Kievan Russia. Zimin examined a broad range of questions: he touched upon the reasons why the *Lay* could have been written in the eighteenth century, described the personality of the hypothetical author, examined the language of the work, in particular, the role of Turkisms in the vocabulary of the *Lay,* and dealt with the relationship of the *Lay* to *The Hypatian Chronicle* and other monuments of Old Russian literature, but paid special attention to the central question—the relationship of the *Lay* to *The Trans-Doniad.*[123]

After this discussion scholars again turned to a profound study of all the questions listed and it emerged that the facts testified indisputably to the authenticity of the work: the connection between *The Trans-Doniad* and the *Lay,* which served as a model for the former,[124] is beyond doubt, and the relationships between the various manuscripts of *The Trans-Doniad* are different (in particular, the White Lake Monastery of St Cyril manuscript does not represent the first redaction of the work, as Zimin argued).[125]

The authenticity of the *Lay* is confirmed by an analysis of its language[126] and a comparison of its grammatical structure with that of *The Trans-Doniad.*[127] The *Lay* is closely connected with the historical reality of its age, and to ascribe it to the eighteenth century gives rise to a number of ideological and source discrepancies that are hard to explain.[128] Even more striking is the aesthetic correspondence of the *Lay* to the spirit of the twelfth century and the obvious difference between its artistic nature and the perception and interpretation of historical subjects in the literature of the eighteenth century.[129] The authenticity of the *Lay* is borne out by its relationship with *The Hypatian Chronicle.*[130] The Turkisms in the *Lay* are archaic.[131] The personality of Archimandrite Joel gives us no grounds whatsoever for seeing him as the possible author of the *Lay.*[132]

In general the most recent discussion on the dating of the *Lay* was a fruitful one, since a more careful study was made of many different facts—textological, historical and linguistic—which confirmed the traditional view of the *Lay* as a literary work of Kievan Russia.[133]

Let us now examine the text of the *Lay.*

The Historical Basis of the Subject of *The Lay of Igor's Host.* The events forming the basis of the subject of the *Lay* are set out in the chronicles in the following form.[134]

On April 23, 1185 Igor, Prince of Novgorod-Seversky,* set off on a campaign against the Polovtsians. He was accompanied by his son Vladimir, who reigned in Putivl, and his nephew Svyatoslav from Rylsk. On the way they were joined by a fourth campaigner, Igor's brother Vsevolod, Prince of Trubchevsk. The eclipse of May 1, 1185 (described in detail in *The Laurentian Chronicle*) alarmed the princes and their men; they saw it as a bad omen, but Igor persuaded his allies to continue the campaign. The scouts sent on ahead also brought bad news: the Polovtsians could not be taken by surprise, so it was necessary either to attack at once or to turn back. But Igor believed that if they returned home without giving battle, they would condemn themselves to disgrace "worse ... than death", and continued to advance towards the Polovtsian steppe.

On the morning of Friday, May 10, they overcame the Polovtsians and seized their tents and wagons. After this victory Igor intended to turn back at once, before other Polovtsian forces arrived. But Svyatoslav, who had ridden far in pursuit of the retreating Polovtsians, objected that his horses were tired. The Russians spent the night in the steppe. Next morning they saw

---

* A town in the east of the present-day Chernigov Region.

that they were surrounded by hordes of Polovtsians. "They had assembled the whole Polovtsian land against themselves," as the chronicle says. A fierce battle was waged all Saturday and Sunday morning. Suddenly the Turkic warriors sent to help Igor by Yaroslav of Chernigov turned and fled. In an attempt to arrest their flight Igor left his band and was taken prisoner. The Russian host suffered a crushing defeat. Only fifteen men managed to get back to Russia.[135]

After defeating Igor the Polovtsians launched a counterattack. They devastated the left bank of the Dnieper, besieged Pereyas-lavl-Yuzhny, which was heroically defended by Prince Vladimir, captured the town of Rimov and burnt down the fortifications of Putivl. A month after the defeat (Boris Rybakov estimates) Igor managed to flee from captivity. These are the events of 1185 as recorded by the chronicle.

The Ideological Content of the *Lay*. The author of the *Lay* turned this isolated, although tragic episode in Russo-Polovtsian warfare into an event of national dimensions. It is no accident that he summons to Igor's aid not only the princes who had a direct interest in this campaign, since their appanages could have become the object of Polovtsian incursions, but also Prince Vsevolod the Big Nest of Vladimir and Suzdal. The author of the *Lay* persistently stresses the main idea of the work: the need for unity between the princes in the struggle against the steppe nomads, the need to put an end to strife and war between the individual feudal lords, in which the princes received assistance from the Polovtsians on this or that side. The author of the *Lay* does not object to the feudal relations of his age that establish the appanage system (with all the unfortunate consequences of a divided Russia). He merely objects to the internecine strife, the violation of other people's lands ("this is mine, and that, too, is mine"),* and argues the need for the princes to live in peace and to obey their senior in rank, the Grand Prince of Kiev. This explains why the victories of Svyatoslav of Kiev are praised so highly in the *Lay*. It is he who reproaches Igor and Vsevolod with having set off to "seek glory" for themselves, and bitterly censures the princes who refuse to help one another in the struggle against the foe. The author of the *Lay* even seeks to stress the seniority of Svyatoslav by the fact that, in spite of their actual relationship, the Prince of Kiev in the *Lay* calls his cousins, Igor and Vsevolod, his *synovtsy* (nephews), and the author calls him their father (Igor and Vsevolod roused the evil which was "put to sleep by their father, the great, the

---

* Quoted from *The Lay of the Warfare Waged by Igor*, Progress Publishers, Moscow, 1981.

The Chronicle Tale of Prince Igor's Campaign. **The Polovtsians Raid the Russian Land and Are Resisted by the Russian Princes.** Illumination from *The Radziwill Chronicle.* 15th century. Academy of Sciences Library, Leningrad

terrible Svyatoslav of Kiev"):[136] because he is their suzerain, their feudal head.

The same idea, the need for princely unity, underlies the historical digressions of the *Lay*. The author reproves Oleg (addressing him as Gorislavich—"of bitter fame"—instead of using his real patronymic, Svyatoslavich) for stirring up internecine strife by his actions. He proudly recalls the age of Vladimir Svyatoslavich, the age of Russian unity, but now the pennons of Rurik and David "float apart".[137] This persistent and clearly expressed patriotic idea of the *Lay* was formulated by Karl Marx as follows: "In essence, the poem is a call for unity on the part of the Russian princes just before the invasion by the Mongol hordes proper." [138]

The genre of the *Lay* is unusual. It is not a military tale in the proper sense of the term. The author does not describe the events of 1185 in detail. He reflects on them, assesses and examines them against the background of a broad historical perspective, almost against the whole of Russian history. And it is these genre peculiarities of the *Lay* that also determine the originality of its composition and its system of imagery.

The Composition of the Lay. The *Lay* begins with a lengthy introduction, in which the author recalls the ancient bard, the wise and skilled Boyan, but nevertheless declares that in his work he will not follow this tradition, but will begin his "song" in accord with the events of his own time, and not with the poetic imagination of Boyan.

Having fixed the chronological span of his narrative, from "Vladimir of old" (i.e., Vladimir of Kiev who died in 1015) to "Igor of our own days", the author tells of the Prince of Novgorod-Seversky's bold intention to lead his hosts against the Polovtsian land, to "drink of the Don water" with his helmet (drinking from an enemy river is a symbol of vanquishing the foe). The author seems to be trying to adapt the poetic manner of Boyan to his theme ("No storm is this that has blown the falcons beyond the rolling plains: the daws are fleeing in flocks towards the Great Don!" or "Steeds neigh beyond the Sula—glory resounds through Kiev!").

In joyous tones the author portrays the meeting of Igor and Vsevolod the Furious Bull, praising the valour of the men of Kursk. All the greater the contrast with the following story about the terrible omens that mark the arrival of Igor's host on Polovtsian soil and presage the tragic outcome of the campaign: these are the solar eclipse, the strange, sinister sounds in the dark night, and the cry of the fantastic creature called the Div. Although he goes on to describe the first victory that brings the

The Chronicle Tale of Prince Igor's Campaign. Mounting the Stirrup. Defending the Battlements. Illumination from *The Radziwill Chronicle.* 15th century. Academy of Sciences Library, Leningrad

Mounting the Stirrup. Detail

Russian princes some rich trophies, the author again returns to the theme of the terrible omens of imminent defeat: "A blood-red dawn foretells the day. Black clouds come up from the sea..."

The account of the second battle, fatal for Igor, is interrupted by a digression. The author recalls the age of Oleg Svyatoslavich, an appanage prince who appears at the end of the seventies, and again in the latter half of the 1090s as the instigator of a series of internecine wars. This historical digression introduces a theme to which the author of the *Lay* returns over and over again, the condemnation of princely strife in which the birthright of "the grandsons of Dazhbog" perishes. But those bloody battles of the past cannot be compared with Igor's battle against the Polovtsian hosts that surround him: "From morning till evening, from twilight till dawn steel-tipped arrows fly, swords clang upon helmets..." And although the battle is taking place in the remote Polovtsian steppe, the consequences of Igor's defeat will be felt all over the Russian land. Nature itself grieves for him: "the very grass droops with pity, and the trees bend down".

Again, leaving the tale of Igor for a while, the author of the *Lay* narrates all the misfortunes of the Russian land, saying that the Russian princes themselves who stir up strife against one another are to blame. Only the unity of all the Russian forces against the nomads will guarantee victory, as can be seen from the defeat inflicted in 1184 on the Polovtsians by Svyatoslav of Kiev when the Polovtsian Khan Kobyak was taken prisoner.

The author goes on to tell of Svyatoslav's dream that predicted grief and death for him. The boyars interpret the dream: the bad omens have already been fulfilled—"two suns have grown dim", Igor and Vsevolod have been defeated and captured. Svyatoslav reproaches the princes for their rash seeking after glory, their untimely campaign, and laments the lack of help from the other princes.

Continuing Svyatoslav's address, as it were, the author of the *Lay* appeals to the most valorous and influential of the Russian princes, praising them and urging them to avenge "the wrong of these days", to avenge Igor. But for many of the princes the time of glorious victories is past, and the reason for this is again the internecine wars. "Lower your banners, and sheathe your blunted swords! Far, far have you fled from your forefathers' fame!" the author urges them. And just as earlier he recalled the age of Oleg, son of Svyatoslav, now he turns to the figure of another militant prince of the past, Vseslav of Polotsk. Vseslav likewise was not victorious, in spite of his temporary triumphs ("with his spear-shaft he touched" Kiev's "golden throne ... burst open the gates of

Novgorod shattering Yaroslav's fame") and even the superhuman qualities ascribed to him (he is able to move from one place to another with incredible speed, has the gift of second sight, and is a prince-werewolf).[139]

Then the *Lay* again turns to the fate of Igor. In Putivl Yaroslavna is praying to nature to help her husband and free him from captivity. It is typical that this lyrical lament, constructed on the basis of a folk lament, contains the social motifs characteristic of the whole work. Yaroslavna is concerned not only about her husband, but about his men. She recalls the glorious campaigns of Svyatoslav of Kiev against Khan Kobyak. Yaroslavna's lament is closely connected with the following account of Igor's escape from captivity. Nature helps him: the River Donets speaks kindly to him, the jackdaws, ravens and magpies are silent so as not to betray the position of the fugitives, the woodpeckers show them the way, the nightingales regale them with their song.

The dispute of khans Konchak and Gza on what to do with Igor's captive son Vladimir continues this account of the prince's flight full of symbols taken from the realm of nature: Igor "flew like a falcon" to his native land, and the khans decide the fate of the young "falcon". It is interesting that here, as in other passages of the work, two types of metaphors are combined—military symbols (the "falcon"—the brave warrior) and symbols from folklore, in this case originating in the symbolism of wedding songs, where the bridegroom is a "falcon" and the bride a "fair maid", a "graceful swan".[140]

When speaking about the present, the author of the *Lay* constantly recalls the past, searching there for edifying examples, analogies. He recalls first Vladimir Monomachos, then Oleg, son of Svyatoslav, then Vseslav of Polotsk.

The epilogue of the *Lay* is festive and solemn: returning to Russia Igor comes to the great Svyatoslav in Kiev; "the hamlets rejoice, the towns are merry". And the *Lay* ends with a toast to the prince.

The Genre of the *Lay*. The composition of the *Lay* is unusual for an historical tale. We see that the author concentrates not so much on a consecutive account of the actual events of the campaign, as on reflections on it, an assessment of Igor's conduct, reflections on the causes of the hard times and sorrow that beset the Russian land and a turning to the past with its victories and misfortunes. All these features raise the question of the work's genre. This question is all the more important, because in Old Russian literature with its strict system of genres, the *Lay* (like a number of other works) would seem to be outside the genre system. Andrei Robinson and Dmitry Likhachev compare the *Lay*

The Chronicle Tale of Prince Igor's Campaign. The First Battle with the
Polovtsians. Illumination from ***The Radziwill Chronicle.*** 15th century. Academy
of Sciences Library, Leningrad

with the genre of the *chanson de geste*, drawing analogies between the *Lay* and the *Chanson de Roland*, for example, or similar works of the West-European feudal epos.[141]

The epic and bookish elements are united in the *Lay*. "The epos is full of appeals to defend the country..." writes Likhachev. "Its 'direction' is characteristic: the appeal seems to come from the people (hence the folklore element), but it is addressed to the feudal lords, the 'golden words' of Svyatoslav, hence the bookish element."[142]

The Poetics of the Lay. The poetics of the *Lay* are so original, its language and style so vivid and distinctive, that the *Lay* may seem at first glance to lie totally outside the sphere of Russian mediaeval literary traditions.

In fact this is not so. In the portrayal of the Russian princes and particularly the main heroes, Igor and Vsevolod, we find features of styles with which we are already familiar from the chronicle narrative: the epic style and the style of monumental historicism. However blameworthy Igor's foolhardy campaign, the hero himself remains for the author the embodiment of princely valour. Igor is courageous, his heart is "whetted ... with valour"; the desire to "drink a helmetful of Don water", the concept of a warrior's honour ("Better to be slain than taken captive") make him scorn the bad omen, the solar eclipse. His brother Vsevolod and his men are equally knightly: they were swaddled to the sound of trumpets, nursed beneath helmets, fed from the spear's point, and in battle seek honour for themselves and glory for their prince.

In general the style of monumental historicism manifests itself in the *Lay* in various profound ways. The action of the *Lay* unfolds against vast distances. The narrator seems to encompass at a glance all the territory from Novgorod the Great in the north to Tmutorokan (on the Taman Peninsula) in the south, from the Volga in the east to Galich and the Carpathians in the west. In his addresses to the princes the author of the *Lay* mentions many geographical points in the Russian land. Svyatoslav's fame spreads far beyond its borders, to the Germans, the Bohemians and the Venetians. The characters in the *Lay* seem to take a panoramic view of the Russian land, as if from a great height. Thus, for example, Yaroslavna's lament from Putivl is addressed not only to the sun and the wind, but also to the far-off Dnieper, which she asks to carry her dear husband back to her from Polovtsian captivity. Yaroslav Osmomysl rules his principality in deliberately stressed "spatial" borders, upbearing the Carpathian Mountains and "sitting in judgment even as far as the Danube" (that is to say, ruling the peoples up to the Danube). The actual battle with the Polovtsians acquires universal dimensions: the black clouds symbolising Russia's enemies come from the very sea.

Mention has already been made of the historicism of the *Lay*, also a characteristic feature of monumental historicism. The events, the actions and the very qualities of the characters in the *Lay* are judged against the background of the whole of Russian history, against the events not only of the twelfth, but also of the eleventh century.

Finally, the ceremonial element, the conventions of the *Lay*, undoubtedly belong to the style of monumental historicism. It is no accident that it contains so many references to such ceremonial forms of the oral tradition as eulogies and laments. And the princes themselves in the *Lay* are portrayed in ceremonial poses: they step into "golden stirrups" (set off on a campaign), raise or lower their banners (which symbolises setting off on a campaign or defeat in battle), after the first victory Igor is brought trophies. Igor's capture is also reported as a ceremonial act: the prince exchanges his golden saddle for the saddle of a slave.[143]

It is also the principles of monumental historicism that determine such a characteristic feature of the *Lay* as the author's historical digressions in which the main theme of the *Lay* stands out in particularly bold relief, namely, the condemnation of princely strife and reflections on the misfortunes of the Russian land subject to Polovtsian incursions. This is why the author breaks off the account of Igor's battle with the Polovtsians at the very climax and recalls the times of Oleg, son of Svyatoslav, which were equally turbulent and tragic for Russia. Between the account of the falling of Igor's banners and the description of Igor's capture is a long discourse on the consequences of the defeat: "Then, my brethren, an evil time set in..." The calamities of the Russian land subjected to a new Polovtsian incursion and even the sorrow felt by other peoples at this, the Germans and Venetians, Greeks (Byzantines) and Bohemians, are mentioned earlier than Svyatoslav's dream which, judging by the symbolism, he had on the fatal night when Igor was defeated.

In short, the author's digressions shift (deliberately and intentionally) the actual course of events, for the author's aim is not so much to recount these events, which were well known to his contemporaries, as to express his attitude towards them and his reflections on what took place. Once having understood these special features of the narrative, we can see that there is no point in discussing precisely when and where Igor and Vsevolod saw the eclipse and how accurately this is recorded in the *Lay*, exactly how the Polovtsians collected tribute or how advisable it was to appeal to Prince Vsevolod the Big Nest, who was only too ready to interfere in South Russian affairs, to come to Igor's aid. The *Lay* is an epic, not a documentary work. It does not so much relate events as meditate upon them.

The epic quality of the *Lay* is of a special kind. It co-exists with the bookish elements. The author's reflections, appeals to the reader and the above-mentioned ceremoniality, are all indisputable features of the *Lay*'s bookish nature. But alongside this is another element—the world of folkore. This world is reflected, as mentioned above, in the eulogies and above all, in the laments (Yaroslavna's lament, the lament of the Russian wives, and the lament of Rostislav's mother). However, the references to eulogies and laments and even the presence of Yaroslavna's lament, which is undoubtedly folkloric in spirit, are by no means the only elements from the world of folklore in the *Lay*. We find there the hyperbole typical of folklore: Vsevolod can drain the Volga by splashing it with his oars and empty the Don by drinking it from his helmet; Vsevolod the Furious Bull embodies, as it were, a whole host—he cleaves his enemies' helmets with "swords of tempered steel"; the images of the battle-feast, and the battlefield that is likened to a peaceful ploughed field, the images of the wolf, the bull, and the falcon to which the heroes in the *Lay* are compared. The author also uses standard epithets characteristic of folklore. At the same time the author of the *Lay*, as Varvara Adrianova-Peretts wrote, "found material for the construction of a literary style of unequalled expressiveness in the popular language which in the twelfth century contained tremendous possibilities for development, and in the devices of the rich treasury of oral poetry already developed by the poetic genius of the people".[144] A study of the poetics of the *Lay*, which combines features of bookish poetics close to oratory, and the poetics of folklore, also leads us to conclude that the *Lay*'s genre is a special one, as mentioned above.

A characteristic feature of the *Lay* is the existence within it of two levels—the realist (historico-documentary) portrayal of personages and events and the description of the fantastic world of forces hostile to the Russians, namely, the bad omens: the eclipse of the sun, the forces of nature that are hostile to Igor or warn him of misfortune, the fantastic Div, and the mythological Karna and Zhlya.

Many episodes in the *Lay* have symbolical undertones, including such apparently naturalistic sketches as wolves howling in ravines or birds waiting in forests for spoils on the field of battle.

Nature takes an active part in Igor's fate and in the fate of the Russian land: the grass bows in pity and the Donets and the birds who dwell in the groves on its banks gladly assist Igor when he is fleeing from captivity.

This does not mean that the *Lay* does not contain any descriptions of nature as such. But it is characteristic that, like other Old Russian works, it lacks static landscapes: the world around is perceived in movement, in various phenomena and processes. We are not told that the night is light or dark—"long lingers the night", the colour of the river water is not described, but we are told that "the rivers run turbid", the Dvina "flows through fens", the Sula "no longer sweeps a silvery stream". The bank of the Donets is not described, but we are told that the river spreads out green grass for Igor upon its silvery banks and drapes him in warm mists beneath the shade of green trees, etc.[145]

It has been said that the whole "literary system of the *Lay* is based on contrasts".[146] One example is the contrasting of metaphors: the sun (light) and darkness (night). This is traditional both for Old Russian literature and for folklore.[147] In the *Lay* it is frequently used in different images. Igor is a "bright light" and Konchak a "black raven", on the eve of the battle black clouds come in from the sea and seek to veil the "four suns". In his prophetic dream Svyatoslav is covered with a black shroud and given blue (black) wine and all night long dark ravens are croaking. The boyars' answer is constructed in accordance with the same metaphorical system: "On the third day darkness fell: the two suns have grown dim, the two purple pillars blaze no more... On the Kayala River the darkness overcame the light." Whereas when Igor is returning to Russia from captivity, once more "the sun lights up the heavens".

The Rhythmic Quality of the *Lay*. Scholars have long since drawn attention to the rhythmic quality of the *Lay* and frequently sought on these grounds to examine it as a work of verse. There is rhythm in the work, without a doubt, it is intentional and part of the author's stylistic tasks, but all the same the *Lay* is not verse, but rhythmic prose; moreover the rhythmical passages in the *Lay* alternate with passages in which the rhythm is either different or completely absent. These features are yet further proof that the *Lay* belongs to the literary school of the twelfth century for we find in it the same features of rhythmic prose as in other works of this period (Hilarion's *Sermon on Law and Grace*, Cyril of Turov's *Sermons*, and others), namely, repetition of similar syntactical constructions, anaphora (when consecutive fragments of the text begin in the same, or a similar, way) and a special "rhythmic balance", when "several short syntactical units are followed by one or two long ones; several long ones finish with one or two short ones."[148]

The Chronicle Tale of Prince Igor's Campaign. The Second Battle with the
Polovtsians and the Defeat of Igor's Host. Illumination from *The Radziwill
Chronicle.* 15th century. Academy of Sciences Library, Leningrad

A special feature of the language of the *Lay* is also the author's striving, as for example Leonid Bulakhovsky has noted, "to combine similar sounding words",[149] to use a distinctive sound pattern.

The Language of the *Lay*. The language of the *Lay* merits careful study not only as the language of a literary work, but also as a specimen of the Russian literary language of the twelfth century. This is all the more important because the sceptics' assertion that the language of *The Lay of Igor's Host* does not correspond to the language of that period plays a most important part in their argument. "The language is the most dangerous thing that they play with without understanding and discredit the work," wrote Academician Alexander Orlov, challenging the sceptics. "All the available data of the work itself must be clarified and examined", and only then will "all the peel and crusts such as modernisms Gallicisms, etc. ... fall off as totally unfounded invention, and the unprincipled, dilettantist game will stop".[150]

In research on the *Lay* considerable attention has been paid to its lexical analysis, the search for lexical and semantic parallels to the *Lay*'s lexemes in works of Old Russian literature, and an analysis of the grammatical structure and orthography of the *Lay*. A most valuable summary of the research done in this sphere up to the 1920s is given in Vladimir Peretts' monograph.[151] But the study of the language of the *Lay* has attracted particular attention in recent decades: in the definitive study of the work's morphological, syntactical and lexical structure by Sergei Obnorsky,[152] the sections on the language of the *Lay* in the histories of Russian literary language by Lev Yakubinsky and Boris Larin,[153] the articles comparing the grammatical and lexical structure of the *Lay* and *The Trans-Doniad*,[154] and numerous other works dealing with individual lexemes and expressions in the *Lay*.

A most important contribution to the study of the *Lay*'s language is made by Varvara Adrianova-Peretts' monograph in which on the basis of extensive material drawn primarily from works of Old Russian literature and documents of the eleventh to thirteenth centuries she shows how well the author of the *Lay* used "all the devices of Old Russian speech, how skilfully and aptly he selected the best means of expression for each element of the complex content of his work, and how organically he merged them into his own truly unique individual style."[155] Adrianova-Peretts' book is also valuable because it shows that the *Lay* has lexemes with the same meanings as those in other works of the period, and also that the *Lay* conformed to the linguistic norms of the period with regard to constructions, expressions and poetic imagery.

The material collected by Adrianova-Peretts proves beyond all doubt that the *Lay* belongs to the literature of the late twelfth century. This has also been confirmed by the research of Victor Franchuk who has discovered an indisputable similarity between the phraseology of the *Lay* and that of *The Kievan Chronicle.*[156]

Together with Varvara Adrianova-Peretts' monograph another definitive work deserves mention, the multi-volume *Dictionary-Handbook to "The Lay of Igor's Host"* which deals with the whole lexical composition of the *Lay*, illustrating each meaning of a word with examples taken from hundreds of sources—monuments of Old Russian literature and official documents, folklore, recordings of various dialects. In addition the *Dictionary* contains all the most important commentaries on the text of the *Lay*, historical information about the characters in the work, data about the etymology and meaning of individual words used in it, and interpretations of obscure passages.[157]

In recent decades many articles and notes have appeared giving lexical and poetic parallels to readings of the *Lay* (the articles by Boris Larin, Nikolai Meshchersky, Dmitry Likhachev, Varvara Adrianova-Peretts, Sergei Kotkov, and others). The comparison of the language of the *Lay* with that of contemporary dialects is particularly important.[158]

All these observations lead to the indisputable conclusion that the *Lay* belongs to those works of Old Russian literature that were created in Kievan Russia in the period of the greatest flowering of its writing and culture—on the eve of the Mongol invasion, at the end of the twelfth century.

The Time When the *Lay* Was Written and the Question of Its Authorship. Research of recent years shows convincingly that the *Lay* must have been written shortly after the events it portrays—Igor's campaign against the Polovtsians. The character of the narrative, the abundant allusions which could have been understood only by people alive when the events took place and the relevance of certain problems to the end of the twelfth century—all this does not permit us to accept the hypotheses of such specialists as Dmitry Alshits and Lev Gumilev, who have suggested that the work belongs to the thirteenth century. Attempts are continuing, however, to date the *Lay* more precisely within the last few decades of the twelfth century. Some researchers believe that the work was written not later than October 1, 1187, the date when Yaroslav Osmomysl died, for he is referred to in the *Lay* as being alive. However, we know that the addresses to the princes in the work are of a rhetorical nature, and the author could have addressed Yaroslav after his death as well for he was alive during

Igor's campaign and captivity. The argument that the toast pronounced at the end of the *Lay* in honour of Vsevolod would have been inappropriate after his death, which was in 1196, and that therefore the *Lay* was written not later than this date is worthy of attention.[159] However, the question of the work's precise date remains an open one.

No less complex is the question of the *Lay*'s author. Numerous attempts to establish precisely who wrote the work have mostly taken the form of searching for people alive at the time of the campaign who might have written it. But we possess no direct or indirect evidence that would enable us to give preference to any of these hypothetical authors. It is characteristic that Boris Rybakov, who has produced the most circumstantial hypothesis concerning the author of the *Lay*, sums up his observations as follows: "We cannot prove beyond a doubt that *The Lay of Igor's Host* and the chronicle of the tribe of Mstislav (a fragment of *The Kievan Chronicle.—O.T.*) were really written by the same person. And it is even harder to prove that this person was the *tysyatsky* (commander of the city militia) of Kiev, Pyotr Borislavich. Here we shall probably always remain in the sphere of hypotheses. But the remarkable similarity, verging sometimes on identity, of almost all the features of the two works (taking into account their different genres) does not permit us to reject entirely the idea that these two equally brilliant works were by the same author."[160] We are bound to agree with his caution. This question remains open for the time being.

We can, however, describe the unknown author. He was a man with broad historical interests and an excellent understanding of the complex political circumstances of his day, who was able to rise above the narrow interests of his principality to the interests of Russia as a whole, a talented writer, who knew and valued Old Russian literature, both translations and original works, and was also well acquainted with folklore... Only the combination of all this knowledge and ability, refined artistic taste, unerring choice of words and sense of rhythm enabled him to create this work which is the pride of Old Russian literature of the earliest period.

The *Lay* and Old Russian Literature. The question naturally arises as to why the *Lay*, the literary merits of which have been so highly regarded in the modern period, attracted so little attention in Old Russian literature, and in particular, why there are so few manuscripts of it.

It is hard to give a difinite answer to this, but we can advance a number of considerations in the light of our knowledge of Old Russian literature in general and the fate of individual Old

Russian works in particular. Firstly, all the works had their own individual fate: in the Middle Ages, particularly in Russia of the eleventh to thirteenth centuries, a period of feudal wars and Polovtsian incursions, followed by the devastating Mongol invasion, a work either disappeared completely because all the copies of it were destroyed, or sank into oblivion, since the few surviving copies of it might remain unknown for a long time for this or that reason. Secondly, after the Mongol invasion the *Lay* lost its political relevance. It was untraditional in form and complex in language—this too could have been a reason why the Old Russian scribes were not particularly anxious to reproduce existing copies of the *Lay*. The rarity of its copies, however, did not prevent the *Lay* from influencing other works of Old Russian literature. Its influence is felt particularly strongly in *The Trans-Doniad*, the tale of the victory over Mamai on Kulikovo Field, written at the end of the fourteenth century (regarded by some scholars as a fifteenth-century work). Imitating a work that was authoritative or noteworthy because of its literary merits, and quoting or retelling it was customary for mediaeval scribes. And this is what the author of *The Trans-Doniad* did. But in making use of the narrative about Igor's defeat by the Polovtsians in his tale of the Russian victory over the Mongols and taking this work with its untraditional, original style as his model, the author of *The Trans-Doniad* did not always manage to adapt the quotations from the *Lay* to suit his text. Firstly, some images from the *Lay* appear out of place in *The Trans-Doniad*. For example, whereas the *Lay* says of Prince Vsevolod, who is nicknamed the "Furious Bull", "You stand at bay, you spray with arrows the host of the foe", in *The Trans-Doniad* description of the fleeing Tartars a completely incomprehensible phrase suddenly appears: "The bulls stood in battle." Secondly, a number of obscure passages in *The Trans-Doniad* can be understood only as the result of the author's misunderstanding and distortion of the text of the *Lay*.[161]

It has also been discovered that the *Lay* influenced a seventeenth-century revision of *The Tale of Akir the Wise*,[162] and several manuscripts of *The Legend of the Battle of the Novgorodians with the Suzdalians*.

The *Lay* in Modern Russian Literature. In modern times the *Lay* has made a great impression on Russian readers. Almost as soon as it was published Russian poets found it rewarding material for imitations and variations on Old Russian themes, and there were endless attempts to produce the best poetic rendering of it. Of the nineteenth-century translations the finest are undoubtedly those of Vassily Zhukovsky (highly regarded by Pushkin), Mikhail Delaryu, Apollon Maikov and Lev Mey; at the beginning of the present century Alexander Blok wrote a poem based on the *Lay* and Konstantin Balmont translated it. Soviet translators and poets have produced some fine renderings, such as those by Sergei Shervinsky, Vladimir Stelletsky, Georgi Shtorm, Ivan Novikov, Nikolai Zabolotsky and others.[163] The *Lay* is also widely known in translations into the languages of the peoples of the USSR, it was translated into Ukrainian by Maxim Rylsky, into Byelorussian by Yanka Kupala and into Georgian by Simon Chikovani. The *Lay* has also been translated abroad into Bulgarian, English,[164] Finnish, French, German, Hungarian, Japanese, Polish, Romanian, Serbo-Croat, Spanish, Turkish and other languages.

Let us now summarise the development of Russian literature from the eleventh to the early thirteenth century.

We shall begin with translated literature. Thanks to the copying of Bulgarian originals and direct translations from the Greek and other languages Russia became familiar with many genres of Byzantine literature (or, to be more accurate, the common Slavonic literature-mediator) and, what is more, the finest classical specimens of them. Russia became acquainted with the Holy Scriptures and liturgical books, patristics in both its forms, ceremonial and homiletic rhetoric, hagiography (*vitae* and paterica), an extensive apocryphal literature and the encyclopaedic genres, such as miscellanies, for example. Russia was introduced to Byzantine chronicles, writings on the natural sciences, the *Hexaëmeron*, *The Physiologos*, and the *Christian Topography* of Cosmas Indicopleustes. Russian scribes also had at their disposal various specimens of historical narrative such as the *Alexandreid*, the *History of the Jewish War* and purely literary works, such as *The Tale of Akir the Wise.*

The fact that Russia became familiar with a considerable part of the Byzantine literary heritage is in itself sufficient reason to speak of Russia's introduction to European culture of the very high level. But scholarship is not yet creation. There is a great difference between the erudite scholar and the writer, the former merely learns, whereas the latter creates, basing himself on the achievements of his predecessors. And this was precisely the case with Russian literature in the early period: it not only learned and absorbed, but created new cultural and historical values itself.

In the course of the eleventh century the rich and expressive Old Russian literary language was finally formed. It was not the Old Slavonic language mechanically transferred to new ground nor the former Eastern Slavonic language of the pre-literary period. Together with the birth of literature a new literary

Section of the palace ensemble in Bogolyubovo where Prince Andrew Bogolyubsky of Vladimir and Suzdal principality resided. 1158-c.1165. Reconstruction by N. N. Voronin

Plan of the extant section of the palace ensemble in Bogolyubovo

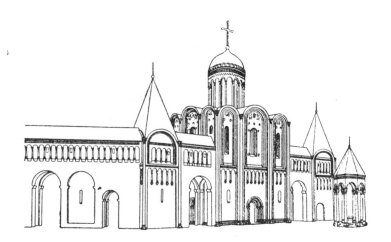

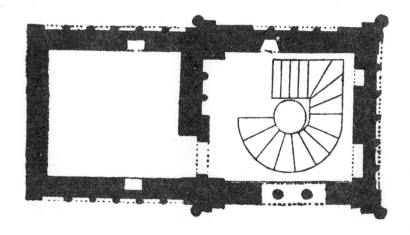

language was formed with the complex interaction of Old Slavonic and Eastern Slavonic linguistic elements at the lexical, semantic, and grammatical levels. This language either took the form of a neutral literary language or, thanks to its diversity, revealed rich possibilities for genre-stylistic gradations.[165]

Something similar took place in literature also. It was not simply that an original Russian literature arose, that in the eleventh and twelfth centuries Russia acquired its own specimens of sermons and religious homilies, its own *vitae* and paterica, its own chronicles and annals. In all the leading literary genres Old Russian writers are by no means imitators copying out imported specimens like good pupils. *The Life of St Theodosius* and *The Tale of SS Boris and Gleb* have an individual, untraditional style that testifies to the high mastery and literary talent of their authors. *The Tale of Bygone Years* does not remind us of a Byzantine chronicle. It is original in both form and sources, and in the style of its exposition, which is less constrained and more lively and vivid than the style of the Byzantine chronicles.

Even the Old Russian translators found the opportunity to compete creatively with the author of the original, the opportunity to add, to embellish, to "better" his style and narrative manner, as we can see in the translation of the *History of the Jewish War*, for example.

By the beginning of the thirteenth century we find Old Russian literature fully mature. In almost each genre it had created original works which themselves could serve as models worthy of imitation and determine the future development of the genre on Russian soil. There were also such masterpieces, as Vladimir Monomachos' *Instruction* or *The Lay of Igor's Host* that stand outside any genre system. Literary styles had been formed, and the Old Russian writers could hold their own in the art of the written word with Byzantine or Bulgarian writers. An example of this is the high literary skill of Cyril of Turov, the author of *The Lay of Igor's Host*, and the authors of the stories about the monks of the Kiev Crypt Monastery.

Not only Kiev and Novgorod, but also Vladimir, Smolensk, Chernigov, Galich, Pereyaslavl-Yuzhny and many other Russian towns had become centres of learning and chronicle-writing and possessed large libraries. The intensive development of urban life promised the further secularisation of culture, the expansion of the range of not merely literate, but broadly educated people. In short, at the beginning of the thirteenth century the prospects for Old Russian culture as a whole and literature in particular were very favourable indeed.

REFERENCES

[1] The earliest surviving Old Russian manuscript book, the Ostromir Gospel transcribed in 1056-1057, was prepared at the request of *posadnik* (mayor) Ostromir of Novgorod. The rich *Miscellany* of 1073 was copied for Prince Izyaslav of Kiev (the later dedication was re-addressed to Prince Svyatoslav). The Mstislav Gospel was copied not later than 1117 for Prince Mstislav of Novgorod.

[2] For a list of extant Slavonic manuscripts of the eleventh to fourteenth centuries in Soviet libraries see the book: *Археографический ежегодник за 1965 г.* Moscow, 1966, pp. 177-272.

[3] Лихачев Д. С. "Своеобразие древнерусской литературы". In the book: Лихачева В. Д., Лихачев Д. С. *Художественное наследие Древней Руси и современность.* Leningrad, 1971, p. 56.

[4] Cyril and Methodius and their pupils appear to have created two Slavonic alphabets, the Glagolitic, which soon went out of general use, and the Cyrillic which, with some modification of the letters and particularly the writing, is still used in modern Russian today.

[5] Мещерский Н. А. "Искусство перевода Киевской Руси". *Труды отдела древнерусской литературы (ТОДРЛ)*, Vol. XV, 1958, pp. 54-72; Мещерский Н. А. "Проблемы изучения славяно-русской переводной литературы XI-XV вв.". *ТОДРЛ*, Vol. XX, 1964, pp. 198-206.

[6] Лихачев Д. С. *Развитие русской литературы X-XVII веков. Эпохи и стили.* Leningrad, 1973, pp. 15-23.

[7] *Compilative* is the term used to describe a work that consists of fragments of other works. This method of creating new texts (particularly historical or theological ones) was widespread in all mediaeval literatures.

[8] For more detail see: Лихачев Д. С. *Развитие русской литературы X-XVII вв.*, pp. 23-24.

[9] Истрин В. М. *Александрия русских хронографов.* Moscow, 1893, p. 348.

[10] The liturgical books include the earliest extant Old Russian manuscripts: the Aprakos Gospel of 1056-1057 copied for Ostromir of Novgorod (also known as the Ostromir Gospel), Novgorodian menologies for 1095-1097, and the Archangel Aprakos Gospel of 1092.

[11] The *Miscellany* of 1073 has been published in phototype: *Изборник великого князя Святослава Ярославича 1073 г.* St Petersburg, 1880; a type-set edition of the *Miscellany* with the Greek parallel text was not completed (see: "*Изборник великого князя Святослава Ярославича 1073 года*". *Чтения в Обществе истории и древностей Российских (ЧОИДР)*, 1882, Book 4). See also: *Изборник Святослава 1073 г.* Moscow, 1971 (a collection of studies by Soviet and Bulgarian specialists).

[12] *Изборник 1076 г.* Compiled by V. S. Golyshenko, V. F. Dubrovina, V. G. Demyanov, G. F. Nefedov. Moscow, 1965; Дубровина В. Ф. "О греческих параллелях к *Изборнику 1076 г.*". *Известия Отделения литературы и языка АН СССР (ИОЛЯ)*, No. 2, 1963, pp. 104-109; Мещерский Н. А. 1) "К вопросу об источниках *Изборника 1076 года*". *ТОДРЛ*, Vol. XXVII, 1972, pp. 321-328; 2) "О некоторых источниках *Изборника 1076 года* в связи с вопросом о

происхождении их переводов". In the book: *Культурное наследие Древней Руси.* Leningrad, 1976, pp. 34-38.

[13] Сперанский М. Н. *Переводные сборники изречений в славянорусской письменности. Исследование и тексты.* Moscow, 1904. See also: Адрианова-Перетц В. П. "Человек в учительной литературе Древней Руси". *ТОДРЛ,* Vol. XXVII, 1972, pp. 3-68.

[14] The compiling of a saint's Life was a necessary condition of his canonisation; the *vita* had to be composed according to a definite scheme (for more about this see the analysis of original Russian *vitae* below).

[15] Безобразов П. "Византийские сказания". Part I. In the book: *Рассказы о мучениках.* Yuryev, 1917.

[16] For the texts of Byzantine *vitae*, see the book: *Византийские легенды.* Prepared by S. V. Polyakova. Leningrad, 1972. On the subjects and artistic features of translated hagiographical literature see: Адрианова-Перетц В. П. "Сюжетное повествование в житийных памятниках XI-XIII вв". In the book: *Истоки русской беллетристики. Возникновение жанров сюжетного повествования в древнерусской литературе.* Leningrad, 1970, pp. 67-88; Адрианова-Перетц В. П. "*Житие Алексея, Человека божия*" в древней русской литературе о народной словесности. Petrograd, 1917.

[17] The Sinai Patericon, the Scete Patericon and, possibly, the Egyptian Patericon were known in Kievan Russia. Some specialists believe that other paterica known only from fourteenth- and fifteenth-century manuscripts date back to translations made in Kievan Russia.

[18] Some apocryphas, for example, reflected the views of the Bogomils, an anti-feudal movement that arose in Bulgaria and Serbia in the tenth century and took on a religious form. According to their teaching the world was created simultaneously by Satan and God: Satan created man's body, and God his soul, and there is a constant struggle between evil (the driving force behind which is Satan) and good (personified in God) in the world.

[19] Some perfectly traditional *vitae* (*The Life of St Basil the New, The Life of St Andrew Salus,* and others) reflect apocryphal views of the end of the world.

[20] For a list of the indexes of proscribed books see: Яцимирский А. И. "Библиографический обзор апокрифов в южнославянской и русской письменности (списки памятников)". In the book: *Апокрифы ветхозаветные.* Petrograd, 1921, pp. 1-75. The oldest manuscript of such an index is in the *Svyatoslav Miscellany* of 1073.

[21] *The Tale of Our Father Agapetus, The Descent of the Virgin into Purgatory,* and some other apocryphal tales are published in *Памятники литературы Древней Руси (ПЛДР). XII век.* Moscow, 1980.

[22] The apocryphal tales *The Paralipomenon of Jeremiah* and *The Journey of Agapetus to Paradise* are included in the famous *Dormition Miscellany.* See: *Успенский сборник XII-XIII вв.* Prepared by O. A. Knyazevskaya, V. G. Demyanov, M. V. Lyapon. Moscow, 1971, pp. 31-37, 466-473.

[23] Истрин В. М. "*Хроника Георгия Амартола*" в древнем славянорусском переводе. Text, study and glossary. Vols. I-III, Petrograd-Leningrad, 1920-1930. See also: Творогов О. В. *Древнерусские хронографы.* Leningrad, 1975. Chapters 1 and 4.

24 Удальцова З. В. "*Хроника Иоанна Малалы в Киевской Руси*". *Археографический ежегодник за 1965 г.* Moscow, 1966, pp. 47-58; Шусторович Э. М. "Древнеславянский перевод *Хроники Иоанна Малалы. История изучения*". *Византийский временник,* Vol. 30. Moscow, 1969. The text of the Slavonic translation of the chronicle was published by V. M. Istrin in a number of periodicals from 1897 to 1914. For information about these publications see the article by E. M. Shustorovich or the book: Творогов О. В. *Древнерусские хронографы,* p. 14.

25 Мещерский Н. А. "Искусство перевода Киевской Руси", pp. 54-72. Творогов О. В. "Беллетристические элементы в переводном историческом повествовании XI-XIII вв.". In the book: *Истоки русской беллетристики,* pp. 124-130.

26 For a study and the text of the work see: Мещерский Н. А. "*История Иудейской войны" Иосифа Флавия в древнерусском переводе.* Moscow and Leningrad, 1958. V. M. Istrin has also published the text of the *History* with a parallel translation into French (see V. M. Istrin. *La prise de Jérusalem par Flavius Jèsephe,* I, Paris, 1934; II, Paris, 1938).

27 Кузнецова Т. И. "Историческая тема в греческом романе. *Роман об Александре".* In the book: *Античный роман.* Moscow, 1969, pp. 186-229.

28 For a study of *The Chronological Alexandreid* with different redactions of its text see: Истрин В. М. *Александрия русских хронографов.* For fragments of the *Alexandreid* with a modern Russian translation see the book: *Изборник (Сборник произведений литературы Древней Руси).* Moscow, 1969, pp. 236-279.

29 *Дигенис Акрит.* Modern Russian translation, articles and commentaries by A. J. Syrkin. Moscow, 1960.

30 In the Old Russian translation it is not clear who Philipapa is. In the Greek poem about Digenes he is a robber chief.

31 *The Deeds of Digenes* was studied in the last century by Alexander Pypin, but the most definitive studies belong to Mikhail Speransky and Vera Kuzmina; it was the latter who discovered the Titov manuscript of *The Deeds of Digenes.* See: Сперанский М. Н. "*Девгениево деяние. К истории его текста в старинной русской письменности".* A study and texts. *Сборник Отделения русского языка и словесности АН СССР* (ОРЯС), No. 7, Vol. XCIX, Petrograd, 1922 (with publication of the text according to the Pogodin and Tikhonravov manuscript copies); Кузьмина В. Д. *Девгениево деяние. (Деяние прежних времен храбрых человек).* Moscow, 1962 (with publication of the reconstructed text of the first and second redactions and photocopies of the manuscripts of the *Deeds*). See also: *Истоки русской беллетристики.* pp. 180-192. The text of the second redaction (with a translation) has also been published in *ПЛДР. XIII век.* Moscow, 1981, pp. 28-65.

32 Armenian, Syrian and Arabic versions exist of this work. The Slavonic translation may have been based on an Armenian original (see: Мартиросян А. А. *История и поучения Хикара Премудрого.* Автореферат на соискание степени доктора филологических наук. Ереван, 1970). Other specialists consider that it was based on a Syrian original (see: Мещерский Н. А. "Проблемы изучения славянорусской переводной литературы XI-XV вв.". ТОДРЛ, Vol. XX, 1964, pp. 205-206.

33 For the oldest redaction of *The Tale of Akir the Wise* see: Григорьев А. Д. "*Повесть об Акире Премудром".* ЧОИДР, Book 3, 1908. Separate edition, Moscow, 1913; *ПЛДР. XII век,* pp. 246-281.

34 The Serbian manuscript copy of 1263 of the *Hexaëmeron* of John, the Bulgarian Exarch was published by *ЧОИДР*, Book 3, 1879. For extracts from the *Hexaëmeron* see: *ПЛДР. XII век*, pp. 184-195.

35 For the text of *The Physiologos*, its translation and commentaries see: *ПЛДР. XIII век*, pp. 474-485.

36 Карнеев А. *Материалы и заметки по литературной истории "Физиолога"*. St Petersburg, 1890.

37 For the text see: *"Христианская топография" Космы Индикоплова*. St. Petersburg, 1886.

38 Лихачев Д. С. "Русский посольский обычай XI-XIII вв.". *Исторические записки*, Vol. 18, 1946, pp. 42-55; Лихачев Д. С. "Устные летописи в составе *Повести временных лет*". *Исторические записки*, Vol. 17, 1945, pp. 201-224; Лихачев Д. С. "Устные истоки художественной системы *Слова о полку Игореве*". In the book: *Слово о полку Игореве*. A collection of studies and articles edited by V. P. Adrianova-Peretts. Moscow and Leningrad, 1950, pp. 5-52.

39 Alexei Shakhmatov's main works on this question are: *Разыскания о древнейших русских летописных сводах*. St. Petersburg, 1908; *Повесть временных лет*, Vol. 1. Introduction. Text. Notes. Petrograd, 1916; "Киевский начальный свод 1095 г.". In the book: *Шахматов А. А. Сборник статей и материалов*. Edited by Academician S. P. Obnorsky. Moscow and Leningrad, 1947, pp. 117-160.

40 Приселков М. Д. *История русского летописания XI-XV вв.*, Leningrad, 1940, pp. 16-44; Лихачев Д. С. *Русские летописи и их культурно-историческое значение*. Moscow and Leningrad, 1947. Chapters 3, 5, 6, 8 and 9. See also: Лурье Я. С. "О шахматовской методике исследования летописных сводов". In the book: *Источниковедение отечественной истории*. Collected Articles. Moscow, 1976, pp. 93-99; Творогов О. В. "*Повесть временных лет* и *Начальный свод*. Текстологический комментарий". *ТОДРЛ*, Vol. XXX, 1976, pp. 3-26; Буганов В. И. *Отечественная историография русского летописания*. Moscow, 1975, pp. 49-64, 130-152, 229-247. For more detail see: Лихачев Д. С. *Текстология на материале русской литературы X-XVII вв.*, Chapter 8.

41 Лихачев Д. С. *Русские летописи и их культурно-историческое значение*, pp. 62-76.

42 Ibid., p. 64.

43 The secondary nature of the legend about Rurik is supported by the fact that in the *Sermon on Law and Grace* by Hilarion, written in the 1030s, the dynasty of the princes of Kiev is traced back to Igor, and not to Oleg or Rurik.

44 Today Soviet scholarship accepts that Norman princes were invited to Russia as leaders of hired armed forces. It is possible that Rurik too was invited to Novgorod in this way. In some cases the invited military leaders seized power in the towns where their armed bands settled (the Norman origin of Rurik, Oleg and Igor is beyond question). However the formation of Russia did not depend on the will of these mercenaries. It was the natural internal process of the emergence of a state of the Eastern Slavs, which began long before the so-called "summoning".

45 This hypothesis is based on the following fact: the ideas mentioned are reflected in a lengthy foreword to a compilation that was preserved in *The Novgorod First Chronicle*. (See: *Новгородская первая летопись старшего и младшего изводов*. Edited and foreword by A. N. Nasonov. Moscow and Leningrad, 1950, pp. 103-104.)

[46] *The Tale of Bygone Years* has been published many times. Of the recent edition provided with commentaries we would mention: *Повесть временных лет.* Part I. Text and translation; Part 2. Appendix. Articles and commentaries by D. S. Likhachev. Moscow and Leningrad, 1950; *ПЛДР. XI-начало XII века,* Moscow, 1978.

[47] This theory is easily disproved by a simple calculation. Even if we allow that Igor was born in the year that Rurik died, Oleg would have been regent at the time when the "infant" prince was already thirty years old. In fact, the three of them, Rurik, Oleg, Prince of Novgorod and later Kiev, and Prince Igor of Kiev, do not appear to have been related.

[48] Лихачев Д. С. *Русские летописи и их культурно-историческое значение,* p. 169.

[49] Мещерский Н. А. "К вопросу об источниках *Повести временных лет".* *ТОДРЛ,* Vol. XIII, 1957, pp. 57-65.

[50] For more detail see: Творогов О. В. "Античные мифы в древнерусской литературе XI-XVI вв.". *ТОДРЛ,* Vol. XXXIII, 1979, pp. 8-11.

[51] Лихачев Д. С. "Комментарии". In the book: *Повесть временных лет.* Part 2, pp. 297-301.

[52] On the sources of *Повесть временных лет* see: Шахматов А. А. *"Повесть временных лет* и ее источники". *ТОДРЛ,* Vol. IV, 1940, pp. 9-150.

[53] Лихачев Д. С. *Поэтика древнерусской литературы.* Leningrad, 1971, pp. 48-50.

[54] On the literary aspect of *The Tale of Bygone Years* see: Еремин И. П. *"Повесть временных лет* как памятник литературы". In the book: Еремин И. П. *Литература Древней Руси. Этюды и характеристики,* pp. 42-97; Лихачев Д. С. *Русские летописи и их культурно-историческое значение.* Chapter 7; Лихачев Д. С. *Человек в литературе Древней Руси.* Moscow, 1970. Chapters 2 and 3; Творогов О. В. "Сюжетное повествование в летописях XI-XIII вв.". In the book: *Истоки русской беллетристики,* pp. 31-66. See also: Лурье Я. С. "К изучению летописного жанра". *ТОДРЛ,* Vol. XXVII, 1972, pp. 76-93.

[55] For more detail see: Лихачев Д. С. *Человек в литературе Древней Руси.* Chapter 3.

[56] We should not, however, trust the "history" of these legends or the events portrayed in them. Thus, for example, the legend of the young tanner states that on the place of his combat Prince Vladimir founded the town of Pereyaslavl, whereas in fact the town existed long before this—it is mentioned in Oleg's treaty with the Greeks.

[57] Лихачев Д. С. *Русские летописи и их культурно-историческое значение,* pp. 215-247.

[58] For a description of the style of monumental historicism see: Лихачев Д. С. *"Слово о полку Игореве* и эстетические представления его времени". *Русская литература,* No. 2, 1976, pp. 24-37.

[59] On literary convention see: Лихачев Д. С. "Литературный этикет Древней Руси (к проблеме изучения)". *ТОДРЛ,* Vol. XVII, 1961, pp. 5-16; Лихачев Д. С. *Поэтика древнерусской литературы.* Third edition, Moscow, 1979,

pp. 80-102; Cf. also: Творогов О. В. "Задачи изучения устойчивых литературных формул Древней Руси". *ТОДРЛ*, Vol. XX, 1964, pp. 29-40.

60 Cf., for example, the obituary description of Vladimir Monomachos. He too was "adorned with kindness", "did not spare his estate, giving to all who asked", and "above all he revered monks and priests, giving them all that they needed". *Полное собрание русских летописей (ПСРЛ)*, Vol I. Second edition, 1927, No. 2, columns 293-294.

61 See, for example. Прохоров Г. М. "*Повесть о нашествии Батыя* в Лаврентьевской летописи". *ТОДРЛ*, Vol. XXVIII, 1974, pp. 77-80.

62 See: "Ипатьевская летопись". *ПСРЛ*, Vol. II, 1962, columns 285-715. *The Hypatian Chronicle* has come down to us in several copies, the oldest of which, the *Hypatian*, dates back to the beginning of the 15th century.

63 For the sources of *The Kievan Chronicle* see: Приселков М. Д. *История русского летописания XI-XV вв.*, pp. 44-57; Насонов А. Н. *История русского летописания. XI-начало XVIII в.* Moscow, 1969, pp. 80-111; Рыбаков Б. А. *Русские летописцы и автор "Слова о полку Игореве".* Moscow, 1972.

64 Еремин И. П. "Киевская летопись как памятник литературы". In the book: Еремин И. П. *Литература Древней Руси. Этюды и характеристики*, pp. 98-131.

65 Приселков М. Д. *История русского летописания XI-XV вв.*, pp. 57-96; Лихачев Д. С. *Русские летописи и их культурно-историческое значение*, pp. 268-280; Насонов А. Н. *История русского летописания. XI-начало XVIII в.*, pp. 112-167. *Летописец Переяславля Суздальского* was published by M. Obolensky in 1851.

66 *Раздзивиловская, или Кенигсбергская, летописъ.* Phototype copy. St Petersburg, 1902; Подобедова О. И. *Миниатюры русских исторических рукописей. К истории русского лицевого летописания.* Moscow, 1965, pp. 49-101.

67 For the text of the chronicle see: *Новгородская первая летописъ старшего и младшего изводов.* Edited and foreword by A. N. Nasonov.

68 See: *Новгородская первая летописъ*, pp. 46-49; for the text and translation of the tale with a commentary see the book: *ПЛДР. XIII век*, pp. 106-113. On the tale see: Мещерский Н. А. "Древнерусская повесть о взятии Царьграда фрягами в 1204 году". *ТОДРЛ*, Vol X, 1954, pp. 120-135.

69 Еремин И. П. "Литературное наследие Феодосия Печерского". *ТОДРЛ*, Vol. V, 1947, pp. 159-184; Еремин И. П. *Лекции по древней русской литературе.* Leningrad State University, 1968, pp. 63-69.

70 Розов Н. Н. "Синодальный список сочинений Илариона—русского писателя XI в.". *Slavia*, roč. XXXII, seš. 2, Praha, 1963, pp. 147-148. The oldest manuscript copy of the *Sermon* is also printed here (pp. 152-175). On Hilarion's *Sermon* see also the book: Лихачев Д. С. *Великое наследие. Классические произведения литературы Древней Руси.* Moscow, 1975, pp. 10-21.

71 Лихачев Д. С. *Русские летописи и их культурно-историческое значение*, pp. 66-70.

72 Никольский Н. *О литературных трудах митрополита Климента Смолятича, писателя XII века.* St Petersburg, 1892. See also: *ПЛДР. XII век*, pp. 282-289.

[73] *The Hypatian Chronicle* under the year 1147. The use of the word "philosopher" suggests that Clement studied in Constantinople and held the academic title of "philosopher". On this point see: Гранстрем Е. Э. "Почему митрополита Климента Смолятича называли 'философом'". *ТОДРЛ*, Vol. XXV, 1970, pp. 20-28; for the text of the *Epistles* see: *ПЛДР. XII век.*

[74] The most comprehensive study and publication of the works of Cyril of Turov is by I. P. Eremin. See: Еремин И. П. "Литературное наследие Кирилла Туровского". *ТОДРЛ*, Vol. XI, 1955, pp. 342-367; Vol. XII, 1956, pp. 340-361; Vol. XIII, 1957, pp. 409-426; Vol. XV, 1958, pp. 331-348; Еремин И. П. "Ораторское искусство Кирилла Туровского". In the book: *Литература Древней Руси*, pp. 132-143.

[75] For a study of the work see: Еремин И. П. "Притча о слепце и хромце в древнерусской письменности". *Известия Отделения русского языка и словесности АН СССР (ИОРЯС)*, Vol. XXX, 1926, pp. 323-352.

[76] Еремин И. П. "Ораторское искусство Кирилла Туровского". In the book: *Литература Древней Руси*, pp. 133-135.

[77] *ТОДРЛ*, Vol. XIII, pp. 415-419.

[78] The text of the *Instruction* is published in *Повесть временных лет* (Part I, Moscow and Leningrad, 1950, pp. 153-167), and also in the book: *ПЛДР. XI-начало XII века*, pp. 392-413, and other sources.

[79] Матьесен Р. "Текстологические замечания о произведениях Владимира Мономаха". *ТОДРЛ*, Vol. XXVI, 1971, pp. 192-201. Even earlier Nikolai Voronin advanced the theory that the prayer belonged to Prince Andrew Bogolyubsky. See: Воронин Н. Н. "О времени и месте включения в летопись сочинений Владимира Мономаха". *Историко-археологический сборник*, Moscow, 1962, pp. 261-271.

[80] Приселков М. Д. "История рукописи Лаврентьевской летописи и ее изданий". *Ученые записки ЛГПИ им. Герцена*, 1939. Кафедра истории СССР, т. XIX, с. 186-188.

[81] See Dmitry Likhachev's commentary on the *Instruction* (*Повесть временных лет*, Part 2, Moscow and Leningrad, 1950, pp. 429-431). For a review of the various points of view on this question see also the book: Орлов А. С. *Владимир Мономах*. Moscow and Leningrad, 1946, pp. 100-107.

[82] Алексеев М. П. "Англосаксонская параллель к *Поучению* Владимира Мономаха". *ТОДРЛ*, Vol. II, 1935, pp. 39-80.

[83] On the *Instruction* see also: Лихачев Д. С. *Великое наследие. Классические произведения литературы Древней Руси*, pp. 111-131.

[84] Адрианова-Перетц В. П. "Сюжетное повествование в житийных памятниках XI-XIII вв.". In the book: *Истоки русской беллетристики*, p. 91.

[85] For the text of the *vita* see: *Успенский сборник XII-XIII вв.* pp. 71-135. Prepared by O. A. Knyazevskaya, V. G. Demyanov and M. V. Lyapon. For a modern Russian translation of the *vita* see: *ПЛДР. XI-начало XII века*. 1978, pp. 304-391.

[86] Бугославский С. А. "К вопросу о характере и объеме литературной деятельности преподобного Нестора". *ИОРЯС*, Vol. XIX, Book I, 1915, pp. 148-155.

[87] On the Byzantine canon see: Дмитриев Л. А. "Литературные судьбы жанра древнерусских житий. (Церковно-служебный канон и сюжетное повествование.)" *Славянские литературы.* (VII Международный съезд славистов. Warsaw, August 1973.) Moscow, 1973, pp. 400-418.

[88] "The Reading Concerning ... Boris and Gleb" was published by Izmail Sreznevsky ("Сказание о святых Борисе и Глебе". *Сильвестровский список XIV века.* St Petersburg, 1860), and Dmitry Abramovich ("Жития св. мучеников Бориса и Глеба и службы им". Petrograd, 1916); see also: *ПЛДР. XI-начало XII века.*

[89] There is a great deal of literature on the *Tale* and *Reading.* We shall merely quote the most important recent works: Воронин Н. Н. "'Анонимное' *Сказание о Борисе и Глебе*, его время, стиль и автор". *ТОДРЛ*, Vol. XIII, 1957, pp. 11-56; Еремин И. П. "'Сказание' о Борисе и Глебе". In the book: Еремин И. П. *Литература Древней Руси*, pp. 18-27; Еремин И. П. "Жития князей Бориса и Глеба". In the book: Еремин И. П. *Лекции по древней русской литературе*, pp. 15-24.

[90] This idea was clearly formulated in Yaroslav the Wise's words on his deathbed (as *The Tale of Bygone Years* gives them under 1054): "I now hand over my throne after me to my eldest son and your brother Izyaslav ... obey him as you would obey me." See also: Лихачев Д. С. "Некоторые вопросы идеологии феодалов в литературе XI-XIII веков". *ТОДРЛ*, Vol. X, 1954, pp. 87-90.

[91] Еремин И. П. *Литература Древней Руси*, p. 25.

[92] Ibid., pp. 21-22.

[93] Ibid., p. 20.

[94] Еремин И. П. *Лекции по древней русской литературе*, p. 21.

[95] Лихачев Д. С. *Поэтика древнерусской литературы.* pp. 102-111.

[96] For the text of the *Patericon* see: *Патерик Киево-Печерского монастыря.* St. Petersburg, 1911 (containing the second Cassian and the Arsenius redactions); Абрамович Д. И. *Киево-Печерский патерик.* Foreword, text, commentaries. Kiev, 1930 (containing the second Cassian redaction). For the text of this redaction with translation into modern Russian, see: *ПЛДР. XII век*, pp. 412-613. On the redactions of the *Kiev Crypt Patericon* see: Абрамович Д. И. "Исследование о Киево-Печерском патерике как историко-литературном памятнике". *ИОРЯС*, Vol. VI, Books 3-4, 1901; Vol. VII, Books 1-4, 1902.

[97] According to the legend these events took place during the time when Princes Svyatopolk and David tricked Vasilko of Terebovl into visiting them and blinded him (this is described in *The Tale of Bygone Years* under 1097).

[98] The story of Rostislav Vsevolodovich's drowning as he crossed the River Stugna is under 1093 in *The Tale of Bygone Years.* Rostislav's death is also mentioned in *The Lay of Igor's Host.*

[99] *The Tale of Bygone Years* mentions the death of Mstislav under 1097, but does not connect it with punishment for murdering the monks of the Crypt Monastery.

[100] Пушкин А. С. *Полное собрание сочинений.* Vol. X, Leningrad, 1979, p. 270.

[101] Адрианова-Перетц В. П. "Задачи изучения агиографического стиля Древней Руси". *ТОДРЛ*, Vol. XX, 1964, pp. 51-63; Адрианова-Перетц В. П.

"Сюжетное повествование в житийных памятниках". In the book: *Истоки русской беллетристики,* pp. 101-107.

[102] The text of *The Pilgrimage* with a modern Russian translation is printed in the book: *ПЛДР. XII век,* pp. 24-115.

[103] Янин В. Л. "Междукняжеские отношения в эпоху Мономаха и *Хождение игумена Даниила". ТОДРЛ,* Vol. XIV, 1960, pp. 130-131.

[104] Данилов В. В. "К характеристике *Хождения* игумена Даниила". *ТОДРЛ,* Vol. X, 1954, pp. 92-94.

[105] The major bibliographical works on *The Lay of Igor's Host* are as follows: *"Слово о полку Игореве". Библиография изданий, переводов и исследований.* Compiled by V. P. Adrianova-Peretts. Moscow and Leningrad, 1940; *"Слово о полку Игореве". Библиографический указатель.* Compiled by O. V. Danilova, E. D. Poplavskaya, and I. S. Romanchenko. Edited and introductory article by S. K. Shambinago. Moscow, 1940; *"Слово о полку Игореве". Библиография изданий, переводов и исследований. 1938-1954.* Compiled by L. A. Dmitriev. Moscow and Leningrad, 1955; Бегунов Ю. К. *"Слово о полку Игореве* в зарубежном литературоведении (краткий обзор). In the book: *От "Слова о полку Игореве" до "Тихого Дона".* A collection of articles to mark the 90th anniversary of N. K. Piksanov. Leningrad, 1969. For a review of the main works on *The Lay of Igor's Host* published over the last twenty-five years see: Дмитриев Л. А. "175-летие первого издания *Слова о полку Игореве.* (Некоторые итоги и задачи изучения *Слова.)" ТОДРЛ,* Vol. XXXI, 1976, pp. 3-13; Творогов О. В. *"Слово о полку Игореве* в советской филологической науке (1968-1977)". *Русская литература,* No. 4, 1978, pp. 177-185.

[106] These words may be taken as echoing the passage in the *Lay* about Boyan, who composed songs "of old Yaroslav, of the valiant Mstislav ... of Roman the Fair, Son of Svyatoslav".

[107] Берков П. Н. "Заметки к истории изучения *Слова о полку Игореве". ТОДРЛ,* Vol. V, 1947, pp. 135-136.

[108] Моисеева Г. Н. *Спасо-Ярославский хронограф и "Слово о полку Игореве".* Leningrad, 1976, pp. 72-73.

[109] Ibid., pp. 51-59.

[110] *Ироическая песнь о походе на половцев удельного князя Новагорода-Северского Игоря Святославича, писанная старинным русским языком в исходе XII столетия с переложением на употребляемое ныне наречие.* Moscow, 1800. The *Lay* has been photocopied several times. One of the best photographic reproductions is in the book: Дмитриев Л. А. *История первого издания "Слова о полку Игореве". Материалы и исследование.* Moscow and Leningrad, 1960, pp. 77-132.

[111] Ibid., pp. 17-56; Дмитриев Л. А. "175-летие первого издания *Слова о полку Игореве",* p. 12.

[112] Творогов О. В. "К вопросу о датировке Мусин-пушкинского сборника со *Словом о полку Игореве". ТОДРЛ,* Vol. XXXI, 1976, pp. 138-140; Моисеева Г. Н. *Спасо-Ярославский хронограф и "Слово о полку Игореве",* pp. 28-33.

[113] Лихачев Д. С. "О русской летописи, находившейся в одном сборнике со *Словом о полку Игореве". ТОДРЛ,* Vol V. 1947, pp. 139-141; Моисеева Г. Н. *Спасо-Ярославский хронограф и "Слово о полку Игореве",* pp. 41-42.

[114] Сперанский М. Н. *Сказание об Индийском царстве.* Ипо РЯС, pp. 369-464.

[115] Творогов О. В. "К вопросу о датировке Мусин-пушкинского сборника со *Словом о полку Игореве*", pp. 159-164.

[116] Дмитриев Л. А. 1) *История первого издания "Слова о полку Игореве"*, pp. 77-132; 2) "Н. М. Карамзин и *Слово о полку Игореве". ТОДРЛ*, Vol. XVIII, 1962, pp. 38-49.

[117] Лихачев Д. С. "История подготовки к печати рукописи *Слова о полку Игореве* в конце XVIII в.". *ТОДРЛ*, Vol. XIII, 1957, pp. 66-89.

[118] Лихачев Д. С. "Изучение *Слова о полку Игореве* и вопрос о его подлинности". In the book: *"Слово о полку Игореве"—памятник XII века.* Moscow and Leningrad, 1962, pp. 8-11.

[119] It is interesting that Alexander Pushkin wrote as early as 1834: *"The Lay of Igor's Host* stands out as a solitary monument in the wilderness of our early literature", (Пушкин А. С. Собрание сочинений, Vol. VII, Leningrad, 1978, p. 211). The discovery of Old Russian literature by Russian philologists took place later, in the middle of the 19th century.

[120] Лихачев Д. С. "Изучение *Слова о полку Игореве* и вопрос о его подлинности", pp. 17-23.

[121] Leger, L., *Russes et slaves, Études politiques et littéraires*, Paris, 1890, pp. 93-102.

[122] *Le Slovo d'Igor par Andre Mazon*, Paris, 1940.

[123] For a brief outline of his idea see the article: Зимин А. А. "Когда было написано *Слово?" Вопросы литературы*, No. 3, 1967, pp. 135-152. See also: "Обсуждение одной концепции о времени создания *Слова о полку Игореве"*. *Вопросы истории*, No. 9, 1964, pp. 121-140. The main theses of Alexander Zimin's view were set out by him in a series of articles: 1) *"Две редакции Задонщины"*. In the book: *Труды Московского историко-архивного института*, Vol. 24, Book 2, *Вопросы источниковедения истории СССР*. Moscow, 1966, pp. 17-54; 2) "К вопросу о тюркизмах *Слова о полку Игореве* (Опыт исторического анализа.)". In the book: *Ученые записки Научно-исследовательского института при Совете Министров Чувашской АССР*, No. 31. Исторический сборник. Cheboksary, 1966, pp. 138-155; 3) "Приписка к псковскому *Апостолу*, 1307 г. и *Слово о полку Игореве"*. *Русская литература*, No. 2, 1966, pp. 60-74; 4) "Спорные вопросы текстологии *Задонщины"*. *Русская литература*, No. 1, 1967, pp. 84-104; "Ипать-евская летопись и *Слово о полку Игореве"*. *История СССР*, No. 6, 1968, pp. 43-67; 6) "*Слово о полку Игореве* и восточно-славянский фольклор". *Русский фольклор*, Vol. XI, 1968, pp. 212-224. See also: Зимин А. А. *"Задонщина* (Опыт реконструкции текста Пространной редакции)". *Ученые записки Научно-исследовательского института при Совете Министров Чувашской АССР*, No. 36. История, этнография, социология. Cheboksary, 1967, pp. 216-239.

[124] Лихачев Д. С. "Черты подражательности *Задонщины*. (К вопросу об отношении *Задонщины* к *Слову о полку Игореве*.)". *Русская литература*, No. 3, 1964, pp. 84-107; Творогов О. В. "*Слово о полку Игореве* и *Задонщина"*. In the book: *"Слово о полку Игореве" и памятники Куликовского цикла. К вопросу о времени написания "Слова"*. Moscow and Leningrad, 1966, pp. 292-343; Дмитриева Р. П., Дмитриев Л. А., Творогов О. В. "По поводу статьи А. А. Зимина 'Спорные вопросы текстологии *Задонщины'"*. *Русская литература*, No. 1, 1967, pp. 105-121.

[125] Roman Jakobson pointed to different relationships between the manuscript copies of *The Trans-Doniad* from those suggested by Alexander Zimin even before the discussion (see: Jakobson, R., and Worth, D. S., *Sofonija's Tale of the Russian-Tatar Battle on the Kulikovo Field.* The Hague, 1963). This question is examined in detail in the following work: Дмитриева Р. П. "Взаимоотношение списков *Задонщины* и текст *Слова о полку Игореве".* In the book: *"Слово о полку Игореве" и памятники Куликовского цикла,* pp. 199-263. See also the above-mentioned article by R. P. Dmitrieva, L. A. Dmitriev and O. V. Tvorogov.

[126] Of special importance is the book: Адрианова-Перетц В. П. *"Слово о полку Игореве" и памятники русской литературы XI-XIII вв.* Leningrad, 1968.

[127] Котляренко А. Н. "Сравнительный анализ некоторых особенностей грамматического строя *Задонщины* и *Слова о полку Игореве".* In the book: *"Слово о полку Игореве" и памятники Куликовского цикла,* pp. 127-196.

[128] See Boris Rybakov's section of the article "Старые мысли, устарелые методы". *Вопросы литературы,* No. 3, 1967, pp. 153-161.

[129] We would refer to Yuri Lotman's article which was published before the discussion, but retains its value, "*Слово о полку Игореве* и литературная традиция XVIII в.-начала XIX в.". In the book: *"Слово о полку Игореве"—памятник XII века,* pp. 330-405, and D. S. Likhachev's articles "*Слово о полку Игореве* и особенности русской средневековой литературы" and "*Слово о полку Игореве* и эстетические представления его времени". In the book: Лихачев Д. С. *"Слово о полку Игореве" и культура его времени.* Leningrad, 1978, pp. 7-39 and 40-74.

[130] See: Fennell, J. L. I., "The *Slovo o Polku Igoreve*: the Textological Triangle". *Oxford Slavonic Papers,* 1968 (New Series), Vol. 1, pp. 126-137. Likhachev, D. S., "Further Remarks on the Textological Triangle: *Slovo o Polku Igoreve, Zadonshchina* and *The Hypatian Chronicle".* *Oxford Slavonic Papers,* 1969 (New Series), Vol. 2, pp. 106-115. See also: Кузьмин А. Г. "Ипатьевская летопись и *Слово о полку Игореве* (по поводу статьи А. А. Зимина)". *История СССР,* No. 6, 1968, pp. 64-87.

[131] Apart from the well-known study: Menges, K. H., *The Oriental Elements in the Vocabulary of the Oldest Russian Epos, "The Igor Tale",* New York, 1951, we would mention a number of more recent studies, for example: Baskakov, N. A., 1) "Polovtsian Reflections in *The Lay of Igor's Host", Ural-Altaische Jahrbücher,* Bd. 48, Wiesbaden, 1976; 2) "Еще о тюркизмах *Слова о полку Игореве".* In the book: *"Слово о полку Игореве". Памятники литературы и искусства XI-XVII веков.* Moscow, 1978, pp. 59-68.

[132] Кузьмина В. Д. "Мог ли архимандрит Иоиль написать *Слово о полку Игореве?" ИОЛЯ,* Vol. XXV, 1966, No. 3, pp. 197-207; Крестова Л. В., Кузьмина В. Д. "Иоиль Быковский, проповедник, издатель *Истины* и первый владелец рукописи *Слова о полку Игореве".* In the book: *Исследования и материалы по древнерусской литературе. Древнерусская литература и ее связи с новым временем.* Moscow, 1967, pp. 25-48.

[133] Лихачев Д. С. "*Слово о полку Игореве* и скептики". In the book: *Великое наследие,* pp. 348-363; Лихачев Д. С., "Когда было написано *Слово о полку Игореве?* (Вопрос о его подлинности.)". In the book: *"Слово о полку Игореве". Историко-литературный очерк.* Moscow, 1976, pp. 147-172.

[134] The most detailed account of the campaign is in *The Hypatian Chronicle* (ПСРЛ, Vol. II, 1962, columns 636-651). *The Laurentian Chronicle (ПСРЛ,* Vol. I,

1962, columns 396-400) has a shorter account of the campaign and some of the details in this verison are thought to be inaccurate. For the texts of the chronicle accounts of Prince Igor's campaign see also a book: *ПЛДР. XII век*, pp. 344-371. See also: Рыбаков Б. А. *"Слово о полку Игореве" и его современники.* Moscow, 1951, pp. 202-293.

135 The precise location of the River Kayala on which the battle with the Polovtsians took place has long been a matter of dispute. See, for example, one of the most recent studies on this question: Гетманец М. Ф. "По следам князя Игоря". *ТОДРЛ*, Vol. 31, 1976, pp. 305-326 (which quotes the main literature on the question).

136 In the account of Igor's campaign in *The Hypatian Chronicle* Svyatoslav calls Igor and Vsevolod "brothers".

137 Natalia Demkova offers an interesting commentary on this passage. In her opinion the *Lay* was written in the mid-nineties of the 12th century. In this case the phrase in question is an allusion to the princes Rurik and David, sons of Rostislav, who co-ruled Kiev and the Kievan lands after the death of Svyatoslav. (See: Демкова Н. С. "Проблемы изучения *Слова о полку Игореве*". In the book: *Чтения по древнерусской литературе.* Yerevan, 1980, pp. 76-77.)

138 Marx, K., and Engels, F., *Collected Works*, Vol. 40. Moscow, 1983, p. 19.

139 Jakobson, R., and Szerftel, M., "The Vseslav Epos". In: Jakobson, Roman, *Selected Writings*. IV. The Hague-Paris, 1966, pp. 301-368.

140 Адрианова-Перетц В. П. *Древнерусская литература и фольклор.* Leningrad, 1947, pp. 117-118.

141 Робинсон А. Н. "Литература Киевской Руси среди европейских средневековых литератур. (Типология, оригинальность, метод.)" *Славянские литературы.* (VI Международный съезд славистов. Доклады советской делегации.) Moscow, 1968; Лихачев Д. С. *"Слово о полку Игореве* и процесс жанрообразования XI-XIII вв.". *ТОДРЛ*, Vol. XXVII, 1972, pp. 69-75; Робинсон А. Н. *Литература Древней Руси в литературном процессе средневековья XI-XIII вв.* Moscow, 1980.

142 Лихачев Д. С. *"Слово о полку Игореве* и процесс жанрообразования XI-XIII вв.", p. 72.

143 For more detail see: Лихачев Д. С. *"Слово о полку Игореве* и эстетические представления его времени"; "Устные истоки художественной системы *Слова*". Both articles are in the book: Лихачев Д. С. *"Слово о полку Игореве" и культура его времени*, pp. 40-74, 150-198.

144 Адрианова-Перетц В. П. "Историческая литература XI-начала XV века и народная поэзия". In the book: Адрианова-Перетц В. П. *Древнерусская литература и фольклор*, p. 43. On the folklore elements in the *Lay* see also: Адрианова-Перетц В. П. *"Слово о полку Игореве* и устная народная поэзия". In the book: Адрианова-Перетц В. П. *Древнерусская литература и фольклор*, pp. 99-119, and the chapter by L. A. Dmitriev on *The Lay of Igor's Host* in the book: *Русская литература и фольклор (XI-XVIII вв.).* Leningrad, 1970, pp. 36-54.

145 For all the conciseness of his sketches of nature in the *Lay* the author is remarkably accurate in his choice of words to define, for example, the sounds made by animals or birds and depict their habits. On this point see: Шарлемань Н. В. "Из реального комментария к *Слову о полку Игореве*". *ТОДРЛ*,

Vol. VI, 1948, pp. 111-124; Шарлемань Н. В. "Заметки натуралиста к *Слову о полку Игореве*". *ТОДРЛ*, Vol. VIII, 1951, pp. 53-57; Шарлемань Н. В. "Заметки к *Слову о полку Игореве*". *ТОДРЛ*, Vol. XI, 1955, pp. 7-12, and others.

[146] Лихачев Д. С. "Слово о походе Игоря Святославича". In the book: "*Слово о полку Игореве*". (Библиотека поэта. Большая серия.) Second edition. Leningrad, 1967, p. 20.

[147] Адрианова-Перетц В. П. *Очерки поэтического стиля Древней Руси.* Moscow and Leningrad, 1947, pp. 20-41.

[148] Лихачев Д. С. "*Слово о полку Игореве*". *Историко-литературный очерк*, p. 114.

[149] Булаховский Л. А. "О первоначальном тексте *Слова о полку Игореве*". *ИОЛЯ*, Vol. XI, No. 5, 1952, p. 443.

[150] Орлов А. С. *Слово о полку Игореве.* Second edition, Moscow and Leningrad, 1946, pp. 212-213.

[151] Перетц В. Н. "*Слово о полку Ігоревім*". *Пам'ятка феодальної України-Руси XII віку.* Kiev, 1926.

[152] Обнорский С. П. *Очерки по истории русского литературного языка старшего периода.* Moscow and Leningrad, 1946, pp. 132-198.

[153] Якубинский Л. П. *История древнерусского языка.* Moscow, 1953, pp. 320-327; Ларин Б. А. *Лекции по истории русского литературного языка (X-середина XVIII в.).* Moscow, 1975, pp. 145-178.

[154] Виноградова В. Л. "Лексическая вторичность *Задонщины* сравнительно со *Словом о полку Игореве*". *ТОДРЛ.* Vol. XII. 1956, pp. 20-27; Котляренко А. Н. "Сравнительный анализ некоторых особенностей грамматического строя *Задонщины* и *Слова о полку Игореве*". In the book: "*Слово о полку Игореве*" *и памятники Куликовского цикла*, pp. 127-196.

[155] Адрианова-Перетц В. П. "*Слово о полку Игореве*" *и памятники русской литературы XI-XIII веков*, p. 43.

[156] Франчук В. Ю. "Мог ли Петр Бориславич создать *Слово о полку Игореве*? (Наблюдения над языком *Слова* и Ипатьевской летописи.)" *ТОДРЛ* Vol. XXXI, 1976, pp. 77-92.

[157] *Словарь-справочник "Слова о полку Игореве".* Compiled by V. L. Vinogradova. Book 1 (А-Г), Moscow and Leningrad, 1965; Book 2 (Д-Копье), Leningrad, 1967; Book 3 (Корабль-Нынешний), Leningrad, 1969; Book 4 (О-П), Leningrad, 1973; Book 5 (Р-С), Leningrad, 1978; Book 6 (Т-Я and addenda). Leningrad, 1984. A concise dictionary of the language of the *Lay* has also been compiled by T. Čiževska, *A Glossary of the Igor's Tale.* The Hague, 1966.

[158] Козырев В. А. "Словарный состав *Слова о полку Игореве* и лексика современных народных говоров". *ТОДРЛ*, Vol. XXXI, 1976, pp. 93-103.

[159] Демкова Н. С. "К вопросу о времени написания *Слова о полку Игореве*". Вестник ЛГУ, 1973, No. 14, Book 3, p. 73. See also: Демкова Н. С. "Проблемы изучения *Слова о полку Игореве*". In the book: *Чтения по древнерусской литературе*, pp. 67-77.

[160] Рыбаков Б. А. *Русские летописцы и автор "Слова о полку Игореве"*, p. 515.

161 For more detail see: Лихачев Д. С. "Черты подражательности *Задон-щины*. (К вопросу об отношении *Задонщины* к *Слову о полку Игореве*.)"; Творогов О. В. *"Слово о полку Игореве и Задонщина"*.

162 Перетц В. Н. *"Слово о полку Ігоревім"*. *Пам'ятка феодальної України-Руси XII віку*, p. 270; Творогов О. В. "Сокол трех мытей в *Повести об Акире Премудром"*. In the book: *Вопросы теории и истории языка. Сборник ·статей, посвященных памяти Б. А. Ларина*, ЛГУ, 1969, pp. 111-114.

163 Стеллецкий В. И. *"Слово о полку Игореве* в художественных переводах и переложениях". In the book: *"Слово о полку Игореве"*. *Поэтические переводы и переложения*. Under the general editorship of V. Rzhiga, V. Kuzmina and V. Stelletsky. Moscow, 1961; Дмитриев Л. А. *"Слово о полку Игореве* и русская литература". In the book: *Слово о полку Игореве*. Second edition, Leningrad, 1967, pp. 69-92.

164 For the best known translation of the *Lay* into English see the Bibliography.

165 Виноградов В. В. "Основные проблемы изучения образования и развития древнерусского литературного языка". *Исследования по славянскому языкознанию*. Moscow, 1961, pp. 4-113; Филин Ф. П. *Истоки и судьбы русского литературного языка*. Moscow, 1981, Chapter 4.

CHAPTER 2

LITERATURE OF THE SECOND QUARTER TO THE END OF THE THIRTEENTH CENTURY

The favourable prospects for the development of Old Russian culture and literature at the beginning of the thirteenth cen-

tury were not destined to be realised. Bitter ordeals lay ahead for Russia, the Mongol invasion and the establishment of Mongol overlordship.

The first clash of the Russians with the Mongols took place in the Polovtsian steppes, near the Sea of Azov, on the small river Kalka. The Russian campaign against this hitherto unknown enemy was a joint one: several princes took part in it. But each of the princes who joined in the campaign was thinking primarily of his own interests, not of the common cause. Therefore the princes did not concert their actions during the battle on the Kalka and in spite of the military prowess and courage of the warriors the Russians suffered a cruel defeat. Feudal strife and the lack of a single leader were the main causes of this defeat. The feudal division and internal quarrels also facilitated the subsequent successes of the Mongols who conquered and subjected most of the Russian lands, although in socio-economic and cultural terms the conquerors were less developed than the people they had conquered.

In the winter of 1237 a vast Mongol host led by Genghis Khan's grandson, Batu, invaded the principality of Ryazan. The Ryazan princes' appeal to Prince Yuri of Vladimir and Prince Michael of Chernigov to join forces against the foreign invaders went unanswered, and the Ryazaners had to confront the enemy with only their own forces. And so, one after another, the Mongols seized first the principalities of North-Eastern Russia, then those of the South-West (Kiev fell in 1240).

Batu's conquest of the Russian lands by bloody battles was accompanied by the devastation and destruction of towns and villages. The merciless cruelty that the nomads showed to Russian warriors and civilians alike features in all the accounts of Batu's invasion of Russia. The accounts from Russian sources are confirmed by historians and writers of other countries.[1] The Mongol invasion did inestimable harm to Russian culture. The human losses were exceptionally great. Many towns in North-Eastern and Southern Russia were destroyed or burnt and with them the architectural monuments, works of handicrafts and the arts, and books. The enemy wiped out the whole population of towns that resisted them and took craftsmen away to the Horde. A whole number of handicrafts ceased to exist. All stone building stopped for a period (the first stone church to be erected after the invasion of Russia was in Novgorod, which the Mongols did not reach, at the end of the thirteenth century).

Having conquered the Russian lands, Batu invaded Eastern Europe, with the intention of subjecting the European states. Weakened by the struggle with Russia, however, his forces were not strong enough to carry out these plans, and at the end of 1242 the conquerors turned back eastwards. Batu settled on the Lower Volga, where a new state grew up, the Golden Horde, with its capital in Sarai. The Russian lands became vassals of the Horde.

The territory of Novgorod-Pskovian Russia was not devastated, but a bitter struggle took place here in the 1240s against German and Swedish invaders.

The role which Russia played in European history by taking upon itself the first blow of the Mongol hordes was brilliantly described by Pushkin: "Russia was destined to play a great role... Its boundless plains sapped the Mongol armies and stopped their invasion on the very brink of Europe; fearing to leave enslaved Russia behind them, the barbarians returned to their eastern steppes. The nascent enlightenment was saved by lacerated, expiring Russia..."[2]

Defeat in the struggle against the invaders and the latter's policy of dividing Russia accelerated the process of feudal disunity and separation into individual principalities. But at the same time the idea of the need to unite the Russian lands, which was most vividly embodied in works of literature, was gradually maturing. This idea was supported by the consciousness of a common language (in spite of all the local dialects), a common religion, history and ethnic roots and the awareness that it was the lack of unity of the Russian principalities that had resulted in defeat and the establishment of foreign dominion.

Spiritually the Russian people was neither destroyed nor enslaved. The struggle against the invaders produced an upsurge of patriotism. And the patriotic theme became the main theme in thirteenth-century literature. Military heroism and courage, devotion to duty, love of one's native land, praise of the former greatness and might of the Russian princes and principalities, grief for the fallen, pain and compassion for all those abased by the enslavers—all this was reflected both in chronicle-writing, hagiography and ceremonial rhetoric. The theme of the need for a strong princely power is stressed urgently in thirteenth-century works, which condemn princely strife and unconcerted action against the foe. The ideal of the strong ruler is the prince, both warrior and wise statesman. In reminiscences of the past Vladimir Monomachos is portrayed as such a prince, and among contemporaries, Alexander Nevsky.

1. Chronicle-Writing

The feudal disunity of Russia, which was particularly strong during Mongol overlordship, promoted the development of local and regional chronicle-writing. This had two consequences. On the one hand, the chroniclers' field of vision became narrower to some extent. On the other hand, the emergence of regional chronicle-writing led to the inclusion of local material in chronicles. At the same time the tradition of beginning a chronicle with *The Tale of Bygone Years* became established and lasted for many centuries (from the eleventh to the sixteenth). This helped to strengthen people's awareness of the unity of Russia. Irrespective of where they were written, the chronicles recount the history of the whole Russian land. In this way they reminded people of the unity of the Russian principalities and aroused memories of the glorious past and former might of Russia.

The development of local chronicle-writing did not mean that the chronicle's interests became limited to the region or land in question. Local chronicle-writers constantly made use of material from chronicles of other principalities in their work. It is by no means always possible to trace and explain the ways in which the chronicle-writing of different principalities, even those hostile to one another, interacted, but the existence of this interaction is indisputable.

The nomadic invasion greatly hampered the development of chronicle-writing. But even in the bitterest years of Mongol overlordship it continued to exist. From the devastated towns it moved to other cities, although it was not carried on so intensively in the principalities that had escaped destruction.

The Chronicle-Writing of North-Eastern Russia. One of the earliest surviving manuscripts of a Russian chronicle is *The Laurentian Chronicle*, which got its name from a note at the end of the manuscript copied in 1377 in the principality of Nizhny Novgorod-Suzdal to the effect that the chronicle was copied by the monk Laurentius and his assistants. This manuscript is a copy of a chronicle compiled in 1305 (for more about the 1305 compilation see below). After analysing the text of *The Laurentian Chronicle*, specialists concluded that, among other things, it reflects the chronicle compilations of Ryazan and Rostov that were made not long after the invasion of Batu and have not survived in manuscript form.

The theory of the existence of Ryazan chronicle-writing was advanced by Vasily Komarovich, who believed that the Ryazan chronicle was compiled shortly after the defeat of Ryazan in 1237 by Batu's forces. The existence of this compilation and its date are deduced from the fact that nearly all chronicle compilations known to date begin their account of Batu's invasion of Russia with Ryazan. In particular, in the episode relating the fate of Ryazan one senses "the voice of a direct observer and even participant in the events described".[3] A characteristic feature of this compilation is the diatribe against the princes: because of the princes' refusal to put the interests of the common cause before their private interests, the Russian hosts, in spite of their heroism, could not withstand the foe. This denunciatory tendency is seen most clearly in the tale of Batu's sacking of Ryazan.

The chronicler exclaims bitterly that even before Batu's invasion "the Lord had taken away our strength and planted folly, and terror, and fear, and trepidation in us for our sins".[4] The "folly", the neglect of common interests for selfish motives, was the cause of the unconcerted actions of princes in the face of the terrible threat. The Ryazan chronicle account of Batu's invasion

Helmet of Prince Yaroslav, son of Vsevolod. Detail

also reflects some oral epic tales of the events. When the nomads invaded Ryazan soil they sent their emissaries to the princes of Ryazan, "a sorceress and two men", to demand "a tithe of everything—people, princes and horses". The oral tales of Batu's invasion of Ryazan and the account of the event in the Ryazan chronicle subsequently formed the basis of *The Tale of Batu's Capture of Ryazan.*[5]

Before Batu's invasion the Grand Prince's chronicle-writing was done in Vladimir. After the destruction of Vladimir it moved to Rostov. Dmitry Likhachev believes that an important role in Rostov chronicle-writing was played by Princess Maria, the wife of Prince Vasilko of Rostov killed during Batu's invasion in 1238 and the daughter of Prince Michael of Chernigov, killed in the Horde in 1246.

In 1262 a series of uprisings against the Horde took place in the towns of the Rostov principality. The chronicle compiled after these events, which Dmitry Likhachev calls the Maria chronicle compilation, "is completely imbued with the idea of standing firm for the faith and independence of the homeland. It is this idea that determined both the content and the form of the chronicle. The Maria chronicle combines a number of tales about the tragic death of Russian princes who refused to compromise with their conquerors."[6] It includes the tale of the death of Maria's husband Vasilko in 1238 in the battle on the River Sit, the account of the moving of Grand Prince Yuri's body to Vladimir (he was killed in the fighting on the Sit, and his body taken from the battle field first to Rostov, then to Vladimir), and the entry under 1246 on the killing of Michael of Chernigov, Maria's father, in the Horde.

The story about Grand Prince Yuri stresses not only his military valour (he rejects the enemy's offer of peace), but also the fact that his death was a martyr's one for the Christian faith.[7]

The idea of boundless devotion to duty and the faith is even stronger in the story about Vasilko and the entry on the death of Michael of Chernigov—they do not betray the Orthodox faith or agree to recognise the pagan faith of the conquerors. The readiness to lay down one's life for Christianity and the refusal to worship pagan gods were a protest against foreign rule in general.

The account of the events of 1262, after which the Maria chronicle was compiled, contains an angry denunciation of a monk called Izosimos who went over to the enemy and helped them. This denunciation contrasts the traitor with the heroes who died a terrible death, but stayed loyal to their homeland: Izosimos also dies, but his death is wretched and inglorious. When the uprisings against the Horde began, writes the chronicler, "this transgressor Izosimos was killed in the town of Yaroslavl. And his body became food for dogs and ravens."

The Galich-Volhynian Chronicle. The Galich-Volhynian principality was in the south-west of Russia. To the west and south-west it bordered on Poland and Hungary, to the east on the principalities of Kiev and Turov-Pinsk. The Galich-Volhynian principality was one of the richest Russian principalities and played an important role in the political life of Old Russia.

The history of the Galich-Volhynian principality was full of inter-feudal wars and a particularly bitter struggle between the princes and local boyars who were a considerable political force. In the thirteenth century the internal strife was complicated by constant clashes with external foes (Hungary, Poland and the Mongols). The feudal wars and the struggle against foreign invaders were accompanied by large-scale revolts by the townspeople and peasants against the alien oppressors and the local boyars. All these events were reflected in *The Galich-Volhynian Chronicle.* This chronicle, compiled in the thirteenth century, has come down to us in *The Hypatian Chronicle,* where it is found immediately after *The Kievan Chronicle* (beginning in 1200). *The Galich-Volhynian Chronicle* is divided into two parts: the first (before 1260) is a description of the life and deeds of Prince Daniel of Galich and the history of the Galich principality, while the second tells of the fate of the Vladimir-Volhynian principality and its princes (Daniel's brother Vasilko, and the latter's son, Vladimir) covering the period from 1261 to 1290. Both the first and the second parts of *The Galich-Volhynian Chronicle* are independent texts, differing from each other in ideology and style.[8]

The first part of *The Galich-Volhynian Chronicle, The Chronicle of Daniel of Galich,* ends with a brief announcement of Daniel's death and a restrained encomium to him. This ending is not in keeping with the chronicle's general attitude to Daniel. On these grounds Lev Cherepnin concluded that "*The Chronicle of Daniel of Galich* was compiled during the prince's lifetime and that the short accounts of his final years and death belong not to Galich, but to Vladimir-Volhynian chronicle-writing."[9] He believes that the *Chronicle* was compiled in 1256-1257. The chronicle was written at the Episcopal See of Kholm.

The Chronicle of Daniel of Galich was a complete work. It does not recount events strictly year by year. This is explained by the fact that its historical narrative is more complete and coordinated than that of the chronicle. The dates now in the *Chronicle,* the first being "in the year of 6709 (1201)", were inserted later, probably by the compiler of the Hypatian manuscript. They were put in an arbitrary order and are as a rule inaccurate, random and approximate.[10] The main idea of the *Chronicle* is the prince's struggle against the rebellious boyars and a denunciation of the boyars' treachery. The second main theme of the *Chronicle* is the glory of Russian military prowess and of the Russian land.

The *Chronicle*, Cherepnin believes, was based on the Galich tale of the fate of the infants Daniel and Vasilko, sons of Prince Roman, *The Tale of the Battle on the Kalka* written by a participant in it, the tale of Daniel's struggle with the feudal boyars, *The Tale of the Battle Against Batu*, an account of Daniel's journey to the Horde to pay homage to Batu, a cycle of military tales about the Jatvingians' struggle, local chronicles, official documents and translated literature. In the *Chronicle* all these sources were moulded into a single narrative with unified themes and style.

The author of the *Chronicle* gives a detailed description of Daniel's struggle for the princely throne of Galich against the Galich boyars and the Hungarian and Polish feudal lords. His narrative of these events opens as follows: "Let us begin to tell of countless battles, of great deeds, of frequent wars, of many conspiracies, of frequent uprisings, and of many rebellions." He does not limit himself to events connected with the history of the Galich principality, but devotes attention to the fate of the whole of Russia as well.

From the different stories about Daniel there emerges the figure of a courageous and bold warrior, a wise and strong ruler. Stressing the prince's nobility and military prowess, the author exclaims that his hero was immensely bold, brave and splendid "from head to foot". But then he describes Daniel's journey to pay homage to Batu in the Horde. And here Daniel appears in the humiliating role of an obedient servitor of Batu, who holds the prince's honour and life in his hands.

Concern for his principality compels Daniel to journey to the Horde, although he knows that shameful humiliation, and perhaps even death, await him there. On the way he stops at the Vydubitsky Monastery and asks the monks to pray for him. Seeing the suffering and oppression of the Russian people Daniel "began to grieve even more in his heart".

When the prince appears before Batu, he is greeted with the words: "Why did you not come before, Daniel? But it is good that you come now." The first part of this address contains a reproach and a threat, the second a gracious pardon. Then Batu asks the prince if he drinks "black milk, our drink, mare's koumiss" and Daniel replies, "I have not drunk it yet. I will do so, if you order."

To which Batu says condescendingly: "You are ours now, a Tartar. So drink our drink."

In spite of the brevity of this dialogue, we have an expressive picture of the abasement of the Prince of the mighty Galich principality before the Khan of the Horde.

Later they do Daniel the honour of bringing him a jug of wine and Batu says, "You are not used to koumiss, drink wine!" But this is the patronising condescension of the ruler to his subject. And the chronicler exclaims sadly: "Oh, Tartar honour, more evil than evil", and proceeds to develop this sad thought as follows: "Grand Prince Daniel, son of Roman, together with his brother ruled o'er the whole of Russia: Kiev, Vladimir, Galich and other lands, but now he kneels and calls himself a slave! The Tartars want tribute, but he does not hope for his life. The storm clouds approach. Oh, evil Tartar honour! His father was ruler in the Russian land, he subjugated the Polovtsian lands and conquered other regions. His son was not vouchsafed this honour. Who else could take it? There is no end to their malice and cunning." Speaking of Daniel's return from the Horde, the narrator describes the feelings of Daniel's sons and brother as follows: "And there was lamenting for his insult and great joy that he was hale."

This story does not degrade Daniel or belittle his virtues as a warrior and prince in the eyes of the Russian reader. But the contrast between the Daniel we see here and the picture of the prince that the reader gets from all the other stories about him stresses most forcefully the tragedy of Russia's subjection.

The Chronicle of Daniel of Galich stands out from all the other works of Old Russian literature with its vivid descriptions of battles and military trappings, its distinctive chivalrous tone. The author's love of military subjects and battle scenes is clearly evident in the care and delight with which he describes military dress, armour and weapons, the way that he portrays the warriors' general appearance as they set off. "...The steeds wore chamfrons and leather crinets and the men shirts of mail, the hosts and glittering weapons shone with a great radiance. Daniel himself rode beside the king, as was the Russian custom. The steed beneath him was most wondrous, his saddle of beaten gold, his arrows and sabre embellished with gold and other precious ornaments: his jerkin of Greek silk trimmed with wide gold braid, his boots of green leather embroidered with gold." These and similar descriptions reveal the author of the *Chronicle* as a man closely connected with military craft, probably a member of the prince's personal bodyguard. He was widely read, familiar with translated works and fond of parading his literary skill. Hence the abundance of

complex bookish forms, the stylistic ornament, lengthy comparisons and rhetorical exclamations.

We must mention that the author of the *Chronicle* was very
familiar with folk epic tales, including Polovtsian ones. The
famous story of the Polovtsian Khan Otrok is based on a
Polovtsian epos. During Vladimir Monomachos' struggle against
the Polovtsians, Otrok fled from the Polovtsian steppes through
the Iron Gates.* When Vladimir Monomachos died, Khan Syrchan
sent the *gudets* Orya (a *gudets* is a singer who accompanies himself
on the *gudok,* a stringed instrument), to Otrok with this message:
"Convey to him my words on the death of Vladimir Monomachos
and sing him Polovtsian songs. If, in spite of your words and the
Polovtsian songs, Otrok does not wish to come home let him smell
some wormwood." The words and songs had no effect on Otrok,
but when he breathed in the scent of his native steppes, he wept
and said: "'Tis better to die on one's native soil, than to find
renown in a strange land" and decided to return home.

Academician Alexander Orlov has given a brief and apt
description of the author of *The Chronicle of Daniel of Galich*: "In
the Galich narrative you sense all the time the educated man of
letters, the diplomat, the warrior who loves the ring and clash of
weapons, the courtier and a kind of knight who understood
history as a succession of wars and revolts." [11]

The distinctive genre features of the *Chronicle* are later
reflected in the literature of North-Eastern Russia, in the
biography of the famous warrior knight and statesman, *The Tale
of the Life of Alexander Nevsky.*

The Volhynian Chronicle, which, according to Igor Eremin,
followed *The Chronicle of Daniel of Galich* "is the work of one and
the same author from beginning to end... Both the content of the
chronicle and its literary structure testify to a single author." [12] *The
Volhynian Chronicle* was compiled as a single complete work in the
1290s. Like *The Chronicle of Daniel of Galich* it does not recount
events strictly year by year. But unlike the *Chronicle* the narrative
in *The Volhynian Chronicle* is in strict chronological order. In this
feature and its stylistic peculiarities *The Volhynian Chronicle* is
closer to the traditions of twelfth-century Kievan chronicle-writing
than *The Chronicle of Daniel of Galich. The Volhynian Chronicle* also
differs from the latter in its simpler exposition. The interests of
the Volhynian principality are in the foreground and it has a more
local nature than the *Chronicle.*

Special attention in *The Volhynian Chronicle* is devoted to

---

* Now Derbent. In the Middle Ages there was a fortress guarding the narrow
passage between the western shore of the Caspian and the Caucasus.

Prince Vladimir, son of Vasilko. He is the ideal prince and ruler. The chronicler stresses his wisdom and justice, and the fact that he is loved by princes, boyars and the whole people. The story of his sickness and death is full of love and compassion.

The chronicler describes in detail the prince's long illness, his final days and death. Vladimir bears his sufferings with brave resignation. In spite of his ill health he continues to rule his land: he draws up a will, carries on negotiations with other princes and takes various decisions aimed at the well-being of the Volhynian principality.

The death of the prince causes universal grief and sorrow. He is mourned not only by all the people of Volhynia, but by other peoples as well. The lament for the dead prince is followed by an encomium to him, which stresses his wisdom, learning and high morals.

The artistic originality of individual episodes and stories derives from the author's well-chosen imagery and detail which is most striking. Here is one example of this vivid detail in the story about Vladimir.

After the prince's death his lands are to go to his brother Mstislav, as agreed between the princes. But there are other claimants to the dying prince's possessions (he had no children). Prince Yuri, the son of Vladimir's cousin, asks Vladimir to bequeath him Berestye (modern Brest). Vladimir refuses, saying to Yuri's envoy: "I cannot break the agreement that I have made with my brother Mstislav." After concluding his talks with Yuri's envoy, Vladimir sends his loyal servant Ratsha to Mstislav to warn his brother of Yuri's claims. Confirming Mstislav's right to his possessions and urging him not to concede any of his inheritance to anyone, Vladimir "took a handful of straw from his bed" and asked Ratsha to give it to his brother and tell him: "If I give you this handful of straw, my brother, do not concede it to anyone else after my death either."

Interest in world history did not wane in the thirteenth century. A large chronological compilation appears to have been written in the second half of the thirteenth century in Galich-Volhynian Russia. It contained Biblical texts, extracts from the *Chronicle* of Georgios Hamartolos, the almost complete text of some books of John Malalas' *Chronicle*, the first redaction of *The Chronographical Alexandreid,* and Josephus Flavius' *History of the Jewish War.* This collection covered events of ancient history from the Creation to the capture of Jerusalem by Titus in 70 A.D.[13]

The chronicles compiled during the Mongol invasion, the chronicle tales and stories of this period, are the sources of our information on the events of those years. But they are equally valuable as records of social thought and works of literature. They not only describe a certain event or record a certain fact, but also provide an assessment of it. The chronicler expresses his attitude towards what he describes. Local chronicles are distinguished by local features, in some cases continuing the older traditions of Kievan Russia and local chronicle-writing, in others introducing something new. But to a greater or lesser extent all the chronicles attempt to throw light on events that concern not only the region or principality in question, but the Russian land as a whole.

2. The *Supplication* of Daniel the Exile

One of the central themes of Old Russian literature was the role of the prince in the life of the country. The need for strong princely power in order to struggle successfully against external enemies and overcome internal contradictions was perfectly clear to those concerned with the fate of their country.

The idea of strong princely power lies at the centre of one of the most interesting works of Old Russian literature—the *Supplication* of Daniel the Exile.[14] This work is interesting not only because of its ideological content and literary qualities, but also because of the mystery that surrounds it. The question of when it was written and who Daniel the Exile was has still not been fully answered, and specialists also disagree strongly on nature of the inter-relationship of the two main redactions.

One redaction is entitled the *Oration* of Daniel the Exile and the other the *Supplication* of Daniel the Exile. The *Oration* is addressed to Prince Yaroslav, son of Vladimir, the *Supplication* to Yaroslav, son of Vsevolod. In the text of the *Oration* the prince is called "the son of the great tsar Vladimir". This wording suggests that the ruler in question was Vladimir Monomachos, but he did not have a son called Yaroslav. Some specialists believe that "Yaroslav" was written by mistake, and that it should be either Yuri the Long-Armed or Andrew the Good (both sons of Vladimir Monomachos). In this case the *Oration* would have been written not later than the 1140s or 1150s (Yuri the Long-Armed died in 1157 and Andrew the Good in 1141).[15] Most specialists take the view that the *Supplication* was addressed to Yaroslav, son of Grand Prince Vsevolod III the Big Nest, who reigned in Pereyaslavl-Suzdalsky from 1213 to 1236.

The view also exists that the *Oration* is a later reworking of the *Supplication*.[16] In spite of the extensive literature arguing both points of view the question of which came first, the *Oration* or the *Supplication*, remains an open one.

The main difference between the *Supplication* and the *Oration* lies in their ideology. In both redactions the power and might of the prince and princely authority are praised equally. But the attitude to the boyars in the *Oration* differs greatly from that in the *Supplication.* In the *Oration* the prince is not contrasted with the boyars, but in the *Supplication* the superiority of the prince to the boyars is stressed strongly.

The chronicle account of the battle on the Vozha in 1378 mentions Daniel the Exile (*zatochnik*). It refers to a certain priest who was banished "into imprisonment on Lake Lacha where Daniel the Exile was." [17] This reference does not solve the question of who Daniel was, however. Most likely it originates itself from the *Oration* or the *Supplication* and merely testifies to the popularity of this work in Old Russia. We cannot even be sure that there really was a person called Daniel who at some time for some reason fell into disfavour with his prince and lived on Lake Lacha (on the north bank of which is the town of Kargopol). The very word *zatochnik* is unclear. The various attempts to identify Daniel in specialist and popular literature are, as a rule, not objective. It is clear from the material of the *Oration* and the *Supplication* and from the author's descriptions of himself that he did not belong to the ruling class. Daniel belonged to the category of prince's "favourites" who came from the most varied strata of bondmen. [18]

Daniel the Exile's work is a collection of aphorisms, each of which or each group of which can be regarded as an independent text. For example: "To help a man in sorrow is like slaking his thirst with icy water on a hot day"; "Gold is melted by heat, but man by misfortune"; "The moth, oh prince, eats away clothes, and sorrow—man", etc. But all these aphorisms, which convey everyday wisdom in extremely condensed form, are united by the figure of Daniel the Exile standing behind them. The eternal, commonplace truths become the peripeteia of the fate of one man, Daniel himself. This makes the work appear not as a collection of aphorisms, but as a narrative about the concrete fate of a concrete person. We do not know whether this is a conscious literary device or whether it is a real Daniel writing about his fate with aphorisms both borrowed and made up by him and portraying the ideal prince and ruler. In either case we can say that here we have a work of considerable literary merit that reflects real life.

The author borrowed aphorisms widely from the Holy Scriptures (Psalms, the Song of Solomon, the Wisdom of Jesus the Son of Sirach, and others) and made use of *The Tale of Akir the Wise*, Gennadius' *Hundred Words* and *The Tale of Bygone Years*, with which he was familiar. At the same time both the *Oration* and the *Supplication* reflect the most varied aspects of Russian life of the period. Daniel makes extensive use of everyday vocabulary and draws on everyday life in his similes and metaphors. And we are presented with thumbnail sketches of the life and customs of the day.

Reflecting on ways to escape poverty, Daniel suggests marrying a rich woman. This leads him to reflect on female spite (a very popular theme in mediaeval writing). Here he makes use of both books as sources and, as he himself says, "worldly parables" (i.e., secular sayings). The wit and common sense of these maxims (Daniel does not attack women in general, only the type of "bad woman" that he finds particularly hateful) create lively scenes. "I saw an ugly woman pressing herself against the mirror and painting her face, and I said to her: 'Look not in the mirror—for you will see the ugliness of your face and grow even more bitter'; "A good wife is her husband's crown and happiness, but a bad wife is woe and ruin to the house."

The author's familiarity with translated and original literature combines well with his extensive knowledge of worldly wisdom. He is not afraid of quoting abundantly from worldly parables and does not avoid colloquial expressions. As Dmitry Likhachev notes: "Daniel flaunts his coarseness, his deliberately low style, as it were, and is not afraid of using everyday words." [19]

This feature of Daniel the Exile's style is explained not only by the fact that he was from the lower strata of society, a bondman, but also by the author's literary position. Daniel's deliberate coarseness and buffoonery are in the tradition of the *skomorokh* (a wandering minstrel-cum-clown).

The combination in Daniel the Exile's work of bookishness and buffoonery, of didactic utterances and "worldly parables" give this work a special character of its own. The *Supplication* also stands out for its attitude to the human personality. By denigrating himself and praising the prince inordinately (one can sense a certain grotesqueness behind this praise), Daniel places intellectual powers above all else and rises to the defence of human dignity. A wise man in dire straits who is seeking to make his way in life cannot and should not compromise his human dignity, act against his conscience. It is interesting that although he stresses the prince's power in all possible ways, Daniel says that however mighty a prince, his actions depend on the counsellors around him: "My lord! It is not the sea that drowns ships, but the winds; it is not fire that makes iron red hot, but the blowing of the bellows; and likewise it is not the prince himself who makes a mistake, but his counsellors who are at fault. If he consults a good counsellor, a prince will win a high throne, but with a bad counsellor he will lose a low one."

Daniel the Exile is an Old Russian intellectual who is fully aware of the evils of his time and tries to find a way of combating them. He stands for the recognition of human merit irrespective of a person's social status and wealth. Vissarion Belinsky, the famous Russian critic, gave a very apt description of Daniel the Exile as a writer: "Whoever Daniel the Exile was, we have good reason to conclude that he was one of those people who, to their cost, are too intelligent, too gifted, who know too much and, unable to conceal their superiority from others, offend proud mediocrity; whose hearts ache and are consumed with zeal for things that do not concern them, who speak when it would be better to stay silent, and stay silent when it would be more advantageous to speak; in short, one of those whom others at first praise and pamper, then plague to death and, finally, having got rid of them, begin to praise again." [20]

3. Tales of the Mongol Invasion of Russia

The Tale of the Battle on the Kalka. In examining the history of thirteenth-century chronicle-writing, we have already mentioned the broad reflection in the chronicles of Batu's invasion and the establishment of Mongol overlordship. Let us now consider the individual works of this type.

The first clash with the invaders, the battle on the River Kalka in 1223, is the subject of a chronicle story the most lengthy version of which is to be found in *The Novgorod First Chronicle.* Comparing this version with shorter ones in other chronicles, one might think that the long form contains later additions inserted when it was included in *The Novgorod First Chronicle,* but for the most part this text "has preserved most fully the popular South-Russian story of the battle on the Kalka which was composed almost immediately after the defeat of the Russians in the period between 1223 and 1228." [21] Let us now examine *The Tale of the Battle on the Kalka* in more detail from the text of *The Novgorod First Chronicle.*[22]

The *Tale* begins by announcing the unexpected appearance of hordes of terrible warriors of a hitherto unknown people. This is punishment sent down by God for man's sins. This view of the cause of the Mongol invasion of Russia, i.e., the standpoint of religious historiosophy, is characteristic of all works of bookish origin.

The author of the tale lists the Mongols' defeat of the peoples who live next to the Russian lands: the Alans, Adygheis and Polovtsians.

Survivors from the defeated Polovtsians come to Russia and

beg the Russian princes to protect them, warning them that with
time the enemy will invade the Russian lands as well. "Today they
have taken away our land, tomorrow they will take yours." The
Russian princes decide to fight the dreaded invaders. Then the
Mongols send envoys to the Russian princes inviting them to
conclude an alliance against the Polovtsians who, as the Mongol
envoys say, "have done you much harm, which is why we are
killing them". But the Russian princes remain true to their word
and embark on a campaign. Lack of unanimity between the
princes, however, means that the military valour of the Russian
warriors is in vain.

The events on the Kalka were as follows. The united Russian
host advanced up to the river and set up camp. The Mongols
suddenly descended on the "camps of the Russian princes" and
the latter, unprepared for battle, turned and fled. Mstislav of
Kiev, whose men were standing apart from the main camp, on
a hill, "saw this disaster and did not move from the spot".

The fact that Mstislav of Kiev did not join in the fighting with
his men determined both the outcome of the battle as a whole and
his own fate. Mstislav's men took refuge behind a stockade and
prepared to defend themselves. But they were able to hold out for
only three days. All those captured were killed, and the princes
(Mstislav had two other princes with him) died a particularly
painful and ignominious death. They were crushed to death by the
wooden table on which the victors were feasting.

The tale ends by saying that the Mongols pursued the Russians
as far as the Dnieper, six princes were killed, and only one in ten
warriors returned home. The defeat on the Kalka aroused
universal grief in the Russian lands.

The Tale of the Battle on the Kalka was written in the tradition
of Russian military chronicle tales of the twelfth century. In a very
short text the author succeeded in conveying the Russian princes'
preparations for the war and their talks with the Polovtsians and
Mongol envoys, narrating how the Russian host marched to the
Kalka, and giving a vivid description of the ill-fated battle.

The Tale of the Battle on the Kalka kept alive the Russian
people's bitter memories of this event for many centuries. It was
constantly recopied and reworked in different chronicles. It also
served as a source for references to this event in other literary
works on the struggle of the Russian people against Mongol
overlordship.

The Lay of the Ruin of the Russian Land. *The Lay of the Ruin
of the Russian Land* has come down to us in two manuscripts, not
as an independent text, but as the foreword to the first redaction
of *The Tale of the Life of Alexander Nevsky.*[23]

Some specialists believe that *The Lay of the Ruin* is the introduction to a secular biography of Alexander Nevsky that has not survived. But a comparison of the style of the *Lay* with that of *The Tale of the Life of Alxander Nevsky* shows that these works are independent of each other and were written at different times. The linking of these texts occurred later in their literary history. Consequently there are more grounds for seeing *The Lay of the Ruin of the Russian Land* as a small fragment of a larger work describing the terrible disaster that befell the Russian lands.[24]

The names mentioned in the *Lay* and the context in which they are found ("up to the Yaroslav of our day and his brother Yuri, Prince of Vladimir"), the echoes of the legends about Vladimir Monomachos and certain South-Russian features in the work give grounds for assuming that *The Lay of the Ruin* was written by an author of South-Russian origin in North-Eastern Russia not later than 1246 (the Yaroslav "of our day" is Yaroslav, son of Vsevolod, and he died on September 30, 1246). The title of the work (which is found in one manuscript) and the phrase on which the text breaks off ("And in those days ... a disaster befell Christian folk") give grounds for regarding this work as a response by an unknown author to the Mongol invasion. Most likely *The Lay of the Ruin* was written between 1238 and 1246.

The surviving fragment of *The Lay of the Ruin*, either the foreword to or first part of a work on the "ruin of the Russian land", is about the horrors of Batu's invasion and the defeat of the Russian principalities. It gives a moving description of the former beauty and wealth of the Russian land, its former political might. This type of foreword to a text about a country's sufferings and misfortunes was quite common. It is also found in other works of early and mediaeval literature that contain a eulogy to the greatness and glory of the author's native land. A specialist who has studied this problem concluded that the *Lay* "is closer not to all patriotic works in other literatures, but only to those that appeared under similar conditions, when the writer's homeland was suffering from war, internal strife and arbitrary rule".[25]

The author of the *Lay* extols the beauty and splendour of the Russian land: "Oh, fairest of fair and finely adorned Russian land! You are renowned for many beauties: you are famed for your many lakes, rivers and sacred springs, your mountains and steep hills ... your wondrous and diverse birds and beasts..." The Russian land is adorned not only with the beauties and gifts of nature, it is also famed for its "mighty princes, honest boyars, and many nobles".

Developing the theme of the "dread princes" who have conquered "pagan countries", the author of the *Lay* portrays the

The Lay of the Ruin of the Russian Land. First page of the manuscript. 16th century. Institute of Russian Literature, Leningrad

ideal Russian prince, Vladimir Monomachos, before whom all neighbouring peoples and tribes trembled. Even the Byzantine Emperor Manuel sent Vladimir gifts so that "he would not take Constantinople away from him". This hyperbolised picture of the "dread" grand prince embodied the idea of strong princely authority and military prowess. At the time of the Mongol invasion and the military defeat of the Russian land a reference to the strength and might of Monomachos served as a reproach to the Russian princes of the day and was also intended to inspire hope for a better future. It is, therefore, no accident that the *Lay* was inserted at the beginning of *The Tale of the Life of Alexander Nevsky*; here Alexander, a contemporary of Batu's, appears as a dread prince.

In its poetic structure and ideology *The Lay of the Ruin of the Russian Land* is close to *The Lay of Igor's Host*. Both works contain a high degree of patriotism, a strong sense of national awareness, hyperbolisation of the strength and military valour of the warrior prince, a lyrical attitude towards nature, and a rhythmic structure. Both works also combine a lament with a eulogy, a eulogy to the former greatness of the Russian land and a lament at its misfortune in the present. Both works have identical stylistic formulae and poetic images. The nature of the titles is similar. The phrase in *The Lay of Igor's Host* from "Vladimir of old to Igor of our own days..." is parallel to the phrase in *The Lay of the Ruin* "From the great Yaroslav to Vladimir, and to Yaroslav of our day..." The authors of both works frequently use collective names of peoples. Other parallel expressions can also be found.[26]

The Lay of Igor's Host was a lyrical call for the unity of the Russian princes and Russian principalities on the eve of the Mongol invasion. *The Lay of the Ruin of the Russian Land* is a lyrical response to this invasion.

The Tale of Batu's Capture of Ryazan. *The Tale of Batu's Capture of Ryazan* is not a documentary account of the struggle of the people of Ryazan in 1237 against the enemy that invaded the principality. Among the participants in the battle many names are mentioned that are unknown in chronicle sources. Some of the princes who, according to the *Tale*, fought against Batu had already died by 1237 (for example, Vsevolod of Pronsk who died in 1208 and David of Murom who died in 1228) and Oleg the Red is said to have died in it (when in fact he was in captivity until 1252 and died in 1258). These deviations from historical fact suggest that the *Tale* was written some time after the actual event, when the real facts had undergone a certain epic generalisation in people's minds. The epic generalisation of the work can also be seen in the fact that all the Ryazan princes who fought in the

battle against Batu are joined together in a single gigantic host
and called brothers in the *Tale.* At the same time we must not date
the writing of the *Tale* too long after the event which it describes.
It was probably written not later than the middle of the fourteenth
century. This, Dmitry Likhachev writes, "is also suggested by the
intensity of the sorrow at the events of Batu's invasion, which has
not yet been softened or diminished by time, and a number of
characteristic details that could have been remembered only by the
closest generations".[27]

We are examining *The Tale of Batu's Capture of Ryazan* together with thirteenth-century works dealing with the Mongol invasion
because it reflects epic legends about Batu's campaign against
Ryazan, some of which may have been created shortly after 1237.

The Tale of Batu's Capture of Ryazan gives the impression of
being an independent work, although in the Old Russian
manuscript tradition it is part of a compilation consisting of texts
about an icon of St Nicholas. This icon was taken to the Ryazan
lands from Korsun (Chersonesus),* the town in which, according
to legend, Vladimir I was baptised and where many Russians lived
before the Mongol invasion. The compilation consists of: 1) *The
Tale of St Nicholas of Zarazsk,* the story of how the icon of St
Nicholas was brought from Korsun to the principality of Ryazan
by the "keeper" of the icon, Eustathius; 2) *The Tale of Batu's
Capture of Ryazan*; 3) *The Encomium of the Princely House of Ryazan*;
and 4) the "family tree" of the "keepers" of the icon.

The first story is based on a subject very common in mediaeval
literature, namely the transfer of sacred objects (a cross, an icon,
relics, etc.) from one place to another. Here this traditional subject
is closely connected with the historical situation immediately
preceding Batu's invasion.

The Tale of St Nicholas of Zarazsk begins with an indication of
when the event took place — "In the year 6733 (1225). In the
reign of the Grand Prince George of Vladimir ... a wonder-
working icon was brought..."[28] St Nicholas appears to Eustathius
several times in a dream and commands his "keeper" to take his
icon from Korsun to Ryazan. Dmitry Likhachev gives the following
answer to the question of why St Nicholas "drove" Eustathius
from Korsun to Ryazan: "Eustathius was driven not by St
Nicholas, of course, but by the Polovtsians who began to move
after the battle on the Kalka, alarmed by the advance of the
Mongol hordes, overran the Black Sea steppes and cut Korsun off
from the Russian north. We should remember that Eustathius'
journey took place in the 'third year after the battle on the Kalka'

_____
* In the Crimea.

and that St Nicholas 'forbade' Eustathius to cross the dangerous Polovtsian steppes. It is also no accident that Ryazan was chosen as a safer place for the 'patron' of trade, St Nicholas. Ryazan's links with the Northern Caucasus and the Black Sea coast can be traced back to early times." [29]

After many misadventures Eustathius eventually arrives in the land of Ryazan. St Nicholas appears to the Ryazan Prince Theodore, son of Yuri (no prince of that name is mentioned in the chronicles), orders him to give his icon a solemn welcome and predicts that the prince, and his future wife and son will gain the "Kingdom of Heaven". The story ends with an account of how St Nicholas' prophesy comes true. In 1237 Theodore was killed "by the godless ruler Batu on the river at Voronezh". Hearing of her husband's death Theodore's wife, Princess Eupraxia, kills herself and her young son Ivan by jumping "from her high palace". After that the icon of St Nicholas became called the icon of St Nicholas of Zarazsk because the pious Princess Eupraxia *zarazilas,* "jumped to her death", with her son, Prince Ivan. Thematically *The Tale of St Nicholas of Zarazsk* is closely connected with the following *Tale of Batu's Capture of Ryazan,* from which we learn how and why Prince Theodore was killed by Batu and what suffering Batu brought to the land of Ryazan.

The *Tale* begins in the manner of a chronicle: "In the year 6745 (1237) ... the godless ruler Batu came to the land of Russia..." Then follows a passage similar to the chronicle account of the coming of Batu saying that Batu demanded a tithe of everything from the people of Ryazan and announcing the refusal of the Grand Prince of Vladimir to go to the aid of Ryazan.

Grand Prince Yuri of Ryazan, not receiving aid from the Prince of Vladimir, consults with his fellow princes and decides to placate Batu with gifts. His son Theodore takes gifts from Ryazan to Batu. Batu accepts them and promises to spare the Ryazan principality. But then he "began to ask the princes of Ryazan for their daughters and sisters to share his bed". One of the Ryazan noblemen out of envy told Batu that Theodore's wife "is of noble birth and fairer in body than all others". In reply to Batu's demand to "taste the beauty" of his wife, the prince "dared to reply to the ruler: 'It is not fitting for us, Christians, to bring our wives to you, impious ruler, for lechery. When you conquer us, then shall you possess our wives also.'" Infuriated by Theodore's bold reply, Batu orders the prince and all those with him to be killed. The death of Eupraxia and her son is described in almost the same words as in *The Tale of St Nicholas of Zarazsk.*

This is the exposition of the *Tale.* Although at first glance this episode seems to be self-contained, it is closely connected with the main theme of the work, namely, that all attempts to mollify the enemy and come to terms with them are pointless and can lead only to total subjection. The only solution is to fight against the invaders, even if this struggle will not lead to victory. The exposition of the *Tale* is linked with the subsequent development of the subject by Yuri's appeal to the princes and men of Ryazan, when the news of his son's death reaches the city: "It were better for us to win eternal glory through death, than to be in the power of pagans." This summons to fight the foe contains the main theme of all the episodes in the work, that death is better than shameful slavery. Yuri's words remind one of Igor Svyatoslavich's address to his men before they set off on their campaign in *The Lay of Igor's Host*: "O brethren and warriors! Better be slain than taken captive!" This is not evidence of a direct link of the *Tale* with the *Lay*. More likely this coincidence is explained by the identical view of military honour, patriotism and civic fervour of the two works.

The men of Ryazan met Batu by the frontiers of the Ryazan land "and fell upon him, and began to fight him hard and bravely, and a cruel and terrible battle ensued. The Russians fought so bravely that even Batu was alarmed. But the enemy forces were so great that there were a thousand of them to each Ryazan man, and each two Ryazan men fought "against ten thousand". The nomads marvelled at the "strength and courage" of the Russians and had difficulty in overcoming them. Listing the princes killed in the battle by name, the author of the *Tale* says that all the other "valiant and daring men of Ryazan" "perished likewise and drained the same cup of death to the dregs".

Having destroyed Yuri's army, Batu began to conquer the land of Ryazan. After a five-day siege his men took Ryazan. "And not a single living soul remained in the town: all died and drained the same cup of death to the dregs." The silence that descended after the fierce battle and terrible slaughter ("There was no groaning and no lamenting there") is eloquent testimony to the mercilessness of the enemy. The same idea is stressed by the words that there was no one to grieve the dead: no fathers and mothers to mourn their children, and no children to mourn the death of their parents, no brothers to mourn their brothers—all lay dead together.

Having sacked Ryazan, Batu advanced on Suzdal and Vladimir, "intending to capture the Russian land". At this time "a certain nobleman by the name of Evpaty Kolovrat from Ryazan" was in Chernigov. Learning of the disaster, he galloped to Ryazan, but it was too late. Then he gathered together a band of "one thousand seven hundred men whom God had preserved outside

The Capture of Ryazan by Khan Batu. Illumination from *The Illustrated Chronicle.* 16th century. Academy of Sciences Library, Leningrad

the town", hurried off "in pursuit of the godless ruler, and managed to catch him up in the land of Suzdal". Evpaty's men fought with such reckless bravery that the enemy "became like drunken or mad men" and "the Mongols thought the dead had come to life".

Evpaty's attack on Batu's immense army with a small band of Ryazan men who had accidentally survived the earlier slaughter ended in defeat. But it was an heroic defeat, symbolising the military valour and selfless courage of the Russian warriors. The enemy managed to kill the "mighty giant" Evpaty only with the help of battering rams. Like a legendary knight, Evpaty felled a vast number of Batu's best men, chopping some in two and cleaving others "to the saddle". The men with him also fought like heroes of folk legends.

The style of the folk epos is felt not only in the figures of Evpaty and his men, but in the whole character of this episode. Batu's men succeed in capturing a few Ryazan men "faint with wounds". When asked by Batu who they are and who has sent them, the captives reply in traditional epic fashion: "We come from Prince Ingvar Ingorevich of Ryazan, to honour you, mighty ruler, and to accompany you with honour and to do you honour." They ask Batu not to "take offence": there are so many of you, they say, that we shall not have time "to fill the cup for such a great Mongol host". The episode ends with the words that Batu "marvelled at their wise reply".

Batu and his generals were forced to acknowledge the immense bravery and unprecedented courage of the Russian warriors. Gazing at the dead body of Evpaty, Batu's princes and generals say that never before have they "seen such valiant and daring men" nor heard from their fathers of such courageous warriors who like "winged men do not know death and fight so hard and bravely, riding on their steeds, one to a thousand and two to ten thousand". Looking at Evpaty's body, Batu exclaims: "If such a man served me, I would hold him right next to my heart." The surviving warriors from Evpaty's band are allowed to leave unharmed with the hero's body. The attack on the foe by Evpaty's men is revenge for the sacking of Ryazan and its dead.

After the Evpaty episode comes an account of the arrival in Ryazan from Chernigov of (according to the *Tale*) the only surviving Ryazan Prince Ingvar. At the sight of the terrible devastation of Ryazan and the death of all his kin Ingvar "shouted with compassion, like a trumpet summoning a host, like a sweet sounding organ". His grief is so great that he falls to the ground "like a corpse". Ingvar buries the remains of the dead and mourns them. In its imagery and phraseology his lament is akin to

2ND QUARTER-END OF 13TH C.

folk laments. The author of the *Tale* makes extensive use in his work of folk epic legends about Batu's sacking of Ryazan. The epic element is most noticeable in the story of Evpaty Kolovrat. Some specialists take the view that the Evpaty episode is in fact an epic song about Evpaty Kolovrat that has been inserted into the text.[30] But the fate of Prince Theodore, his wife and son in the *Tale* are also organic parts of a single, complete narrative. And all these parts are firmly bound together by a single idea, that of the selfless courageous defence of the homeland against the enemy invasion, by the single thought that "it were better for us to win eternal glory through death, than to fall into pagan hands". This central idea of the *Tale* makes it a story of the heroism and greatness of the human spirit.

After *The Tale of Batu's Capture of Ryazan* comes *The Encomium of the Princely House of Ryazan.* "Those sovereigns ... were of Christ-loving lineage, brother-loving, fair of face, bright-eyed, dread of countenance, immeasurably brave, light of heart, kind to their boyars, welcoming to guests, diligent to the church, quick to feast, ready for their sovereign's amusements, skilled in warfare, and majestic before their brothers and envoys. They had a manly mind, dwelt in truth, and observed purity of soul and body without sin..." The *Encomium* stresses the human, spiritual and stately virtues portraying the ideal Russian prince, and the embodiment of this ideal are the Ryazan princes that have been killed. The *Encomium* stands out particularly for its literary mastery.

The Tale of Batu's Capture of Ryazan is a masterpiece of Old Russian literature. The description of Batu's march on Ryazan is of a narrative nature. The reader follows the development of the events with tense interest. He feels the tragedy of what is taking place and the heroic selflessness of the men of Ryazan. The *Tale* is full of a deep patriotism that could not fail to move Old Russian readers, and is also easily understood and shared by readers today. The artistic force of the *Tale* lies in the sincerity with which the author describes the heroism of the men of Ryazan, in the compassion with which he relates the disasters that befell the Ryazan land. The *Tale* shows a high degree of literary perfection. This can be seen, inter alia, in the fact that the author has managed to mould into a single heroic narrative episodes and motifs of oral epic origin and a high bookish culture. The *Tale* combines the folklore genres of the eulogy and the lament. This combination is characteristic of a number of the finest works of Old Russian literature: *The Lay of Igor's Host, The Encomium of Roman Mstislavich of Galich,* and *The Lay of the Ruin of the Russian Land.*[31]

The Chronicle Stories of the Siege and Destruction of Russian Towns. A description of the Russian people's heroic struggle against Batu's forces has survived in accounts of the defence of other towns that were attacked and defeated. They take the form either of brief entries on the capture by the Mongols of a certain town or small stories. In all of them one can sense first-hand knowledge of the period. Thus, for example, in describing the Mongols' campaign against Kolomna, the chronicler exclaims that anyone who experienced it and lived to tell the tale could not restrain his tears. "We bewailed our sins day and night," he continues.[32]

There is a description of the Mongols' siege and capture of Vladimir in both the *Laurentian* and the *Hypatian* chronicles. The account in *The Laurentian Chronicle* is the most detailed.[33] The enemy laid siege to the town when Grand Prince Yuri of Vladimir had gone off to the River Sit with part of his bodyguard. To frighten the besieged inhabitants the enemy brought out Yuri's son, whom they had captured during the fall of Moscow, Prince Vladimir, the brother of princes Vsevolod and Mstislav, whom Yuri had left in Vladimir in his place. The episode with Prince Vladimir makes a very tragic impression. The wretched captive is hauled forcibly by the enemy to the Golden Gate in Vladimir, his native town. "'Do you recognise your princeling Vladimir?' the inhabitants of Vladimir are asked. Vladimir is sorrowful of countenance. But Vsevolod and Mstislav stand on the Golden Gate and recognise their brother Vladimir. Oh, sorrowful spectacle, worthy of tears."

The figure of the young captive prince stands before the inhabitants of Vladimir as the embodiment of the fate that awaits them: death, suffering and slavery.

The account of the fall of the town, like the episode with Prince Vladimir, is full of a sense of doom and hopelessness. The enemy surround the town on all sides. After camping for a while by the walls of Vladimir (during which time the Mongols manage to take Suzdal), they begin to storm the town. The enemy pour into Vladimir from all sides and quickly conquer it. The grand princess, her sisters-in-law and children and a "large multitude of boyars and common people" hide in the huge stone chruch of the Virgin (the Cathedral of the Assumption in Vladimir). The cathedral is set on fire and everyone inside it perishes. After describing the looting of churches and monasteries and the killing of priests, the chronicler concludes his account of Vladimir's sad fate with the words, "The Mongols gave short shrift to all, killing some and leading away others, barefoot and unclothed, dying of cold, to their camps."

The chronicle account of the capture of the town of Kozelsk in *The Hypatian Chronicle* is of a different kind. This story illustrates the bravery and courage of the Russian people.

Batu's forces arrived at the small town of Kozelsk and camped under its walls for seven weeks. When the storm of the town began, the inhabitants decided to a man to fight to the last and not to surrender. The battle was so bloody that the young prince of Kozelsk, Basil, who disappeared without trace, was said to have drowned in the blood. After that, the chronicler says in conclusion, the Mongols referred to Kozelsk as the "evil town".[34]

The story of the siege of Kiev is found in *The Hypatian Chronicle* under the entry for 1240. It contains a striking description of the "great enemy host" that marched up to the town walls. There were so many, the chronicler writes, that people conversing in the town could not hear each other for the creaking carts, grunting camels and neighing horses of the enemy forces surrounding Kiev. The capture of Kiev by Batu's men and their cruel treatment of the inhabitants are described in vivid detail. Archaeological excavations in Kiev confirm this account of the destruction of the town and mass killing of peaceful citizens by the invaders.[35] Tales of the siege and destruction of towns give us not only eye-witness accounts of the cruelty of the conquerors, descriptions of the sacking of Old Russian towns, large and small, and the terrible hardships endured by Russian people in those bitter years. They also present us with a striking picture of the courage, selflessness and patriotism of the Russian people.

The Tale of Mercurius of Smolensk. It is interesting that even in towns that were not attacked by Batu legends grew up about the miraculous saving of the town from this disaster due to the intercession of higher powers. One such legend of this period has survived in *The Tale of Mercurius of Smolensk.* It arose in Smolensk which Batu's forces did not reach.

As a tale the legend of the saving of Smolensk from Batu was composed not earlier than the late fifteenth or early sixteenth century. Two versions of the *Tale* have survived. They are not directly connected, but both of them originated independently from one and the same legend. The first version, which has been preserved in a single seventeenth-century manuscript, would appear to be closest to the legend, although as a literary work it belongs to the seventeenth century. The second version, which has survived in a large number of manuscripts, has several redactions.[36]

The subject of the *Tale* in its first version is as follows. A young man called Mercurius lived in Smolensk. He was god-fearing and prayerful. At this time Batu was advancing on the Russian land, spilling "innocent blood like water". Batu's forces marched on Smolensk. The Virgin Mary appeared to the sacristan of the Crypt Monastery outside the town and ordered him to find Mercurius and bring him to her. The Virgin gave Mercurius her blessing, armed him with a sword and told him to go to Batu's camp and attack the foe boldly. When he had overcome Batu's force a splendid warrior would appear to him, to whom Mercurius must hand over his sword. The warrior would cut off Mercurius' head with this sword and he, Mercurius, would return to the town, holding his head in his hand, and be buried there with great honour in her (the Virgin's) church. Everything came to pass as the Virgin had foretold.

With a few changes, and considerable additions and rhetorical insertions, this subject is repeated in the second version of the *Tale*. Here Mercurius is a Roman nobleman who came to Smolensk some years ago. His head is cut off not by a splendid warrior, but by the son of the Mongol "giant" whom Mercurius kills. According to this redaction of the *Tale* after his burial Mercurius appears to the sacristan and asks that his sword be hung over his tomb to ward off enemies.

Ivan Bunin's story *Sukhodol* testifies to the existence of other versions of the legendary tale of Mercurius of Smolensk. It refers to an old icon of Mercurius of Smolensk and says that "having defeated the Mongols, the saint went to sleep and was beheaded by his enemies".[37]

It is difficult to say what the original legend of Mercurius of Smolensk was like. But we can get a general idea of it from the surviving texts of the tale. The legend reflected the horror and grief felt by the Russian people, and the epic motifs of the people's heroic struggle against the enslavers during the period of the Mongol invasion and overlordship. In spite of the hagiographical, religious nature of the figure, Mercurius appears as an epic hero in both versions of the work: he defeats the enemy forces alone. Batu is terrified by Mercurius' miraculous strength and flees from the walls of Smolensk to Hungary, where he perishes. We can assume that in the original version of the legend the epic element was expressed even more vividly.

4. The Works of Serapion of Vladimir

The Mongol invasion was also reflected in the oratorical genre, one of the main genres of Old Russian literature.

Serapion of Vladimir was a fine master of this genre in the thirteenth century. Very little is known about Serapion's life. We know that up to 1274 he was Archimandrite of the Kiev Crypt Monastery and from 1274 to 1275 (the year of his death) Bishop of Vladimir. Serapion was appointed Bishop of Vladimir-Zalessky on the initiative of Metropolitan Cyril, a highly educated man for his day, who took part in the compilation of *The Chronicle of Daniel of Galich* and *The Life of Alexander Nevsky*. Both Serapion of Vladimir and Metropolitan Cyril were among the thirteenth-century figures who maintained cultural ties between South-Western Russia and the Russia of the north-east.

Five sermons by Serapion have come down to us, but from the description which the chronicler gives of Serapion when announcing his death under the year 1275 and from the works of Serapion himself it is obvious that he wrote far more sermons and homilies. The main theme of Serapion's sermons are the disasters that have befallen the Russian land as a result of the Mongol invasion, which was Divine punishment to Russia for people's sins. According to Serapion, only repentance and moral self-perfectionment can save the Russian land. Serapion's vivid descriptions of the disasters that have befallen the Russian land and his depth of feeling for his people's sufferings, which he himself shared, give his sermons great patriotic meaning.

Four of Serapion's five surviving sermons were written by him in 1274-1275 in Vladimir.[38] One of them, "On Divine Punishments and Battles", was most likely written shortly after the destruction of Kiev by Batu in 1239-1240.

All Serapion's sermons form, as it were, a single cycle in which the author describes with a heavy heart the terrible hardships of the enemy invasion and calls on people to cease their internal strife and cleanse themselves from their sins and shortcomings in the face of the terrible menace. In his *Sermons* he condemns the internecine warfare of the princes, greed, usury and violence.[39]

Both the general theme, central to all Serapion's *Sermons*, namely, the merciless cruelty of the Mongols, and the individual questions with which he deals in them, are developed not in abstract, rhetorical discourses, but in realistic and convincing sketches. At the same time the author's literary talent is evident throughout.

The dramatic solemnity of Serapion's account of the disasters that have befallen the Russian people is achieved by alternating long series of parallel syntactical constructions with phrases in the form of a question: "...They ravaged our land, and captured our towns, destroyed our holy churches, killed our fathers and brothers, and violated our mothers and sisters"; "Is our land not captive? Are our towns not conquered? Have our fathers and brothers not fallen dead upon the ground? Have our women and children not been taken into captivity? Have not those who remained been enslaved with the bitter slavery of the infidels? For nigh on forty years bitter suffering and torment and tribute have lain heavily upon us, and hunger, and the plague has stricken our cattle. And we cannot eat our fill of our bread, and our bones are dried by our groaning and grief"; "Then God did send against us a pitiless people, a cruel people, a people who spare not the beauty of the young, nor the infirmity of the old, nor the infancy of children."

The general idea and sense of the pictures of violence wrought by the invaders and the hardships suffered by the people are similar in all the *Sermons*, but the concrete images and individual details vary throughout. No less vivid and lively are the passages in Serapion's works where he dwells on moral questions and speaks of ignorance and superstition. Thus, for example, he condemns the cruel punishment of people suspected of sorcery and ridicules it most effectively. He says that if people believe that sorcerers can bring hunger or abundance, why burn them? If they really can do this, Serapion exclaims, "Pray to these sorcerers, and worship them, and make sacrifices to them—let them rule the community, and call down rain, and bring warmth, and command the earth to bear fruit!"

Serapion's *Sermons* are a fine example of the noble art of oratory. They continue the traditions of such masters of this genre of Old Russian literature as Hilarion and Cyril of Turov. Unlike the works of these eleventh- and twelfth-century writers, Serapion of Vladimir's *Sermons* convey first-hand impressions of the events of his age more strongly. They are written in simple, clear language.

5. Hagiography

A characteristic feature of hagiography was the desire to observe the canons which had grown up over the many centuries of hagiographic literature. These canons gave the Lives of saints an abstract, rhetorical nature. Historical reality, political tendencies, folk legends and the real facts of the life of the person concerned contradicted the canons of the genre. Real life injected into hagiographical works a publicistic element, literary variety and exciting subject matter. The *vitae* were the form of religious literature which was closest to secular, historical and publicistic literature and in which one could express oppositional and heretical ideas, the influence of the apocryphal tales and folk legend, most easily.

During this period of Old Russian literature this tendency is seen most clearly in the Lives of princes. While preserving many conventional hagiographical images and expressions the Lives of princes to some extent deviated from the canons and violated the genre's conventions. This was because the hero of these Lives was not a zealot of the church, but a statesman. Moreover it was the Lives of princes written during this period that reflected the events of the Mongol invasion and rule. The period in question produced *The Tale of the Life of Alexander Nevsky*, a famous warrior

King David amid Beasts. Reliefs on the south façade of the Church of the Intercession on the River Nerl

and statesman of this period. There were also Lives of princes in which the prince is presented as a martyr for the Orthodox faith, dying a martyr's death in the Golden Horde.

The Tale of the Life of Alexander Nevsky. Alexander (born circa 1220, died in 1263) was Prince of Novgorod from 1236 to 1263 and Grand Prince of Vladimir from 1252 to 1263. Both during his reign in Novgorod and as grand prince he led Russia's struggle against the German and Swedish invaders.

In 1240 Swedish knights invaded the north-west of Russia. They sailed up the river Neva, stopping somewhere near the mouth of its tributary the Izhora (some say at the point where the settlement of Ust-Izhora now stands outside Leningrad, others at the Alexander Nevsky Monastery in Leningrad itself). With a small force of men Alexander attacked the enemy on June 15, 1240 and won a splendid victory over a large force. Hence his nickname, Alexander of the Neva (Nevsky). In 1241-1242 Alexander led the struggle against the Teutonic Knights who had captured the lands of Pskov and Novgorod. On April 5, 1242 on the ice of Lake Chudskoye (Peipus) a decisive battle was fought that ended with the total defeat of the invaders, the famous Battle on the Ice.

Realising that it was futile at that time to launch an attack on the Golden Horde, Alexander maintained peaceful relations with the khan of the Golden Horde and pursued a policy of uniting the lands of North-East and North-West Russia and strengthening the authority of the grand prince. He travelled to the Horde several times and succeeded in releasing Russia from the obligation of providing troops for the Mongol khans. Alexander relied extensively on the assistance of the common people in his defence of Russian lands against external foes, which did not prevent him, however, from cruelly suppressing anti-feudal revolts by the masses (e.g., the uprising in Novgorod in 1259).

The Tale of the Life of Alexander Nevsky is devoted to Alexander as the wise statesman and great military leader. The work was written in the Monastery of the Nativity in Vladimir, where Prince Alexander was buried (he died on his way back from a journey to the Horde).* In composition, manner of describing the battles, individual stylistic devices and certain phraseologisms *The Tale of the Life of Alexander Nevsky* is similar to *The Chronicle of Daniel of Galich.* According to Dmitry Likhachev's convincing argument, this is explained by the fact that Metropolitan Cyril played a part in the writing of both works. "There can be no doubt," he writes, "that Cyril was associated with the compiling of the biography of

---

* Alexander's remains were transferred to St Petersburg in the reign of Peter the Great.

13*

Alexander. He could have been the author, but more likely he commissioned the Life from a Galich writer living in the north."[40] That Cyril had something to do with the compiling of *The Chronicle of Daniel of Galich* is well argued by Lev Cherepnin.[41] The Metropolitan died in 1280, therefore, *The Tale of the Life of Alexander Nevsky* must have been compiled between 1263 and 1280.

As well as being similar the *Tale* and the *Chronicle* also differ in terms of genre. The biography of Alexander Nevsky is a work of the hagiographical genre.[42] This is reflected in many characteristic features of the work. First of all, in keeping with the canons of the genre, the author speaks of himself in the foreword, with exaggerated humility, using stock phrases: "I, a wretched, much-sinning man of little understanding, dare to write the Life of the saintly Prince Alexander..."[43] Secondly, in keeping with hagiographical custom he begins his narrative by announcing the birth of Alexander and his parentage: "He was born of a merciful, loving and, furthermore, meek father, Grand Prince Yaroslav, and of his mother Theodosia." Thirdly, the story of the miracle that happened after Alexander's death is of a clearly hagiographical nature. Finally, the actual text contains constant digressions of an ecclesiastical and rhetorical nature and the prince's prayers.

The story about Alexander Nevsky was intended to show that in spite of the conquest of the Russian principalities by the Mongols, there were still princes in Russia whose courage and wisdom could resist the enemies of the Russian land, and whose military prowess could inspire fear and respect in neighbouring peoples. Even Batu acknowledges Alexander's greatness. He summons Alexander to the Horde: "Alexander, know you not that god has subjected many peoples to me? Why do you alone refuse to submit to me? If you wish to keep your land come quickly to me and you will see the glory of my kingdom." When he meets Alexander, Batu says to his nobles: "It is true what I have been told that there is no prince the like of him."

The author of the *Tale*, as he tells us at the very beginning of his story, knew the prince and witnessed his acts as a statesman and military feats: "I myself was a witness of his age of maturity." Hagiographers often tell us in their works where they obtained information about the life of their hero. The author usually says that he found out about the saint from contemporary accounts, extant records, an earlier Life, or as his contemporary or pupil. It is rare for the author to say that he knew the saint himself; the wording of the *Tale*: "I myself was a witness..." is not found in any other Life. Therefore we have every reason to regard this phrase as documentary proof of the fact that the author was a

The Tale of the Life of Alexander Nevsky. **The Battle on the Neva and the Defeat of the Swedes in 1240.** Illumination from *The Illustrated Chronicle.* 16th century. State Public Library, Leningrad

contemporary of Alexander's and personally acquainted with him.

Both the real figure of the prince, who is close to the author, and the tasks which the author sets himself give this hagiographical work a special military flavour. One can sense the narrator's liking for Alexander and admiration of his military and political activity. This lends a special sincerity and lyricism to the *Tale*.[44]

The descriptions of Alexander in the *Tale* are on various levels. His "Christian virtues" are stressed in keeping with hagiographical canons. The author says that the Prophet Isaiah had in mind such princes as Alexander Nevsky when he said: "He loved priests and monks and beggars, revered the Metropolitan and the bishops and heeded them like Christ Himself."

At the same time Alexander is of majestic and comely appearance, a brave and invincible military leader: "He was comely as no other, and his voice was like a trumpet among the people." He is invincible. In his military operations Alexander is swift, dedicated and merciless. On hearing that the Swedish army has reached the Neva, Alexander "flared up in anger" and sped off "with a small bodyguard" against the enemy. He was in such a hurry that he could not "send news to his father", and the Novgorodians did not have time to rally to his aid. Alexander's impetuosity and military daring are characteristic of all the episodes about the prince's military exploits. Here he appears as an epic hero.

The combination of the emphatically religious and even more clearly expressed secular levels constitutes the distinctive style and originality of the *Tale*. In spite of this multiplicity of levels, however, and the apparently contradictory nature of the descriptions of Alexander, his character is unified. This unity is produced by the author's attitude towards his hero, by the fact that for him Alexander is not only a heroic military commander, but also a wise statesman. For the enemies of the Russian land he is terrible and merciless: "the Moabite women" (meaning the Mongols here) frighten their children by saying "Alexander is coming!" But in his own land Alexander "judges orphans and widows righteously, gives alms, and is kind to his household". He is the ideal prince, ruler and military leader.

In the episode of the battle on the Neva we are told of six heroes who fight alongside Alexander and distinguish themselves in battle. The first, Gavrilo Alexich, tried to ride on horseback onto an enemy boat, fell with his horse into the Neva, climbed out unharmed and went on fighting. The second, a Novgorodian called Zbyslav Yakunovich, slayed a vast number of the enemy with his battle axe. The third, Yakov from Polotsk, felled them with his sword. The fourth, Misha from Novgorod, sank three enemy ships. The fifth, "by the name of Sava from the younger bodyguard" "burst into the royal gold-canopied tent and hacked down the tent post", which caused great rejoicing among Alexander's men. The sixth, Ratmir, fought on foot and died "from many wounds".

This story in the *Tale* is obviously based on a folk legend about the battle on the Neva, or perhaps an heroic song about the six brave men. The inclusion of such a story in a hagiographical text is explained by the heroic epic nature of this work. Nevertheless the hagiographical element is felt in this episode as well. The author merely lists the names of the heroes and mentions briefly, in one or two phrases, the feats of each of them.

The concluding section of the *Tale*, the account of the prince's final days and death, is very solemn, yet full of sincere lyricism.

Alexander went to the Horde to see the khan in order to relieve Russians of the obligation of serving in the Mongol army. As already mentioned, he succeeded in this. After announcing that the prince fell sick on his way back from the Horde, the author gives vent to his feelings in exclamations of grief: "Oh, woe unto you, poor wretch! How can you describe your master's death! How will your very eyes not fall out with tears! How will your heart not be torn from its roots! For a man can take leave of his father, but not of his good master. If it were possible, he would go into the grave with him." After announcing the day on which Alexander died he quotes the words of Metropolitan Cyril and the men of Suzdal, when they heard the sad tidings: "And Metropolitan Cyril said: 'My children, know that the sun has now set on the land of Suzdal!' And the priests and deacons, monks, beggars, rich men and all folk exclaimed: 'We are done for!'"

The *Tale* ends with an account of the "wondrous" and "memorable" miracle that was believed to have happened during the burial of the prince. When they were about to put a scroll with a prayer for absolution into the prince's hand, the dead man "as if alive stretched out his hand and took the scroll from the metropolitan's hand".

In spite of the hagiographical nature of the work, the author makes extensive use of military epic legends and the poetic devices of military tales in his descriptions of the prince's military feats. This enables him to reproduce in a hagiographical work the striking figure of the defender of the homeland, military leader and warrior. Right up to the sixteenth century *The Tale of the Life of Alexander Nevsky* was a kind of model for portraying Russian princes by describing their military feats.

The Life of Michael of Chernigov. In examining the Rostov chronicle above, we mentioned that among the tales of Russian princes who died a martyr's death during the rule of Batu the Princess Maria chronicle of 1263 contains a record of the murder of Maria's father, Prince Michael of Chernigov, in 1246 in the Horde. During Maria's lifetime (she died in 1271) apart from the chronicle entry a short prologue Life[45] was compiled about the murder of Prince Michael and his boyar Theodore in the Horde.[46]

The prologue Life says, that after seizing the Russian land the *inoplemenniki* (literally "those of another tribe"), "began to summon" the Russian princes to pay homage to Batu in the Horde. There the Russian princes were forced "to go through fire (walk between burning bonfires) and bow to the sun and idols".*

The Prince of Chernigov, who had come to the Horde at Batu's command, also had to perform this rite. Michael was prepared to pay homage to Batu, but he refused to walk between the fires or bow to the Mongol gods, for he considered this to be a profanation of the Christian faith. In return for this Batu's nobleman Eldega orders the prince to be "tormented" "with various tortures" and beheaded. The boyar Theodore, who accompanied Michael to the Horde, follows his master's noble example. The death of the prince and his boyar in the Horde is treated in the Life as suffering for the Christian faith. The story ends with the announcement that Princess Maria and her sons are building a church, and a plea to the saints to pray for the Rostov princes Boris and Gleb, Michael's grandsons.

This short prologue Life formed the basis of a whole series of subsequent expanded redactions of *The Life of Michael of Chernigov*. The first of these, whose author is named as Father Andrei in the title, was compiled in the late thirteenth or early fourteenth century. This redaction contains a number of new details making the story more dramatic and psychological.

For example, this is how the culminating episode of Prince Michael's refusal to perform the pagan rite is described.[47] Michael and Theodore stop by the fires between which they have to walk. Batu's envoy, Eldega, rides up to them. He informs the prince that the khan has said if Michael walks between the fires and worships his gods, he will stay alive, return home and continue to rule his principality. If not, he will die. When Michael refuses, Eldega says to the prince: "Know, Michael, that you are dead!" At this time Michael's grandson, Prince Boris of Rostov, is in the Horde, and many other Russian princes. They all try to persuade the prince to submit to Batu's orders and promise to do penance for the prince.

---

* The ritual of walking between burning fires was compulsory for all foreigners who came to the Horde. It was a special ritual: it was thought that if a man passed through the fires unharmed he could not do any harm to the khan.

Theodore the boyar fears that their pleas will shake the prince's resolve to suffer for the faith, that remembering his wife and children the prince will weaken and submit to the khan's demands. But Michael remains firm and resolves to do his duty to the end. Taking off his sumptuous princely cloak, he throws it at the feet of those who are pleading with him, and exclaims: "Take the glory of this world for which you are striving." Then follows an account with much dramatic detail of how Michael and Theodore were brutally killed.

Already in its short prologue form *The Life of Michael of Chernigov* was no abstract account of the sufferings of a saint for the faith, but the story of a Russian prince who dies in the Horde for his religious beliefs. Dying for one's faith in these circumstances was a kind of political protest. The complexity and dramatic tension of the subject in the expanded redaction, the introduction of new details that slow down the development of the action make this work an even more heart-rending story of the cruelty of the conquerors and the resolute pride of the Russian prince who lays down his life for the honour of his homeland. Such a story was of great patriotic significance: it urged people not to reconcile themselves to the Mongol invaders and extolled those who refused to compromise with the foe, elevating them to the rank of saints.

The *Lives* of Zealots of the Church. The Lives of zealots of the Church written in the second half of the thirteenth century can be characterised in general as works which followed the hagiographical canons more strictly than the princely lives of the same period. Examples of this are *The Life of Abraham of Smolensk* compiled by a certain Ephraem in the middle of the thirteenth century and the first redaction of *The Life of Barlaam of Khutyn* that belongs to the latter half or end of the thirteenth century (author unknown).

Ephraem gives an abstract, generalised account of the biography of Abraham, making use of hagiographical conventions, although he was a pupil of Abraham's and could have heard about his life from Abraham himself. *The Life of Abraham of Smolensk* centres mainly on his preaching in Smolensk and his clashes with the local clergy and townspeople. These events, of importance in the life not only of Abraham but of the town in general, are described in hints and allegories. It is impossible to see from this account why Abraham aroused such dislike in the clergy and the townspeople and how he managed to escape being killed. Nevertheless the fact of this inter-clerical strife is most important. It shows that the Church itself was far from united.[48]

The Life of Barlaam of Khutyn is about the founder of the Khutyn Monastery outside Novgorod and provides in condensed form the main facts of his life (in secular life he was the Novgorodian boyar Alexei Mikhailovich). At the time when the first redaction of *The Life of Barlaam* was compiled, the oral tradition in Novgorod contained some legendary tales about Barlaam of a fantastic nature. But these tales were not included in the written text of the Life until later, in the subsequent redactions. In the thirteenth century the hagiographer did not yet dare to include episodes of a secular or legendary nature in the Life of a zealot of the Church.[49]

During the period of Batu's invasion and the establishment of Mongol overlordship the main feature of Russian literature was its strong patriotism. The chroniclers, Serapion of Vladimir, and the hagiographers saw the victory of the Mongols as Divine punishment of the Russian people for their sins. But from the accounts by the same chroniclers of the Mongol invasion and the tales dealing with the same subject it is clear that in the popular consciousness the way to salvation from the enemy was seen as lying not in repentance and praying, but in active struggle. Therefore the literature of the period in question shows a pronounced heroic nature. In the chronicle accounts, *The Tale of the Life of Alexander Nevsky* and particularly *The Tale of Batu's Capture of Ryazan* the strength and cruelty of the enemy are contrasted with the military daring and immense courage of the Russian warriors, the bravery and selflessness of the Russian people.

The second main theme of thirteenth-century literature is the idea of strong princely authority. In the years of struggle against the external foe and the growth of feudal disunity this theme was also of great national patriotic significance: the question of a strong prince who could lead the struggle against external enemies was of the greatest importance for the future destiny of the Russian state.

In the thirteenth century the development of the traditional genres of Old Russian literature continued. Even more intensively than in the preceding century tales were inserted in the chronicle compilations that, although subjected to the overall contents of the chronicle, are nevertheless self-contained. These are the chronicle tales of the struggle against the Mongols, the murder of Russian princes in the Golden Horde, and encomiums of the princes. Traditional *vitae* were also written. At the same time a number of works arose that went beyond the traditional hagiographical framework.

The Chronicle of Daniel of Galich shows a number of features that give it a special place. It is not so much a chronicle, as a prince's biography.

The Tale of the Life of Alexander Nevsky belongs for the most part to the hagiographical genre. But in many respects it does not observe the conventions of this genre and is closer to that of the princely biography, in particular, to *The Chronicle of Daniel of Galich.*

The Tale of Batu's Capture of Ryazan forms part of the cycle of tales about St Nicholas of Zarazsk which, to quote Dmitry Likhachev, is akin to the chronicle compilations: "It is in the nature of a 'compilation', in this case a compilation of different

Ryazan tales that appeared at different times and are connected at different periods with the icon of St Nicholas of Zarazsk."[50] But it is not a chronicle, and its resemblance to chronicle-writing is mainly external. At the same time, however, taken as a whole and in its individual parts, this work cannot be called an historical tale either, although the main section of the cycle, *The Tale of Batu's Capture of Ryazan*, deals with an important historical event. What we have is an historical tale in the making, that has "broken away" from the chronicle, but is still connected with it to some extent. Herein lies the originality and novelty of *The Tale of Batu's Capture of Ryazan.*

Thus, it can be said that the thirteenth century witnessed the intensive formation of new phenomena within traditional literary genres. And the most striking works of this period, although still connected to some extent with the canons of the traditional genres, are in fact already new genres in the making.

REFERENCES

[1] An Arabian historian of the early thirteenth century, Ibn al Athir, described the Mongol invasion as a disaster the like of which history had never known before and wrote that the conquerors "did not take pity on anyone, and killed women, men and infants". (See: Тизенгаузен В. В. *Сборник материалов, относящихся к истории Золотой Орды.* Vol. 1, St Petersburg, 1884, p. 2.)

[2] Пушкин А. С. *Полное собрание сочинений.* Vol. 11, Moscow and Leningrad, 1949, p. 268. A similar idea was repeated by Pushkin in a letter written in 1836 to Pyotr Chaadayev. (See: Ibid., Vol. 16, p. 171.)

[3] Комарович В. Л. "Рязанский летописный свод XIII в.". *История русской литературы (ИРЛ)*, Vol. II, Moscow and Leningrad, 1945, Part I, p. 75.

[4] *Новгородская первая летопись старшего и младшего изводов*, p. 75.

[5] The text of the tale is published in *ПЛДР. XIII век*, pp. 176-203.

[6] Лихачев Д. С. *Русские летописи и их культурно-историческое значение*, p. 285.

[7] "Лаврентьевская летопись". *ПСРЛ*, Vol. 1, 1962, columns 465-471.

[8] The main works dealing with the time and place when the chronicle was compiled, and its ideological and stylistic features are: Черепнин Л. В. "Летописец Даниила Галицкого". *Исторические записки*, No. 12, 1941, pp. 228-253; Еремин И. П. "Волынская летопись 1289-1290 гг. как памятник литературы". In the book: Еремин И. П. *Литература Древней Руси*, pp. 164-184; for the text of *The Galich-Volhynian Chronicle* see: *ПЛДР. XIII век*, pp. 236-425.

[9] Черепнин Л. В. "Летописец Даниила Галицкого", p. 230

[10] This feature was first discovered by M. S. Grushevsky. See: Грушевський М. С. "Хронологія подій Галицько-Волинської літописи". In the book: *Записки Наукового товариства ім. Шевченка*, Vol. XLI, Lvov, 1901, pp. 1-72.

[11] Орлов А. С. *Древняя русская литература XI-XVI вв.* Moscow and Leningrad, 1937, p. 118.

[12] Еремин И. П. "Волынская летопись 1289-1290 гг. как памятник литературы". In the book: Еремин И. П. *Литература древней Руси*, p. 174. There are also different opinions. Mikhail Grushevsky takes the view that *The Volhynian Chronicle* combines texts written by three chroniclers. (Грушевський М. *Історія української літератури*. Vol. III, Kiev and Lvov, 1923, pp. 180-203.) In the opinion of V. T. Pashuto *The Volhynian Chronicle* is the work of two chroniclers. (Пашуто В. Т. *Очерки по истории Галицко-Волынской Руси*. Moscow, 1950, pp. 101-133.)

[13] We can get an idea of this chronological collection from two late manuscript copies of it: the *Archive Chronograph* (late 15th-early 16th century) and the *Vilna Chronograph* (mid-16th century). See: Истрин В. М. *Александрия русских хронографов*, pp. 317-352; Мещерский Н. А. *"История Иудейской войны" Иосифа Флавия в древнерусском переводе*, pp. 5-164.

[14] For the text of the *Supplication* of Daniel the Exile see: *ПЛДР. XII век*, pp. 388-399.

[15] For the most convincing arguments in support of this theory linking the *Oration* with Andrew the Good see: Скрипиль М. О. *"Слово Даниила Заточника"*. *ТОДРЛ*, Vol. XI, 1955, pp. 80-83.

[16] This view is best developed and argued by Nikolai Gudzii in the article "К какой социальной среде принадлежал Даниил Заточник?" In the book: *Сборник статей к 40-летию ученой деятельности академика А. С. Орлова*. Leningrad, 1934; see also: Nikolai Gudzii's chapter on this work in *ИРЛ*, Vol. II, Part I. *Литература 1220-х-1560-х гг.*, pp. 35-45, and his textbook *История древней русской литературы* (first edition, Moscow, 1938; seventh edition, Moscow, 1966).

[17] "Московский летописный свод конца XV века". *ПСРЛ*, Vol. XXV, 1949, p. 200.

[18] Лихачев Д. С. "Социальные основы стиля *Моления* Даниила Заточника". *ТОДРЛ*, Vol. X, 1954, pp. 106-119.

[19] Ibid., p. 111.

[20] Белинский В. Г. "Русская народная поэзия". *Полное собрание сочинений*, Vol. V, Moscow, 1954, p. 351.

[21] Лихачев Д. С. "Летописные известия об Александре Поповиче". *ТОДРЛ*, Vol. VII, 1949, p. 23.

[22] *Новгородская первая летопись старшего и младшего изводов*, pp. 61-63.

[23] One manuscript is in the State Archives of the Pskov Region under the collection of the Pskov Crypt Monastery (15th century), the other (16th century) in the archives of the Institute of Russian Literature of the USSR Academy of Sciences.

[24] For the text of *The Lay of the Ruin of the Russian Land* see: *ПЛДР. XIII век*, pp. 130-131.

[25] Данилов В. В. "*Слово о погибели Рускыя земли* как произведение художественное". *ТОДРЛ*, Vol. XVI, 1960, pp. 137-138.

[26] For similar passages in *The Lay of Igor's Host* and *The Lay of the Ruin of the Russian Land* see: Соловьев А. В. "Заметки к *Слову о погибели Русской земли*". *ТОДРЛ*, Vol. XV, 1958, pp. 109-113.

[27] Лихачев Д. С. *"Повесть о разорении Рязани Батыем"*. In the book: *Воинские повести Древней Руси.* Moscow and Leningrad, 1949, pp. 139-140.

[28] For the text of *The Tale of St Nicholas of Zarazsk* see: *ПЛДР. XIII век,* pp. 176-183.

[29] Лихачев Д. С. *"Повесть о разорении Рязани Батыем"*, p. 126.

[30] Путилов Б. Н. *"Песня о Евпатии Коловрате"*. *ТОДРЛ,* Vol. XI, 1955, pp. 118-139.

[31] Лихачев Д. С. *"Слово о полку Игоря Святославича"*. In the book: *Слово о полку Игореве* (Библиотека поэта. Большая серия.), pp. 33-35.

[32] *ПСРЛ,* Vol. I, 1962, column 515.

[33] The text of the story is in *ПЛДР. XIII век,* pp. 132-149.

[34] *"Ипатьевская летопись"*. *ПСРЛ,* Vol. II, 1962, columns 780-781.

[35] Толочко П. П. *Древний Киев.* Kiev, 1976, pp. 191-202.

[36] For a monographic study of the *Tale* with its printed text see: Белецкий Л. Т. *Литературная история "Повести о Меркурии Смоленском". Исследование и тексты.* Petrograd, 1922. See· also: Буслаев Ф. *"Смоленская легенда о св. Меркурии и ростовская повесть о Петре, царевиче Ордынском". Исторические очерки русской народной словесности и искусства,* Vol. II, 1861, pp. 155-198; Кадлубовский А. *Очерки по истории древнерусской литературы житий святых.* Warsaw, 1902, pp. 44-107; *ПЛДР. XIII век,* pp. 204-209.

[37] Бунин И. А. *Собрание сочинений* в 9-ти томах, Vol. 3, Moscow, 1965, p. 140.

[38] The French specialist M. Gorlin believed that all Serapion's sermons except the last were written not in 1274-1275, but earlier during his time in Kiev (M. Gorlin, "Serapion de Wladimir, prédicateur de Kiev", *Revue des études slaves,* Vol. 24, Paris, 1948, pp. 21-28). Nikolai Gudzii has convincingly refuted this argument. (Гудзий Н. К. *"Где и когда протекала литературная деятельность Серапиона Владимирского?"*. *ИОЛЯ,* Vol. XI, 1952, No. 5, pp. 450-456.)

[39] For the texts of Serapion of Vladimir's *Sermons* see: *ПЛДР. XIII век,* pp. 440-455.

[40] Лихачев Д. С. *"Галицкая литературная традиция в житии Александра Невского"*. *ТОДРЛ,* Vol. V, 1947, p. 52.

[41] Черепнин Л. В. *"Летописец Даниила Галицкого"*. *Исторические записки,* No. 12, pp. 245-252.

[42] The unusual combination in *The Tale of the Life of Alexander Nevsky* of elements of the military tale with ecclesiastical religious elements has provided grounds for arguing that the extant text of the *Tale* was based on a secular biography of the prince. Attempts to extract this secular biography from the surviving texts have not been successful, however.

[43] For the text of the *Tale* see: *ПЛДР. XIII век,* pp. 426-439.

[44] Еремин И. П. *"Житие Александра Невского"*. In the book: *Художественная проза Киевской Руси XI-XIII веков.* Moscow, 1957, p. 355.

[45] A prologue was a collection of hagiographical and morally edifying and didactic essays and sermons which were read on certain days each month. They included short redactions of *vitae,* known as prologue *vitae.*

46 Nikolai Serebryansky believed that the Rostov short prologue *Life of Michael of Chernigov* was written at the time when Princess Maria and her sons instituted the church worship of Michael and his boyar Theodore and built a church in Rostov in their honour. See: Серебрянский Н. *Древнерусские княжеские жития.* Moscow, 1915, p. 111.

47 For the text of the *Life* see: *ПЛДР. XIII век,* pp. 228-235.

48 Ibid., pp. 66-105.

49 For more detail see: Дмитриев Л. А. *Житийные повести русского Севера как памятники литературы XIII-XVII вв.* Leningrad, 1973.

50 Лихачев Д. С. "Повести о Николе Заразском". *ТОДРЛ,* Vol. VII, 1949, p. 257.

CHAPTER 3

LITERATURE FROM THE BEGINNING TO THE THIRD QUARTER OF THE FOURTEENTH CENTURY

In the fourteenth century, as in the preceding period, a bitter struggle continued between the Russian principalities for political

and economic supremacy. This internecine strife profited the Horde, because it undermined the forces that could have resisted Mongol oppression. The khans of the Horde encouraged this internal struggle between the Russian princes and used it to suppress the popular uprisings against the invaders that broke out sporadically.

A prince who succeeded to a princely throne had first to obtain the sanction in the Horde in the form of a special written document or *yarlyk* permitting him to reign. The Russian prince who obtained a *yarlyk* to rule in the grand principality of Vladimir was senior to all the other Russian princes. The competition between the politically and economically strongest princes for sanction to rule the grand principality sometimes led to the killing of one Russian prince while he was visiting the Horde, with the connivance of another.

In the late thirteenth and early fourteenth centuries the principality of Moscow emerged as one of the strongest in North-Eastern Russia. The Moscow princes played an active part in the struggle for supremacy among the Russian princes, and, consequently, for the title of Grand Prince of Vladimir. The main rivals in this struggle at the beginning of the fourteenth century were the princes of Tver and Moscow. At that time when religious ideology was prevalent the support of the Church was extremely important. Moscow was most successful in strengthening its alliance with the Church. In the 1320s during the reign of Prince Ivan, son of Daniel, Metropolitan Peter of All Russia moved from Vladimir to Moscow, and Moscow became the ecclesiastical centre of all the Russian lands.

Mongol dominion put a brake on the country's political and socio-economic development, but it could not arrest the march of history.

The late thirteenth and early fourteenth century saw a gradual revival of handicrafts, expansion of trade between town and countryside and a growth in settlements of traders and artisans. These processes led to the flowering of architecture in Russia, particularly in the middle and latter half of the fourteenth century. Stone churches and fortifications were built in Novgorod, Pskov, and Tver. Stone building began in Moscow in 1326. Four stone churches were built in the Kremlin under Ivan the Money-Bag. White stone walls were erected round it in 1366-1367.

Book production, which had been greatly undermined by the Mongol invasion, also revived. During the destruction of Russian towns a large number of manuscript books had perished. Mongol rule led to a drop in literacy among the population. The revival of book culture was promoted by the appearance in Russia during the second half of the fourteenth century of paper, a cheaper writing material than parchment.

By the beginning of the fourteenth century the disrupted relations of the Russian lands with other countries began to be resumed. Pilgrimages to Jerusalem and Constantinople were resumed, and in this connection the genre of the travel story describing journeys and places visited by pilgrims was also revived.

In the period when Russia was ruled by the Mongols the style of monumental historicism continued but did not produce any great or impressive individual works.

In general, it must be said that in mediaeval literatures of the traditionalist type (i.e., literatures in which tradition and literary convention played the dominant role) there was not the radical change of literary styles within a strictly defined space of time, that we find in literatures of the modern age. Literary styles did not replace one another suddenly in mediaeval literatures, but rather grew gradually out of one another. The features of the new style developed slowly within the old one.

In the fourteenth century the emotional element became stronger in Russian literature. Whereas in the preceding period a strong, majestic emotion pervaded works about the Mongol invasion, which combined in these works with the epic grandeur of the events to create a kind of monumental emotionality, now, in the period of oppressive foreign rule, when, as the chronicler puts it, "you could not swallow bread from fear", the lyrical, emotional element was combined with minor themes, about the day-to-day events of foreign rule: the courage of individual people who perished in the Horde for their homeland and their faith, and popular uprisings. Increasingly more space was devoted in literature to dreams of a better future, of distant happy lands, of an earthly paradise as yet undiscovered. The emotional element was also strengthened by the growing interest in familiar events of the present, in local and regional themes. Inevitably the monumentalism so characteristic of the preceding period gradually weakened as the subject-matter changed and no longer showed its former consistency and unity of stylistic expression.

1. Chronicle-Writing

No substantial changes or new phenomena appeared in chronicle-writing during this period, by comparison with the preceding one. The beginning of the fourteenth century is the date of the Synodal manuscript of *The Novgorod First Chronicle*, a compilation of earlier Novgorodian chronicles brought up to date with additional entries (this is the oldest surviving manuscript of a Russian chronicle; the next oldest is *The Laurentian Chronicle* of 1377). In the late thirteenth and first half of the fourteenth century new chronicle-writing centres emerged: in Tver, Pskov and Moscow. Tver chronicle-writing is reflected in the so-called *Tver Miscellany* and *Rogozh Chronicle*.[1] The extant *Tver Miscellany* and *Rogozh Chronicle* are based on a Tver compilation of 1375. (Both this and the other Tver compilations have been hypothetically reconstructed by specialists on the basis that the Tver text common to *The Rogozh Chronicle* and *The Tver Miscellany* goes up to 1375.) The compilation of 1375 was preceded by earlier ones in Tver, the original source of which was the compilation made in 1305, when Prince Michael of Tver, the first prince to bear the

Page from a Novgorod Psalter with the initial X in the form of a youth drinking from a horn. 14th century. State Public Library, Leningrad

title of Grand Prince of All Russia, received the throne of the Grand Prince of Vladimir. Monuments of Tver chronicle-writing show a special interest in the theme of struggle against foreign oppression.

In all probability the compilation of 1305, which combined the chronicle compilations of both Southern and North-Eastern Russia (Pereyaslavl-Russky, Vladimir, Rostov and Tver), was also of Tver origin. "In relation to subsequent chronicle writing..." writes Yakov Lurie, "the compilation of 1305 is a kind of single nucleus, the basis of all the chronicle accounts from ancient times to the beginning of the 14th century."[2] The text of the 1305 compilation has survived in a copy of 1377, in *The Laurentian Chronicle*.

The surviving Pskov chronicles date back to the end of the fifteenth century and later. But there are grounds for assuming that chronicle-writing began in Pskov at an earlier period: a Pskov chronicle compilation is reflected in Russian chronicle-writing of the mid-fifteenth century (the so-called compilation of 1448, see pp. 303-05). This testifies to the existence of chronicle-writing in Pskov at an earlier period than the extant Pskov chronicles. Specialists date the emergence of local Pskov chronicle-writing to the second half of the thirteenth or the early fourteenth century.

No Moscow chronicles of this period have survived either. On the basis of later compilations specialists date the first Moscow chronicle to the 1340s. It is assumed that this compilation was based on the records of Ivan the Money-Bag's family chronicle and the chronicle of Metropolitan Peter who moved to Moscow from Vladimir.[3]

The Tale of Shevkal. In 1327 there was an uprising in Tver against the khan's *baskak*[4] Chol-Khan (Shevkal, Shchelkan). Chol-Khan was killed together with all the Mongols (Tartars) who had come with him. This event was reflected in chronicle tales.

The earliest *Tale of Shevkal* is in *The Rogozh Chronicle* and in the so-called *Tver Miscellany*, i.e., in chronicles that reflect Tver compilations. The *Tale* was inserted mechanically into the chronicle, its text is interspersed with other chronicle records and the chronicle entries alongside it contain duplicate information (i.e., repetition of one and the same fact). This suggests that the *Tale* originally existed as an independent work.

The story of Shevkal in the *Tale* begins with the announcement that Prince Alexander of Tver received the *yarlyk* in the Horde to rule the grand principality of Vladimir. Incited by the Devil, the Mongols tell their khan that if he does not kill "Prince Alexander and all the Russian princes" he will not have "power over them".[5] Shevkal, the "instigator of all the evil" and "destroyer of Christianity", asks the khan to send him to Russia, boasting that he will kill all the Russian princes and bring much "booty and slaves" to the Horde. "And the khan ordered him to do so." When Shevkal arrives in Tver, he drives the prince "from his court, and himself settled in the court of the grand prince full of pride and fury. And he did wreak great havoc on the Christians—rape, looting, murder and desecration." The people of Tver beseech their prince to defend them, but the prince dares not go against Shevkal and tells them to be patient. The people will not tolerate the cruelty of their oppressors and wait for a suitable opportunity to rise up against them.

One day "on the fifteenth of August, in the early morning, when the market place was assembling" (i.e., when people from the surrounding villages were arriving), the Tartars seize "a young and very fleshy mare" from a Tver deacon "by the name of Dudko" as he is taking her to water in the Volga. Dudko begins to wail: "Don't let them have it, people of Tver!" This wail from an injured townsfellow acts as a signal for an uprising against the invaders: "and they rang all the bells, and held a meeting, and the town rose up". They killed so many Tartars that there was no *vestonosha* left in the town, i.e., someone who could bear the tidings of the slaughter to the Horde.

Nevertheless the news of what had happened did not take long to reach both Moscow and the Horde. Some Tartar herdsmen were tending horses in the fields outside the town and managed to gallop away from the furious townspeople on their fastest steeds. It was they who carried the news of Shevkal's murder to the Horde and Moscow. In revenge the khan sent an army to Tver led by Fedorchuk. Tver was sacked and looted, and Prince Alexander fled to Pskov.

The beginning of the *Tale*, the account of how and why Shevkal marched against Tver, differs in general character and style from the main section. This suggests that the main section, the story of Shevkal's outrages and the uprising, was written earlier and was an independent text. The introduction was added later.

Judging by the details in the main section of the *Tale* we can assume that it goes back to an oral legend written down shortly after the uprising, possibly from the account of an eyewitness who took part in the events. This oral, folk origin would also explain the attitude of the prince in the *Tale*, who is afraid to challenge the oppressors.

Apart from *The Tale of Shevkal* the folk tradition has also preserved a response to the popular uprising of 1327 against the conquerors, namely, the historical song "Shchelkan Dudentievich" of which several versions exist.

A comparison of the different versions of this song enables us to get an idea of its original form and to consider the question of the relationship between the song and the *Tale*.[6] The song, like the *Tale*, has preserved historical memories which suggest that it originated shortly after the events themselves.[7] The song views them in a somewhat different light from the *Tale*, however, and contains different characters. In the song the town is defended by the two brave Borisovich brothers, the chiliarch (*tysyatsky*) of Tver and his brother,[8] and the prince is not even mentioned.

The song, like the *Tale*, has drawn on oral accounts about Shevkal but these accounts came from different sources and the resemblance between the *Tale* and the song is explained by the fact that they are based on the same historical event. *The Tale of Shevkal* resembles the historical song "Shchelkan Dudentievich" in its attitude to the uprising against the foe: the hero that revolts against the Tartars and destroys them is the people in both works. In this respect the song expresses the people's assessment of the event more consistently and strongly: it portrays the enemy with a touch of satire, Shchelkan's death is shameful and humiliating ("One seized his hair, Another his feet, And they tore him asunder"), and the end of the song, contrary to the historical facts, is optimistic—no one suffers for the murder of Shchelkan: "Here he was done to death, No one was punished for it."[9]

The Tale of Shevkal and the song about Shchelkan expressed the popular protest at Mongol oppression and testified to the ordinary people's reluctance to accept the rule of the Horde. The emergence during this period of this type of literary work and song was of great patriotic significance.

2. Hagiography

As with chronicle-writing, in the first half of the fourteenth century we find the same phenomena in hagiography as in the preceding period. *Vitae* of both princes and churchmen were written. The Lives of princes continued the traditions both of the heroic type (the Pskov *Tale of Dovmont*) and of princes martyred in the Horde (*The Tale of Michael of Tver*). One of the earliest works of Moscow literature, *The Life of Metropolitan Peter*, belongs to the second category.

The Tale of Dovmont. In 1266 Prince Dovmont fled from Lithuania because of the princely strife there and went to Pskov with his retinue "and all his kinsmen".[10] In Pskov Dovmont was baptised, christened Timothy and became Prince of Pskov. His reign was marked by successful military operations against

Lithuania and the Teutonic Order, the age-old enemies of Pskov. After his death (1299) Dovmont-Timothy was revered in Pskov as a saint for his military feats.

We have no exact information as to when *The Tale of Dovmont* was written. Some specialists believe it was in the early 14th century,[11] while others date it to the latter half or the end of that century.[12]

The Tale of Dovmont is found in the Pskov chronicles, but it is hard to say whether it was originally intended for a chronicle or included later. There is every reason to believe, however, that the *Tale* was written in those literary circles where the Pskov chronicles were compiled. This can be seen from the similarity of style and descriptive devices in the *Tale* and chronicle accounts of the military feats of the Pskovians.

Individual images and whole sections of the text of *The Tale of Dovmont* are taken from *The Tale of the Life of Alexander Nevsky*. For this reason Nikolai Serebryansky concludes that it is merely a "good literary copy of a very good original, but *The Tale of Dovmont* has hardly any independent literary significance".[13] We cannot agree with this opinion. Making use in an original work of passages from other monuments on a similar subject was a common device in Old Russian literature. By drawing on individual images, situations and fragments of the text of *The Tale of the Life of Alexander Nevsky*, the author of *The Tale of Dovmont* merely wished to elevate Dovmont in a special way, to show that both in appearance and in deeds he resembled Alexander Nevsky. At the same time *The Tale of Dovmont* is original and distinctive in many respects.

The first half of the work, which describes the campaign of Dovmont, already Prince of Pskov, against Lithuania, the battle of Rakovor and the fighting on the River Miropovna, does not depend on literary images. It is full of echoes from heroic accounts by eyewitnesses and participants of these events. In certain passages we can sense its oral epic origin. This is evident in the vocabulary, individual expressions and the rhythm of the narrative. Addressing the men of Pskov before battle, when he is about to enter the fray with them for the first time, Dovmont says: "Brothers, men of Pskov! He who is old is a father to me, and he who is young a brother. I have heard of your courage in all lands. Now, brothers, it is a matter of life or death. Brothers, men of Pskov! Let us stand for the Holy Trinity * and the holy churches, for our homeland."

The *Tale* is full of military heroism. The military prowess of the Pskovians is stressed with dignified restraint. As well as poetic fervour the work contains the practicality and authentic detail typical of Pskovian literature. The text contains local dialect expressions and use is made of poetic epithets from folk poetry.

---

* The main cathedral in Pskov.

The Tale of Dovmont is a fine specimen of Pskovian literature, an original and distinctive work that is at the same time closely connected with the literature of the other Old Russian principalities.

The Tale of Michael of Tver, Son of Yaroslav. In November 1318, during the political struggle between the princes of Tver and Moscow for the grand principality of Vladimir, Prince Michael of Tver was killed in the Horde due to the intrigues of the Moscow Prince Yuri, son of Daniel. This event formed the subject of *The Tale of Michael of Tver, Son of Yaroslav* written in late 1319 or early 1320 by someone who witnessed the prince's murder.[14] Most likely its author was Abbot Alexander of the Page Monastery in Tver. In general character and genre the *Tale* is akin to *The Life of Michael of Chernigov* discussed above. But whereas the latter work stresses the religious nature of the prince's feat (he goes to the Horde to denounce the "impious faith"), the cause of the prince's death is treated differently in *The Tale of Michael of Tver*.

The Prince of Tver, like the Prince of Chernigov, sets off to the Horde knowing that death awaits him, but he goes there to avert the danger that is threatening his principality from the Horde, to sacrifice himself for the well-being of his land. When the boyars and the prince's sons suggest that Michael stay at home and that they go to the Horde in his place, the prince replies that by doing so he would save his life, but not avert the disaster threatening the principality of Tver. "You see, my children," Prince Michael says, "the khan does not summon you, my children, nor anyone else but me to him. It is my head that he seeks."[15]

Michael's sacrifice is a patriotic act. He appears as the ideal princely ruler. In contrast to Michael of Tver, Prince Yuri of Moscow is in league with the Horde and hostile to Tver. This condemnation of the prince of Moscow is particularly obvious in the final episode, the account of Michael's death. The Mongol *temnik* (military commander) Kavgady and Prince Yuri ride up to the naked body of the murdered prince prostrate on the ground. Kavgady is the main denouncer and cunning enemy of the prince in the *Tale*. But even he, on seeing the prince's dead body, says angrily to the prince of Moscow: "Is he not your elder brother, like a father unto you, then why does his abandoned body lie naked?" By putting these accusing words in the mouth of Kavgady the author wishes to stress the baseness of the Moscow prince's act.

The laconic ending of the *Tale*, in keeping with the whole spirit of the work, stresses the main idea of the work very effectively and testifies vividly to its literary perfection. It describes the moving of Michael's body: "And they put the body on a wide plank and laid it in a cart, and bound it firm with rope, and carried it across the river called Adezh, which means 'grief' (in Russian); and indeed, brothers, there is grief today for all those who saw the violent death of our lord Prince Michael at that time."

The Tver story of Prince Michael could not fail to move the Russian reader by its theme and character.

Although created in Tver, *The Tale of Michael of Tver* became firmly established in Moscow chronicle-writing also. But the Moscow chroniclers sensed the anti-Muscovite sentiment in it and with each redaction of their chronicles omitted or revised everything that showed Yuri of Moscow in a bad light, leaving out the author's anti-Muscovite attacks. Thus *The Tale of Michael of Tver* became a story about the death of a Russian prince in the Horde for the land of Russia which was in keeping with the objective historical facts.

The original redaction of *The Life of Metropolitan Peter*. *The Life of Metropolitan Peter* was most likely written in the first half of 1327 by someone close to the metropolitan and the Grand Prince of Moscow. The *Life* was commissioned by Ivan the Money-Bag: it was essential to canonise and extol the person who had transferred the Metropolitan See from Vladimir to Moscow. A *vita* based on the miracles which were said to have been performed straight after Peter's death would confirm the metropolitan's saintliness.[16]

The Life of Metropolitan Peter was of great political and publicistic importance. The choice of Peter by God manifested itself in the miraculous vision which the saint's mother had before he was born. Along the whole of his life's path he was accompanied by Divine protection. And then this prelate elected by God, the Metropolitan of All Russia, out of all the towns in the land of Russia preferred Moscow, in which he chose not only to live, but also to be buried (he began building himself a tomb in the Cathedral of the Assumption). On his death-bed Peter gives his blessing to Ivan the Money-Bag and all his descendants.

The Life of Metropolitan Peter not only extolled the saint, but also to no lesser extent sang the praises of Moscow and the Grand Prince of Moscow. It confirmed the sanctity of the town chosen by God, which was soon to become what Kiev had been at the cradle of Russian history, the main town and centre of all the Russian lands.

3. Translated Tales

During the period of the Mongol invasion and rule Russia's relations with foreign centres of culture became far more difficult, but were not broken off completely, as we can see from the appearance of translated literary works in North-Eastern Russia during this period. We referred above to Bulgarian literature as the intermediary for the literature of Kievan Russia. Now the literature of the Dalmatian coast of the Adriatic also began to play this role. Slavonic, Byzantine and Romance (via Italy) culture met here. In the latter half of the thirteenth and the fourteenth century literary works of Oriental origin began to appear in Russia, some of which may have been translated directly from the Oriental original.

The translated works that may reasonably be dated to the latter half of the thirteenth and the fourteenth century are in keeping with the mood of the age. They are works of a Utopian and eschatological nature. On the one hand, they reflect dreams of lands where justice reigns and life is peaceful and prosperous, and on the other, they express man's fear and insecurity in the face of the disasters and misfortunes around him, his disillusion with the moral foundations of society. These works are characterised by hyperbole of both positive and negative elements. They arouse in the reader admiration and amazement at the variety and wonders of the world and at the same time a disquieting sense of the helplessness of the ordinary mortal threatened by all sorts of unknown dangers.

The Tale of the Indian Empire. Ever since ancient times India was reputed to be a wonderful, immensely rich land inhabited by strange creatures. One legend said that India was ruled by a mighty ruler called John, who was both emperor and presbyter. To the mediaeval mind remote, mysterious India was a land where people knew neither want nor strife. These fantastic, Utopian views of India were reflected in the legendary *Epistle* of Emperor John to the Byzantine Emperor Manuel written in the twelfth century. The Latin version of this *Epistle* formed the basis of a Slavonic translation which is thought to be thirteenth-century. Russian manuscripts of the tale date to the latter half of the fifteenth and the sixteenth century.[17]

The *Tale* paints an enticing picture of far-off India. All a person could desire for himself (wealth, universal abundance, peace and security) and for his country (a strong ruler, an invincible army, honest judges, etc.) are to be found there. All this does not simply exist, but is portrayed with the embellishments of the fairy tale. John writes in his *Epistle* that he is the emperor of emperors, and "three thousand three hundred emperors" are subject to him, his empire is "such that you can walk for ten months in one direction and never reach the other side, for sky and earth meet there". The emperor's palace is splendid beyond compare with ordinary earthly ones ("My court is such that you must walk for five days round it...") and so on and so forth. Apart from ordinary people the Indian empire is inhabited by the strangest creatures (horned, three-legged, many-armed, with eyes in their chest, half-men and half-beasts, etc.). Equally varied and fantastic is the animal kingdom (there is a description of the different birds and beasts and their habits) and many wondrous treasures are to be found in its rivers and below the ground. India has everything, yet there are "no thieves, no robbers, no envious men, because my land abounds in all manner of riches," writes Emperor John.

John's unquestionable superiority over the real rulers with which the mediaeval reader could compare this emperor and presbyter of legendary India can be seen not only in the description of his land's wonders, wealth and power, but also in the foreword to this description. This says that if the Greek Emperor Manuel were to sell his Empire and use the money to buy parchment, the amount of parchment would not suffice even for a description of the wealth and wonders of India.

Some images in *The Tale of the Indian Empire* recall the *bylina* about Dyuk Stepanovich. Arriving in Kiev "from India's rich land" Dyuk boasts of his country's riches.[18] Ilya Muromets and Dobrynya Nikitich set off for India on Prince Vladimir's orders to see for themselves and find that Dyuk is right and that it is impossible for them to describe the wealth of India. After they have spent three years and three days describing the horses' harnesses, Dyuk's mother, "the most venerable widow Marfa Timofeyevna", says to them:

> *Oh, you good men, you valuers!*
> *Go you to the fair town of Kiev,*
> *Even unto the Great Prince Vladimir,*
> *And say to the Great Prince Vladimir,*
> *That though he sell Kiev town for paper*
> *And sell all Chernigov town for ink*
> *'Twill suffice but to describe a few beasts.*

Alexander Veselovsky and Vassily Istrin believe that the similarity between the tale and the *bylina* means they both originated from a common source, a Byzantine poem. One is equally justified in assuming, however, that the *bylina* was influenced by *The Tale of the Indian Empire*.

At first glance the descriptions of the wonders of India in the *Tale* are of a fairy-tale, entertaining nature. However, this fairy-tale nature of the *Tale* also reflected social and worldly dreams and ideas of the splendour and variety of the world in keeping with the times.

The Tale of Macarius of Rome. For the people of the Middle Ages, whose thinking was dominated by religious ideology, paradise must have seemed even more splendid than idyllic India. They longed to see this paradise on earth.

Therefore the search for an earthly paradise was a most popular theme in mediaeval literature. *The Tale of Macarius of Rome* is about such a search. It originated in Byzantium and appears to have come to Russia not later than the beginning of the fourteenth century (an early manuscript is dated fourteenth century).

The *Tale* consists of two parts. The first is the account of the difficult journey of three monks who set out to find the place where "heaven and earth meet".[19] The second is the story of the life of the recluse Macarius of Rome, whom the three travellers meet at the end of their journey.

In their search for an earthly paradise the three monks travel through India and many other wondrous lands. They encounter people and animals similar to those described in *The Tale of the Indian Empire*. Like the hero of *The Alexandreid*, Alexander the Great, they visit places where sinners are writhing in torment. All these descriptions, which show the influence of *The Tale of the Indian Empire* and the *Alexandreid*, are very daunting. They arouse the reader's attention and concern for the fate of the heroes, who are constantly threatened by all manner of dangers. Only Divine protection and wonder-working guides sent by God (a dove and a deer) help the travellers to overcome the difficulties of their journey.

At the end of the three monks' long and dangerous journey is the cell of Macarius. On learning from the travellers the purpose of their wanderings, Macarius tells them that it is impossible to reach the earthly paradise, because it is guarded by terrible sentries appointed by God to keep mortals away. Earthly paradise does exist, but it is not accessible even to the righteous and those favoured by the Lord in this earthly life.

Macarius' account of himself is a typical hagiographical narrative about a pious hermit. It tells briefly of his retirement from the world, his life in the wilderness and friendship with wild beasts, his temptations, sins and repentance.

The Lay of the Twelve Dreams of Emperor Shakhaishi. *The Lay of the Twelve Dreams of Emperor Shakhaishi* originates from an Oriental source. This source is unknown, but motifs of a similar character and content have been found in a Tibetan legend, a Buddhist tale and a number of other Oriental works.[20] The *Lay* became known in the South-Slavonic countries and either came to Russia from there or was translated directly from the Oriental original. This question has not yet been answered.[21] Nor is it known when the work first appeared on Russian soil. We assume that it was in the thirteenth or fourteenth century (the earliest of the known manuscripts is fifteenth-century). The extant manuscripts of the *Dreams of Emperor Shakhaishi* can be divided into two redactions. In many manuscripts the Emperor is called Mamer. In those manuscripts where the Emperor is called Shakhaishi, Mamer is the name of the philosopher who interprets the Emperor's dreams.

According to Mamer's interpretation, Shakhaishi's dreams mean that "bad times" will come in the distant future. Each dream betokens poverty and need, the destruction of the foundations, the collapse of morals, "when those bad times come".[22] There will be rebellion and strife, there will be no truth—people will speak sweetly, but conceal malice in their hearts, the laws will no longer be observed, children will cease to obey their parents and elders, licentiousness and dissipation will be rife, even nature will change its pattern—autumn will come in winter, winter in spring or in the middle of summer, and so on.

Sombre eschatological pictures of the future of the world were widespread in mediaeval literature. These apocalyptic themes usually appeared during troubled times. The mood of *The Lay of the Twelve Dreams of Shakhaishi* corresponded to the period of the Mongol invasion. It is indicative that at a later date this work was widely read by Old Believers persecuted by the tsarist government.

The Old Russian reader's striving to understand the world, his dreams of a just, prosperous life on earth and his philosophical reflections on man's need for

Church of St Theodore Stratilates in Novgorod. 1361

earthly happiness are reflected in literary works like the tales we have examined. These questions were also raised in original works. In particular, the legends about the existence of an earthly paradise were treated in an interesting way in the *Epistle* of Archbishop Basil of Novgorod to Bishop Theodore of Tver.

4. Epistles

The Epistle of Archbishop Basil of Novgorod to Bishop Theodore of Tver Concerning Paradise. The *Epistle* of Basil the Pilgrim, Archbishop of Novgorod, to Bishop Theodore the Good of Tver on earthly paradise is found in *The Sophia First Chronicle* and *The Resurrection Chronicle* under the year 1347.[23]

Basil wrote his *Epistle* in Tver, after learning of the "disagreement" which had arisen among the people of Tver concerning the question of the existence of paradise. "I have heard, brother," he addresses Theodore, "that you say 'the paradise in which Adam dwelt is gone', and there is only the paradise 'of the mind'" (i.e., that Theodore believes there is no earthly paradise, only paradise as a spiritual, moral category). Basil does not agree with this and argues the existence of earthly paradise. He bases his arguments on various texts, making extensive reference to apocryphal works and to the "testimony" of eyewitnesses.

Basil's arguments, which seem naive to the modern reader, reveal the great respect which Old Russian writers had for the written word and also the existence in Novgorod of oral tales by sailors and travellers about distant, mysterious lands, the reality of which their audience did not doubt.

Proof that paradise exists can be found, according to Basil, in the Holy Scriptures and the writings of the Church Fathers. Nowhere is it said that earthly paradise had disappeared. It was created by God, and "all God's works are everlasting". This is indeed so, as Basil has seen for himself: when he was in Jerusalem, he saw with his "own eyes" fig trees planted by Jesus, which "have survived ... to this very day, and not withered or rotted". He was also a "witness", he says, that the town gates closed by Jesus "stand unopened to this very day". All this, Basil sincerely believes, is indisputable proof that earthly paradise exists too. There are also men who have seen the existence of both paradise and hell on earth. They are Novgorodian seafarers. "To this day," Basil writes, "torments (i.e., hell) are to be found in the West." "Many of my spiritual children, the people of Novgorod, have seen it in the Breathing Sea: a worm that never slumbers, and the gnashing of teeth and the seething River Morg, and the water there doth flow into the underworld and come up again three times a day." This vivid description of the Arctic Ocean (the

Breathing Sea is a sea with the ebb and flow of the tide) reflects both legends of the harsh North Sea and a fantastic explanation of strange natural phenomena (the tidal ebb and flow is the water flowing in and out of the underworld). The Novgorodians are said to have seen the very spot where earthly paradise is.

In his *Epistle* Basil recounts the poetic legend of the earthly paradise which the Novgorodians found. Parallels to this subject can be traced in a number of other literatures, but the legend retold by Basil bears the clear imprint of local Novgorodian origin. Like the story of the Breathing Sea, this legend reflects the fantastic tales of Novgorodian seafarers about their voyages. A storm carries some Novgorodians' boats far out to sea, to mountains on which, as those who took part in the voyage relate, the composition of the Deisis [24] was painted "in a marvellous *lazor*" [25] (a very precious bright blue, particularly beloved by the Novgorodians). The spot is bathed in ineffable light, and joyous singing wafts from behind the mountains. The mariners are sent up a mountain and see what lies behind them, clap their hands joyfully and run off. One of them ties a rope round his leg so he can be held back. When they drag him back to the boat, he is dead. The Novgorodians sail away from the spot in terror. Basil gives the names of those who witnessed the event and recounted it: "Moislav and Yakov", and as proof of the truth of their story he notes that the "children and grandchildren" of Moislav and Yakov are "hale and hearty" even now.

Unlike translated works on the search for paradise on earth, which are excessively fantastic, everything in Basil's *Epistle* is simpler, more life-like and more "authentic". Basil is not only arguing the correctness of his philosophical and theological views on the existence of a paradise on earth but also telling an interesting story. One can sense a local patriotism in it for it is not about apocryphal heroes of the distant past from foreign lands, but about Novgorodians who discover an earthly paradise, and whose children and grandchildren are still alive.

In respect of both genre and subject-matter the literature of the first three quarters of the fourteenth century continues the traditions of the preceding period. New centres of chronicle-writing arose, *vitae* were compiled, epistles and homilies written, and foreign works translated.

In this period the chronicle-writing of Tver and Pskov, which began in the late thirteenth century, continued to develop. Moscow chronicle-writing emerged and, with the growth and enhancement of Moscow's political power, acquired a national Russian character. The year 1305 saw the compilation of a chronicle that was to provide the basis in all subsequent chronicle-writing for an account of the history of Russia from earliest times to the beginning of the fourteenth century.

The *vitae* which can be dated to the beginning or first half of the fourteenth century continue the old traditions of the genre for the most part, but a strengthening of the political and publicistic elements can be detected. *The Life of Metropolitan Peter* is acutely political. In *The Tale of Michael of Tver, Son of Yaroslav*, the civic element is enhanced in the Life of the martyr prince. The traditions of the heroic type of princely *vita* acquire a local character in *The Tale of Dovmont* and are simplified to some extent.

The Mongol overlordship oppressing the Russian people determined the choice of translated works that circulated during this period in Russia. There was a heightened interest in eschatological writings and works about happy, prosperous lands and the search for paradise on earth. The latter theme became the subject of an original Russian work, the *Epistle* of Archbishop Basil of Novgorod. However, not only despair and hopeless dreams of wondrous lands and an earthly paradise filled the minds of the people of this age. *The Tale of Dovmont* extols heroism, and *The Tale of Shevkal* tells of the people's struggle against their Mongol overlords.

In the period in question we can detect the interaction, not very significant, but increasing nevertheless, of literature with local, originally oral traditions and the growth of democratic elements in literature. This is seen in the character of Pskov chronicle-writing and in the special features of *The Tale of Dovmont*. Sympathy with the outlook of the popular masses can be seen in *The Tale of Shevkal*. Basil's *Epistle*, although written on a universal subject, bears a clearly expressed local, Novgorodian stamp and reveals the author's interest in Novgorodian folk legends.

The style of monumental historicism did not undergo any significant changes in this period, compared with the preceding one. Nevertheless this style was becoming less elevated, to some extent simpler and more "down to earth". As already mentioned, the features of a new style developed gradually in Old Russian literature, within the old style. The first three quarters of the fourteenth century were precisely such a period of transition. This time saw the gradual maturing of the prerequisites for the expressive-emotional style that replaced monumental historicism and characterised the following stage in the history of Old Russian literature.

Korsun Doors in the Cathedral of St Sophia in Novgorod. 12th century

Self-portrait of the master Avraam. Detail of the Korsun Doors in the Cathedral of St Sophia in Novgorod

REFERENCES

¹ *ПСРЛ*, Vol. XV, 1965. For a short history of Tver chronicle-writing see: Насонов А. Н. "Летописные памятники Тверского княжества. Опыт реконструкции тверского летописания с XIII до конца XV в.". *Известия АН СССР. Отдел гуманитарных наук*, Vol. VII, 1930, No. 9, pp. 709-738; No. 10, pp. 739-772. Nasonov later discovered a third monument of Tver chronicle-writing—a chronicle fragment for 1318-1348. See: Насонов А. Н. "О тверском летописном материале в рукописях XVII века". *Археографический ежегодник за 1957*. Moscow, 1958, pp. 30-40.

² Лурье Я. С. *Общерусские летописи XIV-XV вв.* Leningrad, 1976, p. 34.

³ Приселков М. Д. *История русского летописания XI-XV вв.*

⁴ *Baskak*—an official sent from the Horde to Russian towns and principalities conquered by the Mongols to supervise the collection of tribute and population censuses.

⁵ For the text of *The Tale of Shevkal* see: *ПЛДР. XIV-середина XV века*. Moscow, 1981, pp. 62-65.

⁶ For a detailed description of the different versions of the song and a comparative analysis of them see: Путилов Б. Н. *Русский историко-песенный фольклор XIII-XVI веков*. Moscow and Leningrad, 1960, pp. 116-131.

⁷ Воронин Н. Н. "*Песнь о Щелкане* и Тверское восстание 1327 г.". *Исторический журнал*, № 9, 1944, pp. 75-82.

⁸ Лурье Я. С. "Роль Твери в создании Русского национального государства". *Ученые записки Ленинградского университета*, No. 36, 1939, p. 107. See also N. N. Voronin's article "*Песнь о Щелкане* и Тверское восстание 1327 г.".

⁹ *Древние российские стихотворения, собранные Киршею Даниловым*. Moscow and Leningrad, 1958, p. 32.

¹⁰ For the text of *The Tale of Dovmont* see: *ПЛДР. XIV-середина XV века*, pp. 50-57.

¹¹ Энгельман А. *Хронологические исследования в области русской и ливонской истории в XIII и XIV столетиях*. St Petersburg, 1858, pp. 44-93.

¹² Серебрянский Н. *Древнерусские княжеские жития*, Moscow, 1915, p. 274.

¹³ Ibid.

¹⁴ Кучкин В. А. *Повести о Михаиле Тверском. Историко-текстологическое исследование*. Moscow, 1974.

¹⁵ The text is quoted from *The Sophia First Chronicle* (*ПСРЛ*, Vol. V, St Petersburg, 1851, pp. 207-215). A specialist on the *Tale*, V. A. Kuchkin, divides all its texts into two main categories, one found in the chronicles and the other in miscellanies. Of those in the chronicles the text closest to the original form of the *Tale* is that in the early recension of *The Sophia First Chronicle* and in the Tver chronicles (*The Rogozh Chronicle* and *The Tver Miscellany*). "*The Tale of the Death of Michael* in the early recension of *The Sophia First Chronicle*," writes Vasily Kuchkin, "has retained older features than the text of *The Rogozh Chronicle*." However, as Kuchkin has shown, in relation to the *Tale* of the chronicle type, the text of the miscellanies, referred to by specialists as the Extended Redaction of the *Tale*, is the earliest. For the most part the Extended Redaction is very close to the text of the early recension of *The Sophia First Chronicle*. Since the Extended Redaction has not

been published, we refer the reader to the text of *The Sophia First Chronicle*, although the quotations in Kuchkin's book are from manuscripts of the Extended Redaction.

[16] Кучкин В. А. *"Сказание о смерти митрополита Петра"*. *ТОДРЛ*, Vol. XVIII, 1962, pp. 59-79. Before Kuchkin's study Bishop Prochorus of Rostov was thought to be the author of the *Life*. Prochorus' name is in the title of the second recension of the *Life*. But, as Kuchkin shows, it refers not to the text of the *Life*, but to *The Reading in Memory of Metropolitan Peter* that comes after the *Life* and was compiled and read by Prochorus in the Cathedral of Vladimir during the Vladimir Council of 1327 at which Peter was canonised.

[17] For the text of the *Tale* see: *ПЛДР. XIII век*, pp. 466-473.

[18] *Былины* (Библиотека поэта. Большая серия). Second edition. Leningrad, 1957, pp. 354-365.

[19] The text has been published in the book: Тихонравов Н. *Памятники отреченной русской литературы*, Vol. II, Moscow, 1863, pp. 59-77.

[20] Веселовский А. Н. *"Слово о двенадцати снах царя Шахаиши по рукописи XV в."*. *Сборник Отделения русского языка и словесности АН СССР (СОРЯС)*, Vol. XX, 1879, No. 2, pp. 1-3; Рыстенко А. В. *"Сказание о 12 снах царя Мамера в славяно-русской литературе"*. Odessa, 1904; Кузнецов Б. И. *"Слово о двенадцати снах Шахаиши и его связи с памятниками литературы Востока"*. *ТОДРЛ*, Vol. XXX, 1976, pp. 272-278.

[21] Alexander Veselovsky takes the view that the *Lay* was translated directly from the Oriental original; Alexei Sobolevsky believes it to be a translation from the Greek; A. V. Rystenko traces it to Serbia, and Vasily Istrin to the Dalmatian coast.

[22] The text is quoted from the edition: Веселовский А. Н. *"Слово о двенадцати снах царя Шахаиши по рукописи XV в."*. pp. 4-10.

[23] For the text of the *Epistle* see: *ПЛДР. XIV-середина XV века*, pp. 42-49.

[24] Deisis, or deisus (Greek) means "prayer, supplication". This composition shows Christ at the Last Judgement. The Virgin Mary, on one side, and John the Baptist, on the other, are interceding for sinners, begging Christ to be merciful. Other saints may also be portrayed in the composition.

[25] On the typically Novgorodian character of this image in Basil's *Epistle* see: Лихачев Д. С. *Новгород Великий*. Moscow, 1959, p. 62.

CHAPTER 4

LITERATURE OF THE LATE FOURTEENTH AND THE FIRST HALF OF THE FIFTEENTH CENTURY

In the latter half of the fourteenth and first half of the fifteenth century, under the descendants of Ivan the Money-Bag, Moscow emerged more and more actively as the centre uniting the principalities of North-Eastern Russia. Moscow's struggle for supremacy against rival principalities was accompanied by constant clashes with external enemies—the Horde and the Grand Duchy of Lithuania. The importance of the Moscow grand principality as the only real force capable of achieving the unification of the Russian lands and organising resistance to the Horde is seen most clearly in the 1370s and 1380s.

From 1359 to 1389 the throne of the Grand Prince of Moscow was held by Ivan the Money-Bag's grandson, Dmitry, under whom the political and economic power of Moscow were greatly enhanced. Internal strife within the Horde became very acute at this time, weakening the enemy and assisting Russia's

struggle against Mongol overlordship. Moscow practically ceased to pay tribute to the Horde.

The Mongols took resolute steps to restore their wavering dominion. The *temnik* (military leader) Mamai, who had seized power in the Horde during the internal strife, sent a large force against Moscow in 1378. In a battle on the River Vozha the forces of the Grand Prince of Moscow defeated the enemy. This was the first serious defeat that the Mongols had suffered since the establishment of their rule. Two years later, in 1380, the Battle of Kulikovo was fought. Hordes of Mongols and mercenaries led by Mamai marched on the Moscow principality. As in the battle on the Vozha, the Russians advanced to meet them. Many apanage principalities of North-Eastern Russia allied with Moscow against the foe. A mighty battle, from which Russians emerged victorious, was fought on the Don (after which Dmitry became known as Dmitry Donskoy), on Kulikovo Field.

The rout of Mamai demonstrated the leading role of the Moscow principality and its grand prince in North-Eastern Russia and the military superiority of the united Russian forces to the enemy. The Battle of Kulikovo was of immense national and patriotic importance: it produced an upsurge of national awareness and inspired confidence that the Russians could cast off the hated Mongol supremacy. In 1382, two years later, Khan Tokhtamysh attacked Moscow, defeating it and restoring the payment of tribute. But neither this raid nor the subsequent Mongol incursions could shake the dominance of Moscow and the grand prince in the political life of the country. It is significant that when he bequeathed the grand principality to his eldest son Basil, Dmitry Donskoy was acting independently of the Golden Horde.

In the late fourteenth and first half of the fifteenth century, at the same time as the unification of the lands around Moscow, the number of apanages within the borders of the Moscow principality increased as a result of territory being divided up between a number of heirs. The princes who held these apanages recognised the authority of the grand prince. The grand prince sought to turn them into privileged landowners bound to serve him. This led to the outbreak of a feudal war in the second quarter of the fifteenth century which lasted for almost thirty years. In this war the reactionary apanage princes and boyars opposed the growing authority of the Grand Prince of Moscow. Apart from the apanage princes, the principality of Tver and the Novgorodian boyar republic took an active part in the struggle against Moscow. This feudal war was a bitter, cruel one, complicated by the constant struggle against the Horde. In the end the forces that were progressive at that particular stage in history triumphed: the apanage and boyar opposition was defeated, and the power of the Grand Prince of Moscow consolidated.

All the most important historical events of the period were reflected in the literary works of the age.

To some extent or other the development of human culture is connected with the strengthening and enrichment of the individual element in it. The succession of historical formations mark stages in the liberation of man. In the age of feudalism man was liberated from the power of the clan, and after that in the period of the Renaissance from the power of the corporation and estate. Later he sought to free himself from the oppression of class. This process was assisted by various forms of the "discovery of man", the recognition of his value as an individual.

In the age of early feudalism Old Russian literature was connected with the liberation of the individual from the power of the clan and the tribe. By becoming part of a feudal corporation, man grew conscious of his power. The hero of literary works of this period is a member of a feudal corporation, a representative of his estate. He is a prince, monk, bishop or boyar, and in this capacity he is portrayed in all his grandeur and corporate dignity. Hence the monumental nature of the portrayal of man.

The extent to which a person was valued as a member of a corporation in the period of early feudalism, the tenth and eleventh centuries, can be seen from *Russian Law*, where a blow with the hilt or the flat of a sword, a drinking horn or a goblet was considered several times more offensive than a wound that drew blood, because it expressed extreme contempt for one's antagonist.[1]

But then came an age in Russian history when a person was valued irrespective of whether he belonged to a mediaeval corporation. There was a new "discovery of man", of his inner life, his virtues, his historical significance, etc. In Western Europe this discovery took place with the development of commodity-money relations. At the same time as enslaving man, money in other respects liberated him from the power of the corporation. In principle anyone could acquire money, and it gave one power over others. Money broke down the corporative barriers and made the concept of corporate honour unnecessary.

In Russia the conditions for the liberation of the individual from the power of the corporation were created, on the one hand, by economic growth and the development of trade and handicrafts which led to the rise of the "town-communes" of Novgorod and Pskov, and on the other hand, by the fact that with the military conflicts and the bitter moral tribulations of Mongol overlordship inner qualities became valued increasingly: a person's fortitude, devotion to his homeland and his prince, his ability to resist the offers of advancement with which the foreign authorities constantly tempted people to betray their country. The prince promoted competent military commanders, administrators, etc., irrespective of their origin and membership of a corporation. As we shall see later, the chronicle tells of the Surozh merchants who defended Moscow against Tokhtamysh and describes the bravery of a simple sacrist of the Assumption Cathedral in Vladimir who refused to hand over the church plate to the enemy. There are increasing references to the activity of the populace, the townspeople in particular, in the life of the state.

This explains why literature, and particularly hagiography, describes the inner life of an individual and pays increasing attention to the emotional sphere. Literature is interested in a person's psychology, his state of mind. This leads to expressive style and dynamic description.

The expressive-emotional style develops in literature, and in ideology increasing importance is attached to "silence", solitary prayer outside church, withdrawal to a monastery or hermitage. This seclusion of the individual, his withdrawal from society, was also in keeping with the development of the individual element.

These phenomena should not be identified with the Renaissance, for religion dominated the spiritual culture of Old Russia right up to the seventeenth century. In the fourteenth and fifteenth centuries there was still a long way to go to the secularisation of life and culture: the liberation of the individual took place within the framework of religion in Russia. It was the initial period of a process that, given favourable conditions, usually developed into the Renaissance or in other words the Pre-Renaissance.

The interest in man's inner life, which demonstrated the transience, the vanity of all earthly things was connected with an awakening of historical awareness. History was no longer seen as a simple succession of events. In people's minds at the end of the fourteenth and fifteenth centuries the very nature of the age was changing. This manifested itself, first and foremost, in the attitude to the foreign dominion. The idealisation of Russia's age of independence began. Thinking turned to the idea of independence, art to the works of pre-Mongol Russia, architecture to the buildings of the age of independence, and literature to the works of the eleventh to thirteenth centuries: to *The Tale of Bygone Years,* Metropolitan Hilarion's *Sermon on Law and Grace, The Lay of Igor's Host,* and so on.

Thus, pre-Mongol Russia, the Russia of the period of independence, became a kind of "age of antiquity" for the Russian Pre-Renaissance.

All mediaeval literature is characterised by abstraction, generalisation of phenomena, the urge to single out the general instead of the particular, the spiritual instead of the material, the inner, religious meaning of every phenomenon. The mediaeval method of abstraction acquired special significance during the Russian Pre-Renaissance, determining the method of portraying human psychology. Dmitry Likhachev has defined this feature of the literature of the Russian Pre-Renaissance as "abstract psychologism". "In the late fourteenth and early fifteenth century writers focused their attention on man's psychological states, his feelings, his emotional responses to the events of the external world. But these feelings and states of mind were not yet moulded into characters. Individual manifestations of psychology were portrayed without any individualisation and were not shaped into psychology as such. The connecting unifying element—human character— had not yet been discovered, human character was still restricted by being put into one of two categories—good or bad, positive or negative."[2]

The Pre-Renaissance phenomena that emerged in the first half of the fourteenth century in Russian cultural life became particularly evident at the end of the century and in the first half of the following one. The upsurge of national awareness after the Battle of Kulikovo produced a flowering of culture, arousing intense interest in the country's past and the urge to revive national traditions and to strengthen Russia's cultural contacts with other states. Russia's traditional contacts with Byzantium and the Southern Slav countries were revived.

The monumental stone building that resumed in the first half of the fourteenth century acquired considerable dimensions by the end of the century. The fine arts, which was where Pre-Renaissance ideas manifested themselves most clearly, enjoyed a special flowering in the late fourteenth and first half of the fifteenth century. In the late fourteenth and early fifteenth century the great mediaeval painter Theophanes the Greek worked in Russia, whose painting brilliantly embodied the ideals of the Pre-Renaissance. In the churches of Novgorod, Moscow and other towns in North-Eastern Russia Theophanes painted frescoes that still impress us with their majestic, dynamic and austere figures.

The great Russian painter Andrei Rublev was working at the end of the fourteenth and in the first quarter of the fifteenth century. His activity is connected with Moscow and the towns and monasteries around Moscow. Together with Theophanes the Greek and the elder Prochorus, he painted the frescoes for the Cathedral of the Annunciation in the Moscow Kremlin (1405). With Daniel the Black (his close friend) he painted frescoes and icons in the Assumption Cathedral in Vladimir (1408) and the Trinity Cathedral of the Trinity Monastery of St Sergius in Zagorsk (1424-1426). His famous *Trinity* icon belongs to the period of his work in the Trinity Monastery. Andrei Rublev's painting radiates a profound humanism.

"The painting of this period," writes Dmitry Likhachev, referring mainly to frescoes, "was enriched by new themes. Its subject matter became more complex and narrative, events were given a psychological treatment, painters strove to portray the emotions of the people involved in them, to stress their suffering, grief, longing, fear, joy and ecstasy. Biblical subjects were treated less formally, more intimately and prosaically." [3]

The overall spread of enlightenment, the awakening urge to find a rational explanation for natural phenomena led to the emergence of rationalistic movements in the towns. The Strigolniks' heresy appeared in Novgorod at the end of the fourteenth century. The Strigolniks (Shearers) rejected the church hierarchy and church ritual, and some of them appear not to have believed in the doctrine of the resurrection of the dead and the divinity of Christ. Their protests contained social undertones.

The cultural flowering of the late fourteenth and the fifteenth century led to an expansion of Russian cultural links with Byzantium and the Southern Slav countries (Bulgaria and Serbia). Russian monks frequently spent long periods in the monasteries of Mount Athos and Constantinople and a number of Southern Slavs and Greeks settled in Russia. Among those who played an important role in Russian literature of the late fourteenth and first half of the fifteenth century were the Bulgarians Cyprian and Gregory Tsamblak and the Serb Pachomius the Logothete. Many Southern Slav manuscripts and translations appeared in Russia during this period. Russian literature interacted closely with the literature of Byzantium and the Southern Slavs.

1. Chronicle-Writing

In the late fourteenth and first half of the fifteenth century numerous chronicles were compiled. The compilers collected, revised and redacted local chronicles depending on the political interests that the compilation was intended to serve.

Of great ideological importance was the tradition of including

Andrei Rublev. Icon of the Old Testament Trinity. C. 1408. Tretyakov Gallery, Moscow

Andrei Rublev. Icon of the Old Testament Trinity. Detail

The Tale of Bygone Years or extracts from it in the opening section about the history of Kievan Russia. Thanks to this the history of each principality became a continuation of the history of the whole Russian land, and the grand princes of these principalities appeared as heirs to the princes of Kiev. The compilers of chronicles drew on chronicles from various principalities and also inserted tales, *vitae*, polemical writings and official documents that did not originate in chronicles. Moscow became the centre of chronicle-writing and, most important, Moscow chronicle-writing acquired an all-Russian character.

The Laurentian Chronicle. As mentioned above, in 1377 the monk Laurentius with helpers copied the chronicle compilation of 1305[4] in the Nizhny Novgorod-Suzdal principality. The fact that this was done in 1377 was of considerable ideological and political significance.

The Laurentian Chronicle began with *The Tale of Bygone Years* about the former greatness of the Russian land. It also included the *Instruction* of Vladimir Monomachos, the prince who was the ideal wise statesman and valiant military leader in Old Russia. This work called on all the princes to forget their personal grudges and internal strife in the face of the danger that threatened the Russian land.[5] The accounts of the events in the 1230s were full of lofty patriotism: although Russian princes perished in the unequal struggle, they were courageous and united in resisting the Mongols.

The late 1370s, when Laurentius and his assistants were working on the chronicle, were the eve of the Battle of Kulikovo, a period of particularly tense relations between Moscow and the Horde. The work was commissioned by the Prince of Nizhny Novgorod-Suzdal, then an ally of the Grand Prince of Moscow. Thus, the aim of copying the 1305 compilation in 1377 was to stimulate patriotism and encourage the Russian princes to struggle actively against the Mongols.

Moscow Chronicle-Writing. The first Moscow chronicle compilation about which we can get a concrete idea was that of 1408 (1409) by Metropolitan Cyprian of Moscow. A manuscript copy of this compilation, *The Trinity Chronicle*, was destroyed in the Fire of Moscow in 1812.[6] The 1408 (1409) compilation was begun on the initiative of Metropolitan Cyprian, who may also have taken a direct part in it, and not completed until after his death (he died in 1406).

Cyprian's chronicle compilation was the first All-Russian compilation to be made in North-Eastern Russia. As Metropolitan of All Russia, Cyprian was able to draw on chronicles from all the Russian principalities subject to his ecclesiastical jurisdiction, including those that formed part of the Grand Duchy of Lithuania at this time. Use was made of chronicles of Tver, Nizhny Novgorod, Novgorod the Great, Rostov, Ryazan, Smolensk and, of course, all the earlier Moscow chronicles. Information on the history of Lithuania was also included. There was little revision of the sources, but, nevertheless, Cyprian's compilation tends to be pro-Moscow; it is characterised by a didactic, publicistic tone.

We can consider the next stage in All-Russian chronicle-writing to be the compilation that has survived in the *Novgorod Fourth* and *Sophia First* chronicles, and is usually referred to as the compilation of 1448 (see below, pp. 313).

Tver Chronicle-Writing. The chronicle-writing of the principality of Tver, whose princes, as mentioned above, were the main rivals of the Moscow princes in the struggle for supremacy, ceased temporarily after the defeat of Tver in 1375 by Grand Prince Dmitry of Moscow. It was resumed in 1382 and continued until Tver lost its independence. Tver chronicle-writing reached its height under Grand Prince Boris of Tver (1425-1461). It sought to prove that Tver played the leading role in Russian history, that it was the bulwark of the struggle against the Mongols, and that the grand princes of Tver, experienced military leaders and wise statesmen, were worthy of becoming the autocratic rulers of the whole of Russia.

Novgorod Chronicle-Writing. During this period Novgorod chronicle-writing lost its former democratic spirit and local character and began to lay claim to All-Russian importance. As in Moscow chronicle-writing, the Novgorod chronicles included writings of a narrative, historico-political nature that did not derive from the chronicles and were designed to confirm Novgorod's special role in the history of the Russian land and to contrast Novgorod and Novgorod's age with Moscow. This tendency in Novgorod chronicle-writing is explained by the political and ideological struggle between Moscow and the boyar republic of Novgorod that came to a head in the late fourteenth and first half of the fifteenth century. It is seen most clearly in Novgorod chronicle-writing from 1429 to 1458 when Euthymius II became Archbishop of Novgorod. The Archbishop of Novgorod played a most important part in the town's ideological life. Under Euthymius much material was collected on the town's history, legends and historical stories were revived, chronicle-writing was carried on intensively at the Archbishop's Court and new chronicles were compiled.

The Hellenic and Roman Chronicle. As already mentioned, the Russian readers' interest in world history was catered for by chronographs. Chronographs were collections of stories about the history of different countries and peoples, beginning with Biblical times. The chronographs portrayed history in a more narrative way than the chronicle. The stories in them were often fantastic or didactic. There were far more fables and anecdotes in the chronographs than the chronicles, and they showed a marked urge to moralise.

Describing the difference between the chronograph and chronicle narrative, Dmitry Likhachev writes: "For the chronicler the most important thing was historical truth. The chronicler valued the authenticity of his entries. He carefully preserved the entries of his predecessors and was primarily an historian. The compiler of the chronograph, however, was a writer. He was interested in events not from the historical, but from the edifying point of view."[7]

During this period works produced in the chronograph genre include the first and second redactions of *The Hellenic and Roman Chronicle.* Oleg Tvorogov dates the compilation of the second redaction to the middle of the fifteenth century. He believes that it originates from an archetypal redaction that was compiled in the thirteenth century from three main sources: the text of the *Chronicle* of Georgios Hamartolos, considerable fragments of the *Chronicle* of John Malalas and the first redaction of the *Alexandreid.* Compared with its protograph, the second redaction of *The Hellenic Chronicle* acquired a large number of new texts. The main sources for these texts were as follows: *The Chronograph According to the Great Exposition, The Life of SS Constanine and Helen, The Tale of the Building of Sophia of Constantinople, The Tale of Theophilus* and others.[8] Use was made of information from Russian chronicles. The inclusion in the second redaction of *The Hellenic Chronicle* of lengthy story-like texts and the skilful combining of different sources into a single narrative strengthened the literary, entertaining element in this extensive compilation on world history.

A further strengthening of the literary element is to be found in *The Russian Chronograph* of the late fifteenth and early sixteenth century.

2. Works of the Kulikovo Cycle

The victory of the Russians over the Mongols at Kulikovo Field not only made a great impression on contemporaries of this epoch-making event in Russian history, but also interested Russians for a long time afterwards. This is explained by the fact that the battle against Mamai was the subject of a number of literary works produced at different times, which were copied and revised by Old Russian writers throughout several centuries.

The works of the Kulikovo cycle vary in character and style. The poetic *Trans-Doniad*, the documental-historical original chronicle story, the intensely publicistic Extended Redaction of the chronicle story and, finally, *The Tale of the Battle Against Mamai*, full of military heroism, echoes of folklore and detail.[9]

The Trans-Doniad. *The Trans-Doniad* has already been mentioned above in connection with *The Lay of Igor's Host.* Apart from its independent literary importance and the fact that this work is devoted to such an outstanding event in Russian history as the Battle of Kulikovo, *The Trans-Doniad* is important also as indisputable evidence of the age and authenticity of *The Lay of Igor's Host.*

The Trans-Doniad was most probably written in the 1380s or early 1390s. It is a response to the Battle of Kulikovo and arose under the direct influence of the event itself.[10]

Six manuscripts of *The Trans-Doniad* have survived, the earliest of which (the Euphrosyne MS) dates back to the 1470s, and the latest to the end of the seventeenth century. The work is called *The Trans-Doniad* in the Euphrosyne MS. In the other manuscripts it is called *The Lay of Grand Prince Dmitry, Son of Ivan, and His Brother, Prince Vladimir, Son of Andrew.* The Euphrosyne MS is a condensed version of a non-extant original long text. In the remaining manuscripts the text is full of errors and distortions. Below we shall use the reconstructed text of *The Trans-Doniad* compiled on the basis of all manuscript copies of the work.[11]

The Trans-Doniad expresses the poetic attitude of its author to the events of the Battle of Kulikovo. The narrative (as in *The Lay of Igor's Host*) moves from one place to another: from Moscow to Kulikovo Field, back to Moscow, to Novgorod and back to Kulikovo Field. The present intertwines with reminiscences of the past. The author himself describes his work as "a lament and eulogy to Grand Prince Dmitry, son of Ivan, and his brother, Prince Vladimir, son of Andrew". The lament (*zhalost*) is for the fallen, and the eulogy (*pokhvala*) is for the courage and military valour of the Russians.

The whole text of *The Trans-Doniad* is related to *The Lay of Igor's Host:* we find repetitions of whole passages from the *Lay,* identical descriptions and similar poetic devices. But the author of *The Trans-Doniad* makes creative use of the *Lay.* In taking it as the model for his work, Dmitry Likhachev writes, his purpose was not simply to imitate his model, but "to draw a deliberate comparison

The Trans-Doniad. Euphrosyne's autograph. 1470s. State Public Library, Leningrad

The Trans-Doniad. Euphrosyne's autograph. Detail

between the events of the past and present, the events portrayed in *The Lay of Igor's Host* and those of his day. And both the former and the latter are symbolically contrasted in *The Trans-Doniad*".[12] This comparison made it clear that lack of unity in the actions of the princes (as in the *Lay*) led to defeat, while the uniting of all in the struggle against the foe was the pledge of victory. At the same time this comparison showed that a new age had arrived and that now it was the "pagan Tartars, the infidels" who were being defeated, not the Russians.

This comparison of the past with the present, of the events described in the *Lay* with those of 1380, runs right through the text. It is expressed vividly already in the introduction and is of profound significance. The author dates the beginning of the disasters that have befallen the Russian land to the ill-fated encounter on the Kayala and the Battle of the Kalka: Russia's enemies "overcame the tribe of the Japhetites (i.e., the Russians) on the River Kayala. Since then the land of Russia has been joyless; from the Battle of the Kalka to the rout of Mamai it has been consumed with anguish and grief." The victory over Mamai was a turning point in the fate of the Russian land: "Brothers and friends, sons of the land of Russia! Let us gather together, put word to word, gladden the land of Russia, and cast off sorrow to the Eastern lands."

Describing Dmitry Donskoy setting off on his campaign, the author of *The Trans-Doniad* says that "the sun shone brightly for him in the East and showed him the way". In *The Lay of Igor's Host* the departure of Igor's army is accompanied by an eclipse of the sun. ("Then Igor gazed up at the bright sun and he saw a shadow from it overcasting all his host.") Describing the advance of Mamai's forces to Kulikovo Field, the author of *The Trans-Doniad* presents a picture of natural phenomenon that bode ill: "And their destruction (the Tartars) was awaited by winged birds hovering in the clouds, the ravens cawed ceaselessly, and the jackdaws spoke in their tongue, the eagles screeched, the wolves howled menacingly and the foxes yelped, sensing bones." In the *Lay* the same bad omens accompany the advance of the Russian host.

There are some poetical features of *The Trans-Doniad* that distinguish it from the *Lay*. *The Trans-Doniad* has far more imagery of a religious nature: "For the land of Russia and for the Christian faith", "he stepped into his golden stirrup, mounted his swift steed, took his sword in his right hand, and prayed to God and to His Virgin Mother", and so on. The author of *The Lay of Igor's Host* made use of devices of folk poetry and adapted them creatively, fashioning his own original poetc images with material from folklore. The author of *The Trans-Doniad* simplifies many of these images. His poetic devices deriving from folk poetry are closer to their prototypes. A number of original epithets in *The Trans-Doniad* are clearly of oral origin.

The Trans-Doniad has a mixed style. Poetic passages alternate with prose passages that remind one of official documents. It is highly likely that this mixture is due to the condition of the surviving manuscripts of the work: those passages where the style resembles officialese may be the result of later additions and not reflect the author's original text of the work.

It is generally believed that *The Trans-Doniad* was written by Sophonius of Ryazan: this name is mentioned as the name of the author in the title of two manuscripts of the work. However, Sophonius of Ryazan is also called the author of *The Tale of the Battle Against Mamai* in a whole series of manuscripts of the main redaction of the *Tale*. The name of Sophonius of Ryazan is also mentioned in the text of *The Trans-Doniad*, and the nature of this reference suggests that we should probably regard Sophonius not as the author of *The Trans-Doniad*, but as the author of another poetic work on the Battle of Kulikovo which has not survived and which the author of *The Trans-Doniad* and the author of *The Tale of the Battle Against Mamai* used, independently of each other.[13] We do not possess any other information about Sophonius of Ryazan apart from the mentions of his name in *The Trans-Doniad* and *The Tale of the Battle Against Mamai*.

The Trans-Doniad is an extremely interesting work of literature created in direct response to a major event in Russian history. It is also of interest because it reflects what was a progressive political idea for its time: namely, that Moscow should stand at the head of all the Russian lands and that the unity of the Russian princes under the power of the Grand Prince of Moscow was a sure pledge for freeing Russia from Mongol overlordship.

The Chronicle Story of the Battle of Kulikovo. The chronicle story of the Battle of Kulikovo has survived in two versions: the short and the extended. The short chronicle story is found in chronicles that originate from the Cyprian compilation (*The Trinity Chronicle*). The extended story in its earliest form is in the *Novgorod Fourth* and *Sophia First* chronicles, i.e., it must have been in the protograph of these chronicles.

The short chronicle story, which appears to have been written shortly after the event (in any case not later than 1408 or 1409, the date when the Cyprian chronicle was compiled), gives the main historical facts about the Battle of Kulikovo. To take vengeance on Prince of Moscow for the defeat on the River Vozha, Mamai sets off against Russia with a large army. Grand Prince Dmitry of

Moscow marches out to meet him. A bloody battle lasting a whole day is fought on the Don. The Russians are victorious. Mamai flees for his life with a small band of men. The names of the Russian princes and generals who lost their lives are listed. "Standing on their bones" Prince Dmitry pays tribute to the Russian warriors. The Russians return home with much booty. Mamai gathers together the remains of his host and prepares to march against the Grand Prince of Moscow again. But Khan Tokhtamysh attacks Mamai himself. Mamai is defeated and killed, and Tokhtamysh becomes the ruler of the Horde.

Here we have a brief list of the events in chronological order. Most of the work is devoted to what happened after the Battle of Kulikovo. The battle itself is described briefly in the stock phrases of military tales: "And they sped into the fray, and the two forces met, and there ensued a long, merciless battle and cruel slaughter." There are a few details, it is true, in the short story as well. For example, it says that the Russians pursued the enemy "to the river Mecha and there slayed a great number of them and others ... jumped into the water and drowned". The author's attitude to what is described and his evaluation of it are expressed in brief epithets describing the Russians and Mongols and in references to Divine aid to the Russians. Mamai is "godless, impious and pagan", Dmitry goes out to fight the enemy "for the Holy Church, and for the true Christian faith, and for the Russian land", "And God helped Grand Prince Dmitry", the enemy are "pursued by the wrath of the Lord", etc.

The extended story is several times longer than the short one. It contains the text of the short one in full with a few textual changes in the first part and word-for-word reproduction of the second, main part. The extended story contains some new historical data. It describes the assembling of the Russian army in Kolomna, the arrival of Prince Andrew of Polotsk and Prince Dmitry of Bryansk, sons of Grand Prince Olgierd of Lithuania, to help the Prince of Moscow, the message sent to the grand prince on the battle field from Abbot Sergius, the crossing of the Don by the Russian army. There is a more detailed account of the battle. It says that the grand prince fought at the head of the army and that "all his armour was rent and smashed, but there was not a single wound upon his body". There are also details and names that are not mentioned in the short chronicle story. However, the increased length of the text is due not so much to the inclusion of additional historical information and a more detailed account of this information, as to literary reasons.

The author of the extended story includes lengthy rhetorical discourses on the events he describes, drawing on religious texts for this purpose. The role of Dmitry of Moscow as the defender of Russian Orthodoxy is greatly enhanced, the contrast between the Russian army as a Christian host and the host of the "impious Mongols" is sharper and more wordy, and the negative characteristics of the latter are enhanced and expanded. The author includes several prayers by Dmitry and describes the Divine aid to the Russians in greater detail and length. The short version merely says that Oleg of Ryazan was on the side of Mamai. In the extended version this theme is developed extensively. The author returns to Oleg several times, giving details of his relations with Mamai and frequently breaking into lengthy invectives against the Prince of Ryazan. He denounces Oleg for his treachery, threatens him with retribution, and compares him to Judas and Svyatopolk the Accursed.

Until recently specialists believed the short story to be a condensation of the extended one. Marina Salmina, who has made a special study of this question, argues convincingly that the short story came first, however.[14] She believes that the extended story was compiled for the compilation of 1448, from which the *Novgorod Fourth* and *Sophia First* chronicles originate (for more about this chronicle see below).

Almost all the additional historical information in the extended story can be found in some form in *The Tale of the Battle Against Mamai*. It is generally assumed that the *Tale* was created on the basis of the extended story, and, therefore, appeared later than the chronicle story. There is no convincing proof of this, however. And there are equal grounds for assuming the reverse, namely, that the extended story was written when the *Tale* already existed, and was influenced by it. It is quite possible also that some of the similarities in the *Tale* and the extended story can be explained by the influence on the various works of the Kulikovo cycle of a non-extant *Lay of the Battle Against Mamai*, the existence of which is argued by Alexei Shakhmatov. This question remains unsolved and requires further study.

The Tale of the Battle Against Mamai. *The Tale of the Battle Against Mamai* is the most lengthy work of the Kulikovo cycle. It contains the most detailed account of the events of the Battle of Kulikovo.

The *Tale* describes the preparations for the campaign and the *uryazhenie* or deployment of the detachments, the order of battle and the military tasks assigned to each detachment. It contains a detailed description of the advance of the Russian army from Moscow via Kolomna to Kulikovo Field. At this point there is a list of the princes and military leaders who took part in the fighting and an account of the Russian forces crossing the Don. Only from

The Battle of Kulikovo in 1380. Illumination from *The Illustrated Chronicle.*
16th century. Academy of Sciences Library, Leningrad

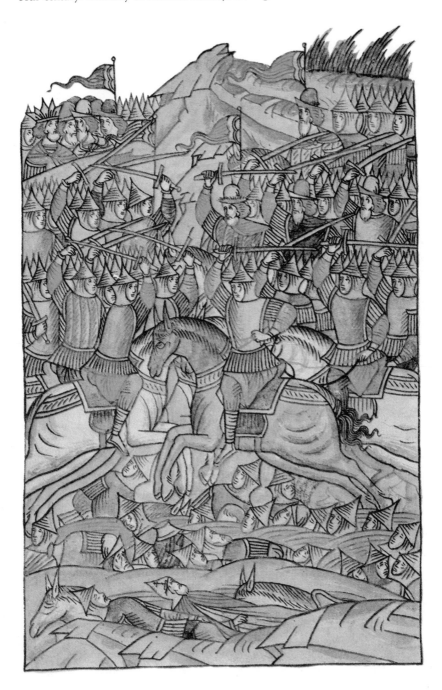

the *Tale* do we learn that the outcome of the battle was decided by a detachment led by Prince Vladimir of Serpukhov: just before the battle began he was told to wait in ambush, and his unexpected attack from the flanks and the rear on the enemy after they had broken into the Russian lines inflicted a resounding defeat on them. It is also from the *Tale* that we learn that the grand prince was found unconscious when the battle was over. These details and a number of others, including some from legendary sources (the story of the combat of the monk Peresvet with a Mongol warrior before the battle, the episodes about help given by Russian saints, etc.), have come down to us only in *The Tale of the Battle Against Mamai*.

The *Tale* was frequently copied and revised right up to the beginning of the eighteenth century and has survived in eight redactions and a large number of versions. The many illuminated manuscripts of it bear witness to its popularity with the mediaeval reader as a work intended for individual reading.[15] The main hero of the *Tale* is Dmitry Donskoy. The *Tale* is not only a story about the Battle of Kulikovo. It was also intended to extol the Grand Prince of Moscow. The author portrays Dmitry as a wise and brave leader, stressing his military prowess and valour. All the other characters in the work are grouped around Dmitry. Dmitry is the senior Russian prince, and the other princes are his loyal helpers, his vassals, his younger brothers.

Dmitry's campaign is blessed by Metropolitan Cyprian in the *Tale*. In fact Cyprian was not in Moscow in 1380. This is not an error on the part of the author, but a literary, publicistic device. For publicistic considerations the author of the *Tale*, who set out to present the Grand Prince of Moscow as the ideal ruler and leader of all the Russian armies, had to show him in firm alliance with the Metropolitan of All Russia. In a literary work he could, of course, take the poetic licence of adding Metropolitan Cyprian's blessing of Dmitry and his host particularly as Cyprian was formally Metropolitan of All Russia at that time.

At the time of the Battle of Kulikovo Prince Oleg of Ryazan and Prince Jagiello of Lithuania, the son of Grand Prince Olgierd of Lithuania who died in 1377, allied with Mamai. The *Tale*, however, describing an event that took place in 1380, says that Olgierd was Mamai's Lithuanian ally. As in the case of Cyprian's blessing this is not an error, but a conscious literary, publicistic device. For the Russian reader of the late fourteenth and early fifteenth century, and for Muscovites in particular, the name of Olgierd was associated with memories of his campaigns against the principality of Moscow. He was a wily and dangerous enemy, whose military cunning is mentioned in the chronicle record of his death. Olgierd could be called Mamai's ally instead of Jagiello only at a time when his name was still fresh in people's memories as that of a dangerous enemy of Moscow. At a later period this change of names would have been pointless.[16]

By calling Olgierd Mamai's ally, the author of the *Tale* enhanced both the publicistic and the literary aspects of his work: Moscow was attacked by the most cunning and dangerous enemies, but they too were defeated. There was also another reason for this change of name: Andrew and Dmitry, Olgierd's sons, allied with Prince Dmitry of Moscow. Thus Olgierd's own children were shown to be fighting against him, which also enhanced the publicistic and narrative elements of the work.

Mamai, the enemy of the Russian land, is portrayed by the author of the *Tale* in a highly negative light. Whereas Dmitry is the embodiment of light, the leader of a noble cause, whose actions are guided by God, Mamai is the personification of darkness and evil—behind him stands the Devil. The principle of abstract psychologism is seen very clearly here.

The heroic nature of the event portrayed in the *Tale* explains why the author turned to oral legends about the battle against Mamai. The episode of the combat before the battle between Peresvet, a monk from the Trinity Monastery of St Sergius, and a Mongol warrior probably originated in oral legend. The epic element is felt in the story about Dmitry of Volhynia's "testing of omens"; the experienced leader Dmitry of Volhynia rides out with the grand prince at nightfall on the eve of the battle, into the steppe, between the Russian and Mongol armies, and Dmitry hears the earth weeping for the Mongol and the Russian warriors: there will be many dead, but the Russians will win the day. An oral legend probably was behind the statement in the *Tale* that before the battle Dmitry put his princely armour on his beloved commander Mikhail Brenok, and attiring himself in the clothing of a common warrior was the first to rush into battle with an iron cudgel in his hand.

The influence of oral folk poetry on the *Tale* can be seen in the author's use of representational devices from the folk tradition. The Russian warriors are compared to falcons and gerfalcons, the Russians smite the enemy "as if they were felling timber, or mowing grass with a scythe". The lament of Grand Princess Eudoxia after parting with the prince who is going off to fight the Mongols can also be regarded as an example of the influence of folklore. Although the author presents this lament in the form of a prayer, one can still detect elements of the popular lament in it.

The descriptions of the Russian host are vivid and striking. It is possible that here the author of the *Tale* was influenced by the poetics of *The Galich-Volhynian Chronicle*: "And the armour of the sons of Russia was like water streaming in the wind, the gold helmets on their heads shone like the morning sunrise in clear weather, and the pennoncels of their helmets fluttered like a fiery flame." In the descriptions of nature one detects a lyrical quality and the urge to link these descriptions with the events. Some remarks by the author are deeply emotional and realistic. For example, describing the wives bidding farewell to the warriors as they are leaving Moscow to fight the enemy, the author writes that the wives "could not say a single word for their tears and heartfelt cries", and adds that "the grand prince himself, barely holding back his tears, did not weep before the people".

The author of the *Tale* made extensive use of the poetic imagery and devices in *The Trans-Doniad*. The interaction of these two works was two-way: in late manuscripts of *The Trans-Doniad* we find insertions from *The Tale of the Battle Against Mamai*.

The question of when the *Tale* was written is a difficult one and, in spite of the extensive literature on it (a large number of works appeared on this subject recently in connection with the 600th anniversary of the Battle of Kulikovo), it still remains open. We take the view that the work was written in the first quarter of the fifteenth century.[17] The special interest in the Battle of Kulikovo at this time can be explained by the increased tension in the relations with the Horde and, in particular, Jedigei's attack on Russia in 1408. Jedigei's attack, which was successful because of the lack of unity among the Russian princes, made people aware of the need to restore unity under the leadership of the Grand Prince of Moscow in order to fight the external foe. This is the main idea in the *Tale*.

No matter how long after the event itself the *Tale* was written (and a number of recent works tend to date it some time after),[18] there can be no doubt that it reflects stories about the Kulikovo epic that date from the time of the actual event and are based on the reports of participants and eyewitnesses.

The Tale of the Battle Against Mamai was of interest to readers because it gave a detailed description of the Battle of Kulikovo. However, this was not its only attraction. In spite of its rhetoric, the *Tale* has the elements of an exciting story. Not only the actual event, but also the fate of the individual characters and the development of the plot produced an emotional response to the account. In some redactions the narrative episodes are more numerous and detailed. All this makes *The Tale of the Battle Against Mamai* not only an historical and publicistic work, but also a stirring tale.

3. Tales of Mongol Attacks
on Russia After the Battle of Kulikovo

The Tale of Tokhtamysh's Campaign Against Moscow. After
Mamai's defeat at Kulikovo Field Khan Tokhtamysh seized power
in the Horde. Realising that the victory over Mamai could mean a
radical change in the attitude of the Russian princes to the Horde,
Tokhtamysh undertook a campaign against Moscow in 1382. Due
to the unconcerted action of the Russian princes, the depletion of
the Russian forces as a result of the Battle of Kulikovo and some
tactical errors, Moscow was captured by the Mongols and cruelly
devastated. After a short time in Moscow, Tokhtamysh returned to
the Horde, devastating the principality of Ryazan on the way,
although the Prince of Ryazan had assisted Tokhtamysh when his
army was advancing on Moscow. Tokhtamysh's invasion is the
subject of a chronicle tale in several versions.

The chronicle of 1408, as we can see from extant chronicles
that derive from this compilation (for example, *The Rogozh
Chronicle*), contained a short chronicle tale. The compilation of
1448, as can be seen from extant chronicles originating from it
(the *Novgorod Fourth, Sophia First* and a number of others),
contained an extended chronicle tale.[19]

The chronology and correlation of the above-mentioned compilations are such
that the short chronicle tale appears to be primary.[20] However, the reverse may be
the case. In certain parts of the short tale one can detect the condensation of a
fuller primary text (i.e., the text of the extended story). The details of
Tokhtamysh's invasion found in the extended chronicle tale and absent in the short
one suggest not later inventions, but the testimony of a contemporary or even
eyewitness of what is being described. Stylistically the extended tale is a
self-contained text. Thus, there are equal grounds for seeing the short story as a
condensation of the extended one. That is to say, we can assume that *The Tale of
Tokhtamysh's Campaign Against Moscow* was created independently of the chronicles
and only included in them later: its short form in the compilation of 1408 and its
extended form in that of 1448. The short chronicle tale with some rearrangements
and slight textual variations is included in full in the extended one.

The extended tale begins by describing a sign from heaven that
"foretold the evil coming of Tokhtamysh to the land of Russia".[21]
Tokhtamysh embarks on his campaign against Russia secretly,
rapidly and suddenly. In spite of this, the Prince of Moscow learns
of it in advance. Dmitry Donskoy does not have time to assemble
an army, however, and he leaves Moscow. The town, behind
whose stone walls not only Muscovites seek refuge but also the
inhabitants of the surrounding villages, waits anxiously for the
enemy. For three days the Mongols besiege Moscow to no avail.
On the fourth day they assure the Muscovites "with false speeches
and false words of peace" that if they come out to greet the khan

The Capture of Moscow by Khan Tokhtamysh in 1382. Illumination from *The Illustrated Chronicle.* 16th century. Academy of Sciences Library, Leningrad

The Capture of Moscow by Khan Tokhtamysh in 1382. Detail

"with honour and gifts", they will receive "peace and love" from him. The trick works and the enemy captures the town. After a detailed description of the slaughtering of the inhabitants and the terrible sacking of the town, the author exclaims: "Up till then Moscow had been for all a great city, a wondrous city, a populous city, with many people, many lords, and all manner of riches. And its appearance changed in a single hour, when it was captured, sacked and burnt. There was nothing on which to look, only earth and dust, and remains, and ashes, and many dead bodies, and the holy churches stood in ruins, as if orphaned, as if widowed."

The extended *Tale of Tokhtamysh's Campaign Against Moscow* is a most interesting work of Old Russian literature in which the role of the people in the events that take place is shown in greater detail than in any other work of this period. The story of the siege describes the courageous resistance of the townspeople. The author notes bitterly that they have to face an adversary far better versed in the art of warfare. Here is a description of the skill of the Mongol archers: "Some shot standing, others were taught to shoot at the run, while some shot on horseback at full gallop, right and left, backwards and forwards, never missing." But among the townspeople unversed in warfare there are some real heroes. The author describes one of them in detail. "A certain Muscovite standing on the Frol Gate,* a clothier by the name of Adam, after noticing and picking out a well-known Mongol of high birth, the son of a prince in the Horde, did pull his cross-bow and let fly an arrow unexpectedly, which pierced the Mongol's cruel heart and brought him a quick death. This grieved all the Mongols sorely, so that even the ruler was sorrowed by what had taken place."

At the beginning of his account of the siege of Moscow the author gives a vivid description of the events in the town. Following the grand prince, who goes north to muster an army, the most high-ranking boyars hurriedly leave the town and Metropolitan Cyprian also departs. The townspeople try to stop the Metropolitan and the boyars from leaving. The author does not approve of such actions by the common people and says of the latter that they are "rebellious, bad men, seditious folk". But he does not express any sympathy with the Metropolitan and the boyars who left Moscow, however. The people for whom the unknown author of this work feels most sympathy are the merchants and tradesmen. This can be seen not only from the fact that the hero Adam is a clothier, but from a number of other

---

* On the site where the Spassky Tower of the Moscow Kremlin now stands.

details as well. At the very beginning of the tale we are told about the fate of the merchants who were visiting the Horde when Tokhtamysh decided to march on Moscow (he had them all imprisoned and their wares confiscated). Speaking of the destruction of Moscow the author mentions that the merchants' wealth, together with the prince's treasury and the property of the boyars, was looted. He speaks of himself in the first person: "But Prince Oleg of Ryazan ... not wishing us well, but helping his own principality", "Woe is me! 'Tis terrible to hear, but 'twas more terrible then to see."

All this gives grounds for assuming that the author was a Muscovite, someone connected with the trading world, who witnessed the events which he describes and did not have to borrow from the chronicle-writing of the prince or the Metropolitan. The vivid narrative combining lively descriptions of real events with rhetorical passages, the stylistic repetitions and contrasts testify to the literary talent of the unknown author of the *Tale.*

The Tale of Temir Aksak. In 1395 Timur's army invaded the Russian principalities. Timur (also known as Tamerlane or Timur i Leng), the famous Oriental conqueror, was Emir from 1370 to 1405 of a state that had its capital in Samarkand. His large, well-organised armies waged constant warfare and were famed for their cruelty. The very name of Timur struck terror into the peoples of Asia and Europe. After a bitter struggle against Tokhtamysh, Timur defeated the Golden Horde and subjected it to his rule. He then invaded Russia. His army captured the principality of Elets and advanced to the borders of Ryazan. After standing on the frontier of the Ryazan lands for two weeks, Timur left Russia.

The Tale of Temir Aksak, which has survived in several redactions and versions, in both chronicles and miscellanies, tells the story of Timur's campaign against Russia and Russia's deliverance from the terrible conqueror.

The most recent researcher on the *Tale,* Vassily Grebenyuk, dates the writing of the original work to the period between 1402 and 1408.[22] Of the published texts the one closest to the original is that in *The Sophia Second Chronicle.*

The *Tale* opens with the strife in the Horde and the arrival of Temir Aksak.[23] Then follows an account of who he is and why he is called by that name. Temir Aksak, we learn, "was not of royal birth: not a ruler's son, nor of a ruler's house, nor a prince's, nor a boyar's, only the lowliest of the low ... by trade he was a blacksmith, by temper and disposition pitiless, a robber, a violator, and a plunderer..." Temir Aksak's master got rid of him for "depravity". Having no sustenance Temir Aksak began to steal. One day he stole a sheep and was caught. He was almost beaten to death and had one of his legs broken. Temir Aksak "bound his broken leg with iron, which is why he limped and was nicknamed Temir Aksak, because 'Temir' means 'iron' and 'Aksak', a 'lame man'". Then it describes how Temir gathered a small band of young men as desperate as himself that grew and grew until eventually he began to conquer lands and was called a ruler.

The story of Temir Aksak forms the first half of the *Tale,* and is of oral origin. In the *Tale* this story was intended to draw a contrast between the lawful power of the Grand Prince of Moscow and the unlawful dominion of the rulers of the Horde.

The second part of the *Tale* describes the preparations in Moscow to resist the enemy, the transfer of the icon of the Virgin from Vladimir to Moscow and Temir Aksak's flight from Russia. In order to protect Moscow against the danger it is decided to bring the icon of the Virgin of Vladimir from Vladimir to Moscow. This icon, which was taken from Kiev to Vladimir by Andrew Bogolyubsky, was regarded as the patron icon of the Russian land.* The *Tale* describes the farewell to the icon in Vladimir "with lamenting and with tears" and its solemn reception in Moscow by the whole population. Then, on "the very day when the icon of the Holy Virgin was brought from Vladimir to Moscow, on the same day Temir Aksak, the ruler, took fright, and was struck with horror and dread, and fell into disarray, and fear and trepidation did come upon him, fear crept into his heart and terror into his soul, and trepidation into his bones". Overcome by this fear and trepidation, Temir Aksak fled with his army from the land of Russia.

The main ideological tendency of the *Tale* was to show how wisely the Prince of Moscow and the Metropolitan had acted in bringing the icon from Vladimir to Moscow, and to demonstrate that the wonder-working icon was particularly favourably disposed towards Moscow, thereby enhancing the national importance of Moscow. All this was of great political significance, not only for the historical episode in question, but for enhancing Moscow's national importance in the future.

In the latter half of the sixteenth century, on the basis of the different redactions and versions of the *Tale* a large compilation was made entitled *The Tale of the Icon of the Virgin of Vladimir*. Apart from *The Tale of Temir Aksak* the author of this work drew on a considerable number of other sources.

4. Hagiography

As in the preceding periods, together with chronicle-writing, hagiography remains one of the main literary genres which underwent a number of important changes during this period.

In the late fourteenth and early fifteenth century in the Slav countries (Bulgaria, Serbia and Russia) there was a flowering of the expressive-emotional style which we have already mentioned. Reflecting a common philosophical conception conditioned by Pre-Renaissance tendencies, this style, which originated in Byzantine traditions, was embodied in different ways in each country. It manifested itself most strikingly in hagiographical works.

Of considerable significance for the emergence and development of the panegyric style in Russia was the contact of Russian literature with that of Bulgaria and Serbia. But the emergence of this style in Russia cannot be explained solely as a result of the influence of South Slavonic literature on Russian literature (the so-called "Second South Slav Influence"). The process of the formation and development of the panegyric style took place amid the mutual interaction of the Slavonic cultures. A major part in this process was also played by these countries' relations with Byzantine culture both directly and (to an even greater extent)

---

* Now in the Tretyakov Gallery in Moscow.

through the Slavonic-Byzantine cultural centres: the monasteries of Constantinople, Thessalonica and the Holy Mountain (Mount Athos).[24]

In Russian hagiography the first manifestations of the expressive-emotional style are associated with the name of Metropolitan Cyprian. The style found most perfect and most original expression in the work of Epiphanius the Most Wise. The third representative of this literary trend was Pachomius the Logothete.

Cyprian. Cyprian, a Bulgarian, was a very learned man. He received an ecclesiastical and scholarly education in his homeland, in Byzantium and at Mount Athos. He was closely associated with his fellow-countryman Euthymius of Tyrnovo (1330-1402), the Bulgarian Patriarch, who was the founder and theoretician of the panegyric style in Bulgarian literature and reformed the orthographic system of the Bulgarian language.

In 1375 the Patriarchal Assembly of Constantinople appointed Cyprian Metropolitan of Lithuania with the right to inherit, after the death of Metropolitan Alexis, the Metropolitan See of All Russia. In 1378, the year of Alexis' death, a struggle began between several claimants for the metropolitan see, in which Cyprian took an active part. He was finally established as Metropolitan of All Russia in Moscow during the reign of Dmitry Donskoy's son in 1390.

Cyprian began to engage in literary activity when he was at Mount Athos and continued it right up to the end of his life (he died in 1406). As already mentioned, he played an important part in the compilation of the first All-Russian chronicle, translated from Greek, copied books and composed liturgical texts.

During his struggle for the metropolitan throne Cyprian turned to literature as a means of political struggle. On his initiative and, it would appear, with his direct participation *The Tale of Mityai* directed against Cyprian's main rival was written.[25] Politico-publicistic considerations also dictated Cyprian's new redaction of *The Life of Metropolitan Peter*, his major literary work. He wrote it in the 1380s, i.e., the period of struggle for the metropolitan throne.[26]

As a basis for his work Cyprian took the 1327 redaction of *The Life of Metropolitan Peter*. Under his pen the original short *vita*, written concisely and simply, without any rhetorical embellishment, was considerably lengthened and acquired a sumptuous literary form. In his brief foreword to the *Life* Cyprian defined the purpose of his work, saying that it was a eulogy to Peter. In keeping with the canons of the genre Cyprian added a foreword and conclusion, which did not exist in the original.

Cyprian's redaction of the *Life* is close to the *vitae* of the panegyric style. But first and foremost his work had political and publicistic aims. Here, even more strongly than in the 1327 redaction, the greatness of Moscow is stressed and its national importance as the political and ecclesiastical centre of the Russian lands. Cyprian not only extols Peter and the Prince of Moscow, but also seeks to assert his right to the metropolitan throne of All Russia. Cyprian's life had much in common with Peter's (competing for the metropolitan see, clashes with opponents after his appointment as metropolitan, and the transfer from Lithuania to Moscow), and by so doing he seems to be ranking himself with Peter. In the eulogy to Peter, which concludes the *vita*, Cyprian recounts the story of Peter's appointment as metropolitan in detail, depicting Peter as his protector and patron. This "autobiographical element" in Cyprian's *Life of Metropolitan Peter* reflects the new attitude in literature towards the author.

Cyprian's *Life of Metropolitan Peter* was clearly publicistic. But in terms of structure, imagery and language it is akin to the works of the expressive-emotional style.

Epiphanius the Most Wise. Epiphanius was born in Rostov in the first half of the fourteenth century. In 1379 he became a monk in a Rostov monastery. Later he moved to the Trinity Monastery of St Sergius. He visited Jerusalem and Mount Athos and most probably travelled in the Orient. He died in the 1420s. Because of his erudition and literary skill he became known as "the Most Wise". Two *vitae* belong to his pen: *The Life of St Stephen of Perm*, written in 1396-1398, and *The Life of St Sergius of Radonezh*, written between 1417 and 1418.

In the author's foreword to *The Life of Metropolitan Peter*, as already mentioned, Cyprian says that the *vita* was to serve as an embellishment for the saint. Epiphanius' *Life of St Stephen of Perm* is a fine example of the *vita* embellishment, the eulogy to a saint.

In this work Epiphanius' views on the literary tasks of the hagiographer are reflected most fully and clearly. Ordinary words are incapable of expressing the greatness of the deeds done by holy men to the glory of Christ, but the author of a story about a saint is a common mortal. And so, appealing to God for help and relying on the protection of the saint whom he is extolling, the hagiographer strives to use the ordinary devices of language so as to make the reader see the saint as a person of a completely different spiritual type from other people. Therefore linguistic artifice is not an aim in itself but a device with the help of which the author is able to extol the hero of his narrative in worthy fashion.

At the beginning of the *vita* (and this is particularly characteristic of works in the panegyric style) the author speaks of his literary talents in the most self-denigrating terms. In one such tirade he writes that he is "coarse of mind" and thick of tongue, that he is not versed in rhetoric, philosophy, or bookish wisdom, the "braiding of words" and, to put it simply, he is full of ignorance.[27] The author's professed lack of learning and ignorance contradict the rest of the text, in which his erudition and ability to use the devices of rhetoric manifest themselves fully. This is a clever literary device with the same aim, that of praising and extolling the saint. If the author of a *vita*, whose writing showed him to be highly learned and a master of the art of rhetoric, never tired of saying how worthless he was, the person who read or heard the *vita* was bound to feel even more worthless before the saint's greatness. Moreover the author's confession of his ignorance and literary inability which contradicted the actual text was intended to create the impression that what he had written was a kind of Divine revelation, inspiration from on high.

In *The Life of St Stephen of Perm* Epiphanius achieves true virtuosity in his eulogy of Stephen. His selection of poetic devices and the compositional structure of the text are a well-planned, carefully elaborated literary system.[28] In his writing the traditional poetic devices of mediaeval hagiography are made more complex and enriched with new shades. The frequent use of amplification, the strings of similes and metaphors, the speech rhythms, and assonance make the text very moving and expressive.

Epiphanius on several occasions defines the nature of the writer's work as the "braiding of words". This definition conveys very well the ornamental nature and verbal refinement of Epiphanius' style and the expressive-emotional style in general.

The "braiding" of the eulogy to the saint is the main purpose of *The Life of St Stephen of Perm*. Nevertheless this eulogy to the missionary of the Perm lands also contains lifelike sketches and historical facts. These are particularly evident in the descriptions of the ordinary life of the people of Perm, the stories about their idols and their hunting skill, and Epiphanius' discourses on the relations between Moscow and Perm. The long central section of the *Life*, the story of Stephen's struggle against the Perm magician Pam, is like an adventure story full of vivid sketches and lively scenes.

Epiphanius' second work, *The Life of St Sergius of Radonezh*, is of a more narrative nature than *The Life of St Stephen*. It is far simpler stylistically and contains more factual material. Many episodes in *The Life of St Sergius* have a distinctive lyrical quality (the story of the childhood of the boy Bartholomew, who took the name of Sergius when he became a monk, the episode in which Bartholomew's parents beg him not to enter a monastery until

Epiphanius the Most Wise Compiling the Life of St Sergius of Radonezh.
16th-century illumination. State Lenin Library, Moscow

they die, so that he will be able to look after them in their old age, etc.) [29]

Whereas in *The Life of St Stephen of Perm* Epiphanius shows himself to be a brilliant stylist, in *The Life of St Sergius* he appears as a master of the narrative. *The Life of St Sergius* was extremely popular in mediaeval times and later due largely to Sergius' remarkable moral qualities which won him great authority in Old Russia (as we know Dmitry Donskoy came to him at the Trinity Monastery before the Battle of Kulikovo for approval of his decision to do battle with Mamai), and has survived in a large number of manuscripts.

Pachomius the Logothete. In the works of Epiphanius the Most Wise the expressive-emotional style reached its height. In the third exponent of this style in hagiography, Pachomius the Logothete, it acquired an official nature. The *vitae* written by Pachomius became models for all subsequent official hagiographies. We cannot deny Pachomius' literary ability. He was a very prolific writer. He was perhaps Russia's first professional writer: the chronicle tells us that Pachomius received remuneration for his literary activity and was invited to work in various centres of learning. The mediaeval scholars admired his hagiographical skill. But Pachomius' writing was very rational in nature. He aimed at standardising the exposition in hagiographical works and bringing their texts into line with the formal requirements of the genre.

Born in Serbia, Pachomius the Logothete began his literary activity in the 1430s in Novgorod, under Archbishop Euthymius II of Novgorod. Later he worked in Moscow, the Trinity Monastery of St Sergius and the White Lake Monastery, subsequently returning to Novgorod. He is thought to have died in the 1480s. He is the author of several original *vitae*, of which the best is *The Life of St Cyril of the White Lake*. Apart from *vitae*, he also wrote a number of eulogies and services for saints. Pachomius' main activity as an hagiographer, however, was his reworking of existing *vitae* with the aim of making them more rhetorical and closer to the canons of the genre.[30]

As Vasily Klyuchevsky points out, "Pachomius the Logothete laid down set devices for the biography of a saint and for his glorification in church and gave Russian hagiography many examples of the smooth, slightly cold and monotonous style that was easy to imitate with a very limited amount of scholarship."[31]

5. Panegyrical Works

The Eulogy of the Life and Death of Grand Prince Dmitry, Son of Ivan. Stylistically *The Eulogy of the Life and Death of Grand Prince Dmitry, Son of Ivan, and Tsar of Russia* belongs to hagiographical works of the expressive-emotional style. It is a eulogy to Dmitry Donskoy. At the end of his work the author announces with the self-denigration customary for the genre: "But I, unworthy one, because of the poverty of my mind have been unable to compose a eulogy worthy of a prince and a Christian."[32] In style and composition the *Eulogy* is akin to the works of Epiphanius the Most Wise.[33]

There are different opinions about when the *Eulogy* was written. Most specialists date it to the 1390s, assuming that it was written by someone who witnessed the death and burial of the prince (who died in 1389). Varvara Adrianova-Peretts suggests the 1420s, and Marina Salmina the end of the 1440s, linking its appearance with the 1448 compilation.[34] These dates are hypothetical and so far it is impossible to give preference to any of them.

The author shows little interest in biographical facts about Dmitry Donskoy and historical information. At the beginning he traces Dmitry's parentage back to Grand Prince Vladimir I and stresses that he was related to the princes Boris and Gleb. The Battle on the Vozha and the Battle of Kulikovo Field are mentioned. Both in these and other sections of the *Tale* which deal with concrete events, there is not so much an account of them as a generalised description. The main content of the *Eulogy* are eulogies to Dmitry and the author's complex philosophical discourses on the prince's greatness. He compares his hero with Biblical characters, stressing his superiority to them. In these comparisons Dmitry is represented as the greatest ruler that the world has ever known.

The lament by Dmitry's wife, Princess Eudoxia, is deeply lyrical and shows the influence of the traditional widow's lament: "How could you die, my precious life, leaving me a lonely widow! Why did I not perish earlier? The light has gone out of my eyes! Where have you gone, treasure of my life? Why do you not speak to me, dear heart, to your wife?" Eudoxia's lament was very popular with Old Russian scribes, who often reworked it introducing tales about the death of other princes.

The character and content of *The Eulogy of the Life of Grand Prince Dmitry* were determined by the style of *The Book of Degrees of the Tsar's Genealogy,* one of the most important ideological literary works of the sixteenth century.[35] In its panegyric style *The Eulogy to Prince Boris of Tver* resembles the *Lay*.

Embroidered cloth on the tomb of St Sergius of Radonezh. 1424. Zagorsk State
Museum-Preserve of History and Art

The Eulogy to Prince Boris of Tver by the monk Thomas. The mid-fifteenth-century specimen of Tver literature, *The Eulogy to Prince Boris of Tver* written by the monk Thomas, is a striking example of the expressive-emotional style. In its lofty rhetoric and certain literary devices it resembles *The Eulogy of the Life of Grand Prince Dmitry.* But Thomas departs even further than the author of the latter from the hagiographical genre and greatly enhances the publicistic element in his work. It is a eulogy to the greatness and might of Prince Boris of Tver (1425-1461) and the principality of Tver. We know nothing of Thomas himself. He wrote the *Eulogy* circa 1453.[36]

The *Eulogy* consists of six parts (the sixth part breaks off after the first few lines).[37] Thematically and compositionally each part is independent. They are joined by a single idea and a single style. The main idea of all the parts is that Prince Boris of Tver is an "autocrat" worthy of ruling the whole Russian land. He possesses all the virtues, cares for his subjects, and is a bold and skilled military commander. Like the author of *The Eulogy of the Life of Grand Prince Dmitry,* Thomas compares Boris of Tver with famous historical figures and Biblical characters, rating him above them.

In his work Thomas seeks to stress the complete agreement between Tver and Moscow, to persuade the reader that there was friendship between Prince Boris of Tver and Grand Prince Basil the Blind of Moscow. The Prince of Tver plays the dominant role in this alliance.

The *Eulogy* is written in a lofty rhetorical style. Yet behind the skilfully constructed rhetorical passages one senses real human feeling and drama. Take the episode when Basil, who has been blinded and driven out of the principality of Moscow, arrives in Tver from Vologda. The two princes weep on meeting. Basil is moved by Boris' charity, and Boris grieved by the degradation of the Prince of Moscow: "Formerly he had beheld his brother, the Grand Prince Basil, handsome and comely, adorned with a sovereign's dignity, but now he was humiliated and impoverished, profaned by his own brothers." The wives of the princes also weep. Their lament continues even at table: "In the same way did the Grand Princess Anastasia with the Grand Princess Maria take each other by the hand and go to the same feast and sit down to eat. But when they should have been eating and drinking and making merry, they did shed tears instead of merry-making."

The *Eulogy* shows that its author, the monk Thomas, was extremely well-read. He makes use of images and expressions from many works of different periods and styles, for example, *The Tale of Bygone Years,* Hilarion's *Sermon on Law and Grace,* Cyril of Turov's *Sermons, The Life of Alexander Nevsky,* the works of the Kulikovo cycle and other monuments.

Thomas the monk's *Eulogy* reflects the idea of the creation of an autocratic Russian state, but the ideal autocrat here is the Prince of Tver, to whom the Grand Prince of Moscow is junior. This explains why the *Tale* was not included in official Moscow literature and has survived in one manuscript only thanks to sheer luck.

6. Historical Legends

In terms of genre the historical legends that were widespread in the fourteenth and first half of the fifteenth century stand somewhere between the *vita* and the tale. Dealing with a single person and in a single text, they were read and intended as *vitae.* An example is *The Life of Archbishop John of Novgorod.* At the same time some episodes in Lives of saints had arisen independently and were inserted in these Lives later as historical legends, such as many of the episodes in the expanded redaction of *The Life of St Barlaam of Khutyn.* In historical legends real events are given a mystical interpretation. Below we shall examine the cycle of historical legends about Archbishop John of Novgorod as an example of this genre.

The Cycle of Legends About John of Novgorod. The Archbishop of Novgorod played an important role in the political and ideological life of the republic. The first Novgorodian Archbishop (before him the highest church dignitary there was the bishop) was John. John (Archbishop from 1165 to 1186) was extremely popular with the people of Novgorod both during his lifetime and after his death. Several legends belonging to different periods are connected with him. These are *The Legend of the Battle of the Novgorodians with the Suzdalians, The Legend of John's Journey to Jerusalem on a Devil's Back, The Legend of the Finding of John's Relics* and *The Legend of the Church of the Annunciation.* We shall examine the first two, which are the most interesting in terms of literary merit.[38]

The Legend of the Battle of the Novgorodians with the Suzdalians. The subject of this legend is the campaign against Novgorod in 1170 by the Suzdalians led by Mstislav (the son of Andrew Bogolyubsky), which ended in the victory of the Novgorodians. It is based on a folk legend and the short chronicle record of this event in *The Novgorod First Chronicle.* As a written work it appeared in the 1340s or 1350s.[39]

Novgorod was besieged by the Suzdalians. Archbishop John prayed at night in his cell for the town to be saved. He heard a voice telling him to carry onto the town battlements the icon of Our Lady from the church in Ilyina Street (the Church of Our Saviour in Ilyina Street with frescoes painted by Theophanes the Greek in the late fourteenth century). During the storming of the town the icon, which had been placed on the town wall facing the besiegers, was hit by arrows. It turned to face the town and wept.[40] Darkness descended upon the Suzdalians, and they killed one another.

The *Legend* gives a striking description of the church procession that carried the icon onto the battlements of the besieged town. The arrogance and complacency of the Suzdalians is stressed by the statement that they had already divided up the streets of Novgorod between themselves for looting and killing the townspeople. To stop the Virgin's tears falling on the ground John collects them in his robe.

These striking images made a strong impression on all those

who read or heard the *Legend*, as can be seen from the portrayal of this subject in Old Novgorodian painting. We know of two fifteenth-century icons and several later ones in which this subject is depicted. On the icons (which are known as the *Sign from the Icon of the Virgin* to specialists) the episodes are depicted in chronological order. The finest artistically is the icon of the middle or latter half of the fifteenth century now in the Novgorod Museum.[41]

The Legend of John of Novgorod's Journey to Jerusalem on a Devil's Back. The legend of John's journey on a devil's back appears to have arisen very early, but it is impossible to establish when the story based on this legend was written (it was probably not later than 1440, when John was made a locally revered saint).

One night when John is praying in his cell a devil decides to frighten him and distract him from his devotions: he creeps into the saintly man's water-pot and begins splashing about in it.* John makes the sign of the cross over the water-pot and trapped the devil inside it. In return for his release the devil carries John to Jerusalem and back in one night on condition that John shall not tell anyone about the journey. But John accidentally lets out the secret, although he does not mention his own name. The devil gets his revenge on the saint: assuming the guise of a young maiden he walks out of the Archbishop's cell for all to see, and when some high-ranking townspeople come to visit John, the devil bewitches them into thinking they can see some articles of female apparel in the Archbishop's cell. The Novgorodians accuse their spiritual pastor of fornication and decide to drive him out of the town. John is put on a raft and the raft pushed off down the River Volkhov. But the raft, although unnavigated, floats upstream to the St George Monastery. Persuaded of John's innocence and realising that their suspicions were the work of the devil, the Novgorodians walk along the bank after the raft, begging John to return to Novgorod.

The legend of how John trapped a devil with the sign of the cross and made him serve him originated in Old Russian folklore. This motif is widespread in the folklore of many countries.

The *Legend* reflects features of Novgorodian everyday life and is full of local colour. It stands out for its dynamic, exciting plot and realistic portrayal of events. The fact itself is miraculous, but it is conveyed with lively, realistic detail. This brings the story of John's journey on a devil's back close to the realm of fairy tale.

---

* An old copper water-pot said to have belonged to John is now in the Novgorod Museum in the Cathedral of St Nicholas in the Dvorishche.

The Battle of the Novgorodians with the Suzdalians. Second half of 15th century. Detail of another icon

The description of the devil's revenge is very reminiscent of the fairy tale in its humour and cunning.

The episode of a devil being trapped in a vessel is also found in the Old Russian *Life of Abraham of Rostov* (fifteenth century). There is an account of a devil's revenge which is similar in a number of respects to the corresponding section of John's journey on a devil's back, in the Old Russian *Tale of Bishop Basil of Murom* (mid-sixteenth century). Both these monuments are secondary in relation to *The Legend of John of Novgorod*.

A characteristic feature of Novgorodian historical legends is their peculiar "authenticity". They not only tell of concrete historical personages and events, but are confirmed by "material evidence", e.g., the icon that was carried onto the town walls in 1170 and John's water-pot.

The historical legends of old Novgorod have survived mostly in *vitae* and the Novgorodian chronicles. As Dmitry Likhachev remarks, the most popular and widespread legends that everyone knew "did not need to be recorded and written down in manuscript form... Only the need to use a legend in the liturgy or in the chronicle, to give it literary form, could save it from oblivion." [42] This gives us grounds for assuming that in oral tradition, and possibly in a written form no longer extant, there was a vast number of legends of which only a few have survived in the form of historical legends.

The literature of the fourteenth and the first half of the fifteenth century reflects the events and ideology of the period when the principalities of North-Eastern Russia were uniting around Moscow, the period of the formation of the Russian nation and the gradual emergence of the Russian centralised state.

As in the preceding periods the main literary genres were chronicle-writing and hagiography. The travel genre was revived. The genre of historical legends, that brought the hagiographical genre closer to the fictional narrative, became widespread. Historical tales and legends were created both in chronicle-writing and independently of it and are most widely represented by the works of the Kulikovo cycle.

During this period chronicle-writing developed intensively and the political and publicistic importance of chronicles grew. Chronicle-writing assumed an All-Russian character, and Moscow became its centre. The Moscow chronicles included much material from chronicles of all the Russian lands and also non-chronicle material, such as tales, legends, *vitae* and official documents. Chronicle-writing became a powerful ideological weapon in the political struggle to unify the Russian lands around Moscow and create a single centralised state.

The works of the Kulikovo cycle occupy a special place in the literary history of this period. These works are noteworthy not only because they reflect such an important event in Russian history, but also because of their literary significance. *The Trans-Doniad* revived the poetic traditions of the greatest work of Old Russian literature, *The Lay of Igor's Host*, while *The Tale of the Battle Against Mamai* marked the beginning of a new type of historical narrative, the lengthy, non-chronicle story of an historical event, a story which combined hagiographical, military-heroic, rhetorical and publicistic elements together with an attempt to make the event depicted appear as exciting as possible.

Pre-Renaissance features of this period are felt most strongly in hagiography. Interest in man and his spiritual world led to a growth of the subjective element in literature, the desire to portray man's psychological state. The expressive-emotional style emerged in hagiography.

Interest in the hero's inner world did not yet lead to attempts to portray individual human character. The revealing of the hero's psychological states and emotional experiences did not become a reflection of the individual in question, but remained an abstract expression of the qualities that the person was supposed to possess as the representative of a certain class, as the bearer of good or evil. This explains the oversimplified, one-sided descriptions of heroes and their behaviour. But at the same time writers did introduce elements of a concrete, personal nature in the portrayal of this or that generalised image.

The characteristic features of the literature of the fourteenth and first half of the fifteenth century were to find further development and even greater flowering in the second half of the fifteenth and beginning of the sixteenth century.

REFERENCES

[1] For more detail see: Лихачев Д. С. "Возрождение в средневековье". *Русская литература*, No. 4, 1973, pp. 114-118.

[2] Лихачев Д. С. *Развитие русской литературы X-XVII веков. Эпохи и стили*, p. 91. For more detail about the Russian Pre-Renaissance see the above-mentioned work by Dmitry Likhachev and his study *Поэтика древнерусской литературы* and *Человек в литературе Древней Руси*.

[3] Лихачев Д. С. *Культура Руси времени Андрея Рублева и Епифания Премудрого*. Moscow and Leningrad, 1962, p. 116.

[4] On the text of *The Laurentian Chronicle* see: Приселков М. Д. "Лаврентьевская летопись (история текста)". *Ученые записки Ленинградского университета*, No. 32, Book 2, 1939, pp. 76-142; Насонов А. Н. "Лаврентьевская летопись и Владимирское великокняжеское летописание первой половины XIII в.". *Проблемы источниковедения*, No. II, 1963, pp. 428-480.

[5] The only known copy of Vladimir Monomachos' *Instruction* is in *The Laurentian Chronicle*. None of the other surviving chronicles deriving from the 1305 compilation contain the *Instruction*.

[6] The hypothetical text of *The Trinity Chronicle* has been reconstructed by Mikhail Priselkov on the basis of passages quoted from it by Nikolai Karamzin, extracts from it published before the fire of 1812, and information in the *Laurentian, Simeon* and *Resurrection* chronicles. See: Приселков М. Д. *Троицкая летописъ. Реконструкция текста.* Moscow and Leningrad, 1950. *The Vladimir Chronicle* and *The West Russian (Byelorussian First) Chronicle* can now be used for reconstructing *The Trinity Chronicle*. See: Лурье Я. С. "Троицкая летопись и московское летописание XIV в.". *Вспомогательъные исторические дисциплины,* Vol. VI, 1974, pp. 84-91.

[7] Лихачев Д. С. *Русские летописи и их кулътурно-историческое значение,* p. 346. See also: Творогов О. В. "К истории жанра Хронографа". *ТОДРЛ,* Vol. XXVII, 1972, pp. 203-226.

[8] Творогов О. В. *Древнерусские хронографы.* Chapters 1 and 5.

[9] For the texts of the works of the Kulikovo cycle see: *Сказания и повести о Куликовской битве.* Edited by L. A. Dmitriev and O. P. Likhacheva; *ПЛДР. XIV-середина XV века,* pp. 96-189.

[10] For a detailed study of the question of the date of *The Trans-Doniad* see: Дмитриев Л. А. "Литературная история памятников Куликовского цикла". In the book: *Сказания и повести о Куликовской битве,* pp. 309-311, 324-330.

[11] Many attempts have been made to reconstruct the text of *The Trans-Doniad.* The text is quoted from the edition: *Сказания и повести о Куликовской битве.* See also: *ПЛДР. XIV-середина XV века,* pp. 96-111.

[12] Лихачев Д. С. *Национальное самосознание Древней Руси.* Moscow and Leningrad, 1945, p. 76.

[13] The theory that apart from the surviving works of the Kulikovo cycle there was *The Lay of the Battle Against Mamai*, which did not survive and was reflected in both *The Trans-Doniad* and the *Tale*, belongs to Alexei Shakhmatov. See: Шахматов А. А. *Отзыв о сочинении С. К. Шамбинаго. "Повести о Мамаевом побоище".* St Petersburg, 1910. The view that Sophonius of Ryazan could not have been the author of *The Trans-Doniad*, but was the author of *The Lay of the Battle Against Mamai* is argued by Rufina Dmitrieva. See: Дмитриева Р. П. "Был ли Софоний автором *Задонщины?*" *ТОДРЛ,* Vol. XXXIV, 1979, pp. 18-25.

[14] Салмина М. А. "Летописная повесть о Куликовской битве и *Задон-щине*". In the book: *"Слово о полку Игореве" и памятники Куликовского цикла,* pp. 344-384.

[15] For the illuminated manuscripts of *The Tale of the Battle Against Mamai* see: Дмитриев Л. А. "Миниатюры *Сказания о Мамаевом побоище*". *ТОДРЛ,* Vol. XXII, 1966, pp. 239-263; Дмитриев Л. А. "Лондонский лицевой список *Сказания о Мамаевом побоище*". *ТОДРЛ,* Vol. XXVIII, 1974, pp. 155-179; Дмитриев Л. А. Introductory article to the book: *Сказание о Мамаевом побоище. Лицевой список конца XVII века.* Leningrad, 1980, pp. 5-26; Лихачев Д. С. "Куликовская битва в миниатюрах XVI века". In the book: *Повестъ о Куликовской битве. Из Лицевого летописного свода XVI века.* Leningrad, 1980, pp. 171-177.

[16] It is interesting that already in the early period of the history of the work the name of Olgierd was replaced by that of Jagiello in some redactions of the *Tale*

in the interests of historical accuracy. For more detail see: Дмитриев Л. А. "О датировке *Сказания о Мамаевом побоище*". *ТОДРЛ*, Vol. X, 1954, pp. 185-199.

¹⁷ Дмитриев Л. А. 1) "О датировке *Сказания о Мамаевом побоище*"; 2) "Литературная история памятников Куликовского цикла". In the book: *Сказания и повести о Куликовской битве*, pp. 306-359.

¹⁸ Салмина М. А. "Летописная повесть о Куликовской битве и *Задонщина*". In the book: *"Слово о полку Игореве" и памятники Куликовского цикла*, pp. 344-384; Салмина М. А. "К вопросу о датировке *Сказания о Мамаевом побоище*". *ТОДРЛ*, Vol. XXIX, 1974, pp. 98-124; Бегунов Ю. К. "Об исторической основе *Сказания о Мамаевом побоище*". In the book: *"Слово о полку Игореве" и памятники Куликовского цикла*, pp. 477-523; Мингалев В. С. *"Сказание о Мамаевом побоище" и его источники*. Abstract of a dissertation for the degree of Candidate of Historical Sciences. Moscow and Vilnius, 1971; Кучкин В. А. "Победа на Куликовом поле". *Вопросы истории*, No. 8, 1980, pp. 3-21.

¹⁹ There are also other types of chronicle tales about Tokhtamysh's campaign that are older in origin than the two above-mentioned forms of the work. Thus, for example, *The Ermolin Chronicle* has a condensed version of the extended version of the *Tale*.

²⁰ This point of view is argued in a special article by M. A. Salmina. See: Салмина М. А. *"Повесть о нашествии Тохтамыша"*. *ТОДРЛ*, Vol. XXXIV, 1979, pp. 134-151.

²¹ For the text of *The Tale of Tokhtamysh's Campaign* see: *ПЛДР. XIV-середина XV века*, pp. 190-207.

²² Гребенюк В. П. *"Повесть о Темир-Аксаке* и ее литературная судьба в XVI-XVII веках". In the book: *Русская литература на рубеже двух эпох (XVII-начало XVIII в.)*. Moscow, 1971, pp. 185-206.

²³ For the text of the *Tale* see: *ПЛДР. XIV-середина XV века*, pp. 230-243.

²⁴ Лихачев Д. С. *Культура Руси времени Андрея Рублева и Епифания Премудрого*, pp. 30-93; Мошин В. А. "О периодизации русско-южно-славянских литературных связей X-XV вв.". *ТОДРЛ*, Vol. XIX, 1963, pp. 28-106; Дуйчев И. С. "Центры византийско-славянского общения и сотрудничества". *ТОДРЛ*, Vol. XIX, 1963, pp. 107-129; Дмитриев Л. А. "Нерешенные вопросы происхождения и истории экспрессивно-эмоционального стиля XV в.". *ТОДРЛ*, Vol. XX, 1964, pp. 72-89.

²⁵ Прохоров Г. М. *"Повесть о Митяе". (Русь и Византия в эпоху Куликовской битвы.)* Leningrad, 1978.

²⁶ Дмитриев Л. А. "Роль и значение митрополита Киприана в истории древнерусской литературы". *ТОДРЛ*, Vol. XIX, 1963, pp. 215-254.

²⁷ *Житие святого Стефана, епископа пермского, написанное Епифанием Премудрым*. Published by the Archaeographical Commission. St Petersburg, 1897.

²⁸ Коновалова О. Ф. *Панегирический стиль русской литературы конца XIV-начала XV века (на материале "Жития Стефана Пермского", написанного Епифанием Премудрым)*. Abstract of a dissertation for the degree of Candidate of Philological Sciences. Leningrad, 1970.

²⁹ For the text of the *Life* see: *ПЛДР. XIV-середина XV века*, pp. 256-430.

³⁰ For a monograph study of Pachomius see: Яблонский В. *Пахомий Серб и его агиографические писания*. St Petersburg, 1908; see also: Орлов Г. "Похомије Србин и његова књижевна делатност у Великом Новгороду". Прилози на књижевност, језик, историју и фолклор, кн. XXXVI, св. 3-4, Belgrade, 1970.

[31] Ключевский В. О. *Древнерусские жития святых как исторический источник.* Moscow, 1871, p. 166.

[32] For the text of the *Tale* see: *ПЛДР. XIV-середина XV века,* pp. 208-229.

[33] Адрианова-Перетц В. П. *"Слово о житии и о преставлении великого князя Дмитрия Ивановича, царя русьскаго".* *ТОДРЛ,* Vol. V, 1947, pp. 73-96. Developing Varvara Adrianova-Peretts' idea of the similarity of the *Tale* to Epiphanius' writing, Alexei Soloviev concluded that the *Tale* was written by Epiphanius in the 1390s, before he wrote the *vitae* of St Stephen and St Sergius. See: Соловьев А. В. *"Епифаний Премудрый как автор Слова о житии и о преставлении великого князя Дмитрия Ивановича, царя русьскаго".* *ТОДРЛ,* Vol. XVII, 1961, pp. 85-106.

[34] Салмина М. А. *"Слово о житии и о преставлении великого князя Дмитрия Ивановича, царя русьскаго".* *ТОДРЛ,* Vol. XXV, 1970, pp. 81-104. On the compilation of 1448 see below, pp. 303-05.

[35] Орлов А. С. *Древняя русская литература XI-XVI вв.,* p. 216.

[36] All the historical information in the *Tale* is not later than this date. It mentions Shemyaka's flight to Novgorod, but does not refer to his death (he died on July 17, 1453). See: Инока Фомы *"Слово похвальное о благоверном великом князе Борисе Александровиче".* A communication by N. P. Likhachev, published by *Общество любителей древней письменности (ОЛДП).* See also: Лурье Я. С. *"Роль Твери в создании Русского национального государства".* *Ученые записки Ленинградского университета,* 1939, No. 36, Book 3, pp. 85-109.

[37] For the text of the *Eulogy* see: *ПЛДР. Вторая половина XV века.* Moscow, 1983, pp. 268-333.

[38] For the texts of legends about John of Novgorod see: *ПЛДР. XIV-середина XV века,* pp. 448-467.

[39] Дмитриев Л. А. *Житийные повести русского Севера как памятники литературы XIII-XVII вв.* Leningrad, 1973, pp. 129-131.

[40] Dmitry Likhachev suggests a rational explanation for this. The icon of Our Lady of the Sign (which is now in the Novgorod Museum) was fixed to a pole and carried onto the town wall as a patronal icon. It really was hit by an arrow (of which it still bears the traces), and the blow could have made the icon swivel on its axis.

[41] Порфиридов Н. Г. *Древний Новгород.* Moscow and Leningrad, 1947, p. 296; Лазарев В. Н. *Новгородская иконопись.* Moscow, 1969, pp. 35-36, tables 51-53; Смирнова Э. С., Лаурина В. К., Гордиенко Э. А. *Живопись Великого Новгорода. XV век.* Moscow, 1982.

[42] *История русской литературы,* Vol. II, Part 1, Moscow and Leningrad, 1945, p. 261.

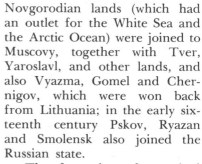

CHAPTER 5

LITERATURE OF THE SECOND HALF OF THE FIFTEENTH CENTURY

The second half of the fifteenth century saw the formation of a united Russian state. Novgorod and the extensive

Novgorodian lands (which had an outlet for the White Sea and the Arctic Ocean) were joined to Muscovy, together with Tver, Yaroslavl, and other lands, and also Vyazma, Gomel and Chernigov, which were won back from Lithuania; in the early sixteenth century Pskov, Ryazan and Smolensk also joined the Russian state.

The formation of a united national state, the abolition of feudal disunity, and the strengthening of the monarchy were not only characteristic of Russia in the fifteenth century: the same processes took place at that time in England, France, Spain, Denmark and other states. This is roughly the period of the Renaissance and a little later the Reformation in Western Europe. The Renaissance was, first and foremost, the victory of the secular trend in culture over the religious, the widespread introduction of secular subjects (including comical and satirical ones) from folklore into written literature, and a turning to the pre-Christian culture of Greece and Rome. A little later the widespread movement within the Catholic Church known as the Reformation began (in Germany, England and the North European countries, and in parts of France and Poland), the main consequence of which was the destruction of the monasteries and monasticism and the simplification and translation into national languages (from Latin) of church services.

Was the formation of a single state in Russia in the fifteenth and sixteenth centuries connected with the Renaissance and Reformation movements? The political changes of the fifteenth and sixteenth centuries coincided with profound changes in Russian culture. The fifteenth century saw the flowering of Russian architecture. The stone Moscow Kremlin which stands today is almost entirely a creation of the late fifteenth and the early sixteenth century. Icon-painting developed (the great Dionysius painted at the end of the fifteenth century). Important changes also took place during this period in Russian letters: expensive parchment was finally replaced by the much cheaper paper; it is in paper manuscripts no earlier than the fifteenth century that nearly all the works of Old Russian secular literature have survived. We have already noted Pre-Renaissance features in Russian culture of the fourteenth century. By the end of the fifteenth certain phenomena in Russian literature distinctly resembled those of the Renaissance and Reformation in Western Europe.

The fifteenth century, particularly the second half, saw a sharp increase in the number of secular works in Old Russian literature. There appeared translations (mostly Russian adaptations of South Slavonic texts) of mediaeval tales of chivalry and adventure. The first original works of Russian fictional narrative appeared.

We even know the name of a man who lovingly collected and copied this secular literature. It was a monk at the White Lake Monastery of St Cyril, the talented late-fifteenth-century scribe Euphrosyne. It was he who transcribed the oldest extant manuscripts of *The Trans-Doniad*, and *The Tale of the Indian Empire* and also a number of fifteenth-century works of fictional narrative: *Solomon and Kitovras*, the *Alexandreid, The Tale of Dracula*, verse condemning drunkenness, etc. In some cases Euphrosyne has obviously revised the work, compiling his own versions of chronicles and chronographs. Well aware that many of the works that came into his possession were considered "of little use" and "false" and even included in the special lists of books proscribed by the church, Euphrosyne copied these works notwithstanding, advising his readers not to read them in company and not to show them to "many". Euphrosyne does not appear to have been a heretic or opponent of the church, but the range of his interests extended far beyond the limits set by official church ideology. In Euphrosyne's manuscripts we also find tales of utopian lands inhabited by happy people (Brahmins) who have "no king, no nobles, no theft and no robbery..." [1]

The fifteenth century was a time of heretical activity in Russia. Already by the late fourteenth and early fifteenth century the heresy of the Strigolniks (Shearers) appeared in Novgorod and Pskov, which attacked the greed of the clergy and appointment to ecclesiastical office in return for bribes. The name of this heresy would appear to be connected with the fact that its supporters did not recognise the former taking of monastic vows *(postrig)* and took them afresh.[2] In the late fifteenth and the early sixteenth century heresy became widespread in Novgorod and Moscow. Novgorod and Pskov, where heresy first arose, were free cities, feudal republics where the townspeople were very active and played an important part in political life. In Novgorod heresy was widespread mainly among the lower clergy and minor church officers who had close links with the urban populace. Then heresy spread to Moscow and other cities. In Moscow it found support mainly in secular circles, beginning with the grand prince's secretary Fyodor Kuritsyn and including some lower-ranking members of the administration. We know that they included a merchant. The heretics not only strove for reform of the church, but also showed great interest in secular culture; the books that circulated among them included Greek and Roman works. One of the chief heretics, Fyodor Kuritsyn, who dealt with foreign policy matters under Ivan III, was the author of a philosophical and grammatical treatise entitled *The Laodicean Epistle.*[3]

A most important element of Novgorodian-Muscovite heresy in the late fifteenth and the early sixteenth century was the rejection of monasticism and monasteries (in so doing the heretics quoted the Bible which contains no references to monasticism) and also criticism of the doctrine of the Trinity and the worship of icons. Some of the bolder heretics even went so far as to deny life in the hereafter, i.e., views of an almost atheistic nature.[4]

The influence of heresy on the culture of the late fifteenth century was considerable. In his *Laodicean Epistle* Fyodor Kuritsyn argued that man's soul was "autonomous", and was defended by faith. But what does this "autonomy" mean? Another work similar to *The Laodicean Epistle* and entitled *The Writing on Literacy* says that a person's "autonomy" is realised in literacy: "Literacy is autonomy."[5] It is possible that Kuritsyn was also the author of one of the oldest known extant works of Old Russian fictional narrative, *The Tale of Dracula* (see below).

For a while the heretical movement in Russia received the support of the grand prince, who was himself striving to wrest the large land holdings away from the monasteries. But in the final analysis heresy seemed to threaten princely power too. The heretics were attacked by the leading churchmen of the late

fifteenth and the early sixteenth century, Abbot Joseph of the Volokolamsk Monastery and a monk of the White Lake Monastery of St Cyril, Nilus of Sora. The literary work of these two men differed greatly. Joseph was, first and foremost, a defender of monasticism and supporter of large monasteries where the monks were not supposed to have any personal possessions and lived at the expense of the villages and peasants that belonged to the monastery. Nilus of Sora favoured a different form of monastic organisation: small retreats with separate cells for two or three people. Above all he concerned himself with perfecting the monastic way of life and studying the monks' inner psychological state. In the struggle against heresy they were united, however, and Nilus of Sora even helped Joseph to write his main anti-heretical work, *The Enlightener.*

The early reformationist movement in Russia was unsuccessful because the basis of the reformationist movements of the late Middle Ages (as can be seen from West European history) were the towns, and in the fifteenth and sixteenth centuries Russian towns were not sufficiently developed. In 1504 the heretical movement was defeated and heretics punished. The isolated humanist elements in Russian culture did not lead to a Renaissance in Russia.

This fact must be borne in mind if one is to understand the development of Russian literature in the second half of the fifteenth and the sixteenth century.

1. Historical Narrative

As in the preceding period the main works of historical narrative in the fifteenth century were the chronicles, the compilations of Russian history.

Fifteenth-Century Chronicle Compilations. Unlike those of previous years, the fifteenth-century compilations have come down to us not only in later manuscripts, but often in the original or in redactions made shortly afterwards. The similarity of the main text of these redactions enables us to establish with reasonable accuracy their common sources, the chronicle compilations.

The finest work of fifteenth-century Russian chronicle-writing that influenced the whole subsequent development of All-Russian and Novgorodian chronicle-writing was the compilation which formed the basis for two chronicles (the *Sophia First* and the *Novgorod Fourth*) and is known to specialists as the compilation of 1448. The text of the two chronicles coincides up to 1418-1425, consequently their common protograph (source) must have been compiled after 1425, i.e., probably during the bitter struggle for the throne of Muscovy between Grand Prince Basil II (the Blind) and his relatives, the Galich princes Yuri and Dmitry Shemyaka and Prince Ivan of Mozhaisk. It was this struggle which made the chronicler (who was probably connected with one of the metropolitans of Russia) attack princely feuding with special fervour, appeal for unity in the struggle against Mongol overlordship that had still not been cast off, and combine extensively in his compilation the chronicle-writing of Novgorod and North-Eastern Russia (Vladimir and Moscow). Already chronicles of earlier times had contained information about events in neighbouring principalities but these were only isolated reports, often very brief (very little was said in Vladimir and Moscow chronicles about events in Novgorod, and even less in Novgorodian chronicles about the affairs of Vladimir-Suzdal; the chronicle-writing of Tver and Pskov developed in isolation). The compilation of 1448 combined Novgorodian and Vladimir-Moscow chronicle-writing, with large passages from the chronicles of Tver and Pskov and reports from Suzdal and Rostov. We have already mentioned the tale of Michael of Chernigov, the Tver account of Michael, son of Yaroslav, and of Shchelkan, the Pskov tale of Dovmont and the Novgorodian account of the battle on the Lipitsa. In All-Russian chronicle-writing all these accounts were included in the compilation of 1448 and borrowed from it for other chronicles of the fifteenth and sixteenth centuries. The compilation of 1448 made use of a number of chronicle sources (Novgorodian, Vladimir, Southern and, possibly, Rostov chronicles) to give lengthy accounts of the battle on the Kalka (with a reference to the *bogatyr* Alexander Popovich and the "ten brave men" who perished with him) and Batu's invasion. The extended accounts of the struggle against the Mongols under Dmitry Donskoy, the Battle of Kulikovo, the invasion of Tokhtamysh, and the Life of St Dmitry Donskoy, appeared for the first time in the compilation of 1448. Taking as a basis the brief and completely factual account in *The Trinity Chronicle* of the Battle of Kulikovo, the compilation of 1448 stressed in particular the treachery of Oleg of Ryazan, a "villainous murderer" and "Moslem accomplice", contrasting him with the figure of the pious Dmitry. The original short account of Tokhtamysh's invasion in 1382 was also rewritten: concrete details of the town's defence were added, for example, the story about the cloth merchant Adam who caught sight of a high-born Mongol from the town wall and with one shot from his cross-bow "sent an arrow through his wrathful heart", and the description of the underhand way in which the Mongols captured the city.

A single idea runs through all the stories in the compilation of 1448 that were borrowed from other compilations or included in chronicle-writing for the first time, namely, the need to renounce fratricidal feuding and unite against the external enemy. This is why the short account of Svyatopolk's murder of his brothers Boris and Gleb in earlier compilations was replaced here by a detailed *vita* text, the story of the murder of Andrew Bogolubsky is supplemented by a condemnation of the murderers who acted against their "benefactor and master", and the account of the battle on the Lipitsa is supplemented by an imaginary speech by the boyar Tvorimir on the need to submit to the senior in line; the same ideas were expressed in *The Life of Michael of Tver* and other tales in the compilation of 1448. Against the background of the feudal war of the mid-fifteenth century all this was of great political relevance.

Compiled before the final conclusion of the feudal war, the compilation of 1448 began to be revised shortly after it appeared. Its text has been conveyed most closely by *The Sophia First Chronicle*; however the final section of the 1448 compilation, that contained an account of the feudal war and presumably reflected the neutrality of the chronicler on the question of Basil II's struggle against his rivals, has been altered even in *The Sophia First Chronicle*. After Basil the Blind's victory the concluding section of the compilation of 1448 describing his reign and struggle with his rivals was omitted (earlier redaction) or greatly condensed (later redaction). In *The Novgorod Fourth Chronicle* different changes were made. This chronicle was compiled in Novgorod, which by then had adopted a hostile attitude to Moscow and gave refuge to Basil the Blind's defeated rival, Dmitry Shemyaka. The basic text of the compilation of 1448 was supplemented by many purely Novgorodian additions (about mayors of Novgorod and events in Novgorod), and the long stories were abridged.[6]

The first extant chronicle compilations of the grand princes of Moscow date back to the 1470s.

The earliest is a compilation of the early 1470s which has survived in the *Nikanor* and *Vologda-Perm* chronicles. Taking as its basis the compilation of 1448, the grand prince's chronicle carefully removed all references in it to the fact that the Novgorodians invited the princes they liked to rule and drove out those who displeased them. Instead of "they enthroned him in Novgorod" or "they drove him out of Novgorod" it says that such-and-such a prince "came to Novgorod" or "left Novgorod". Moreover, the grand prince's chronicle of the early 1470s contains an account of Basil II's struggle for the throne that is highly sympathetic to this prince. The story of the conspiracy of his opponent Dmitry Shemyaka and Ivan of Mozhaisk, who imprisoned Basil in 1446, is described particularly vividly (and possibly based on Basil the Blind's own recollections). Basil hid in the church of the Trinity Monastery, but not expecting to be allowed to take refuge there, himself came out, "praying and shouting fit to choke". Ivan of Mozhaisk called to one of his boyars, "Seize him." Basil was thrown into a "bare" (uncovered) sledge and taken to Moscow to be blinded.[7]

In 1479 a new grand prince's Moscow compilation was made. By now Novgorod was finally joined to Moscow; unlike the compilation at the beginning of the decade, that of 1479 did not conceal the existence of Novgorod's former liberties, but noted and condemned them outright: "For such was the accursed custom of these treacherous folk." The Moscow compilation of 1479 ended with an account of the final submission of Novgorod and the building of Moscow's main church, the new Cathedral of the Assumption.[8]

Apart from the chronicle-writing of the Moscow grand principality in the latter half of the fifteenth century, local chronicle-writing continued (in Novgorod up to the 1470s, in Tver up to the 1480s and in Pskov up to the sixteenth century), together with chronicles compiled independently of the grand prince, most probably in the monasteries. The most striking of the latter is *The Ermolin Chronicle*, the only extant manuscript of which appears to have been commissioned by the eminent Moscow architect and builder Vasily Ermolin (it contains a list of the buildings erected by him). *The Ermolin Chronicle* and others similar to it (abridged compilations of the late fifteenth century) appear to be based on a compilation made in the White Lake Monastery of St Cyril in 1472. This compilation did not oppose the unification of the Russian state by the princes of Moscow. On the contrary, it regarded the Prince of Moscow as "the great sovereign of the universe"; but it strongly condemned the prince's cruelty and his military commanders' abuses. Thus, it relates how Dmitry Shemyaka fled after his defeat to Novgorod and was poisoned by his own cook, at the instigation of a secretary from Moscow. When Basil the Blind heard that his enemy had been killed he was so delighted that he promoted the messenger to a higher rank. Here too it describes how mercilessly Basil dealt with the courtiers of Prince Basil of Serpukhov whom he had imprisoned—he ordered them to be "executed, beaten and tortured, and dragged around by horses". But the most outraged account in *The Ermolin Chronicle* is of the annexation of the Yaroslavl lands, which the grand prince seized for himself, giving the princes of Yaroslavl possessions in other, more remote areas. The chronicler begins this account by mentioning a quite different subject. He describes how the relics of local saints "appeared" (i.e., were found) in Yaroslavl, and how these relics began to "forgive", (i.e., heal the sick and crippled by supposedly forgiving them their sins). But then the chronicler remarks that "the appearance of these miracle-workers did not bode well for the princes of Yaroslavl: for they bade farewell to their patrimonies forever". He adds wrily that then a "new miracle-worker" appeared in Yaroslavl, the grand prince's lieutenant, whose "miracles" it is impossible to "describe or count" for he was "the very *tsyashos* incarnate" (the word *tsyashos* was an euphemism for "devil").[9] The opening part of the White Lake Monastery of St Cyril compilation of 1472 (up to 1425) is not found in *The Ermolin Chronicle*: it has been almost completely replaced by a text similar to the Moscow compilation of 1479. But we can get some idea of this part of the White Lake Monastery of St Cyril compilation from the abridged compilations of the late fifteenth century: for example, they contain a fuller version than the *Sophia First* and *Novgorod Fourth* chronicles of the Rostov tales about the *bogatyrs* Alexander Popovich and Dobrynya, who are said to have fought not only in the Battle on the Kalka, but also in the battle on the Lipitsa in 1216.

Another chronicle compilation that was independent of the grand prince and compiled at the end of the 1480s has survived in the *Sophia Second* and *Lvov* chronicles. This compilation was highly critical of Grand Prince Ivan III, in particular, his attempts to remove the head of the Church, Metropolitan Gerontius, from office, but the compilation was not a metropolitan chronicle: the metropolitan himself is also criticised here (for lack of respect for the burials of his predecessors). It includes a number of literary works, among them *Afanasy Nikitin's Voyage Beyond Three Seas*. It also condemns Ivan III's oppression of his brother princes and the boyars of Tver, the help which Ivan gave to the Crimean khan who looted Kiev (then part of Lithuania) and Ivan's indecision during the final invasion by Ahmat, the khan of the Horde. When Ivan decided against doing battle and returned to Moscow, the townspeople voiced their discontent with a prince who was handing them over "to the khan and the Mongols". Possibly fearing that the townspeople would plot against him, Ivan III marched against the khan (the latter was forced to retreat, marking the end of the Mongol overlordship in 1480).[10]

In the late 1480s independent chronicle-writing ceased in the Russian state (except in Pskov); from then onwards all Russian chronicles were based on the chronicle compilations of the grand princes of Moscow.[11]

Chronicle Stories of the Victory Over Novgorod. The most noteworthy of the fifteenth-century chronicle stories are those of Moscow's victory over Novgorod in 1471. Several of these stories have survived. One of them is Novgorodian (in a redaction of *The Novgorod Fourth Chronicle*) and two are Muscovite: the story in the grand prince's compilations of 1472 (the *Nikanor* and *Vologda-Perm* chronicles) and 1479 (the Moscow compilation of the late fifteenth century), and the separate *Selected Passages from Holy Writings*, which served as a kind of supplement to the compilation of 1448 and completed the later redaction of *The Sophia First Chronicle*.

In the Muscovite stories we find features reminiscent of *The Life of Alexander Nevsky* of the chronicle story of the Battle of Kulikovo. The enemy (the Novgorodians) have grown proud and unruly, forgetting the exhortations of the Scriptures: the grand prince (Ivan III) grieves, sheds tears, and prays to God, and only when his cup of endurance is full does he give battle. The victory of the grand prince's army is portrayed in many respects as a miracle that takes place with Divine assistance. In the *Selected Passages from Holy Writings* the tempting of the Novgorodians by the Devil is seen, inter alia, in the fact that they were led by an "accursed woman", the mayor's widow, Martha Voretskaya, who is barely mentioned in the other chronicles and who became known to historians and writers (Martha the Mayor's Wife figures constantly in scholarly works and fiction of the nineteenth and twentieth centuries) from this very source. In the *Selected Passages* miracles accompany the Muscovite army all the way to Novgorod: God makes the marshes dry up, helps the Muscovites to cross deep rivers, and at the sight of the grand prince's forces the Novgorodians stagger "like drunken men" and flee. They are terrified "by the invisible power of the living God and the aid of the great Archangel Michael, the commander of the heavenly hosts"; everywhere, even when no one is chasing them, the Novgorodians seem to hear the word "Moscow", the terrible battle-cry of the grand prince's men.

In the story in the grand prince's compilations the miraculous aspect is not so obvious, but here too the outline of the story is the same: the Novgorodians themselves are made to speak of the miraculous nature of the victory, saying that as well as the

Muscovite army they saw some "other hosts"—"and then did terror come upon us, and fear seized us, and trepidation gripped us". The stories of the campaign against Novgorod differ somewhat from those of the Battle of Kulikovo and similar tales in that in the latter it is usually the "infidels" and persecutors of Christianity who are the enemy; but the chronicler assures us that by plotting with the Catholic Prince of Lithuania (against the Grand Prince of Moscow) the Novgorodians had lapsed into Catholicism and apostasy.

The account of Moscow's victory over Novgorod is quite different in the Novgorod chronicle which was compiled shortly before Novgorod became part of the Russian state (at the end of *The Novgorod Fourth Chronicle* which continues the compilation of 1448). Here the Novgorodians see no sign of a miracle in the grand prince's victory; they find the cause of their defeat on the ground, not in the heavens. The Archbishop of Novgorod, who was traditionally in charge of the cavalry, dared not "raise his hand against the grand prince". There was also some outright treachery: a certain Upadysh, who supported the grand prince, put five Novgorodian cannons out of action by thrusting iron bars down them. Describing the strife and "mutiny" in his native town, the chronicler relates how during the battle the Novgorodians "howled" at their "important people", to demand a decisive battle or complain about the poor arms: "I am a young man, fallen into poverty, and have not a good steed nor armour." [12]

The Russian Chronograph. Interest in world history, evident in Russia from the eleventh century when the Russian scribes first acquired translations of the Byzantine chronicles of Georgios Hamartolos and John Malalas, was particularly strong in the late fifteenth and early sixteenth centuries. It was during this period that the lengthy *Russian Chronograph* was compiled, which continued to be copied in its various redactions right up to the middle of the eighteenth century. The first redaction of *The Russian Chronograph* [13] contains an outline of world history from the Creation to 1453, the year when Constantinople fell to the Turks, marking the end of the Byzantine Empire.

About half of the *Chronograph* text is taken up with a brief exposition of the Bible (mainly stories and information about the history of the kingdom of Judaea). This is followed by the history of the Orient, the history of Rome and a detailed history of Byzantium. The final section of the *Chronograph* contains information on the history of Russia from early times to the mid-fifteenth century, and also accounts of the history of Bulgaria and Serbia. The *Chronograph* also includes a somewhat condensed version of *The Chronographical Alexandreid* (supplemented from *The Serbian Alexandreid*) and *The Tale of the Trojan War*.

The *Chronograph* was of great interest not only as an historiographical, but also as a literary work. Russian scribes were particularly impressed by the stories about Byzantine emperors which the compiler of *The Russian Chronograph* had taken from a translation of the Byzantine *Chronicle* of Constantine Manasses. The emotional style, the vivid descriptions of historical personages, and the many strifing scenes, all these features were later to have a great influence on the style and manner of the Russian historical narrative, for example, *The History of Kazan* or the tales about the Time of Troubles, the events at the beginning of the seventeenth century.[14]

The Tale of Tsargrad (Constantinople).[15] One interesting specimen of historical narrative was *The Tale of Tsargrad*, whose author humbly describes himself as "the much-sinning and wayward Nestor-Iskander". In the sixteenth century the *Tale* was included in an additional section of *The Russian Chronograph* of 1512; but it has also survived separately.

The Tale of Tsargrad dealt with a major event in fifteenth-century world history, the final collapse of the Byzantine Empire and the capture of its capital Tsargrad (Constantinople) by the Turks in 1453. The author of the *Tale* says of himself that still as a child he was captured by the Turks and converted to Mohammedanism. He describes the siege from two points of view, as it were. Scenes taking place in the Turkish camp alternate with scenes in the besieged city. It is difficult to say how much of what the author says of himself is actually true, but the early origin of the tale (latter half of the fifteenth century or beginning of the sixteenth) is beyond question.

The characteristic features of *The Tale of Tsargrad* are the dynamism and tension of the narrative. The author reduces the story of the siege, which lasted six months, to a few brief scenes, a description of five or six of the tensest days in its defence.

The narrative begins with a description of the storming of the city, which took place on the fourteenth day of the siege. The Turks bombarded the city and stormed the walls. There was hand-to-hand fighting. The battle continued until nightfall, when the Turks were forced to retreat and the exhausted defenders slept like the dead.

The Turks again prepared to storm the city, but new forces appeared to aid its defenders, namely an Italian called Justinian with his army (Nestor-Iskander calls them the "600 brave men"), the only one to respond to Emperor Constantine's appeal for help. He becomes the true leader of the Greeks during the second storming. The huge cannon on which the Turks have been relying makes a breach in the most vulnerable part of the city wall which Justinian is defending. At night Justinian manages to block up the breach by building a wooden barrier. Next morning the Turks bombard the place again and destroy the barrier, but Justinian "takes aim with his cannon", returns their fire, and destroys the breech of the Turks' big cannon. The infuriated sultan cries *yağma* (charge!) and divides up the city in advance for plundering. Again there is hand-to-hand fighting and again the besiegers retreat and the city's defenders sleep like the dead.

The third storming of the city begins again with bombardment by the big cannon bound with strips of iron, but after the very first shot it "broke into many parts". The besiegers fill in the ditches and roll up battering rams, but at this moment the townspeople explode some mines and send the Turks flying. This failure causes the sultan to lose heart and he decides to "retreat and go home", but then the Greeks make a peace offer to the sultan, thereby revealing their weakness, and the hostilities are resumed.

During the fourth storming the Turks manage to destroy a large section of the wall. This time the defenders cannot repair the damage; they only manage to build a tower behind the destroyed section. Some Turks break in and nearly kill Justinian, who is saved by a Greek general. But just as the Turks are about to rush into the city with victorious cries, the Greeks begin to fire cannons "secretly" placed in the tower. The emperor himself joins in the battle. Alone "with sword in hand", he drives the enemy back through the breach and out of the city.

Incensed by the failure of their fourth attempt, the Turks prepare a new assault. At this point an event takes place that presages the imminent destruction of the capital: fire comes out of the windows of Hagia Sophia and rises up to the heavens. The patriarch explains to the emperor that this means the Holy Spirit has left Constantinople. When the fifth assault comes all seems lost, but the emperor and Justinian do not consider the battle over "for the hour of judgment was not yet nigh".

The Turks manage to destroy the tower put up by Justinian, and when he tries to erect it again, he is shot in the chest by a cannon-ball. But the physicians manage to get him back on his feet, and no sooner has he recovered than he sets about building the tower again. He is again hit by a stray cannon-ball. The emperor weeps over the dying Justinian, but does not lose heart and drives the Turks out of the city for the last time.

Even on the eve of the city's collapse, its destruction does not seem inevitable. The sultan again considers raising the siege. But a "great darkness" gathers over the city and it rains blood, a sign that Constantinople is about to fall.

The day of the fall of Constantinople arrives. In spite of his courtiers' exhortations to leave the city, the emperor rushes into the final battle on the streets of Constantinople and dies under the swords of the Turks, thus making an old prediction about Constantinople come true: "It was founded by Constantine and with Constantine it will end." (The first emperor to rule in Constantinople was Constantine the Great and the last Constantine XI.) The *Tale* ends with a description of the sultan's triumphal entry into the city and a reminder of the prophesy that Constantinople will be liberated by *rusy rod*, which can be interpreted as blond-haired people or Russians.

The Tale of Tsargrad is rich in factual details and evidently based on the authentic recollections of an eyewitness or eyewitnesses (in this connection the author's stories about himself as someone who participated in these events are worthy of attention). At the same time, however, the tale shows the clear influence of Russian military tales, *The Tale of Batu's Capture of Ryazan* and others. We find stylistic phrases here that are characteristic of these tales ("the battle was a great and terrible one", the blood was running "in torrents", etc.), although unlike most Russian tales there is no sharp distinction in the portrayal of the belligerent parties, no outright condemnation of the "infidels" (the Turks) and sharp contrasting of them with the Christians (the Greeks). The author is respectful towards both sides. In terms of genre *The Tale of Tsargrad* is a work of historical narrative, and at the same time a fictional tale similar to those which, as we shall see, occupy an important place in Russian literature of the latter half of the fifteenth century.

2. Hagiography

The hagiographical works of the latter half of the fifteenth century are closely linked with those of the preceding period. The traditions of Epiphanius the Most Wise were continued by hagiographers throughout the century; one of the most important representatives of this tradition, Pachomius the Logothete, continued to write until the end of the century. The latter half of the fifteenth century, however, is marked by certain new features in hagiographical literature not found in the preceding period.

In the latter half of the fifteenth century we find, on the one hand, "unadorned" *vitae* that appear to have been written by people who actually witnessed the lives of eminent churchmen, as material for hagiography, and, on the other hand, *vitae*-cum-tales that are based on the stories and legends of the oral tradition.

The record of the last days of Paphnutius, abbot of the Borovsk Monastery, written by his servant Innocentius, is an example of the first type.

It is an ingenious, lively, authentic account of the sickness and death of the founder and abbot of a large monastery closely connected with the grand prince. Wordly concerns have not entirely left this powerful and active old man, but he already senses that ahead lies "another matter ... that brooks no delay", the destruction of the union of body and soul. People still come to see him on business; he already has no desire to receive visitors, but the humble Innocentius is intimidated by the influential personages and keeps bothering the old man with their requests. "What are you thinking of?" Paphnutius exclaims irritatedly and not at all "meekly" (as befitted a saint). "You won't give me a single hour's rest from this world!" For sixty years, Paphnutius says, he has tried to please "the world and worldly folk, the princes and the boyars", "interfering" in their affairs. "And to what avail I do not know. Now I have understood that all this is of no avail to me!" [16]

This figure of the dying old man has the authenticity of a "human document" created by someone who is undoubtedly a gifted writer, but does not observe the hagiographical canons. Innocentius' ability to discern and record lively details and speech was most important for the literature of later periods, not only hagiographical, but also historical and narrative.

The Life of St Michael of Klopsk. Unlike the record of Innocentius, the Novgorodian *Life of St Michael of Klopsk* was not an account by an eyewitness, but a story based on oral legends about the life and miracles of this Novgorodian saint and *yurodiviy* (fool-in-Christ) who supported the princes of Moscow. But this *vita* too is not similar to the traditional Lives of saints: it is far closer to the folk tale-cum-*novella*.

The *Life* opens in an unusual way for a hagiographical work. It begins not with the usual account of the birth and upbringing of the saint, but with a description of the mysterious appearance of an unnamed person in the Klopsk Monastery near Novgorod. What we have here is a "closed" plot, as it were, the denouement of which is not known to the reader and arouses his curiosity.

At nightfall on St John's Day the priest Ignatius returns to his cell to find it unlocked. Inside is "an old man sitting on a chair with a candle burning in front of him". The startled priest fetches Abbot Theodosius; this time the cell is locked. The abbot looks through the window and greets the stranger with a prayer; the stranger repeats the prayer. This happens three times. "Who are you? Man or demon? What is your name?" the abbot then asks him. "Man or demon? What is your name?" the stranger repeats. The abbot asks again: "Man or demon?" The stranger repeats his words again; this happens a third time also. Then the abbot has them tear down part of the roof of the lobby and begins to burn incense; the old man shields himself from the smoke of the censer, but crosses himself. This reassures the abbot, and the stranger is admitted to the monastery. The secret of his origin is not discovered until later, when Prince Constantine, son of Dmitry, visits the monastery and tells the monks that the stranger is a person of rank, related to the prince. [17]

Michael of Klopsk was a fool-in-Christ and this explains the eccentric nature of the stories about him to a large extent. This feature of the *Life* links it with secular literature of the kind that

Illumination from **The Life of St Michael of Klopsk** in a 17th-century manuscript copy. Institute of Russian Literature, Leningrad

Men Fishing. Detail of the illumination from *The Life of St Michael of Klopsk*

we shall be discussing later, for example, the legends about Solomon and Kitovras, in which, like Michael, the "wondrous beast" Kitovras can "see through" the present and future of people he talks to and conceals a profound wisdom behind his "foolishness". The unusual structure of *The Life of St Michael* was noted by readers and subsequent redactors of the *Life*. In the sixteenth century when the *Life* was included in the large compilation of religious literature called *The Great Menology* (Church calendar readings), it was revised. The redactors tried to get rid of the unusual "closed" plot, in which the narrative began in the middle, as it were (with the arrival of the unknown old man in the monastery). They arranged the text in the traditional order for a hagiographical work and omitted the mysteries. True, the redactors apologised for the fact that they did not know "whence this wondrous teacher came from" and who his parents were, but immediately explained that he was no stranger, but "the wondrous Michael" who had decided to give up worldly things and find a fitting place for meditation. The unusual dialogue with which the first redaction of the *vita* began, when Michael repeats the abbot's words, was also omitted. The redactor simply stated that Michael repeated what he heard from the abbot. Other scenes were altered in the same way. Instead of being shown, portrayed dramatically, the events were merely described.

Thus, the official hagiographers of the next century did not recognise the type of *vita*-cum-tale to which *The Life of St Michael* belonged. But this type did have its supporters, a fact that can be seen from the existence of other *vitae* that centred round an unusual hero whose wisdom is revealed in an unexpected way to those around him and to the reader. An example is *The Life of SS Peter and Febronia of Murom*, which has come down to us in a sixteenth-century redaction, but probably dates back to the fifteenth century.[18]

The Tale of Peter of the Horde. *The Life of St Peter, Prince of the Horde* was also a *vita*-cum-tale, based on oral tradition. The hero is a pious Mongol prince who lived in the Horde, heard a sermon by an Archbishop who had come to visit the Mongols, and was baptised and given the Christian name of Peter. Peter moved to Rostov. On the shore of Lake Nero the Apostles appeared to him in a dream, gave him two sacks of gold and ordered him to erect a church with the money. The Apostles also appeared to the Bishop of Rostov in a dream and ordered him to help Peter. To build the church Peter needed the permission of the Prince of Rostov, but the latter demanded in payment for the land on which the church was to be built the number of gold coins that could be placed along the edge of the land. Peter agreed. He acquired a pie-

ce of land by the shore of Lake Nero, dug a ditch round it, as was
the custom in the Horde, and placed so many coins along the
boundaries of his land (taking them from the magic sacks), that
they filled the carts and chariots sent by the prince. When the
church was built the prince persuaded Peter to marry and live in
Rostov. After Peter's death "at a ripe old age" a monastery was
built on the spot where the Apostles had appeared to him. The
rest of the *vita* tells of the fate of this monastery and Peter's
descendants and describes the disputes between them and the
townspeople of Rostov over the lake which was on the monastery's
land.[19]

Both the plot, which lacks the martyrdom and suffering for
the faith typical of *vitae,* and its individual images are far removed
from traditional Lives. The figure of the Rostov prince who gives
Peter the land for the church and the monastery is very
interesting. Unlike the devout Mongol prince, he is a shrewd,
cunning politician. To the "horror" of Peter and the Archbishop
of Rostov he derides the appearance of the Apostles, openly
mocking Peter: "The archbishop will build you a church, but I
won't give you a place for it. What can you do about that?" Free
from earthly cares, Peter replies meekly: "At the command of the
Holy Apostles, Prince, I shall buy from you however much land
your grace will grant unto me." Hearing these words and seeing
the sacks of money in Peter's hands, the prince decides privately to
profit as much as possible from the "horror" of the other two
men and extract lots of money (which he does). His subsequent
behaviour is of an equally practical nature, i.e., the decision to
keep the christened Mongol in Rostov: "If that man, the kinsman
of rulers, goes back to the Horde, it will be a loss to our town...
Peter, shall we get you a bride?" Peter accepts the offer and stays
in Rostov.

One of the main motifs in the tale, the excessive price asked by
the prince for the plot of land and the magical way in which Peter
complies with this condition, is obviously derived from folklore.
The same applies to the account of the dispute over the lake in
the second part of the *vita.* This dispute begins with an unusual
contest between the fishermen from the town and the monastery
(Peter's) fishermen. The monastery fishermen catch more fish
than the town fishermen. Peter's men cast their nets almost
playfully and bring in a great haul of fish, but the town fishermen
labour hard and catch nothing. Incensed by the insult to their
fishermen, the prince's descendants decide to deprive Peter's
descendants (the owners of the monastery's land) of the right to
fish there, arguing that their forefather sold Peter the land, but
not the lake. The settlement of this dispute is again typical of oral

tradition. The Mongol khan's envoy appears in the role of the fair arbiter. He asks the Rostov princes if they can take the water away from the land granted to Peter. "The water is our patrimony, but we cannot take it away, Sir," the princes reply. "If you cannot take the water away, then why do you call it yours?" the envoy concludes.

Like *The Life of St Michael of Klopsk, The Life of St Peter of the Horde* was revised in the next century. The redactors were troubled by the unusual figure of the Prince of Rostov, Peter's patron. Whereas in the original redaction he spoke of his desire to "extract" lots of money from the Mongol prince, in subsequent revisions he himself gasps "with terror" at the vision seen by Peter and the archbishop, although he demands an exorbitant price from Peter for his land. His desire to keep Peter in Rostov is explained not by practical considerations, but by the pious fear that Peter will renounce Christianity.

But these were later revisions of the hagiographical tales. In the fifteenth century the *vitae*-cum-tales were a fairly widespread type of Life: their engaging plot, humour, folklore and motifs from everyday life brought them closer to the secular tales of the fifteenth century.

3. Translated Tales

Fifteenth-century tales, unlike earlier ones, not only tell of historical events and famous figures in Russian history, but of all sorts of people whose lives contain events of interest to the reader. They were works of fictional prose, intended for reading, without any official or religious purpose. Translated works of this type had been known in Russia earlier (*The Tale of Akir the Wise,* for example), but in the fifteenth century there were far more of them than before.

The Serbian Alexandreid. Of all the translated tales that appeared in Russia in the latter half of the fifteenth century, mention must be made, first and foremost, of the so-called *Serbian Alexandreid,* a romance about the life and adventures of Alexander the Great.[20] This romance came to Russia in the fifteenth century and became more popular than *The Chronographical Alexandreid.*

The earliest Russian manuscript of *The Serbian Alexandreid* was transcribed by a monk in the White Lake Monastery of St Cyril, Euphrosyne. *The Serbian Alexandreid* appears to derive from a Greek original of the third or fourth century, but it came to Russia in a South Slavonic (Serbian) version. *The Serbian Alexandreid* differed from *The Chronographical Alexandreid* in several important respects. In the *Serbian* version Alexander is credited with the conquest of Rome and Jerusalem. He also visits Troy and pays tribute to the heroes of Homer's *Iliad*, but at the same time he worships the one and only God and is friendly with the Old Testament prophet Jeremiah. The features of the mediaeval romance were greatly enhanced in *The Serbian Alexandreid*: the theme of the love of Alexander and Roxana (which is not found in *The Chronographical Alexandreid* or other tales about Alexander) is a major one here: Alexander tells his mother that this love that "conquered" his heart made him think for the first time of domestic matters and the Macedonians. When Alexander dies, Roxana kills herself.

The tale opens with a description of Alexander's "miraculous" birth. As in *The Chronographical Alexandreid*, his father is not Philip of Macedonia, but the Egyptian King and magician Nectanebes. At his birth it is predicted that Alexander will be king of the whole universe known for his "piety, joy, and wisdom", but will live not more than forty years.

After Philip's death Alexander becomes an "autocrat", conquering "Athens the Wise" and other Greek lands, then waging war against King Darius of Persia.

In the romance Alexander is constantly putting himself in perilous situations, challenging fate "sticking his neck out", as his generals put it. He dresses up in other people's clothes, now in the guise of a close friend, now as his own envoy. He even makes so bold as to visit Darius himself, dressed up as the Macedonian envoy, on the eve of the decisive battle with the Persians. At the feast in Darius' palace the disguised king drinks the wine offered to him and hides the goblet under his robes. After deceiving the Persians, he hurries to leave the palace and uses the goblet to help him to get through the gates. "Here, take this goblet! King Darius has sent me to inspect the guard," he says curtly to the gate-keepers, who believe him and let him through.

The account of Alexander's visit to Darius is followed by a description of the decisive battle between them. Darius is beaten, and his treacherous counsellors stab him and leave him by the wayside. There he is found by Alexander and carried to the royal palace. Whereas in the scenes describing Alexander's adventures and exploits the speech of the characters is laconic and expressive, in the scenes portraying strong emotions it is lengthy and rhetorical. On being found more dead than alive by Alexander Darius can "barely breathe", but this does not stop him from speaking in a most protracted, high-flown fashion. Eventually, "after much weeping", Darius gives his daughter Roxana to Alexander in marriage and dies. Alexander buries Darius with

The Battle of Alexander the Great and King Porus. Illumination from a
17th-century manuscript copy of the *Alexandreid.* State Public Library, Leningrad

"great honour" and executes his murderers. After his victory over Darius Alexander is equally successful in defeating the Indian ruler Porus and then sets off to journey round some strange lands. During this journey he visits, among other things, the cave of the dead, where he meets his vanquished opponents, Darius and Porus.

The twists and turns in the hero's fate could not fail to enthral the reader of the *Alexandreid*. Not knowing the outcome of Alexander's adventures, the reader lived every moment of them in thrilled suspense and rejoiced when they ended happily. At the same time the theme of the transience and impermanence of all human achievements is constantly reiterated in the romance. The successes won with such difficulty and danger amount to nothing in the end, and the early death predicted for Alexander at his birth is not to be avoided. During his travels Alexander visits the Brahmins who live close to paradise and are called *nagomudretsi* ("naked wise men"), because they are *nagi* ("naked"), i.e., completely lacking not only in clothes, but in all belongings and "all passion". Alexander offers to give them anything they do not have in their land. "Then give us immortality, King Alexander, for we are mortal!" exclaim the Brahmins. "I am not immortal; how shall I give you immortality?" the king replies. The only thing the Brahmins need is something that Alexander does not possess either. "Go in peace, Alexander, conquering the whole earth, yet in the end you yourself will lie in it," the Brahmin elder says to him. This theme recurs over and over again in the romance. "Oh, most wise of men, Alexander," Darius asks in the cave of the dead, "are you too doomed to join us?" At the end of the romance the prophet Jeremiah appears to Alexander in a dream to announce that his death is nigh, and Alexander has a final inspection of his army. The description of this inspection is one of the most powerful scenes in the work. Past the doomed general march his victorious soldiers: Greeks, Macedonians, Egyptians, all the peoples that make up his army. Looking at them, Alexander shakes his head and says: "Do you see them all? Fifty years hence they will all be in their graves!"

Although the time of Alexander's death has been foretold in advance, its cause is unexpected. Alexander is treacherously poisoned by his cup-bearer. Like the description of Darius' death, the account of Alexander's last days is high-flown and moving. The poisoned emperor grows numb and begins to "tremble", but still utters lengthy speeches to his generals, Roxana and even the wicked cup-bearer. When he dies, Roxana laments her "Macedonian sun" and stabs herself to death over her husband's coffin. Alexander and Roxana are buried together.

The main idea consistently and very expressively developed throughout the narrative is that of the vanity of all earthly greatness. For the reader, however, who could undoubtedly appreciate the hero's bravery and nobility and love him for it, Alexander's fate after death remained unclear. The author made Alexander believe in a single god, but could not turn him into a Christian or a believer in Judaism in his religious views. Does the hero go to heaven or hell? The compiler of the Russian redaction adds a typical note that was not in the Greek and South Slavonic texts, saying that after Alexander's death an angel appeared and carried away his soul.

Trojan Tales. The *Alexandreid* was not the only work in Old Russian literature that had classical roots. In the late fifteenth and the early sixteenth century, several lengthy tales about the Trojan War came to Russia. Before the fifteenth century the myths of the Trojan cycle as retold in Book Five of the *Chronicle* of John Malalas had been known, but we can assume that this book was not very widespread in Old Russia. In the fifteenth century the Byzantine *Chronicle* of Constantine Manasses became known in Russia in a Bulgarian translation, which gives a detailed account of the events of the Trojan War. Some manuscripts with this translation also include a separate story about the Trojan War known as *The Tale of Kings*. The compiler of *The Russian Chronograph* at the beginning of the sixteenth century created his own *Tale of the Creation and Capture of Troy* combining passages from the main text of Manasses' *Chronicle* and *The Tale of Kings*. This tale was included in one of the chapters of the 1512 redaction of the *Chronograph*, and was also included in miscellanies as a separate work.

In the late fifteenth or the early sixteenth century, evidently from a German printed edition of the late fifteenth century, a translation was made of another lengthy story about the Trojan War written at the end of the thirteenth century by the Sicilian Guido da Colonna. This story gives a detailed account of the events preceding the Trojan War (the voyage of the Argonauts, Jason's winning of the Golden Fleece in Colchis with the help of the priestess Medea and the first destruction of Troy by Jason and Hercules), the campaign of the Greeks against Troy, the capture of the town after a ten-year siege, and the fate of the main heroes of the Trojan War—Agamemnon, Odysseus (Ulysses) and Pyrrhus. In Guido da Colonna's romance, alongside the descriptions of battles, combats, military stratagems and noble exploits, considerable space is devoted to the "romantic subjects" characteristic of mediaeval tales of chivalry: the love of Medea and Jason, and Paris and Helen, the fickle Briseida beloved by Prince Troilus, and Achilles' love for Priam's daughter Polyxena. These themes were rare in Old Russian literature (if one does not count the above-mentioned *Serbian Alexandreid*), but undoubtedly aroused great interest among readers—all these subjects have been preserved even in the short reworkings of Guido da Colonna's *Trojan History* that had appeared already by the sixteenth century, but were particularly widespread later, in the seventeenth.[21]

Tales of Solomon and Kitovras. *The Serbian Alexandreid* and *The Trojan History* are examples of the "high" courtly literature that entered Russian letters in the fifteenth century. But during the same period several other works of quite a different nature, close to the oral tradition of the Middle Ages, also appeared in Russia. One of the first specimens of this genre was the tales of King Solomon and the beast Kitovras that are mentioned in mediaeval lists of proscribed books (indexes), but from the end of the fifteenth century were included in the Old Russian *Interpretive Paleya* which set out and explained Bible stories.[22]

The prototype of mediaeval legends about Solomon was the Old Testament story of how King Solomon settled a dispute between two women who both claimed to be the mother of the same infant. The king ordered the child to be cut in half: when one of the women agreed to hand over the child to the other rather than let it be killed, the king immediately knew that she was the real mother. This Bible story provided the model for the *Judgements of Solomon,* which was not part of the Bible, but was included in the *Interpretive Paleya.* One of the chapters of the *Judgements* tells about three people who accuse one another of stealing purses of gold while the two others were asleep. They appeal to Solomon and he tells them a parable. A certain girl was betrothed to a young man who went away to another land and forgot about her. Time passed and the girl's father decided to give her in marriage, but she confessed to her bridegroom that she was already betrothed. The bridegroom agreed to go with his bride to her betrothed, who freed the girl from her vows. On the way back a robber attacked the young couple, but when the girl told him her story he let them go unharmed. After hearing the parable, one of the people said that the betrothed had behaved best, another the bridegroom, while the third praised the robber, but said that he should have taken the belongings of the bridegroom and the girl. "You covet the possessions of others, my friend, it was you who took the purse..." said Solomon.[23]

The tales about Kitovras are similar to those about Solomon, but here the king has a rival who is even wiser than he. These tales tell how King Solomon decided to build the temple in Jerusalem and needed the help of a "fleet-footed beast", Kitovras (the legendary centaur, half-man and half-beast). Thinking it would be impossible to persuade him, Solomon's counsellors decide to capture Kitovras by a clever ruse. They fill some wells with wine and honey; Kitovras drinks from them and falls asleep. The counsellors fetter him and take him to the king. The captured Kitovras surprises everyone by his behaviour: he laughs at a man in the market who is choosing himself a pair of boots to last seven years and at a fortune-teller sitting on the ground, and cries at the sight of a wedding; later it transpires that the buyer of the boots had only seven days to live, that the bridegroom was to die shortly as well and that the fortune-teller did not know that there was some treasure buried under the spot where he was sitting. Kitovras tells them how to get the *shamir* stone needed to polish the slabs for the future temple. The temple is built, but the king doubts Kitovras' wisdom, for it did not save the "fleet-footed beast" from being captured by men. Then Kitovras asks the king to take off his chains and carries Solomon away to the ends of the earth where his wise men and scribes have to seek for him. After that the king is so afraid of Kitovras that he has sixty brave warriors stand guard by his bedside every night.

Apart from this tale about Kitovras, several more have survived. The miscellany of the White Lake Monastery of St Cyril scribe Euphrosyne contains a short but very interesting tale in which the capture of Kitovras is due to the cunning wife, whom the "fleet-footed beast" conceals in his ear. But his wife manages to tell "her young lover" about the wells from which Kitovras usually drinks; and after this they put wine in them. The meeting of Kitovras and Solomon is described differently here. "What is the finest thing in the world?" asks the king. "Freedom," replies Kitovras, breaking everything and leaping free. A third tale about Kitovras, which has survived only in manuscripts of the seventeenth century and later, also includes the theme of female cunning. Here the victim is not Kitovras but Solomon. With the help of a magician Kitovras steals Solomon's wife. Solomon sets off to get her back, but due to his wife's treachery falls into Kitovras' hands. The king is sent to the gallows, but asks permission to play on his horn. In reply to a triple call from Solomon's horn his army appears; the king is freed and executes Kitovras, his wife and the magician.[24]

There is no evaluation of the character of Kitovras in the tales about him: we cannot say whether he is good or evil. He helps Solomon to build the temple, but he also takes him to the ends of the earth. The reader had to decide for himself what he thought of this main character.

Stefanit and Ikhnilat. The absence of a clearly expressed moral and an appropriate ending is characteristic of another work that entered Russia from South Slav literature in the latter half of the fifteenth century, the book of fables entitled *Stefanit and Ikhnilat*.[25] The structure of the plot was rather complex. Deriving from the Arabic book of fables entitled *Kalilah and Dimnah* (and

through it to the Indian *Panchatantra*), this work, like the collection *Arabian Nights*, was a cycle of stories or, rather, a group of cycles, in which the text of the main stories includes shorter stories. Already in the Greek, and later in the South Slav translation, pride of place was given to the story of two animals, in the Arabic version Kalilah and Dimnah and in the Graeco-Slavonic Stefanit and Ikhnilat (in the Arabic text they were jackals and in the Graeco-Slavonic texts unspecified "beasts"). This story took up the first two chapters of the cycle; the subsequent chapters, which contained other stories, were gradually abridged and sometimes simply omitted altogether. The main plot of the chapters about Stefanit and Ikhnilat, after whom the whole cycle is called, is as follows. One day a cart drawn by bullocks is driving through the forest. One of the bullocks gets stuck in a quagmire. The owner of the cart does not try to get it out, but drives on leaving the Bullock to its fate. The Bullock does not perish, however. It climbs out of the quagmire, begins to eat the lush grass and grows big and strong. Its powerful bellow deafens the whole forest in which the Lion reigns, but this king does not show the courage, bravery and virtue characteristic of the kings in the *Alexandreid* and *The Trojan History*. On the contrary, he is "arrogant and proud and lacking in wisdom". This king is surrounded by flattering courtiers, and the two wise beasts, Stefanit and Ikhnilat, live far from the king's palace, in disfavour. The bellowing of the mysterious "loud-voiced beast" frightens the Lion; contrary to his custom, he even refrains from "violence". The wily Ikhnilat comes to the Lion and promises to find out the source of the terrible bellowing.

For all his slow-wittedness the Lion is not over-confident about the loyalty of his subjects. After sending Ikhnilat to find out who is bellowing, the Lion immediately regrets having done so: recalling that Ikhnilat was the wisest of the king's counsellors before he fell into disfavour, and concluding that if he were to find out that the "loud-voiced beast" was stronger than the Lion "he would worm his way into his favour and tell him of my weaknesses". Even when Ikhnilat returns to him and says that the mysterious beast is a Bullock and can cause no harm, the Lion continues to be afraid—the unknown beast did not touch the lowly Ikhnilat, but who knew how he would behave towards King Lion.

The Bullock comes to the court, and for a while the king forgets his suspicions. He makes the Bullock his head counsellor; the wily Ikhnilat is again dismissed from court. So he decides to take advantage of his ruler's suspicious nature and slander the Bullock. He makes the Lion suspicious of the Bullock, and the

Bullock of the Lion. The king and his favourite meet, each suspecting the other, and both detect hostile intentions. The Lion kills the Bullock.

Then urged by his closest courtiers the repentant Lion takes Ikhnilat to court. Here, too, Ikhnilat shows resourcefulness and quick-wittedness. He agrees that "as the Lion's friend" he told him his suspicions about the Bullock. But who can prove that Ikhnilat deliberately slandered the Bullock? Perhaps he really did suspect him of treachery? Ikhnilat rightly compares his accusers to unskilful physicians: none of them can make any definite accusation against him. A "certain nobleman" demands that Ikhnilat shall confess all with a pure heart; the Lion's mother says the wily beast is "cunning and brutal"; the king's head cook points out that Ikhnilat's "left eye is too small and screwed up" and that he "hangs his head" when he is walking, which, he insists, are sure signs of a slanderer. Ikhnilat brushes aside these accusations with no difficulty at all, even proving that the cook himself looks no better than him. He is covered with "foul-smelling scabs" and dares to come before the king and touch the king's food with his hands. "If I do not defend myself," Ikhnilat says, "who will defend me?" He defends himself so well, that he makes fools of all his accusers. The outcome of the trial is by no means a triumph of justice. The Lion, who killed the Bullock because of his ill-founded suspicions, shows himself to be not a fair judge, but a spineless weak-willed despot easily influenced by others. "Conceding to his mother's demands, the Lion ordered Ikhnilat to be executed." This is how the story of the trial of Ikhnilat ends.

The other fables and tales that the characters in the book tell one another are very reminiscent of the story of Stefanit and Ikhnilat. Thus, there is one about an old lion who can no longer catch beasts and demands that they should bring one of their number to him each day to be eaten. It is now the lot of the hare, who suggests to the other beasts a way of getting rid of the lion. He comes to the hungry lion late and unaccompanied. Then he explains to the lion, who is furious at being kept waiting, that he was bringing "his friend, the hare", to him to be eaten, when another lion fell upon them on the way and took the hare, although he had been told for whom it was intended. The king demands to be shown the guilty lion. Then the hare takes him to a deep well and shows him their reflection in it. The enraged lion jumps into the well and is drowned.

A sick lion no longer able to hunt is found in another subsidiary fable. Among his subjects are a wolf, a fox, a raven and a camel "from other lands" that has lost its way and wandered into this kingdom. Unable to persuade the lion to make short work of the camel, the wolf, fox and raven devise a cunning ruse: each in turn offers himself to be eaten by the lion, while the others say that he is not edible. Expecting the same response, the camel also boasts about how "sweet" his flesh is and offers himself as a victim. "Truly said, oh, camel!" cry the others and tear him to pieces.

It is easy to detect the common feature in these tales—the strong triumph over the weak, and it is the wily, not the righteous, who can get the better of them. Unlike most works of Old Russian literature there are no completely positive (or negative) characters in *Stefanit and Ikhnilat*. In the main story of the cycle Stefanit does not take part in Ikhnilat's cunning ruses and tries to dissuade him from them, but nevertheless he values his friend's wisdom and is truly devoted to him. In the Graeco-Slavonic version of the tale (unlike the Arabic one) Stefanit comes to a tragic end: deeply grieved to hear of Ikhnilat's imprisonment he kills himself even before his friend's execution. "He went and took poison and died." Learning of Stefanit's death, Ikhnilat weeps bitterly: "It is not fitting that I should live having lost such a loyal and beloved friend!" This feature makes the character of Ikhnilat even more complex: he turns out to be capable of noble feelings as well.

The structure of the main story of the *Stefanit and Ikhnilat* cycle, like that of most of the inserted fables, was thus different from the stories where all the characters were divided into heroes and villains. In many respects the "small Ikhnilat book" (as it was called in Russia) was similar to another cycle about a crafty animal, not known in Russian literature but popular in Western Europe in the Middle Ages, the stories about Reynard the Fox, or Reineke Fuchs.

The unusual nature of *Stefanit and Ikhnilat* compared with most works of Old Russian literature produced different attitudes towards it on the part of readers.

The text of *Stefanit and Ikhnilat* first appeared in Russia in the fifteenth century and already at this time an attempt was made to give the fables a religious, ascetic moral which was by no means in keeping with them. Thus, one of the fables was about a crane who found it difficult to catch fish. "Through much grief doth it befit us to enter the kingdom of heaven," the commentator "explains" (although there is nothing in the story about the crane's "grief" or the salvation of his soul, only about how he outwitted the fish). Other explanations were of a similar nature. But there were also other Russian readers and scribes who removed the moral interpretations by their predecessors from the manuscript (together with some of the moral reflections that were in the Greek and Arabic texts). Thus the tale had an active life in literature—it had demanding readers who sought to "improve" the text and others who regarded these "improvements" as unnecessary.

4. Original Tales

Alongside the translated tale, which was fully mastered by Russian literature in the fifteenth century, the same period saw the creation of original tales in Russia. These tales were extremely varied in content and character. They included stories about real and comparatively recent historical events (similar to *The Tale of the Battle Against Mamai* already mentioned), historical legends and works which can be regarded as the first specimens of Russian secular fictional narrative.

The Tale of Babylon. The tale of the town of Babylon, which appeared in Russian literature in the fifteenth century, became extremely widespread in the following centuries together with a number of publicistic works extolling the greatness of the Russian state. In its original form, however, the *Tale* was a narrative, rather than a publicistic work. It told the story of how the Orthodox Emperor Basil resolves to bring from Babylon the "signs" belonging to the three holy youths (mentioned in the Old Testament Book of Daniel)—Hananiah, Azariah and Mishael. He sends three youths, the Greek Gugry, the Georgian Yakov and the Russian Lavr. This choice is not an accidental one, as we see later. The envoys reach the ruins of Babylon overgrown with weeds and are confronted by an enormous sleeping dragon. Above the dragon is a notice written in three languages, Greek, Georgian and Russian, which can be read only by envoys who know these languages. From the notice they find out how to get past the dragon and reach the treasure. In the deserted royal palace they find the crowns of King Nebuchadnezzar, precious stones and goblets, drink from the goblets and become intoxicated. On the way back one of them, Yakov, touches the dragon "and the dragon's scales did rise up like waves on the sea". The envoys manage to reach their horses and put their booty on them. Meanwhile the dragon awakes and gives a terrible whistle which makes them fall to the ground as if dead. The action moves to the place where the Greek Emperor Basil is awaiting his envoys. The dragon's whistle reaches Basil's camp, which is fifteen days' march away, and makes him and his men collapse lifeless. The emperor thinks his envoys have perished, but decides to wait a few days longer for them. On the sixteenth day, when all the periods of waiting are up, the three envoys, who have come to their senses "as if from a dream", appear before the emperor and present him with crowns and "signs from Babylon".

In its character *The Tale of Babylon* is a rather complex and heterogeneous work. It is both a legend about the winning of the emperor's "signs", linked with the Old Testament story of the three youths, and an intriguing tale about the exciting adventures of its heroes whose names (Gugry, Yakov and Lavr) had no historical associations for the reader and sounded like the names of heroes from folk tales (or fictional works of the modern period). The style is also mixed: sometimes it reminds the official style of ambassadorial reports ("they travelled three weeks to Babylon", "they were fifteen days' journey from Babylon"), sometimes a lively narrative. The narrative is written in the third person except for one point, when the narrator changes to the first person: "but we did drink from the goblet and grow merry".[26]

Thus, *The Tale of Babylon* is an interesting work of a transitional genre—from the legend to the fictional narrative. In the subsequent fate of the work its legendary character played an important part—it was included in the hagiographical collection of *The Great Menology* and joined the political legends of the sixteenth century.

The Tale of the Monk Who Asked for the Hand of the King's Daughter. This tale has an even more pronounced folk-tale character.

The subject matter is simple. It tells of a certain monk who is puzzled by the New Testament words in St Matthew: "Ask, and it shall be given you; seek, and ye shall find; knock, and it shall be opened unto you." He goes to the king's palace and seeks admittance; the king lets him in. Delighted to have confirmation of the New Testament words, the monk asks the king: "You have a daughter, Sire. Give her to me!" "I shall give you an answer in the morning, father," replies the king equally briefly. He does not refuse the monk's request, but says that he must first fetch a "precious stone". In the cave of a dead hermit on the seashore the monk finds a glass vessel in which "something was buzzing, like flies". It is a demon who has been trapped inside the vessel by a cross on the top (a motif also found in hagiographical literature, cf., the legend about John of Novgorod's journey on a devil's back). The monk agrees to let the demon out of the vessel if it promises to get him a "bright precious stone" from the sea. The demon becomes enormous, like a great oak, "jumps into the sea", stirs it up "with great winds and strong waves", brings out the stone and gives it to the monk. The monk asks the demon if it can grow small again and get back into the vessel. The demon shrinks and "jumps onto his palm"; whereupon the monk traps it in with the cross again. The story has an unexpected ending. True to his promise the king agrees to give the monk his daughter when he has received the stone from him. But the monk refuses to take her. He had only wanted to test the truth of the New Testament words. "Keep your daughter and the precious stone," he says to the king and returns to his meditations.[27]

In *The Tale of the Monk* the dual nature is felt even more strongly than in *The Tale of Babylon*. The tale is a didactic one—it confirms the New Testament words. But in fact the events have only a formal correspondence to this homily: the king's behaviour does not bear out the words "ask and it shall be given you" at all, for he agrees to comply with the monk's request only if the monk performs an obviously impossible task—to fetch treasure from the bottom of the sea; in order to do so the monk has to seek the assistance of a demon. The subject of the tale—the performance of a difficult task with the help of a supernatural assistant—clearly belongs to the folk tale.

Readers of the tale about the monk, like the readers of *Stefanit and Ikhnilat*, reacted in different ways to it. Some were upset by the anonymity of the characters (a monk, a king and a demon), which is customary in the folk tale but not in Old Russian literature, and they invented names for them; others were disturbed by the monk's deception of the demon and sought an explanation for this (in one version the monk even begs the demon's forgiveness).

The Tale of the Monk resembled the tales, well known to the fifteenth-century reader, of the stranger who appears at (or is brought to) the king's palace and succeeds in performing an apparently impossible task. In this respect the hero of the *Tale* resembled the heroes of such translated works as *Solomon and Kitovras* (Kitovras) and *Stefanit and Ikhnilat* (Ikhnilat). Yet *The Tale of the Monk* was no translation, but an original Russian work. The finest specimens of the original Russian tale of this period were *The Tale of Dracula* and *The Tale of Basarga*.

The Tale of Dracula. *The Tale of Dracula* is based on legends about the Wallachian (Rumanian) prince of the middle of the fifteenth century Vlad Ţepeş (Dracula) famed for his cruelty. These legends circulated and were written down in the neighbouring countries of Hungary and Germany that bordered on Wallachia. The Russian *Tale of Dracula* was composed in the 1480s by a member of the Russian embassy who travelled in Moldavia and Hungary during these years. Most likely its author was Fyodor Kuritsyn, the head of the embassy, an eminent statesman who held heretical beliefs. The Russian *Tale of Dracula* was not a translation of the foreign stories about him, just as the foreign texts do not derive from the Russian tale. The common basis for all the stories about Dracula are the oral anecdotes about him recorded in different ways in Russian, Italo-Hungarian and German texts; the Russian *Tale of Dracula* is an original rendering of "itinerant" plots.[28]

The Tale of Dracula was not regarded as an historical tale in Russia; the author makes no mention of the period, the circumstances of the reign and the real name of the main character, Vlad Ţepeş, and calls him Dracula (dragon, devil), the nickname by which this prince was called outside Wallachia.

The tale begins with a brief statement that "in the land of Wallachia" there was "a Christian *voevoda* by the name of Dracula in Wallachian, meaning the devil" and that this *voevoda* was "evil-wise" both in name and in way of life. As in *The Life of St Michael of Klopsk*, the author begins his story not at the beginning of the main character's life, but in the middle: he tells how Turkish envoys came to Dracula and refused to take off their caps. They said that this was a law of their land. "I wish to uphold your law, that you may observe it well," Dracula announced and ordered their caps to be nailed to their heads. After this comes a story about Dracula's war with the Turkish Sultan, during which he frequently defeated the Sultan and covered him with shame. Then follow a number of anecdotes about Dracula's "evil-wiseness". There is a description of Dracula's defeat in a war against a neighbouring ruler, King Matthias Corvinus of Hungary and his captivity in Hungary. At the price of renouncing Orthodoxy and embracing Catholicism, Dracula got back his crown and again embarked on war against the Turks. It was in this war that he perished: during a battle he left his soldiers "and rode up a hill for joy"; some Wallachian soldiers took their sovereign for a Turk and stabbed him to death with their spears.

Like the tales of *Solomon and Kitovras, The Tale of Dracula* consists for the most part of disconnected episodes and, again as in *Solomon and Kitovras,* this fragmented structure does not mean the absence of a single theme. Episode by episode we are shown the "evil-wiseness" of the Wallachian prince, a strange combination of refined cruelty and sharp-wittedness. These episodes take the form of anecdotes, many of which were composed like riddles with a metaphorical meaning. Dracula does not simply execute the people who fall into his hands—he puts them to the test, and the slow-witted and "unrefined" (lacking in cunning) who cannot "pay him back in kind" pay a tragic price for their "lack of refinement". This is seen most clearly in the episode with the beggars. Having assembled "a vast multitude of beggars and wanderers" from all over his land and given them food and drink in a "great mansion", Dracula asks them: "Do you not wish that I should deliver you from the cares of this world, so that you will not need for anything?" Not understanding the sinister hidden meaning of his words, the beggars agree joyfully. Dracula delivers them "from poverty" and "from disease" by locking them in the church and burning them. He behaves in a similar way with the Turkish Sultan, promising to "serve" him. The Turkish Sultan takes these words literally and is overjoyed; Dracula devastates the Turkish possessions and informs the Sultan that "he has served him as much as he could". The first episode of the tale is also based on the same ambiguity. Dracula promises the Turkish envoys to "uphold" their custom of not removing their headgear to anyone and does so by nailing their caps to their heads.

The theme of testing which runs through all these episodes is a favourite motif of mediaeval literature and folklore. This motif was well known in Old Russian literature as well: Olga "tests" the Drevlyane envoys in *The Tale of Bygone Years* just as cruelly as Dracula; and the testing motif is also found in *The Tale of Akir the Wise.*

What then was the purpose of *The Tale of Dracula*? What did the author want to convey in presenting his "evil-wise" hero to the reader? All manner of answers to this question have been proffered by specialists[29]: some see the tale as a condemnation of tyranny and believe that it was popular with the nobility hostile to absolute monarchy; others believe, on the contrary, that the tale was written in support of a strong, just monarchy and the punishment that the feudal state meted out to its enemies. The possibility of such conflicting interpretations is explained by the fact that the subject of *The Tale of Dracula,* like that of *Solomon and*

Kitovras and *Stefanit and Ikhnilat* cannot be reduced to any single conclusion or homily. Dracula performs many wicked acts, burning beggars to death, killing monks, women and the coopers who make him barrels for hiding treasure; he dines among stakes on which the dead bodies of the executed are rotting. But he also wages war against the Turks, an heroic struggle which was bound to arouse the reader's approval, and perishes in this struggle. He hates evil, puts an end to theft and sets up a fair and impartial judiciary in his state: "And Dracula so hated evil in his land that if any man did commit a crime, steal or rob, or deceive, he was sure to die. Whether he was a nobleman, or a priest, a monk, or a common man, even if he possessed countless riches, he could still not escape death."

We can see the author's attitude towards Dracula by comparing his tale with Western works about the same character. Whereas the authors of German tales described only the cruelty of a "great monster", the Italian humanist Bonfini, who wrote in Hungary, stressed, like his Russian confrère, the combination in Dracula of "unprecedented cruelty and justice". But unlike Bonfini's chronicle, *The Tale of Dracula* was a work of fictional narrative, not a publicistic work, which is why the author does not evaluate his hero directly, but gives a most unusual and vivid portrait of the prince. Dracula is not simply a villain, yet nor does he resemble the just ruler, who was portrayed as kind and pious in mediaeval works. Dracula is a monster who amuses himself by putting his victims to the test (such monsters are found in certain folk tales). Totally unusual for the *vita* or heroic military tale, Dracula was closer to the main characters of translated fictional narrative than the hero of *The Tale of the Monk*. Kitovras in *Solomon and Kitovras* was wise; Ikhnilat in *Stefanit and Ikhnilat* was clever and cunning. Dracula's self-justification concerning the killing of the beggars or the execution of the envoys is in many respects reminiscent of Ikhnilat's cunning arguments during his trial.

As with *Solomon and Kitovras* and *Stefanit and Ikhnilat,* the reader himself has to decide what to think of the hero.

As a result this tale has been even more diversely interpreted than other similar works. In the sixteenth century *The Tale of Dracula* was not transcribed and disappeared from the manuscript tradition. In addition to the general reasons for the disappearance of secular tales which is discussed in the following chapter, this was also because the tale gave too frank a picture of the cruelty of "terrible" rule. In the seventeenth century the tale reappeared, but in many copies changes were made in an attempt to simplify the complex, ambiguous character of Dracula—he was turned either into a completely cruel or into a completely wise ruler.

The Tale of Basarga and His Son Quick-Wit. The plot
structure of *The Tale of Basarga and His Son Quick-Wit* is not as
complex as that of *The Tale of Dracula*. It is not a combination of
anecdotes, but one long story.[30]

It tells how the merchant Basarga and his seven-year-old son
Quick-Wit set off on a journey from Constantinople; a storm
drives their ship to the town of Antioch. The heretical sovereign
Nesmeyan, a Catholic, who rules in this town, demands that
Basarga give him the answers to three riddles, if not the merchant
must become a Catholic or be executed. Returning to his ship
after the conversation with Nesmeyan, "weeping and sobbing
bitterly" in the expectation of "death for himself from the
sovereign", Basarga finds his son engaged in his "child's games":
he is galloping round the deck "on a stick, as if on a horse", "for
such is the custom of children engaged in play". But although he
plays "child's games", young Quick-Wit turns out to be wise
beyond his years: he offers to solve the sovereign's riddles,
Basarga takes Quick-Wit with him, and the boy really does solve
them. The first is "How far is it from east to west" (answer—one
day by the sun's path); the second: "What loses one-tenth of itself
in the day and regains it at night" (answer—in the day one tenth
of the water in the seas, rivers and lakes is dried up by the sun
and comes back in the night). In order to solve the third riddle
("What must you do to stop infidels mocking Orthodox Christians?"), the boy asks them to give him a sovereign's robes and a
sword and assemble the people of Antioch. He asks the people of
Antioch which faith they wish to espouse. "We want to believe in
the Holy Trinity, Sire!" they all "shout in unison". "Here is the
answer to your third riddle! Do not mock us, Orthodox Christians,
infidel!" says the "child". He chops off the wicked sovereign's
head, frees Antioch and becomes the ruler there.

The single subject of *The Tale of Basarga* is similar to the
anecdotal episodes of *The Tale of Dracula*: it too is based on the
answering of riddles: the hero is put to the test and emerges with
honour, having outwitted his adversary. *The Tale of Basarga* is
based on a story very widespread in folklore and world literature
and usually referred to in folklore studies[31] as the story of "the
emperor and the abbot". As in all tales on this subject, the riddles
set by a cruel ruler are answered not by the person to whom they
are addressed (the merchant Basarga), but by a "simpleton" who
takes his place, in this case the seven-year-old Quick-Wit.

Unlike *The Tale of Dracula*, the attitude towards the characters
is clear and unambiguous in *The Tale of Basarga*: the reader's
sympathy is entirely on the side of the wise youth who outwits the
infidel emperor. Here, too, however, the exciting narrative

prevails over the didactic element. Quick-Wit who gallops round the deck on a stick is quite unlike the usual hagiographical heroes who renounce children's games and "empty pastimes"; nor did this hero fit into the framework of the usual historical narrative.

The translated and original tales that became fairly widespread in Russian literature in the latter half of the fifteenth century in many respects broke with the literary traditions of the preceding period. These tales introduced new, unusual themes (subjects from Greek history and mythology, the theme of love treated without the traditional moral condemnation), and new heroes. The deliberate inventing of literary characters was not typical of mediaeval literature. The readers of the fifteenth century did not doubt that the heroes of narrative literature were real historical figures, for example: Alexander the Great, the Emperor Constantine and the general Justinian, nòr, most likely, did they doubt that Dracula was a real person, but Nesmeyan, the nameless monk in *The Tale of the Monk*, the three youths from *The Tale of Babylon*, Basarga and Quick-Wit were more likely to remind them of characters in folk tales, than historical personages. It was even more complicated in the case of tales in which the heroes were clearly legendary creatures, such as Kitovras, or animals behaving as humans, in *Stefanit and Ikhnilat*. In structure *Solomon and Kitovras*, and particularly *Stefanit and Ikhnilat*, may have reminded readers brought up on mediaeval literature of religious fables in which the characters and their actions were of a symbolical nature. They were not fables, however, but stories about animals, and when scribes tried to interpret the fables of *Stefanit and Ikhnilat* unambiguously and added homilies to them, they were clearly spoiling and distorting the work.

The tales that appeared in Russian literature in the second half of the fifteenth century had one more characteristic feature. They all had a plot: the author's ideas contained in them were expressed not in the form of direct preaching, but indirectly, through the unfolding of the events that happened to the characters. Thus, the central theme of the *Alexandreid*, that all men are mortal, unfolded before the reader on its own as the story developed. While sympathising with the hero and admiring his bold feats, the reader nevertheless arrived at the idea that in the end all his brilliant achievements were pointless, for death inexorably claimed Alexander in the end. In a number of fifteenth-century tales the characters were psychologically complex and the portrayal of them ambiguous. Kitovras, Ikhnilat and even the "evil-wise" Dracula were not simply heroes or villains. The ending of *Solomon and Kitovras, Stefanit and Ikhnilat* and *The Tale of Dracula* was also ambiguous, it was not a triumph of justice.

The plot structure of a number of translated and original tales of the second half of the fifteenth century set them apart from most works of Old Russian literature, in which the main ideas were usually expressed directly and unambiguously by the author in person. But this structure brought these tales closer to the oral narrative, the folk tale, in which the plot—the story of the hero's adventures—also played an important part and in which the characters were clearly imaginary, sometimes strange beasts. Barely linked with traditional religious literature, many fifteenth-century tales reflected "secular" subjects which became widespread in Western literature of the late Middle Ages and Renaissance. The *Alexandreid, The Trojan Tales, Solomon and Kitovras, Stefanit and Ikhnilat, The Tale of Dracula* and *The Tale of Basarga*—all these works are similar in many respects to West European works of the fourteenth to sixteenth century. This was not the result of direct borrowing; the similarity is explained by the fact that both in Western and Eastern Europe "itinerant" oral legends began to be copied down on paper and found their way from folklore into literature; translations of Oriental cycles of fables (such as *Stefanit and Ikhnilat*) also appeared.

In the second half of the fifteenth century literature in Russia developed along a path that in many respects resembled that of literature in the West. In the sixteenth century, as we shall see, these paths diverged sharply.

5. Afanasy Nikitin's
Voyage Beyond Three Seas

The *Voyage Beyond Three Seas* by the Tver merchant Afanasy Nikitin is a work that stands alone in the literature of the fifteenth century. Outwardly it resembles the accounts of pilgrimages to the Holy Land which had existed since the twelfth century or the description of journeys to church councils. Nikitin's voyage was not a pilgrimage to Christian lands, however, but a trading mission to distant India and could not be regarded as an act of piety worthy of a corresponding description.

Afanasy Nikitin's journey to India in the late 1460s and early 1470s was not undertaken at anyone's request. It was the merchant's private initiative. In setting off for the "Shirvan land" (the Northern Caucasus) with letters from his sovereign, the Prince of Tver, Nikitin hoped to join the caravan of the Moscow merchant Vasily Papin, but failed to meet up with him. At Astrakhan Nikitin and his companions were robbed by the Nogai Tartars; he appealed for help in Derbent to the local prince and the Muscovite envoy who had arrived earlier, but did not receive any. "And we wept and dispersed; those of us who owned something in Rus left for Rus, and those who had debts there went wherever they could." [32] *

Among those who had debts in Russia and for whom the way home was evidently closed for fear of ruin and servitude, was Afanasy Nikitin. He went from Derbent to Baku, thence to Persia and then via Hormuz and the "Indian Sea" to India. Having set off for India because of "the many misfortunes", Nikitin does not appear to have done any successful trading there. The item that he was hoping to sell in India, a horse transported by him with great difficulty, brought him more misfortune than gain: the khan took the horse away from him, demanding that Nikitin should adopt the Islam faith, and only the assistance of a Persian merchant with whom he was acquainted helped the voyager from Tver to regain his property. When Nikitin, six years after beginning his voyage, eventually returned to Russia with great difficulty (he died somewhere near Smolensk before reaching his native town of Tver), he was hardly more capable of repaying his debts than at the beginning of his journey. The only fruits of Nikitin's wanderings were his notes.

Preserved in a miscellany of the late fifteenth or early sixteenth century, and also in an independent chronicle compilation of the 1480s (the *Sophia Second* and *Lvov* chronicles), Nikitin's *Voyage Beyond Three Seas* was a completely unofficial piece of writing; consequently it was entirely lacking in the features characteristic of religious or official secular literature. Only a few points linked it with the "voyages" and "pilgrimages" of preceding centuries: the listing of geographical place-names with an indication of the distances between them and notes on the riches of this or that country. In fact, however, Nikitin's *Voyage* was a travel diary, notes about his adventures, while writing which the author did not know how they would end: "Four Easter Sundays have already passed in the Moslem land, but I have not forsaken the Christian faith; and God knows what may yet happen... In Thee I trust, O God, save me, O Lord! I know not my way. Whither shall I go from Hindustan?" Later Nikitin set off back to Russia and found a way "from Hindustan", but here too the record of his wanderings follows the course of his journey closely and breaks off with his arrival in Caffa (Theodosia) in the Crimea.

In recording his impressions abroad, the Tver merchant was probably hoping that his *Voyage* would one day be read by his

---

* Quoted from *Afanasy Nikitin's Voyage Beyond Three Seas*, Raduga Publishers, Moscow, 1985.

"Christian brothers of Rus". Fearing hostile eyes, he wrote his most daring thoughts in a language other than Russian. But he saw these readers as appearing in the future, perhaps after his death (which was in fact the case). For the time being Nikitin simply recorded his experiences: "And that is where the land of India lies, and where everyone goes naked; the women go bareheaded and with breasts uncovered, their hair plaited into one braid. Many women are with child... The men and women are all dark. Wherever I went I was followed by many people who wondered at a white man."

The merchant from Tver by no means understood all that he saw in that strange land. Like most people who find themselves abroad, he was prone to see everything, even the most unusual things, as an example of strange local customs. A certain gullibility is evident in his accounts of the "ghuggû" bird spitting fire and a "monkey prince" who has his own army and sends hosts of warriors against his enemies.

When Afanasy Nikitin is basing his notes not on stories that he has been told, but on his own observations, his views are sober and reliable. The India that Nikitin saw by no means resembled the land "full of all manner of riches" from *The Tale of the Indian Empire*, in which everyone was happy and there were "no thieves, no robbers, no envious men". The India that Nikitin saw was a distant land with its own scenery and its own customs, but its system was the same as that of all the other lands with which the Russian voyager was familiar: "The land is very populous; the countrymen are very poor, but the boyars are rich and live in luxury." Nikitin was clearly aware of the difference between the conquerors, the Moslems, and the indigenous population, the people of Hindustan. He also noticed that the Moslem ruler "rides on men", although "he has many elephants and fine horses", and "the people of Hindustan go on foot ... and are all naked and barefoot". A foreigner with no rights and insulted by a Moslem ruler, Nikitin informed the Indians that he was not a Moslem. He notes, not without a touch of pride, that the Indians who carefully concealed their everyday life from the Moslems, "did not hide from me when eating, trading, praying, or doing something else, did not conceal their wives".

Nikitin was lonely and homesick in foreign parts, of course. The theme of nostalgia for one's country is perhaps the central one in the *Voyage*. It is present not only in Nikitin's words about there being no other land like Russia "although the princes of Russia are not like brothers to each other..." (this remark was written in a Turkic tongue to be on the safe side), but also in other passages where his homesickness is expressed indirectly, rather than directly. Nikitin curses the "Moslem dogs" who assured him that there were "a lot of wares" (i.e., wares suitable for sale in Russia) in India, and urged him to make this difficult journey. He complains about how expensive everything is: "And to live in Hindustan would mean to spend all that I have, because everything is expensive here; alone I spend on food two and a half *altins* a day. As for wine or mead, I have drunk none of it here." The thing that oppressed Nikitin most of all was being far away from his native language and his faith, which for him was indissolubly linked with his native land and the way of life to which he was accustomed. He was depressed not only by the direct attempts to convert him to Islam, but also by the impossibility of observing his native customs abroad: "I have nothing—no book; we took books with us from Rus, but when I was robbed the books were seized too." Particularly striking are the meditations into which Nikitin falls after one of his Moslem companions tells him that he is not a Moslem but nor does he know Christianity: "And then I thought it over a great deal, and said to myself: 'Woe to me, miserable sinner, for I have strayed from the true path and knowing no other, must go my ways. Almighty God, Maker of heaven and earth, turn not Thy face from Thy servant who sorrows... God and Protector, Most High, Merciful and Gracious. Praise be to God...'" The last few words are written in Persian. After beginning by addressing God in Russian, Nikitin goes over to a Moslem prayer.

Similar addresses to Allah in Oriental languages and also the Moslem prayer with which the *Voyage Beyond Three Seas* ends have even led some specialists to suggest that the Moslems were eventually successful in converting Nikitin to Islam.[33] This is unfounded. We have no reason to doubt the truth of Nikitin's frequent statements in his notes that despite all the pressure from the Moslems, he remained true to Christianity. His contact with other religions did exert a certain influence on Nikitin's outlook, however. After describing the successes of the Moslem Sultan and the "Mohammedan faith" in India, Nikitin wrote: "As for the true faith, God alone knows it, and the true faith is to believe in one God, and to invoke His name in purity in every pure place." This viewpoint of the merchant from Tver would certainly not have been regarded as orthodox in his homeland and might have got him into serious trouble (as might his statement that there was "little justice" in the land of Russia), had he not died on the return journey home.

Written for himself, Nikitin's notes are one of the most individual works of Old Russia: we know Afanasy Nikitin and can imagine his personality far better than that of most Russian writers from early times to the seventeenth century. The autobiographical and lyrical elements in the *Voyage Beyond Three Seas*, which conveys the emotional suffering and mood of the author, were new features in Old Russian literature and characteristic of the fifteenth century. In its directness and concreteness the *Voyage Beyond Three Seas* is reminiscent of Innocentius' account of the last days of Paphnutius of Borovsk discussed above. But Afanasy Nikitin is a much more striking and interesting figure than Innocentius, of course. The personal nature of the *Voyage,* the author's ability to show us his emotions, his inner world, all these features of Afanasy Nikitin's diary re-emerge two centuries later in one of the finest monuments of Old Russian literature, the *Life* of Archpriest Avvakum.

REFERENCES

[1] On Euphrosyne see: Лурье Я. С. "Литературная и культурно-про-светительная деятельность Ефросина в конце XV в.". *ТОДРЛ*, Vol. XVII, 1961, pp. 130-168; Дмитриева Р. П. "Приемы авторской правки книгописца Ефросина (к вопросу об индивидуальных чертах Кирилло-Белозерского списка *Задон-щины*)". In the book: "*Слово о полку Игореве*" *и памятники Куликовского цикла.* pp. 264-291; Каган М. Д., Понырко Н. В., Рождественская М. В. "Описание сбор-ников XV в. книгописца Ефросина". *ТОДРЛ*, Vol. XXVI, 1980, pp. 3-300.

[2] In specialist literature a different explanation of the term Strigolniks has been advanced, namely, that it derives from the cutting of cloth (see: Лихачев Д. С. "К вопросу о происхождении названия псковско-новгородских еретиков *стриголь-ники*". In the collection of reports and communications of the Linguistics Society of Kalinin University, Vol. IV, 1974, pp. 130-132).

[3] *ПЛДР. Вторая половина XV века*, pp. 538-539.

[4] For sources on the history of the heretical movements see the book: Казакова Н. А., Лурье Я. С. *Антифеодальные еретические движения на Руси XIV-начала XVI в.* Moscow and Leningrad, 1955.

[5] Клибанов А. И. "*Написание о грамоте.* Опыт исследования просветительно-реформационного памятника конца XV-первой половины XVI века". In the book: *Вопросы истории религии и атеизма*, Vol. 3, Moscow, 1956, pp. 325-374; Fine, J.V.A., "Feodor Kuritsyn's *Laodikijskoe poslanie* and the Heresy of the Judizers" *Speculum*, Cambridge, Mass., Vol. 41, 1966, pp. 500-504; Freydank, D., "Der Laodicenerbrief". *Zeitschrift für Slawistik*, Bd. 11, Berlin, 1966, S. 355-370; Kämpfer, F., "Zur Interpreta-tion des *Laodicenischen Sendschreibens*". *Jahrbücher für Geschichte Osteuropas*, Bd. 16, Jg. 1968, S. 566-569; Maier, J., "Zum jüdischer Hintergrund des sogenanten *Laodicenischen Sendschreibens*". Ibid., Bd. 17, Jg. 1969, S. 1-12; Haney, J.V., "*The Laodicean Epistle:* Some Possible Sources". *Slavic Review*, Vol. 30, 1971, No. 4, pp. 832-842; Lilenfeld, F.v., 1) "Das *Laodikijskoe poslanie* des grossfürstlichen D'jaken Fedor Kuricyn". *Jahrbücher für Geschichte Osteuropas*, Bd. 24, Jg. 1976, S. 1-22; 2) "Иоанн Тритемий и Федор Курицын". In the book: *Культурное наследие Древней Руси. Истоки. Становление. Традиции.* Moscow, 1976, pp. 116-123; 3) "Die *Häresi* des Fedor Kuricyn. *Forschungen zur Osteuropäischen Geschichte*, Bd. 24, Wiesbaden, 1978,

S. 39-64. Cf. Luria, J., 1) "L'heresie dite des judaisants et ses sources historiques". *Revue des études slaves,* t. 45, Paris, 1966, p. 49-67; 2) "Zur Zusammenfassung des *Laodicenischen Sendschreiben". Jahrbücher für Geschichte Osteuropas,* Bd. 17, Jg. 1968, S. 66-69; 3) "Unresolved Issues in the History of the Ideological Movements of the Late Fifteenth Century". In: *Medieval Russian Culture.* Ed. H. Birnbaum and M.S. Flier. University of California Press. Berkeley-Los Angeles-London, 1984, p. 150-163.

[6] *The Sophia First Chronicle* is published in ПСРЛ, Vols. V-VI, 1851-1853 (with gaps); ПСРЛ, Vol. V. Second edition, 1925 (not to the end); *The Novgorod Fourth Chronicle* is published in ПСРЛ, Vol. IV, 1915-1925.

[7] *The Nikanor Chronicle* is published in ПСРЛ, Vol. XXVII, 1962, pp. 17-161; *The Vologda-Perm Chronicle,* in ПСРЛ, Vol. XXVI, 1959.

[8] Chronicle compilation of 1479 (in a redaction made in the 1490s) is published in ПСРЛ, Vol. XXV, 1949.

[9] *The Ermolin Chronicle* is published in the ПСРЛ, Vol. XXIII, 1910; the abridged compilations of the late fifteenth century in ПСРЛ, Vol. XXVII, 1962, pp. 163-367; ПЛДР. *Вторая половина XV века,* pp. 410-443.

[10] *The Sophia Second Chronicle* is published in ПСРЛ, Vol. VI, 1853 (the account of 1480 is on pp. 230-231).

[11] On fifteenth-century chronicles see: Лурье Я. С. *Общерусские летописи XIV-XV вв.* Leningrad, 1976.

[12] ПСРЛ, Vol. IV, Part I, 1925, No. 2, pp. 446-449; see also: ПЛДР. *Вторая половина XV века,* pp. 404-409.

[13] A. A. Shakhmatov's dating of the first redaction of *The Russian Chronograph* to 1442 has now been revised. See: Клосс Б. М. "О времени создания *Русского хронографа". ТОДРЛ,* Vol. XXVI, 1971, pp. 244-255; Творогов О. В. *Древнерусские хронографы,* pp. 190-192. In a review of this book B. M. Kloss expressed the view that the first redaction of *The Russian Chronograph* was compiled in 1516-1522. (*История СССР,* No. 3, 1977, p. 183.)

[14] For an analysis of the style of *The Russian Chronograph* see: Лихачев Д. С. *Русские летописи и их культурно-историческое значение,* pp. 331-354; Творогов О. В. "К истории жанра хронографии". *ТОДРЛ,* Vol. XXVII, 1972, pp. 203-226.

[15] For the text of the *Tale* see: *Русские повести XV-XVI вв.* Moscow and Leningrad, 1958, pp. 55-78. Cf. Сперанский М. Н. "Повести и сказания о взятии Царьграда турками". *ТОДРЛ,* Vol. X, 1954, pp. 138-165; Скрипиль М. О. "'История' о взятии Царьграда турками Нестора Искандера". *ТОДРЛ,* Vol. X, 1954, pp. 166-184; ПЛДР. *Вторая половина XV века,* pp. 216-267.

[16] The Innocentius' record is printed in the book: Ключевский В. О. *Древнерусские жития святых как исторический источник,* pp. 439-453; ПЛДР. *Вторая половина XV века,* pp. 478-513.

[17] *Повести о житии Михаила Клопского.* Preparation of texts and article by L. A. Dmitriev. Moscow and Leningrad, 1958; ПЛДР. *Вторая половина XV века,* pp. 334-349.

[18] Р. П. Дмитриева. *Повесть о Петре и Февронии Муромских.* Leningrad, 1979, pp. 99-101, 118. On *The Tale of Peter and Febronia* by Ermolai-Erasmus, see below, pp. 354-59.

[19] "Повесть о Петре Ордынском". In the book: *Русские повести XV-XVI вв.,* pp. 98-105; ПЛДР. *Конец XV-первая половина XVI века.* Moscow, 1984, pp. 20-37.

[20] "Александрия". *Роман об Александре Македонском по русской рукописи XV века.* Prepared by M. N. Botvinnik, Y. S. Lurie and O. V. Tvorogov. Moscow and Leningrad, 1965; ПЛДР. *Вторая половина XV века,* pp. 22-177.

[21] For the study and publication of the text of works on the Trojan War see the book: *Троянские сказания. Средневековые рыцарские романы о Троянской войне по русским рукописям XVI-XVII вв.* Preparation of texts and article by O. V. Tvorogov. Commentaries by M. N. Botvinnik and O. V. Tvorogov. Leningrad, 1972; *ПЛДР. Конец XV-первая половина XVI века*, pp. 222-267.

[22] *"Сказание о Соломоне и Китоврасе".* In the book *Изборник (Сборник произведений литературы Древней Руси).* Moscow, 1969, pp. 370-375; *ПЛДР, XIV-середина XV века*, pp. 68-73.

[23] For *"Суды Соломона"* see the book: *Памятники отреченной русской литературы, собранные Н. С. Тихонравовым*, Vol. I. St Petersburg, 1863, pp. 259-265; *ПЛДР. XIV-середина XV века*, pp. 66-67, 76-78.

[24] *Памятники старинной русской литературы. Ложные и отреченные книги русской старины, собранные А. Н. Пыпиным.* St Petersburg, 1862, No. 3, pp. 59-61; Cf: Ярошенко-Титова Л. В. *"Повесть об увозе Соломоновой жены* в русской рукописной традиции XVII-XVIII в". *ТОДРЛ*; Vol. XXIX, 1974, pp. 257-273; see also Luria, J., "Une légende inconnue de Solomon et Kitovras dans un manuscript du XV-e siécle". *Revue des études slaves,* t. XLIII, f. 1-4, Paris, 1964, p. 7-11.

[25] For the publication and study of *Stefanit and Ikhnilat* see the book: *"Стефанит и Ихнилат". Средневековая книга басен по русским рукописям XV-XVII вв.* Edited by O. P. Likhacheva and Y. S. Lurie. Translations from the Greek by E. E. Granstrem and V. S. Shandrovskaya. Leningrad, 1969; *ПЛДР. Конец XV-первая половина XVI века*, pp. 152-221.

[26] For the text of the oldest version of *The Tale of Babylon* see: Скрипиль М. О. *"Сказание о Вавилоне-граде". ТОДРЛ*, Vol. IX, pp. 142-144; republished in the book: *Русские повести XV-XVI вв.*, pp. 85-87; *ПЛДР. Вторая половина XV века*, pp. 182-187.

[27] For the study and publication of *The Tale of the Monk Who Asked for the Hand of the King's Daughter* see: Дурново Н. Н. *"Легенда о заключенном бесе в византийской и старинной русской литературе".* In the book: *Древности. (Труды Славянской комиссии Московского археологического общества*, Vol. IV, No. 1.) Moscow, 1907, pp. 103-153. The *Tale* is also published in *ПЛДР. Вторая половина XV века*, pp. 182-187.

[28] *Повесть о Дракуле.* Study and preparation of texts by Y. S. Lurie. Moscow and Leningrad, 1964. *ПЛДР. Вторая половина XV века*, pp. 554-565. Recent years have seen the publication of a number of foreign works examining the Dracula legends, including the Russian fifteenth-century tale: Giraudo, G., *"Dracula". Contributi alla storia delle idee politiche nell' Europa Orientale alla svolta del XV secolo.* Venezia, 1972; Ronay, G., *The Truth About Dracula* (English edition: *The Dracula Myth*). New York, 1972; Florescu, R., and McNally, R.T., *Dracula. A Biography of Vlad the Impaler, 1431-1476.* New York, 1973; Berza, M., "Vlad Ţepes, ses regnes et sa legende en marge de deux livres recentes". *Revue des études sudest europeennes,* t. XV, 1977, No. 2, p. 325-354. Cf.: Luria J. "Probleme der gegenwärtigen 'Draculiana'". In: *Osteuropa in Geschichte und Gegenwart. Festschrift fur Günter Stökl zum 60 Geburtstag.* Köln-Wien, 1977, S. 316-327.

[29] Черепнин Л. В. *Русские феодальные архивы XVI-XV веков*, Part 2, Moscow and Leningrad, 1951, pp. 310-312; Адрианова-Перетц В. П. "Крестьянская тема в литературе XVI в.". *ТОДРЛ*, Vol. 10, 1954, p. 203; Морозов А. А. "Национальное своеобразие и проблема стилей". *Русская литература*, No. 3, 1967, pp. 111-118; Лурье Я. С. "Еще раз о Дракуле и макиавеллизме". *Русская литература*, No. 1, pp. 142-146; Лихачев Д. С. *Человек в литературе Древней Руси*, p. 13.

30 *Повѣстъ о Дмитрии Басарге и о сыне его Борзосмысле.* Study and preparation of texts by M. O. Skripil. Leningrad, 1969; the *Tale* and a modern Russian translation of it are also published in *ПЛДР. Вторая половина XV века,* pp. 566-577.

31 Anderson, W., *Keiser und Abbot,* Helsinki, 1923; for the Russian text of the first part of this book see: Андерсон В. *"Император и аббат". История одного народного анекдота,* Part 1, Kazan, 1916.

32 *"Хожение за три моря" Афанасия Никитина.* 2 изд., доп. и перераб. Л., 1986 (Сер. "Литературные памятники"). See also: Лурье Я. С. "Подвиг Афанасия Никитина. (К 500-летию начала его путешествия.)" *Известия Всесоюзного географического общества,* Vol. 99, No. 5, pp. 435-442; Семенов Л. С. *Путешествие Афанасия Никитина,* Moscow, 1980; Трубецкой Н. С. *"Хождение за три моря Афанасия Никитина, как литературный памятник".* In the book: N. S. Trubetskoj, *Three Philological Studies,* Michigan Slavic Materials, 3, 1963; Lennhoff, Gail, *"Beyond Three Seas:* Aphanasij Nikitin's Journey from Orthodoxy to Apostasy". *East European Quarterly,* Vol.XIII, No. 4, Dec. 1979, pp. 431-447. For publication of the text see: *ПЛДР. Вторая половина XV века,* pp. 444-477.

33 Lennhoff, G., op. cit.

CHAPTER 6

LITERATURE OF THE SIXTEENTH CENTURY

1. The Main Ideological Phenomena of the Sixteenth Century

The sixteenth century was the period of the final formation and establishment of the Russian centralised state. During

this period Russian architecture and painting continued to develop and book printing began. At the same time the sixteenth century witnessed the strict centralisation of culture and literature—the various chronicle compilations were replaced by the single national chronicle of the grand prince (later the tsar), and a single compendium of religious and some secular literature was set up known as *The Great Menology*, tomes in which the reading material was arranged according to months. The heretical movement that had been put down at the beginning of the sixteenth century re-emerged in the middle of the century after the large-scale popular revolts of the 1540s. And again heresy was cruelly repressed. One sixteenth-century heretic, a nobleman by the name of Matfei Bashkin, concluded boldly from the New Testament behest to love your neighbour that no one had the right to own "Christ's servants" and freed all his serfs. Another heretic, a serf called Theodosius Kosoy, went even further by declaring that all people were equal irrespective of nationality and creed: "All people are equal before God, both Tartars, and Germans, and all other peoples." Theodosius Kosoy fled from prison to Lithuanian (West) Russia where he continued to preach his beliefs, together with the boldest of the Polish-Lithuanian and West-European Protestants.

Official ideology opposed the anti-feudal movements. The formation of this ideology can be traced from the early decades of the sixteenth century. Almost simultaneously, in the early 1520s, two most important ideological works appeared: *The Epistle on the Monomachos Crown* by Spiridon-Savva and *The Epistle Against the Astrologers* by the Pskovian monk Philotheus.

The Epistle on the Monomachos Crown and **The Tale of the Princes of Vladimir.** *The Epistle on the Monomachos Crown* by Spiridon-Savva contains a legend that played a most important part in the development of the official ideology of the Russian autocratic state. It is the legend about the descent of the ruling dynasty of grand princes in Russia from the Roman emperor Augustus and the confirmation of its dynastic rights by the Monomachos crown, said to have been given to Prince Vladimir Monomachos of Kiev by the Emperor of Byzantium. This legend went back to the fifteenth century and may have been connected with the claims to the "emperor's crown" made in the middle of that century by Grand Prince Boris of Tver. In 1498 Ivan III's grandson Dmitry (who was descended from the princes of Tver on his mother's side) was proclaimed co-ruler with his grandfather and crowned with the Monomachos cap. This was the first appearance of the crown which was subsequently used at the coronation of the rulers of Russia. Legends to substantiate this coronation may have existed even then, but the earliest written record of such legends that we know is Spiridon-Savva's *Epistle on the Monomachos Crown.*

A monk of Tver, who was appointed Metropolitan of All Russia in the fifteenth century in Constantinople and whom the Grand Prince of Moscow refused to recognise and subsequently imprisoned, Spiridon-Savva was a highly educated man for his day. He began his *Epistle on the Monomachos Crown* with an account of Old Testament history and the division of the universe under Augustus, in which the towns on the rivers Vistula and Neman were given to his kinsman Prus; one of Prus' descendants was Rurik, who was thus "of the line of the Roman Emperor Augustus". Then followed the legend about the summoning of the Varangians and an account of Vladimir Monomachos' campaign against Constantinople and the presentation to him by the emperor of the Imperial crown that belonged to Augustus, and other gifts. This story is followed by an account of the lineage of the princes of Lithuania, who are said to be descended from the "slave-groom" Hegiminicus, who served Prince Alexander of Tver, the prince who restored the Russian lands after Batu's invasion. Thus, the legend about the descent of the Russian rulers from the Emperor Augustus is connected here with Tver dynastic legends.

The Epistle on the Monomachos Crown provided the basis for one of the most popular sixteenth-century works, *The Tale of the Princes of Vladimir.*

For the most part its text was close to that of Spiridon's *Epistle,* but the "Lineage of the Princes of Lithuania" was set apart in a special section and the role assigned by Spiridon to the princes of Tver was attributed to Prince Yuri of Moscow and his descendants; at the end there was a reference to Dmitry Donskoy's victory over Mamai.

In 1547 an event of great importance for the history of the Russian state took place: the young Grand Prince Ivan IV was crowned with the Monomachos cap and proclaimed Tsar of All Russia. In this connection a special *Coronation Order* was compiled, the introduction to which made use of *The Tale of the Princes of Vladimir.*

The ideas of the *Tale* were expounded in diplomatic missives and are reflected in the chronicles, the sixteenth-century *Book of Degrees* and *The Royal Genealogy.* They even appeared in representational art: scenes from *The Tale of the Princes of Vladimir* are carved on the doors of the Royal Seat (the wooden partition for the throne of Ivan IV) in the Cathedral of the Assumption in Moscow.[1]

Philotheus the Monk's Theory of "Moscow as the Third Rome". Around 1524 Philotheus, a monk in the Pskov Crypt Monastery, wrote an *Epistle Against the Astrologers* addressed to the Secretary Misiur Munekhin attacking the German physician and philosopher Nikolai Bulev (Bülow), a Catholic who served at the court of Basil III and circulated a German almanach with astronomical and astrological predictions in Russia. Protesting against this, Philotheus expressed the view, quite common in Russian publicistics, that the whole Latin (Catholic) world was sinful and that the "first Rome" and the "second Rome" (Constantinople) had lapsed into heresy and ceased to be the centres of the Christian world. They would be replaced by Russia, the "third Rome": "For two Romes have fallen, a third stands, and a fourth there will not be."[2]

The same idea is expressed in two more epistles connected in the manuscript tradition with the name of Philotheus and addressed to Grand Prince Basil III and Grand Prince Ivan IV. The names of these princes are mentioned only in later copies, however (not before the seventeenth century), and we do not know what these copies were: other epistles by Philotheus or later revisions of his *Epistle Against the Astrologers.*

No matter how many epistles Philotheus may have written, the theory of "Moscow as the third Rome" belongs to him. This

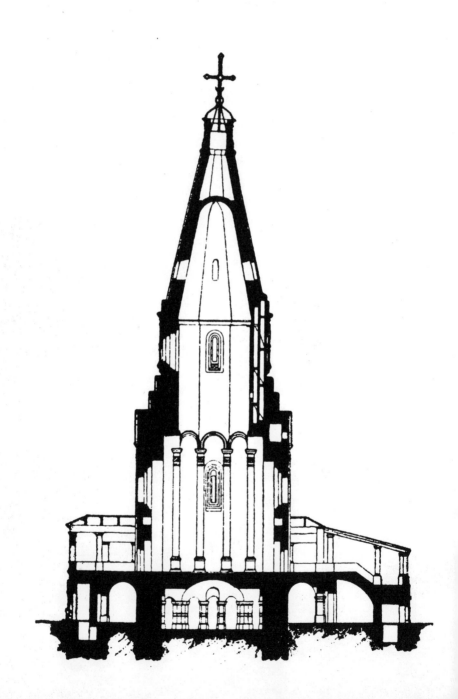

theory was based on ideas expressed as early as the fifteenth century. Shortly before the capture of Constantinople by the Turks the Byzantine Emperor and Patriarch, wishing to obtain help from the West, agreed to a union of the Greek Orthodox Church with the Latin Catholic Church. This union did not save Constantinople, and in 1453 it was captured by the Turks. The union was not recognised in Russia, and the fall of Constantinople was seen as Divine punishment of the Greeks for renouncing Orthodoxy. In 1492 Metropolitan Zosimus proclaimed that the place of the "first", the Greeks, was being taken by the "last", the Russians, and called Moscow "the new city of Constantine". Unlike Zosimus Philotheus was opposed to heretical movements and would not entertain the idea of any reform of the ecclesiastical system, but he expanded the idea of "Moscow as the new city of Constantine", proclaiming Moscow to be the spiritual centre of the whole of Christendom.

All these works shared the idea, which was gradually becoming a fundamental principle of official ideology, that Russia had a special role as the only Orthodox country in a world that had lost true Christianity.

In 1551 a Church Council was held in Moscow and its decisions published in a special book consisting of the tsar's questions and the council's answers to these questions. The book had one hundred chapters, hence the name of the book and of the council that published it. The Council of the Hundred Chapters reaffirmed the ecclesiastical cult established in Russia as inviolable and final (its decisions, as we shall see, later played an important part in the religious schism of the seventeenth century). At the same time the council's decisions were aimed against all reformatory heretical doctrines. In his epistle to the "fathers" of the council Ivan the Terrible called upon them to defend the Christian faith "from murderous wolves and all manner of enemy snares". The council condemned the reading and dissemination of "impious" and "heretical proscribed books" and spoke out against *skomorokhs,* (i.e., minstrels and buffoons), and icon-painters who paint not "from the ancient models" and ignore the accepted canons.

A number of literary undertakings of a generalising nature in the sixteenth century were connected with the official ideological policy of Ivan the Terrible in the period of the Council of the Hundred Chapters. These include the compilation of *The Hundred Chapters* and such outstanding literary works as *The Great Menology* and the *Household Management.*

The Great Menology. *The Great Menology* was compiled under the supervision of Macarius, Archbishop of Novgorod and later

Relief carving on Ivan the Terrible's throne in the Assumption Cathedral of the Moscow Kremlin depicting subjects from *The Tale of the Princes of Vladimir.* 1551

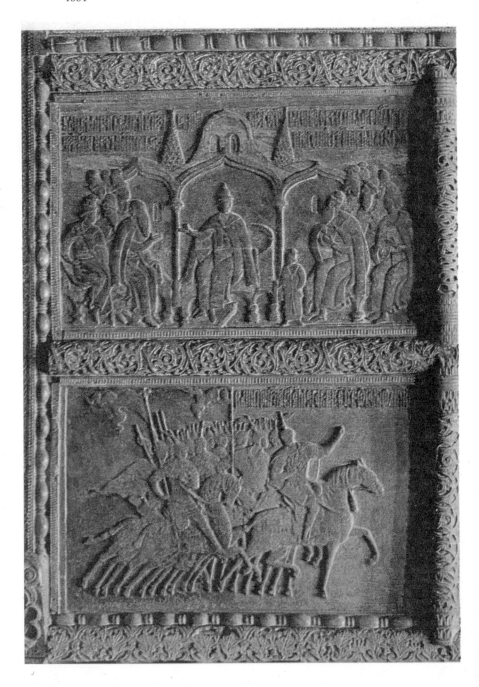

Metropolitan of All Russia. This impressive compilation consisted of twelve volumes, one for each calendar month. It has survived in three versions, *The Sophia Menology*, compiled in the 1530s and early 1540s, and the *Assumption* and *Tsar's* menologies of the early 1550s. Each volume contained the Lives of all the saints whose feast days came in that particular month and all the literature directly or indirectly linked with these saints. It was Macarius' intention that *The Great Menology* should include not only Lives of the saints, but "all books of reading" (i.e., all books intended for reading) "that there are in the Russian land". Alongside *vitae*, the codex drawn up by Macarius included works by Greek Church Fathers (patristics), religious polemical literature (for example, Joseph of Volokolamsk's book against heretics, *The Enlightener*), religious rules and even such works as the *Christian Topography* (description of the world) by Cosmas Indicopleustes, the tale *Barlaam and Josaphat, The Tale of Babylon*, etc. Thus, *The Great Menology* was to cover all the works (apart from chronicles and chronographs) that were permitted reading in Old Russia. Each of its huge volumes (in folio) contains 1,000 printer's quires. It is such an enormous work that, although publication of a scholarly edition began in the middle of the nineteenth century and continued up to the early twentieth, it has not yet been completed.[3]

The *Household Management*. *The Hundred Chapters* contained the basic rules for religious worship and ritual in Old Russia, and *The Great Menology* determined the Russian's range of reading, the *Household Management* offered a similar set of rules for private, domestic life. Like other works of the sixteenth century, the *Household Management* was based on an earlier literary tradition. This tradition included, for example, such an outstanding work of Kievan Russia as Vladimir Monomachos' *Instruction*. Russia had long possessed homiletic miscellanies containing instructions and remarks on questions of everyday conduct (such as *The Emerald* and the *Chrysostom* collections). The sixteenth century saw the appearance of a work entitled the *Household Management* (i.e., rules for domestic life) and consisting of three parts: on worship of the Church and the Tsar, on "wordly management" (relations within the family) and on "household management" (economy). The first redaction of the *Household Management*, compiled before the middle of the sixteenth century, contained (in the descriptions of everyday life) some very vivid scenes of Moscow life, for example, the story of the procuresses who tempted married gentlewomen.[4] The second redaction of the *Household Management* belongs to the middle of the sixteenth century and is linked with the name of Sylvester, a priest who belonged to the narrow circle of most influential people close to the tsar, a circle later referred to (in the writings of Andrew Kurbsky, who was closely associated with it) as the Select Council. This redaction ended with Sylvester's epistle to his son Anfim.[5] At the centre of the *Household Management* is the sixteenth-century household, self-contained and cut off from the outside world. This household is in a city and reflects the life of the prosperous city-dweller, rather than the landowning nobility. The master is a thrifty, practical man with retainers and servants, bondmen or hired freemen. He acquires all the basic objects at the market, combining trading and craftsmanship with money-lending. He fears and respects the tsar and the powers-that-be. "He who opposes the sovereign, opposes God too."

Sylvester removed from the *Household Management* the most striking scenes of everyday life found in the first redaction, but preserved the main theme: austerity and strictness in private life, compulsory handiwork for members of the family, thriftiness even to the point of stinginess, guarding against dangerous relations with the outside world and the strictest keeping of all family secrets. Moderation and caution are prescribed in all things; in particular, in corporal punishment of one's wife, children and servants: "strike courteously with the lash, holding both hands ... and do so not in anger, but let no man know or hear of it..."

The creation of *The Hundred Chapters*, *The Great Menology* and the *Household Management* was largely for the purpose of controlling the development of culture and literature. The well-known literary historian, Nikolai Tikhonravov, rightly remarks that these measures "speak eloquently to us of the arousing of conservative elements in the intellectual movement of Muscovite Russia of the sixteenth century".[6] This control over culture and literature became particularly strict during the Oprichnina established by Ivan the Terrible in 1564. The tsar, to quote his enemy Kurbsky, "locked up his tsardom as if in an infernal fortress", not allowing any literature from Western Europe where the Renaissance and Reformation were developing at this time. Book printing, which had begun in the 1550s and 1560s, ceased in somewhat unclear circumstances: due to harassment "from many superiors and churchmen" who accused him of "heresy", the first Russian printer, Ivan Fyodorov, was forced to flee to Western Russia (Ostrog and later Lvov).[7]

But the change of direction in the development of Russian culture in the sixteenth century did not mean that this development ceased. The sixteenth century was an unfavourable time for fiction or what was then called "useless tales". Many tales known in the fifteenth century stopped being copied altogether in the sixteenth, such as *Stefanit and Ikhnilat*, *The Tale of Dracula*, the *Alexandreid* and the tales about Solomon and Kitovras. But the "useful" (from the viewpoint of official ideology) tales of an historical and religious-didactic nature continued to develop. Many *vitae* arose, both in *The Great Menology* and independently. Chronicle-writing, although now centralised, was carried on with great care right up to the middle of the 1560s. A new type of literature, particularly characteristic of the sixteenth century, also became widespread, namely, secular publicistics, which discussed the most important questions of the day.

2. Hagiography. *The Tale of Peter and Febronia*

One of the main types of literature in the sixteenth century was still hagiography, the *vitae*. The sixteenth century saw the canonisation by the Russian Church of many persons who had formerly been worshipped only in certain areas and principalities, and also a number of churchmen of the recent past.

The sixteenth-century *vitae* have survived in separate texts, in miscellanies and, most characteristic of this period, in large compilations—paterica and *The Great Menology*. Many of the *vitae* in this period were about the founders of monasteries in the late fifteenth and sixteenth centuries.

Many sixteenth-century hagiographical works are linked with the Volokolamsk Monastery, the founder of which, Joseph of Volokolamsk, was the main "denouncer" of Novgorodian and Muscovite heresy. The Volokolamsk *vitae* were assembled in a special compilation of "tales of the former fathers" of the Borovsk and Volokolamsk monasteries, known as *The Volokolamsk Patericon*. It was compiled by Joseph of Volokolamsk's nephew and supporter, the writer and icon-painter Dositheos Toporkov.[8]

The hagiographical traditions of the Josephites, Joseph of Volokolamsk's followers, were continued by Metropolitan Macarius. Macarius was originally a monk in the Borovsk Monastery where Joseph also began his activity. *The Great Menology*, compiled under his guidance, as we already know, was intended to encompass the whole range of people's reading in the sixteenth century, but it was based on *vitae*. Moreover, in spite of its size *The Great Menology* by no means included all the *vitae* known in Russian literature up to the sixteenth century. The compilers of *The Great Menology* clearly gave preference to "ornate" Lives, such as those written in the fifteenth century by Pachomius the Logothete. The fifteenth-century *Life of St Michael of Klopsk*, written in a style uncommon in hagiography, was considerably revised by one of the redactors of *The Great Menology*, Vasily Tuchkov; its unexpected beginning was replaced by the traditional hagiographical introduction, etc.[9]

Apart from the *vitae* included in *The Volokolamsk Patericon* and *The Great Menology*, others continued to be created and transcribed separately. Thus, separate miscellanies have preserved *The Life of Peter of the Horde*, radically revised in *The Great Menology*. It was in the sixteenth century that the extant redaction of such a fine work of Old Russian literature as the Life of SS Peter and Febronia was made.

The Tale of Peter and Febronia. The hagiographical *Tale of Peter and Febronia* has come down to us in the work of the sixteenth-century writer and publicist Ermolai-Erasmus.[10] There is scant information about this writer's life. He came to Moscow from Pskov in the middle of the sixteenth century and became an archpriest in the court cathedral in Moscow, by the early 1560s took monastic vows (under the name of Erasmus) and possibly left the capital. His most important publicistic work was a treatise, in which he expresses the idea that peasants are the foundation of society: "First of all, the peasants are essential: from their labours comes bread, and from them most good things... and the whole country from the tsar down to the common folk is fed." Believing the social inequality by which the peasant feeds his masters to be an inevitable phenomenon, Ermolai nevertheless suggests that the peasant's payments and taxes should be strictly defined and that he should be protected from oppression by state land surveyors and tax collectors. Such measures, in his opinion, would reduce "all manner of rebellion".[11]

As well as publicistic works Ermolai-Erasmus also wrote hagiographical ones, *The Tale of Bishop Basil of Ryazan* (later included in *The Life of Prince Constantine of Murom*) and *The Tale of Peter and Febronia*, which appear to have been based on a fifteenth-century *vita*.

The existence of a story of Peter and Febronia compiled before the end of the fifteenth century can be deduced from the fact that there is a fifteenth-century church service dedicated to Prince Peter of Murom who killed a dragon and to his wise wife Febronia, with whom Peter was buried in the same coffin. Evidently the basic subject of the tale dates back earlier than Ermolai-Erasmus.

The plot is as follows. Prince Paul's wife is visited by a dragon in the guise of her husband. Paul's brother, Peter, fights the dragon and kills it; but Peter is stricken down by the dragon's blood that spurts onto him and his body is covered with sores.

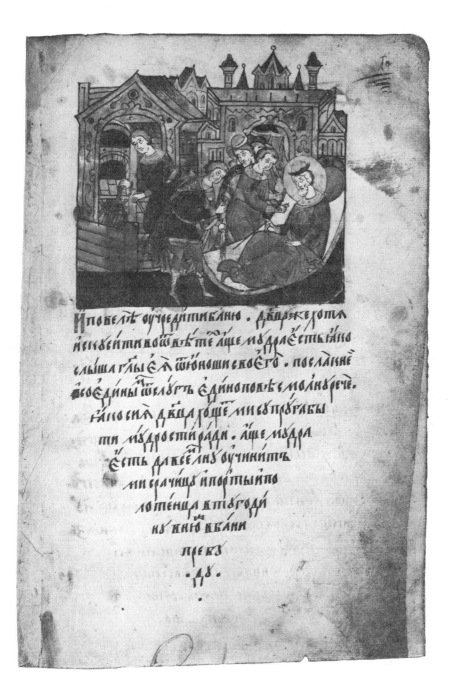

The Maid Febronia Healing Prince Peter. Detail

Peter is cured by a wise peasant girl called Febronia; as a reward she asks the prince to make her his wife.

The subject-matter of the tale is reminiscent of many works in Russian and world folklore; it is also reflected in mediaeval written sources. In the famous West European (Celtic, Romance) legend of Tristan and Isolde the story also begins with the hero (Tristan) killing the dragon; he is cured by the heroine (Isolde).

However, the similarity between the subject matter of *The Tale of Peter and Febronia* and that of *Tristan and Isolde* stresses even more the difference in the respective treatment of the characters. Unlike the legend of Tristan and Isolde *The Tale of Peter and Febronia* is a story not about love, not about the all-consuming passion of the main characters, but about faithful conjugal life, and the main motif in the tale is the heroine's quick-wittedness, her ability to outwit her adversaries, a feature which makes her akin to Olga in *The Tale of Bygone Years.*

Febronia appears in the tale after the sick Peter has sent messengers all over the land of Ryazan in search of physicians to heal him. During this search one of his servants comes to the village of Laskovo (meaning "tender"), which still exists to this day, and sees a girl at her loom; in front of her a hare is frisking about. In reply to the youth's question as to the whereabouts of the other members of the household, she replies that her parents have gone "to weep to their credit", and her brother "to look death in the eye through his legs". The youth cannot make head or tail of these words, but the girl explains to him that her parents have gone to weep for the dead; when they die, people will weep for them too, so they are weeping to their credit; her brother is a wild-honey farmer who gets honey from trees and looks down through his legs so as not to fall to his death. Having ascertained that Febronia (the girl's name) is very wise, the youth begs her to cure his prince. Febronia agrees on condition that Peter makes her his wife.

How are we to understand this condition? The reader who regarded the tale solely as a hagiographical work and Febronia, first and foremost, as a saint, could see this as a manifestation of her wisdom—she knew in advance that Peter was ordained to be her husband. But people brought up on folk tales, where such a condition is often met, could regard this motif in a different way, on a purely prosaic level. Living in her village of Laskovo. Febronia was unlikely to have even seen Peter before she was asked to cure him. The reader would naturally conclude that she was drawn to Prince Peter not by love (in the legend of Tristan and Isolde there is a reference to a love potion) but simply by the desire not to let her good luck slip through her fingers.

Febronia shows the same quick-wittedness and ability to outwit in her dealings with Peter. At first the prince puts her to the test: he sends her a piece of flax and asks her to weave him a robe from it. But Febronia counters this impossible demand with one of her own*; she agrees to do as Peter asks on condition that the prince makes her a loom out of a splinter of wood. Peter cannot, of course, so he withdraws his request. After he has been healed Peter tries to break his promise to marry the peasant girl. But Febronia had prudently rubbed all his sores with ointment except one, and as a result of Peter's treachery from "that sore many other sores began to appear on his body"; in order to be completely healed Peter has to keep his promise.

Peter marries Febronia, but the noblemen of the land of Murom do not want a princess who was a peasant girl. She agrees to leave Murom on condition that she is allowed to take what she wants with her. The noblemen agree and the princess wants "only my husband, Prince Peter".

Peter and Febronia leave Murom together on a boat with other passengers. Among them is a certain married man who, egged on by an evil spirit, looks lustfully at the saintly woman. Febronia advises him to scoop up and drink some water first from one side of the boat, then from the other. "Is that water the same or sweeter than the other?" she asks him. He replies that the water is the same. "And woman's essence is the same also. So why leave your own wife and covet another man's?" Febronia asked.

How are we to understand these scenes? Like the story of Peter's marriage to Febronia, they too can be regarded in different ways: both as an indication of the heroine's wisdom and as proof of her cunning. Febronia foresees that the stupid noblemen will not know what she is going to ask them for. In the same way her answer to the importunate fellow-traveller on the boat is witty and edifying, rather than openly didactic; one of the heroines of Boccacio's *Decameron* (Day I, story 5) replies to the importunate advances of the French King in similar fashion.

The exile of Peter and Febronia does not last for long: the rebellious noblemen begin to quarrel and fight among themselves and prove incapable of retaining power, so Peter and Febronia are again summoned back to Murom.

The final scene is deeply poetic. As old age approaches the hero and heroine take monastic vows and wish to die together. Peter is the first to feel the approach of death and calls Febronia to "depart" together. Febronia is embroidering a special cloth for the chalice. She embroiders the saint's head only, then sticks her

---

* This countering of something absurd with something equally absurd is characteristic of mediaeval literature. For example, Akir in *The Tale of Akir the Wise* does precisely the same.

needle into the cloth, winds the embroidery thread round it, and dies together with her husband.

After the death of Peter and Febronia they are buried apart, but are miraculously reunited in the same coffin.

The Tale of Peter and Febronia was closely connected with folklore and also related to the "itinerant subjects" of world literature. With regard to Russian folk tales it is closest to *The Seven-Year-Old Girl* and *The Shorn Maid* which are also about the marriage of a person of noble birth to a peasant girl who proves her wisdom by solving difficult tasks; here too is the motif of exiling the heroine who takes her dearest possession—her husband.[12] But in Russian tales (which have survived only in manuscripts of the modern age) we do not find the theme of the illness and healing of the high-born husband. It is obvious, however, that this motif was also present in the folklore subject used by Ermolai-Erasmus. In one of the stories of *The Decameron* (Day III, story 9) the heroine receives a courtier as a husband in return for healing the King of France. The unequal marriage brings her grief and banishment, but, as in the Russian tale, the heroine's wisdom helps her to triumph. The same subject is also used by Shakespeare in his comedy *All's Well That Ends Well.* The combination of the themes of the unequal marriage and the healing of the hero by the heroine was obviously also known in Russian folklore of the fifteenth and sixteenth centuries. The end of the tale of Peter and Febronia is also linked with folklore motifs and again reminds us of *Tristan and Isolde,* where the love of the two main characters is stronger than death (a rose bush grows out of Tristan's grave linking it with the grave of Isolde).

The untraditional nature of the hagiographical *Tale of Peter and Febronia* evidently made it unsuitable for the hagiographical canons of the sixteenth century. Although created at the same time as the final version of *The Great Menology* (the *Assumption* and *Tsar's* menologies), it was not included in them. The folklore elements in the tale, its brevity, and lack of conventional features made it unsuitable for the hagiographical school of Metropolitan Macarius. But it is precisely these features that make *The Tale of Peter and Febronia* one of the finest works of Old Russian literature.

3. Historical Narrative

In the sixteenth century Russian chronicle-writing became centralised. Chronicles could be compiled in both the metropolitan and the grand prince chancelleries, but all records of current events were standardised. Consequently, if there was a change in the policy of the grand prince, these records were revised accordingly.

Two large All-Russian chronicles have survived from the sixteenth century—the *Nikon* and the *Resurrection* chronicles; on the basis of *The Nikon Chronicle* the multi-volumed sixteenth-century *Illustrated Chronicle* was compiled. Alongside All-Russian chronicle-writing local chronicle-writing continued in Pskov; individual chronicles were also compiled in Novgorod and the north of Russia, the Dvina lands and Kholmogory.

After the suppression of the heretical movements in 1504 a considerable role in the development of Russian literature was played by the victors, the "militant churchmen", whose main citadel was the Volokolamsk Monastery founded by Joseph; after Joseph's death his pupil, Daniel, became abbot of the Volokolamsk Monastery. In 1522 Daniel was appointed metropolitan, head of the Russian Church. At the same period two very similar chronicles were compiled with the direct participation of Daniel: *The Josaphat Chronicle*, which covers the years from 1437 to 1519 (it is called Josaphat after Metropolitan Josaphat to whom it later belonged), and the chronicle that later became called *The Nikon Chronicle* by historians. *The Nikon Chronicle* was extremely large in size and complex in content; in its compilation use was made of an early fifteenth-century chronicle similar to *The Trinity Chronicle*, Tver and Novgorodian chronicles, a chronicle compilation transcribed in the Volokolamsk Monastery, and so on. But in the final section, which covers the history of the early sixteenth century, *The Nikon Chronicle* reproduced the official chronicle-writing of the grand prince.

A little later, in the 1530s (the period of Ivan IV's infancy and "boyar rule"), a chronicle appeared which specialists now call *The Resurrection Chronicle*. It was compiled in the grand prince's court and based on a Moscow grand prince's compilation of the late fifteenth century.

In the middle of the sixteenth century, during the reforms of Ivan IV, the Council of the Hundred Chapters and the conquest of the Kazan Khanate, a special official *Chronicle* was compiled extolling the young ruler who had been crowned tsar a few years earlier. It bore the title of *The Chronicle of the Beginning of the Reign of the Tsar and Grand Prince Ivan, Son of Basil*. This chronicle soon acquired a lengthy preceding section based on *The Nikon Chronicle* of the 1520s.

Thus we have the second redaction of *The Nikon Chronicle*, taken up to the 1550s.[13]

In the 1560s the last and most official redaction of *The Nikon Chronicle* with a large number of miniatures was compiled— *The Illustrated Chronicle*. This compilation consisted of nine volumes, three dealing with world history and based on the Bible, *The Hellenic Chronicle* and *The Russian Chronograph*, and six based on *The Nikon Chronicle* supplemented from *The Resurrection Chronicle*. Of particular interest is the fate of the last volume dealing with the reign of Ivan IV himself, but continued much further than *The Chronicle of the Beginning of the Reign*—up to 1567. There are two extant versions of this volume, one incomplete and not illuminated, which is called *The Tsar's Book*. The last volume of *The Illustrated Chronicle* shows traces of work by a redactor, who deleted the previous text and inserted in its place a new text in cursive script quite different in content. Many of these amendments attacked persons who suffered under Ivan IV. One of them (which we shall discuss later) describes events during the illness of Ivan the Terrible. The authorship of these amendments is a matter of dispute between historians: it could have been the tsar or his secretary Ivan Viskovaty, but in any case they were official and reflected the policy of the period of the Oprichnina. Some of them were made in the main text of the new version of the last volume of *The Illustrated Chronicle.* The incompleteness of *The Illustrated Chronicle* which breaks off in 1567 and the cessation of official All-Russian chronicle-writing after this date were obviously connected with the drastic political changes in the years of the Oprichnina.[14]

A number of stories contained in the Russian chronicles of the sixteenth century are of literary, as well as historical value. These include the accounts of the end of Pskov's independence, Basil III's death in 1533 and Ivan IV's illness in 1563.

Tales of the Capture of Pskov. Two accounts of the annexation of Pskov have survived, in the *Pskov First* (1547 compilation) and *Pskov Third* (1567 compilation) chronicles. The first account begins with a lament for Pskov: "O, most renowned of cities, great Pskov! Why do you mourn, why do you weep?" To which Pskov replies: "How can I not mourn, how can I not weep? A many-winged eagle did swoop down on me ... and lay waste our land..." But further on this lament turns into a caustic description of the activity of the Moscow lieutenants (*namestniks*). "And as to the lieutenants, and their stewards and the secretaries of the grand prince, their truth, their promises, have flown up to heaven, and falsehood has begun to walk among them..." Later on it says that these lieutenants drank "heavily of Pskovian blood", which is why all the foreigners chose to flee abroad; "only Pskovians have remained, but the earth will not open, and they cannot fly up to the heavens". In the second account Moscow's abuse of power is condemned even more strongly. Clearly challenging his fellow-countryman Philotheus, who extolled the realm of Muscovy as the Third Rome, the compiler of *The Pskov Third Chronicle*, compares it to the realm of Anti-Christ and writes: "That realm shall grow and the evil thereof increase."[15]

The Tale of the Death of Basil III. The account of the death of Basil III appeared in chronicle-writing almost immediately after the event itself, in 1534.[16] The account of the grand prince's last days was undoubtedly written by someone who witnessed his death. There is a detailed description of Basil's illness ("a small sore on the left side of the thigh ... the size of a pin-head" which caused blood poisoning). The sick prince was taken from the Trinity Monastery, where he happened to be, to Moscow. He asked his court physician Nikolai Bulev (with whom Philotheus disputed in his epistle on the "Third Rome") whether there was any remedy, "an ointment or anything else" to ease his affliction.

"My art is helpless without God's aid," replied the physician. Basil realised that his condition was hopeless. "Brothers! Nikolai has divined my illness well—it is incurable," he said to his courtiers.

The account of the death of Basil III was compiled during the reign of his widow Yelena Glinskaya (who ruled as regent for her infant son Ivan), and she naturally played a particularly honourable role in it. It was she whom Basil charged to rule "like former grand princesses". Custom demanded that he send for his son on his death-bed but Basil, who had become a father late in years and was very concerned about the health of his three-year-old son Ivan, was afraid of alarming him: "I do not wish to call my son, Grand Prince Ivan, for he is too little. I lie in my great affliction, and do not wish that my son should fear me." "Do not let my son Ivan out of your sight for a moment, Ographena," he cautions the nanny. Other words and actions of the dying prince are equally natural and moving, such as his attempts to conceal the gravity of his affliction from his young wife, who sobbed so bitterly that Basil could not give her his parting instructions—"because of her cries he did not manage to give her a single word of instruction", and the conversation with his brother about the last days of their father, Ivan III.

The account of Basil III's death was amended several times in the chronicle-writing of the sixteenth century. In *The Resurrection Chronicle*, compiled after the death of Basil III's wife, Yelena, the reference to her being charged to rule was omitted and replaced by a eulogy to the boyars (uttered by Basil III) for their loyalty; at the same time many details in the account of the Grand Prince's illness and death were also omitted. In *The Chronicle of the Beginning of the Reign* (and in some of the manuscripts of *The Nikon Chronicle*) new amendments were made. The eulogy to the boyars was omitted and a reference inserted to the effect that Basil presented the infant Ivan IV with "the tsar's crown and royal diadems, with which Vladimir Monomachos was crowned". And finally, in the last volume of *The Illustrated Chronicle* (in *The Tsar's Book*) the earlier account of the death of Basil III was restored (plus the addition of the "Monomachos crown") together with the details of the grand prince's last days typical of this account.

The Account of the Illness of Ivan the Terrible. The special interest which the compiler of *The Tsar's Book* showed in the account of Basil III's death would appear to be linked with the following circumstance. The lengthy amendment to *The Tsar's Book* contained an account of the tsar's illness, Ivan IV's illness in 1553, in the course of which the tsar, like his father before him, wished to hand over the throne to his infant son and demanded that the boyars swear allegiance to the child and his mother. In spite of its unusual form (it is scribbled in the margins of the manuscript), this account is very striking and in many respects similar to the account of Basil III's death. The replies of the boyars who refuse to swear allegiance to a "babe-in-arms" are most expressive. Fyodor Adashev, the father of one of Ivan IV's closest boyars, Alexei Adashev, who fell into disfavour in the early 1560s, said, according to *The Tsar's Book*, that they would be willing to swear allegiance to the infant prince, but feared the rule of his mother's relatives: "Your son is still in swaddling clothes, Sire, but it is the Zakharins who will govern over us ... and we have already seen great misfortune from the boyars before you came of age." "If you do not swear allegiance to my son Dmitry, you wish to have another sovereign!" cried the ailing tsar. "And I cannot talk much with you, but you have forgotten about your souls, and you do not wish to serve me and my children..." "But you, Zakharins, why are you afraid?" he cried to his wife's relatives. "Or do you think the boyars will spare you? You will be the first to die from the boyars! You would do better to die for my son and for his mother, and not to give my wife to be profaned by the boyars." [17]

The account of the events of 1553 in *The Tsar's Book* was not a simple record of authentic conversations. It was created many years later and has a definite political purpose (to slander those who have fallen into disfavour). What we have here is deliberate invention, but invention that is of literary, as well as political significance.

The Book of Degrees. The existence of deliberate invention in historical narrative is seen most clearly in the semi-official, mid-sixteenth-century work *The Book of Degrees of the Tsar's Genealogy*.[18] *The Book of Degrees* was compiled in 1560-1563 in the Macarius' circle that produced *The Great Menology* and was similar to it in structure. It set out the whole history of Russia in the form of lives "of the God-appointed sceptre-holders shining in piety" and the life of each of these "sceptre-holders" or princes was seen in the form of a "rung" on the "ladder" to heaven, like the ladders described in Bible stories or hagiographical literature. All the Russian princes (ending with Ivan IV himself) appeared in *The Book of Degrees* as men full of "virtues pleasing to the Lord". The desire to ascribe "piety" to all of them made it necessary to "amend" Russian history to a far greater extent than this was done in chronicle-writing. Under the influence of "political passions and worldly interests" chronicle writers frequently introduced changes into the accounts written by their predecessors, but such changes usually affected recent history only; they were more cautious about tampering with accounts of the distant past. Not so with the compilers of *The Book of Degrees*. Seeking to extol the whole dynasty of Kiev-Vladimir-Moscow princes, they turned boldly to the distant past, radically revising the descriptions of Ivan the Terrible's ancestors and removing everything that did not fit in with a eulogy to them.

The attitude of the compilers of *The Book of Degrees* to historical material is seen not only in the changing of individual events described in the chronicles, but also in the creation (or borrowing from oral tradition) of new stories not found in chronicle sources. Such stories include, for example, the legend about Princess Olga which was put at the very beginning of *The Book of Degrees* as a kind of introductory story. Making use of legends not found in the literature of the preceding centuries and evidently derived from folklore, the author of *The Book of Degrees* began his account with the scene of the first meeting of the heroine who is "not of royal, nor of noble birth, but from the common folk", with the young Prince Igor. Out hunting in the "Pskov region", Igor wanted to cross a river. Seeing a boat, he summoned the rower to the bank and got into it. Only when they had set off from the shore did he notice that it was a girl, young but "comely and brave"; "and he did burn with desire for her, and uttered some bold words to her". But Olga cut short his importunate speech, reproaching him "with a wisdom far beyond her years" and uttered a long speech: "Do not be tempted on seeing me, a young girl all alone..." This scene reminds one of the similar episode in *The Tale of Peter and Febronia*, but in the tale the heroine's answer is mocking and witty, whereas in *The Book of Degrees* it is solemn and didactic. Olga's words of wisdom caused Igor to change his "youthful" behaviour; but when the time came for them to find him a wife, "as is the custom of the state and tsardom", Igor "remembered the most wondrous of maidens", Olga, sent for her, "and they were joined together in holy matrimony".[19]

In spite of the insertion of individual light-hearted scenes, *The Book of Degrees* is, first and foremost, an official, publicistic work. Its theme is the extolling of the ruling dynasty, its style—solemn and monumental.

The History of Kazan. This combination of literary and publicistic invention is found not only in *The Book of Degrees* but in other sixteenth-century works of historical narrative. It is seen most clearly in *The History of Kazan*. Written in 1564-1566,[20] *The Short Legend About the Beginning of the Realm of Kazan* differed from the chronicle compilations and *The Book of Degrees* in its more concrete nature—for it dealt mainly with the capture of Kazan in 1552; but at the same time *The History of Kazan* was not a separate historical tale like *The Tale of the Battle Against Mamai*. The author sought to give an account not only of the capture of Kazan under Ivan IV, but of the whole history of the Kazan state. He began this history with a legend which is not found in Russian historical narrative and appears to have been borrowed from the Tartar feudal lords of Kazan, about the legendary ruler Sain of the Horde, who marched against the Russian land after the death of Batu, delivered a place "on the Volga, on the very border of

Russia", from a terrible two-headed dragon and set up a rich kingdom—flowing with milk and honey—Kazan.

The History of Kazan combines several different literary influences. A number of threads link the work with official publicistics of the sixteenth century, *The Tale of the Princes of Vladimir* and the epistles of Ivan the Terrible. It was also close to the historical narrative of the preceding period—it contains direct borrowings from *The Tale of Tsargrad (Constantinople)* by Nestor-Iskander and *The Russian Chronograph* of 1512. And, finally, this "fine new tale", as the author called it, also resembled such works of fictional prose as the *Alexandreid* and *The Trojan History.*

The mixture of literary influences was bound to affect the style of the *History.* Specialists have already noted the "blatant flouting of literary convention" characteristic of this work: contrary to the canons of the military tale, the enemy is shown in heroic colours—"a single Kazaner fought a hundred Russians, and a pair two hundred"; the "fall of the brave Kazaners" is accompanied by the looting of mosques, murders and cruelties committed by Russian warriors. But the portrayal of the ruler of the Khanate of Kazan, Queen Sumbeka, is most unexpected. Sumbeka is far from a positive figure in the *History.* The author tells of "the illicit love of the khan's relative Koshchak and the queen", of the queen's readiness in concert with her lover "to kill her son, the young prince", and how after being forced to marry Shigalei, Sumbeka tries several times to poison her second husband. Nevertheless, Sumbeka is not only an adulteress and criminal for the author of the *History.* For all this she still remains the wise queen, "fair as the sun", and when she is deposed this is lamented by the whole realm—both "honest wives and fair maidens" and "the whole royal court"; "and hearing this lament, the people came from all over to the royal palace and likewise wept and sobbed inconsolably". The deposed Sumbeka even recalls her beloved first husband, Sapkirei and, as befits heroines in Old Russian literature, addresses him through her tears; she also remembers "her infant son" (although it is said earlier that she planned to kill him).

There were political reasons for this idealised picture of the Tartar Queen in *The History of Kazan.* In the period of the Oprichnina many of the generals who helped to take Kazan in 1552 fell into disfavour and were executed; to counter the old noble families Ivan IV created a new aristocracy of Tartar descent. In his desire to extol Sumbeka, the author attributes to her certain features of heroines from translated fictional literature, those of the beautiful Helen in *The Trojan History* or even Roxana in the *Alexandreid* (cf. her lament over her husband's coffin is similar to that of Roxana over Alexander).

But the use of fifteenth-century tales in *The History of Kazan*, as in *The Book of Degrees*, was somewhat superficial and artificial. These historical works were, first and foremost, official works, whose authors were deliberately seeking to inculcate certain political ideas in the reader. The style of these works is also in keeping with their official nature, e.g., the use of conventional formulae that had ceased to be expressive. The authors readily made use of rhetoric, artificial phrases and expressions: the Volga in *The History of Kazan* is called "the gold-streamed Tigris" (after the river in Babylon), Ivan IV is "strong-handed" and his soldiers are "fierce-hearted". Similar high-flown rhetorical expressions are found in *The Book of Degrees*, for example, in the eulogy to Prince Vladimir, son of Svyatoslav: "That Vladimir is a valiant, pious branch! That Vladimir is an Apostolic zealot! That Vladimir is the affirmation of the church!", etc.

In such works as *The Book of Degrees* and *The History of Kazan* the emotional style that developed in Russian literature of the Pre-Renaissance is formalised. "Individual devices become ossified and begin to be repeated mechanically." A high-flown, pompous, yet dry and formal style arose, which is known as the "second monumental style" in Old Russian literature.[21]

What proved to be fruitful for the development of Russian literature in the following period was not these semi-official works, in spite of their authors' attempts to introduce diverting elements into the narrative, but the expressive elements that found their way into historical narrative from live observations. It could have been the record of an eyewitness, as in the chronicle account of the death of Basil III, or a tale by a talented publicist who created the illusion of authenticity, as in the description of Ivan IV's sickness in *The Tsar's Book*. These lifelike elements can be found in other sixteenth-century works, particularly publicistic ones.

4. Tales

Secular tales were less widespread in the literature of the sixteenth century than in that of the second half of the preceding century. They also differed radically from the tales of the preceding period in character also.

The tales of the sixteenth century are predominantly didactic, openly instructive. Examples are *The Dispute of Life and Death* and *The Tale of Queen Dinara*. The tale written at the end of the century about an important historical event, the defence of Pskov against King Stephen Bathory of Poland in 1581, occupies a somewhat special place.

The Dispute of Life and Death. In sixteenth-century manuscripts we find very few translated tales, either those known in Russia in the fifteenth century or new ones. The only work of a similar genre that became fairly widespread in the sixteenth century is *The Dispute of Life and Death* translated in 1494 (from the German original) in the circle of a well-known opponent of heresy, Archbishop Gennadius of Novgorod. This work was readily transcribed in the sixteenth century in the main centre of church life, the Volokolamsk Monastery of St Joseph.[22]

In form *The Dispute of Life and Death* was a dialogue between Everyman and Death. Everyman asks Death to spare him; Death refuses. Here we have a work close to the dramatic genre (in the German original *Everyman* was a play acted by the German *Fastnachtsspiel* (Shrovetide carnival theatre), but there is no dispute and hardly any action in it. Everyman begs Death to spare him for a short while: "Oh, Death, spare me until morning that I may repent and put my lfe in order." Death refuses and explains to the reader at length that one must repent and pray at all times, for Death can come for any man at any time. At the end Death takes Everyman.

The Tale of Queen Dinara. *The Tale of Queen Dinara* has come down to us in a miscellany of works connected with the circle of Metropolitan Macarius (the tales of the Crimean invasion and the Moscow fire of 1547), and evidently appeared in the first half of the sixteenth century.[23] The main heroine is the Queen of Iveria (Georgia); her prototype appears to have been the famous Queen Tamar of Georgia who ruled in the late twelfth and the early thirteenth century. The plot of *The Tale of Dinara* is simple. It is briefly as follows: the King of Persia demands that the young Queen of Iveria shall submit to him; she refuses. Angered by her refusal, the king invades the land of Iveria (Georgia) with his army. Dinara's noblemen hesitate, but the queen urges her warriors on and promises to present Persian treasures that they win to the Convent of the Virgin. When the Persian army approaches the queen at the head of her army gallops out with a spear in her hand to meet them. The Persians flee in terror. After defeating the Persians the queen keeps her promise, presents the treasures "to the house of God" and reigns happily for many years.

The difference between sixteenth-century tales, such as *The Tale of Dinara,* and the tales of the second half of the fifteenth century was clear to people of that day; it was even specially emphasised. Whereas the works proscribed by the Church in the late fifteenth century were called "useless tales", *The Tale of Dinara* was given the special subtitle of "a very useful tale of great worth".

The tales listed (and the first redaction of *The Tale of the White Mitre*) evidently appeared not later than the middle of the sixteenth century. No tales have survived from the second half of Ivan the Terrible's reign: the period of the Oprichnina was evidently not particularly conducive to the development of literature.

The Tale of the Campaign of Stephen Bathory Against Pskov. The last sixteenth-century tale appeared after the death of Ivan the Terrible. It is the historical *Tale of the Campaign of Stephen Bathory Against Pskov.* Like the historical tales of the fifteenth century, it had a single theme. That theme was the siege of Pskov by King Stephen Bathory of Poland in 1581.[24]

After a short account of the beginning of the war the author turns to the siege of Pskov by Polish-Lithuanian forces. The king, whom the author of the tale portrays like a "ferocious monster" out of a folk tale, encircles the city and is gloating prematurely over his victory. The enemy bring up siege towers and manage to capture the Intercession and Swine towers: the Polish flag is hoisted on both of them. But the people of Pskov pray, and God hears their prayers. The Russians attack the Swine Tower, put gunpowder under it and blow it up. "Are my nobles in the castle yet?" asks Bathory. "No, Sire, they are under the castle," is the reply. Not understanding this, the king decides that they must be by the city walls, fighting the Russians. "Sire! All those in the Swine Tower have been killed and burnt to death, and lie in the moat," he is told. The enraged king orders his men to advance through the breach in the wall and take the city. But the Russians resist the assault, monks and women fighting together with the men, and drive the enemy out of the city. Pskovian women help their husbands by dragging abandoned Lithuanian arms into the city.

The first assault has been unsuccessful, but the boyars and commanders remind the people of Pskov that fresh battles lie ahead. Having failed to take Pskov directly by siege, Stephen fires a message over the city walls on an arrow, inviting the townspeople to surrender "the city without bloodshed" and threatening "all manner of cruel deaths" if they do not. The people of Pskov reply in the same vein declaring that "not even the most feeble-minded in the city of Pskov" would accept this advice.

The king begins to dig underground passages under the town; the Pskovians learn of this from enemy soldiers who have been captured or changed sides. The Russians dig underground passages and blow up the enemy's passages. The last assault on the city, over the ice of the River Velikaya, is also unsuccessful. The king withdraws from Pskov, leaving his chancellor (Zamoisky) in his place. Not expecting to overcome the Pskov *voevoda* Ivan Shuisky in fair combat, the chancellor resorts to a foul trick. He sends Shuisky a casket, assuring him that it contains money. But the trick does not work. Shuisky orders one of his men to open the casket some distance away from his headquarters, and it is found to contain gunpowder with a "self-firing" device. The chancellor withdraws from Pskov "in great haste"; the siege is lifted, and the city gates, closed at the beginning of the siege, are opened.

Stylistically *The Tale of the Campaign of Stephen Bathory Against Pskov* is very reminiscent of such sixteenth-century works of

historical narrative as *The Book of Degrees* and *The History of Kazan.* Here too high-flown conventional formulas are used, rhetorical addresses to the characters and the reader, and so on. But for all its traditional elements *The Tale of the Campaign of Stephen Bathory,* like other works of historical narrative, was to some extent influenced by the fictional literature of the fifteenth century (the author of the tale quotes the *Alexandreid* and *Stefanit and Ikhnilat.*

5. Polemical Writings

In the sixteenth century in Russia a new type of literature became widespread, namely, works dealing with current political issues, or, to use a later term, polemical works.

Joseph of Volokolamsk. The first work of sixteenth-century Russian polemics was a book written at the very beginning of the century that played a most important role in the history of Russian social thought. This was *The Book Against the Novgorodian Heretics* (later entitled *The Enlightener*) by the abbot of the Volokolamsk Monastery Ivan Sanin (Joseph of Volokolamsk). It was the main work attacking Novgorodian-Moscow heresy of the late fifteenth and the early sixteenth century, which served as a kind of bill of indictment in the condemnation of heretics at the council of 1504.[25] At the end of the fifteenth century Joseph of Volokolamsk and his followers did not enjoy the support of the grand prince in the struggle against the heretics; this was connected with Ivan III's plans for restricting monastery landownership. In his early works written at the end of the fifteenth century Joseph even urges opposition to the "torturer tsar" who has insulted the Christian faith. He supported Ivan III's opponent, the appanage Prince of Volok. But after the suppression of the heretics in 1504 the former denouncer of tsardom became its zealous protector and declared that "in power the tsar is like unto God, the Most High". A few years later Joseph broke with his former patrons, the appanage princes of Volok, and announced that his monastery would henceforth be under the direct authority of the grand prince. Joseph of Volokolamsk's last writings attack the Prince of Volok and his protector, Archbishop Serapion of Novgorod.

Joseph of Volokolamsk is, first and foremost, a polemicist and denouncer; his style is high-flown and lofty. In his defence of Orthodox religious doctrine, Joseph bases his arguments entirely on Holy Writ and the works of Byzantine religious writers; quoting them as his authority, he develops his arguments logically and consistently. His logic and extensive reading in theology enable us to see Joseph as a kind of Russian representative of mediaeval scholastics. The principle of

Pskov. Gremyachaya Tower. 1525

White Lake Monastery of St Cyril. 16th-17th centuries. General view **375**

systematic analysis of all points raised by his adversaries was later borrowed from Joseph by other sixteenth-century polemicists (Ivan the Terrible, for example).

There are passages in Joseph's writing in which one senses the colloquial speech of the day. Thus, in an epistle to the *okolnichy** Boris Kutuzov, Joseph very vividly and expressively accuses the appanage Prince Theodore of Volok, who persecuted the monastery, of robbing "town and country folk". He describes, for example, how Prince Theodore extorted money from the widow of a "trading man": "And Prince Theodore bade them torture her. And she told them everything, where she kept what, and he took all her money..." Joseph begged the prince not to leave the widow penniless. The prince promised to send her something. But all he sent her was "five fritters from dinner, and four fritters for the morrow, and did not give her back any of the money. And her children and grand-children still go begging round the houses to this day..." 26

Daniel. The polemical tradition of Joseph of Volokolamsk was continued by Daniel, who first succeeded Joseph as abbot of the Volokolamsk Monastery, then became Metropolitan of All Russia. Daniel is the author of a large *Miscellany* of sixteen sermons and also of many epistles to individuals. Unlike Joseph, Daniel was dealing with vanquished adversaries; consequently his writings are in the nature of homilies, rather than lively disputes. Satire is also found in his work.

In one of his homilies, for example, he describes a dandy trying to catch the eye of some loose women. Daniel ridicules his dress, the fashionable narrow boots, "very fine and far too small, so that your feet suffer great constraint from their tightness", and says to the dandy: "You parade, prance, bray, and neigh like a stallion... You not only cut your beard and flesh with a razor, but tear and pluck it out by the roots, shamelessly, envious of women, and change your man's face into a woman's..." 27

Vassian Patrikeyev and the Non-Possessors. Joseph of Volokolamsk and Daniel were opposed by polemicists of a more independent nature. The most talented of the polemicists who opposed the Josephites was undoubtedly Vassian Patrikeyev, a prince who had been forced to become a monk in the White Lake Monastery of St Cyril by Ivan III. At the beginning of the sixteenth century Vassian became the founder of the movement of the Non-Possessors, who opposed monasteries owning land. Vassian's teacher, Nilus of Sora, paid little attention to concrete questions of social organisation. Like Joseph of Volokolamsk, he waged theoretical disputes with heretics, possibly even helped to write *The Enlightener,* and preached the moral perfectionment of monks. Only towards the end of his life, in 1503, did Nilus indirectly reveal his standpoint on practical questions by supporting Ivan III, when the latter suggested depriving the monasteries of land at a church council. Precisely how Nilus justified this support of the prince, we do not know. Unlike his teacher, Vassian

---

* *Okolnichy*—a court post and rank in Old Russia.

White Lake Monastery of St Cyril. Fortified tower

White Lake Monastery of St Cyril. Fortifications

was primarily a polemicist and a politician. He wrote a great deal about monastic landowning, arguing that the monasteries should not own "villages with peasants", but should subsist on state allowance and their own labours.[28]

Yet Vassian was not a heretic or a supporter of the Reformation. Unlike all the Reformation figures he did not cast doubt on the teaching of the Church Fathers or attack monasticism. On the contrary, he sought to perfect it. Nor did he support religious toleration. He agreed that heretics should be punished. He objected only to the mass reprisals which began to be used after 1504 not only against free-thinkers, but also against their supporters—both real and imaginary. Vassian declared that one could be indulgent towards heretics who repented and opposed capital punishment. Joseph of Volokolamsk argued that for the saints of old it was all the same "if a sinner or heretic were killed with hands or prayer". To which Vassian replied that Joseph himself did not act like the saints of old: he did not perform miracles or wish to be bound to the stake with heretics and remain unharmed. "We would greet you ... as you stepped out of the flames," he wrote in an ironical epistle to Joseph of Volokolamsk on behalf of the "elders of St Cyril".

Ridicule was also this prince-monk's strongest weapon in his polemic against Metropolitan Daniel who had Vassian tried by a church tribunal (as a result of which he was found guilty and subsequently put to death). In reply to Daniel's accusation that Vassian did not regard Macarius of Kalyazin and other miracle-workers recently canonised by the Church as saints, Patrikeyev remarked with feigned simplicity: "I knew him, a simple man; ... but whether he is a miracle-worker or not is for you to decide..." Daniel objected that in that case anyone could be a saint, a tsar or a priest, "a freeman or a bondman". "That, Sir, only God and you and your miracle-workers know," replied Vassian with venomous humility.

Irony is not the only feature of Vassian's polemical writing, however. In disputes with his adversaries he could also be extremely solemn and eloquent, for example, when he was accusing the Possessors of cupidity and of oppressing their "wretched brothers", the peasants: "The Lord says: 'Give to the needy'," wrote Vassian, contrasting this New Testament behest with the behaviour of landowners who extorted more and more interest from the peasants and drove penniless debtors with their wives and children off their land, "after taking their cow and horse from them".

Maxim the Greek. The subjects raised by Vassian Patrikeyev attracted other sixteenth-century publicists as well. The most

educated among them was undoubtedly Michael-Maxim Trivolis, who became known in Russian as Maxim the Greek. Today we know quite a lot about the life of this educated monk. Acquainted with many eminent Greek and Italian humanists of the Renaissance, Michael Trivolis went to live in Italy in 1492 and worked with the famous publisher Aldo Manucci. Shortly afterwards he renounced his humanist interests and entered a Dominican monastery. A few years later he returned to the Orthodox Church, became a monk at Mount Athos with the name of Maxim and in 1518 was summoned by Basil III to Moscow.[29]

Maxim the Greek did not forget about his humanist past: in Russia he wrote of the Aldo Manucci printing-house and the University of Paris; he was the first to announce the discovery of America in Russia. But he was now strongly opposed to the ideas of the Renaissance. He cursed the "pagan doctrine" embraced by the humanists, from which he himself might have perished had not God "visited" him with "his grace".[30] The warnings that Maxim delivers to his Russian readers against taking an interest in Greek writers (Homer, Socrates, Plato, and the Greek tragedies and comedies) are worthy of attention. They testify to the fact that such interests existed among certain Russian scribes of the period (Theodore Karpov, for example, with whom Maxim corresponded). But for the officials of the Russian Church (such as Metropolitan Daniel) Maxim himself seemed a highly suspicious character: he was twice tried by a church tribunal (in 1525 and 1535), imprisoned and exiled. Maxim was charged with heresy and with refusing to acknowledge that the Russian Church was independent of the Patriarch of Constantinople, and he was exiled first to the Volokolamsk Monastery, and then to Tver. Only after the death of Basil III's widow, Yelena, and the retirement of his main persecutor, Metropolitan Daniel, was Maxim able to resume his literary activity and declare his innocence, but all his requests for permission to return to Mount Athos remained unanswered. In the early 1550s Maxim was moved from Tver to the Trinity Monastery and virtually rehabilitated; he was drawn into the struggle against the heresy of Matvei Bashkin. He died in the middle of the 1550s.

An important role in Maxim the Greek's fate was played by his close connections with the Russian Non-Possessors and their leader, Vassian Patrikeyev; the trial and sentencing of Maxim took place shortly after Vassian's fall from grace.

The ideas of the Non-Possessors are expressed in a number of Maxim the Greek's writings. Among them is *The Awesome and Edifying Tale of the Monk's Life of Perfection, The Discourse of the Mind and the Soul, The Sermon on Repentance* and *The Dispute of the*

Maxim the Greek. Illumination from 17th-century manuscript. Academy of Sciences Library, Leningrad

Trinity Monastery of St Sergius. 15th-18th centuries

Covetous Man with the Non-Covetous Man. In them he described, inter alia, the sad lot of the peasants whom the monasteries drove off their lands for non-payment of debts, or sometimes refused to let them leave, demanding that they work the land and pay "the fixed quit-rent". If any of them, Maxim wrote, exhausted from "the heavy burden of labour and toil constantly imposed upon them by us, wishes to move to another place, we do not let him go, alas, if he has not paid the fixed quit-rent..."

Whereas Maxim's themes are in many respects reminiscent of Vassian's, the literary styles of the two polemicists are not alike. Maxim eschews the irony to which Vassian has recourse, and also his everyday touches. Maxim's language is a literary, bookish. It is not colloquial speech, but a foreign tongue which the Greek monk learned in middle age. Long phrases of complex construction are typical of it.

Ivan Peresvetov. The writer to break most sharply with the traditions of earlier writing was the West Russian *voinnik* (professional soldier) Ivan Peresvetov.[31] He was a completely secular writer. Arriving in Russia in the late 1530s (he had previously lived and served in Poland, Hungary and Moldavia), when Ivan IV was still a child and the boyars were ruling for him, Peresvetov became a firm opponent of the arbitrary rule of the boyars. All his works denounce the "idle rich" and eulogise the poor, but brave *voinniki*. Peresvetov's writings include works of various genres, ranging from petitions to the tsar containing predictions by "Latin philosophers and doctors" about the glorious future of Ivan IV to tales about the rulers of Greece and Turkey. Peresvetov's works written in the form of epistles, his *Lesser* and *Greater* petitions, differed greatly from each other. *The Lesser Petition* was a typical petition of the time. It was a request from Peresvetov to the tsar to defend him from the arbitrariness of his neighbours and permit him to set up the shield-making workshop that Peresvetov wanted to open in the 1530s, but could not due to the unrest in the period of boyar rule. *The Greater Petition* is a petition in form only. In content it is a publicistic work in which Peresvetov suggests that Ivan IV should introduce some major political reforms (the creation of a standing army, the abolition of the lieutenants, the abolition of debt-servitude, and the conquest of Kazan). Ideas similar to those in *The Greater Petition* were expressed in two tales by Peresvetov: *The Tale of Magmet* and *The Tale of the Emperor Constantine*; a collection of Peresvetov's works also included *The Tale of Constantinople* by Nestor-Iskander, slightly revised by Peresvetov and used by him as a foreword to a collection of his writings.

Peresvetov's ideology was somewhat complex. A professional

soldier, Peresvetov can in many respects be regarded as a member of the service gentry. He hated the rich boyars and dreamed of a "terrible" strong tsar. But in Peresvetov's writings we also find bold ideas that are unlikely to have occurred to most members of the sixteenth-century service gentry. He condemns debt-servitude and enslavement; declares that all debt-servitude comes from the devil; believes that truth (justice) is higher than faith, and states that there is still no truth in the tsardom of Muscovy, "and if there is no truth, then there is nothing at all".

Many of the features of Peresvetov's work remind one of the fifteenth-century *Tale of Dracula*. Like the author of *The Tale of Dracula*, Peresvetov believed in the merits of "terrible" power and its ability to destroy "evil": "A king cannot be without terror. A kingdom without terror is like a king's horse without a bridle." Like the author of *The Tale of Dracula*, Peresvetov did not regard "true faith" as an absolute condition of "truth" in a state. (There was no "truth" in the empire of Constantine, in spite of the "Christian faith". It was the "Anti-Christ" Magmet who succeeded in introducing "truth".) But *The Tale of Dracula* was a fictional work, whose author left it to his readers to draw their own conclusions from the stories, and these conclusions could vary. Peresvetov was, first and foremost, a publicist. He did not doubt the value of "terrible" power and expressed this idea directly.

The influence of folklore and oral speech can be seen clearly in Peresvetov's works. His aphorisms are constructed like proverbs: "A kingdom without terror is like a king's horse without a bridle"; "God loves not faith, but truth", "A soldier is like a falcon. You must look after him well and keep him cheerful." There is a macabre humour in Peresvetov's writings (which also reminds one of *The Tale of Dracula*). When the wise ruler Magmet finds out that his judges are taking bribes, he does not rebuke them, but orders them to be flayed alive, saying: "If their flesh grow round them again, their guilt shall be forgiven." And he orders their skins to be stuffed and the following words to be written on them: "Without such terror it is impossible to bring truth into the kingdom."

The fate of Peresvetov's proposals is rather interesting. The programme of this publicist who valued truth more than faith and condemned debt-servitude was not accepted by autocracy. Peresvetov himself soon disappeared without trace from the historical scene. Judging from a reference to "Peresvetov's black record" in the tsar's archives (a common way of referring to records of court proceedings), Peresvetov may have been subjected to repressions. His idea of royal terror was realised in the sixteenth century, although probably not quite as its author had assumed it would be.

This idea was taken up by Tsar Ivan IV, to whom Peresvetov addressed himself and who was to go down in history as Ivan the Terrible.

6. Ivan the Terrible and Andrew Kurbsky

Ivan the Terrible. The role of Ivan the Terrible, son of Basil III, in Russian history and literature is a complex and contradictory one. The first tsar of All Russia, Ivan IV, was one of the most terrifying figures in the country's history. His tyrannical features affected his writing also: the strings of clearly fantastic accusations against his opponents and growing fury of his tirades are typical of a ruler dictating to scribes (Ivan appears to have dictated, not written, his works). The constant repetition of the same idea was noticed by the tsar himself who agreed that he used "the same word" "all over the place". But he invariably blamed this on his enemies, whose "evil-spirited machinations" forced him to return to the same questions time and time again.

However, Ivan's works do not only reveal the absolute monarch with a persecution complex. Ivan IV had an artistic nature of a kind and was fairly well educated for his day: his younger contemporaries referred to him as a "man of wondrous reasoning". In spite of his Josephite education and participation in the activity of the Hundred Chapters Council, which attacked "mockers" and "gibers", the tsar permitted the buffoonery of the *skomorokhs* (as he himself admits in one of his epistles) and was evidently fond of them. Ivan's "buffoon-like" tastes and predilection for biting and occasionally coarse ridicule, are also found in his writings.

Ivan tried his hand at various types of literature: we have his "speeches"—a dispute with the Protestant preacher Jan Rokita[32] and talks with foreign diplomats; and it is likely that a religious work, the canon to the Terrible Angel, signed by the name of Parfeny Yurodivy (Parthenius the Fool-in-Christ)[33] also belonged to Ivan IV. But the main genre in which Ivan IV wrote was the epistle. We have his polemic epistles, including those to Kurbsky and the White Lake Monastery of St Cyril, and his diplomatic epistles.[34] But even in the latter (which have survived in the sixteenth-century *Diplomatic Records*) one constantly finds polemics (for example, the epistles to King Johann III of Sweden and Stephen Bathory, the epistles sent to Sigismund Augustus II on behalf of the boyars, etc.) and features of his distinctive style—lively argument with his opponent, rhetorical questions, ridiculing of his opponent's arguments, and frequent appeals to

Portrait of Ivan the Terrible. Woodcut by an unknown West-European master. 16th century. State Public Library, Leningrad

his reason ("judge for yourself"). These features are characteristic of the tsar's early and later epistles (from the 1550s to the 1580s), yet we cannot name a single person close to Ivan who retained his favour throughout his reign. Evidently they are features of Ivan's style as a writer.

The Epistle to the White Lake Monastery of St Cyril. *The Epistle to the White Lake Monastery of St Cyril* was written by Ivan IV in 1573 in reply to a document sent to the tsar by the abbot of the monastery. A dispute had arisen within the monastery between two influential monks: Sheremetev, a former Moscow boyar, and Sobakin, a member of one of the families that had risen to power during the Oprichnina (thanks to the tsar's marriage to Martha Sobakina). The tsar pretended that the dispute was above him—he began his epistle with a humble refusal to aspire to such "heights" as monastery affairs. "Alas, sinner that I am! Woe is me, accursed one! Oh, base wretch! Who am I to brave such heights?" But as the tsar's strong temperament gets the upper hand over his "humble" pose, the letter becomes more and more threatening. Ivan IV is deeply angered by the fact that the monastery is "cajoling the boyars" and trying to please the boyar-monk Sheremetev who has incurred the tsar's disfavour. Do not tell me "those shameful words", the tsar declares. "If we wish to have nothing to do with the boyars, the monastery will receive no endowments." The "humble" epistle ends with a strict reprimand to the monks and an order not to trouble the tsar with "trifles". "Decide yourselves, how you wish to treat him, it is no business of mine! And in future do not trouble me with it; verily, I will not answer any more of your questions."

The Epistle to Vasily Gryaznoy. Unlike the epistle to the White Lake Monastery of St Cyril and the epistles to Kurbsky, Ivan IV's epistle to Vasily Gryaznoy, who was captured by the Crimean Tartars, has survived in one copy only, in the *Crimean Records* of diplomatic correspondence with the Crimean Khanate. Obviously this epistle was not intended for circulation, but only for the person to whom it was addressed. In 1574 Vasily Gryaznoy, an Oprichnik and favourite of the tsar, was captured by the Crimean Tartars. He wrote to the tsar from captivity asking him to pay his ransom, but Ivan IV considered the sum asked by the Crimean Tartars to be excessively high. "You write that you were captured for your sins, Vasyushka. Well, you should not have gone off to the Crimean nomads so recklessly. You thought you were going out with the hounds to hunt hares, but the Tartars tied you to the saddle..." During the Crimean campaign of 1571-1572 the Oprichnina had proved ineffective and been abolished. The tsar's displeasure with the Oprichniks is reflected in the epistle. Ivan writes that he promoted "slaves" such as Gryaznoy only because "the princes and boyars of my father and me began to betray me". For the sake of his former favourite the tsar agrees to pay a ransom, but fifty times less than what the Tartars want. The style of the epistle, its somewhat coarse humour, is very reminiscent of the *skomorokh* traditions popular during the Oprichnina. "Or did you think that it was the same in the Crimea as joking at dinner with me," asked the tsar. In his reply (also in the *Crimean Records*) Gryaznoy declares that he is a complete nonentity. "If it were not for Your Majesty's favour, what sort of a man would I be? You, Sire, are as God—you make all things, great and small."

The Diplomatic Epistles of Ivan the Terrible. Of Ivan IV's diplomatic epistles the most interesting as literary works are those to King Johann III of Sweden and the epistle to King Stephen Bathory of Poland.

The epistles to Johann III were written after unsuccessful attempts to conclude a military alliance between Ivan the Terrible and King Eric XIV of Sweden. In 1568, when the Russian envoys who had come to conclude the alliance were staying in Stockholm, Eric XIV was deposed and his brother Johann III, who supported an alliance with Poland and was the sworn enemy of Moscow, came to the throne. "Robbed and dishonoured", the Russian envoys were first imprisoned for several months, then sent back to Russia; there could, of course, be no question of an alliance now. *The First Epistle to Johann III*, written in 1572, reflects Ivan the Terrible's anger at the change in Swedish foreign policy and the robbing of his envoys. The tsar points out that originally he had no intention of negotiating with Johann, and wanted to fight, but then decided to give the king time to think the matter over. But the king had made no moves. "There is no word of your envoys even now, whether you are to send any or not." Making no distinction between the deposed Eric and the new king Johann, the tsar declares all Swedish kings to be deceivers who use the pretext of a *coup d'état* to avoid the performance of their duties: "In autumn they said that you had died, in spring they said that you had been banished from the state... Now your deception is revealed: like a reptile, you don different guises." Johann III's reply to this was equally sharp: "most unbecoming" was the comment in the *Diplomatic Records*. In 1573 Ivan the Terrible sent Johann III a second epistle, one of his most outspoken works. He declared the whole line of Swedish kings to be a "line of peasants". As proof he recalled that when "our traders came with bacon fat and wax to Sweden" Johann's father, Gustav Vaza, "put on gloves" and tested the quality of the bacon fat and wax. In contrast the tsar referred proudly to the descent of his ancestors "from Augustus Caesar", quoting from *The Tale of the Princes of Vladimir*. This epistle too ended most acerbically: "And now about your barking at us ... if you wish to take a dog's mouth and bark for your amusement, such is your base custom ... but if you want someone to bark with, find a slave like yourself ... and bark at him."

In 1581 Ivan the Terrible wrote another diplomatic epistle, *The Epistle to King Stephen Bathory of Poland*. It was written in entirely different circumstances. Elected to the Polish throne in 1576 Stephen Bathory radically changed the military state of affairs in the Livonian war; nearly all the Russian conquests in Western Russia and southern Livonia were lost. Consequently Ivan the Terrible could not address the Polish King as arrogantly as he addressed the King of Sweden a few years earlier. He intended to write "humbly", but did not manage this very well. Already in his opening title, after listing all his possessions, he called himself a ruler "by the will of God, and not by the much-rebellious will of mankind". This was an allusion to the fact that, unlike Bathory, he was an hereditary ruler, not an elected monarch. The main theme of the epistle was the need for peace and the impermissibility of "shedding Christian blood", which benefited only the Moslems. Here too there is a somewhat insulting allusion to the fact that Bathory enjoyed the support of the Sultan of Turkey in his election to the throne. Accusing Bathory of aiding and abetting Mohammedanism was particularly significant because the tsar was negotiating with the Pope about Papal mediation in the conclusion of a peace "for the good of Christendom". This accusation emerges gradually at the beginning of the epistle: by constantly referring to the "Christian customs" that he observes Ivan contrasts them with the customs of the Moslems. At the end, as if forgetting about his peaceful intentions, Ivan declares outright: "It is clear what you are doing, betraying Christianity to the Moslems!.. You call yourself a Christian, and utter the name of Christ, yet you wish to overthrow Christianity!"

The Correspondence of Ivan the Terrible with Kurbsky. The most important place in Ivan the Terrible's writing belongs to his correspondence with Kurbsky. Born of a noble family (related to the princes of Yaroslavl) and a member of the governmental group of the 1550s known as the Select Council, who took part in the Kazan campaign, Andrew Kurbsky fled from Russia in 1564, fearing the tsar's disfavour. From Polish Livonia he wrote a denunciatory epistle to the tsar accusing him of unjustly persecuting the loyal generals who had conquered "the proudest of realms" for Russia. The tsar replied with an epistle almost as long as a book; and that was the beginning of this famous correspondence.[35]

A feature of this correspondence, distinguishing it from most epistles of preceding centuries, addressed to concrete people, that only later became the object of widespread reading, is that from the very beginning it was of a publicistic nature. In this respect it resembles an earlier epistle, namely, that of the "elders of St Cyril's" (by Vassian Patrikeyev) to Joseph of Volokolamsk. Of course, the tsar replied to Kurbsky, and Kurbsky to the tsar, but neither expected to persuade the other to change his views. They were writing, first and foremost, for their readers, like the authors of "open letters" in modern literature. Ivan IV's First Epistle to Kurbsky was called an epistle "to the Russian state" against "those who sin against the cross" (i.e., traitors, perjurers).

In his dispute with "sinners against the cross", the tsar was naturally guided by the purpose of this polemic. Readers "throughout the Russian state" had to be shown how criminal the boyars denounced in the epistle were.

In reply to the tsar's First Epistle Kurbsky wrote a brief caustic missive, ridiculing the style and length of Ivan's epistle; he was unable to send it, however. In 1577 the tsar waged a long and successful campaign in Livonia, conquering numerous towns along the Western Dvina and advancing right up to Riga. After capturing the town of Wolmar (Walmiera) where Kurbsky had fled thirteen years earlier, Ivan sent him a Second Epistle from there. In 1579 during a Polish-Lithuanian counter-offensive Kurbsky wrote his Third Epistle to the tsar.

In his dispute with Kurbsky the tsar defended the idea of absolute monarchy, arguing that the intervention of the boyars and clergy in government was detrimental to the state. The tsar blames his adversary for boyar rule of the 1530s and 1540s, although Kurbsky, who was about the same age as the tsar, could not have taken part in politics at that time. In fact both adversaries were proceeding from the same ideal—the ideas of the Hundred Chapters Council that reaffirmed Russian "purest of pure Orthodoxy" and were merely disputing as to which of them was most faithful to these ideals. Both the tsar and Kurbsky readily appealed to "the Divine Judge" in this dispute. Ivan declared in 1577 that his military successes were proof that Divine providence was on his side, and two years later Kurbsky explained the tsar's failures in exactly the same way, as Divine judgement.

An important place in the polemics (particularly in Ivan's First Epistle) was played by lengthy references to religious literature. But in attempting to prove to readers "throughout the Russian state" that he was right and that "sinners against the Cross" were criminals, the tsar could not confine himself to lengthy quotations from the Church Fathers and rhetorics. He needed vivid, striking examples of the "insults" he had suffered.

And find them he did, painting a moving picture of his orphaned childhood in the period of boyar rule, when the rulers "fell upon one another" and "tossed our mother's coffers into the State Coffers and kicked out wildly with their feet". Many of these scenes resemble or are identical to descriptions in the amendments to *The Illustrated Chronicle*.

The scenes of the tsar's orphaned childhood are particularly vivid; they have frequently been used by historians and artists. The tsar declared that he lacked food and clothing and, most important, the care and attention of elders: "I remember how we would play our children's games, while Prince Ivan Vasilyevich Shuisky sat on a bench with one elbow resting on our father's bedstead and his foot up on a chair", taking no notice of young Ivan and his brother.

This picture can hardly be historically authentic, but its effectiveness, and consequently its literary significance, are not to be denied. Kurbsky did not ignore this passage in his reply. As well as being Ivan IV's political opponent, he opposed him in literary matters as well. Mocking the "loud-mouthed and noisy" First Epistle of the tsar, Kurbsky criticised him strongly for introducing these everyday scenes or, as he called them "babblings

First Epistle of Prince Andrew Kurbsky to Tsar Ivan the Terrible. 17th-century manuscript copy. State Public Library, Leningrad

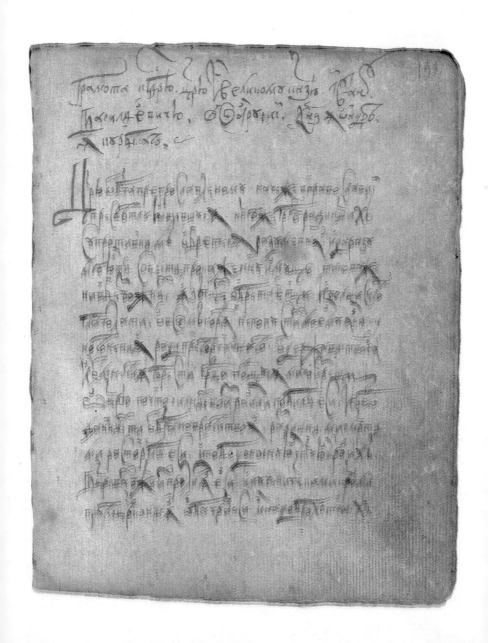

First Epistle of Tsar Ivan the Terrible to Prince Andrew Kurbsky. 17th-century manuscript copy. State Public Library, Leningrad of foolish women" into literature. The political polemic between the two opponents was accompanied by a purely literary polemic—about the limits of the "scholarly" and "barbaric" in literature.

Andrew Kurbsky. Kurbsky was no less educated than Ivan the Terrible. His grandfather was Vassily Tuchkov, one of the redactors of *The Great Menology.* It was from the writers of Macarius' circle that Kurbsky got the idea that literature should be serious and solemn.

We have already noted that in the dispute between Ivan and Kurbsky both opponents had some common points of departure (without such common premises the dispute itself would have been impossible). Both believed that in the middle of the sixteenth century (the time of the Hundred Chapters Council) the Russian state was the land of "most pure Orthodoxy" and each considered himself to be true to this "most pure Orthodoxy" and accused the other of departing from it. That is why Kurbsky called Russia "the Holy Russian Tsardom" and, when he was in Western Russia, defended the Orthodox Church against both Catholics and Russian heretics (such as Theodosius Kosoy) who had fled into Lithuanian Russia and joined the Reformation movement there.

Similar in his social outlook to the Non-Possessors of the first third of the sixteenth century, Kurbsky was nevertheless alien to the literary manner of Vassian Patrikeyev with its humour and colloquial speech. Kurbsky was closer to another writer of the sixteenth century, Maxim the Greek (whom Kurbsky knew before he fled from Russia and deeply respected). Kurbsky's high-flown rhetoric and complicated syntax are reminiscent of Maxim the Greek and the Graeco-Roman models that he imitated. His epistles to Ivan are a brilliant specimen of the rhetorical style. It is no accident that Kurbsky included a work by the great Roman orator Cicero in one of them. The author's speech in the First Epistle is written all in one breath, as it were. It is logical and consistent, but completely void of all concrete detail. "Why, oh, Tsar, have you struck down the strong men of Israel and surrendered the generals, given to you to fight your enemies, to all manner of deaths? Why have you shed their victorious, holy blood in God's churches and made the porches crimson with their martyr's blood? Why have you thought up unheard-of torments and deaths and persecution for those who wish you well and have laid down their lives for you? Why have you wrongfully accused true Orthodox believers of treason and magic, trying your utmost to turn light into darkness and to call bitter that which is sweet?" Kurbsky asks: "Did they not destroy proud kingdoms and make them subject to you in all realms where our forbears were their slaves? Did they

not give you by the efforts of their minds from God the invincible
German towns? Have you acted justly in rewarding us, poor
creatures, by destroying us in whole families?"[36] The lofty
oratorical feeling of this address has been brilliantly conveyd by
Alexei Konstantinovich Tolstoy, who included a poetic rendering
of it in his ballad *Vasily Shibanov*.

The tsar's reply, as we know, was not couched in such austere
language. Ivan was not afraid of using openly the *skomorokh* brand
of coarse humour. To Kurbsky's grief-stricken words, "You will
not set eyes on my face until the Day of Judgement", the tsar
replies caustically: "Who wants to see an ugly face like that
anyway?" As we know, Ivan also included scenes from everyday
life in his epistle.

Kurbsky regarded such a mixture of styles and the introduction of "coarse" colloquialisms as the height of bad taste. "It is
absurd and ridiculous," he declared in his reply, to send such an
epistle "to scholarly, learned men", and particularly to a "foreign
land where some men are skilled not only in grammar and
rhetoric, but also in dialectics and philosophy". He condemned as
improper the references to the tsar's bedstead on which Prince
Shuisky was leaning and another passage saying that until Shuisky
stole the tsar's money he had only one fur coat—"green cotton
fabric on marten, and pretty tattered at that..." "And at the same
time you speak of beds, and body-warmers and countless other
things like the babblings of foolish women; and so barbariously..."
Kurbsky comments.

What we have here is a real literary polemic, a dispute as to
which style befits an epistle. But whereas in political disputes
Kurbsky frequently got the better of the tsar, ridiculing the most
absurd of the accusations made against his now executed advisers,
in the literary debate he can hardly be considered the winner. He
undoubtedly sensed the power of the tsar's "barbarous" arguments and showed this in another work that he wrote in an
entirely different form, that of the historical narrative.

The History of the Grand Prince of Moscow. This work was
The History of the Grand Prince of Moscow written by Kurbsky in
1573, when Poland was without a king, with the direct political
aim of preventing the election of Ivan IV to the Polish throne.[37]

Kurbsky composes his narrative in the form of an answer to a
question put by "many learned men": how is it that the Prince of
Moscow, once "good and deliberate", has fallen into such villainy?
In order to explain this, Kurbsky tells of the emergence of "evil
habits" in Ivan's ancestors: the forcing of Basil III's first wife to
take the veil and Basil's "unlawful" marriage to Yelena, Ivan IV's
mother, the imprisonment of the "holy man" Vassian Patrikeyev,

Second Epistle of Prince Andrew Kurbsky to Tsar Ivan the Terrible. 17th-century manuscript copy. State History Museum, Moscow

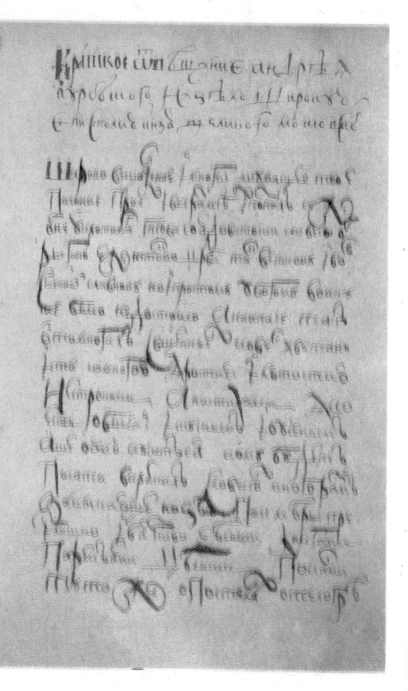

Second Epistle of Tsar Ivan the Terrible to Prince Andrew Kurbsky. 17th-century manuscript copy. State Lenin Library, Moscow

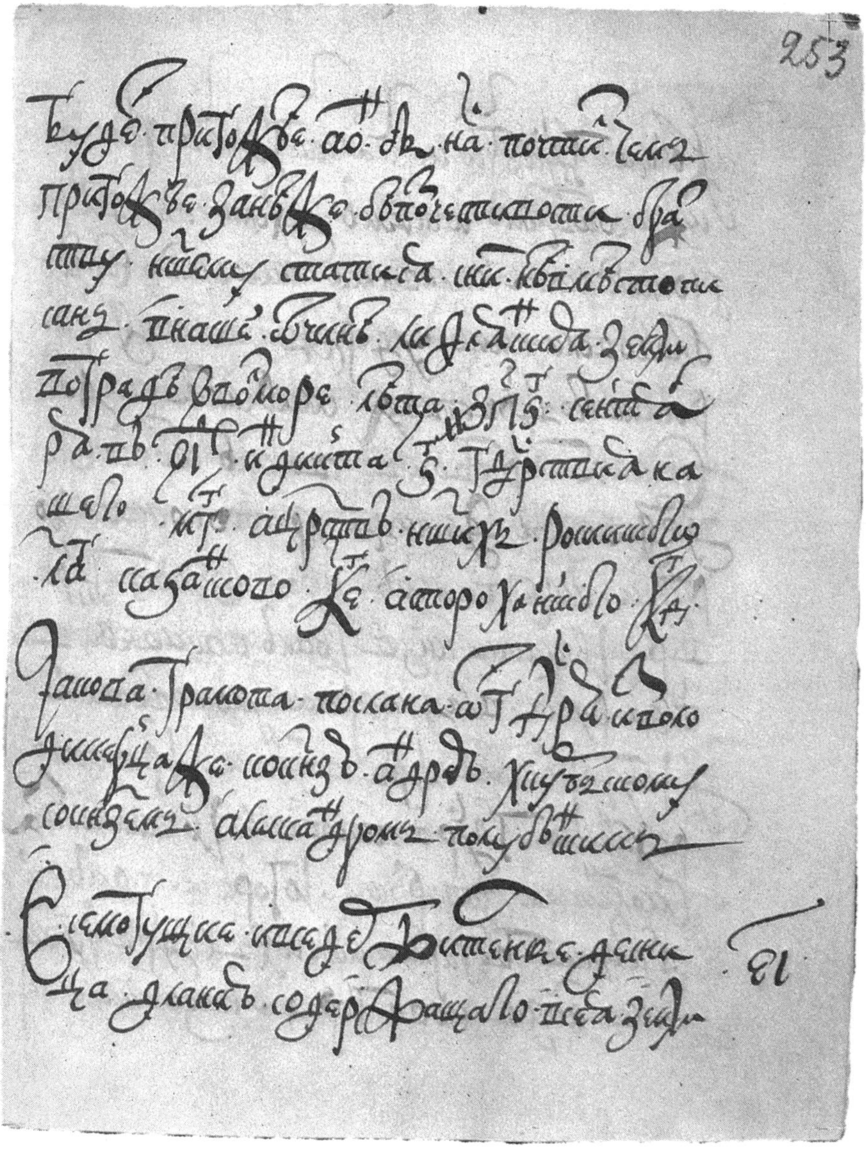

the birth "of the present Ivan in unlawfulness" and "voluptuousness" and his "nefarious deeds" in his youth. Having thus disclosed the original "sin" that gave rise to subsequent "sin", Kurbsky goes on to speak of the "two learned men" who succeeded in turning to piety and military valour "the young tsar, brought up in evil passions and wilfulness without a father, who was most savage and had already tasted all manner of blood". These two men are the Presbyter Sylvester of Novgorod, who began to instruct the young tsar during the "unrest" in 1547 and the "noble youth" Alexei Adashev; it was they who turned the tsar away from the companions of his revelries, "parasites and idlers", and brought him into the company of "men of good sense and perfection", the Select Council. The natural consequences of the beneficial influence of the Select Council, according to the *History*, were Ivan IV's military successes, first and foremost, the conquest of Kazan, which is described in detail by Kurbsky as an eyewitness and participant in the war.

This was only the first half of the reign of the "Grand Prince of Moscow". After the "glorious victory" at Kazan and the "burning ailment" that afflicted the tsar in 1553, a sudden change took place in him. This change was assisted by a monk who was one of the Josephites (Joseph of Volokolamsk's followers whom Kurbsky accused of killing Vassian Patrikeyev), the former Bishop Vassian Toporkov, who advised the tsar not to have any counsellor wiser than himself if he wished to be an autocrat. Filled "with such death-dealing poison from the Orthodox bishop", Ivan IV began to surround himself with "scribes" from the "common people" and persecute the "grandees". He did not follow their good advice to continue the war against the Moslems and ignored their plans for the cautious and peaceful subjection of the land of Livonia.

The advice of Vassian Toporkov and the influence of "contemptible counsellors" led the tsar to cast aside and disgrace Sylvester and Adashev and persecute his own, formerly "most beloved" supporters. At this point Kurbsky ends his story about the Grand Prince of Moscow and turns to the second part of his pamphlet, a list of the "boyar and service gentry families" and "holy martyrs" destroyed by Ivan.

Such was the content of *The History of the Grand Prince of Moscow*, a work which Kurbsky sought to compose as a stylistically austere and elegant narrative, intended for readers well-versed in grammar, rhetoric, dialectics and philosophy. Nevertheless the author was unable to maintain this stylistic unity throughout and on at least two occasions had recourse to the device that he himself had so severely censured, namely, the portrayal of everyday scenes and the use of colloquial speech. Condemning the Lithuanian

nobility for not being sufficiently militant in the early years of the Livonian war, Kurbsky describes how the "rulers" of the Lithuanian land, having partaken of "all manner of rich wines", loll "on their thick feather-beds, then, after sleeping almost until noon, rise with bandaged heads heavy from drinking, barely alive and seek to regain their wits". Without noticing it himself, he describes "beds", which he had criticised Ivan for mentioning earlier. Kurbsky commits the same "sin" again when, clearly in response to Ivan's description of his childhood, he gives his own version of the same events. He argues that the "great proud *pany*, in their language (Russian) the boyars", who brought Ivan up, did not offend him, but, quite the reverse, pandered "to his every whim and passion". And he tells how already in childhood Ivan began "to shed the blood of defenceless (animals), hurling them down from lofty places, or in their language from porches or from the upper storeys of houses..." Kurbsky does his utmost to avoid the prosaic detail of "foolish women": he turns dogs or cats into abstract "defenceless creatures", and porches into "lofty places", but nevertheless he could not resist one lively detail—the description of the early cruelty of the orphaned prince who, later as tsar and writer, depicted his orphaned childhood so movingly.

Thus, the two major publicists of the sixteenth century eventually introduced observations from real life into their narrative.

Created in hard and unfavourable conditions the literature of the sixteenth century nevertheless represents an important stage in the history of Old Russian literature as a whole. The Renaissance elements found in works of the late fifteenth century could not develop in the age of Ivan the Terrible, when all subjects, from the most high to the most low, were regarded as the sovereign's "slaves" without any rights. But in spite of the numerous obstacles new phenomena can be detected in sixteenth-century literature. In this literature, particularly the publicistic works of this period, the personality of the author is clearly felt. Almost all the writers of the sixteenth century are striking individuals, known to us by name and most unlike one another, such as Joseph of Volokolamsk and Vassian Patrikeyev, Daniel and Maxim the Greek, Ermolai-Erasmus and Peresvetov, Kurbsky and Ivan the Terrible.

For all the great differences between them, the publicists of the sixteenth century share one common feature characteristic of the European Renaissance, faith in human intellect, in the possibility of building society and the state on certain rational foundations. Many of them also took a secular view of the purpose of the state

Ivan Fyodorov's **The Book of Apostles,** the first book to be printed in Russia. 1564

ПА҃ , К҃З . М҃А .   ПА́ВЕЛЪ ПОСЛА́ННИКЪ

КТІ́ЖꙊЕ ВТ́ОРОЕ ПОСЛА́НЇЕ СТ҃ГО АП҃ЛА ПА́ВЛА

П АВЕЛЪ ПОСЛА́ННИКЪ І҃С Х҃ВЪ , ВО́ЛЕЮ
Б҃ЖЇЕЮ , ПО ОБꙊ́ТОВА́НЇЮ ЖИ́ЗНИ Ꙗ́ЖЕ
Ꙋ Х҃ТꙊ І҃С. ТИМОѲЕ́НꙊ ВОЗЛЮ́БЛЕННОМꙊ
ЧА́ДꙊ, БЛГОДА́ТЬ МЛ҃ТЬ И МИ́РЪ , ѿ Б҃ГА
ѻ҃ЦА , И Х҃А ІС҃А ГА҃ НА́ШЕГО . ПРЕСТꙊ́ПН,
   ПА҃ . БЛГОДАРꙊ́ БГ҃А   ЕМꙊ́ЖЕ СЛꙊ́ЖꙊ
ѿПРАРО́ДИТЕЛЕН , ЧИ́СТОН СО́ВꙊСТІИ . Ꙗ́КО НЕ
ПРЕСТА́ННꙊН И́МА ѻ́ ТЕБꙊ́ ПА́МАТЬ ВЪ МЛ҃ТВА
МОИ́ХЪ ДН҃Ь И НО́ЩЬ , ЖЕЛА́Ꙗ ВИ́ДꙊ́ТИ ТꙖ , ПО
МИНА́Ꙗ СЛЕЗЫ́ТВОꙖ , ДА РА́ДОСТИ НСПО́ЛНИСꙖ .
ВОСПОМИНА́НЇЕ ПРІЕ́МЛꙖ ѻ́ СꙊ́ЩЕН В ТЕБꙊ́ НЕЛИ
ЦЕМꙊ́РНꙊН ВꙊ́РꙊ́ . Ꙗ́ЖЕ ВСЕЛИ́СꙖ ПРЕ́ЖДЕ ВБА́
БꙊ́ ТВОЮ ЛО́ИДꙊ́ . И ВЪ М҃ТРЬ ТВОЮ ЕВНИКІ́Ю .
ОУ́ПОВА́Н ЖЕ Ꙗ́КО И В ТЕБꙊ́ . Е́ꙖЖЕ РА́ДИ ВИ́НЫ ВО
СПОМИНА́Ю ТЕБꙊ́ ВОЗГРꙊ́ВА́ТИ ДА́РЪ Б҃ЖІИ , ЖИ
ВꙊ́ЩІИ В ТЕБꙊ́ ВОЗЛОЖЕ́НІЕМЪ РꙊКꙊ́ МОЕ́Н .
НꙊ́СТЬ БО НА́МЪ ДА́ЛЪ Б҃ГЪ Д҃ХЪ СТРА́ХꙊ , НО СИ́ЛЫ

СТО́МꙊ А́ПЛꙊ ТИМО́ . ЧА́ДО ТИМО́ , БЛГОДАРꙊ́ БГ҃А

as an institution that served the common good (Ermolai-Erasmus and Peresvetov). Even Ivan the Terrible, who in practice tended towards the most unbridled use of force, in theory considered himself obliged to discuss measures without which "all realms would be racked by discord and internecine strife".

In spite of the suppression of the Reformationist, humanist movements and the disappearance of "useless tales" (fictional, narrative), the literature of the sixteenth century reveals new features not characteristic of mediaeval literature. These new features were developed in the literature of the following century.

REFERENCES

[1] Дмитриева Р. П. *Сказание о князьях Владимирских.* Moscow and Leningrad, 1955.

[2] Philotheus' epistles are published in the book: Малинин В. П. *Старец Елизарова монастыря Филофей и его послания.* Kiev, 1901 (Appendix). Cf. Гольдберг А. Л. "Три 'послания Филофея' (Опыт текстологического анализа)". *ТОДРЛ,* Vol. XXIV, 1974, pp. 68-97; "Идея 'Москва—третий Рим' в цикле сочинений первой половины XVI века". *ТОДРЛ,* Vol. XXXVII, pp. 138-149; Kämpfer, F., "'Sendschreiben Filofeis' oder 'Filofei-Zyklus'? Argumente gegen die Ergebnisse Alexander Goldbergs". *Canadian-American Slavic Studies.* 1979, Vol. 13, Nos. 1-2, pp. 126-138.

[3] *"Великие Минеи Четии", собранные митрополитом Макарием.* St Petersburg and Moscow, 1868-1917. *The Great Menology* for September, October, November (1-25), December (1-24 and 31), January (1-11) and April have been published.

[4] For the text of the first redaction of the *Household Management* see: *"Домострой" по списку ОИДР.* Moscow, 1882, pp. 73-75.

[5] For the text of the second redaction of the *Household Management* see: *"Домострой" по Коншинскому списку и подобным.* Prepared for publication by A. Orlov. Moscow, 1908. On the *Household Management* see: Зимин А. А. *И. С. Пересветов и его современники. Очерки по истории русской общественно-политической мысли середины XVI в.* Moscow, 1958, pp. 55-57, 64-70; Адрианова-Перетц В. П. "К вопросу о круге чтения древнерусского писателя". *ТОДРЛ,* Vol. XXVIII, 1974, pp. 24-29.

[6] Тихонравов Н. С. *Сочинения,* Vol. I, Moscow, 1896, pp. 92-93.

[7] Тихомиров М. Н. *Русская культура X-XVIII вв.* Moscow, 1968, pp. 292-345; Зернова А. С. *Начало книгопечатания.* Moscow, 1947.

[8] *"Волоколамский патерик". Семинарий по древнерусской литературе высших женских курсов.* Moscow, 1915, No. 5.

[9] Дмитриев Л. А. *Житийные повести русского Севера как памятники литературы XIII-XVII вв.,* pp. 264-265.

[10] The dispute about the dating of the extant text of the *Tale* has now been settled thanks to the discovery of the autograph of the *Tale* (see: *Повесть о Петре и Февронии.* Preparation of texts and study by R. P. Dmitrieva. Leningrad, 1979, pp. 95-118).

[11] Ржига В. Ф. "Литературная деятельность Ермолая-Еразма". *Летописъ занятий Археографической комиссии (ЛЗАК)*, Vol. 33, 1926, pp. 103-200.

[12] Дмитриева Р. П. "О структуре *Повести о Петре и Февронии*". *ТОДРЛ*, Vol. XXXI, 1976, pp. 247-270.

[13] *The Resurrection Chronicle* is published in the *ПСРЛ*, Vols. VII-VIII, 1856-1859; *The Nikon Chronicle* in *ПСРЛ*, Vols. IX-XIII, 1862-1910 (Phototype reproduction. Moscow, 1965); *The Chronicle of the Beginning of the Reign...* in *ПСРЛ*, Vol. XXIX, 1965, pp. 9-116; *The Josaphat Chronicle* is published separately under the editorship of A. A. Zimin: *Иоасафовская летопись*. Moscow, 1957; See: Клосс Б. М. *Никоновский свод и русские летописи XVI-XVII вв.* Moscow, 1980.

[14] For the text of the final volume of *The Illustrated Chronicle* (Synod manuscript and *The Tsar's Book*) see: *ПСРЛ*, Vol. XIII, 1904-1906. (Phototype reproduction. Moscow, 1965.); cf., Альшиц Д. Н. "Иван Грозный и приписки к лицевым сводам его времени". *Исторические записки*, Vol. 23, pp. 251-289; Альшиц Д. Н. "Происхождение и особенности источников, повествующих о боярском мятеже 1553 г.". *Исторические записки*, Vol. 25, pp. 266-292; Андреев Н. Е. "Об авторе приписок в лицевых сводах Ивана Грозного". *ТОДРЛ*, Vol. XVIII, 1962, pp. 117-148; Веселовский С. Б. *Исследования по истории опричнины*. Moscow, 1968, pp. 265-291; Зимин А. А. "О методике изучения повествовательных источников XVI в.". In the book: *Источниковедение отечественной истории*. No. 1, Moscow, 1973, pp. 187-196; Протасьева Т. Н. "К вопросу о миниатюрах Никоновской летописи (Син. № 962)" In the book: *Летописи и хроники*. Moscow, 1974, pp. 271-285; Амосов А. А. "Датировка и кодикологическая структура в 'Истории Грозного' в 'Лицевом летописном своде'". *Вспомогательные исторические дисциплины*, Vol. XIII, Leningrad, 1982, pp. 155-193.

[15] *Псковские летописи*. No. I, Moscow and Leningrad, 1941, pp. 95-97; No. 2, Moscow, 1955, p. 226.

[16] See: *ПСРЛ*, Vol. VI, 1853, pp. 269-276. A similar account is found in the Novgorodian compilation of 1539 in *ПСРЛ*, Vol. IV, 1929, pp. 552-564.

[17] *ПСРЛ*, Vol. XIII, Part 2, 1906 (Phototype reproduction. Moscow, 1965.), pp. 524-525.

[18] Cf.: Васенко П. Г. *"Книга Степенная царского родословия" и ее значение в древнерусской исторической письменности*. Part I, St Petersburg, 1904, pp. 218-240.

[19] *ПСРЛ*, Vol. XXI, Part I, pp. 7-8.

[20] *Казанская история*. Text prepared by G. N. Moiseyeva. Moscow and Leningrad, 1954; Cf.: Кунцевич Г. З. *История о Казанском царстве, или Казанский летописец*. St Petersburg, 1905, pp. 176-179.

[21] Лихачев Д. С. *Развитие русской литературы X-XVII вв.*, pp. 133-137.

[22] *Повести о споре жизни и смерти*. Study and preparation of texts by R. P. Dmitrieva. Moscow and Leningrad, 1964.

[23] "Повесть о царице Динаре" published by M. O. Skripil in the book: *Русские повести XV-XVI вв.*, pp. 88-91 (for the article by M. O. Skripil see pp. 414-419). Cf.: Сперанский М. Н. "Повесть о Динаре в русской письменности". *ИОРЯС*, Vol. XXXI, 1926.

[24] *Повесть о прихожении Стефана Батория на град Псков*. Preparation of text and article by V. I. Malyshev. Moscow and Leningrad, 1952.

²⁵ *Просветитель, или Обличение ереси жидовствующих. Творение преподобного отца нашего Иосифа, игумена Волоцкого.* Kazan, 1904. On the date of *Просветитель* see: Лурье Я. С. *Идеологическая борьба в русской публицистике конца XV-начала XVI в.* Moscow and Leningrad, 1960, pp. 95-110, 458-474.

²⁶ *Послания Иосифа Волоцкого.* Moscow and Leningrad, 1959.

²⁷ Daniel's works have been published in the appendix to the book: Жмакин В. *Митрополит Даниил.* Moscow, 1881.

²⁸ Казакова Н. А. *Вассиан Патрикеев и его сочинения.* Moscow and Leningrad, 1960.

²⁹ The identity of Maxim the Greek and Michael Trivolis is proved by E. Denissoff in his work: Denissoff, E., *Maxime le Grec et l'Occident*, Paris-Louvain, 1943. The fact of Maxim's conversion to Catholicism is confirmed by documentary evidence found by E. Denissoff (See: Denissoff, E., *L'influence de Savonarole sur l'église russe expliquée par un MS. inconnu du couvent de St Marc a Florence. Scriptorium*, Bruxelles, 1948, t. 11, f. 2, p. 252-256).

³⁰ *Сочинения Максима Грека*, parts 1-3, Kazan, 1859-1862; Иванов А. И. *Литературное наследие Максима Грека. Характеристика, атрибуции, библиография.* Leningrad, 1969; Синицына Н. В. *Максим Грек в России.* Moscow, 1977; Haney, J. V., *From Italy to Muscovy. The Life and Works of Maxim the Greek.* München, 1973; Буланин Д. М. *Переводы и послания Максима Грека. Неизданные тексты.* Leningrad, 1984.

³¹ *Сочинения И. Пересветова.* Text prepared by A. A. Zimin. Moscow and Leningrad, 1956. Cf.: Зимин А. А. *И. С. Пересветов и его современники. Очерки по истории русской общественно-политической мысли середины XVI в.* Moscow, 1958.

³² "Ответ царя Ивана Васильевича Грозного Яну Роките". See: *Древнерусские полемические сочинения против протестантов.* Book I. Moscow, 1878. For the most recent edition from the Russian manuscript of the sixteenth century in Harvard University see: *Tsar Ivan IV's Reply to Jan Rokita* by V. A. Tumins. The Hague-Paris, 1971.

³³ Лихачев Д. С. "Канон и молитва Ангелу Грозному Парфения Юродивого". In the book: *Рукописное наследие Древней Руси. По материалам Пушкинского дома.* Leningrad, 1972, p. 10.

³⁴ *Послания Ивана Грозного.* Text prepared by D. S. Likhachev and Y. S. Lurie. Translation and commentaries by Y. S. Lyrie. Edited by V. P. Adrianova-Peretts. Moscow and Leningrad, 1951. On the literary work of Ivan IV, see the book: Лихачев Д. С. *Великое наследие*, pp. 265-288, 333-348; Лурье Я. С. "Был ли Иван IV писателем?" *ТОДРЛ*, Vol. XV, 1958, pp. 505-508.

³⁵ *Переписка Ивана Грозного с Андреем Курбским.* Text prepared by Y. S. Lurie and Y. D. Rykov. Leningrad, 1979; Moscow, 1981. In recent years several works have appeared on the correspondence of Ivan IV and Kurbsky in connection with Edward Keenan's claim that the correspondence was a seventeenth-century "apocrypha". Cf: Keenan, E. L., *The Kurbskii-Groznyi Apocrypha. The XVIIth Century Genesis of the "Correspondence" Attributed to Prince A. M. Kurbskii and Tsar Ivan IV.* Cambridge, Mass., 1971; Скрынников Р. Г. *Переписка Грозного и Курбского. Парадоксы Эдварда Кинана.* Leningrad, 1973; for a review of Edward Keenan's book see: Андреева Н. *The Slavonic and East European Review*, Vol. LIII, 1975, No. 133, pp. 582-588; for reviews of R. Skrynnikov's book see: Fennell, J., *Russia Mediaevalis*, Vol. II, München, 1975, pp. 188-198; Keenan, E., *Kritika*, Cambridge, Mass, Vol. X, 1973, No. 1, pp. 1-36; Лихачев Д. С. "Существовали

ли произведения Курбского и Грозного?" In the book: Лихачев Д. С. *Великое наследие*, pp. 333-348; Зимин А. А. "Первое послание Курбского Ивану Грозному". *ТОДРЛ*, Vol. XXXI, 1976, pp. 176-201; Скрынников Р. Г. "К вопросу о происхождении сходных мест в Первом послании Курбского Ивану IV и сочинениях Исайи". *Русская литература*, No. 3, 1977, pp. 65-76; Лурье Я. С. "О возникновении и складывании в сборники переписки Ивана Грозного с Курбским". *ТОДРЛ*, Vol. XXXIII, 1978, pp. 204-218; Rossing, N., Rønne, B., *Apocryphal—Not Apocryphal? A Critical Analysis of the Discussion Concerning the Correspondence Between Tsar Ivan IV and Prince Andrey Kurbski*, Gopenhagen, 1980.

[36] *Переписка Ивана Грозного с Андреем Курбским*, p. 7.

[37] Зимин А. А. "Когда Курбский написал 'Историю о великом князе Московском'?" *ТОДРЛ*, Vol. XVIII, 1962, pp. 305-308.

CHAPTER 7

The beginning of the seventeenth century was a time of profound social and political crisis for Russia. The increasing

LITERATURE OF THE FIRST HALF OF THE SEVENTEENTH CENTURY

social contradictions produced many uprisings of peasants, bondmen and urban townsfolk. The most important of these was the Peasant War led by Ivan Bolotnikov, the first peasant war in Russian history. The Polish intervention led to the loss of Smolensk and other southwestern territories. The Swedes blocked Russia's outlet to the Baltic. The crisis in the social and state structure was accompanied by a dynastic crisis. The people of that day and subsequent generations called this difficult period the Time of Troubles.

Ivan the Terrible's son Theodore, the last tsar from the house of Grand Prince Ivan the Money-Bag, died in 1598 leaving no heir. His brother-in-law Boris Godunov, who had in fact ruled Russia under Theodore and was a member of the junior line of the old Moscow boyar family of Saburovs, acceded to the throne. Although his accession was represented as an "election by the whole people", the authority of the autocracy began to decline rapidly. After Boris' death (on April 13, 1605) the cap of Monomachos became a plaything in the hands of numerous pretenders, lost as easily as it was won. Boris Godunov's son Theodore held the title of sovereign of All Russia for six weeks only, before being killed by the supporters of Pseudo-Dmitry I.* Pseudo-Dmitry I was murdered before a year had passed. And two days after his death, on 19 May, 1606, Prince Vasily Shuisky, the leader of the plot, came to the throne, the last of the line of Rurik to accede to the throne of Moscow.

But Russia did not want to acknowledge this "boyar tsar". It was rumoured that "Dmitry" had escaped death and that someone else had been killed in his place. Before the new pretender had even appeared, the towns of Putivl, Chernigov, Ryazan and Tula rose up in support of him. Vasily Shuisky hastily assembled an army to put down the revolt, but it was overwhelmingly defeated at the battle of Kromy. The insurgents were led by a boyar's bondman called Bolotnikov, a brave and skilled soldier who had been captured by the Tartars, sold as a slave to row in Turkish galleys, and then, after being freed, gained military experience in Europe.

Although Bolotnikov was fighting for the "natural tsar Dmitry" he represented the interests of the lower social strata and urged them to give short shrift to the ruling estate. The poor townsfolk, peasants and fugitive bondmen flocked to his banners. Bolotnikov won many victories over the tsar's forces and advanced almost to the gates of Moscow. However the treachery of noblemen's contingents from the southern regions caused him to retreat, first to Kaluga, then to Tula. Only after a long siege of Tula did Vasily Shuisky succeed in defeating the peasant army.

The breathing space gained by the government was short-lived, however. A new enemy threatened it—Pseudo-Dmitry II. Supported by detachments of Polish soldiers of fortune and Cossacks he advanced as far as Moscow in the summer of 1607, largely thanks to the Polish interventionists. Pseudo-Dmitry II made the village of Tushino outside Moscow his capital and was nicknamed the Tushino thief or Tushino *tsarik*. From here he dispatched his agents and soldiers round the Russian towns. He was recognised by Pskov, Suzdal, Vladimir, Rostov, Yaroslavl and Vologda. For

---

* Ivan the Terrible's infant son Dmitry died in Uglich during the reign of Theodore. (Rumour had it that Boris Godunov was responsible for his death, but it is more likely that the boy died as the result of an accident.) At the beginning of the seventeenth century this gave rise to a spate of pretenders claiming to be Dmitry, who, they said, had managed to escape death.

almost three years Moscow and Tushino threatened each other, and neither side could gain the upper hand.

Vasily Shuisky was forced to turn to the Swedes for assistance.

The pretenders, or *tsariks* as they were called, provided a strange background to the kaleidoscopic changes of tsars. They began with Pseudo-Dmitry I (there were no pretenders in Russian history prior to the seventeenth century). This "playing the tsar" reflected a most important change: the Russian people had ceased to believe in the Divine origin of autocratic power, in the idea that there could be only one tsar "by the Will of God" in the country. The very number of pretenders is significant in itself. During the Time of Troubles more than ten of them appeared, and they came from different social strata. Pseudo-Dmitry I was from the Otrepyev family of the service nobility; Pseudo-Dmitry II or the Tushino thief was the son of a priest; and "Prince" Peter, who claimed to be Tsar Theodore's son and fought together with Bolotnikov, was a bondman. This shows clearly that at this time of crisis not only the nobility, but also the lower strata hoped to sieze power and put a "just" tsar on the throne from their own estate.

Participation by all estates is characteristic not only of the political and social struggle. It is a common feature of the Time of Troubles in general and is clearly seen in the sphere of literature also. The role of the spoken and written word increased greatly. The victory of Pseudo-Dmitry I was secured not so much by arms, as by "anonymous sheets", skilful propaganda that won popular opinion over to his side. All rulers and pretenders to the throne, Vasily Shuisky, Pseudo-Dmitry II and the Boyars' Duma, circulated appeals. King Sigismund III of Poland flooded Russia with "enticing sheets" on behalf of himself and his son Władysław who also had designs on the throne of Moscow. Many agitational *gramotas* were issued from Bolotnikov's camp, particularly at the beginning of the war of liberation. The "brothers of the Moscow state" (the towns and the Trinity Monastery of St Sergius) urged one another "to stand together with the whole land and fight the Lithuanians to the death".

The *gramota* is an official genre aimed at providing information about certain events, conveying facts, forbidding or ordering something to be done. But the *gramotas* of the Time of Troubles not only informed. They also sought to persuade, to act not only on the reader's mind, but also on his heart. They are characterised by a heightened emotionality that is not usually found in official document writing and is always present in fictional texts. The authors of these *gramotas* wrote rhythmic and rhyming prose, had extensive recourse to rhetorical devices, painted pictures of the common folk's misfortunes and included "laments" in their texts.

As a result information was relegated to the background, and the *gramota* became a product of rhetoric, oratory. Thus the agitational literature of the Time of Troubles paved the way for the artistic reinterpretation of official genres which is one of the literary discoveries of the first half of the seventeenth century.

The participation by all estates also explains why the circle of writers became broader. Whereas before it consisted mainly of learned monks who engaged in literary activity, now laymen of all different ranks and estates took up the pen, princes, nobility from the capital and the provinces, and government officials. Whereas before there had been a division between the oral and written tradition, now folklore found its way into manuscript books. From the first half of the seventeenth century we have some very old specimens of *rayeshnik* verse, an extremely old collection of incantations, the manuscripts of the oral poetic *Tale of the Kievan Bogatyrs* and songs about Grigory Otrepyev.

As Russian society broke up into various parties and camps, governmental and church control of literature became impossible. The Time of Troubles was also a time of no censorship. The writer's freedom did not depend on non-literary factors. The writer began to reflect freely on the behaviour of the people he portrayed, rejecting the traditional mediaeval scheme of good or bad and discovering for himself the diversity, complexity and contradictory nature of human character.

This period also witnessed a cultural reorientation in Russia. Up to the seventeenth century Russian literature had been oriented primarily on the literature of South-Eastern Europe (the Greeks and the Balkan Slavs). Now contacts with the Ukraine, Byelorussia and Poland became paramount. One of the consequences of the Brest Church Union of 1596, aimed at making the Orthodox population of the Polish-Lithuanian state adopt Catholicism, was that Ukrainian and Byelorussian intellectuals emigrated to Moscow. At the beginning of the century their experience and knowledge were used extensively. They worked at the Moscow Printing House and translated from Greek and Polish. With regard to Poland, with whom Russia was waging a long and exhausting struggle, literary contacts did not cease even in these difficult years. The Poles who inundated Russia were not only soldiers of fortune out to loot and plunder; they also included some highly-educated scholars. The eminent Polish philosopher Sebastian Petrycy, who came for the wedding of Marina Mniszech and was exiled after the murder of Pseudo-Dmitry I, wrote some poetic variations on themes of Horace while "in Moscow captivity". In this book (published in Cracow in 1609) there are hundreds of lines about Moscow.

Polish works very soon began to predominate in translated literature. Polish literature played the role of an intermediary literature: through it the themes and characters of European culture began to circulate in Russia. The "turning to Western Europe" is reflected in the *Chronograph* of 1617, which contains far more information about Greek mythology (some existed before), renderings of the myths about Chronos, the struggle of the gods and the titans, Heracles, Perseus, Dedalus and Icarus, King Midas and Orpheus. Drawing on the Polish *Chronicle of the World* by Martin Bielski, the redactor of the *Chronograph* of 1617 compiled chapters on the history of Poland and the Holy Roman Empire and included information about the popes. The *Chronograph* was intended as a model for imitation, its viewpoint being that of official historiography. By drawing on European material, the *Chronograph* was instrumental in bringing about the Europeanisation of Russian culture.

In 1618 Russia and Poland signed the armistice of Deulino. Patriarch Philaret, the father of Tsar Michael, returned to Moscow from Polish captivity. The chief ideologist by virtue of his office, Philaret also became the virtual ruler of the state. His aim was to restore the former ideological status destroyed by the Time of Troubles. Philaret proclaimed isolationism, banning the importing, possession and reading not only of Polish works, but also of books of the "Lithuanian press" and publications of Orthodox Ukrainian and Byelorussian printers.

But no bans could turn back the clock. There could no longer be any question of universal submission, unquestioning obedience. The experience of the Time of Troubles had not been in vain. Philaret himself, incidentally, took this experience into account. His isolationist programme was cut according to the Polish pattern. He also borrowed a great deal from the Counter-Reformation, with which he had become familiar during his captivity and which was waging an ideological offensive, because by the beginning of the seventeenth century the position of Catholicism in Poland had been gravely weakened. Protestants of all kinds (Lutherans, Calvinists, etc.) were opening more and more new schools and printing houses, flooding Poland with their writings. The oppositional writing of the lower strata was also finding its way to the printing press: from time to time works of semi-folklore satire kept appearing on the book market, which ridiculed and rejected the hypocritical world of official culture. The Counter-Reformation began a campaign both against religious free-thinking and against popular culture. In 1617 Bishop Martin Szyszkowski published an index of proscribed books. The "control of people's minds" was becoming a reality.

Like the Counter-Reformation in Poland, the Moscow Patriarchate was also fighting on two fronts. While setting up obstacles to contacts with the West, Philaret at the same time declared war on the *skomorokhs*, the confraternity of wandering minstrels and jesters who were the professional bearers of folk art, their skits, songs and street shows. The *skomorokhs* are known from Russian sources as far back as the eleventh century. From the outset the Orthodox Church had denounced their "play-acting, diabolical singing and blasphemous mockery" (there is an old Russian proverb that say "God created the priest, and the Devil the *skomorokh*"), but right up to the seventeenth century the Church tolerated the *skomorokhs*, not regarding them as particularly dangerous. Patriarch Philaret was the first to turn from words to deeds, from denunciation to direct persecution. Moscow *skomorokhs*' musical instruments were confiscated, put into carts, taken down to the River Moscow and burnt. The persecution of the *skomorokhs* was a sign of the weakness, not the strength of the Church, a sign that it had begun to fear "secular" culture as an ideological rival.

The attempts to restore ideological equilibrium did not lead to stagnation, nor to turning back the clock. The principle of dynamism, the principle of constant change, not only quantitative, but also qualitative, was already firmly established in Russian literature.

1. Polemical Writings of the Time of Troubles

The works which contain a record of the Time of Troubles can be divided into two main groups.[1]

The first consists of works that appeared before 1613, that is, before the election of Michael Romanov to the throne. They are direct responses to events, the direct impression of social and political passions and biases. They are polemical writings in which everything is subordinated to a concrete agitational task. The texts of the second group were also written by people who had witnessed and taken part in the Time of Troubles, but they were written after it was over, in more or less peaceful times. Their authors are already attempting to interpret philosophically, historically and artistically the "evil years" that Russia has just endured.

Minor genres are more suitable for agitation. The publicists of the Time of Troubles were no exception to this rule: one of the main genres in their repertoire is "visions".[2] The canonical structure of the "visions" can be seen from *The Tale of the Vision to a Certain Holy Man* compiled in the autumn of 1606 when Bolotnikov's army was approaching Moscow.

The Tale of the Vision to a Certain Holy Man of **Archpriest Terentius.** It tells how a certain man in the capital dreamed that the Virgin, John the Baptist and the Holy Saints were praying to Christ in the Cathedral of the Assumption to spare the Orthodox people who had fallen into sin and therefore been made to suffer the horrors of the Time of Troubles. In the end Christ is moved by His Mother's tears and says in a quiet voice: "For your sake, Mother, I shall spare them if they repent. But if they do not repent, I shall show them no mercy." After this a saint bids the hero: "Go, you who have found favour with Christ, and tell what you have seen and heard!" The hero tells his vision to Archpriest Terentius of the Kremlin Cathedral of the Annunciation, who then writes a tale about it "and gave it to the Patriarch, and told it to the tsar".

The same compositional stereotype provides the basis for visions described in Nizhny Novgorod, Vladimir, Veliky Ustyug and other towns. The local details and characters vary considerably in works of this genre: in the vision Christ may appear, or the Virgin, or a "wondrous woman" in shining robes with an icon in her hands (the Vladimir vision). Grigory Klementyev of Ustyug heard the voices of the patron saints Procopius and John (the tale about this vision was appended to *The Life of St Procopius of Ustyug* as another miracle). The conditions of salvation also vary and may be of a general nature ("let them fast and pray with tears") or more concrete. In the Nizhny Novgorod vision as well as three days of fasting the Lord orders that a church be built and adds: "Let them place an unlit candle and blank paper on the altar." If all these conditions are fulfilled to the letter, "the candle will be lit by fire from Heaven, the bells will peal out on their own, and on the paper will be written the name of him who is to rule the Russian state".

For all the variations in these visions they have a lot in common, and not only in their composition. Use is often made of everyday detail creating an illusion of authenticity. Here are the opening lines of one of the Moscow visions: "In the year 115 (1607), on the twenty-seventh day of February, on Friday night, the head watchman Istoma Mylnik, son of Artemy, was told to spend the night in the porch of the Cathedral of the Archangel Michael; but in his place his son Kozma did spend the night there, and with him six watchmen from the Vegetable Row: Obramko Ivanov, Vaska Matfeyev, Andriushka Nikitin, Pervushka Dmitriyev, Pervushka Matfeyev, and Grishka Ivanov." Of particular interest here is the reference to the fact that the head watchman's place was taken by someone else ("but in his place his son Kozma did spend the night there"). This simple detail enhances the impression of the authenticity of the vision itself. There can be no doubt that all the watchmen listed were real traders "from the Vegetable Row".

In *The Tale of the Vision to a Certain Holy Man* we are told that the hero hears not the pealing of bells in general, but the strokes from one particular bell "the big bell ... which was made in the reign of Tsar Boris". When the hero goes to the Kremlin, he notices that the streets are dry and smooth, although it is October, the month of autumn rains. The hero observes Christ and the Virgin from a definite vantage point—through the "West doors, from the Patriarch's Court".

In times of war and unrest "visions" and "heavenly signs" are always observed and recorded with care by the people of the day. Five years after the election of Michael Romanov the Thirty Years War broke out in Europe. A comet was commonly thought to have presaged the war. Visions and prophesies enthralled Catholic and Protestant countries alike. They were believed by kings, generals and monks, simple folk and learned scholars.

In this respect the literature of the Time of Troubles is no exception. Prince Ivan Chvorostinin, a favourite of Pseudo-Dmitry I and a theologian, historian and poet, recalling the sudden death of Boris Godunov and the six-week reign of his ill-fated son Theodore, remarked in *Tales of the Days and Tsars and Prelates of Moscow*: "There were many signs through comets: sometimes in the shape of a spear, sometimes two moons, one conquering the other."

The visions of the Time of Troubles played an important part in the political struggle. At the bidding of Tsar Vasily Shuisky *The Tale of the Vision to a Certain Holy Man* of Archpriest Terentius was read on 16 October, 1606 in Russia's main church, the Kremlin Cathedral of the Assumption "out loud to all the people, and there was a great gathering".[3] At the same time a special week of fasting was declared, "and prayers were sung in all the churches ... that the Lord God might turn his righteous anger from us and still the internecine strife and bring peace and harmony to all the towns and lands of the Moscow state". In 1611 the Nizhny Novgorod and Vladimir tales of visions spread to other Russian towns. The people of Ustyug heard of the Nizhny Novgorod vision from the townsfolk of Yaroslavl and passed it on to Vychegodsk, from whence it went appended to a special letter to Perm.

The "vision" is a very old genre, adopted in Russia together with Christianity. In the period of the Time of Troubles, however, it acquired new functions and came to the fore, ousting other genres. Similar changes took place in other genres also: the Time of Troubles breathed new life into such traditional form of official writing as the *gramota*.[4]

During this period agitation by means of *gramotas* was unusually intensive. The *gramotas* combine an official style with rhetoric. They not only contain calls for unity, but also pictures of the devastation of the Moscow state, the despoiling of national relics by the Polish invaders, and so on.

All this prepared the way for the appearance of so-called false *gramotas*, strange literary hoaxes. For example, there is a *Gramota* of 1611 purporting to be written by Smolensk "captives" who had "surrendered to the Lithuanians without any resistance" and were living in a camp behind the lines of King Sigismund III of Poland who had laid siege to Smolensk.[5] "All of us," says the text, "have perished without exception and without mercy and have not found favour or mercy." This literary hoax betrays ignorance of the details of the siege of Smolensk and a remarkably detailed knowledge of Moscow affairs, which one would hardly expect from a captive far from the capital. The *Gramota* appears to have been written in the Trinity Monastery of St Sergius, which led the patriotic movement during the Time of Troubles. Its aim is clear from the following appeal in the text: "Cast off your fear! What favour and mercy do you hope to find? If you do not unite with the rest of the land now, you will perforce weep bitter tears and sob in eternal, inconsolable lament." The authors of the hoax thought that an appeal for unity would be more effective if it were put in the mouths of people who had drunk the cup of the enemy's "favour" to the full.

The New Tale of the Most Glorious Russian Tsardom. *The New Tale of the Most Glorious Russian Tsardom*, written in 1610-1611, is based on a literary reinterpretation of official genres. The anonymous author calls his work a "letter" (*pismo*) (which is a synonym for *gramota*): "And may you read this letter without any doubt... And he who takes this letter and reads it, let him not keep it to himself, but pass it on to his brethren, Orthodox Christians, to read briefly ... and not to those who ... have turned from Christianity and become our enemies ... do not tell them of it and do not give them it to read."

In his appeal to free the realm from the Polish invaders, the anonymous writer concentrates on his agitational task. He is interested only in the alignment of political forces at the end of 1610. His sympathies and antipathies are expressed clearly, and consequently the characters in the *New Tale* are either patriots

Cathedral Square in the Moscow Kremlin. Illumination, 1672-1676

and heroes, or villains. The author is ardent in his praise of Patriarch Hermogenes. He is an unshakeable pillar supporting the vaults of the "great chamber"—of the Russian land. Its arch-enemy is Sigismund III, the "wicked and strong godless one", who is seeking to win himself a bride by force—Moscow. The bride's "kinsfolk" and well-wishers are the people of Smolensk, who will not surrender to the Poles, and the leaders of the embassy to Sigismund, Philaret Romanov and Prince Vasily Golitsyn, who are acting for the whole of Russia. The "cursed bride-groom" Sigismund is helped by traitors, the seven boyars who are ruling Moscow and have sworn allegiance to Sigismund's son, Prince Władysław.

One of these boyars, the treasurer Fyodor Andronov, is compared in the *New Tale* to Ikhnilat, the crafty royal counsellor in *Stefanit and Ikhnilat.* In order to debunk this puppet ruler, the author creates a comic effect with the use of rhymed speech (on the comic effect of rhyme in Old Russian culture see the section entitled "Versification").

Федор Андронов "ни от царских родов, ни от боярских чинов, ни от иных избранных ратных голов; сказывают, что от смердовских рабов. Его же, окаяннаго и треклятаго, по его злому делу не достоит его во имя Стратилата, но во имя Пилата назвати, или во имя преподобнаго,—но во имя неподобнаго, или во имя страстотерьпца,—но во имя землеед-ца, или во имя святителя,—но во имя мучителя, и гонителя, и разорителя, и губителя веры христианьския".

Fyodor Andronov is "not of royal birth, nor of boyar rank, nor from a great general's family. They say he is of bonded peasant stock. Cursed and damned, he should be named not after Stratilates,* but after Pilate; not the Reverend, but the irreverend, not a martyr, but a man-eater, not a prelate, but a predator, and persecutor and destroyer of the Christian faith."

As a literary device rhymed speech is most effective in texts intended for declamation. The author of the New Tale was undoubtedly well aware of this: his "letter" was intended to be read out at meetings "of his brethren", so rhymed passages were particularly suited to it. The author is striving to make his readers and listeners actively resist the foreign invaders. He is an agitator, not an historian. Therefore he deals only with matters of the moment and does not reflect on the past or on the reasons for Moscow's struggle.

---

* St Theodore Stratilates, in whose honour Andronov was given the Christian name of Fyodor—the Russian form of Theodore.— *Tr.*

The Lament on the Capture and Final Destruction of the State of Muscovy. One of the first attempts to establish the causes of the Time of Troubles was made in another work written at the same time as the *New Tale.* This work was written in the genre of the lament. As well as laments for the dead and fallen, Old Russian literature also has laments for realms and cities. These were composed in times of hardship and tribulation. The unknown author of *The Lament on the Capture and Final Destruction of the State of Muscovy* was writing at the time when Minin and Pozharsky were already forming a national levies, but Moscow was still in the hands of the Poles (i.e., before the autumn of 1612). No one could yet predict the outcome of the struggle against the invaders, and therefore the main themes of the *Lament* are sorrow, mourning and grief at the former might and greatness of Russia, and calls to repentance and prayer, "that God ... might spare what remains of the Christian family".

"What precious royal chambers there were," the author exclaims, "adorned with gold inside! How many wondrous treasures, royal diadems and fine royal mantles and robes of purple!" After beginning with the appearance of the first pretender, "the forerunner of the Anti-Christ" and "the son of darkness", the author touches upon the many sad events of the later years. He condemns the invaders and their Russian accomplices, but does not place the blame for Russia's sufferings entirely on them. In his opinion, it was internal strife, "brother hating brother", and the domestic crisis caused by general moral decline, that produced the Time of Troubles. "Truth had grown scarce in people," the author of the *Lament* writes sadly, "untruth reigned ... evil bared itself, and we were covered in falsehood".

This discourse on the causes of the Time of Troubles suffers from religious-moral abstraction, of course. The author himself is aware of that. "Alas, woe is me! How has such a tower of piety fallen, how has the God-planted garden been laid waste?" the author asks rhetorically and cannot provide a clear answer. The traditional collection of authoritative sources for the Orthodox scribe do not help either. "Such punishment and wrath were let loose, that it is worthy of no little amazement and many tears. And not a single theological work, no *vitae,* philosophical books, writings on different reigns, chronographs, histories, or other works tell of such punishment of any monarchy, tsardom or principality as that which befell most exalted Russia." So one had to rely on one's own powers of reasoning. The author of the *Lament* seems to be inviting the reader to reflect on the causes of the Time of Troubles.

2. Historical Works on the Time of Troubles

The task of providing an historical explanation of the Time of Troubles fell to writers of the period after the Time of Troubles and the election of Michael Romanov to the throne in 1613, that is, the remaining years of that decade and the following one. These writers belonged to various estates, for the participaton of all estates found in the period of the Peasant War and Polish intervention had not yet ceased. They included churchmen and laymen, government officials and aristocrats.

The *Tale* of Abraham Palitsyn. One of the most popular and lengthy works on the Time of Troubles was written by the monk Abraham Palitsyn, cellarer of the Trinity Monastery of St Sergius (the cellarer was in charge of the monastery stores or its secular affairs in general). His *Tale*[6] consists of seventy-seven chapters dealing with different periods. The first six chapters were written in 1612, although the work was not completed until 1620. The central part deals with the famous siege of the Trinity Monastery of St Sergius. Then the account is continued up to the Deulino armistice of 1618, in the conclusion of which Abraham Palitsyn himself took an active part.

Abraham Palitsyn was a prominent figure in the events of the Time of Troubles (his conduct in these difficult years was not entirely without reproach, however, for he served Pseudo-Dmitry II). He constantly stresses his own importance, as, for example, in his account of how he went to the Hypatian Monastery in Kostroma to fetch Michael Romanov, how he met him later in the Trinity Monastery of St Sergius and so on.

In the *Tale* Abraham Palitsyn paints a terrible picture of the people's sufferings: "Then people hid in dense thickets and in the heart of dark forests, and in secret caves, and in the water among the bushes. And they sighed, and wept, and prayed to the Lord their Maker that night cover them and that they might rest a little in a dry place. But there was no peace for the fugitives neither day nor night, nor did they find a secluded spot. Instead of the pale moon the fields and forests were lit up at night by fire, and no one could move an inch: the enemy lay in wait like wild beasts for those who left the forest."

The *Annals* of Ivan Timofeyev. Another writer of this period, the head of a central government department Ivan Timofeyev, depicts Russian history from Ivan the Terrible to Michael Romanov in his *Annals*,[7] written in 1616-1619. By virtue of his office Ivan Timofeyev was constantly dealing with affairs of state.

He had access to many important documents, which explains why the *Annals* contains much historical information not recorded by any other writer. Moreover, Timofeyev describes many events that he witnessed personally. When the people went to the Novodevichy Convent to ask Boris Godunov to accept the royal crown, he "had in his hands a cloth that he used to wipe off sweat ... and he did wind this cloth around his neck, gesturing that he would hang himself if the petitioners did not cease their supplications". Apart from this hypocritical gesture by Boris Godunov, Ivan Timofeyev noticed other interesting details characteristic of the atmosphere surrounding Boris' "voluntary" election to the throne. A certain young boy, who had been so directed, climbed up to the window of Tsarina Irina's cell and shouted right "in her ear", begging her to bless her brother's coronation. These are insignificant details, but their very insignificance is typical, for here Ivan Timofeyev reveals himself as a writer of memoirs, a private individual, and not an historian.

Ivan Khvorostinin. The third author, Prince Ivan Khvorostinin, descended from the house of Yaroslavl appanage princes. In his youth he was closely associated with the Pseudo-Dmitry I, who appointed him royal carver (*kravchiy*) and, according to another contemporary, held this callow youth in great favour, in which the youth in question gloried greatly and did permit himself everything. This shameful fact was known to all, and it was important for Khvorostinin to vindicate himself in the eyes of his contemporaries and heirs. Therefore in his *Tales of the Days and Tsars and Prelates of Moscow*, which Khvorostinin appears to have written shortly before his death (he died in 1625), he introduces elements of self-justification. One day, he writes, when the pretender was boasting about one of his edifices, "a certain youth stood there, who enjoyed his favour and who always and above all others was concerned for his salvation." This youth, Khvorostinin himself (the narrative continues in the first person), is said to have dared denounce the Pseudo-Dmitry's vain pride, reminding him that God "flouts in all manner of ways the boastings of the proud". In another passage Khvorostinin states that he was valued by Patriarch Hermogenes himself, who led the resistance to the Polish invaders. One day when he was instructing those assembled, the Patriarch singled out Khvorostinin who was present for special mention: "You have laboured above all others in your studies, you understand, you know!" Whether this conversation really took place we do not know, as there is no reference to it in other sources.

Semyon Shakhovskoy. Prince Semyon Shakhovskoy was related to Ivan Khvorostinin. His life was full of the sudden changes and vicissitudes so typical of the Time of Troubles. In 1606, when the towns of Putivl, Chernigov, Yelets and Kromy rose up against Tsar Vasily Shuisky, Semyon Shakhovskoy was serving at Yelets. Here his first fall from favour occurred: he was taken to the capital and without any explanation exiled to Novgorod (where there was an outbreak of plague). On the way there, however, they turned off into a village. In 1608-1610 he was back in service in Moscow, where he fought for a while against the Tushino army and then went over to it. His second and again short fall from favour came in 1615 as a result of Shakhovskoy's own petition in which he complained that he was "tormented by being sent from one office to another." At the end of 1619, after the death of his third wife, Shakhovskoy married a fourth time, which was forbidden by the church. This incurred the wrath of the Patriarch Philaret. In his *Supplication* to Philaret, Shakhovskoy justifies himself by saying that he lived three years with his first wife, only eighteen months with his second, and a mere nineteen weeks with his third. He lived to a ripe old age (some sources mention him still in the 1650s) and was quite frequently in disgrace.

A man of great learning, Shakhovskoy left a considerable literary heritage. The Time of Troubles is the subject of two of his tales: *The Tale in Memory of the Holy Martyr, the Devout Prince Dmitry* and *The Tale of How a Certain Monk Was Sent by God to Tsar Boris to Avenge the Blood of the Righteous Prince Dmitry.* It has recently been proved that Shakhovskoy was the author of one of the most important works on the history of the Time of Troubles, the so-called *Tale of the Book of Former Years.* This condensed, but comprehensive work on the history of the Time of Troubles has survived in the *Chronograph* of the Tobolsk nobleman Sergei Kubasov. It was thought to be the work of Prince Ivan Katyrev of Rostov, because the *Tale* ends with the following two lines:

Есть же книги сей слагатай
Сын   предиреченнаго   князя   Михаила   роду   Ростовского
сходатай.

The author of this book/Is the son of the above-mentioned Prince Mikhail of the princely house of Rostov.

Mikhail Katyrev of Rostov, the well-known general who is referred to most favourably in the *Tale,* had one son, namely, Ivan Katyrev. Ivan's first wife was the daughter of the future Patriarch Philaret and the sister of Michael Romanov. Tsar Vasily Shuisky exiled Ivan Katyrev to Tobolsk for "vacillating" in the struggle against the "Tushino thief". Only in 1613, during the election of his brother-in-law as tsar, did he reappear in Moscow.

A School. Engraving from the printed **ABC** by Vasily Burtsov. Moscow. 1637. Academy of Sciences Library, Leningrad

A. School. Engraving from the printed *ABC* by Vasily Burtsov. Detail

An early manuscript, dating back to the late 1620s-early 1630s, of the original redaction of the *Tale* has recently come to light.[8] A postscript states directly that the author was the "most sinful among men Semyon Shakhovskoy". In this redaction the *Tale* has no title, and the lines are as follows:

Есть же книги сей слагатай
Рода Ярославского исходатай.

The author of this book / Is descended from the princes of Yaroslavl.

Thus, the Time of Troubles was written about in the 1610s and 1620s by a monk, a head of a government department, and two princes of the house of Rurik, although of the junior line. From this list it will be clear that the literary milieu of the first few decades of the seventeenth century was a very motley one. This tells us that there were not yet any professional writers; it also shows that there was not yet a monopoly on writing, that anyone could become a writer.

Naturally enough, the outlook and literary manner of these writers varied. They had certain important things in common, however. The main one was the enhancement of the individual element, the striving for a kind of self-expression. We have already seen how Abraham Palitsyn stressed his role in events of national importance; how Ivan Khvorostinin sought to vindicate himself by quoting conversations with the Pseudo-Dmitry and Patriarch Hermogenes, conversations which are most likely fictitious. Even in *The Tale in Memory of Prince Dmitry*, in which Shakhovskoy adheres strictly to hagiographical canons, one can detect autobiographical touches. Having announced that Prince Dmitry was the son of Ivan the Terrible by his sixth wife, Tsarina Maria, i.e., an heir of dubious legitimacy, Shakhovskoy continues: "Let no one condemn this birth not of the first marriage." By defending the prince, the author of the *Tale* was also defending himself, or rather the rights of his children by his fourth wife.

The enhancement of the individual element is not found in autobiographical allusions and scenes alone. It is also expressed in the comparatively free discussion of the causes of the Time of Troubles and the behaviour of the main personages irrespective of their position in the hierarchy and in social relations. All historians of the Time of Troubles see the cause of the natinal disaster as lying in "the sin of all Russia". This is only natural, for they could not yet reject the religious view of history. It is important, however, that they do not confine themselves to a general reference to this "sin", but seek to analyse it. And it is most significant that this analysis varies from author to author.

Ivan Timofeyev and Abraham Palitsyn both agree that the

Time of Troubles resulted from the "wordless silence", or "the foolish silence of the whole world", in other words, slavish submission to unjust rulers. But then each of them goes his own way. According to the *Annals* the influx of foreigners was responsible for the moral decline; their pernicious role in Russia's misfortunes is stressed by Ivan Timofeyev over and over again.

Abraham Palitsyn, however, in speaking of the signs of general moral decline, from tsar to bondman, from boyar to churchman, is not inclined to place the blame on the foreigners. He stresses the social contradictions on the eve of the Time of Troubles. Under Boris Godunov there were bad harvests for three years running and many thousands died of starvation. It became known that the rich had concealed vast stores of grain: "The old granaries were not empty, the fields were covered with ricks, and the barns were filled with stacks that had piled up over the fourteen years before the troubles of the Russian land ..." Abraham Palitsyn puts the blame for the civil unrest on the rich: "Thus must we understand the sin of all Russia, the reason why it has suffered from other peoples: for during the time of Divine tribulation and Divine wrath (i.e., the three years of bad harvests) they did not have mercy on their brothers ... And just as we were merciless, so have our enemies been merciless to us."

Historians of the autocratic state cannot be content with depicting "the sin of the people". Their sphere of attention must also include "the powers-that-be". All the authors writing about the Time of Troubles provide a description of the tsars, from Ivan the Terrible to Michael Romanov. These descriptions reveal most clearly the literary discovery that Dmitry Likhachev has termed "the discovery of character".[9] According to him, this is, briefly, as follows.

In mediaeval historiography man is "absolutised", that is to say, he is for the most part (but not always, as we have already seen) either absolutely good or absolutely evil. The authors of the beginning of the seventeenth century no longer regard the good and evil elements in a person's character as something fixed and immutable. Character changes and contrasts no longer upset the writer; on the contrary, he indicates reasons for these changes. They are, alongside human free will, the influence of other people, vanity and so on. Man combines all sorts of traits, both good and bad.

This discovery can be illustrated by the descriptions of Boris Godunov that abound in works on the Time of Troubles. It is interesting that in their discussion of Boris none of the authors can help qualifying their remarks. "Although he was skilled in ruling the realm," Abraham Palitsyn writes of him, "he was not versed in the Holy Scriptures and hence did not observe the commandment about brotherly love." Khvorostinin writes: "Although he was not learned in the Scriptures and scholarly things, yet he possessed a firm natural wit." Even Shakhovskoy, discussing him as the murderer of Prince Dmitry, thought it necessary to say a few good words about the "most wise and sensible mind" of Boris Godunov!

For Ivan Timofeyev the combination of good and bad in one person acquires the importance of an aesthetic principle: "Insofar as we have told of Boris' evil doings, it behoves us not to keep silent about his good deeds to men."

This literary principle is proclaimed and established in the 1617 redaction of the *Chronograph.* Here a contradictory and changeable character is typical of the overwhelming majority of the personages, from Ivan the Terrible to the Patriarch Hermogenes and Boris Godunov, Vasily Shuisky, Kozma Minin and Ivan Zarutsky, one of the Cossack leaders. The compiler of the 1617 *Chronograph* gives this feature theoretical substantiation: "No one has a blameless life." The *Chronograph* was to some extent an official work to be emulated. Its authority helped to establish the "discovery of character" in Russian literature.

3. Hagiographical-Biographical Tales

The "discovery of character" meant that writers of the first half of the seventeenth century began to assess their personages regardless of mediaeval convention, their status in the hierarchy. A personage was assessed as an individual, not as a tsar, a general or a prelate. From here it was but a step to recognition of the value of the individual in general. The first attempts at the biography of a private person appeared. The authors of these attempts still write with one eye on hagiographical canons (for *vitae* remained the school of the biographical genre). But these canons were greatly modified, as we can see from the North Russian Lives of saints.[10] Feats of piety were replaced by strange happenings that stretched the imagination. The stories centred round some extraordinary event. For example, as a guest at a banquet Nikodim Kozheozersky accidentally partakes of some poison prepared by a wicked wife for her husband. Varlaam Keretsky kills his wife in a fit of rage, thereby condemning himself to a terrible ordeal: he sails along the shore of the Kola Peninsula in a boat, alone with the corpse, until "the dead body began to rot away". Persecuted by his superiors, Kirill Velsky drowns himself in the river in protest. Thus even a person who had committed

suicide and whom the Church would not allow to be buried on
consecrated ground or have prayers said for him, was associated in
the popular mind with saintliness!

One of the main functions of hagiography was to portray
examples for emulation. In the North Russian *vitae* this function
is relegated to the background: it is difficult to imagine anyone
deciding to emulate Varlaam Keretsky or Kirill Velsky. Saintliness
is replaced by human suffering, the story arousing sympathy for
the heroes, tears of compassion. North Russian locally revered
saints are an early version of the literary type embodied in
Dostoyevsky's "insulted and humiliated".

At the same time Platon Karatayev's* predecessor, the "good
man" type, appeared in hagiographical prose, for example, the
heroine of *The Tale of Juliana Osorgina* written between 1620 and
1630.[11]

The Tale of Juliana Osorgina. At first glance this work is a
vita of a locally revered saint. Take the typical hagiographical
heading, for example: *In the Month of January on the Second Day Is
the Dormition of Saint Juliana the Wonder-Worker of Murom.* The tale
makes use of many stereotypes of the hagiographical genre. The
heroine's noble parents live "in piety and purity". Juliana herself
is from childhood "diligent in prayer and fasting", meek and
quiet, "refraining from laughter and all games". After marrying,
she gives alms and cares for widows and orphans, washing them
"with her own hands and giving them food and drink". When her
husband refuses to let her go to a convent, Juliana mortifies her
sinful flesh by sleeping on logs and putting nut shells and
potsherds in her boots. As befits a holy person, Juliana overcomes
evil spirits. Her demise is a blessed one. It is not death, but going
to sleep. Summoning her children and servants, she instructs them
"in love, prayer, alms-giving, and other virtues". Her last words
are those of a hagiographical heroine: "Glory be to God. Into The
hands, Oh Lord, I commit my spirit. Amen!" Those who were
present at her dormition, the author tells us, saw "a gold nimbus
around her head, like unto that painted round the heads of saints
on icons". Bells are heard when Juliana's relics are found, and her
coffin is full of chrism that gives off a sweet fragrance; the chrism
turns out to have healing properties. This shows that Juliana is a
wonder-worker.

True, after mentioning her posthumous miracles, the author
immediately breaks off the narrative. The final sentence reads as
follows: "We dared not write this, for it has not yet been
examined." Thus the author had a practical purpose in writing

---

* A character in Lev Tolstoy's *War and Peace.*

this tale: he was hoping that the Orthodox Church would canonise
Juliana. The tale was intended as the first step in the canonisation
procedure. We do not know whether Juliana was canonised, or
whether she remained a locally revered Murom saint.

These hagiographical elements, however, constantly contradict
the author's designs and the development of the plot. Let us
examine the scene of the finding of Juliana's relics, for example.
Juliana died in 1604. A "warm" church (i.e., one heated in winter)
was built over her grave shortly afterwards. Eleven years later her
son Georgi died. He was naturally buried next to his mother, in
the church porch. When this new grave was being dug, Juliana's
coffin appeared "on top of the earth whole and quite undam-
aged". "And they did marvel," writes the author, "and wonder
whose it was, for there had not been any burials here for many a
year." The hagiographical "marvelling", which invariably accompanied the "discovery of relics" is out of place here. For the *Tale*
was composed by Juliana's other son, Druzhina, whose Christian
name was Calistratus and who must have buried Georgi too. He
could not have forgotten where his mother's body lay!

Druzhina Osorgin, Juliana's other son, held a senior post in the
local chancery from 1625 to 1640. The story of the pious Juliana
reveals the author's personal attitude towards her clearly. It is full
of filial love and reverent admiration. Only a son who had lived
side by side with the devout Juliana could have observed her
dozing while she told her beads: "Many a time did we see her
sleeping, while her hand told the beads." What Druzhina wrote
was not a conventional hagiographical account, but a biography
with elements of a family chronicle of the Osorgins, Nedyurevs,
Arapovs and Dubenskys, noble families in Moscow and the
provinces.

Juliana's house, family and servants are not merely the
backcloth to the action, as in a typical *vita*. Her whole life is
devoted to her family. She is idealised as a wife, mother, and
daughter-in-law, a thrifty and fair mistress of the household, a
lady of the manor who gives refuge to the homeless and cares for
the needy.[12] Among the good deeds essential for saving the
Orthodox soul, the author gives pride of place to Juliana's
indefatigable household labours. Because of them she has no time
to go to church: "And the priest of that church ... did hear a voice
from the icon of the Virgin saying unto him: 'Go and ask the
gracious Juliana why she does not come to church to pray. Her
prayers uttered at home are pleasing to the Lord, but not as
pleasing as prayers uttered in church. But revere her, for she is no
less than sixty now, and the Holy Spirit dwells within her.'" As we
can see, the author tries to present even the fact that Juliana does

not go to church as a reason for glorifying the heroine. However, Juliana did not go to church even before she was married (there was no church in the village where she grew up), nor did she go after she married. Thus, Juliana's piety was by no means exceptional.

A person may deserve to enter the kingdom of heaven without leaving the daily round of earthly pastimes—this is the logic of the tale. Although Druzhina Osorgin may not have intended to implant this "free-thinking" idea in the reader, the latter could not help arriving at it. This idea was also suggested by the main literary device in the tale, namely, the clash of the practical and the conventional hagiographical explanations of one and the same fact. When there was a bad harvest Juliana "took the food from her mother-in-law intended for the morning and midday meals" and secretly gave it to the hungry. This amazed her mother-in-law: in times of plenty her daughter-in-law would fast and refuse food, and now, when food was scarce, she had suddenly changed her habits. Juliana explained that before she had children she did not feel hungry, but now, the heroine says, "I cannot have enough to eat, I often crave food not only by day, but also by night, yet I am ashamed to ask you."

Another episode relates to these hungry years, the fatal three years of bad harvests in the reign of Boris Godunov. Juliana has to mix goose-foot and bark with the flour, "and her bread was sweet from prayer. She gave it to the needy, and did not send a single beggar away without alms, although at that time there was a great multitude of them." The neighbouring landowners jeered at the beggars: "Why are you going to Juliana's house? She's dying of hunger herself!" "We have been to many villages and received good bread," the beggars replied, "but none so sweet as hers; that widow's bread is sweetest." Juliana's neighbours also decided to try her bread, and began praising her bakers: "How skilled her servants are at baking bread!" "They did not understand that her bread was sweet from prayer," the author explains. Here the reader was left to decide for himself what made the bread sweet—prayer or skilful baking. The author insisted on the religious explanation, but the reader could choose the prosaic one.

There is a most important idea in The Tale of Juliana Osorgina. It is that "salvation" in this world lies not in religious zeal, but in the family, in family love, meekness and piety. This idea was of great importance in the first half of the seventeenth century, when the Russian Church was going through a deep crisis. The idea of "salvation in the world" inspired the activity of the "God-lovers" in the 1630s and 1640s, Ivan Neronov, Stefan Vonifatiev and Avvakum. In the final analysis this idea promoted the secularisation of literature, as we can see from the work of the Murom senior official, Druzhina Osorgin, who wrote the biography of his mother.

4. Versification

New Russian literature uses two forms of literary speech—prose and verse. The same forms are also characteristic of folklore, where prosaic and poetic genres have developed since time immemorial. In oral popular poetry the text is, as a rule, closely connected with a melody. The performer sings, rather than declaims. But in Russian folklore there was also "oral-speech" verse, for example, the *rayeshnik* which had an unlimited number of syllables in each line, no fixed stress and compulsory plain rhyme at the end of the line. The term *rayeshnik* comes from the popular picture theatre (*rayek*) which used this type of verse. It was also used in the ditties chanted by the showmen at fairs, street-vendors, traders, pedlars, and in particular, by the *skomorokhs.*

The Russian literary language of the Middle Ages was different. In Old Russian literature verse, i.e., a text divided into lines of equal length, is found only in exceptional cases.[13] The few verse works known to Old Russia were written either from Byzantine models or under the influence of oral folk poetry. The influence of Byzantine metrics is obvious in the early Slavonic poems using the principle of syllabic symmetry (a set number of syllables in each line) that were written by Cyril the Philosopher and the early generations of his followers in Greater Moravia and in Bulgaria in the ninth and tenth centuries.[14] These include the foreword in verse *(proglas)* to the translation of the Gospels, and an *ABC prayer*, which consists of twelve lines with an alphabetical acrostic (each line beginning with the next letter of the Slavonic alphabet), and the services for Cyril and Methodius. The activity of the early Slavonic writers was dictated to a large extent by the idea that the language of the Slavs as a language of religious worship and culture was equal to Greek and Latin. Therefore from the very outset Slavonic literature sought to master all the achievements of Byzantine literature, including the poetic genres.

The literature of Kievan Russia included early Slavonic verse. The scribes preserved and the readers were aware of its syllabic nature. In the twelfth century, however, some major changes took place in the Russian language. The reduced vowels ъ and ь ceased to perform a syllabic function in a weak position. As a result lines ceased to have the same number of syllables. In new translations from the Greek the metrics of the original was not preserved. The thirteen-syllable lines of the collection of sayings entitled *The Wisdom of Menander the Wise* in the Slavonic version that appeared in the thirteenth century became lines of different length, ranging from eleven to sixteen syllables. This "translation into prose" was the result not of technical ineptness, but of the aesthetic premise that one should translate the "inner meaning" of the text, without bothering about precese observance of the form.

The author of *The Lay of the Ruin of the Russian Land* made use of "oral-speech" verse:

> О светло светлая и украсно украшена
>   Земля Руськая!
> И многими красотами удивлена еси:
> Озеры многыми удивлена еси,
> Реками и кладязьми месточестьными,
> Горами крутыми, холми высокыми,
> Дубравоми частыми, польми дивными...

Oh, most radiant and finely adorned / Land of Russia! / You are renowned for your many beauties: / You are famed for your many lakes, / Your revered rivers and springs, / Steep mountains, high hills, / Dense oak groves, wondrous plains...

This splendid text shows that Old Russian scribes possessed a sense of poetry. This sense was satisfied by both folklore, which in the Middle Ages was shared by all, and literature. Almost completely ignorant of verse in the modern meaning of the world, Old Russian literature made extensive and exclusive use of rhythm.[15]

In Metropolitan Hilarion's *Sermon on Law and Grace* and the ceremonial rhetoric of Cyril of Turov the rhythm is deliberate and often so consistent that the texts of these authors can be considered as the meeting point of prose and verse. The "braiding of words" of the fourteenth and fifteenth centuries, in which words with the same root and similar sounds are repeated like elements of ornament, creating a rhythmical impulse, is also non-prose. The writers of the sixteenth and seventeenth centuries, Maxim the Greek, in particular, used the expression "to compose", "to braid" and "to weave" verse as synonyms. Thus, in their mind the "braiding of words" was a special form of literary speech different from "ordinary" prose.[16]

The rhythmic movement is particularly strong in hymnology, where the text and the melody form a single entity. Hymnology is lyrical, because its subject is man's emotional life, but this lyricism is constricted by the framework of Divine worship. Towards the beginning of the sixteenth century, however, a form of lyricism appeared that was independent of liturgical service but based on the hymnological tradition, the so-called verses of repentance.[17] They are no longer directly connected with church services, although still associated with them in subject matter (particularly with the Lenten cycle). In these verses of repentance the themes of sin and repentance, death and the last judgement, of leaving this world for the "beautiful wilderness" prevail:

> Прими меня, пустыня,
> Как мать чадо свое,
> В тихие и безмолвные
> Недра свои...[18]

Take me, wilderness,/ As a mother her child,/ Into your still and silent/ Depths...

The verses of repentance very soon became an independent genre. In song manuscripts of the sixteenth century we find large selections of several dozen texts. Then the verses of repentance were swelled by the addition of new works in which secular themes were heard. Thus, during the invasion by the Poles and Swedes, they reflected the theme of defence of the homeland:

> Придите, все русские люди,
> Верующие и благочестивые,
> И храбрые воины...
> Станем, братья,
> Против полков языческих,
> Не убоимся часа смертного...[19]

Come, all ye Russian folk/ Faithful and pious,/ And valiant warriors.../ Let us stand, brothers,/ Against the pagan hosts,/ Let us not fear the last hour...

The verses of repentance are not prose, of course, but nor are they poetry in our understanding of the word. They were not recited, but chanted "in eight voices", like hymns, and the melody played a very important part. Even the final ъ, not normally pronounced, was often marked with a note and, consequently, chanted.

Versification as a conscious form of literary speech, distinct from prose in general and rhythmic prose and hymns in particular, arose in the first decade of the seventeenth century, in the Time of Troubles. In manuscript books of that time we find both folklore metres (*rayeshnik* verse and accentual verse) and also borrowed Ukrainian-Polish syllabic verse.[20] This marks the beginning of the history of Russian poetry of the West-European type.

The Epistle of One Nobleman to Another. The verse section of *The Epistle of One Nobleman to Another* (1608-1609) is written in *rayeshnik* verse. The author of the *Epistle*, a landowner by the name of Ivan Funikov, was in Tula, which had been captured by Ivan Bolotnikov, when it was besieged by Vasily Shuisky. Food supplies ran out and the besieged went hungry. The rebels held Ivan Funikov in prison on the suspicion that he was concealing grain. In the *Epistle* Funikov describes his misadventure:

> Сидел 19 недель,
> А вон из тюрьмы глядел.
> А мужики, что ляхи,
> Дважды приводили к плахе,
> За старые шашни
> Хотели скинуть с башни.
> А на пытках пытают,
> А правды не знают.
> Правду-де скажи,
> А ничего не солжи.
> А я божился,
> И с ног свалился,
> И на бок ложился:
> Не много у меня ржи,
> Нет во мне лжи...[21]

For nineteen weeks I sat in jail,/ And through the window did I look/ And twice the peasants, like the Poles,/ Did take me to the chopping block,/ For sins as old as old can be/ They wanted to throw me off a tower./ And oh, how bad they tortured me,/ Because the truth they did not know./ Tell us the truth, they all did cry,/ But mind you do not tell a lie./ And I did tell them and did swear,/ Down on my knees and lying there:/ Alas, I have but little rye/ And, 'pon my soul, I do not lie. The comic ring of these lines led some specialists to suspect that Ivan Funikov was not the author of *The Epistle of One Nobleman to Another*, that it had been wrongly ascribed to him and that a person could not write in such a humorous vein about his own sufferings! But the fact is that the *rayeshnik* verse, which Funikov uses, is designed to produce a comic effect. The semantic aura of the *rayeshnik* is comicality. It is the buffoonery of the *skomorokhs* accentuated by rhyme. The rhyme "distorts phenomena, by making the dissimilar similar ... depriving the account of its seriousness and making a joke even of hunger",[22] suffering and torture. This joking is a kind of psychological defence against real phenomena that can damage the psyche. In making use of *rayeshnik* verse, the author has to reckon with its semantic inertia. Therefore, Ivan Funikov willy-nilly adopts the pose of the joker. There are also prose passages in the *Epistle*, incidentally, and they do not contain a trace of humour: the semantic inertia of the *rayeshnik* does not operate here.

Evstraty. Whereas Funikov made use of the verbal art of the *skomorokhs*, the traditions of the wandering minstrels, showmen and jesters, a contemporary of his, the poet Evstraty, who was a supporter of Vasily Shuisky, borrowed from the poetic culture of Western Europe in his prayer in verse of 1621. This prayer, written in syllabic verse with alternate rhyme, is prefaced by the author with the Latin words *serpenticum versus*, i.e., "serpentine verse". And Evstraty's poem is indeed represented graphically in the form of a serpent. This is done as follows: the common elements (inflexions) are omitted from neighbouring lines and written between the lines. As a result the lines form a zigzag, or serpentine pattern, otherwise it is quite impossible to read them. Take, for example, the two consecutive quatrains: *To God in God,/ to the light from the light,/ in plain words/ in all time,/ be praise and glory, honour, worship,/ extolling, power,/ and thanksgiving.* In Evstraty's manuscript they appear like this (with a syllabic system of 4-5-4-5; 8-6-8-6):

All manner of "curious" verse was common in European poetry of the sixteenth and seventeenth centuries, for example, palindromes, which read the same from left to right and right to left. There was also a special genre of representational epigram in which the text was set out in the form of a cross, a star, a goblet, the sun's rays or tongues of flame, a heart, and so on. Evstraty's poem is a typical example of this "verbal alchemy".

The poems of Ivan Funikov and Evstraty were at opposite ends of the extremely broad spectrum within which Russian poetry of the seventeenth century was to develop. From buffoon-like ridiculing of the world to the meditative lyric, from clowning to "theology in verse", from the *rayeshnik* to strict syllabic verse, these were its thematic and metric possibilities, which can be seen already in the Time of Troubles. It was the realisation of these possibilities that Russian poets of the seventeenth century took upon themselves.

One constant factor was the influence of the poetry of the

Ukraine, Byelorussia and Poland. As we know, the Pseudo-Dmitry introduced music and singing at his court and set up court posts in the Polish manner. He evidently did not forget the post of court poet (Polish poets of that period included many noblemen, because the art of composing verse was part of a Polish nobleman's education). More likely than not he intended to bestow this post upon his favourite, Prince Ivan Khvorostinin.

The Verse of Ivan Khvorostinin. Already during the time of Patriarch Philaret, in late 1622 or early 1623, Khvorostinin was persecuted for "vacillating in faith" (he forbade his servants to go to church, saying that "praying is useless and won't raise the dead"). They confiscated Khvorostinin's manuscripts containing "all manner of reproaches against various people of the state of Muscovy", among which there were notebooks with verse. Of these only one couplet has survived, quoted in a decree of the Tsar and the Patriarch: "Moscow folk sow the earth with rye, but all of them do live a lie." Khvorostinin was banished to the White Lake Monastery of St Cyril, where he was put in a separate cell under strict supervision. In order to prove his loyalty to Orthodox faith, Khvorostinin had to write his *Discourse Against Heretics and Vilifiers,* a long treatise in verse consisting of 1,300 lines, in which he denounced Catholicism and various heresies.[23] Khvorostinin's *Discourse* was not an original work. It was a translation (or, rather, a rendering) of a Ukrainian polemical work, also in verse.[24] In spite of this, Khvorostinin's treatise provides most interesting material for evaluating early attempts at Russian written poetry.

From the late sixteenth century two systems of versification were used in Ukrainian and Byelorussian books, the parisyllabic and the imparisyllabic, in both cases with plain rhyme.[25] Whereas Evstraty inclined towards parisyllabic rhyme, Khvorostinin gave preference to imparisyllabic. It was along the path chosen by Khvorostinin that Russian poetry of the first half of the seventeenth century developed. The early generations of Moscow poets wrote imparisyllabic verses, calling it "two-lined harmony", thus stressing the principle of plain rhyme.

In certain important respects "two-lined harmony" coincided with *rayeshnik* verse. In both cases each line was a complete phrase intonationally and syntactically. In both cases alongside the prevailing feminine rhyme considerable use was made of masculine and dactyllic rhyme. In Khvorostinin we find the following final rhymes: *Рим—дым, сотворил—одарил, ловец—овец, бог—мног* (masculine rhyme), *отвращаемся—утверждаемся, писание—прочитание, учители—мучители* (dactyllic rhyme). For all his westernisms, Khvorostinin was clearly influenced by the *skomorokhs'* art. The couplet "Moscow folk sow the earth with rye, but all of

them do live a lie" is a paraphrase of an old proverb: "Beautiful is a field with rye, and speech with a lie" known from miscellanies of the seventeenth and eighteenth centuries. It should be
noted that the same rhyme is used in Ivan Funikov's *Epistle* and
later in the *Polite Epistle to a Foe* and in other works of *rayeshnik*
verse.

Thus, in the early stages the folklore tradition and the
Ukrainian-Polish influence acted together. Very soon, however,
these streams divided, when a certain hierarchical principle began
to operate in written poetry. The "two-lined harmony" became
identified with "highbrow", serious versification, and the inherent-
ly comic *rayeshnik* with "low-brow", popular versification. This
hierarchical division led to changes in the technique of "two-lined
harmony", which can be seen clearly in the verse of the so-called
Chancery School.

The Verse of the Chancery School. Until recently it was
thought that the versification of the first half of the seventeenth
century was a random collection of a few disconnected and
immature attempts at writing verse. An analysis of manuscript
material has shown, however, that by the late 1620s and early
1630s a poetic school had emerged in Russia that functioned
actively over two decades right up to the reforms of Patriarch
Nikon.[26] It consisted of up to ten versifiers—the Secretaries Alexei
Romanchukov and Pyotr Samsonov, the Under-Secretary Mikhail
Zlobin, the redactors of the Moscow Printing House Savvaty,
Stefan Gorchak, Mikhail Rogov and others. For the most part,
they were government officials, not of noble descent, whose
families had only recently, in the first or second generation, won
themselves a place on the administrative ladder. Which is why this
literary group is called the Chancery School.

At that time the most educated members of the Russian
intelligentsia had posts in the Printing House and the Moscow
chanceries, particularly the Ambassadorial Chancery, the central
office dealing with foreign affairs. Literary work was the main
profession of the redactors in the Printing House. The ability to
wield the pen was also essential for the secretaries and under-
secretaries of the chanceries. They had to receive foreign envoys
and carry out various commissions abroad, so they were accustomed to have contact with European culture. One of the most
distinguished and also typical members of the Chancery School
was the Secretary Alexei Romanchukov, who was in charge of the
Russian embassy to Persia from 1636 to 1638. The Russians
travelled together with the Holstein trade mission, whose members
included some famous writers, such as the great German Baroque
poet Paul Fleming. Alexei Romanchukov was in constant contact

with him (and, incidentally, managed to learn Latin during the journey). A reminder of this encounter is his own verse entry, an acrostic, in the album of the Holstein physician Hartmann Gramman (who later went into Russian service, becoming court physician to Tsar Michael):

Не дивно во благополучии возгоржение,
единай добродетель — всего благого совершение.
Дом благой пускает до себя всякого человека
и исполняет благостыню до скончания века.
Вина всяким добродетелем — любовь,
не проливается от нее никогда кровь...[27]

'Tis no wonder that folk grow proud in prosperity,/but there is a single virtue — to pursue goodness./A good home is open to every man,/goodness dwells within it forever./The origin of all virtues is love./Love prevents the spilling of blood...

This verse is a kind of landmark in the history of Russo-European cultural contacts: in 1638 the lines of a Moscow poet appeared for the first time in the manuscript of a European.

The Chancery School poets had intensive personal and creative contacts. A popular expression with them was "spiritual alliance" (a variation on "amorous alliance"), a term which they applied to themselves as a body. What professional qualities should a poet who belonged to the "spiritual alliance" possess? Above all, "wit".

In that period the word "wit" did not bear any relation to the ability to think up an apt expression. "Wit" was knowledge, intellect. But the Chancery poets gave the term a special meaning. From their point of view "wit" was the ability to use oratorial language. A favourite device of oratorial language is comparison. In their search for material for comparison the poets turned, for the most part, to the Russian tradition, the miscellanies of *The Physiologos* (Bestiary) and *ABC,* from which they borrowed information about animals, plants, stones and trees.

Есть в море хитрый зверь, он ныряет на большую глубину,
Так же ритор и философ мудро рассуждает о природе вещей...
Мы просим у тебя любви, как просят воды жаждущие онагры...
Камень хризолит по виду подобен золоту,
Этому камню и ты подобен своим разумом...
Камень карбункул зелен цветом,
А твоя, государь, царская душа прекрасна перед богом
                                                        молитвами...

There lives in the sea a cunning beast, he dives to a great depth,/Likewise the rhetorician and philosopher discourse wisely on the nature of things.../We ask you for love, as thirsty onagers ask for water.../The chrysolite stone is like unto gold in appearance,/And you are like unto this stone in intellect.../The carbuncle stone is green in colour,/And your royal soul, Tsar, is fair with prayer before God...

The poet had to possess an associative mind. "Wit" is the ability to find new associative links. Association is the focal point of the language of the Chancery School. The search for new associations is something that it shares in common with the artistic style that prevailed in Europe in the seventeenth century, Baroque. The Moscow versifiers avoided outlandish associations, however, contenting themselves with traditional metaphors and symbols. The information about magnets, onagers (wild donkeys), chrysolite and carbuncle was taken from books long popular in Russia.

From the 1620s to 1640s versification was still a new occupation for Russian writers. It was regarded as a kind of literary game. It is no accident that among the genres used by the Chancery poets, the epistolary one prevailed. They wrote epistles mainly to one another, but also to Tsar Michael and those who were close to him, Ivan Romanov, brother of Patriarch Philaret, Prince Dmitry Pozharsky, and others. These epistles, as a rule, contained little information (usually centring around a request for patronage), but they were often fairly lengthy (a hundred lines or more). It is obvious that the Chancery poets were concerned not so much with the content, as with showing off their ability to write "two-lined harmonies".

Like all budding poets, they showed exaggerated concern for the technique of versification, first and foremost, for the acrostic. Their epistles literally abound in acrostics. The first letters of each line form a phrase containing the name of the recipient and the name of the author. The author invariably points out in the text that he has made use of an acrostic and indicates where it ends. There was no need to conceal the name of the author and the recipient because the epistles were handed to real people.

Thus, the acrostics in the epistolography of the Chancery School are also element of the literary game, a sign of literary "elegance". But the acrostic had another function as well. It distinguished the "two-lined harmony" of Moscow intellectuals from the "low-brow" *rayeshnik* (it should be noted that Chancery epistles and comic *rayeshnik* messages were included in the same collections). The division was further widened by the difference in rhyming technique. In the *rayeshnik* we find sound rhymes, including root and compounded rhymes. What predominates in the works of the Chancery poets are grammatical or suffixalinflexional rhymes formed by the consonance of suffixes and inflexions, when verb rhymes with verb, adjective with adjective and noun with noun in the same grammatical form. This is not to say, of course, that the Chancery poets were technically imperfect.

By preferring grammatical rhymes and renouncing sound rhymes, they set themselves apart from the *rayeshnik*. It is interesting that this disdain of sound (particularly compounded and punning) rhyme was preserved in the "high-brow" genres of Russian poetry right up to the beginning of the twentieth century.

The Chancery poets very soon turned from literary games to serious poetic pursuits. Savvaty wrote a cycle of didactic poems *On Light, On the Flesh,* and *On the Womb,* in which he developed the theme of the vanity and transience of human life, a traditional theme in Christian culture and a major one in European Baroque. He tried to get this cycle published at the Printing House, then the only printing house in Russia. Other verse texts were also prepared for printing: a condensed version of Hamartolos' *Chronicle* and prefaces to several Moscow publications. But none of these texts were printed. They remained in manuscript form. Evidently the authors of the "two-lined harmonies" had not only protectors, but some influential enemies as well.

The Chancery School ceased to exist in the 1650s. When Patriarch Nikon began to introduce his ecclesiastical reforms, the leading poets of the Chancery School, Savvaty included, joined the supporters of the "old belief". And that was the end of the Chancery School.

5. New Literary Areas (Siberia and the Don)

In the first half of the seventeenth century the "geography" of Russian literature expanded somewhat, as the remote borderlands of the state, Siberia and the Don, in particular, joined in the literary movement.

The beginning of Siberian literature is connected with the founding of the Tobolsk archbishopric in 1621. Before moving to Tobolsk the first Archbishop of Siberia, Cyprian Starorusenkov, was archimandrite of the Khutyn Monastery in Novgorod. In fact almost all Siberian archbishops in the seventeenth century came from Novgorod. At that time Siberia was being settled mainly by pioneers from the northern and White Sea provinces of European Russia. Consequently early Siberian literature drew primarily on Novgorodian and North Russian literary traditions.[28]

Cyprian was well aware that the role of the clergy was more

important in Siberia than in the central regions. The nobility, which was represented only by military commanders and exiles, could not become the dominant or even a major force in the economy and culture of Siberia. In conflicts between the administration and the Church in Siberia the Church invariably came out on top. Sensing itself to be the all-powerful and uncontrolled master of this huge area far from Moscow, the Tobolsk archbishopric showed a clear tendency towards separatism, cultural separatism included. It was on this basis that Siberian literature developed.[29]

There is an account of the literary ventures of the first Archbishop of Tobolsk in *The Esipov Chronicle* which was compiled fifteen years after the founding of the archbishopric: "In his second year as archbishop he (Cyprian) remembered the ataman Ermak and his band and had them enquire of Ermak's Cossacks how they came to Siberia, where they fought battles with the infidels, who was slain by the infidels in these skirmishes and where. The Cossacks brought him a manuscript... And he ... ordered the names of those slain to be written in the Synodical of the Cathedral of St Sophia and to have prayers said in remembrance of them on Orthodox Sunday together with others who had died for Orthodoxy."[30] The Cossacks' written account has not survived, but the Synodical compiled from it has been preserved in a number of chronicles, and the original has also come to light,[31] i.e., the actual manuscript from which prayers were said in the Tobolsk Cathedral of St Sophia in memory of Ermak's Cossacks in the first week of Lent (Orthodox Sunday).

The Synodical for Ermak's Cossacks. The Synodical did not only contain the "names of the slain," i.e., it was more than a simple list of names. Cyprian included the Synodical in the *Feast of Orthodoxy* ritual according to which praises were sung in Lent for people revered by the Church and heretics and sinful people were anathematised. Short narrative passages and stories were allowed in the *Feast of Orthodoxy* ritual. There are many such historical insertions in the version of this work that was preserved in the Tobolsk Cathedral of St Sophia. There are also narrative passages in the Synodical for Ermak's Cossacks. It is, in fact, a brief account of the Siberian campaign, with a list of the main battles and a description of Ermak's death. Here we find clearly formulated an idea that was later preached extensively by official Siberian literature, namely, that the Cossacks came to Siberia with the "shield of the true faith", and that they shed their blood for the triumph of Orthodoxy to bring Christianity to this pagan land.

The Esipov Chronicle. This idea forms the basis of *The Esipov Chronicle,* named after its writer, Savva Esipov, who completed work on it in 1636. Savva Esipov was in charge of the Chancery of the Archbishop of Tobolsk (he had the post of archbishop's secretary). Naturally Esipov, who was probably acting on direct instructions from the ecclesiastical authorities, had at his disposal both the Synodical and other documents in the library and archives of St Sophia which are unknown to us.

His chronicle was conceived and written as a history of Siberia. After beginning with an account of the countryside, peoples, local rulers and princes, Esipov then concentrates on two figures, Kuchum and Ermak. He portrays Kuchum in the traditional mediaeval guise of the proud pagan ruler who tried the Lord's patience sorely. Ermak is the instrument of the Lord, a "two-edged sword". God chose a simple Cossak ("not of an illustrious line" the chronicle tells us), to put Kuchum to shame. Ermak as a person does not interest Esipov, only Ermak as the instrument of the Lord. The Siberian chronicler had not yet "discovered character". The chronicle ends with an account of the founding of the Tobolsk archbishopric. This event testifies to the triumph of Orthodoxy in Siberia.

The "Historical" Tale of the Capture of Azov. In 1637, one year after the completion of *The Esipov Chronicle,* another work about the Cossacks was written in a different borderland region of Russia, the Don. It was the first of the Azov cycle of tales, which consists of an "historical", a "poetic" and a "folk" tales. The events described by this "historical" tale are designated in the title: *A Work on the Town of Azov, and on the Coming of the Atamans and Cossacks of the Great Don Army, and on Its Capture.*[32]

For the Don Cossacks Azov, a strong Turkish fortress at the mouth of the Don, the river which the Cossacks regarded as the "bastion" of their free lands and called respectfully "Don Ivanovich", had always been a great obstacle. In the spring of 1637, taking advantage of a favourable balance of forces (the sultan was engaged in a war against Persia), the Cossacks laid siege to Azov and took it after two months.

The tale that describes this episode was written by a man who worked in a Cossack chancery. This left its mark both on the composition, which is that of the official military report of the capture of Azov, and on the style of the work. Here in documentary form and great detail with much enumeration we find descriptions of the preparations for the campaign, the undermining of the fortress walls, the storming of the Turkish stronghold and the fate of the captured. The author does not confine himself to purely documentary tasks, however. He says as much in the concluding lines: "And we have written this that Christian folk might remember it ... and to the shame and disgrace of impious peoples of pagan stock for present and future generations." The ideas of the "historical" tale are in harmony with those of *The Esipov Chronicle*: the Don Cossacks marched on Azov in order to "replant the Orthodox Christian faith" there.

Like any writer, the author of the "historical" tale was addressing not only future generations, but also his contemporaries. And he sought to ensure that their response was favourable to the Cossacks. Every reference in the text to Tsar Michael is highly respectful. Even in the account of the undermining of the Azov fortress, the author does not forget to mention that the Cossacks got their gunpowder from Moscow:

Ermak's Journey Along the Siberian Rivers. Drawing for *The History of Siberia* by S. U. Remezov. The end of 17th century. Academy of Sciences Library, Leningrad

Ermak's Journey Along the Siberian Rivers. Detail

"And they dug a second passage for four weeks and put gunpowder supplied by the Sovereign under the wall." This detail would be unnecessary if the tale were intended for Cossack readers only; it becomes relevant if the author was addressing himself to Muscovites as well. The Cossacks took Azov without the tsar's permission and without even informing Moscow. The author is seeking to vindicate their wilful conduct.

The Cossacks realized that they could not hold Azov without the assistance of Moscow. Therefore, throughout the four-year struggle for Azov, which was followed with great interest by the Moslem and the Christian world alike, the Don Cossacks sought to put Azov under the protection of the tsar. Fearing a large-scale war with the Ottoman Porta (peace with the Turks was a firm principle of the foreign policy of the early Romanovs), the Moscow government refrained from sending troops to help the Cossacks and officially disowned them through its ambassador in Istanbul. At the same time it sent the Cossacks arms and ammunition and did not prevent volunteers from joining the Azov garrison.

In August 1638 Azov was besieged by Crimean and Nogai Tartar cavalry, but the Cossacks sent them packing. Three years later the fortress had to repulse another attack, this time from the Turkish Sultan's huge army equipped with powerful artillery. A large naval fleet blockaded the town from the sea. Mines were put under the walls and cannons destroyed the fortress. Everything that could burn was burnt to cinders. But a handful of Cossacks (all that remained of more than five thousand at the beginning of the siege) withstood the four-month siege, repulsing twenty-four assaults. In September 1641 the sultan's battered army was forced to retreat. The disgrace of this defeat was a bitter blow to the Turks: the inhabitants of Istanbul were forbidden to utter the word "Azov".

It was clear that the sultan would not give up Azov and that it was only a question of time before he launched a new campaign. Moscow, too, realised that the time had come to cease its ambiguous policy. In 1642 a National Assembly (*Zemsky sobor*) was convened to decide whether to defend the fortress or hand it back to the Turks. It was attended by a delegation of elected envoys from the Don Cossacks. The *esaul* (the assistant of the ataman who led the delegation) was Fyodor Poroshin, formerly a slave of Prince Nikita Odoyevsky who had fled from his master's service. In all probability it was he who wrote the "poetic" tale of the siege of Azov, the finest work of the Azov cycle.

The "Poetic" Tale of the Siege of Azov. The "poetic" tale was aimed at winning Moscow public opinion for the Cossacks and influencing the National Assembly. Through the mouths of the

Turks it uttered truths most unpalatable for the Moscow authorities: "And to you, rebels, we declare that you will receive no help or support from the Tsardom of Moscow, not from the Tsar, nor from the Russian people." The Cossacks in the tale agree with this warning: "We know full well ourselves without you, curs, what we are worth in the Moscow state in Russia, they have no use for us there... We are held in less respect than a stinking cur in Russia. We flee ... from eternal toil, from forced slavery... Who cares a jot for us there? They are all too glad to see the end of us. And never have we received food or support from Russia."

The exaggeration here is deliberate: Moscow did, in fact, send generous supplies of provisions and gunpowder to the Don. Evidently the author no longer believed in support from the Tsar and leading boyars. The bitter reproaches from the Cossack defenders of the fortress are intended for the National Assembly, their last hope.

The "poetic" tale was composed by a highly educated person. He used a wide range of written sources, in particular *The Tale of the Battle Against Mamai*, whence he borrowed devices for describing the enemy host. However, it is not paraphrases or concealed quotations that determine the artistic character of the work. There are two main principles in its poetics: the artistic reinterpretation of chancery genres and the use of folklore. The author makes use of the oral tradition of the Cossacks. From written sources he also borrowed primarily folklore motifs.

The tale begins like an extract from an official report: the Cossacks "compiled an inventory of their siege and submitted the inventory to the Ambassadorial Chancery in Moscow ... to a state secretary ... and the inventory ran as follows..." Then follows a long list of the forces dispatched to Azov by Sultan Ibrahim, a list of the infantry regiments, cavalry and artillery, the Crimean and Nogai Tartar nobles, the mountain and Circassian princes, the European mercenaries and even the peasants whom they have assembled "on this side of the sea ... with spades and with shovels, so as to bury us, Cossacks, alive by their great numbers in the town of Azov and cover us with a great mountain of them".

The last phrase is out of keeping with the dry, official style. This is no accident, but a literary device. For the list of forces, which appears at first glance to be cold and factual, actually contains emotional undertones. By listing more and more Turkish detachments, the author builds up an impression of terror and hopelessness. He himself seems to be in the grip of these feelings. He is horrified by what he has written, and the pen drops from his hand: "And there were countless thousands of them assembled against us, simple folk, so many that the pen cannot say."

These are the words of a person who is perfectly aware of the favourable outcome of the siege. He is not a clerk or a chronicler. He is a writer. He is aware that contrast creates emotional tension. The more hopeless the beginning seems, the more effective and impressive the happy ending. This contrasting picture is the author's main, but remote aim. For the time being he prepares the ground for the transition from official style to the semi-folkloric style of the military tale, the hyperbolic conventional portrayal of vast enemy hordes. It is here that he turns to *The Tale of the Battle Against Mamai.*

The Turkish hordes "sowed the empty plains with their bodies". Where there had once been open steppe, there rose up forests "of their multitudes". From the size of the infantry and cavalry "the ground ... around Azov quaked and shook, and out of the river ... out of the Don, the water rose onto the banks from such great weights." The firing of the cannon and muskets is compared to a storm—"like a great storm and terrible lightning coming from the clouds, from the heavens". The sun was covered with gunpowder smoke, "and a great darkness descended". "And a mighty fear of them seized us at the time," the author exclaims, "we beheld the untold and terrible and awful coming of the Mohammedans with dismay and wonder!"

The shifts from an official style to a folklore style continue to be the most characteristic feature of the author's writing. Here is the farewell of the Cossacks exhausted from their bloody skirmishes: "Farewell, shady forests and leafy groves! Farewell, open plains and quiet waters! Farewell, blue sea and fast-flowing rivers!.. Farewell, our quiet Lord Don Ivanovich, we shall no longer travel along you, our ataman, with a fearful host, shoot wild beasts in the open plain, nor catch fish in the quiet Don Ivanovich." This is an almost perfect reproduction of the style of Don folk songs, as we know them from later manuscripts.

The author does not only alternate between the official and folkloric styles, he also combines them, filling the officialese with folklorism and thus artistically reinterpreting it. The most striking examples of this reinterpretation is the imaginary speeches which the Turks and Cossacks exchange. The words of the Turkish commander contain the real demands of the sultan. The orator both threatens and flatters the Cossacks, but folklore imagery is intertwined in the threats and flattery. "You can see for yourselves, foolish rebels," he says, "a vast, immense ... force ... a soaring bird could not fly over our Turkish host, it would be seized with terror at the multitude of our hosts, and would fall from on high to the ground." He goes on to say that if the rebels abandon the fortress, the Turks will call them "holy Russian bogatyrs" now and forever more.

The Cossacks reply in similar vein. They rebuke the sultan for excessive pride and are not inhibited in their choice of words. The sultan is a "foul swineherd", a "stinking cur", and a "niggardly dog". This abuse is similar to the "literary abuse" that one finds in many seventeenth-century works, which also reinterpret the official genres artistically, in the legendary correspondence of Ivan the Terrible with the Turkish Sultan, then the Zaporozhye and Chigirin Cossacks.

The stylistic range of the tale stretches from the lyricism of the song to "literary abuse". It is based entirely on contrasts, because its historical basis was also a contrast, the contrast between the handful of men defending Azov and the vast host of besiegers. The tale ends with the Cossacks repulsing the final assault and storming the Turkish camp. The Turks flee in terror. Whereas earlier the Cossacks shamed the sultan with words, they now shame the Turks with deeds: "Our weak hand and the free Don Cossacks have shamed (the Turks) forever before all lands, rulers and kings."

The National Assembly was the scene of some heated disputes, but the tsar's opinion prevailed: Azov must be handed back to the Turks. The surviving rebels left the fortress. In order to relieve the bitter impression that this "sentence" had on the Don Cossacks, the tsar presented lavish gifts to those Cossacks who had attended the Assembly. Only one exception was made: the author Fyodor Poroshin, a fugitive slave and writer, was exiled to Siberia.

The "poetic" tale of Azov was fittingly appreciated by the people of the day. It circulated in many manuscripts and was constantly being reworked. On the basis of this tale and the "historical" tale of the siege of Azov, a "folk tale" about Azov was created in the second half of the seventeenth century, which belongs to a new genre in Russian literature, the genre of historical fiction.

REFERENCES

[1] Платонов С. Ф. *Древнерусские сказания и повести о Смутном времени как исторический источник.* St. Petersburg, 1888; Назаревский А. А. *Очерки из области русской исторической повести начала XVII столетия.* Kiev, 1958. For the publication of texts see the book: *Памятники древней русской письменности, относящиеся к Смутному времени* (Русская историческая библиотека). Second edition, Vol. XIII, St. Petersburg, 1909. All works about the Time of Troubles are quoted from this edition unless otherwise indicated.

[2] Прокофьев Н. И. "Видения как жанр в древнерусской литературе". *Ученые записки МГПИ им. В. И. Ленина*, Vol. 231, 1964; Лихачев Д. С. *Развитие русской литературы X-XVII веков. Эпохи и стили*, p. 141.

[3] Копанев А. И. "Новые списки *Повести о видении некоему мужу духовному*". *ТОДРЛ*, Vol. XVI, 1960, pp. 477-480.

[4] Дробленкова Н. Ф. *"Новая повесть о преславном Российском царстве" и современная ей агитационная патриотическая письменность*. Moscow and Leningrad, 1960. *The New Tale* is quoted from this edition.

[5] Платонов С. Ф. *Статьи по русской истории (1883-1902)*. St Petersburg, 1903, p. 193-198.

[6] For the publication and study of this work see: *Сказание Авраамия Палицына*. Preparation of text and commentaries by O. A. Derzhavina and E. V. Kolosova. Moscow and Leningrad, 1955.

[7] For publication of the text see: *"Временник" Ивана Тимофеева*. Preparation of text, translation and commentary by O. A. Derzhavina. Moscow and Leningrad, 1951.

[8] Кукушкина М. В. "Семен Шаховской—автор *Повести о Смуте*". In the book: *Памятники культуры. Новые открытия. Письменность. Искусство. Археология (Ежегодник 1974)*. Moscow, 1975, pp. 75-78.

[9] Лихачев Д. С. *Человек в литературе Древней Руси*, pp. 7-26.

[10] Дмитриев Л. А. *Житийные повести русского Севера как памятники литературы XIII-XVII вв.* Leningrad, 1973.

[11] For publication of the text see: Скрипиль М. О. *"Повесть об Улиянии Осорьиной"*. *ТОДРЛ*, Vol. VI, 1948, pp. 256-373.

[12] Лихачев Д. С. *Человек в литературе Древней Руси*, pp. 116-117.

[13] On the reasons for this see: Лихачев Д. С. "Система литературных жанров Древней Руси". In the book: *Славянские литературы*. (V Международный съезд славистов. Sofia, September 1962.) Moscow, 1963, pp. 65-68; Панченко А. М. "Изучение поэзии Древней Руси". In the book: *Пути изучения древнерусской литературы и письменности*. Leningrad, 1970, pp. 126-129; Матхаузерова С. *Древнерусские теории искусства слова*. Prague, 1979.

[14] Соболевский А. И. *Церковнославянские стихотворения конца IX-начала X века*. St Petersburg, 1892; Лавров П. А. *Материалы по истории возникновения древнейшей славянской письменности*. Leningrad, 1930; Панченко А. М. "Перспективы исследования истории древнерусского стихотворства". *ТОДРЛ*, Vol. XX, 1963, pp. 263-264.

[15] Сазонова Л. И. "Принцип ритмической организации в произведениях торжественного красноречия старшей поры". *ТОДРЛ*, Vol. XXVIII, 1973, pp. 30-46.

[16] Матхаузерова С. "'Слагати' или 'ткати'? (Спор о поэзии XVII в.)" In the book: *Культурное наследие Древней Руси*, pp. 195-200.

[17] The texts of the verses of repentance are quoted from the book: Бессонов П. Д. *Калики перехожие*. Moscow, 1861-1863. See also: Перетц В. Н. "К истории древнерусской лирики (стихи 'умиленные')". *Slavia*, Roč. XI, Nos. 3-4, Praha, 1932, pp. 474-479; Малышев В. И. "'Стих покаянны' о 'люте' времени и 'поганых' нашествии". *ТОДРЛ*, Vol. XV, 1958, pp. 371-374; Позднеев А. В. "Древнерусская поэма—'Покаянны на осмь гласов'". *Československá-Rusistika*, XV, No. 5, Praha, 1970, pp. 193-205.

[18] Фролов С. В. "Из истории древнерусской музыки. (Ранний список стихов покаянных.)" In the book: *Культурное наследие Древней Руси.* p. 168.

[19] Text quoted from the edition in the book: Малышев В. И. *Древнерусские рукописи Пушкинского Дома. Обзор фондов.* Moscow and Leningrad, 1965, p. 187.

[20] A general impression of seventeenth-century poetry can be obtained from the following two anthologies: *Демократическая поэзия XVII века.* Introductory article by V. P. Adrianova-Peretts and D. S. Likhachev. Preparation of text and notes by V. P. Adrianova-Peretts. Moscow and Leningrad, 1962; *Русская силлабическая поэзия XVII-XVIII вв.* Introductory article, preparation of text and notes by A. M. Panchenko. Second edition, Leningrad, 1970.

[21] Quoted from the edition in the book: *Русская демократическая сатира XVII века.* Preparation of texts, articles and commentaries by V. P. Adrianova-Peretts. Moscow and Leningrad, 1954. Second edition, enlarged, Moscow, 1977, p. 183.

[22] Лихачев Д. С., Панченко А. М. *"Смеховой мир" Древней Руси.* Leningrad, 1976, p. 27.

[23] The text of the *Discourse* was published by V. I. Savva in the book: *Вновь открытые полемические сочинения XVII в. против еретиков.* St. Petersburg, 1907, pp. 7 et seq.

[24] *Українська поезія. Кінець XVI-початок XVII ст.* Edited by V. P. Kolosova and V. I. Krekoten. Kiev, 1978, pp. 54-55.

[25] Перетц В. Н. *Историко-литературные исследования и материалы,* Vol. 1. *Из истории русской песни.* St Petersburg, 1900, pp. 5 et seq.; Холшевников В. Е. "Русская и польская силлабика и силлаботоника". In the book: *Теория стиха.* Moscow and Leningrad, 1968, pp. 27-31.

[26] Панченко А. М. *Русская стихотворная культура XVII века.* Leningrad, 1973, pp. 34-102, 242-269; Шептаев Л. Л. "Стихи справщика Савватия". *ТОДРЛ,* Vol. XXI, 1965, pp. 5-28.

[27] Here and elsewhere the verse of the Chancery School poets is quoted from the book: Панченко А. М. *Русская стихотворная культура XVII века,* pp. 35, 51, 52-53.

[28] Ромодановская Е. К. *Русская литература в Сибири первой половины XVII в.* Novosibirsk, 1973, pp. 17-20.

[29] On Siberian literature, apart from the above-mentioned work by E. K. Romodanovskaya, see: Бахрушин С. В. *Научные труды,* Vol. III, Part 1; *Очерки по истории колонизации Сибири в XVI в. и XVII вв.* Moscow, 1955; Андреев А. И. *Очерки по источниковедению Сибири.* Second edition, Moscow and Leningrad, 1960, No. 1; Лихачев Д. С. *Русские летописи и их культурно-историческое значение,* pp. 411-417; Дергачева-Скоп Е. И. *Из истории литературы Урала и Сибири XVII века.* Sverdlovsk, 1965; Дворецкая Н. А. "Археографический обзор списков повестей о походе Ермака". *ТОДРЛ,* Vol. XIII, 1957, pp. 467-482; Сергеев В. И. "У истоков сибирского летописания". *Вопросы истории,* No. 12, 1970, pp. 45-60.

[30] *Сибирские летописи.* St Petersburg, pp. 163-164.

[31] Ромодановская Е. К. "Синодик ермаковым казакам". *Известия Сибирского отделения АН СССР. Серия общественных наук,* No. 9, 1970, Book 3. The term "Synodical" (Sinodik) is used in Old Russian Literature to designate three types of works. Firstly, it is a *pomyannik,* a book in which the names of the dead are written for remembrance in the church. Secondly, it is the term used for the *Feast*

of *Orthodoxy* ritual (see text). And thirdly, in the 17th century a special miscellany appeared which was also called a Synodical: apart from a general list of names of the dead and sick, it also contained theological articles and narrative passages. The *Synodical for Ermak's Cossacks* is first and foremost a *pomyannik.* But because it was intended to be put together with another Synodical, the *Feast of Orthodoxy* ritual, it also contained narrative elements.

[32] The main works on the Azov cycle belong to Alexander Orlov and Andrei Robinson. See: Орлов А. С. *Исторические и поэтические повести об Азове (взятие 1637 г. и осадное сидение 1641 г.). Тексты.* Moscow, 1906; Орлов А. С. "Сказочные повести об Азове. 'История' 1735 года". *Русский филологический вестник,* Book 4, 1905; Books 1-4 1906; Робинсон А. Н. "Из наблюдений над стилем поэтической повести об Азове". *Ученые записки Московского университета,* No. 118, Book 2, 1946, pp. 43-71; Робинсон А. Н. "Повести об азовском взятии и осадном сидении. Исследование и тексты". In the book: *Воинские повести Древней Руси.* Edited by V. P. Adrianova-Peretts. Moscow and Leningrad, 1949, pp. 47-112, 166-243, The tales of the Azov cycle are quoted from this work.

CHAPTER 8

LITERATURE OF THE SECOND HALF OF THE SEVENTEENTH CENTURY

T he seventeenth century has gone down in Russian history as an age of revolt. Between the Time of Troubles and 1698, the

year of the last revolt by the Streltsy,* there were several large-scale popular uprisings, and many minor ones. They were particularly strong and frequent in the middle and latter half of the century. In fifty years Russia witnessed the uprisings of 1648-1650 in Moscow, Novgorod and Pskov, the "copper revolt" of 1662, the peasant war led by Stepan Razin, the rebellion of the Solovetsky Monastery in 1668-1676, and the famous *Khovanshchina* of 1682, when the Streltsy rebelled and held Moscow for practically a whole summer.

These revolts, which reflected the insoluble social contradictions of pre-Petrine Russia, compelled the government to introduce half-hearted reforms. The re-

---

* *Streltsy*—members of a military corps instituted by Ivan IV, who enjoyed special privileges in the Muscovite State in the 16th and 17th centuries.

forms were invariably in the interests of the upper estates and, therefore, in the final analysis merely aggravated the social ills. In response to the Moscow uprising of 1648 the famous Code of 1649 was introduced, a collection of laws passed quickly by the National Assembly and printed by the Moscow Printing House. The Code gave certain rights to the urban middle strata (the strata that had revolted in 1648). It made the tradesfolk a privileged estate. But most of all it benefited the nobility, against whom the revolt had been directed. The estates which the service gentry had previously held for their lifetime only were turned into hereditary holdings which they could bequeath, and the peasants were bound once and for all to the land. The period during which fugitive peasants could be brought back to their masters was no longer limited as before. This intensification of oppression immediately produced peasant revolts. Thus the revolts produced reforms, and the reforms fresh revolts.

Russian culture of the seventeenth century was also a culture of "revolt", that had lost the external unity and monolithic quality characteristic of the Middle Ages. Culture split into several trends, either autonomous or directly opposed. The greatest blow to cultural unity was dealt in the 1650s by the church reforms of Patriarch Nikon, who introduced many changes into liturgical practice and ritual, in particular, the Creed, the number of fingers used in making the sign of the cross, etc. This led to a Schism in the Russian Orthodox Church; historians reckon that between a quarter and a third of the population remained true to the old rites. Those who did not accept Nikon's reforms and adhered to the pre-reform, "old" rules and customs became called the Old Believers. The Old Believers constituted the most powerful religious movement in the whole of Russian history.

On the eve of Nikon's reforms the Church was experiencing a profound crisis. The bishoprics and monasteries (whose serfs constituted eight per cent of the population of Russia) had accumulated great wealth, whereas the lower ranks of the clergy, the country parish priests, subsided in poverty and ignorance. All educated and thinking people realised that the Church needed reform. The idea of transforming church life inspired the movement of the God-lovers, which reached its height in the first seven years of the reign of Tsar Alexis, son of Michael, who came to the throne in 1645. This was a revolt of the lower ranks of the clergy against the bishops, of the parish priests, who in terms of possessions and way of life did not differ greatly from the urban tradesmen and artisans or even the peasants.

The God-lovers' preaching contained a strong social element, in Christian attire, of course. The God-lovers did not urge people to enter hermitages and monasteries. They offered "salvation in the world", set up schools and almshouses, preaching in churches and in the streets and squares.

This social element links the God-lovers' movement with the Reformation in Western Europe. Yet there was also a great difference between them. For the God-lovers, the zealots of the old belief, the transformation of the Church meant the total subjection of Russian life to the Church. They saw the church during a service as the living embodiment of the kingdom of heaven on earth. The imaginary "holy Russia", for the return of which they fought so passionately, was envisaged by them in the likeness of a church where pious souls communed with the Lord. For this reason the reforming of the liturgy was a matter of special concern to both the future Patriarch Nikon and the Archpriest Avvakum, who at first worked side by side in the God-lovers' movement, but later became sworn enemies. This external, ritual aspect greatly influenced the Schism in the middle of the century.

When Nikon, a personal friend of the young Tsar Alexis, was made patriarch, it transpired that he had a totally different understanding of the subjection of life to the Church from his recent allies. The latter saw Russia as the last bulwark of "immaculate" Orthodoxy and sought to protect it from foreign influence. They looked with suspicion on Orthodox Greeks, Ukrainians and Byelorussians, convinced that under the rule of Turks and Poles these people could not have preserved their faith intact. Nikon, however, opposed isolationism and dreamed of Russia leading world Orthodoxy. He firmly supported the attempts of Bogdan Khmelnitsky to join the Ukraine to Russia, although he realised that this would inevitably involve war with Poland. He dreamed of the liberation of the Balkan Slavs, and even dared to think of conquering the "second Rome", once Constantinople, now Istanbul.

It was this idea of a world Orthodox empire under the aegis of Russia that led to the reform of the Church. Nikon was worried about the differences between Russian and Greek rites, which he regarded as an obstacle to Moscow's supremacy. So he decided to standardise ritual taking as a basis Greek practice, which had recently been introduced in the Ukraine and Byelorussia. Just before Lent in 1653 the Patriarch sent a "memorandum" to all the Moscow churches prescribing the use of three fingers instead of two for making the sign of the cross. Then followed the revision of liturgical texts. Those who refused to accept the changes were excommunicated, exiled, imprisoned or executed. The Schism had begun.

The Campaign by the Moscow Streltsy Against Stepan Razin. Detail of a scroll. 1670s. State Public Library, Leningrad

The Campaign by the Moscow Streltsy Against Stepan Razin. Detail

In preferring seventeenth-century Greek ritual, Nikon was proceeding from the belief that the Russians, who adopted Christianity from Byzantium, had themselves distorted this ritual. History has proved him to be wrong. During the reign of St Vladimir the Greek Church used two different sets of rules, the Studion and the Jerusalem rules. Russia adopted the Studion rules (prescribing two fingers) which were completely ousted with the time in Byzantium by the Jerusalem rules.

Like Nikon, the zealots of the old belief were also poor historians (although in the dispute concerning ritual they were right). It was not the desire for historical truth, but offended national pride that led them to oppose the reforms. They regarded the break with age-old tradition as a violation of Russian culture. They detected the Westernising tendencies in Nikon's reforms, and protested against them, fearing to lose their national distinctiveness. The very idea of reforming Orthodoxy smacked of Westernising to the God-lovers.

The imperious and harsh Nikon had no trouble in removing the God-lovers from the helm of the Church. But his victory was short-lived. His claims to unlimited power angered the tsar and boyars. By 1658 the differences were so acute that Nikon suddenly vacated the patriarchal throne. He spent eight years in his New Jerusalem Monastery, until the Church Council of 1666-1667 pronounced sentence on him and the leaders of the Old Believers, at the same time as approving his reforms.

The nobility supported the reforms for various reasons. The reforms promoted the ideological and cultural drawing together of Russia and the Ukraine which had recently joined Russia. The nobility did not want the subjection of Russian life to the Church in the form advocated by the God-lovers or by Nikon, who believed that "the Church is higher than the State". On the contrary, the nobility's ideal was restriction of the rights and privileges of the Church and secularisation of life and culture, without which Russia as a European power could not hope for progress, an ideal later embodied in the activity of Peter the Great. In this connection it is indicative that the nobility barely played any part in defending the old beliefs. The few exceptions (the boyar's wife Fedosia Morozova and Prince Khovansky) merely prove the rule.

It was only natural, therefore, that the Old Believers' movement very quickly turned into a movement of the lower classes, the peasants, Streltsy, Cossacks, poorer artisans and tradespeople, lower ranks of the clergy, and a section of the merchants. It produced its own ideologists and writers who combined criticism of reforms and defence of the national past with dislike of the whole policy of the tsar and the nobility and even went as far as calling the tsar Anti-Christ.

So the upper classes of Russian society chose the path of Europeanisation, the path of reorganising the cultural system inherited from the Middle Ages. The purpose and form of this reorganisation was understood differently by the different groups of thinkers of that day; hence the "vacillation" among the upper strata continued. Already at the Church Council of 1666-1667 two hostile parties emerged, the Graecophile ("Old Muscovite") and Westerniser ("Latiniser") parties. The former was led by the Ukrainian Epiphanius Slavinetsky, and the latter by the Byelorussian Simeon of Polotsk, both pupils of the Kievan school. But Epiphanius studied at this school before Metropolitan Peter Mogila gave it a Latin trend, basing it on the Polish Jesuit collegia. Simeon of Polotsk, however, was educated as a devoted Latinist scholar and Polonophile. Both parties agreed that Russia needed enlightenment, but set themselves different tasks.

Epiphanius Slavinetsky and his followers enriched Russian letters with numerous translations, including dictionaries and medical textbooks. But for writers of this type enlightenment was merely the quantitative accumulation of knowledge. They did not entertain the thought of a qualitative reorganisation of culture, believing that it was dangerous to break with national traditions. The "Latinisers" and Simeon of Polotsk, however, made a firm break with this tradition. They sought their cultural ideal in Western Europe, above all in Poland. It was the "Latinisers" who first transplanted to Russian soil the great European style of the Baroque in its Polish version adapted to Muscovite conditions. It was with the "Latinisers" that disputes began in Russia—literary, aesthetic and historico-philosophical debates.

It was the "Latinisers" who created the professional community of writers in Moscow. For all the differences in the individual biographies of the members of this literary fraternity, it produced a special type of writer fashioned on the Ukrainian-Polish model. The professional writer engaged in pedagogical pursuits, who collected an extensive private library, took part in publishing ventures, studied foreign authors and knew at least two foreign languages, Latin and Polish. He regarded writing as his main pursuit in life.

After the death of Epiphanius Slavinetsky and Simeon of Polotsk, during the regency of Sophia (1682-1689), there was an open clash between the "Latinisers" and Graecophils. The latter emerged victorious with the support of Patriarch Joachim. They managed to gain control of Moscow's first establishment of higher education, the Slavonic-Graeco-Latin Academy, founded in 1686.

The Execution of the Rebellious Streltsy in Moscow in 1698. Engraving from the Vienna edition of Johann Korb's **Diary**. C. 1700. Academy of Sciences Library, Leningrad

After Sophia was overthrown they succeeded in sending the leader of the "Latinisers", the poet Sylvester Medvedev, to the scaffold. This victory did not put an end to professional literature, however. Professional writing was now firmly established in Russia.

The percentage of authorial works rose sharply in seventeenth-century literature. The anonymous stream that reigned supreme in the Middle Ages did not dry up. But whereas during that period the anonymity or, at least, the playing down of the personal element was characteristic of all literary production in general, now it was primarily fiction that was anonymous, while poetry, rhetoric and publicistics bore the name of the author. The anonymous stream was nourished, in particular, by links with Western Europe. From there Muscovy received all manner of entertaining "popular books", cheap, mass-produced publications. The stream of fiction in the seventeenth century was spontaneous and uncontrollable. Anonymous works of fiction showed the same artistic and ideological diversity as authorial works. The links with Europe produced the translated tales of chivalry and *novella.* The first original works in these genres also appeared, as, for example, *The Tale of Vasily the Golden-Haired* and *The Tale of Frol Skobeyev.* A reassessment of the traditional genre schemes led to the creation of qualitatively new, complex compositions, such as *The Tale of Savva Grudtsyn* with its Faustian theme. The artistic treatment of history is reflected in the cycle of stories about the founding of Moscow and the tale of the Page Monastery in Tver.

The social basis of literature was constantly expanding. The democratic literature of the lower strata of society was beginning to appear. These strata, the poor clergy, the street scribes and the literate peasants, spoke out in the independent and free language of parody and satire.

1. Translated Tales of Chivalry and Adventure

Among the translations of the seventeenth century the tales of chivalry occupied an important place and interest in them grew constantly. Whereas in the first half of the century the reader knew only *The Tale of Bova, the King's Son* and *Eruslan Lazarevich,* by the end of the century there were no less than ten works of this genre in circulation. The tale of chivalry satisfied the readers' demand for "unofficial" private reading. It did not exhort, but entertained. It is no accident that the epithets "amazing" and "worthy of amazement" are found regularly in the titles of the Russian versions. As a rule, tales of chivalry were translated from

Polish. Exceptions to this rule are rare: for example, the plot of
Eruslan Lazarevich is Turkic in origin, and *Bruncvik* is borrowed
from Czech literature.

Many of the motifs found in translated tales of chivalry were
well known to the Russian reader. The fight with the dragon, the
husband at his wife's wedding, recognition by a ring, prophetic
dreams and supernatural helpers of the hero, the man sewn into
the skin of an animal and the bird who carries him away, the love
potion and the self-cutting sword—all these things were familiar
partly from written works, but mainly from the oral epos, in
particular, the fairy tale. However, the artistic meaning of
translated tales of chivalry cannot be understood by dividing them
up under these headings. Motifs are only the bricks of the
building. Its architecture is determined by the plot, and the plot is
not simply the sum total of the motifs. The plot depends upon the
conception of reality. What conception of life did the tale of
chivalry bring to Russia in the seventeenth century? What was new
about it and how did it attract the reader?

The classical writers of the mediaeval tales of chivalry,
Chrétien de Troyes, Hartmann von Aue and Wolfram von
Eschenbach who wrote in the second half of the twelfth and the
early thirteenth century, and later authors also basically created
two types of narrative, two branches of this genre. One tells of a
knight's love for a lady, and the other of the search for the Holy
Grail, the platter used by Christ at the Last Supper in which
Joseph of Arimathea later collected drops of the crucified Christ's
blood (according to early legends Joseph of Arimathea brought
Christianity to Britain, and it was in Britain that the cycle of tales
of chivalry arose connected with the court of King Arthur). The
first type depicted earthly love, the second ideal, mystical love, the
aim of which is to find the source of wondrous grace. Common to
both types was a code of chivalry, a set of rules that governed the
behaviour of a noble knight, and also the description of numerous
adventures and battles.

Russia of the seventeenth century became acquainted with
romances that were far removed from their classical mediaeval
prototypes. The so-called chap-books, cheap pamphlets published
in large editions all over Europe and sold to the common people
at fairs or by pedlars, were translated into Russian. The heroes of
chap-books are pale shadows of the knights of the classical type.
They pursue entirely earthly aims. They are less active. Often it is
not they who command fate, but fate that commands them. They
are victims of fatal twists of fate. Whereas in the classical courtly
romance there is a balance between the noble hero who strictly
observes the code of chivalry and the adventurous plot, in the

chap-book the centre of gravity moves to the action, the adventures. It is the action, not the hero, the plot and not character, that attracted the seventeenth-century Russian readers. In the chap-book they found great exploits, exotic journeys and amorous intrigues. The apotheosis of the great exploit is *The Tale of Bova, the King's Son.*[1]

The Tale of Bova, the King's Son. Legends about the deeds of the knight Bovo d'Anton, which grew up in mediaeval France, spread throughout Europe. This tale reached Russia in the following fashion: in the middle of the sixteenth century in Dubrovnik, a Slav republic on the shores of the Adriatic, the publications of neighbouring Venice circulated widely, including books with the Italian version of the romance of Bovo d'Anton. The Serbo-Croat translation made here was retold in Byelorussian, also in the sixteenth century. All the Russian manuscripts can be traced back to the Byelorussian version.

The Tale of Bova is first mentioned in a Russian source of the second quarter of the seventeenth century. The manuscripts of the work belong to an even later period. However, the evidence suggests that it became popular long before the Time of Troubles. It may have been transmitted to Russia orally, first as an epic tale, and written down later. An indication that it was popular in the sixteenth century can be found in the so-called secular names (by which people were called in addition to their Christian names). In the middle of the century in Ryazan there lived a certain Bova Vorobin (the Vorobins were a branch of the old Moscow boyar family of Shevlyagins, related to the Romanovs and Sheremetevs).[2] In the 1590 an official by the name of Bova Gavrilov arrived with documents from the Terek to Moscow. Ten years later a nobleman Bova Ivanov, related to the Skriptsyns, made a donation to the Trinity Monastery of St Sergius. In 1604 a certain Lukoper Ozerov (Lukoper is one of the characters in the tale, a knight and Bova's rival) delivered an official communication from Moscow to Nizhny Novgorod. How early and how firmly the tale became established in Russian culture can be seen from the manuscript English-Russian dictionary of the physician Mark Ridley who served at the Moscow court at the end of the sixteenth century. For "a knight" he gives as the Russian equivalent "licharda", and Licharda is the name of one of the characters in the *Tale.*

Bova lived a long life on Russian soil. No less than seventy copies of the work have survived. For two hundred years, from the time of Peter the Great right up to the beginning of the twentieth century, it circulated in numerous chap-books. There was an intensive reworking and russification of the text.

The Byelorussian version was a courtly romance with a

complex plot. The hero's jousting in tournaments and ceremony of knighting are described. Bova's love is portrayed as the love of a knight for his lady. But on Russian soil the features of the courtly romance were gradually erased, and the tale grew closer to the Russian epic. Most indicative in this respect is the third redaction of the tale (as classified by Vera Kuzmina).[3]

The main features of the plot are retained. At the beginning of the tale we are told about Bova's wicked mother, Queen Militrice, who kills her husband an marries King Dodon. Militrice also tries to kill her son, but he manages to escape and enter the service of King Zenzevey. Then we are introduced to the love theme that runs throughout the tale: Bova falls in love with Zenzevey's daughter Druzhnevna. She is wooed by various suitors, and all Bova's numerous subsequent adventures are struggles against his rivals. The reader learns of Bova's duels with other knights and battles in which he overcomes large hosts single-handed, about the treachery of his rivals, Bova's capture and imprisonment, etc. Eventually Bova is united with Druzhnevna who bears him two sons, but then fate parts them again. The adventures continue up to the happy ending when Druzhnevna and Bova are reunited and he avenges his father by killing Dodon and his wicked mother.

"In a certain kingdom, in a mighty realm..." begins this redaction of the tale. This is a traditional fairy-tale opening, and the rest of the narrative is in the same key, that of the Russian epic tale. Here Lukoper resembles Idolishche in the heroic epos: "His head is like a beer cauldron, his eyes are a good span apart, a bow's length separates his ears, and he measures seven feet from shoulder to shoulder." The heroes live in towns with gold-roofed chambers, hunt with falcons, make obeisances to one another and, in general, observe Russian customs. At a feast Druzhnevna "carves a swan", and her father, King Zenzevey, greets one of her suitors as follows: "He took him by his lily-white hands and kissed his sugar-sweet lips and called him his beloved son-in-law." The main hero has turned from a European knight into a *bogatyr*, a defender of the true faith, who does not forget to stress that he is a Christian. This is how Bova, concealing his name and rank, presents himself to seafarers whom he happens to meet: "I am not of Tartar stock, but of Christian stock, the son of a sexton, and my mother was a poor woman who washed clothes for fine ladies in order to feed herself."

The tale had come so close to the folk tale, that it became folklore. As we know, the romance "is a product of the folk tale. Here the development follows the stages: folk tale—romance—folk tale."[4] *Bova* traversed the whole of this path, and by the end of the seventeenth century it had gone the full circle. The tale with illustrations was one of the books given to Peter the Great's son, Tsarevich Alexis. His tutors evidently regarded it as a children's story. On 3 December 1693 the Secretary Kirill Tikhonov took out of the tsarevich's rooms "an entertaining book with illustrations in folio about Bova the king's son, many pages of which were torn out and spoiled, and ordered the book to be repaired".[5]

The characters in the tale are forever in motion, but this motion is chaotic, weakly motivated and basically aimless. The characters are as static internally as they are active externally. Their reactions to their surroundings can be reduced to a primitive selection of the simplest emotions. They remain in the power of literary convention, mediaeval or folk-tale, and it is significant that the seven-year-old Bova, "a little childe" behaves like an adult, falling in love and fighting battles, something which did not disconcert the Russian translators and redactors in the slightest. There is no character in *Bova*, for character is sacrificed to adventurous action. This is the rule in the courtly romance where character was replaced by general declarations; it was considered perfectly sufficient to speak of the hero's irreproachable bravery and loyalty to duty. Very few characters are an exception to this rule.

The Tale of Bruncvik. This is the Czech Prince Bruncvik, to whom Russian readers appear to have been introduced in the second half of the seventeenth century.[6] *The Tale of Bruncvik* is a translation of a Czech work of the same name. It tells of the adventures of a fictitious prince in exotic "unknown lands". The Czech details are limited to two or three references to Prague and the statement that Bruncvik sets off on his wanderings to win a new coat-of-arms. At the end of the tale the eagle on the Czech standard is replaced by a lion (this change is historically accurate).

The Russian reader was able to connect this change in the coat-of-arms with various translated cosmographs which said that the Czech sign of the zodiac was Leo and that was why the Czechs "are alike in their way to the lion—and in their courage, their heart ... their pride and their majesty ... do portray their lion's nature".[7] The *Tale* was not regarded as a source of information about the Czechs, however. The average seventeenth-century Russian reader took little interest in this land. Enslaved by the Hapsburgs, the Czechs existed in the Russian mind not as an independent political and cultural unity, but as one of the lands of the Holy Roman Empire. Russian scribes, who were not looking for any historical information in the tales, would replace the very name of the Czech land by "a certain land", "a great land", "the

Greek land" or even "the French land". The adventures that happened to the hero could have happened to a person of any nationality.

After leaving Prague, Bruncvik goes down to the sea, finds a ship and sails off where his fancy takes him. The ship is drawn to a magnetic mountain, at the foot of which he is forced to disembark with all his men. An old knight tells the prince that there is only one way to escape from this god-forsaken spot: once a year the "nog" bird comes to the island (this is the gryphon, the mythical creature with a lion's body and eagle's wings, known to the Slavs from *The Chronographical Alexandreid*). You must wrap yourself into a horse skin and the bird will carry you up into its nest. This is what Bruncvik does. After being carried away to the gryphon's nest and killing its greedy young, he continues on his journey. In some deserted mountains, he suddenly sees a lion fighting a losing battle with a ten-headed dragon. Bruncvik helps the lion who then becomes his rescuer's loyal servant. They visit many strange lands of people with dog's heads and other monsters, and overcome many great perils, before they return to Prague. Bruncvik lives another forty years and dies a peaceful death. The lion dies on his master's grave.

The Tale of Bruncvik is a work based on descriptions of a person's wanderings in strange lands. Like Bruncvik, Bova also journeys, but in kingdoms inhabited by people, not monsters. Like Bruncvik, Bova also fights, but mainly with flesh-and-blood knights. The magical element plays a very small part in *Bova*, whereas Bruncvik is constantly confronted by a mysterious, fantastic world. The link between the hero's adventures, between the descriptions of people with dog's heads, sea monsters, exotic islands and mysterious mountains that rise up suddenly out of the sea, is a conventional link of a "geographical" nature. The waves bear Bruncvik's ship to an unknown shore, and the readers learn about the evil, death-dealing magnetic mountain, then the gryphon carries the hero into wild, uninhabited mountains and the fight with the dragon follows; the raft bearing Bruncvik and the lion is carried out to sea and the astonished prince sees before him the shining mountain of Carbunculus.

It has long since been remarked that Bruncvik is the least heroic of all the characters in translated romances of the seventeenth century.[8] He is timid and even tearful. A "great terror" seizes him in almost every episode. Bruncvik frequently refuses to do battle. The pleas for help with which he pesters the Lord are not a devout prayer for strength before battle that befits a Christian knight, but rather the ramblings of a lost and terror-stricken soul. Occasionally these scenes strike a comic note.

After the victory over the dragon Bruncvik does not trust the lion for a long while. In an attempt to get rid of it, he climbs up a tree with a store of acorns and apples. The lion sits under the tree for three days and three nights, waiting in vain for its rescuer to come down. Eventually the lion loses its patience and roars so loudly that the luckless Bruncvik falls down from the tree in fright, injuring himself badly.

Thus, Bruncvik was no knight *sans peur et sans reproche*. Yet nor was he a negative figure. The magnetic mountain, the gryphon and the fire-breathing dragon were far more "imaginable" and less exotic for Russian and European readers in the Middle Ages than for us. There is no doubt that most people believed they were real. Therefore seventeenth-century man regarded the story somewhat differently from the way in which we regard it. We are inclined to assign Bruncvik more of a compositional (his presence links the individual episodes) than an heroic role. We forget about the great conflict that forms the basis of the tale, the conflict between man and the forces of nature.

The main hero is man in general, an abstract representative of the human race void of all national and social features. His exalted position on the social ladder neither helps nor hinders him. The fact that Bruncvik is a sovereign ruler may be considered as merely a feature of mediaeval literary convention which limited the choice of personages to a certain estate. Knowing that Bruncvik was a prince and seeing that he was frightened and lost, the seventeenth-century reader would believe that all men were equally helpless before nature, that princes and kings were no different in this respect from ordinary people. Herein lies the special democratic flavour of this Robinsoniana of the transition period.

The Tale of Peter of the Golden Keys. This tale belongs to the genre of the courtly romance[9] (the hero conceals his identity for a long time, believing that he can only reveal it when he has performed some noble deeds; "and they called him the Knight of the Golden Keys, because he had two gold keys attached to his helmet"). This work is thought to have originated in the fifteenth century at the magnificent Burgundian court. Its theme is a knight's love for his lady and their fidelity throughout a long parting. This theme remains the main one in the Russian version, which is separated from the original by several intermediary links: the Russian translation was made in 1662 from a Polish edition.

The Russian version preserved the chivalrous spirit of the original in many respects. It introduced the reader for the first time to Sir Launcelot, the most famous of King Arthur's Knights of the Round Table: Peter gets the better of Launcelot at a tournament, "He did knock Launcelot and his steed to the ground, and put his arm out of joint." Peter of the Golden Keys is a most courtly hero. He observes the rules of chivalry. At tournaments he is noble and courteous to his adversary. He chooses his lady (his future bride Magilena), swears to serve her until death—and keeps his word. He never sits in the presence of a woman. He is devout and attends Mass, where Magilena sends her confidante to him. All these are courtly features. But there is also a gallant sensitivity in Peter's character. This is found in many European romances of the seventeenth century. In Russia it is characteristic of the cavaliers of Peter's day; this gallant sensitivity ensured the popularity of the *Tale* in the Petrine period.

So after many ordeals, captivity and serving the sultan, Peter of the Golden Keys is on his way home. He sails over the sea and is "sick from the sea crossing". "And, stepping onto the shore, he did stroll along the bank and found a fine meadow, and in that meadow were many sweet-smelling flowers. And Prince Peter lay down in that meadow among the flowers. And the fresh breeze revived him after the sea journey, and he began to look at the flowers, and saw among them one small flower fairer and more fragrant than all the others, and he did pluck it. And looking at the small flower he recalled the beauty of Queen Magilena, the fairest of the fair. And ... he began to weep bitterly..."

Magilena is a match for Peter of the Golden Keys in this respect too: she frequently swoons and weeps, curses her bitter fate, sighs and laments. These are not so much real feelings, as gallant sensitivity. But they conceal a true and noble love.

The mainspring of the action is the clash of courtly love and carnal passion. Describing the secret meetings of the hero and heroine and conveying their impassioned outpourings, the author stresses constantly that Peter and Magilena retain their chastity. They decide to elope and "trusty steeds" are ready, when Peter makes a solemn vow to his beloved: "I vow before the Lord God ... to protect thy maidenly honour until the wedding night." It is the breaking of this vow that leads to their parting. One day when resting Peter "forgot himself and began to conceive a different, evil plan". But the heavenly protector was not asleep, and intervened immediately. A ravan suddenly appeared and carried away three precious rings, Peter's gift to Magilena. Peter set off in pursuit and was parted from his beloved for many years to come.

Peter sinned, but Magilena atoned for his sin. She made a pilgrimage to Rome, "visited the relics of the Holy Apostles Peter and Paul, and prayed for three months that the Lord God would unite her safely with her dear friend". Then she founded the convent of St Peter and St Magilena with an almshouse. And it was here that the hero and heroine were reunited and held a splendid wedding feast. In all these episodes of the tale the Catholic influence is most evident: everyone knew that in Rome there was the Pope, the sworn enemy of Orthodoxy, and that there was no St Magilena among Orthodox saints. But this did not worry the Russian translators and readers unduly. They were not looking for "edification" in fiction and were not afraid of obvious digressions from it. The emancipation of literature from the Church had come a long way, and the translated courtly romance did much to assist this process.

In spite of the tremendous popularity of Western romances of love and adventure in Russia, we find only a small number of these works in original Russian literature of the seventeenth century. Evidently the paucity of original works in this genre was still not felt to be a deficiency. Readers' needs were met by the oral tradition—the folk tale and heroic epos. These began to be written down and reworked for the first time in the seventeenth century. One such reworking is *The Tale of Sukhan* in verse, which has survived in a single manuscript of the last quarter of the seventeenth century.[10]

The Tale of Sukhan. According to the records of folklore specialists of the nineteenth and twentieth centuries, the heroic poem about Sukhan is known in two versions. One focuses on the social aspect, portraying the unjust prince's quarrel with Sukhan. The other concentrates entirely on the heroic theme, on Sukhan's heroic feat. It is this latter version that forms the basis for *The Tale of Sukhan*. The *Tale* tells how the Kiev *bogatyr* rides out unarmed to hunt with his gerfalcon and meets a mighty Tartar host advancing on Russia, how he uproots a tree in a forest and brandishes it to defeat the Tartars; how the Tartar ruler "ordered them to load three *poroks*" (battering rams or catapults), and how the Tartars launched a third attack on Sukhan:

> And they fired from the third and killed the bogatyr
> Hitting his brave heart,
> Cutting its very roots.
> But he forgot his mortal wound,
> Fell upon them shouting,
> And slayed the Tartars one and all.

Sukhan returned to Kiev and died, mourned by his prince and his mother.

In addition to the heroic poem, the author of the *Tale* made use of literary works on the struggle against the Tartars, in particular, *The Tale of the Battle Against Mamai*. He also drew on the military practice of his day. For seventeenth-century Russia the theme of the struggle against the Tartars was not merely an historical one: the Nogai and Crimean hordes were a constant threat to the southern borders. This is why the author gives Sukhan the features of a seventeenth-century member of the service gentry. For Sukhan the defence of the Russian borders was an "affair of state" of "serving the sovereign".

The Tale of Vasily the Golden-Haired, Prince of the Czech Land.[11] This tale belongs to the adventure genre, but the question of its origin is not yet clear. It may derive from a non-extant Czech source,[12] which was adapted by a Russian scribe with a good knowledge of Greek. The constant epithet "golden-haired" is a Graecism. The Greeks used the corresponding Greek equivalent both in relation to strong barbaric peoples and to themselves. In the latter case "golden-haired" meant handsome, noble and clever. In the seventeenth century this epithet-cum-symbol was well known to the educated Russian. Some copies of the tale retain the original versions of the hero's name: *Valaomikh, Valamikh* and *Valamem*. These versions derive from Greek words meaning "rejected" or "anyone who so desires". Both meanings, as we shall see, are fully in keeping with the function of this character. The heroine Polimestra also has a Greek name which means "much-wooed".

In the tale use is made of the theme of folk tales about the fastidious maid. The proud French princess refuses the match-makers who press the suit of Vasily the Golden-Haired, because she does not want to marry a vassal. So the hero sets off for France incognito. There, with the help of his psaltery playing, he succeeds in seducing the inquisitive Polimestra and the princess is forced to beg this "commoner" to marry her. After refusing twice Vasily agrees. Although the tale reworked considerably its folk tale stereotype (omitting, for example, the father's driving out of his dishonoured daughter compulsory for the folk tale), in general it is extremely close to Russian folklore. The similarity between its plot and that of the *bylina* about Solovei Budimirovich and Zabava Putyatishna was pointed out long ago.[13] Solovei also sails off to win his bride, seduces her by playing the psaltery and dishonours her. Yet, there is more to the artistic aspect of the tale than the adventure and folklore elements. The real life details are very strong and bring the tale close to the *novella*. In folklore and early literature a crystal floor was traditionally used for the hero to recognise secret signs from the heroine. But the author of *Vasily the Golden-Haired* used this motif to make fun of Polimestra and transfers it to the level of daily life: when Vasily gives the fastidious princess a good hiding, she "got badly bruised ... because it (the floor) was so smooth and slippery".

The everyday element is reflected in the style also. In rejecting the matchmakers who come from Vasily the Golden-Haired, Polimestra uses the language of a lively tradeswoman: "It's not ground, so it can't be a loaf, it's not tanned, so it can't be a strap, it's the wrong boot on the wrong foot." In punishing the dishonoured princess, Vasily reminds her of this allegorical reply, continuing it as follows: "...Will a commoner's son take the king's daughter for his wife? It will never come to pass, that a commoner's son takes the king's daughter for his wife."

Vasily the Golden-Haired himself resembles the hero of a *novella*. Although the theme of getting a bride resounds at the beginning and end of the tale, most of the time the hero has a different aim: he wants to punish Polimestra for insulting him, his purpose is "revenge for ridicule". Vasily is very far removed indeed from the ideal courtly knight. His enterprise and lack of fastidiousness about the means remind one of the characters in a picaresque *novella*. He resembles his "literary kinsman" Frol Skobeyev. Whereas *Ivan the Sexton's Son* was a timid, weak exercise in a new genre borrowed from Western Europe, *Vasily the Golden-Haired* heralded creative attempt at the adventure story. This work shows that Russian writers were learning remarkably luckily from Europe. The courtly romance brought the theme of love to Russia, no traditional Christian love, but secular, wordly love. It cultivated a taste for adventure and for the "gallant sensitivity" that became so prevalent in Russian culture of the Petrine period.

2. *The Tale of Savva Grudtsyn*

In the seventeenth century the genre system of Russian prose underwent a radical change. As a result of this change it lost its official functions and its ties with ritual and mediaeval literary convention. The "fictionalisation" of prose took place, turning it into free fictional narrative. The *vita* gradually lost its former significance as a "religious epos" and acquired features of secular biography. The translated courtly romance and translated *novella* greatly increased the proportion of entertaining subjects. Prose began to acquire new complex compositions in which use was made of several traditional genre schemes.

An example of this is *The Tale of Savva Grudtsyn*,[14] written in the 1660s in the form of an episode from the recent past. The tale begins in 1606 and covers the Russian siege of Smolensk in 1632-1634. The anonymous author of the tale writes not about Russian history, however, but about the private life of a Russian merchant's son, Savva Grudtsyn. Using Russian material the tale develops the theme of a man selling his soul to the devil for earthly joys and delights.

Savva Grudtsyn, a young man from a rich merchant family, is sent on business by his father from Kazan to a town in the region of Sol Kamskaya, where he is seduced by a married woman. He almost finds the strength to resist her advances on Ascension Day, but his lascivious mistress takes cruel revenge upon him: first she beguiles him with a love potion, then she rejects him. The tormented Savva is ready to do anything to get her back, even to sell his soul. "I would serve the Devil," he thinks. And straightway there appears beside him his "sham brother", the Devil, who proceeds to accompany him everywhere and with whom Savva makes a contract to sell his soul (in an attempt to excuse the hero's conduct the author writes that Savva did not realise the "sham brother" was the Devil). Savva's mistress returns to him. Together with the Devil he goes carousing, joins the army and is dispatched from Moscow to Smolensk. Here (with the Devil's assistance, of course) he performs miraculously brave feats, slaying three giants one after the other and returning to the capital as a hero. But the time of reckoning comes. Savva falls mortally ill and is seized with terror, for his soul is doomed to eternal torment. He repents, vows to become a monk and begs the Virgin Mary for forgiveness. In the church where the sick Savva has been taken the "God-rejecting missive" falls from above. It is blank for the writing has been "erased". So the contract is no longer valid, and the Devil loses his power over Savva's soul. The hero recovers and enters the Chudov Monastery in the Kremlin. This is the plot in brief.

The Tale of Savva Grudtsyn makes use of the structure of the "miracle", the religious legend. This genre was one of the most widespread in mediaeval literature. It is widely represented in seventeenth-century prose also. The religious legend has a didactic aim: to prove some Christian axiom, for example, the effectiveness of prayer and repentance or the inevitability of Divine punishment for sin. As a rule the legend has three stages. It begins with the sinning, misfortune or falling ill of the hero. Then follows repentance, prayer, turning to God, the Virgin or a saint for assistance. The third stage is absolution, healing and salvation. This form of composition was compulsory, but a certain amount of artistic freedom was permitted in its concrete application. The writer could use his discretion in the choice of the hero or heroine and the time and place of action and introduce as many minor characters as he liked.

The sources of the subject matter of *The Tale of Savva Grudtsyn* were religious legends about a young man who sinned, sold his soul to the Devil, then repented and was forgiven.[15] In one of these legends, *The Lay and Legend of a Certain Merchant*,[16] the action took place in Novgorod, the hero was a merchant's son, and the Devil took the guise of the hero's servant. This *Lay and Legend* appears to have served as the direct literary source for *The Tale of Savva Grudtsyn.* It is most important that the characters of both the

Lay and the *Tale* belong to the merchantry. The merchants were the most mobile of the Old Russian estates. They frequently went on long journeys around Russia and abroad. They knew foreign languages, were in constant contact with foreigners at home and abroad, bought, read and imported foreign books. The merchantry was less backward and parochial than the other estates in Old Russian society, more tolerant of foreign culture and open to outside influences. How wide the range of interests of the finest members of this estate was can be seen from Afanasy Nikitin's *Voyage Beyond Three Sees* with its remarkable tolerance and respect for other beliefs and traditions. This "mobility" of estate is also reflected in literature—in works where the heroes were merchants. Here the reader found descriptions of perilous voyages with storms and shipwrecks, stories about testing the fidelity of the wife during her husband's absence and other adventure and romance motifs. The "pressure of literary convention" in works about merchants is far weaker than in works about "official" heroes, religious zealots, princes, tsars and military leaders. By choosing a merchant's son as the hero of his tale, the author of *The Tale of Savva Grudtsyn* was able to draw on this tradition.

The tale had one more source—the folk tale.[17] The scenes in which the Devil acts as a magical helper, "granting" Savva "wisdom" in the art of warfare, supplying him with money and so on, are redolent of the folk tale. And Savva's combats with the three giants by Smolensk clearly derive from folklore, particularly the symbolism of the number three. Another link with the folk tale is found in the "tsar" theme. In the scenes leading up to the denouement it is constantly emphasised that the tsar "showers mercy" upon Savva, caring for him and commiserating with him. When the hero is suffering from "devilish languor" and everyone is afraid that he will take his life, the tsar sends guards to watch over him and food to sustain him. The tsar orders the suffering man to be taken to church. And the tsar questions Savva about his life and adventures. From the point of view of the plot the tsar's patronage is quite logical, for it comes after Savva's heroic performance at Smolensk. The patronage is given to the brave hero, the invincible warrior. The ruler's solicitations are no whim or accident, but a reward for valour in the field of battle.

Yet the author speaks of Savva's connection with the tsar much earlier, before the Smolensk campaign, when the reader does not yet know that the dissipated merchant's son will become a hero. "For some reason the tsar himself got to know of him," writes the author about Savva, when he comes to Moscow with his "sham brother". Here the boyar Semyon Streshnev, the tsar's brother-in-law, takes a friendly interest in Savva. For some reason Streshnev's patronage infuriates the Devil. "And the Devil said angrily to Savva: 'Why do you want to scorn the tsar's grace and serve his slave? You have become his equal now, and are known to the tsar himself.'" What does this mean? Why does the Devil say that Savva has become the equal of the tsar's relative? The answer is to be found in the folk tale.

The author seems to avoid giving an explanation, but this does not mean that the seventeenth-century reader did not understand the allusion here. For people in Old Russia the folk tale was a close and constant companion right from childhood. And it is the folk tale that explains this episode. It usually ends with the hero marrying the tsar's daughter and acceding to the throne. It is usually a son-in-law, a relative by marriage, who accedes to the throne, and not a son or other blood relative of the ruler. This is what the Devil has in mind: why bow to the tsar's brother-in-law, if Savva is to become the tsar's son-in-law? What follows seems to be leading up to a triumphal folk-tale ending. The author transfers the action to Smolensk to give Savva the chance to distinguish himself. He becomes a hero, having performed something in the nature of a folk-tale feat, i.e., killing the three giants in single combat. But here the author breaks off the folk-tale development of the action and returns to the theme of the "miracle". He describes the illness (a consequence of sinning), repentance and, finally, healing and forgiveness. In the artistic respect these shifts from one prototype to the other, from the religious legend to the folk tale and then back to the religious legend are extremely important.

This device was not characteristic of the Middle Ages, when convention prevailed in literature and when one familiar situation led to another equally familiar one. Such a device belongs to the art of the modern age, which valued the unexpected, unfamiliar and new. The author of *The Tale of Savva Grudtsyn* disregards mediaeval convention, because he keeps the reader in constant suspense, switching from one subject line to the other.

It would be wrong to see this as a literary game or as inconsistency. *The Tale of Savva Grudtsyn* is not a mosaic of fragments from different compositions crudely thrown together. It is a well thought-out, ideologically and artistically integrated work. Savva is not destined to find a happy folk-tale ending, because God is the judge, and Savva has sold his soul to the Devil. The Devil, who so resembles the magical helper in the folk tale, is actually the hero's antagonist. The Devil is not all-powerful, and he who relies on him suffer for it. Evil begets evil. Evil makes a person unhappy. This is the moral clash in the tale, and in this clash the Devil plays a major role.

The theme of the Devil in *The Tale of Savva Grudtsyn* is the tragic theme of duality. The Devil is the hero's "brother", his "second self". The Orthodox Christian believed that every living person was accompanied by a guardian angel, also a kind of double, but an ideal, heavenly one. The author of the *Tale* treats this theme in a negative way. The Devil is the hero's double. He embodies Savva's sin, the dark side of his nature—his levity, weak will, vanity and lust. The forces of evil are helpless in the struggle with a just man, but a sinner is an easy prey, for he chooses the path of evil. Savva is a victim, of course, but he himself is to blame for his misfortunes.

The Tale of Savva Grudtsyn is full of signs of the "age of revolt", when the pillars of Old Russian life were collapsing. The author seeks to impress upon the reader that his work is not fantasy, but that it is true. This illusion of authenticity is supported, in particular, by the surnames of the characters. The rich family of Grudtsyn-Usovs held a distinguished place in the merchant estate of the seventeenth century. It is quite possible that the tale reflected some real misfortunes that befell this family. It is also quite possible that some dissolute young fellow from that line seduced a merchant's wife (or vice versa). It is even possible that the young stripling tried to beguile the merchant's wife with the help of Satan: we know from eighteenth-century sources [18] that there were many cases of making a "pact with the Devil", and the most frequent cause was an unhappy love affair. The unfortunate person wrote on a sheet of paper that he agreed to sell his soul (signing in blood was not compulsory), wrapped the paper round a stone (to weigh it down) and threw it into a mill pond where a devil was thought to reside (cf. the Russian saying "Devils dwell in still waters"). If this was done in the eighteenth century, it was even more likely to have happened a century earlier. Nevertheless the use of a real family, a real name and a real address is, first and foremost, a literary device. It was not the truth of the event being described, but the truth of his work, its authority, weight and significance that the author was seeking to establish in this way.

The author attached great importance to the idea of the endless variety of life. The young man is captivated by its inconstancy. But the perfect Christian should resist this delusion, because for him life on earth is a dream, decay, the vanity of vanities. The author was so strongly obsessed with this idea that he permitted an inconsistency in the structure of the plot.

Savva Grudtsyn makes a pact with the Devil in order to satisfy his sinful passion for Bazhen II's wife. The Devil carries out his part of the bargain: Savva's mistress returns to him. But then a letter arrives making it clear that Savva's father has learnt of his son's debauchery and wants to bring him home. At this point Savva suddenly forgets about his demonic, all-consuming passion and abandons his mistress forever. He never gives her another thought, and the reader hears nothing more about her. Why then did he sell his soul? Surely Savva did not cool towards her because he was afraid of his father? Surely the all-powerful "sham brother" could have fixed everything, detained his father? Let us see what the Devil has to say about this: "Brother Savva, how long are we to tarry in this small town? Let us go and make merry in other cities." "Well said, brother," Savva replies approvingly. So Savva Grudtsyn sold his soul not only for love, but also to be able to "make merry" in different Russian towns, to see the world, enjoy life and taste its inconstancy and variety. Thus the inconsistency of the plot is redeemed by the logic of the main character.

In his views the author of the tale is a conservative. He is horrified by carnal passion and the mere idea of enjoying life, for it is sin and destruction. But the power of earthly love and the attraction of life in all its variety have already gripped his contemporaries and become part of the flesh and blood of the new generation. The author opposes these new attitudes and judges them from the standpoint of religious morality. But as a true artist he recognises that these attitudes have become firmly rooted in Russian society.

3. *The Tale of Woe-Misfortune*

The Tale of Woe and Misfortune, and How Woe-Misfortune Led a Youth to Monkhood[19] in verse has survived in one copy only. Its fate resembles that of many fine Old Russian works: only one manuscript has survived of *The Lay of Igor's Host*, Vladimir Monomachos' *Instruction* and *The Tale of Sukhan*, and only two of *The Lay of the Ruin of the Russian Land*. Like these works, *The Tale of Woe-Misfortune* stands outside the traditional genre system. It arose at the meeting-point of the folklore and written traditions. It was nourished by folk songs about Woe and verse of repentance.[20] Some of its motifs are taken from apocryphal tales. Like the *bylinas*, *The Tale of Woe-Misfortune* is composed in accentual verse without rhyme.[21] On the basis of all these sources the unknown author has created a splendid work, a fitting crown for seven centuries of Old Russian literary development.

The tale links two themes, human destiny in general and the fate of a Russian of the "age of revolt", a nameless youth. In accordance with mediaeval custom the author of *The Tale of Woe-Misfortune* places every individual event in the perspective of world history, beginning his narrative with an account of the fall from grace of Adam and Eve, who eat of the forbidden fruit from the "tree of the knowledge of good and evil". Yet this account is not the canonical story, but an apocryphal version which differs somewhat from the Bible story:

> *The human heart is wild and foolish*
> *Adam and Eve were tempted,*
> *They forgot the Lord's command,*
> *And ate of the grape*
> *From the wondrous great tree.*

From the Old Testament it is not clear what the "tree of the knowledge of good and evil" in the Garden of Eden was like. It is usually thought to be an apple tree. But in apocryphal tales it is sometimes a grape vine. "Adam's transgression was from the vine," maintains the Bogomil tradition.[22] Linking together the Old and New Testament, they compared this with the well-known story of the wedding feast at Cana in Galilee. At this feast Christ turned the water into wine, removing the eternal curse from it, as it were. However, the apocryphas maintain, the wine "still retained something of its original evil, for he who drinks of it without measure ... falls into much sin".[23]

In *The Tale of Woe-Misfortune* these apocryphal motifs form, as it were, the foundation of the plot. Every seventeenth-century reader knew the story of the fall from grace. He was aware of the parallels between it and the tale, including those that were only inferred. God forbade Adam "to eat of the fruit of the vine", Adam disobeyed and was cast out of the Garden of Eden. The story of the nameless Russian youth seems to echo these remote events. His parents give their son the same instructions as God, the "parent" of the first man, gave Adam. The parents tell the young man:

> *Dear child of ours,*
> *Heed your parents' teaching.*
> *Heed their sayings*
> *Good, and clever, and wise.*
> *And you will never know great need.*
> *And you will never know great poverty.*
> *Go not to feasts and revelries, child.*
> *Sit not above your station,*
> *And drink not two cups at a time, child!*

In the Garden of Eden Adam and Eve were tempted by the serpent, which, according to the Bible, was "more subtile than any beast of the field". The Russian youth was also tempted by a "serpent" that finally destroyed him:

> And that youth did have a friend most dear—
> Who called himself a sworn brother
> And tempted him with fine words,
> Lured him into a tavern yard,
> Led him into a tavern house,
> Brought him a cup of hard liquor
> And a mug of strong beer.

Adam and Eve, having learnt the meaning of shame, are made to leave the Garden of Eden. The youth also becomes a voluntary exile and flees in disgrace "to a distant, unknown, foreign land". Up to this point the author creates two parallel and similar series of events—from the Old Testament, on the one hand, and from Russian life of his day, on the other. The idea of the parallel, as we shall see, is also reflected later in the plot of *The Tale of Woe-Misfortune*.

But what the youth endures now is no longer directly linked artistically with the events of the Bible. The youth chooses his fate himself.

In the Middle Ages the individual was dominated by lineage, the corporation and the estate. Although the Orthodox religion taught that a man's life was determined not only by "Divine intent", but also by the "free will" of the person himself, in literature the idea of an individual destiny was not developed. The behaviour of characters in mediaeval literature is determined totally by convention, and their fate depends on either the behests of lineage, or on a corporative (princely, monastic, etc.) code of morality and behaviour. Not until the seventeenth century, the age of the decline of mediaeval culture, did the idea of the individual fate, the idea that a person chooses his life's path himself, become established. The *Tale of Woe-Misfortune* was an important step in this direction.[24] The youth chooses a "bad lot", an evil fate.

This evil, luckless fate is personified in the figure of Woe.

Woe appears to the hero at the moment when he decides to do away with himself after being degraded yet again.

> And at that moment by the swift river
> Woe jumped out from behind a rock:
> Barefoot and without a stitch of clothing,
> With a rope in place of a belt,

And he cried out in a loud voice:
"Stop, youth; you cannot escape from me, Woe!"

Woe-Misfortune is the evil spirit, the youth's tempter and double. This fatal companion is not to be avoided. The hero cannot escape from his power, because he himself has chosen his "bad lot".

The youth flew off as a grey dove,
And Woe pursued him as a grey hawk.
The youth raced across the plain as a grey wolf,
And Woe pursued him with swift hounds.
The youth turned into feather-grass in the plain,
And Woe came with a sharp scythe.
Then Misfortune mocked the youth saying:
"'Tis your fate to be mown down, little grass,
'Tis your fate to lie mown down, little grass,
And to be blown away by the wind's blasts."

Why is Woe-Misfortune so inescapable? For what terrible sins of the hero has Woe been granted such power over him, power that is truly demonic if the only way that he can escape from it is by going into a monastery. At the end of the story the hero retires into a monastery, "and Woe is left by the Holy Gates and will trouble the youth no more!"

When the youth leaves home, he goes to a foreign land, grows rich and finds himself a bride. The "transgression with the wine" does not lead to total destruction. So it is some other sin that decides his fate. In order to find out precisely what, let us return to the historiosophical introduction to *The Tale of Woe-Misfortune*.

The author portrays original sin with Olympian calm. We can understand the author both as a Christian (for the Bible says that Christ redeemed Adam's sinning), and as a thinker: if it were not for sin, there would be no human race. After casting Adam and Eve out of the Garden,

God created a lawful commandment:
He ordered that there should be marriages
For human birth and for beloved children.

The youth is guilty of violating this commandment! As long as he was true to his bride, as long as he was thinking of "human birth" and "beloved children", Woe was helpless. But then it played a cunning trick, appearing to the youth in a dream as the Archangel Gabriel and persuading him to abandon his bride. This was the hero's final undoing. He received an individual fate, because he had rejected his kith and kin. He became an outcast, a renegade, a homeless vagabond. It is no accident that we find reflected in the *Tale* the reckless philosophy of the hero of "satirical literature", for whom the tavern is home, and drinking his only joy. This philosophy of the dissolute is set out in one of Woe-Misfortune's monologues:

> *Or do you know nothing of nakedness*
> *And barefootedness without measure, youth,*
> *Of great levity and recklessness?*
> *All you buy gets sold for drink!*
> *But you, bold fellow, can live as you are.*
> *The naked and barefooted are not beaten or persecuted,*
> *They are not driven out of paradise,*
> *Nor are they sent back from the next world.*
> *No one bothers with the man who is naked and barefoot,*
> *And brigandage doth entice him.*

Yet in the noisy throng of "merry-makers" the young man seems out of place, a chance guest. He is now merry, now sad. He is no stranger to the moral recklessness of the tavern. But the hero of the *Tale* is a penitent sinner who often suffers from his own debasement.

The Tale of Woe-Misfortune is dramatic. One of its finest features is sympathy for the fallen hero. Although the author condemns the youth's sins and preaches fidelity to one's kith and kin, loyalty to the ideals of the *Household Management*, he is nevertheless not satisfied with the role of denouncer. He believes that a man is worthy of sympathy for the simple reason that he is a man, albeit a sinner. Such is the humanistic conception of *The Tale of Woe-Misfortune*. It is a new conception, for up till now literature did not so much commiserate with a sinful person, as denounce him.

4. Translated and Original *Novellas*

The translated *novella* was gradually absorbed by Russian literature throughout the whole of the seventeenth century. The intermediary country through which European *novella* subjects reached Russia was Poland.

The History of the Seven Wise Men. Already in the first half of the seventeenth century Russian readers had access to *The History of the Seven Wise Men* in a translation from the Polish, possibly through an intermediate Byelorussian version.[25] Based on an ancient Indian source,[26] *The History of the Seven Wise Men* was extremely popular under various titles in the East and in Europe. European redactors changed the Eastern legends into a typical Renaissance *novella*. The *History* is a collection of *novellas* united by a "framework" that was developed in Euripedes' *Hippolytus* and Seneca's *Phaedra*, and in the case of the Eastern and Southern Slavs in *Stephanit and Ikhnilat*, for example. *The History of the Seven Wise Men* tells how a king's son who had been brought up by seven wise men and compelled to keep silent for seven days (the position of the heavenly bodies predicts death for him if he utters a single word), repulses the advances of his lustful mother-in-law. The latter takes her revenge by lying to the king about him, who orders his son to be executed. The seven wise men have an interesting dispute with the mother-in-law in the king's presence. They tell the king a story showing how harmful it is to make hasty decisions, and the mother-in-law a story about human cunning and baseness, hinting that the prince is depraved. The execution is postponed again and again. Thus seven days pass and eventually the king's son is able to plead his innocence.

Facetiae. The largest collection of *novellas*, consisting of several dozen individual texts, was translated from Polish in 1680. It is the *Facetiae*,[27] which combines both classical European *novellas*, beginning with Boccacio, and the "minor genres" of comic literature (usually called "simple forms"), namely jokes, witticisms and anecdotes. It is the "simple forms" that provided nourishment for the *novella*. By the seventeenth century the Latin word *facetiae* had entered many European languages with the meaning of "witticisms, humorisms". In Russia, this word was translated as *uteshitelnaya* or *smekhotvornaya izdyovka* (comforting or ridiculing mockery), stressing that *facetiae* were not "edifying", but amusing, entertaining. The *Facetiae* introduced the Russian reader to the "historical" anecdote that derived from the Greek tradition, with such anecdotal personages as Diogenes and such traditional anecdotal couples as Socrates and Xanthippe.

The famous Cynic Diogenes, on being asked what was the best time to dine, replied: "For a rich man whenever he likes. For a poor man whenever he has something to eat." The same Diogenes, who led a truly dog-like, "Cynical" life, once began to eat in the market place amid a crowd of people. Someone laughed at him: "Why do you not eat at home, like a man, instead of in the market place like a cur?" To which Diogenes replied: "When a man eats, the curs always gather round him." One day when Socrates' wife Xanthippe scolded her husband for a long time, as was her wont, and finished by pouring some slops over him, Socrates said: "Thunder is always followed by rain..."

The combination in a single collection of "simple forms" and longer *novellas* was perfectly logical, because their poetics had much in common. All of them are characterised, first and foremost, by a single theme: the plot is limited to a single event (even if this event consists of several episodes). It is only natural, therefore, that the anecdote and the *novella* have few characters. This is a laconic genre. The characters always pursue definite, unambiguous aims. They are shown in action. They are like marionettes. Their life outside the event in question is not shown. It depends entirely on the event. Therefore the character of the heroes is void of psychological complexity or contradictions. It is unambiguous, portrayed with a single brush stroke.

Let us take as an example one of the *novellas* in *The History of the Seven Wise Men* (the seventh story of the mother-in-law) on the theme of love. A certain queen, whose jealous husband keeps her locked up, sees a knight in a dream and falls in love with him. The knight also dreams of the locked-up queen. He enters the king's service and finds a way of getting into the queen's chambers. The lovers meet constantly. One day the knight forgets to remove the ring given to him by the queen. The king becomes suspicious. But the knight manages to communicate with his mistress before her husband sees her, gives her the ring and she is able to lull her husband's suspicions. In the end the king gets so confused that he accidentally marries his vassal and the queen, sends them off in a boat and does not realise until he gets home that he has been tricked. Here the number of personages is reduced to a minimum—the classical triangle. Their characters are unambiguous—determined by a single trait. About the king we know only that he is jealous (this is necessary for the structure of the plot), about the queen only that she is in love and unfaithful to her husband, and about the knight only that he is the lover of a married woman. Their aims are clear: the king wants to keep his wife, and the lovers want to be united. Their behaviour is governed by these aims.

The *novella* neither condemns nor justifies. This genre does not try to be didactic, sententious or edifying. At its base lies entertainment, unexpected twists and turns of the plot, novelty (the Italian word *novella* actually means "something new"). These qualities of the *novella* and its dynamic plot were one of the discoveries of seventeenth-century Russian literature.

In the *Facetiae* we find historical personages: Hannibal, Scipio Africanus, Demosthenes, Alfonso of Spain, Charlemagne, Michelangelo (naturally, their words and actions belong for the most part to the realm of pure fantasy). We also find "certain" people who are not given a name: "a certain rich and fine man", monks, merchants, barbers; rogues, "two maidens", "a certain peasant", "an old woman", "our next-door neighbour". But in fact there is no difference between the characters with historical names and the anonymous personages. Emperors, philosophers, generals and poets behave like people from the third estate. The reason for this is simple: the *novella* is an urban genre and selects only everyday incidents (what the "next-door neighbour" is doing), which do not depend on the code of behaviour and prejudices of the different estates. The *novella* as a genre is democratic. It does not stand in awe of the powers-that-be.

The chance to use material from everyday life artistically was immediately appreciated by Russian writers. The seventeenth century produced many attempts at the original *novella*, from "simple forms" to complex subjects.

The Tale of the Drunkard. The closest to the "simple forms" is *The Tale of the Drunkard*, the oldest copies of which date back to around the middle of the seventeenth century.[28] It is a string of anecdotes all constructed on the same model. A drunkard who praises God "with every cup" knocks at the Heavenly Gates after his death. The Old Testament kings David and Solomon, the Apostles (Peter, Paul and John the Theologian) and a saint (Nicholas the Wonder-Worker) all announce in turn: "Paradise is closed to drunkards." (One of the main theses of the religious teaching condemning drunkenness says: "Drunkards shall not inherit the Kingdom of Heaven.") Revealing an excellent knowledge of church history, the drunkard discovers sinful acts in the earthly life of each of those who refuse to let him in and "puts them to shame". He reminds Peter that he denied Christ thrice, Paul that he took part in the stoning of Stephen the Martyr, Solomon that he worshipped idols, David that he sent Uriah to his death in order to take Uriah's wife Bathsheba into his bed. Even in the life of Nicholas the Wonder-Worker, the most popular saint in Russia, the drunkard finds something with which to vilify him, recalling that Nicholas gave the heretic Arius a slap in the face. "Do you remember..." the drunkard says, "that you once raised your hand to the mad Arius. It is not fitting for prelates to raise their hands. In the Scriptures it is written: thou shalt not kill, but you smote the thrice-accursed Arius with your hand!"

In the dialogue with John the Theologian, who declared that for drunkards "there is prepared torment with fornicators and with idolaters and with robbers", the hero behaves somewhat differently. He knows of no sin committed by his saintly interlocutor, and therefore points to a moral contradiction between John's words and behaviour. "In the New Testament you have written: if we love each other, God will preserve the two of us. Why then, Mr John the Theologian and Evangelist, do you love yourself and refuse to let me into Paradise? Either remove your words from the New Testament, or deny that these words are yours." After this St John opens the Gates of Heaven to the drunkard, saying: "Come join us in Heaven, dear brother."

A *novella* only becomes a *novella* when it ends with some unexpected development in the plot. In the final scene of the oldest copies of *The Tale of the Drunkard* the reader found maxims reminiscent of the denunciations of drunkenness widespread in mediaeval literature: "And you, my brothers, sons of Russia ... do not drink yourselves silly, do not take leave of your sense and you shall inherit the Kingdom of Heaven." This maxim openly contradicted the artistic meaning of the text, and for this reason it was omitted and replaced by the unexpected denouement typical of the *novella*. "And the drunkard went into Heaven and sat down in the best seat. The Holy Fathers began to say: 'Why have you, a drunkard, come into Heaven and taken the best seat? We did not dare approach it.' And the drunkard replied: 'Holy Fathers! You know not how to talk to a drunkard, nor to a sober man!' And all the Holy Fathers said: 'May you be blessed with this seat for now and ever more, drunkard. Amen.'" Thus the drunkard and the Holy Fathers have changed places, as it were. At first the rascal makes them open the Gates of Heaven to him. Then, after being disgraced, they acknowledge his superiority.

The Tale of Shemyaka's Trial. One of the best-known seventeenth-century *novellas* is *The Tale of Shemyaka's Trial*, the title of which has become a popular saying ("Shemyaka's trial" means an unfair trial). Apart from the prose texts of the tale, there are also some verse renderings. In the eighteenth and nineteenth centuries the tale was reproduced in wood-cut prints, transposed into drama, and reflected in oral stories about the rich and poor brothers.

The first part of *The Tale of Shemyaka's Trial* describes a number of tragicomic misfortunes that befall a poor peasant. The hero is given a horse by his rich brother, but no collar, so he has to tie the sledge to its tail, and the horse's tail is pulled off in a gateway. The hero spends the night on the sleeping-bench at the priest's house, but is not called to have supper. Looking down from the bench at the table below covered with food, he topples over and crushes the priest's infant son to death. The wretched peasant comes to town for the trial (he is to be tried for the horse and the baby), and decides to take his life. He jumps off a bridge over a moat. But under the bridge a townsman is taking his old father to the bath-house on a sledge; the hero "crushes the son's father to death", but himself remains uninjured.

These three episodes can be regarded as "simple forms", as unfinished anecdotes or an exposition. In themselves they are amusing but not complete, for they lack a denouement. The denouement awaits the reader in the second part of the tale, where the unfair judge Shemyaka appears, a cunning and mercenary pettifogger. This part is more complex in composition. It is divided into the judge's verdicts and the "framework", which has an independent and complete plot of its own. The "framework" tells how the defendant, the poor peasant, shows Shemyaka a stone wrapped in a cloth, how the judge thinks it is a bribe, a bag of money, and decides the case in favour of the poor brother. When Shemyaka learns of his mistake he is not upset, but gives thanks to the Lord that he has "judged according to Him", otherwise the defendant might have "smitten down" the judge, as he did the infant and the old man, only this time on purpose, not accidentally.

The verdicts for each of the three indictments form the denouement of the three episodes in part one, producing complete anecdotes. The comic effect of these anecdotes is enhanced by the fact that Shemyaka's verdicts are a reflection, as it were, of the poor brother's misadventures. The judge orders the rich brother to wait until the horse grows a new tail. He advises the priest: "Give him your wife for a while until he and she beget you a child. And then take back your wife from him and the child too." A similar type of decision is made concerning the third matter also. "Go onto the bridge," Shemyaka tells the plaintiff, "jump off it yourself, and kill him like he killed your father." It is not surprising that the three plaintiffs prefer to settle the matter out of court: they pay the poor peasant not to make them carry out the judge's verdicts.

Reading this tale Russian people of the seventeenth century naturally compared Shemyaka's trial with the legal practice of their day. According to the legal code of 1649 punishment reflected the crime. For murder people were executed, for arson they were burnt, for minting forgery they had molten lead poured down their throat. So Shemyaka's trial was a parody of Old Russian legal proceedings.

Thus, apart from the "framework" in *The Tale of Shemyaka's Trial* there are three independent *novellas*: the conflict with the brother—the trial and buying off; the conflict with the priest—the trial and buying off; and the conflict with the townsman—the trial and buying off. Formally the anecdotal collisions are outside the "framework", although in the classical type of story about a trial (for example, the trial of Solomon) they are included in the narrative about the pleading. In these classical stories, which were very popular in Old Russia, the events are narrated in the past tense. In *The Tale of Shemyaka's Trial* the anecdotes are split up. This overcomes the static nature of the narrative and creates a dynamic novellistic plot abounding in unexpected twists and turns.

In dividing the seventeenth-century *novellas* into translated and original works, we must bear in mind that this division is a conventional one. *The Tale of the Drunkard* has been traced back to the European anecdote about the peasant and the miller who argue with the saints by the Gates of Heaven. Students of *Shemyaka's Trial* have found parallels in Tibetan, Indian and Persian works. It has often been remarked that in Polish literature a similar subject was treated by the famous sixteenth-century writer Mikolaj Rej who is called the "father of Polish literature". In this connection specialists have drawn attention to the fact that certain manuscripts of the Russian *Tale of Shemyaka's Trial* say that the tale "was copied from Polish books".

However none of these searches have revealed the direct sources of the Russian *novellas*. In all cases we can speak only of a general resemblance and of analogous plots, but not of direct textual dependence. In the history of the *novella* the origin of works is not of decisive importance. The "simple forms", jokes, witticisms and anecdotes, out of which *novellas* developed, cannot be considered the property of any one people. They travelled from country to country or, since everyday happenings are often very similar, arose in different places at one and the same time. The poetic laws of the *novella* are universal, which is why it is difficult, and sometimes unfair, to distinguish between borrowed and original texts. It should be remembered that just as analogous plots do not necessarily indicate borrowing, so national features do not always make a *novella* totally original, as we shall see from *The Tale of Karp Sutulov*.[29]

The Tale of Karp Sutulov. This tale is known from one manuscript only which has unfortunately been lost (the collection in which the tale was included consisted of several quires some of which have not survived). As he sets off on a trading voyage, the Russian merchant Karp Sutulov tells his wife Tatiana that if she needs money she should ask his friend Afanasy Berdov, also a merchant. When Tatiana does so, her husband's unworthy friend makes importunate advances to her. Tatiana seeks advice from the priest, who turns out to be no better than Afanasy Berdov, and then from the bishop. But this prelate, sworn to celibacy, also becomes inflamed with sinful passion. Tatiana pretends to agree and makes an assignation with all three at her house. The first to appear is Afanasy Berdov. When the priest knocks at the gate, Tatiana tells Afanasy that her husband has come home, and hides her first visitor in a trunk. She gets rid of the priest and the bishop in similar fashion—in the case of the latter it is her servant-maid who by prior arrangement arrives in the nick of time. The story ends with the three disgraced visitors being pulled out of the trunks in the governor's court.

This is a typical folk-tale *novella* with delayed action, constant repetition, the triple construction characteristic of folklore, and the unexpected, amusing ending: after the three importunates are disgraced the "strict" governor and the "chaste" Tatiana divide up their money. The Russian detail in the *novella* is merely a superficial veneer. The Sutulovs and Berdovs really were famous Russian families in pre-Petrine Russia. Tatiana's husband goes off "to do trade in the land of Lithuania", along the trade route to Vilna often used in seventeenth-century Russia. The action takes place in the governor's court—also a Russian touch. All these details do not affect the construction of the plot, however. The Russian names and details are the backcloth of the action. They can easily be removed or replaced, and we get a "universal" itinerant plot, not connected directly with Russian urban life of the seventeenth century. In terms of its plot *The Tale of Karp Sutulov* is a typical picaresque *novella* similar in mood to Boccacio.

The Tale of Frol Skobeyev. However the century spent in assimilating the West European *novella* and producing independent works in this genre did yield a totally original and outstanding work, namely, *The Tale of Frol Skobeyev*. There are good grounds for assuming that it was written already in the reign of Peter the Great.[30] The anonymous author constructs his narrative as a story about the past[31] (in some manuscripts the action is placed in 1680). The lively official style of the tale clearly reflects the age of Peter the Great's reforms: frequent use is made of borrowings from West European languages, such barbarisms as *kvartira* (apartment), *reestr* (register) and *persona* (in the sense of "personage"; in the reign of Tsar Alexis, the word *persona* meant a portrait). Although separately all these barbarisms can be found in seventeenth-century Russian documents, in particular, the archives of the Ambassadorial Chancery, taken together they are typical of the texts of the Petrine period.

The comparatively late dating of *The Tale of Frol Skobeyev* does not place this work outside the limits of the Old Russian *novella.* The mediaeval literary tradition did not break off abruptly. It continued even under Peter the Great, giving way to the new type of literature slowly and not without a struggle. *The Tale of Frol Skobeyev* was more the end result of a definite tendency that formed in the seventeenth century, than the beginning of a new stage in the development of literature.

The Tale of Frol Skobeyev is a picaresque *novella* about a cunning rogue, an impoverished nobleman who cannot make a living from his patrimony or estate and is therefore compelled to make money by engaging in malicious litigation and petitioning on behalf of other people's cases. Only a large-scale successful swindle can make him a full-fledged member of the noble estate once more, so he uses his cunning to abduct and marry Annushka, the daughter of the rich and high-ranking chamberlain Nardin-Nashchokin. "I'll end up a general or a corpse," the hero exclaims and eventually achieves his aim.

Compositionally the tale falls into two parts of almost equal length. The dividing line between them is the hero's marriage: after his marriage Frol still has to mollify his father-in-law and get the dowry.

In part one there are few genre scenes and even fewer descriptions. Everything here is subject to the swiftly developing plot. It is the apotheosis of the adventure, presented as a gay, and not always decorous game. Frol Skobeyev's growing intimacy with Annushka is like a kind of mummery, and the hero himself is even portrayed as a mummer in part one: wearing female dress he manages to slip into the Nardin-Nashchokin's country house at Christmastide, and in coachman's attire, sitting in the driving seat of someone else's carriage, he abducts Annushka from her father's house in Moscow.

In part two of the tale the plot develops more slowly. It is slowed down by dialogues and static situations. As a rule love stories end with marriage in literature. The author of *Frol Skobeyev* did not confine himself to this customary ending, but continued the narrative, shifting it to another level. In part two the author shows exceptional skill in the portrayal of characters.[32]

Having enlisted the support of the chamberlain Lovchikov, Frol Skobeyev prepares to ask his father-in-law for forgiveness. Service has just finished in the Assumption Cathedral. The chamberlains are conversing sedately in Ivan Square in the Kremlin, opposite the bell-tower of Ivan the Great. Frol, known to everyone and despised by all, prostrates himself at Nardin-Nashchokin's feet in front of everyone and says: "Gracious master, head chamberlain, forgive the guilty one, like a slave, who has dared to take such a liberty!" The old chamberlain whose sight is failing tries to raise Frol with his stick: "Who are you and what do you want?" But Frol will not get up and keeps repeating: "Grant me forgiveness." Then the good Lovchikov comes forward and says: "It is the nobleman Frol Skobeyev who lies before you and begs your forgiveness."

This splendid scene stands outside the framework · of the *novella* plot. It is not actually necessary for the structure of the *novella*. The characters have already been sketched in part one: Frol is a rogue, Annushka is the submissive mistress, Annushka's duenna, the rogue's mercenary accomplice, and Nardin-Nashchokin, the deceived father. This simple treatment is fully in keeping with the laws of the *novella*. But whereas in dynamic part one the author is interested in the plot, now he is concerned with the psychology of the characters. Part one is a kaleidoscope of events, but in part two it is the characters' emotions, not their actions, on which attention is focused.

This can be seen from the individual quality of the direct speech, the deliberate way it is distinguished from the speech of the narrator. *The Tale of Frol Skobeyev* is the first work in Russian literature in which the author distinguishes the words of the characters from his own in respect of form and language. From the remarks of the characters the reader learns not only about their actions and intentions, but also about their emotional state. Annushka's parents send their son-in-law an icon in a sumptuous casing and bid their servant: "Tell that rogue and thief Frol Skobeyev not to squander it." Nardin-Nashchokin says to his wife: "What are we to do, my dear? That rogue will be the death of Annushka: how will he feed her, he's as hungry as a wolf himself. We must send six horses with provisions for them." Eventually Frol and Annushka are summoned to her parents' home, and Nardin-Nashchokin greets his son-in-law thus: "Why do you stand, rascal? Sit down at once! Will you have my daughter, rogue that you are?" In these lines we detect a grudge against Annushka and Frol, parental love and concern, and an old man's peevishness and anger, which is helpless and just for show, because in his heart the father has already become reconciled to the disgrace and is ready to forgive. The narrator often passes over the characters' emotions in silence: but their dialogues are enough to convey these emotions to the reader.

The contrasting structure of *The Tale of Frol Skobeyev* is a conscious and deliberate device. It does not indicate contradiction or artistic lack of skill. By creating a composition based on contrast the author wanted to show that he was capable of solving different tasks, of constructing a dynamic plot and of portraying human psychology.

5. Historical Fiction. The "Folk" Tale of Azov, the Tales of the Founding of Moscow, and *The Tale of the Page Monastery of Tver*

One of the most important elements in the history of literature is the history of literary invention. This is a matter not so much of the authenticity or lack of authenticity of the information conveyed by the text, as of the evolution of the author's premises and the reader's response. Generally speaking this evolution is as follows.

In mediaeval literature the author aimed at persuading the reader of the truth of what he was describing. And the reader, for his part, believed wholly and unquestioningly in this truth ("it was so"). If the text aroused doubts in him for some reason ("it was not so"), he classed it as false and did not regard it as having any spiritual value. Neither the composing nor the reading of such a work could be regarded as morally justified.

The literature of the modern age preached a different principle. It valued not truth (understood as factual authenticity), but the illusion of truth, verisimilitude. Literature was seen as a phenomenon with an independent spiritual value and could therefore not be judged in terms of being "true" or "false". The author and the reader began to realise that literary authenticity and verisimilitude were not the same thing. In other words, a different system of values was set up in which artistic invention held a most important place.

Mastering the art of invention was a complex and lengthy process. It is seen most clearly in the "historical mythology" of the seventeenth century, in fiction on historical themes. A typical example is the "folk" tale of Azov, written in the 1670s, which enables us to see how historical fiction freed itself from historiography.[33]

The "Folk" Tale of Azov. Its plot combines both episodes in the story of Azov—the capture of the fortress by the Don Cossacks in 1637 and its defence against the Turks in 1641 (see p. 448). Moreover the author had at his disposal both the "historical" and the "poetic" tales about these events. He borrowed only a few phrases from the former, however. It is clear that the documental description of the preparation for the campaign, the undermining of the fortress and the assaults on it did not interest him. He replaced this description by two motifs which had been connected with the themes of war and siege ever since the times of the *Iliad.*

These were, firstly, the motif of the abduction of a high-born lady. We are told that the Azov Pasha gave his daughter in marriage to the Crimean Khan and that the Cossacks hid their light boats in the rushes by the sea-shore and captured the ship that was bearing the young bride. She was spared and "they did her ... no harm", but obtained a large ransom for her and "grew rich from that wedding". This introductory episode is of no consequence for the plot, but it would be wrong to regard it as either self-sufficient or superfluous. It fulfils the function of an exposition: the reader is warned, as it were, that the author wishes to entertain him.

The second is the motif of the "Trojan horse". Cossacks

disguised as Astrakhan merchants, with a forged letter from the *voevoda* of Astrakhan to the Pasha of Azov, enter the fortress with one hundred and thirty carts. Thirty are loaded with merchandise, but each of the others contains four Cossacks who capture the fortress. As we can see, the reader was not disappointed. The further he read, the more entertaining the story became.

What is the origin of these two motifs that replace the documental "historical" tale? Their direct source would appear to be the Don songs in which the capture of Azov is portrayed in a very similar way (the Cossacks hide in carts).[34] It is most important that both motifs are found in one and the same song. A similar text ("On the Island of Buzan") is included in Kirsha Danilov's *Old Russian Verses*.[35] Here the Cossacks led by Ermak capture Turkish ships with merchandise and a "beautiful maiden", the Murza's daughter, in the Caspian Sea. Then they set sail for Astrakhan where they pretend to be merchants.

In the folklore and literature of various peoples both motifs, basically autonomous, are combined so regularly that this suggests a kind of artistic law. Evidently there exists a stereotype of adventure story that is constructed from a limited number of typical situations. This stereotype appears in a similar way in the *Iliad* (the abduction of Helen and the gifts of the Danaans), in *The Tale of Bygone Years* when Prince Oleg the Seer captures Kiev after disguising himself as a merchant, in the "folk" tale of Azov, in legends about Stepan Razin (the capture of the town of Farabad and the famous "princess" whom he throws into the river at the insistence of his men), in Walter Scott, Gogol's *Taras Bulba* and the historical novels of Dumas and Sienkiewicz.

The author of the "folk" tale could, of course, sense the difference between the officialese of the "historical" account of the capture of Azov and the expressive quality of his second source, the "poetic" tale of the siege. This can be seen albeit from the fact that he borrowed the imaginary dialogue between the janissaries and the Cossacks. The author knew that he was dealing with fiction and not fact, but nevertheless he made some use of it. Why? Because in the "poetic" tale the main artistic leitmotif was feeling (hence the heightened attention to style). In the "folk" tale the accent moves to adventure, exciting situations. The plot is the pivot of seventeenth-century historical narrative.

The latter retains only the external devices, the shell of mediaeval historicism. The authors draw their characters from the chronicles and chronographs, but no longer take pains to ensure that their actions correspond in the slightest to what is said about them in these sources. The source no longer constricts the writer's imagination. Only the name remains historical. The bearer of this name becomes what is in effect an imaginary hero. His actions no longer depend either on the facts contained in the source, or on mediaeval "conventional behaviour".

This can be seen most clearly in the cycle of stories about the founding of Moscow.[36] The most popular of these were two works: *The Tale of the Founding of Moscow* written in the second quarter of the century and *The Legend of the Killing of Daniel of Suzdal and of the Founding of Moscow* (composed between 1652 and 1681). A comparative analysis of these works dealing with the same subject shows how literary invention was becoming established.

The Tale of the Founding of Moscow. The first of these tales begins with a reference to the well-known idea that "Moscow is the Third Rome". Without indulging in reflections on Moscow as the last invincible bulwark of Orthodoxy, the author makes use of one motif only that accompanied this traditional idea, the motif of the sacrifice. This motif goes back to the rites of primitive peoples and is based on the belief that no building would stand for long unless a human life was sacrificed at its founding. The author of the tale writes the following about Moscow: "This town is indeed called the Third Rome, for at its founding there was the same sign as at the founding of the First and Second...—bloodshed." Rome and Constantinople were said to have been founded on blood. And the future capital of Russia was also founded on blood. Turning to the theme of sacrifice, the author announces straightway that he is not an historian, but a writer of fiction; for the seventeenth century this motif was not so much an historico-philosophical, as an artistic one.

The action of the tale begins in 6666 "from the Creation of the world" (that is to say in 1157-1158).* Ever since the Gospel times the number 666 had been considered the "number of the beast", the Anti-Christ. By choosing an almost apocalyptic number, the author may have wanted to stress that a fatal predestination was involved in the founding of Moscow, that the age itself demanded blood, as it were. In this year Prince Yuri the Long-Armed, halting on his way from Kiev to Vladimir on the high bank of the River Moskva, killed the local boyar Kuchka who "did not show the Grand Prince due respect". Then the prince is said to have ordered the building here of "a fortress with wooden walls, and to call it Moscow from the name of the river that flows by it". He gave Kuchka's daughter in marriage to his son Andrew Bogolyubsky. Her handsome brothers were also sent to Andrew.

The blood of the boyar Kuchka was not sufficient. One

---

* In fact Moscow already existed in 1147.

murder was not enough. The blood of Andrew Bogolyubsky was also required. This pious prince, as the tale describes him, a builder of churches, devout in prayer and fasting, thought only of heavenly things and soon renounced "carnal conjugation" with Kuchka's daughter. She incited her brothers to kill her husband. "Like watch-dogs" they burst into the prince's chambers one night, dealt him a cruel death, and threw his body into the water. Andrew's brother avenged his death by killing the murderers and his wife. This is the plot of *The Tale of the Founding of Moscow.* However, in keeping with the manuscript tradition some historical notes were added to the work that were only indirectly connected with the theme of Moscow, namely, references to Andrew Bogolyubsky's brother, Vsevolod the Big Nest, Batu's invasion of Russia, Alexander Nevsky, his son Daniel of Moscow and his grandson, Ivan the Money-Bag. The number and content of the additions to the manuscripts vary. This shows that the tale as a genre had not yet split off from the historical works with which it was related. Like any chronicle *The Tale of the Founding of Moscow* was not a self-contained subject. Like a chronicle, the *Tale* could be continued with records of later events.

However, *The Tale of the Founding of Moscow* is only formally linked with the chronicle (in the structure of the final stories and the placing of the events under years). The author is not in the least interested in Andrew Bogolyubsky's political conflict with the boyars, a conflict which the chronicler used to explain the prince's murder. The author of the tale deliberately ignores the historical and political significance of the chronicle account, concentrating on its fictional background, on the chronicler's obscure hints at a connection between the conspirators and Andrew Bogolyubsky's wife. This "fictional impulse" is developed with the help of the *Chronicle* of Constantine Manasses, with which he was familiar from the 1512 *Chronograph.* One of the sections in the Manasses' *Chronicle* gave the author of *The Tale of the Founding of Moscow* the motif of sacrifice, and from another he borrowed the conflict between the lustful Byzantine empress and her pious husband, transferring it to a Russian setting.

The Legend of the Killing of Daniel of Suzdal and of the Founding of Moscow. The second work in the cycle represents a new step in the development of historical fiction, the mastery of artistic invention. In the *Legend* the subject receives a consistently fictional treatment. Here Moscow is not called the "Third Rome", and the motif of sacrifice is firmly rejected. If one can speak of a philosophy of history in the *Legend,* it is a philosophy of historical accident. This is stated in the opening lines: "And why was Moscow to be a realm, and who knew that Moscow would be a state? Here on the River Moskva stood the fair, fine villages of the boyar Stefan Ivanovich Kuchka." The element of chance can also be sensed in the closing scenes which actually speak of the founding of Moscow: "And God did plant a thought in the prince's heart; these fair villages and settlements greatly pleased him, and he thought that it was fitting to build a city here... And ever since that day ... the city of Moscow has been renowned." In this case the phrase "God did plant a thought in the prince's heart" simply means that the hero admired the beauty of this spot on the River Moskva and decided to build a fortress here, and nothing more than that.

By renouncing the idea of Divine predestination, the author of the *Legend* gave full rein to artistic imagination. Pure fantasy dominates in the *Legend.* There are very few authentic historical details. They are the statements that Daniel, the youngest son of Alexander Nevsky and the founder of the Muscovite principality, was the brother of Andrew who reigned as Grand Prince of Vladimir, and had a son called Ivan, the future Ivan the Money-Bag. In fact there was no bloody drama in Daniel's family. The author made it up. The manuscripts of the *Legend* also show a total lack of concern for historical facts. In different redactions of the work the heroes bear different names: instead of Prince Daniel we find Prince Boris and the wicked princess is sometimes called Ulita and sometimes Maria. Whereas *The Tale of the Founding of Moscow* still preserves the characters' historical names, in the *Legend* we find a transition to invented names.

This fact is extremely important. It shows that free narrative had finally triumphed over history in historical prose, that the subject had freed itself from the chronicle or chronograph source. The following point also illustrates the shift of attention to entertainment, fiction: while freely varying the "historical" details from manuscript to manuscript, from redaction to redaction, the *Legend* left all the details of the plot untouched. Thus invention was given priority over history.

When Prince Daniel forced the two handsome sons of the boyar Kuchka into his service ("there were none so fine in the whole Russian land"), they immediately caught the eye of the princess. "And the Devil did kindle lust in her, and she became enamoured of the beauty of their faces, and at the Devil's instigation an amorous liaison arose between them. And they thought to kill Prince Daniel." Out hunting the brothers attack their master, but he abandons his horse and manages to escape from them. "The prince ran to the River Oka, to the ferry. And he had nothing with which to pay the ferryman but a gold ring on his hand. The ferryman rowed close to the shore and put out his oar for the prince to place the ring on it. The prince placed his ring on the oar, but the ferryman took it, then pushed off his boat and would not row the prince over." Prince Daniel ran on. The dark autumn night found him in a forest. "And he knew not where to shelter: it was a wild spot in the depths of the forest. And he found a wooden tomb where a dead man lay. And the prince hid in the grave, overcoming his fear of the body. And the prince slept through the dark autumn night until morning."

Meanwhile the disheartened Kuchka brothers told the princess of their failure, and she gave them the following advice: "We have a certain hound. When Prince Daniel went off to the war he would tell me: 'If the Tartars or Crimean folk kill me or capture me alive ... send your men to search for me with this dog ... the dog will be sure to find me.'" So the Kuchka brothers followed the hound and it led them to the wretched fugitive: "The dog stuck its head into the wooden tomb and saw its master ... and began to fawn upon him." Then Daniel met a cruel death. And the princess rejoiced.

But Prince Andrew avenged his brother. First he executed the widow, then her lovers who were hiding at their father's place. It was then that Andrew had the idea of building Moscow on the site of the ill-fated boyar Kuchka's fair villages.

As we can see, the plot of the *Legend* has been put together from "evergreen" motifs: here we find the sudden attack during the hunt, the flight, the dark autumn night in the forest, the treacherous ferryman, the night spent in a wooden tomb and the faithful hound who unwittingly betrays its master to the murderers. In the modern day these motifs are well known to any writer and reader. But a Russian writer of the seventeenth century could not base himself on tradition. He himself was creating it.

An analysis of the individual elements of the *Legend* enables us to reconstruct the diverse masterly devices used to compose the plot. The author of the *Legend* knew not only the earlier *Tale of the Founding of Moscow* with its single theme, but also its sources. Turning once more to the *Chronicle* of Constantine Manasses, he found a love triangle in one of its chapters, where the Empress Theophania kills her husband in order to marry Tzimisces, the pretender to the Byzantine throne. Whereas *The Tale of the Founding of Moscow* was content with the conflict between the pious husband and his lustful wife, the *Legend* complicated this conflict with the motif of the heroine's unlawful passion for her husband's vassals.

The scene with the ferryman did not require much effort on the part of the author. It was a simple adaptation of an old legend about Metropolitan Alexis, a contemporary of Dmitry Donskoy.

According to the legend, Metropolitan Alexis was travelling to the Horde, when, like Prince Daniel in the *Legend,* he was robbed and tricked by ferrymen (here the Metropolitan's gold cross takes the place of the ring).

The story of one of the main incidents in the plot, the episode of the faithful hound, is more complicated. *The Tale of the Founding of Moscow* compares the Kuchka murderers to dogs; they fall upon their victim "like watch-dogs". This is a typical mediaeval comparison of the functional, dynamic type.[37] In "function" the despicable murderers are like dogs: in the Middle Ages the dog was a symbol of someone disgraced or outcast, the fool-in-Christ, the buffoon or the executioner.

Another source of this episode was Russian life of the seventeenth century. During this period the number of bondmen and tied peasants who sought to flee their masters reached vast proportions. Their masters thought up all manner of ways to get them back, including sending hounds after them, who would follow their scent and unwittingly betray them by fawning upon them joyfully.[38]

Thus, the author of *The Legend of the Killing of Daniel of Suzdal and of the Founding of Moscow* made use of both written sources and real life. He sought to combine motifs of different types. This weaving together of episodes is done by the hand of the artist, however, not the compiler: the individual motifs merge into an organic whole in the structure of the plot.

The Tale of the Page Monastery of Tver. Another specimen of historical fiction is *The Tale of the Page Monastery of Tver,* one of the finest tales of the seventeenth century.[39] It is the legendary story of the founding of the Page Monastery under the first Grand Prince of Tver, Yaroslav (died 1271), son of Yaroslav and grandson of Vsevolod the Big Nest. The attitude to history here is different from that in the Moscow cycle.[40] The author does not approve of free treatment of the facts. If he makes a mistake, it is not because he is aiming at a fictional treatment of the material, but because of ignorance: for the simple reason that he transposes the topography and architecture of his own day to the thirteenth century. Hence the anachronisms in which the tale abounds. Incidentaly, it is thanks to these anachronisms that we can confidently date the work to the middle or second half of the seventeenth century.

The author had very little documentary information at his disposal, however. Perhaps only the fact of Prince Yaroslav's marriage to a woman by the name of Xenia can be regarded as authentic. We know from the chronicle that she was the prince's second wife and that he married her in 1266, in Novgorod, when

he reigned there. Apart from this the rest of the tale cannot be
historically verified. All the circumstances that accompany the
marriage, including the bride's humble origins, are probably
invented, a literary adaptation of an old Tver legend. The world
of folklore is strongly reflected in the plot and the poetics of
the work. It is not surprising that history plays a secondary role
in it.

The Tale of the Page Monastery of Tver is a love story. Its three
main characters form the classic triangle. The daughter of a
village sexton, Xenia, whom the prince's page Gregory wants to
marry, suddenly rejects him on their wedding day and marries the
prince instead. The broken-hearted Gregory runs away and
becomes a hermit, founds the Page Monastery, takes monastic
vows and dies there.

It is interesting that this drama is not presented to the reader
as a typical conflict between good and evil.[41] There are no "evil"
characters in it at all. Its action takes place in an ideal principality,
where the subjects live in peaceful harmony with their sovereign.
The main characters are young and handsome. Even after the
tragic denouement the happy couple and the rejected "page"
Gregory do not cease to love one another. The tale has an aura of
majestic beauty and solemnity that reminds one of the work of the
great Old Russian painter Andrei Rublev: "peace on earth and
goodwill to men." Why in this land of love, peace and harmony is
happiness the lot of some and suffering the fate of others?

The author (for the first time in Old Russian literature) seeks
the answer to this question in the sphere of sentiment. It is no
one's fault that two fine young men are in love with the same
beautiful maiden. Nor is Xenia, who has to choose between them,
to blame. Love is a source of both happiness and suffering. True,
the author realises that there is a dubious element in the tale: for
it is the master, not the servant, who emerges victorious, as one
might expect. Was it perhaps not only love, but some other, less
exalted consideration that led the bride to make that particular
choice?

In order to dispel any possible doubts on the part of the
reader, the author introduces the idea of fate. Like the "wise
maidens" of folklore, Xenia knows in advance that she is "fated"
to marry the prince, and not the page. So she does not act. She
simply waits for the time to come. This inactivity of the heroine
stems not from passivity, but from submission to fate. The prince
suspects nothing before his meeting with Xenia. He is a laything
of fortune. But his fate too is sealed.

After giving his consent to Gregory's marriage to the sexton's
daughter and promising to come to the wedding, the prince has a

prophetic dream: he goes out falcon-hunting and lets loose "his favourite falcon on a flock of birds; the falcon drives away the flock, catches a dove whose beauty is more radiant than gold, and brings it to him". The whole of this dream is based on Russian matchmaking ritual. For example, when the bride is promised in marriage they sing this song:

> Many bright falcons flew up,
> And the falcons sat down at oaken tables,
> At oaken tables with damask table-cloths,
> And the falcons did eat and drink,
> They ate, drank and made merry,
> One falcon only did not eat or drink,
> He ate not and drank not, but sat sadly...[42]

The reader is sure that the dove must be Xenia and the falcon Gregory. Incidentally, Xenia's almost total silence is probably also an echo of a ritual: at the matchmaking ceremony the bride-to-be is supposed to remain silent. But the favourite falcon brings the dove to his master. This is the first hint at the unexpected denouement. The prophetic dream goes on to repeat itself, and then comes true, as it were, in the scenes of the real falcon hunt in which Prince Yaroslav engages on his way to his dear page's wedding. "The same falcon of the grand prince, tired of sporting, flew off to the village. The grand prince galloped after it and quickly came to the village, forgetting about the wedding; the falcon alighted on the church... At that time a crowd of people gathered to watch the bride and bridegroom go to the wedding. Hearing about this from the villagers, the prince ordered his servants to lure down the falcon. The falcon would not fly down to them, but sat preening its feathers. The grand prince went into the courtyard where his page was... Such was the will of God."

At this moment the action reaches its climax. As soon as the prince sets foot on the threshold, Xenia says to Gregory: "Go you from me and make way for your prince, for he is greater than you, he is my bridegroom, and you were my matchmaker." In other words, Gregory is being sent away, as a false bridegroom. So it transpires that the reader was mistaken and interpreted the wedding symbols wrongly. The falcon is not the bridegroom, but the matchmaker (wedding ritual poetry allows both interpretations). The true bridegroom is the prince (in wedding songs the bridegroom is called a prince, and the bride a princess). Seeing the beautiful Xenia, the prince's "heart was inflamed with passion and his mind confused" and he led her to the altar. When the young couple came out of the church, "then his beloved falcon ... sitting on the church, began to tremble, as if for joy and kept looking at the prince... And the prince called to it. The falcon flew down straightway to the grand prince and settled on his right hand, looking at the two of them, the prince and the princess."

It would be wrong to suppose that the idea of predestination detracts from the idea of love, that if feelings are predestined, they are somehow tarnished and depreciated. The author is saying quite the reverse. The prince's love is so great and splendid, that it becomes his fate. The fate of the prince and Xenia is a splendid, blessed one, because their fate is their love. The tale does not have two separate themes, the theme of love and the theme of fate. It has one theme only, namely, love-fate or fate-love.

After losing earthly love, the page Gregory gains heavenly love instead. He is rejected by the "wise maiden" Xenia, but accepted by the Virgin, who appears to him in a dream, orders him to found a monastery and promises to put an end to his sad days on earth: "When you have done all and built that monastery, you will live there for a little while, then leave this abode for the Lord."

After losing Xenia, Gregory "was consumed by great sorrow, and did not eat or drink". The sorrow turned him into a hermit and then a monk who renounces all earthly pleasures. The prince and Xenia are happy, but he is unhappy. Thus the heavenly love acquired by the "page" does not compensate for the loss of earthly love. This conclusion evidently followed in spite of the Christian author's intentions. But that is characteristic of "free narrative": a subject transferred to the sphere of feeling develops according to its own laws and sometimes leads to an unexpected artistic conclusion.

6. Democratic Satire

In the seventeenth century a whole category of works arose that were independent of official literature and became known as "democratic satire" (*The Tale of Ruff Ruffson, The Tale of Savva the Priest, The Kalyazin Petition, The ABC of a Poor and Naked Man, The Tale of Foma and Erema, The Tavern Service, The Tale of the Cock and the Fox, The Tale of the Good Life and Merrymaking* and others).[43] They were written both in prose, often rhythmical prose, and *rayeshnik* verse. They are closely linked with folklore in respect to both artistic features and mode of existence. The works that constitute democratic satire are for the most part anonymous. Their texts are fluid and have many versions. Their subjects are generally known both in written works and in the oral tradition.

The Tale of Ruff Ruffson. Democratic satire is full of the spirit of social protest. Many of its works openly denounce feudal customs and the church. *The Tale of Ruff Ruffson*, which appeared in the early decades of the seventeenth century (in the first redaction the action takes place in 1596), is about a lawsuit brought by Bream and Chub against Ruff. Bream and Chub "who dwell in the Rostov lake" bring a suit against "Ruff Ruffson, thief, brigand and trickster ... a wicked, unkind man". Ruff asked them to let him into the Rostov lake "to live and find something to eat there for a little while". The simple-hearted Bream and Chub believe Ruff and let him into the lake, but once there he multiplies and "takes over the lake by force". The story continues in the form of a parody on the legal proceedings by relating the mean tricks and base actions of Ruff, an "inveterate cheat" and "notorious thief". Eventually the judges decide that Bream and Chub are right and hand Ruff off to them. But here too Ruff manages to escape punishment: "he turned his tail towards Bream, and said: 'If they have given you my head, then you, Bream, and your friend, swallow me from my tail.' Seeing Ruff's cunning, Bream thought to swallow him from the head, but his head was bony and his tail covered with spikes, like sharp bear-spears or arrows, so he could not be swallowed at all. And they let Ruff go free."

Bream and Chub refer to themselves as "peasants", but Ruff, it transpires at the trial, is from "the minor nobility who are nicknamed Vandyshevs" (*vandyshi* is a collective name for very small fish). In the second half of the sixteenth century, i.e., the period when the landed estates gradually became hereditary holdings, the landowners gained far more power over the peasants and often abused it. This sort of situation, in which a nobleman took land from the peasants by trickery and force, is reflected in *The Tale of Ruff Ruffson*. Here, too, is a reflection of the complete impunity with which landowners broke the law, not even fearing a court sentence.

The Tale of Savva the Priest. Church life of the 1640s and 1650s is reflected in *The Tale of Savva the Priest* which makes use of *rayeshnik* verse. At this time there were no schools for training priests in Russia. Peasants and townsfolk selected candidates who were sent for training and ordination to the towns that were diocesan centres, and "apprenticed" to local priests. The latter, of course, bullied them, extorted money and other bribes from them, and often issued them with a certificate of ordination without teaching them a thing, in return for a bribe. In the middle of the seventeenth century Patriarch Joseph decreed that ordinands must be trained in Moscow. Thus the Moscow priests acquired additional ways of getting rich.

The main character in *The Tale of Savva the Priest* is a parish priest in the Church of SS Cosmas and Damian in the Kadashevsky settlement of Zamoskvorechye (opposite the Moscow Kremlin on the other side of the River Moskva).

> *He ... scours the squares,*
> *Looking for ordinands,*
> *And talks much with them,*
> *Enticing them over the river to him.*

It is unlikely that the real prototype of this character bore the name of Savva. This name is a kind of satirical, comic pseudonym, because in the Old Russian burlesque tradition, many names in proverbs and sayings were associated with traditional rhymes that produced a comic effect.

Savva rhymed with *khudaya slava* ("of ill-repute"). Filya with the verbs *pili* and *bili* meaning drank and beat. The name Spirya rhymed with the word *styril* (stole) and Fedos *lyubil prinos,* i.e., liked presents.

The sad life of these helpless, downtrodden ordinands is portrayed in the *Tale* in the blackest of colours:

> *And he keeps his ordinands,*
> *Until they have spent all their money,*
> *And sends some home*
> *After they have sworn in writing*
> *To come back to Moscow,*
> *And bring Savva the Priest wine.*
> *And should anyone bring him mead too,*
> *He will accept it gladly,*
> *For he likes to drink, and having drunk all,*
> *He roars at them:*
> *'Don't hang around here doing nothing,*
> *Go and water the cabbages...'*
> *He sends the ordinands to take the Eucarist,*
> *While he stays in bed.* (In the original Russian this is all in rhymed prose).

It was probably one of these unfortunate ordinands who took up his pen to avenge himself on the hated priest.

The satirical element is very strong in this work; the satire is aimed, first and foremost, at the main character.

Another kind of satire typical of the texts that form the category of democratic satire is that directed "at oneself". In keeping with the specific nature of mediaeval humour[44] not only the object, but also the subject of the narrative is ridiculed. Irony turns into self-irony and extends to both the readers and the author himself. The laughter is also directed at those who are laughing. This creates a kind of aesthetic counter-balance to official culture with its pious, deliberately serious "edification", a literary "world inside out", a burlesque anti-world.

The Kalyazin Petition. The characters inhabiting the burlesque anti-world live by special laws. If they are monks, they "turn inside out" the rigid monastic rules that demand strict observance of fasts and attendance of church services, hard work and vigils. *The Kalyazin Petition* is a satirical complaint by the monks of the Trinity Monastery of Kalyazin (on the left bank of the Volga opposite the town of Kalyazin) supposedly addressed to Archbishop Simeon of Tver and Kashin. They are complaining about their Archimandrite Gabriel who is "vexing" them. The Archimandrite, they complain, "has given orders for ... our brethren to be woken up and for them to go to church frequently. But we, your devout servants, are at this moment sitting with no pants on round a keg of beer". Then follows a folkloric description of the "carefree monastery" in which the monks drink and guzzle instead of performing their monastic duties. Here both the drunken plaintiffs and the hypocritical life of Russian monasteries is satirised.

The Tale of the Good Life and Merrymaking. The Utopian ideal of the "world inside out" had nothing in common with the Kingdom of Christ on earth or in Heaven. It was a dream of an imaginary land of plenty which is free for all. This paradise of gluttons and drunkards is described in *The Tale of the Good Life and Merrymaking* (it has survived in a single, rather late manuscript): "And there is a lake, not a very big one, full of strong vodka. And anyone who likes can drink without fear, two mugs at a time. And nearby is a pond of mead. And anyone who comes can drink his fill, with a ladle or a bowl, on his knees or with his hands. And nearby is a whole marsh of beer. And anyone who comes can drink from it, pour it over his head and wash himself and his horse in it, and no one will reproach him or say a word."

Seen against a West European background this group of works appears as a Russian version of the satirical culture of the Middle Ages, Renaissance and Baroque, which includes such classics as Rabelais' *Gargantua and Pantagruel,* Erasmus of Rotterdam's *In Praise of Folly* and Grimmelshausen's *Simplicissimus. The Tale of the Good Life and Merrymaking* shows the existence of connecting links between the West European and Russian traditions. The *Tale* contains an "absurd" route "to that merrymaking" (that land).

This route winds through Lesser and Greater Poland, Sweden and Livland, and many Ukrainian towns, but does not go into Russia. It begins in Cracow. Evidently it was there that the original *Tale* arose, for the Russian text contains several polonisms, "birth-marks" of the original. This is no accident for Cracow, and Lesser Poland in general, was the focal point of Polish satirical literature in the seventeenth century; it was both written and printed there. Among the Polish and Ukrainian works of this period we find many similar to *The Tale of the Good Life and Merrymaking,* satirical "anti-utopias" that portray a country of "roast pigeons", a land of gluttons and drunkards.

The characters in Russian satirical literature of the seventeenth century are akin to the German Eulenspiegel, the Polish Sowizdzal and the Czech Franta, but also very different from them. The European tradition followed the rule: "it is funny, so it is not frightening". In Russian culture laughter is indissolubly linked with tears, "it is funny, so it is frightening".[45] This is bitter laughter. The Russian characters are pessimists who have lost all hope of happiness. Such is the collective hero, the nameless youth, who expresses his attitude to the world most fully and precisely in *The ABC of a Poor and Naked Man.*

The ABC of a Poor and Naked Man. This work, which appeared not later than the middle of the seventeenth century, has come down to us a number of very different redactions, but all of them are constructed according to the same plan: the remarks of the nameless hero, which taken together form a kind of monologue, are set out in alphabetical order from *az* to *izhitsa* (the names of the first and last letters in the Old Russian alphabet, *Az* also meaning "I" in Old Russian).

The choice of form is no accident. Ever since ancient times the alphabet was considered to be a model of the world: the individual letters reflected individual elements of the universe, and the letters taken together the world as a whole. *The ABC of a Poor and Naked Man* also offered the reader a concise and all-embracing picture of the world, but an "inside-out" picture, a caricature, at once comic and bitter. The outlook of the hero is that of the outcast injured by life. There is no place for him in Old Russian society with its strictly regulated estates and rigidity. "I am hungry and cold, and naked and barefoot... My yawning mouth has not eaten all day and my lips are stiff and blue... I see people living in plenty, but they give us, hungry ones, nothing, the devil knows what they are saving their money for." The hero who utters this "alphabet monologue" has been cast out of the world of the well-fed and has no hope of entering it: "Barefoot and naked— that is my beauty."

The Tale of Foma and Erema. Popular woodcut. 18th century. Museum of Fine Arts, Moscow

The Tale of Foma and Erema. Detail

The Tale of Foma and Erema. The comic *Tale of Foma and Erema,* a fable about two unfortunate brothers, is full of despair.[46] Here use is made of the most widespread device in mediaeval art, that of contrast. When a zealot is contrasted with a sinner, for example, they are portrayed in two colours only, black and white, without any nuances or semi-tones. Foma and Erema are also contrasted with each other, but it is a pseudo-contrast, a caricature contrast. The author makes use of the adversative conjunction "but" to link synonyms instead of antonyms. He gives the following portraits of the two brothers: "Erema had one eye, but Foma had a cataract, Erema was bald, but Foma was mangy." They go to church: "Erema began to yell, but Foma began to howl." The sexton chases them out of the church: "Erema tore out, but Foma ran out." Life is not easy for the brothers. Fortune never smiles upon them. After being chased out of the church, they are driven away from a feast: "Erema hollers, but Foma squeals." Their death is as absurd as their life: "Erema fell into the water, Foma sank down to the bottom."

One of the manuscripts ends with a pseudo-denunciatory exclamation: "Ridicule and disgrace to both the stubborn fools!" This accusation of "foolishness" should not be taken at its face value. It must be remembered that Old Russian humour is universal, that in satirical literature the borderline between the author and the hero, the narrator and his characters, the ridiculer and the ridiculed is blurred and conventional. Therefore the acknowledgement of Foma and Erema as "stubborn fools" is also an acknowledgement of universal "foolishness", including that of the narrator himself. The satirical texts of the seventeenth century abound in this. "Greetings from your son, God-given and long a fool," the author of a *rayeshnik* epistle describes himself.[47] This is mock self-denunciation and self-abasement, a "mask of foolishness", a fool's grimace, because the "poor and naked" outcast of satirical literature chooses the role of the fool.

He turns his rags into a fool's cap and bells. In *The ABC of a Poor and Naked Man* we read: "I had some fine *feryazi* (loose tunics) made of matting with long laces of bast, and those cruel folk took them in payment of a debt and left me quite naked." Matting and bast were traditional features of the fool's attire. Thus, the hero here has adopted the pose of the fool. And it is no accident that this statement comes under the letter *fert* (Ф): *fert* was considered a kind of pictogram for the poseur, the dandy, the conceited, worthless person, who stands hands on hips, showing off.

In the language of the seventeenth century the word "fool" had the meaning of "jester" as well. The court appointments of

Tsar Alexis included fools, and the Tsarina Maria Miloslavskaya had female fools and male and female dwarfs who used to amuse the royal family.[48] The main paradox of the fool's philosophy is that the world is full of fools and the greatest fool is the man who does not realise that he is one. Hence it follows that in a world of fools the only wise man is the jester who plays the fool, pretends to be a fool. Thus the ridiculing of the world is a kind of philosophy (and not only a literary device), which develops from contrasting one's own bitter experience with the "edifying nature" of official culture. The powers-that-be insist that order reigns, but any unprejudiced observer can see that there is constant, insuperable discord between state laws, between Christian precepts and everyday life, and that what reigns is not order, but absurdity. Acknowledging reality to be absurd, satirical literature constructs artistic reality in accordance with the laws of the absurd.

This is clearly evident in the style of satirical literature. Its favourite stylistic device is the oxymoron and oxymoronic combination of phrases (the conjoining of contradictory terms or contradictory sentences).[49] Thus, in satirical texts the deaf are invited to hear, those without hands, "to play the psalter" and the legless "to leap about".

Satirical literature does not invent new genres. It parodies compositions long established in folklore and letters. In order to understand and properly appreciate the parody, the reader and hearer must be well acquainted with the parodied genre. For this reason it is the most common genres that are chosen, the ones that the Old Russian encountered every day, the court case (*The Tale of Ruff Ruffson*), the petition (*The Kalyazin Petition*), the book of home remedies, the epistle, the church service.

The Tavern Service. The model of the church service is used in *The Tavern Service*, the oldest manuscript of which is dated 1666. It is about drunkards, frequenters of the tavern. They have their own religious service, which is held not in church, but in the tavern. They compose hymns and canons not to the saints, but to themselves. They ring "small goblets" and "five-gallon beer kegs", instead of bells. Here we find mock prayers from the service books. One of the most common prayers: "Holy God, strong and immortal, have mercy on us" is replaced by the following exclamation by the tavern drunkards: "Bind us, O vine, bind us stronger, bind the drunk and all those drinking, have mercy on us, beggars." This version imitates the rhythm and sounds of the original with great subtlety. The prayer *Our Father* appears in *The Tavern Service* in this form: "Our Father, which art sitting at home, hallowed by thy name. Come and join us. Thy will be done in the tavern as in Heaven. Give us this day bread in the stove.

And forgive us our debts, creditors, as we forgive the tavern what we have squandered on drink, and lead us not into flogging (the punishment for insolvent debtors), for we have nothing to give, but deliver us from prison."

We should not take the parodies of prayers for blasphemy. The unknown author of the introduction to one of the manuscripts of *The Tavern Service* says so openly: "If anyone should think that these merry lines are blasphemy, and if this should trouble his conscience gravely, let him not force himself to read, but let those who can read and enjoy." Mediaeval Europe had a vast number of such parodies (*parodia sacra*) both in Latin, and in the vernacular languages. Right up to the sixteenth century parodies on the psalms, New Testament readings and church hymns were included in the scenarios of the "festivals of fools" that were held in churches, and the Catholic Church allowed them. The fact is that the mediaeval parody, the Old Russian parody included, was a special type, which did not aim at ridiculing the parodied text. "In this case the laughter is directed not at another work, as in parodies of the modern age, but at the very thing that is being read or listened to. It is the 'laughter at oneself' typical of the Middle Ages, including laughter at the work that is being read at this particular moment. The laughter is immanent to the work itself. The reader laughs not at some other author or some other work, but at that which he is reading." [50] It is not the prayer *Our Father* that is funny, but the parody of it. Not the saints that are ridiculous, but the drunkards who are worshipping the tavern.

Neither religious belief nor the church as a whole is discredited by satirical literature. Unworthy servants of the Church are very often ridiculed, however. Describing how drunkards bring their belongings to the tavern, the author of *The Tavern Service* places the clergy and the monks at the head of the "ranks of drunkards": "The priests and deacons bring skull-caps and other headwear, caftans and prayer books; the monks bring their robes and cassocks, *klobuks* (headgear), jackets and all the things from their cells; and the sextons bring books and ink." The priests and deacons say: "Let us drink and be merry in exchange for our dark-green caftan, nor will we spare the light-green one, and we will pay the rest in money given to us for prayers for the dead... Thus the drunken priests thought to rob a dead man." This cynical "easy bread philosophy" is found in European satirical literature too: the hero of the famous Spanish picaresque novel, Lazarillo de Tormes, admits to the reader that he prayed to God that at least one person should die each day, so that he could eat and drink at the funeral breakfast.

33*

The Tale of the Cock and the Fox. *The Tale of the Cock and the Fox* is pointedly anti-clerical. This work, which is mentioned in sources as early as 1640, has survived in prose and verse redactions, and also in mixed and folk-tale versions. The oldest is the prose redaction. It parodies the subject of the religious legend. The main features of the plot in the religious legend (the sinning, followed by the sinner's repentance, then salvation) are distorted here and become comic. The cock turns out to be a mock sinner (he is accused of polygamy), and his "most wise wife the fox" is a mock righteous person. What awaits the repentant cock is not salvation but destruction. The confessor in the *Tale* is replaced by a cunning mock confessor who is literally "dying for someone to eat".

The parodied plot is supported by a parodied theological dispute: the cock and the fox quote the Scriptures in turn, competing in witty theological casuistry.

The comic situation created by *The Tale of the Cock and the Fox* is characteristic not only of Old Russian, but also of European culture.[51] The early Middle Ages regarded the fox as the embodiment of the Devil. The Russian *Physiologos* and the European bestiaries explained this symbol as follows: the hungry fox pretends to be dead, but as soon as the hens and cock get near enough he tears them to pieces. Thomas Aquinas, interpreting the Old Testament text "Take us the foxes, the little foxes, that spoil the vines: for our vines have tender grapes" (Song of Solomon, 2, 15), wrote that the foxes are Satan and the vines are Christ's Church. From the twelfth century, after the appearance of the French *Roman de Renart,* a different interpretation began to prevail: the fox was considered the living embodiment of cunning, hypocrisy and sanctimoniousness. In the ornament of Gothic churches we find a fox preaching from a pulpit to hens or geese. The fox is often wearing a monk's dress and is sometimes in bishop's robes. These scenes originated in the story of Renardin, the son of the hero of the *Roman de Renart,* who flees from a monastery and lures geese by reading them "edifying" sermons. When the trusting and inquisitive listeners are close enough, Renardin gobbles them up.

The Russian *Tale of the Cock and the Fox* is familiar with both of these symbolical interpretations. The first (the fox as the Devil) is of secondary importance and is reflected directly in one sentence only: "The fox ground his teeth, and, casting a harsh look at the cock, like the Devil at a christian, remembered the cock's sins and grew angry with it." An echo of this interpretation can be found in the fact that the fox is called "the most wise wife". According to the mediaeval Christian tradition, the Devil can disguise himself as a "most wise wife" or "most wise maid". The second interpretation (the fox as the hypocrite, depraved confessor, and false prophet) becomes an element in the structure of the plot and serves to produce a comic situation.

Who wrote the works of democratic satire? To what sections of the population did the anonymous authors of these works belong? We can assume that at least some of the satirical works came from the lower clergy. In *The Kalyazin Petition* we read that a Moscow priest served as a "model" for the merry brotherhood of this provincial monastery: "In Moscow ... an inspection was made of all the monasteries and taverns, and after the inspection the best revellers were found, the old clerk Sulim and Kolotila the priest from the Intercession who has no certificate of ordination, and they were sent forthwith to the Kalyazin Monastery as models." What is a "priest without a certificate"? We know that in the seventeenth century by the Church of the Intercession of the

Virgin in Moscow there was a patriarchal office where priests who had no certificates of ordination were appointed to parishes. The sources say that these "priests without certificates" used to assemble by the Spassky Bridge causing "great disorders" and disseminating satirical works.[52] In this restless, half-drunk crowd rumours and gossip were rife and proscribed manuscript books were sold surreptitiously. In the late 1670s and early 1680s by the Spassky Bridge you could easily get hold of the writings of the Pustozersk prisoners, Avvakum and his followers, that contained "great abuse of the tsar's house". And satirical works were sold here too.

Russian satire did not arise in the seventeenth century. Daniel the Exile, a writer of the pre-Mongol period, also belongs to it. However, in the Middle Ages satire rarely got as far as manuscripts, remaining within the confines of the oral tradition, and only at the beginning of the seventeenth century did it acquire to a certain extent its rightful place in literature. After that the number of satirical texts grew rapidly. In the eighteenth century they were printed on wood-cut pictures and wall-sheets. What was the reason for this late activity of satire?

The Time of Troubles was a period of "freedom of speech". It created conditions for the writing down of comic and satirical works. The Polish influence clearly accelerated this process, because the flowering of Polish satirical literature took place in the first half of the seventeenth century. But the main reason for this late activity was the state of affairs in Muscovy.

In the seventeenth century the masses were so poor that the burlesque anti-world became too much like real life and could no longer be apprehended only aesthetically, as a world of make-believe. Traditional comic situations were present in everyday life. For many the tavern became a home, the fool's nakedness became real nakedness, and the fool's bast clothes the usual attire for both workdays and holidays. "He who is drunk boasts of riches," wrote the author of *The Tavern Service*. And indeed only in his cups could a poor man imagine himself to be rich. "We have come to love our homeless life," they sing in *The Tavern Service*. "No matter if you are naked, your birthday suit does not fall into tatters, and your navel is bare. Cover yourself with your hand, if you are ashamed. Praise be to God, that's the end of it. Nothing to think about now. Just sleep, don't stand. Just fight off the bugs. It's a merry life, and a hungry one." In the seventeenth century this comic situation had also become a reality: crowds of carousers who had neither a home nor possessions wandered around the towns and villages of Muscovite Russia. The comic, absurd, distorted world became the tragic world of everyday life. Hence the keen sense of despair that breaks through the drunken laughter. Hence also the bitter ridicule of naive Utopias.

Let us recall *The Tale of the Good Life and Merrymaking*. It is an anti-Utopia, i.e., a parody on the genre of the Utopia. In the sixteenth and seventeenth centuries this genre was cultivated by such distinguished European thinkers as Campanella and Thomas More (it was More's book *Utopia* that gave the genre its name). Russian literature of the sixteenth and seventeenth centuries did not create or master the Utopias. Right up to the reign of Peter the Great the reader continued to make use of the mediaeval legends about an earthly paradise, the empire of Presbyter John, and the Brahmin ascetics, which were still in circulation. What then is parodied in *The Tale of the Good Life and Merrymaking* on Russian soil? For a parody in itself makes no sense. It always exists together with that which is parodied.

Although seventeenth-century Russian literature was not familiar with the genre of the Utopia, Russian oral culture was. In seventeenth-century Russia there were many rumours of distant free lands, of Mangazey, the "gold and silver isles", Dauria, and a rich island "on the Eastern ocean". There you could find "grain and horses, and cattle, and pigs, and hens, and they make liquor there and weave and spin as folk do in Russia, and there is much unploughed land and no one levies taxes".[53] The belief in these legends was so strong that in the second half of the seventeenth century thousands of poor people, whole villages, would leave hearth and home and flee they knew not where. These flights assumed such proportions that the government became alarmed: special pickets stopped the fugitives after they had crossed the Urals, and the Siberian governors made fugitives who had become Cossacks swear on the cross not to go to the land of Dauria without permission.

Against the background of these legends *The Tale of the Good Life and Merrymaking* stands out particularly clearly. The land described in it is a caricature of the fantasies about a free country. Naive and ignorant people believe in this land, but the author of the *Tale* destroys this belief. The author is a hungry man, an outcast, an unfortunate insulted by life and excluded from the world of the well-fed. Nor does he try to enter this world, knowing that is impossible. But he takes his revenge by ridiculing it. After beginning with a deliberately serious description of fabulous abundance, he then takes this description to absurd lengths only to prove that it was all make-believe. "The taxes levied there are light, for merchandise, bridges and ferrying—a horse for every shaft-bow, a man for every cap, and the people from every cart train." It is the illusory wealth that the tavern carousers dreamt of in their drunken haze. In the image of comic illusory wealth we find real poverty, the eternal "nakedness and barefootedness".

The satirical literature of the seventeenth century stands in sharp contrast not only to the official untruth about the world but also to folklore with its Utopian dreams. It tells the "naked truth" through the mouth of a "poor and naked" man.

7. The Writings of Archpriest Avvakum

Whereas mediaeval literature is characterised by a relative unity of artistic system and artistic taste, a kind of "style of the age", in the seventeenth century this unity is destroyed. The individual element is felt increasingly strongly in art. Literature turns into an arena for conflicting ideas, and the writer becomes an individual, with his own, unique creative manner.[54]

Most vividly of all the individual element is found in the writing of Archpriest Avvakum (1621-1682). This famous leader of the Old Believers became a writer somewhat late in life. Before the age of forty-five he took up his pen rarely. Of all his writings that have so far come to light (about ninety),[55] barely ten belong to this early period. All the rest, including his famous *Life*, the first lengthy autobiography in Russian literature, was written in Pustozersk, a small town at the mouth of the River Pechora, in "the freezing, treeless tundra". It was here on 12 December, 1667, that Avvakum was brought and imprisoned, here that he spent the last fifteen years of his life, and here, on 14 April, 1682, that he was burnt to death "for greatly abusing the tsar's house".

In his younger years Avvakum had not intended to devote himself to literature. He chose a different field, that of fighting against the abuses committed by Church and State, the field of the spoken sermon, of direct contact with people. The robe of the priest (which Avvakum received at the age of twenty-three, when he was still living in his native parts "within the bounds of Nizhny Novgorod"), and then of archpriest made such contact possible for him. People filled his life. "I had many spiritual children, five or six hundred by then. And I, poor sinner, toiled without rest in churches, and in folk's homes, and on journeys, preaching around towns and villages, and in the capital, and in the land of Siberia."

Avvakum never changed his convictions. In spirit and temperament he was a fighter, a polemicist, a denouncer, and he exhibited these qualities throughout his life and labours. His first clash with the church authorities came in 1653, when he was serving in the Kazan Cathedral in the Kremlin ("I liked it in the Kazan Cathedral. I read books to the people there. Lots of folk used to come.") On the eve of Lent Nikon, who had been made Patriarch a year before, sent a "memorandum" to the Kazan Cathedral, and then to the other Moscow churches instructing people to cross themselves with three fingers instead of the usual two. This memorandum marked the beginning of the Church reform. Avvakum disregarded Nikon's order and, naturally, could no longer serve and preach in the Kazan Cathedral. So he assembled the parishioners in a barn. His supporters said openly: "There are times when a stable is better than a church." [56] The recalcitrant archpriest was enchained in the Andronicus Monastery in Moscow. This was Avvakum's first taste of imprisonment: "They cast me into a dark place in the ground and I sat there for three days, neither eating nor drinking; sitting chained in darkenss I bowed, not knowing whether it was to the east or the west. No one came to me but mice and cockroaches, and the crickets chirped, and there were plenty of fleas."

Shortly afterwards he was sent to Siberia with his wife Nastasia Markovna and their children, first to Tobolsk, then to Dauria. But exile in Siberia (which lasted eleven years) did not break Avvakum, just as all the terrible suffering that fell to his lot later did not break him either.

Meanwhile Avvakum's enemy, Nikon, was forced to relinquish the patriarchal throne in 1658, because Tsar Alexis no longer could or would tolerate the high-handed tutelage of his former personal friend. When Avvakum was brought back to Moscow in 1664, the tsar sought a reconciliation with him: he needed the support of this man whom the people already acknowledged as their protector. But nothing came of this attempt. Avvakum hoped that the removal of Nikon would mean a return to the "old belief", but the tsar and the leading boyars had no intention of renouncing the Church reform, because it was an essential link in the irreversible process of the Europeanisation of Russia. The tsar soon realised that Avvakum was a danger to him, and the recalcitrant archpriest was again deprived of his freedom. Then followed new exiles, monastery imprisonments, defrocking and excommunication by the Church Council of 1666-1667 and, finally, incarceration in Pustozersk.

It was here that the preacher became a brilliant writer. In Pustozersk he had no congregation. He could not preach to his "spiritual children", and there was nothing left for him but to take up his pen. The ideas that he had conceived way back in his youth and that he had sought to impress upon the people in "the bounds of Nizhny Novgorod", the Kazan Cathedral, the Moscow barn and Dauria, he now defended staunchly in his writings.

In Pustozersk Avvakum lived with three other exiled leaders of the Old Believers—Epiphanius, a monk from the Solovetsky Monastery, Lazarus, a priest from the town of Romanov, and Theodore Ivanov, a deacon from the Cathedral of the Annunciation in Moscow. Together they were burnt to death. They were all writers. Avvakum was very close to Epiphanius, his confessor. At first the Pustozersk prisoners lived comparatively freely and were able to communicate with one another. They quickly established contact with their followers in Moscow and other towns. The Streltsy, who sympathised with these sufferers for the "old belief", willingly helped them. "And I told them to make a secret hole in the handle of a Strelets' pole-axe," Archpriest Avvakum wrote to the boyar's wife Feodosia Morozova in 1669, "and with my own poor hands put the missive in the pole-axe ... and bowed low to

Pustozersk Miscellany. The end of the *Life* of Archpriest Avvakum and the beginning of the *Life* of Epiphanius. Autographs. Late 17th century. Institute of Russian Literature, Leningrad

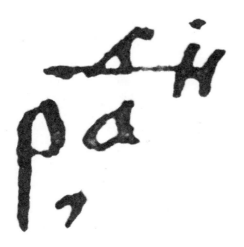

him and asked him to take it, protected by the Lord, to my son (his son was imprisoned on the River Mezen—*A.P.*) and the elder Epiphanius made the secret hiding place in the axe." Epiphanius, who could turn his hand to anything, also made many wooden crosses with secret compartments in which he hid "letters" sent "into the world".

These seditious writings were sent of to the Mezen, where Avvakum's family was living, and from there went further afield. Avvakum even managed to establish contact with the Solovetsky Monastery, which refused to accept Nikon's "innovations" and was besieged by tsar's troops in 1668. In 1669-1670 he wrote to the Mezen, where his devoted pupil, Theodore the Fool-in-Christ, was living with Avvakum's family: "Let Theodore conceal these letters and go to the Solovetsky Monastery, enter it secretly and deliver the letters."

Seeking to put an end to the activities of the "great four", the authorities resorted to punitive measures. Ivan Elagin, a high-ranking officer, was sent to the Mezen and to Pustozersk. On the Mezen he hanged Theodore and in Pustozersk in April 1670 he "meted out punishment" to Epiphanius, Lazarus and the deacon Theodore: their tongues were cut out and their right hands severed. Avvakum was spared. "And I wouldn't abide that and wanted to die of hunger," wrote Avvakum, "and I did not eat for eight days or more, but the brethren bade me eat."

After that the conditions of his imprisonment deteriorated sharply. The guards, Avvakum wrote, "placed timber frames around our pits and filled them up with earth ... leaving us each one small opening through which to get food and firewood." Avvakum described his "large room" with bitter irony: "Both I and the Elder (Epiphanius) have a large room ... where we eat and drink, and ... defecate too, yes, on a spade, and then out of the window! I think the Tsar Alexis, son of Michael, does not have such a spacious chamber."

But the intolerable conditions of this "pit prison" did not weaken the Pustozersk exiles' urge to write, particularly as the demand for their works was tremendous. The words of Avvakum and his followers possessed great moral authority for Old Believers. They were surrounded by the aura of martyrdom for the faith. Their works were copied and disseminated secretly. The "great four" laboured hard, writing more and more new works.

In Pustozersk Avvakum wrote a large number of petitions, letters and epistles, as well as such lengthy works as *The Book of Talks* (1669-1675) which contains ten discourses on different dogmatic subjects; *The Book of Interpretations* (1673-1676) which contains Avvakum's interpretations of the Psalms and other Old Testament texts; and *The Book of Denunciations, or the Eternal Gospels* (1679), containing Avvakum's theological polemic with the deacon Theodore, his co-prisoner. In Pustozersk Avvakum also produced his monumental autobiography, the splendid *Life* (1672), which he revised several times.[57]

In origins and in ideology Avvakum belonged to the common folk, the lower strata of society. Both his sermons and his literary work were full of democratic spirit. His long and bitter experience had convinced Avvakum that life was hard for common folk in Russia. "Even without the flogging a man finds it hard to keep going," he writes in his *Life*, recalling his enforced journey to Dauria. "But the slightest excuse and he gets a touch of the stick: 'Stay where you are, fellow, die on the job!'" The idea of equality is one of Avvakum's favourite ideas: "There is one heaven, and one earth, and bread belongs to all, and water too." He saw Russian people as his brothers and sisters "of the spirit", not recognising any differences of estate. "Are you any better than us because you are a boyar's wife?" he asks Feodosia Morozova. "The Lord has spread out the sky for all of us, and the moon and the sun shine alike for each and every one, and the earth, the waters, and all that grows at the Lord's behest does not serve you more or me less."

Here, of course, Avvakum is quoting the letter and spirit of the Gospels. But in relation to Russian life of the seventeenth century the idea of equality acquires a secular, rebellious note. For Avvakum Christians are the common people, and he accuses the Church pastors and secular rulers of Nikonianism, saying they have turned into wolves that devour their "hapless victims". "Not only for the changing of the holy books," writes Avvakum, "but also for secular truth ... it is proper to lay down one's life."

Avvakum's ideology is full of democratic spirit. The same democratic spirit imbues his aesthetics, determining the linguistic standards, representational means, and writer's standpoint in general. Avvakum constantly has the reader before him as he writes. He is either a peasant or artisan with whom Avvakum had dealings in his younger years. He is Avvakum's spiritual son, careless and diligent, sinful and righteous, weak and strong at one and the same time. He is a "true son of his people", like the archpriest himself. Such a reader would find it difficult to understand the intricacies of Church Slavonic. You have to speak to him simply, and Avvakum makes the vernacular his stylistic principle: "Readers and hearers, do not despise our popular speech, for I love my native Russian tongue... I shall not concern myself with rhetoric and do not disparage my Russian tongue."

It must be said that in all his works, the *Life* in particular, Avvakum shows exceptional skill as a stylist. He has an extraordinarily free and flexible command of the "native Russian tongue". One of the reasons for this is that Avvakum feels he is talking, not writing ("But why say so much?", "But that's enough talk!", "Shall I tell you another story, my friend?"). He is talking to his audience, continuing the work of preaching in his distant "pit prison". He calls his manner of exposition "blathering" and "growling".

Avvakum's style is highly emotional. Sometimes he addresses his reader-hearer affectionately as "father", "dear one" "poor creature", "my dear", "Alexei dear", "dear Simeon", and sometimes he rebukes him, as he rebukes the deacon Theodore, his opponent on theological questions: "You're a real fool, Theodore!" A sad pathos echoes in his words to the boyar's wife Feodosia Morozova, who was dying of hunger in prison in Borovsk: "Are you still breathing, my light? Are you still breathing, dear friend, or have they burnt you, or strangled you? I know not and hear not; I know not if you are alive or they have put an end to you! Child of the Church, my dear child, Feodosia Prokopievna! Tell me, an old sinner, but one word: are you alive?" But nor does he eschew humour—he ridicules both his enemies, calling them "unfortunates", "poor wretches", and "fools", and himself, even when he is describing the most tragic episodes of his life.

Recalling in the *Life* how he was defrocked, "shorn", Avvakum writes about it with humour: "They tore my hair out like dogs, leaving nothing but a tuft, like the Poles have, on my forehead!" This is what he has to say about his sufferings in Dauria: "For five weeks we travelled in sledges over the bare ice. I was given (by the governor Afanasy Pashkov) two nags to carry the children and our poor belongings, and me and the wife went on foot, stumbling over the ice. It's a wild country and the natives are a savage lot; we dared not fall behind the horses, but we couldn't keep us with them, hungry and tired as we were. The poor wife trudged along and kept falling down, it was so slippery! One day she fell down and some poor tired fellow stumbled over her and fell; the two of them were shouting for help and couldn't get up. 'Forgive me, mistress!' the man cried. 'Why did you knock me down, man?' cried the wife. I came up, and the poor woman reproached me, saying: 'How long must we bear this torment, Archpriest?' And I said: 'Till death itself!' Then she sighed and answered: 'Very well, let's be on our way then.'" This episode gives a good idea of the nature of Avvakum's humour. On the one hand, it is "fortifying laughter" at the most difficult moments, healing laughter that helps one endure tribulations with dignity. On the other hand, it is gentle self-mockery that saves one from self-conceit and false pride.[58]

This is essential from the point of view of both Avvakum and his reader, because Avvakum's main hero is himself. This is the first time in Old Russian literature that the author writes so much about his own hardships, about how he "grieves", "sobs", "sighs", and "laments". This is the first time that a Russian writer dares to compare himself to the first Christian writers—the Apostles. "Perhaps I should not have spoken about my life, but I have read the Acts of the Apostles and the Epistles of Paul—and the Apostles did speak of themselves after all." By quoting the authority of the Apostles, Avvakum willy-nilly declared himself also to be an Apostle. He called his *Life* "the book of eternal life", and this was no slip of the tongue. As an Apostle Avvakum could write about himself. He was free in his choice of themes and personages, free to use "popular speech" and to discuss his and others' actions.

In writing his *Life* Avvakum observed the hagiographical canon to some extent. The exposition, as the canon required, contains an account of the parents and childhood of the hagiographical hero. It also describes the first sign that the hero received, the "vision of a ship": "And then I saw ... a ship, adorned not with gold, but with many colours—red, white, blue, black and grey—the human mind cannot encompass how fair and sound it was. And a radiant youth sat at the stern steering it... And I cried out: 'Whose boat is this?' And the youth replied: 'It is your boat! Go sail in it with your wife and children, if you so wish!' And I began to tremble and thought to myself: 'What can this mean? And where shall I sail?'" The sea is life and the ship a man's fate. These are mediaeval images, and they run all through the *Life*. Behind every event Avvakum sees a hidden, symbolic meaning, and this too brings him close to Old Russian hagiography. The *Life* ends with a description of the punishment of 1670 in Pustozersk. But this is followed by episodes from Avvakum's life that are not connected with the main plot and in composition and subject matter recall the "miracles" that are always appended to the Old Russian *vita*.

Nevertheless Avvakum radically reforms the hagiographical scheme. For the first time in Russian literature he unites the author and the hero of the hagiographical narrative in the same person. From the traditional viewpoint this is impermissible for it is sinful pride to extol oneself. The symbolism of the *Life* is also personal. Avvakum gives a symbolical meaning to "transitory" everyday details, that mediaeval hagiography generally ignored.

Speaking of his first imprisonment in 1653, he writes: "I had not eaten for three days and felt hungry. After vespers someone appeared before me. I did not know whether it was an angel or a man, and do not know to this day; only he prayed in the darkness and, putting his hand on my shoulder, led me with the chain to a bench and sat me down on it. And he put a spoon into my hand, and a little bread, and gave me cabbage soup to eat—it was so good and tasty! And he said to me: 'Eat and fortify yourself.' And then he was gone. The door did not open, but he was gone! That is strange if it was a man, but what if it were an angel? Then it is not surprising, for nothing bars his way." The "miracle of the cabbage soup" is an "everyday miracle", like the story of the black hen that fed Avvakum's children in Siberia: "Each day it laid two eggs for our children to eat, helping us in our need at the Lord's behest, for the Lord so ordained."

The symbolical interpretation of everyday details is extremely important in the system of ideological and artistic principles of the *Life*. Avvakum fought hard against Nikon's reform not only because Nikon had violated the Orthodox ritual hallowed by centuries. He also regarded the reform as a violation of Russian customs, the whole Russian way of life. For Avvakum Orthodoxy was firmly bound up with this way of life. If Orthodoxy were destroyed, Russia would perish too. That is why he describes Russian life so affectionately and vividly, particularly family life.

Avvakum's *Life* is not only a sermon, but also a confession.[59] One of the most striking features of this work is its sincerity. This is not only the standpoint of the writer, but also of the sufferer, the "living corpse", who has settled his account with life and for whom death is a blessed release. "What do I need, sitting in my prison, as in a coffin? Can it be death? Truly, it is so." Avvakum detests falsehood and pretence. There is not a single false note in his *Life*, nor in the rest of his writing. He writes nothing but the truth, that truth which his "enraged conscience" dictates to him.

Avvakum does not vary his sincerity in relation to the reader, the person he is addressing. In this respect his wife, the boyar's wife Morozova and the tsar himself were all the same to him. "And I shall order that Tsar Alexis be called to judgment before Christ," wrote Avvakum. "Let him be scourged with copper lashes."[60] When Tsar Alexis died and the throne went to his son Theodore, Avvakum sent the new ruler a petition in which he requested: "Have mercy on me, who have no refuge and am estranged from God and from people for my sins, have mercy on me, son of Alexis, fair child of the Church!" But even in this petition Avvakum did not fail to rebuke the late tsar—in his letter to the son who had just lost his father! "God will be the judge between me and Tsar Alexis. For I have heard from the Saviour that he sits in torment."

In order to judge Avvakum as a fighter, a rebel, we should recall his connection with the act of protest of the Moscow Old Believers during the traditional ceremony of the Blessing of the Waters in 1681. When a large crowd of people had assembled in the Kremlin, the Old Believers "shamelessly and furtively threw down blasphemous scrolls that dishonoured the tsar's dignity" [61] from the bell-tower of Ivan the Great, and smeared tar on the church robes and tsars' tombs in the Cathedral of the Assumption. Among the "furtive scrolls" were writings by the Pustozersk prisoners. Avvakum, who could draw as well as write, also portrayed "their majesties the tsars and high-ranking church leaders" on birch bark with "abusive captions" and "highly forbidden" words. It was these caricatures that the Old Believers distributed during the tsar's procession to the hole in the ice of the River Moscow during the ceremony.

Having lost faith not only in Tsar Alexis, but also in his heir and realising that the Moscow rulers had renounced the "old belief" once and for all, Avvakum turned to openly anti-governmental propaganda. This is why he was burnt at the stake—not only for the Schism, but also "for greatly abusing the tsar's house".

8. Baroque in Russian Literature of the Late Seventeenth Century

In the literature of the seventeenth century, unlike that of the Middle Ages, it is impossible to discern common stylistic principles. The seventeenth century is the age of the emergence, establishment and struggle of different literary schools and trends, both those deriving from Russian traditions and those based on West European practice. From Europe, primarily Poland, through the Ukraine-Byelorussian intermediacy, Russia borrowed Baroque that was destined to be the style of Moscow *courtly* culture for the last third of the seventeenth century. What were the specific features of this style?

In Europe Baroque replaced the Renaissance. Whereas man held pride of place in the Renaissance system of values, Baroque returned to the mediaeval idea of God as the first cause and purpose of earthly existence. Baroque heralded a whimsical synthesis of the Middle Ages and the Renaissance. This whimsicality, artificiality, is present in the very term "Baroque", whether it is seen as deriving from jewellery in which *barroco* was the word for a strangely shaped pearl, or from logics in which it denoted one of the irregular figures of a syllogism.

By turning once again to the Middle Ages, the art of Baroque revived mysticism, the *danse macabre*, the themes of the Last Judgement and infernal torment. At the same time Baroque (in theory at least) did not break with the heritage of the Renaissance or renounce its achievements. The antique gods and heroes remained the personages of Baroque writers, and antique poetry retained for them the importance of a high and unattainable model.

The "dual" nature of European Baroque was of great importance for the assimilation of this style by Russia. On the one hand, mediaeval elements in Baroque aesthetics helped Russia, for whom mediaeval culture was by no means a thing of the distant past, to accept the first European style in its "post-Horde" history relatively easily. On the other hand, the Renaissance element that fertilised Baroque determined the special role of this style in the development of Russian culture: in Russia Baroque performed the function of the Renaissance.[62] Russia is indebted to the style of Baroque for the emergence of regular syllabic poetry and the theatre.

Simeon of Polotsk. The founder of an unbroken tradition of syllabic poetry in Moscow was the Byelorussian Samuil Sitnianovich-Petrovsky (1629-1680), who at the age of twenty-seven took monastic vows and the name of Simeon and became known in Moscow as Simeon of Polotsk, his native town where he had tought in the school of the Orthodox "fraternity" there. In the summer and autumn of 1656 the young teacher had the opportunity of attracting the attention of Tsar Alexis. The tsar visited the Russian army units stationed outside Riga and twice stayed at Polotsk where he heard welcoming verses composed by Simeon. In 1660 Simeon visited Moscow, again presenting the tsar with his verses. A year later Polotsk was captured by the Poles, and in 1664 Simeon moved to Moscow, this time to stay.

Thus, at the source of Baroque stood an Orthodox Byelorussian, who had studied the "seven free arts" in the Kiev-Mogila Academy and may have attended a course of lectures at the Vilna Jesuit Academy, the best educational establishment of the so-called "Lithuanian province" of the Jesuit Order and the only one of its kind. The origins and education of Simeon of Polotsk show clearly whence and how the Baroque style came to Russia.

In Moscow Simeon of Polotsk continued the profession of teacher begun in his native land.[63] He educated the tsar's children (one of whom, the future Tsar Theodore, he taught to write syllabic verse), and opened a Latin school not far from the

Page from a printed *Tale of SS Barlaam and Josaphat* by Simeon of Polotsk. 1680, Moscow

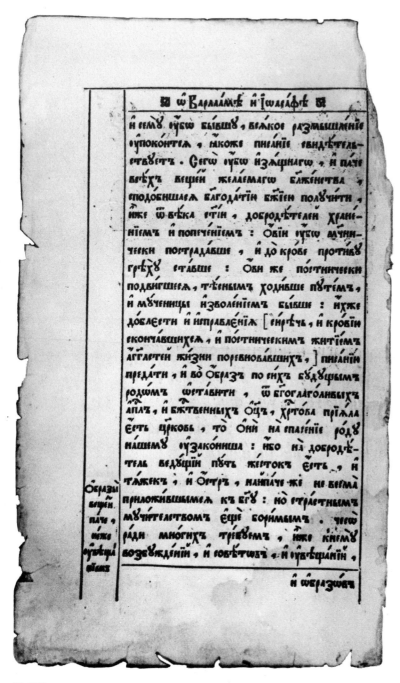

Page from a printed *Tale of SS Barlaam and Josaphat.* Detail

Kremlin in the Monastery Behind the Icon of the Saviour, where the young scribes of the Privy Office, Tsar Alexis' own chancery, studied. Simeon of Polotsk also set up and held another post, that of court poet, which had hitherto been unknown in Russia. Any event in the tsar's family, such as marriages, saint's days, and births, gave Simeon of Polotsk an opportunity to write verses "for the occasion". These verses, which belong to the *silva* genre, were collected by the poet towards the end of his life in the huge *Rhymologian* (which has survived in draft form and been published in extracts only).

Simeon of Polotsk's heritage is very big. It is estimated that he left at least fifty thousand lines of poetry.[64]

Apart from *The Rhymologian,* there are *The Rhyming Psalter* (a verse rendering of the *Psalter,* printed in 1680) and the vast collection, as yet unpublished, entitled *The Garden of Many Flowers* (1678), a kind of poetic encyclopaedia in which the verses are arranged in alphabetical order. *The Garden of Many Flowers* contains 1,155 headings, a single heading sometimes comprising a whole cycle, from two to twelve poems.

From an account by Sylvester Medvedev (1641-1691), a pupil and favourite of Simeon of Polotsk, we know how the latter worked. In the Monastery Behind the Icon of the Saviour the teacher and his pupil lived in neighbouring rooms connected by a common lobby. Sylvester Medvedev, a constant eyewitness of Simeon's work, recalled that the latter "was in the habit of writing half-a-quire of quarto each day, and his handwriting was very small and compact", i.e., each day he covered eight pages of quarto paper with small handwriting. This prolific output was not graphomania; it reflected Simeon of Polotsk's main creative aim. As a European-oriented person, he did not rate Old Russian literature very highly. He believed that his task was to create a new literary culture for Russia.

Such a culture needed readers capable of appreciating and understanding it. Well aware that these readers would have to be trained, Simeon of Polotsk sought to "inundate" life at the tsar's court and among the aristocracy of the capital with syllabic verse. On public holidays his verses in the genres of the "recitation" and "dialogue" were read in public by the author himself and specially trained youths. His panegyrics were also read in public. Judging from the composition of *The Rhymologian* and from the author's notes in the margin, Simeon of Polotsk took advantage of every possible occasion to deliver speeches in verse. He composed these speeches both for himself and for others, commissioned or as a present. They were read at official royal banquets, in boyars' chambers and in church during festivals.

The Garden of Many Flowers was a different sort of work. It was an encyclopaedia of poetry in which Simeon of Polotsk sought to give the reader a broad range of knowledge, first and foremost, on antique and mediaeval West European history. Here we find mythological subjects and historical anecdotes about Caesar, Augustus, Alexander the Great, Diogenes, Justinian and Charlemagne. In many poems he makes use of Pliny the Elder's *Natural History*. *The Garden of Many Flowers* provides information on fantastic and exotic creatures, the phoenix, the crocodile, the ostrich, precious stones, etc. Here we also find an exposition of cosmogonic views and excursions into the sphere of Christian symbolism. In the words of Igor Eremin, the poems of *The Garden* "create the impression of an unusual museum, in whose show-cases all manner of things, often rare and very old, are arranged in a set order... Everything that Simeon, the well-read bibliophile and lover of 'rarities' and 'curiosities', managed to collect in his memory throughout his life is displayed here for inspection." [65]

This "museum of rarities" reflects some of the basic motifs of Baroque, first and foremost, the idea of the "variety" of the world, the inconstancy of all things, and also the penchant for the sensational that is typical of Baroque. However, the unusual feature about this "museum" is that it is a museum of letters. Simeon of Polotsk sees the development of culture as a kind of verbal procession, a parade of words.

At first glance objects too appear to take part in this procession. But Simeon of Polotsk is not interested in the sphinx and the salamander, the phoenix and the siren, the pelican and the centaur, the magnet or amber, as such. It is only their cognisable essence, the word concealed in them, that interests him, for he is convinced that the word is the main element in culture.

According to his point of view, the poet is a "second God": just as God made the world with the Word, so the poet with his word conjures up people, events and ideas out of non-being. Simeon sees the world in the form of a book or alphabet, and the elements of the world as parts of the book, its pages, lines, words, type:

> Мир сей преукрашенный — книга есть велика,
>   ежесловом написа всяческих владыка.
> Пять листов препространных в ней ся обретают,
>   яже чюдна писмена в себе заключают.
> Первый же лист есть небо, на нем же святила,
>   яко писмена, божия крепость положила.

Introduction in prose to **The Garden of Many Flowers** by Simeon of Polotsk.
1670s-1680s. Academy of Sciences Library, Leningrad

тоа̀, нєпаменлїетсѧ слабы чл҃овѣчєскїѧ, сицѐ ѿ тѣсѐ
єстѐ ѡ вєличаєми: Какѡ вы можетє вѣроваτи,
слабы дрꙋгъ ѿ дрꙋга прїємлюще, и̑ слабы ꙗже
ѿ є̑динагѡ б҃га нєищєте. Возмєздїетсѧ прѣмѣ-
ннοе, потолинѧ ми тщателнο, по єлику нꙋждꙋ ест
дополномъ прєпитанїю мєнє грѣшнагѡ, и̑ трꙋды
всєгда полагающихъ о̑ моихъ потрєбахъ.
Нο то попрєданицѣй матти и̑ прємногими щедротаⷨ
стопочивашагѡ ѡ б҃зѣ бг҃а ст҃ыѧ и̑ блаженныѧ па-
мѧти Благочεстивѣйшагѡ тишайшагѡ и̑ самодє-
ржавнѣйшаго̑ вεликагѡ гдⷭ҇рѧ цр҃ѧ и̑ вєликагѡ кнѧⷥ
Алεѯїа Михаиловича всеѧ̀ вεликїѧ и̑ малыѧ и̑ бѣ-
лыѧ рѡссїи самодєржца, нєсадноε, но дополноε
по моεмꙋ чинꙋ изъѧвити чрεзъ лѣтꙑε тринадεсѧⷮ
и̑ мѣⷮ, прεрадостнѡ во цр҃тъующємъ и̑ бг҃оспа-
саεмомъ градѣ Москвѣ прεмнихъ, прикнѡ пο
гдⷭ҇ь бг҃ꙋ теплыѧ моѧ и̑ мⷮвы о̑ нεмъ вεликомъ
гдⷭ҇рꙋ возсылаѧ, и̑ трꙋды трꙋдꙗмъ: ѡвꙑ попода-
лѣтнїю началствꙋющихъ, ѡвꙑ помоεмꙋ своистѣ-
нномꙋ бл҃гохотѣнїю, да нεпраздниц жизни моεѧ̀
вотищε нεкждꙋт врεмѧ, прилагаѧ. Пο блаженно̑
же εгѡ прⷭ҇свꙗтагѡ вεличεства воишѣствꙗ ѡ̑шε-
стꙗи, прикнѡ во моихъ ниночествихъ молεбꙑⷯ мо-
люⷭ҇ и̑ до послѣдⷩ҇нѧгѡ моεгѡ издꙑханїѧ и̑малⷨ нε
имѣннѡ гдⷭ҇а бг҃а молити о̑ εже простититиⷭ҇ вса-
номꙋ εгѡ согрѣшεнїю, и̑ въселититисѧ дш҃и εгѡ в сε
лεнїѧ прикнагѡ вεсεлиѧ, и̑ жизни бεзконεчнꙑⷯ
со бъхꙑ нεбᲀꙑми, и̑ дш҃ами вεстⷯѯ правεдниⷯ ѡⷮ вεкⷮ
бл҃гоꙋгодивⷳихъ гдⷭ҇и. Εгоже бл҃гочεстивагѡ и̑
прикнѡ памѧтнагѡ самодεржца пꙗꙗ вопамꙗ-
ти ѡшεствꙗи ѿ мира содεржꙗ, и̑ аки бл҃года
рномъ срⷣци дши наꙗтвεрдомъ адамантⷯ прε-
мнοꙗ εгѡ цр҃скаꙗ пο мнѣ бл҃готворεнꙗꙗ напи-
санная читаꙗ, нεпозможεстилⷨ никогдаже вεсεлꙗю мѣста во срⷣцⷮ моεмъ дати. Аще нεбꙑ
ми пεчалнагѡ ꙋма лꙗчεсꙗ матти и̑ щεдрωтⷮ
свοихъ позεꙋꙗдалε пο вεсεлꙗю, ѡ εгоже цр҃сꙗꙗ
кⷭ҇рⷯ радниⷮ добротвориꙗ нꙗмꙗ свⷯтлⷯε
возсꙗꙗшꙗ и̑ слꙗнцε, и̑ на εгоже цр҃стεмⷮ
прεстолⷮ бг҃ωмпосꙗждεнный сн҃ъ εгѡ, а на̑

Второй лист огнь стихийный под небом высоко,
в нем яко писание силу да зрит око.
Третий лист преширокий аер мощно звати,
на нем дождь, снег, облаки и птицы читати.
Четвертый лист—сонм водный в ней ся обретает,
в том животных множество удобь ся читает.
Последний лист есть земля с древесы, с травами,
с крушцы и с животными, яко с письменами.

This finely adorned world is a great book,/That the Lord of all wrote with the Word./In it there are five vast sheets/Containing within them wondrous letters./

The first sheet is the heavens on which the Divine power/Hath placed heavenly bodies like letters./The second sheet is the fire of the elements that covers/The heavens and appears to the eye as writing./The third sheet we can call the broad ether/And read rain, snow, clouds and birds upon it./The fourth sheet is the watery element, in which/We can easily read many living creatures./The last sheet is the earth with trees, grasses,/Ores and beasts like letters.

The word was seen as the instrument for transforming the world, a means of creating a new, European culture. Consequently Simeon of Polotsk's plans for enlightenment were, first and foremost, the plans of a humanitarian. It was Sylvester Medvedev who sought to implement these plans in the 1680s.

Sylvester Medvedev. Born in Kursk, Sylvester Medvedev was a scribe in the Privy Office who later, urged by Simeon, took monastic vows.[66] After the death of his teacher, Sylvester inherited his post, that of court poet. He also inherited Simeon's library and his plans. The main plan was to found a university in Moscow. The charter drawn up for it in the tsar's name was inspired by the Kiev-Mogila Academy and stipulated that the university would have the right to guide Moscow culture. In presenting a draft charter to tsarevna Sophia in January 1685, Sylvester Medvedev wrote:

Мудрости бо ти имя подадеся,
богом Софиа мудрость наречеся.
Тебе бо слично науки начати,
яко премудрой оны совершати.

(You have been given the name of wisdom,/For Sophia was named wisdom by God.

It befits you to begin the sciences,/To pursue them, most wise one!

His reliance on Sophia's support were in vain. The European-oriented tendency that Sylvester Medvedev represented aroused strong opposition from the Church leaders under Patriarch Joachim himself. Sophia did not´ want to quarrel with the patriarch, and the Slavonic-Graeco-Latin Academy founded in 1686 fell into his hands. There could be no question of university autonomy now that everything depended on the will of the patriarch.[67] When Sophia's regency came to an end in 1689, Sylvester Medvedev was found guilty of conspiracy. "In the year 199 (1691), on the eleventh day of the month of February the monk Sylvester Medvedev departed from this life..." his brother-in-law Karion Istomin recorded in his diary. "He was beheaded ... in Red Square, opposite the Spassky Gate. His body is buried in the almshouse in a pit with vagabonds."[68] Sylvester Medvedev's works were strictly proscribed. All lists of them were ordered to be burnt on pain of heavy punishment. This would appear to explain why so little of his verse has survived.

Karion Istomin. Like Sylvester Medvedev, Karion Istomin (Zaulonsky) (mid-seventeenth century-after 1717) was born in Kursk.[69] He came to Moscow not later than 1679, having already taken monastic vows. Here he worked as a redactor at the Printing House. The turbulent events of 1689 had little effect on Karion Istomin's career, but the last decade of the seventeenth century was the time of his greatest success. He became firmly established under Patriarch Adrian and on 4 March 1698 was given the important appointment of head of the Printing House. Karion Istomin is a very prolific and little studied poet. He is known for his pedagogical writings (the engraved *ABC* of 1694 and the type-set *ABC* of 1696). In fact he wrote panegyrics (beginning with a book presented to Sophia in 1681), verses for "coats-of-arms", epitaphs, epistles to friends and even tried his hand at the genre of the heroic poem, in thirteen-syllable verse describing the second Crimean campaign of Prince Vasily Golitsyn (1689). Istomin was particularly successful at meditative lyrical poetry, reflections on the vanity of earthly life, the human soul, and death:

> Воззрю на небо—ум не постигает,
>   како в не пойду, а бог призывает.
> На землю смотрю—мысль притупляется,
>   всяк человек в ту смертью валяется.
> По широте ли ум где понесется—
>   конца и края нигде доберется,
> Тварь бо вся в бозе мудре содержится,
>   да всяка душа тому удивится.
> Что небо держит, кто землю строит,
>   человеку како благу жизнь усвоит?

I gaze up at the heavens and know not:/How to get there, yet God calls./I look at the earth and my wits are dulled,/For every man is cast down there

Page from a printed **ABC** by Karion Istomin. 1692. Moscow

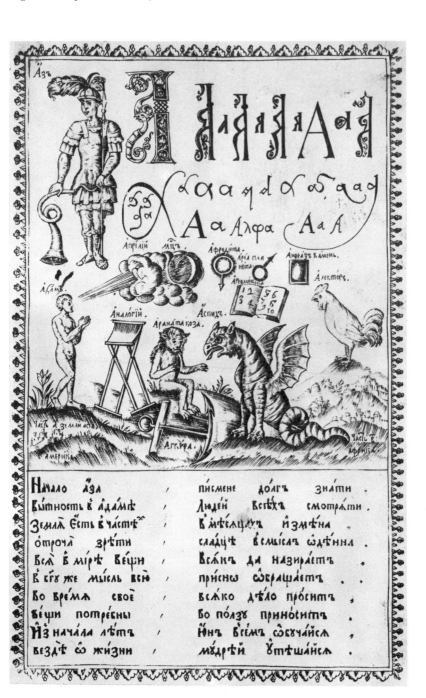

Page from a printed **ABC** by Karion Istomin. Detail

*by death./If my mind should fly around the wide world,/Nowhere will it
reach the end./All creatures are kept by God in His wisdom,/And all souls
do marvel at this:/What keeps the heavens, who makes the earth,/And how
is a man to master a life of piety?*

The Emergence of Russian Drama and the Theatre. The
Russian professional theatre appeared in 1672, the year of Peter
I's birth, as a court theatre.[70] Already in the early 1660s Tsar
Alexis made attempts to hire in the "German lands" and settle in
Moscow a troupe of actors, "masters to make comedy" (the word
"comedy" at that time was used to denote any dramatic work and
theatrical production). These attempts were not successful, and
eventually the founding of the theatre was entrusted to Johann
Gottfried Gregory, the pastor of the Lutheran Church in the
foreigners' quarter, or German settlement, in Moscow. On the
tsar's orders he was commissioned to "make a comedy (theatrical
production), and in the comedy to enact the Book of Esther from
the Bible".[71]

It took several months for Pastor Gregory to compose a play in
German verse about the Old Testament story of the beautiful and
meek Esther who attracts the attention of King Artaxerxes of
Persia, becomes his wife and saves her people; for the translators
of the Ambassadorial Chancery to put the play into Russian; and
for the foreign actors, students of Gregory's school, to learn their
parts, male and female, in Russian. During this time a "comedy
chamber" (theatre building) was erected in the village of
Preobrazhenskoye, where the tsar had a country residence. The
first production, *The Comedy of Artaxerxes*, was performed here on
17 October 1672. It was watched by the tsar, high-ranking
members of the Boyar's Council, and the tsar's closest advisers.
The Tsarina Natalia together with the royal children watched the
performance from a special box behind a lattice partition.

The Comedy of Artaxerxes was performed several times. In
February 1673 a new play was shown, *Judith* (*The Comedy of
Holofernes*), about the Biblical heroine who kills the pagan
Holofernes, leader of the army that besieges her native town. The
repertoire of the court theatre was constantly being added to
(performances were given sometimes in Preobrazhenskoye and
sometimes in the Kremlin, in a chamber over the court apothec-
ary). Alongside the plays on Biblical and hagiographical themes it
included an historical drama about Tamerlaine who conquered the
Sultan Bayazid (*The Comedy of Temir-Aksak*), a play which has not
survived about Bacchus and Venus and the ballet *Orpheus*, about
which we have only some very scanty information.

The actors included not only foreigners from the German
settlement, but also Russian youths, mainly young scribes from the

Ambassadorial Chancery. The new royal entertainment was provided for most lavishly. There was instrumental music in the theatre (in Old Russia only singing was officially recognised, musical instruments being regarded as attributes of the wandering minstrels). There was singing and dancing on the stage. For each play "frames of perspective painting" were executed (painted sets with linear perspective, which was also a new phenomenon in Russian art). The most expensive materials and fabrics were obtained from the treasury or specially purchased for props and costumes, Persian silk, Hamburg cloth and Turkish satin.

The court theatre was Tsar Alexis' pet creation and did not survive its founder. After his sudden death on 30 January 1676, the performances stopped, and towards the end of the year the new ruler Theodore ordered that "all comedy (theatrical) paraphernalia" be put under lock and key.

All the plays of the first Russian theatre were based on historical subjects. But they were no longer the stories about the past so familiar to readers of the Holy Scriptures, chronicles, *vitae* and tales. This was a showing, a visual portrayal, a kind of resurrection of the past. Artaxerxes, who, to quote the play "had been confined in his grave for more than two thousand years", utters the word "today" three times in his monologue. Like the other personages "confined in the grave" he comes to life on the stage, speaks and moves, punishes and pardons, weeps and rejoices. For a modern audience there would be nothing remarkable about "bringing to life" a long dead potentate: this is an accepted dramatic convention. But for Tsar Alexis and his boyars, who had not received a West European theatrical education, the "resurrection of the past" in the "comedy chamber" was a real revolution in their ideas about art. It turned out that one could not only narrate the past, but also bring it to life, portray it as the present. The theatre created the artistic illusion of reality, divorcing the spectator, as it were, from reality and carrying him into a special world, the world of art, the world of history come to life.[72]

According to contemporary accounts, the tsar watched the first performance for ten whole hours without leaving his seat (the boyars, excluding the members of the tsar's family, stood for the self-same "ten whole hours", for it was not permitted to sit in the monarch's presence). From this it is clear that *The Comedy of Artaxerxes* was performed without intervals, although the play was divided into seven acts and a large number of scenes. No intervals were allowed because they might have destroyed the illusion of "resurrected history" and brought the spectator back from the "artistic present" to the real present, whereas it was precisely to create this illusion that the first Russian theatre-lover had built the "comedy chamber" in the village of Preobrazhenskoye.

It was not easy to get used to theatrical convention. This can be seen albeit from information about the costumes and props. They used not theatre trumpery, but expensive cloths and fabrics, because at first it was hard for the audience to grasp the essence of acting, the essence of the "artistic present", difficult for them to see Artaxerxes as both a real "resurrected potentate" and a German mummer from the foreigners' settlement. The author of the play found it necessary to mention this in the foreword which was addressed directly to the tsar:

"Thy sovereign word makes Artaxerxes, as it were, alive, in the form of a youth..."

The foreword was written specially for the Russian audience and "recited by a special character called Mamurza ('the tsar's orator'). Mamurza addresses the most important member of the audience, Tsar Alexis, and explains the artistic essence of the new entertainment to him: the problem of the artistic present, how the past becomes the present before the tsar's eyes. Mamurza has recourse to the concept of "glory" which had long been associated in Old Russia with the idea of the immortality of the past. Clearly and intelligibly he explains to Tsar Alexis that his glory too will remain forever, like the glory of many historical heroes... In order to help the tsar perceive people of the past as being alive, the author makes these people feel that they have been resurrected. Not only do the audience see historical figures before them ... but the figures themselves see the audience, marvel at how they got there, and admire the tsar and his realm... In his brief explanation of the content of the play, Mamurza does his best to draw the audience into the unfamiliar atmosphere of the theatre and stress the marvellous nature of the repetition of past events in the present." [73]

So the theatre created the artistic illusion of life. But what kind of life did the Russian spectator see before him? What sort of people did he see on the stage? Although they were "resurrected" from the past, they bore a remarkable resemblance to those who were sitting (or standing) in the "comedy chamber". The characters were in perpetual motion. They were remarkably active and energetic.[74] They urged one another to "hurry", "tarry not", "effect quickly", "make haste", "waste not time". They were not meditative. They "knew their job well", "got down to work", and "despised the slothful". Their life was packed to the full. "Resurrected history" was portrayed as a kaleidoscope of events, an endless chain of actions.

The "active man" of early Russian drama was in keeping with

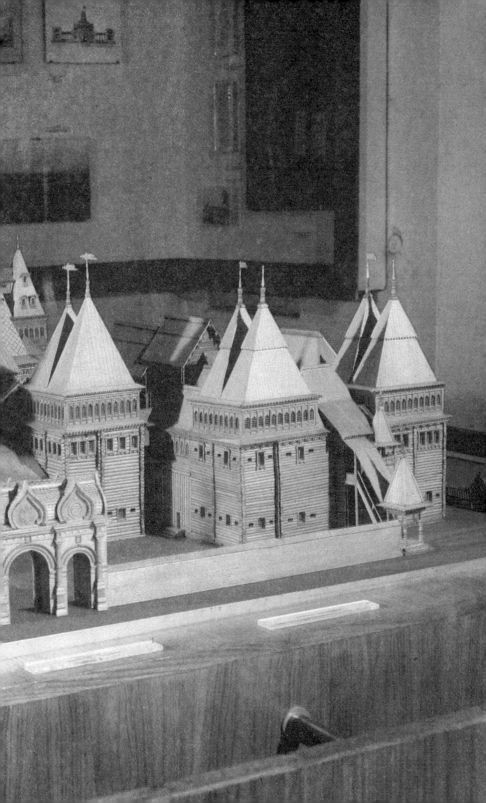

the style of behaviour that arose on the eve of and particularly during the period of the Petrine reforms. During this period the old ideal of "comeliness", "propriety" and "decorum" collapsed. Whereas in the Middle Ages it was considered proper to act calmly and deliberately (*kosno*) without "intense and bestial zeal", now it was positive to be energetic. It was in the latter half of the seventeenth century that the word *kosnost* acquired a pejorative meaning.

Tsar Alexis chose efficient men and demanded constant diligence from them: "Be ever assiduous and vigilant all the while, constantly on the alert and keep your wits about you." [75] In carrying out their sovereign's commands, his "close" advisers, such as Afanasy Ordin-Nashchokin or Artamon Matveyev, laboured ceaselessly "without respite".

The life that the visitors to the court theatre watched on the stage was certainly not conducive to repose. It was a motley, changeable life, in which transitions from grief to joy, merriment to tears, hope to despair and vice versa were quick and sudden. The characters in the plays bemoaned "fickle", "accursed", "treacherous" luck, Dame Fortune whose wheel raises some and casts down others. The "resurrected world" consisted of contradictions and antitheses.

The tsar's new amusement was not only entertainment ("comedy can cheer a man and turn all human care into joy"), but also a school in which one could "learn many good ... lessons in order to renounce wrong-doing and embrace that which is good". The theatre was a mirror in which the spectator recognised and understood himself.

Many ideas of European Baroque were reflected in this mirror, first and foremost, its favourite postulate that life is a stage and people are the actors. In the mirror one could also see a certain reflection of Russia in the process of Europeanisation, as with extraordinary energy she joined in concert with the great European powers on equal terms. The official culture of the latter half of the seventeenth century shows a high degree of confidence in Russia's success and in the greatness of its historic mission. This explains why Russian art of this period, in drawing on the experience of European Baroque, took mainly that which was positive and optimistic. The world of court poetry and court drama is a fickle world, full of conflicts and contradictions. But in the final analysis good and justice triumph, harmony is restored and peoples and countries rejoice and prosper.

The type of professional writer and convinced humanitarian represented by Simeon of Polotsk, Sylvester Medvedev and Karion Istomin did not immediately disappear in the Petrine age. Stefan

Yavorsky (1658-1722), *locum tenens* of the patriarchal throne and later president of the newly instituted Synod, was such a person, a brilliant orator and poet, who in his youth had been crowned with the title of poet laureate at the Kiev-Mogila Academy. So was Dimitry of Rostov (1651-1709), a playwright, composer of fine lyrical verse, and prolific prose writer, who is famous for the multi-volume *Great Menology*. But gradually Peter the Great relegated the Baroque humanitarians into the background. He had no need of them for a variety of reasons.

The very type of Baroque writer from the "Latiniser" school seemed to Peter to be an obstacle to transforming Russia. According to the Baroque philosophy of art, the poet was accountable only to God. Dimitry of Rostov, who compiled *The Great Menology* as he had vowed he would, ordered that the draft of this great work be placed in his coffin, so that he could use it to justify himself in his future life. Peter, however, believed that poets were answerable not to God, but to the tsar, that they did not form the elite of the nation and were no different from any other subject. All inhabitants of Russia were accountable to Peter and the state.

Peter broke with the "Latinisers" also because the culture that they fostered was of an exclusively humanitarian nature. Peter's reforms were imbued with the idea of usefulness, and there was no usefulness, no direct, immediate, palpable benefit from the "Latinisers". Peter advanced a different type of writer. The intellectual, who composed in keeping with a vow or his inner convictions, was replaced by the servant who wrote when commissioned or ordered. Peter promoted a new type of culture. Whereas for the "Latinisers" who created Moscow Baroque poetry was the queen of the arts, now in the Baroque of St Petersburg it was the servant of the natural sciences and practical disciplines. Poetry turned into an embellishment of "useful" books, such as Leonty Magnitsky's *Arithmetic* in which mathematical rules were attired in rhythmical speech.

Whereas in the time of Simeon of Polotsk and his pupils the whole world, all the elements of the universe, including man, were perceived as the Word, now the word too became a thing. From Simeon of Polotsk's "Museum of Rarities" to the St Petersburg Kunstkammer, a real museum of monstrosities and curiosities— this was the evolution of Russian Baroque. The Word was the symbol of Moscow Baroque, but the symbol of St Petersburg Baroque was the Thing.

Under Peter Russia produced many new things for the first time in its history—a fleet, a theatre open to the general public, an Academy of Sciences, parks and park sculpture; it also produced new clothes, new manners, a new style of social behaviour, and even a new capital. The production of things replaced the production of words, which is why the Petrine period is sometimes called the "most unliterary" period in Russian history. Did this mean the decline of literature? The answer is yes, it did, in a certain sense.

There was naturally a deterioration in style, language became macaronic and borrowing and barbarisms abounded. The world of the Russian was in a state of rapid transformation. These changes had to be recorded immediately, more and more new things had to be "given names", and this was done by "bad" style. Literature ceased to be professional. Whereas under Tsar Alexis writing was the prerogative of people with a good humanitarian education, under Peter a tribe of dilettantes multiplied rapidly. The following example illustrates the extent of this dilettantism: in the Petrine period poems (in the genre of the love elegy) were composed by society ladies in St Petersburg from such noble families as the Cherkasskys, Trubetskoys, etc. The Empress Elizabeth herself was active in the field of pursuit of poetry. Dilettantism is a symptom of decline.

Yet there were also positive elements in all this. The secularisation of culture, its freeing from the tutelage and control of the Church, resulted in the liberation of subject matter and plot. Literature not only served practical aims; it also entertained, and under Peter the bans were lifted on humour, merrymaking and the theme of love, which were topical not only in the Middle Ages, but also in the period of Moscow Baroque. Outside state commissions a writer was free in his choice of themes and plots, in so far as he was not bound by religious ideology. This "literary step forward" was also a reform in its way, and a reform with far-reaching consequences.

REFERENCES

[1] For a study of this work see: Кузьмина В. Д. *Рыцарский роман на Руси. Бова, Петр Златых Ключей.* Moscow, 1964.

[2] Веселовский С. Б. *Ономастикон.* Moscow, 1974, p. 42.

[3] For publication of the text of the third redaction see: *Изборник (Сборник произведений литературы Древней Руси).* Moscow, 1969 (серия "Библиотека всемирной литературы"), pp. 516-541. The text is quoted from this edition.

[4] Пропп В. Я. "Трансформация волшебных сказок". In the book: *Поэтика. Временник отдела словесных искусств.* Vol. IV, Leningrad, 1928, p. 82.

[5] Забелин И. Е. *Домашний быт русских царей и цариц в XVI и XVII столетиях.* Part II, Moscow, 1915, p. 181.

[6] For publication of the text see: Петровский М. *"История о славном короле Брунцвике". Памятники древней письменности*, Vol. XXV, St Petersburg, 1888, pp. 31-57; Polívka, Jiři, "Kronika o Bruncvíkoví v ruské litertuře". *Rozpravy České Akademie*, R. I., tr. 3, č. 5, Praha, 1892, pp. 19-133. For a study and bibliography of the tale see: Панченко А. М. *Чешско-русские литературные связи XVII века*. Leningrad, 1969, pp. 85-136. The text is quoted from J. Polívka's Prague edition.

[7] Попов А. *Изборник славянских и русских сочинений и статей, внесенных в хронографы русской редакции*. Moscow, 1869, p. 486.

[8] *История русской литературы*. Vol. II, Part 2, Moscow and Leningrad, 1948, p. 374. "Bruncvick is a gentle Slav prince ready to 'follow the example of his forebears' and fight for the glory of his land, but confounded by every unexpected encounter". (Петровский М. *История о славном короле Брунцвике*, p. 9.)

[9] For the published text see: Кузьмина В. Д. *Рыцарский роман на Руси*, pp. 275-331. The text is quoted from this edition.

[10] For a study and the text see: Малышев В. И. *"Повесть о Сухане". Из истории русской повести XVII века*. Moscow and Leningrad, 1956.

[11] For publication of the text see: Шляпкин И. А. *"Повесть о Василии Златовласом, королевиче Чешской земли". ПДП*, Vol. XXI, St Petersburg, 1882, pp. 1-27. The Shlyapkin edition, as Vladimir Budaragin has established, contains many errors ("О происхождении *Повести о Василии Златовласом, королевиче Чешской земли". ТОДРЛ*, Vol. XXV, 1970, pp. 268-275.).

[12] *Povidka o Vasiliji Zlatovlasem ...* Přel. a uvodem opetřila S. Mathauserová. Praha, 1982.

[13] Халанский М. Г. *Великорусские былины киевского цикла*. Warsaw, 1885, pp. 144-166; Халанский М. Г. *Южнославянские сказания о кралевиче Марке в связи с произведениями русского былевого эпоса*. Part II, Warsaw, 1894, pp. 327-335; Орлов А. С. *Переводные повести феодальной Руси и Московского государства XII-XVII вв*. Leningrad, 1934, pp. 134-136.

[14] The tale is quoted from the edition by Mikhail Skripil. *ТОДРЛ*, Vol. V, 1947, pp. 225-308. For a summary of information on the subject see: Скрипиль М. О. *"Повесть о Савве Грудцыне". ТОДРЛ*, Vol. II, 1935, pp. 181-214; *ТОДРЛ*, Vol. III, 1936, pp. 99-152.

[15] See: D. S. Likhachev's observations in the book: *Истоки русской беллетристики*, pp. 525-536.

[16] For publication of the text see: Перетц В. Н. "Из истории старинной русской повести". *Киевские университетские известия*, No. 8, 1907, pp. 33-36.

[17] *ТОДРЛ*, Vol. XXVII, 1972, pp. 290-304.

[18] Покровский Н. Н. "Исповедь алтайского крестьянина". In the book: *Памятники культуры. Новые открытия (Ежегодник 1978)*. Leningrad, 1979, p. 53.

[19] The text is quoted from the edition in the book: *Демократическая поэзия XVII века*.

[20] Ржига В. Ф. *"Повесть о Горе-Злочастии и песни о Горе". Slavia*, Roč, X, seš 1, Praha, 1931, pp. 40-66; *Slavia*, Roč, X, seš. 2, 1931, pp. 288-315; Малышев В. И. "Стихотворная параллель к *Повести о Горе и Злочастии* (стих 'покаянны о пьянстве')". *ТОДРЛ*, Vol. V, 1947, pp. 146-148.

[21] The *Tale* is written in three-bar stressed accentual verse with inter-stressed intervals ranging between one to three syllables. Mikhail Gasparov calls this type of verse "folk time" verse (see: Гаспаров М. Л. *Современный русский стих. Метрика и ритмика.* Moscow, 1974, pp. 352-371).

[22] Веселовский А. Н. "Разыскания в области русского духовного стиха. X. Западные легенды о древе креста и Слово Григория о трех крестных древах". *СОРЯС,* Vol. XXXII, No. 4, 1883, p. 396.

[23] Ibid., p. 397.

[24] Лихачев Д. С. *Развитие русской литературы X-XVII веков. Эпохи и стили,* pp. 149-150.

[25] For publication of the text see: Булгаков Ф. И. *"История семи мудрецов".* *ПДП,* Vols. XXIX, XXXV, Nos. 1-2, 1878-1880.

[26] Гринцер П. А. *Древнеиндийская проза (обрамленная повесть).* Moscow, 1963.

[27] For publication of the text see: Булгаков Ф. И. "Сборник повестей скорописи XVII в.". *ПДП,* Vol. I, 1878-1879, pp. 94-152; Державина О. А. *Фацеции. Переводная новелла в русской литературе XVII века.* Moscow, 1962, pp. 104-185. Olga Derzhavina's book contains a study of the sources and the literary history of the *facetiae.*

[28] For publication of the texts of *The Tale of the Drunkard, The Legend of the Peasant's Son, The Tale of Shemyaka's Trial,* and *The Tale of Karp Sutulov* see the book: *Русская демократическая сатира XVII века.*

[29] For publication of the text and a study see: Соколов Ю. М. *"Повесть о Карпе Сутулове. (Текст и разыскания к истории сюжета)". Труды Славянского Московского археологического общества,* Vol. IV, No. 2, 1914, pp. 3-40.

[30] Бакланова Н. А. "К вопросу о датировке *Повести о Фроле Скобееве". ТОДРЛ,* Vol. XIII, 1957, pp. 511-518. The text of the *Tale* is quoted from the edition in the book: *Изборник.* Moscow, 1970.

[31] *История русской литературы.* Vol. II, Part 2, M.-L., 1948, p. 238.

[32] See D. S. Likhachev's observations in the book: *Истоки русской беллетристики,* pp. 558-561.

[33] The text is quoted from the edition of Alexander Orlov. (*Русский филологический вестник.* Warsaw, 1906, Books 3-4, pp. 137-174.)

[34] Ibid., p. 42.

[35] *Древние российские стихотворения, собранные Киршею Даниловым.* Moscow, 1977, pp. 64-68.

[36] For the publication and study of the texts of this cycle see: Салмина М. А. *Повести о начале Москвы.* Moscow and Leningrad, 1964. The texts are quoted from this edition. Cf. also: Шамбинаго С. К. "Повести о начале Москвы". *ТОДРЛ,* Vol. III, 1936, pp. 59-98; Тихомиров М. Н. *Древняя Москва (XII-XV вв.).* Moscow, 1947, pp. 11-14, 209-223; Тихомиров М. Н. "Сказания о начале Москвы". *Исторические записки,* Vol. 32, 1950, pp. 233-241; Пушкарев Л. Н. *"Повесть о начале Москвы".* In the book: *Материалы по истории СССР.* Vol. 2, Moscow, 1955, pp. 211-246. The works in this cycle are known by various titles. We use the terminology proposed by Marina Salmina.

[37] On types of similes see: Лихачев Д. С. *Поэтика древнерусской литературы.* Second edition, Leningrad, 1971, pp. 193-202.

[38] Ключевский В. О. *Сочинения.* Vol. III, Moscow, 1957, p. 188.

[39] For publication of the text see: *Изборник*, pp. 675-683. The text is quoted from this edition.

[40] Дмитриева Р. П. *"Повесть о Тверском Отроче монастыре и исторические реалии"*. *ТОДРЛ*, Vol. XXIV, 1969, pp. 210-213. Ржига В. Ф. *"Из истории повести"*. *Известия Тверского педагогического института*, No. IV, 1928, pp. 97-117.

[41] *Истоки русской беллетристики*, pp. 491-500.

[42] *Лирика русской свадьбы.* Compiled by N. P. Kolpakova, Leningrad, 1973, p. 31.

[43] The credit for discovering "democratic satire" as a literary phenomenon must go to Varvara Adrianova-Peretts, who was responsible for the academic publication and study of the main works in this category. See: Адрианова-Перетц В. П. *Очерки по истории русской сатирической литературы XVII века.* Moscow and Leningrad 1937; *Русская демократическая сатира XVII века*; *Демократическая поэзия XVII века.*

[44] Бахтин М. М. *Творчество Франсуа Рабле и народная культура средневековья и Ренессанса.* Moscow, 1965; Лихачев Д. С., Панченко А. М. *"Смеховой мир" Древней Руси.* Leningrad, 1976.

[45] Лотман Ю. М., Успенский Б. А. *"Новые аспекты изучения культуры Древней Руси".* *Вопросы литературы*, No. 3, 1977, pp. 148-167.

[46] Богатырев П. Г. *Вопросы теории народного искусства.* Moscow, 1971, pp. 401-421.

[47] Демин А. С. *"Демократическая поэзия XVII в. в письмовниках и сборниках виршевых посланий".* *ТОДРЛ*, Vol. XXI, 1965, p. 77.

[48] Забелин И. Е. *Домашний быт русских царей в XVI и XVII ст.* Third edition, Part 1, Moscow, 1895, p. 375.

[49] Богатырев П. Г. *Вопросы теории народного искусства*, pp. 453-454.

[50] Лихачев Д. С. *"Древнерусский смех".* In the book: *Проблемы поэтики и истории литературы.* A collection of articles in honour of the 75th anniversary of M. M. Bakhtin. Saransk, 1973, p. 78.

[51] Flinn, J., *"Roman de Penat" dans la litterature française et dans les litteratures étrangères au Moyen Age,* Paris, 1963.

[52] Забелин И. Е. *История города Москвы.* Part 1, Moscow, 1905, pp. 630-634.

[53] Чистов К. В. *Русские народные социально-утопические легенды XVII-XIX вв.* Moscow, 1967, pp. 290-294.

[54] Лихачев Д. С. *Развитие русской литературы X-XVII веков. Эпохи и стили,* pp. 138-164; Робинсон А. Н. *Борьба идей в русской литературе XVII века.* Moscow, 1974.

[55] Archpriest Avvakum's literary heritage is constantly being enlarged by new discoveries. Recent finds include a new autograph of his *Life.* (See: *Пустозерский сборник. Автографы сочинений Аввакума и Епифания.* Prepared by N. S. Demkova, N. F. Droblenkova, L. I. Sazanova, Leningrad, 1975; Малышев В. И. "Об изучении наследия протопопа Аввакума". *Русская литература*, No. 4, 1968, pp. 89-92; Демкова Н. С. "Неизвестные и неизданные тексты из сочинений протопопа Аввакума". *ТОДРЛ*, Vol. XXI, 1965, pp. 211-239.) The fullest

selection of Avvakum's writings is that compiled by Y. L. Barskov in the book: *Памятники истории старообрядчества XVII в.* Book 1, No. 1, Leningrad, 1927. (*Русская историческая библиотека*, Vol. 39.) See also the following authoritative publications: *"Житие протопопа Аввакума, им самим написанное", и другие его сочинения.* Under the general editorship of N. K. Gudzii, Moscow, 1960; Робинсон А. Н. *Жизнеописания Аввакума и Епифания. Исследование и тексты.* Moscow, 1963. *"Житие протопопа Аввакума, им самим написанное" и другие его сочинения.* Irkutsk, 1979. Avvakum's works are quoted from the 1960 edition.

[56] *Материалы по истории раскола за первое время его существования.* Edited by N. I. Subbotin. Vol. 1, Moscow, 1875, pp. 28-31.

[57] For an account of the writing of the *Life* see: Демкова Н. С. *Житие протопопа Аввакума (творческая история произведения).* Leningrad, 1974.

[58] Лихачев Д. С., Панченко А. М. *"Смеховой мир" Древней Руси,* pp. 75-90.

[59] Робинсон А. Н. "Исповедь-проповедь (о художественности *Жития* Аввакума)" In the book: *Историко-филологические исследования.* A collection of articles on the 75th anniversary of Academician N. I. Konrad. Moscow, 1967, pp. 358-370.

[60] Quoted from the article: Малышев В. И. "Два неизвестных письма протопопа Аввакума". *ТОДРЛ.* Vol. XIV, 1958, p. 420.

[61] Quoted from the article: Малышев В. И. "Новые материалы о протопопе Аввакуме". *ТОДРЛ*, Vol. XXI, 1965, p. 343.

[62] See general works on the Russian version of European Baroque: Еремин И. П. "Поэтическиий стиль Симеона Полоцкого". *ТОДРЛ*, Vol. VI, 1948, pp. 125-163; Морозов А. А. "Проблема барокко XVII-начала XVIII в. (Состояние вопроса и задачи изучения)". *Русская литература*, No 3, 1962, pp. 3-38; Лихачев Д. С. *Развитие русской литературы X-XVII веков. Эпохи и стили,* pp. 165-214.

[63] Simeon of Polotsk's biography set out in the book: Татарский И. А. *Симеон Полоцкий (его жизнь и деятельность).* Moscow, 1886; Майков Л. Н. *Очерки из истории русской литературы XVII и XVIII столетий.* St Petersburg, 1889.

[64] Simeon of Polotsk's poetry-writing is presented most fully in the following works: *Вирши. Силлабическая поэзия XVII-XVIII веков.* Edited by P. N. Berkov, introductory article by I. N. Rozanov. Leningrad, 1935; *Симеон Полоцкий. Избранные сочинения.* Preparation of text, article and commentaries by I. P. Eremin. Moscow and Leningrad, 1953; *Русская силлабическая поэзия XVII-XVIII вв.* The texts of Simeon of Polotsk, and also Sylvester Medvedev and Karion Istomin published in these works are quoted without references.

[65] Еремин И. П. "Поэтический стиль Симеона Полоцкого", p. 125.

[66] Simeon of Polotsk believed that a writer should not burden himself with a family, and saw the vow of celibacy as the best solution. "Truly, it is irksome to read a multitude of books and carry out the wishes of a wife in the home!.. Incline yourself to books, to a quiet place. Seek to live out your days without the misfortunes of matrimony."

[67] On Sylvester Medvedev see: Прозоровский А. "Сильвестр Медведев (его жизнь и деятельность)". *ЧОИДР*, Books 2-4, 1896; Козловский И. *Сильвестр Медведев.* Киев, 1895.

[68] *ЧОИДР*, Book 3, 1896, section IV, pp. 373-374.

[69] On Karion Istomin see: Браиловский С. Н. *Один из пестрых XVII столетия.* St Petersburg, 1902.

[70] For an account of the beginning of the Russian theatre and its repertoire see the first two volumes of the series *Ранняя русская драматургия (XVII-первая половина XVIII в.): Первые пьесы русского театра.* Prepared by O. A. Derzhavina, A. S. Demin, E. K. Romodanovskaya. Edited by A. N. Robinson. Moscow, 1972; *Русская драматургия последней четверти XVII и начала XVIII в.* Prepared by O. A. Derzhavina, A. S. Demin, V. P. Grebenyuk. Edited by O. A. Derzhavina. Moscow, 1972. The texts of the plays are quoted from these editions.

[71] Богоявленский С. К. *Московский театр при царях Алексее и Петре.* Moscow, 1914, p. 8.

[72] Лихачев Д. С. *Поэтика древнерусской литературы,* pp. 321-330.

[73] Ibid., pp. 324-326.

[74] Демин А. С. *Русская литература второй половины XVII-начала XVIII века. Новые художественные представления о мире, природе, человеке.* Moscow, 1977, p. 100.

[75] Ibid., p. 100.

Let us now attempt to sum up Russian literary development.

Like most other European peoples, Russia bypassed the

CONCLUSION

slave-owning stage. For this reason Russia did not have an antique stage in the development of its culture. The Eastern Slavs went straight from the communal-patriarchal stage to feudalism. This transition took place remarkably quickly over the vast territory inhabited by Eastern Slav tribes and various Finno-Ugrian peoples.

The absence of this or that stage in historical development demands "compensation". This is usually provided by ideology and culture that draw strength from the experience of neighbouring peoples.

The emergence of literature, moreover, a literature highly developed for its day, could take place only with the cultural assistance of the neighbouring countries of Byzantium and Bulgaria. The special importance of the cultural experience of Bulgaria must be stressed. The written language and literature appeared in Bulgaria a century earlier in

similar conditions: Bulgaria did not have a slave-owning formation either and assimilated the cultural experience of Byzantium. Bulgaria assimilated Byzantine culture in circumstances similar to those that obtained a century later in Russia when Russia assimilated Byzantine and Bulgarian culture: Russia acquired Byzantine cultural experience not only in its direct state, but also in a form "adapted" by Bulgaria to the needs of a society that was becoming feudal.

The need for accelerated cultural development explains why Russia was able to assimilate the cultural phenomena of Byzantium and Bulgaria. It was not just a matter of necessity, but of the fact that Old Russian culture of the tenth and eleventh centuries was young and flexible, and therefore, had little trouble in assimilating the experience of other cultures. The absence of deep-rooted traditions of class culture during the rapid development of class relations compelled Russian society to absorb and assimilate outside elements of class culture and to create its own. The genre system of Bulgarian literature, both that which had been translated from the Greek and that which was Bulgarian in origin, was reorganised in Russia. This reorganisation took two forms: the selection of those genres that were essential and the creation of new genres. The former took place in the actual transfer of literary works to Old Russia. The latter required considerable time and took several centuries.

The system of Byzantine genres was transferred to Russia in an interesting, "condensed" form. Russia needed only those genres that were directly connected with the Church or of a general philosophical nature in keeping with the new attitude to nature.

On the other hand, however, genres were needed that did not exist in either Byzantine or Bulgarian literature.

The genres of mediaeval Russian literature were closely connected with their use in everyday life, both secular and religious. This distinguishes them from the literary genres of the modern age.

In the Middle Ages all the arts, literature included, were of an "applied" nature. Divine service required specific genres for specific parts of the religious worship. Certain genres were intended for the complex monastic life. Even the monks' private reading was strictly regulated. Hence certain types of *vitae*, certain types of canticles, certain types of books regulating Divine service, church and monastic life, etc. The genre system even included such unique works as the Gospels, the Psalms, the Epistles of the Apostles, and so on.

Even from this brief and extremely generalised list of religious genres it will be clear that some of them could develop new works (for example, the *vitae*, which were required to be written in connection with the canonisation of new saints), whereas some genres were strictly limited to the existing works and the creation of new works within them was impossible. Both the former and the latter, however, could not change: the formal features of the genres were strictly determined by their use and by tradition.

The secular genres that came to Russia from Byzantium and Bulgaria were somewhat less constrained by external formal and traditional requirements. These secular genres were not connected with special uses in everyday life and were therefore freer in their external, formal features.

The genre system transferred to Russia from Byzantium and Bulgaria served the highly regulated and ceremonial life of the Middle Ages, but did not satisfy all demands for the artistic word.

The upper layers of feudal society had at their disposal both bookish and oral genres. The illiterate mass of the people satisfied their need for the artistic word with oral genres. Books were accessible to the mass of the people only through Divine service.

The literary-floric genre system of mediaeval Russia was in some respects more rigid, in others less, but taken as a whole it was very traditional, highly formalised, closely connected with ritual and not susceptible to change. The more rigid it was, the more it was subjected to change in connection with changes in historical reality, everyday life, ritual and practical requirements. It had to react to all the changes in real life.

The early feudal states were very insecure. The unity of the state was constantly threatened by the internecine strife of the feudal lords that reflected the centrifugal forces of society. In order to maintain its unity a high level of public morality was needed, a strong sense of honour, loyalty and self-sacrifice, deep patriotism and a highly developed literature—the genres of political writing, genres that extolled love of one's country, lyrical-epic genres.

In the absence of strong economic and military relations, the unity of the state could not exist without the intensive development of personal patriotism. What was needed were works that would testify clearly to the historical and political unity of the Russian people. Works that would strongly condemn princely strife. One striking feature of Old Russian literature of this period is the awareness of the unity of the Russian land without any tribal differences, the awareness of the unity of Russian history and the Russian state.

These features of the political life of Old Russia differ from the political life of Byzantium and Bulgaria. The ideas of unity differed albeit in the fact that they concerned the Russian land, and not Bulgaria or Byzantium. This is why Russia needed its own works and its own genres.

This explains why, in spite of the existence of two mutually complementary systems of genres, the literary and the folkloric, Russian literature of the eleventh to thirteenth centuries was in a process of genre formation. In various ways and from different sources works constantly emerged that stood apart from the traditional genre systems and violated or creatively combined them. As a result of the search for new genres in Russian literature and folklore many works appeared that cannot easily be ascribed to any of the firmly established traditional genres. They stand outside the genre traditions.

Breaking with traditional forms was quite customary in Old Russia. All the more or less outstanding literary works based on profound inner needs broke out of the confines of traditional forms.

In this process of intensive genre formation certain works are unique in respect of genre (Daniel the Exile's *Supplication* and Vladimir Monomachos' *Instruction, Autobiography* and *Letter to Oleg Svyatoslavich*), while others were steadily continued (*The Primary Chronicle* in Russian chronicle-writing, and *The Tale of the Blinding of Vasilko of Terebovl* in subsequent tales of princely misdeeds), and a third group was followed by isolated attempts to continue them in respect of genre (*The Lay of Igor's Host* in *The Trans-Doniad*).

The absence of strict genre limits promoted the appearance of many interesting and highly artistic works.

The processes of genre formation led to the intensive use in this period of the experience of folklore (in *The Tale of Bygone Years* and other chronicles, *The Lay of Igor's Host, The Lay of the Ruin of the Russian Land*, Daniel the Exile's *Supplication* and *Sermon*, etc.). The process of genre formation that took place from the eleventh to thirteenth centuries was resumed in the sixteenth century and fairly intensive in the seventeenth century as well.

The absence of the antique stage in cultural development increased the importance of literature and art in the development of the Eastern Slavs. Literature and the other arts, as we have seen, acquired a most responsible role, that of supporting the accelerated development of Russian society from the eleventh to the early thirteenth century and of mitigating the negative aspects of this accelerated development, namely, princely strife and the disintegration of the Russian state. This is why the social role of all forms of art was extremely great in that period for all the Eastern Slavs.

The sense of historical unity, appeals for political alliance, condemnation of the abuse of power spread over this vast territory with its large and variegated population and its numerous semi-independent principalities.

The level of the arts corresponded to the level of social responsibility that fell to their lot. But these arts did not have their own antique stage, only echoes of an alien one via Byzantium. Therefore, when in the Russia of the fourteenth and the early fifteenth century the socio-economic conditions were created for the emergence of the Pre-Renaissance, and this Pre-Renaissance did in fact appear, it was immediately faced with unusual and unfavourable conditions from the historico-cultural viewpoint. The role of "Russian Antiquity" was ascribed to pre-Mongol Russia, Russia of the period of its independence.

The literature of the late fourteenth and the early fifteenth century turned to the works of the eleventh to the early thirteenth century. Certain works of this period are a mechanical imitation of Metropolitan Hilarion's *Sermon on Law and Grace, The Tale of Bygone Years, The Tale of Batu's Capture of Ryazan* and, above all, *The Lay of Igor's Host* (in *The Trans-Doniad*). In architecture we find a similar return to the monuments of the eleventh to thirteenth centuries (in Novgorod, Tver and Vladimir). The same phenomenon is found in painting, political thought (the desire to revive the political traditions of Kiev and Vladimir Zalessky), and folk art (it was this period that witnessed the intensive formation of the Kiev cycle of *bylinas*). But all this was insufficient for the Pre-Renaissance, and therefore the strengthening of relations with countries that had been through the antique stage of culture acquired great importance. Russia revived and strengthened its links with Byzantium and the countries of Byzantine cultural influence, first and foremost, the Southern Slavs.

One of the most characteristic and significant features of the Pre-Renaissance, and later, to an even greater extent, the Renaissance itself, was the emergence of historical awareness. The static nature of the earlier perception of the world was replaced by a dynamic attitude in this period. This historicism is connected with all the main features of the Pre-Renaissance and the Renaissance proper.

First and foremost, this historicism is organically connected with the discovery of the value of the individual and with a special interest in the historical past. The idea of the historical changeability of the world is linked with interest in man's inner life, with the idea of the world as motion, and with dynamism of style. Nothing is finished, so it cannot be expressed in words; passing time cannot be caught. It can only be reproduced to some extent by a stream of words, by a dynamic and prolix style, a mass of synonyms, shades of meaning, associative sequences.

The Pre-Renaissance in Russian representational art is associated, first and foremost, with the work of Theophanes the Greek and Andrei Rublev. They are two radically different artists, but precisely because of this they are most characteristic of the Pre-Renaissance when the role of the artist's personality came into its own and individual differences became typical phenomena of the age. The Pre-Renaissance is felt less strongly in literature. Characteristic of this period are the "philological" interests of the scribes, the "braiding of words", the emotional style, etc. When, in the middle of the fifteenth century, the main prerequisites for the formation of the Renaissance began to collapse one after another, and the Russian Pre-Renaissance did not develop into Renaissance, the struggle against heresy ended in a victory for the official Church. The formation of the centralised state took up a great deal of spiritual strength. Relations with Byzantium and Western Europe weakened as a result of the fall of Constantinople and the conclusion of the Florence Union, which heightened mistrust of Catholic countries.

Every great style and every world movement has its own historical functions, its own historical mission. The Renaissance was connected with the liberation of the human individual from the mediaeval corporation. Without this liberation there could have been no modern age in culture and, particularly, in literature.

The fact that the Pre-Renaissance did not develop into the Renaissance in Russia had serious consequences: the as yet immature style soon began to grow formal and rigid, and the turning to "antiquity", the constant returning to the experience of pre-Mongol Russia, to the period of independence, soon acquired features of that special conservatism that played a negative role in the development not only of Russian literature, but of Russian culture in general in the sixteenth and seventeenth centuries.

The transition to the modern age became slow and drawn-out. There was no Renaissance in Russia, but there were certain features of the Renaissance throughout the sixteenth, seventeenth and part of the eighteenth century.

The main difference between the Renaissance and the Pre-Renaissance was the former's secular nature, the liberation from the all-pervading religiousness of the Middle Ages.

In the sixteenth century the theological view of human society gradually and cautiously began to recede into the past. The "Divine laws" still retained their authority, but alongside references to the Holy Scriptures there appeared Renaissance-type references to natural laws. Several sixteenth-century writers refer to the order of things in nature as a model for imitation by man in his social and political life. The projects of Ermolai-Erasmus rested on the idea that bread was the basis of economic, social and spiritual life. Ivan Peresvetov makes hardly any use of theological arguments in his writings. The development of polemical writing in the sixteenth century is connected with belief in the power of argument, the power of the written word. Never before had there been so much disputing in Old Russia, as in the late fifteenth and the sixteenth century. The development of polemical writing rode the crest of the upsurge of belief in reason.

The development of publicistic thought led to the emergence of new forms of literature. The sixteenth century is characterised by complex and many-sided searchings in the sphere of artistic form, genres. The set scheme of genres collapsed. Forms employed in official documents began to enter literature, and literary elements found their way into official documents. The new themes are those of vital, concrete political struggle. Many of the themes, before finding their way to lilerature, had formed the content of official documents. Diplomatic epistles, council resolutions, petitions, and lists of enactments became the forms of literary works.

The use of official document genres for literary purposes meant both the development of fantasy, previously very limited in literary works, and also the endowing of this fantasy with the outer appearance of authenticity. The emergence of fantasy in sixteenth-century chronicles was connected with the inner requirements of the development of literature as it broke away from practical functions and was stimulated by the insistent publicistic demands made upon the chronicle at the time. The chronicle had to convince readers of the infallibility and sanctity of state power, and not only register (albeit in most biassed form) individual historical facts. The chronicle became a school of patriotism, a school of respect for state power.

The political legend made itself felt most powerfully in history. Russian people began to meditate more and more on questions of the world-wide importance of their country. In particular, Philotheus' theory of Moscow as the third and last Rome became extremely widespread.

The political legend was one of the manifestations of the strengthening of artistic fantasy in literature. Old Russian literature of the preceding period feared the fantastic and imaginary as lies and falsehood. It sought to write about real fact, or at least what was taken to be real fact. The fantastic could come from outside, in translations of the *Alexandreid, The Tale of the Indian Empire, Stefanit and Ikhnilat,* and others. Moreover the fantastic was regarded either as the truth or as a fable, a parable, genres that also existed in the Gospels.

The development of Old Russian literature throughout all its stages is the gradual struggle for the right to artistic "untruth". Artistic truth gradually ousted the truth of everyday reality. Literary fantasy became legitimate, permissible from the viewpoint of the new attitude to literature and the world. But while coming into its rights fantasy wore the guise for a long time of that which had really existed or did really exist. This is why in the sixteenth century the genre of the official document as a form of literary work entered literature at the same time as fantasy.

The movement of literature towards the document and the document towards literature was the natural process of "breaking down" the borders between literature and official writing. This process in literature was linked with the administrative life of the Russian state, with the concurrent process of the growth and development of genres of state correspondence and record keeping and the appearance of archives. It was highly necessary for the breaking down of the old and development of the new system of genres, for the "emancipation" and secularisation of literature.

All the changes in literary styles are linked with the developments in the ideological and genre aspects of literature. The emotional style that appeared in the late fourteenth and the early fifteenth century was unable to develop into the style of the Renaissance in the late fifteenth and the sixteenth century. Therefore the fate of this style, that had been artificially arrested in its development, was an unfortunate one. It became highly formal, individual devices grew rigid and were used and repeated automatically, literary convention became extremely involved, and as a result ceased to be used properly. A certain "conventional mannerism" appeared. Everything was very elaborate, but also dry and lifeless. This coincided with the increased official nature of literature. The conventional and stylistic formulae and canons were used not because the content of the work demanded them, but depending on the official, i.e., state and church, attitude to this or that phenomenon described in the work. Works and their individual parts became very large. Beauty was replaced by dimensions. There developed a taste for monumentality, which, unlike that of the pre-Mongol period, was distinguished primarily by large dimensions. The authors sought to impress their readers by the size of their works, the length of their eulogies, the amount of repetitions and the complexity of their style.

The seventeenth century was an age of preparation for radical changes in Russian literature. A reorganisation of the structure of literature as a whole began. The number of genres increased greatly due to the introduction into literature of forms of official documents, which were given purely literary functions, at the expense of folklore and translated literature. The works became more entertaining and descriptive, with a wider range of themes and plot. All this is explained mainly by the enormous growth in the social experience of literature, the richer social themes and the widening of the social range of readers and writers.

Literature spread out in all directions and the centripetal forces that lay at the basis of its stability grew weaker. Centrifugal forces developed in literature. It became more flexible and ready for reorganisation and the creation of a new system, the literary system of the modern age.

Of particular importance in this reorganisation were historical changes. The events of the Time of Troubles shook and changed Russian people's view of historical events as dependent on the will of princes and sovereigns. At the end of the sixteenth century the Moscow ruling dynasty came to an end, the peasant war began, and with it came the Polish and Swedish intervention. The participation of the common people in the fate of their country was unusually strong in this period. They made themselves felt not only by revolting, but also by taking part in the discussions about who should accede to the throne.

The historical works about the Time of Troubles testify to the rapid growth in the social experience of all classes of society. This new social experience made itself felt in the secularisation of historical literature. It was at this time that the theological view of human history, state power and man himself was finally ousted from political practice, although it still remained in the sphere of official declarations. Although historical writings on the Time of Troubles speak of this period as the punishment of people for their sins, firstly, the sins themselves are seen on a very broad social scale (the main fault with the Russian people is their "wordless silence" and their social tolerance of crimes by the authorities), and secondly, there is a desire to discover the real reasons behind these events, primarily in the characters of historical personages. In the descriptions of these personages one finds a hitherto unusual mixture of good and evil features and the idea emerges that a person's character is formed under the influence of external circumstances and is able to change. This type of new attitude to man is not only reflected unconsciously in literature, but also begins to be defined. The author of the Russian articles in the 1617 *Chronograph* states openly his new attitude to the individual as a complex combination of good and bad qualities.

One more feature marks the new approach to themes by the writers of the early seventeenth century: it is their subjective interpretation of events. These writers were for the most part active participants in the Time of Troubles. Therefore their works are in part memoires. They write about what they have seen and seek to justify the standpoint which they adopted at this or that time. In their works we find the beginning of the writer's interest in himself which was to become very strong throughout the seventeenth century.

There can be no doubt that the features of Renaissance which made themselves felt in the sixteenth century influenced historical narrative of the first quarter of the seventeenth century. It was not the only element that affected seventeenth-century Russian literature, however. There were also earlier ones. The weak pulse of lyrical feeling for man continued to throb in the seventeenth century. This lyrical attitude continued from the fourteenth and fifteenth centuries, from the Pre-Renaissance elements that had "survived" in Russian culture reappearing in *The Tale of Martha and Mary, The Tale of Juliana Osorgina* and *The Tale of the Page Monastery of Tver*. This is perfectly natural: after being artificially checked, lyrical element continued to be felt for another three centuries, challenging the pressure of the hard and "cold" sentiments of the "second monumentalism".

The social spread of literature affected both its readers and writers. In the middle of the seventeenth century democratic literature appeared. It was the literature of the exploited class. Thus, the differentiation of literature began.

The so-called "literature of the townsfolk (*posad*)" was written by democratic writers, read by democratic readers, and dealt with subjects of interest to the democratic milieu. It was close to folklore, to colloquial and business speech. It was often anti-government and anti-clerical and belonged to the burlesque culture of the people. In many respects it was similar to the popular book in the Western Europe, but it contained a very powerful explosive element that destroyed the mediaeval system of literature.

Democratic works of the seventeenth century are important for the historico-literary process in another respect also. Literary development, even when it is very slow, is never smooth. It proceeds in fits and starts, and these fits and starts are always connected with an extension of its field of activity.

The first major extension of this kind took place in the fifteenth century with the invention of a cheaper writing material than parchment. Paper led to the appearance of mass forms of literature: collections intended for widespread individual reading. The reader and the scribe were often one and the same person: the scribe copied works that he liked, compiling miscellanies for private, "unofficial" reading.

In the seventeenth century works of a democratic nature provided a new stimulus towards mass literature. They were read so widely that literary historians of the nineteenth and the early twentieth century considered them cheap and unworthy of study. They were written in an untidy or office cursive and rarely bound straightway, remaining in quires and circulating among people of little means. This was the second "stimulus towards mass literature". The third came in the eighteenth century, when literature began to be printed on a large scale and journalism developed with its new, European genres.

The features typical of seventeenth-century democratic literature can also be observed outside these limits. There are many echoes of it in translated literature, in particular, translations of pseudo-tales of chivalry. Democratic literature does not stand apart in the historico-literary process of the time.

The changes in foreign influences that took place in Russian literature of the seventeenth century are also characteristic of this period of transition to the literature of the modern age. It is usually considered that the original orientation of Russian literature on Byzantine literature was replaced in the seventeenth century by orientation on Western Europe. But the orientation on the West European countries is less important than the orientation on certain types of literatures.

Russian literature, like any great literature, was always closely connected with the literatures of other countries. In Old Russia this connection was just as considerable as in the eighteenth and nineteenth centuries. We can even say that until the seventeenth century Russian literature formed a kind of unity with the literatures of the Southern Slavs, although this unity was limited to certain genres, mainly religious ones. With the development of national principles in all the Slavonic literatures by the seventeenth century South Slavonic and Byzantine-Slavonic connections with

Russian literature became somewhat weaker and literary relations with the Western Slavs grew more intense, although of a different type. These relations developed not so much along the line of religion, as along the line of fiction and literature intended for individual reading. Consequently, the type of foreign work to which Russian literature turned also changed. Formerly it had turned primarily to works of the mediaeval type, to genres already traditional in Russian literature. Now interest grew in works characteristic of the modern age. This is particularly evident in drama and poetry. However, initially it was not the finest works that were translated, not the literary innovations, but works that were old and to some extent of local value (in drama, for example). But it was not long before Russian literature entered into direct contact with literature of a higher order, with first-rate writers and their works. This was in the eighteenth century.

It was not just a question of the types of literature to which Russia turned, but of how it turned to them. We have seen that in the eleventh to fifteenth centuries literary works of the Byzantine sphere of influence were transplanted to Russia and continued to develop there. It cannot be said that this type of foreign influence disappeared in the seventeenth century, but a new type of influence also appeared, typical of the literature of the modern age. In the seventeenth century not so much works, as style, literary devices, trends, aesthetic tastes and ideas were transplanted.

Russian Baroque can be seen as one of the manifestations of the new type of influence. Russian Baroque was not just individual works translated from Polish or brought from the Ukraine and Byelorussia. It was, first and foremost, a literary trend that emerged under Polish-Ukrainian-Byelorussian influence. It consisted of new ideological trends, new themes, new genres, new intellectual interests and, of course, a new style.

Any more or less significant influence from outside makes itself felt only when inner requirements arise that shape this influence and incorporate it in the historico-literary process. Baroque, too, came to Russia as a consequence of national requirements, and fairly strong ones at that. Baroque, which in other countries had replaced the Renaissance as its antithesis, was close to the Renaissance in its historico-literary role in Russia. It was of an enlightening nature, in many respects promoted the liberation of the individual and was connected with the process of secularisation, unlike in Western Europe, where in some cases in its initial stages Baroque signified precisely the opposite—a return to the Church.

Nevertheless Russian Baroque was not the Renaissance. It could not be compared with the West European Renaissance in scale or importance. Its temporal and social limitations are no accident. They are due to the fact that the preparations for the Russian Renaissance, which took Baroque forms, went on too long. Individual Renaissance features began to appear in literature before they could merge into a definite cultural movement. The Renaissance "lost" some of its features on the way to its emergence.

Therefore the importance of Russian Baroque as a kind of Renaissance, a transition to the literature of the modern age, is limited to the role of the "final stimulus" that brought Russian literature close to the type of literature of the modern age. The personal element in literature, which prior to Baroque had appeared sporadically and in various spheres, developed into a definite system. The secularisation of literature that had been taking place throughout the sixteenth century and the first half of the seventeenth century and manifested itself in different aspects of literary creativity, was completed in the Baroque period. It was in the Baroque period that the new genres which had been accumulating and the changing significance of the old genres led to the development of a new system of genres, the system of the modern age.

The emergence of a new system of genres was the main feature of the transition of Russian literature from the mediaeval type to the type of the modern age.

Not all historians and specialists in literature and the arts recognise the existence of the Pre-Renaissance and subsequent individual Renaissance phenomena in Old Russia. This is primarily because the Italian Renaissance is regarded as the "ideal model". It is considered to be unique. But in fact the Renaissance as an age or the Renaissance phenomena that spread over a long period of time, were the natural transition from the Middle Ages to the modern age, a transition which is traditionally regarded as the crowning phase of the Middle Ages. Moreover, the Renaissance is not an evaluatory category. There is not only the Italian Renaissance, but the North European Renaissance, the Czech Renaissance, the Polish Renaissance and many others. In its classical mediaeval period, the eleventh to the early thirteenth century (prior to the Mongol invasion), Russia was on the same level as other European cultures, whereas in the period of the Pre-Renaissance and the subsequent period, when individual Renaissance elements gradually emerged in Russian literature preparing its transition to the modern age, we can say it was

"lagging behind". We use the term "lagging behind" convention-
ally, since cultures cannot be compared and each culture has its
own lasting values.

All in all we can sum up as follows: the whole historico-literary
process from the eleventh to the early eighteenth century is a
process of the formation of literature, but of literature that exists
not for itself, but for society.

Literature is an essential component of a country's history.

The uniqueness of Old Russian literature lies not only in the
character of its individual works, but also in its special path of
development, a path that is very closely linked with Russian history
and in keeping with the requirements of Russian reality. Old
Russian literature was always concerned with the broad social
problems of its day.

INTRODUCTION

§ I

Ленин В. И. *О литературе и искусстве.* М., 1976; Маркс К., Энгельс Ф. *Об искусстве.* т. 1-2, М., 1976; Белинский В. Г. "Статья о народной поэзии" *Полное собрание сочинений,* т. 5, М.,

BIBLIOGRAPHY

RUSSIAN AND SOVIET LITERATURE

1954; Добролюбов Н. А. "О степени участия народности в развитии русской литературы". *Собрание сочинений* в 9 томах. М.-Л., 1961, т. 2; Горький М. *О литературе. Литературно-критические статьи.* М., 1955; М., 1961.

§ II. READERS AND ANTHOLOGIES

Воинские повести Древней Руси. Вступит. статья. Л. А. Дмитриева. Л., 1985; Гудзий Н. К. *Хрестоматия по древней русской литературе XI-XVII веков.* 8-е изд. М., 1973; *Древняя русская литература. Хрестоматия.* Сост. Н. И. Прокофьев. М., 1980; *Изборник (Сборник произведений литературы Древней Руси).* М., 1969 (Библиотека всемирной литературы, сер. I, т. XV); *Изборник: Повести Древней Руси.* М., 1986; *Памятники литературы Древней Руси (ПЛДР).* Сост. и общая ред. Л. А. Дмитриева и Д. С. Лихачева: 1) *Начало русской литературы. XI-начало XII века.* М., 1978; 2) *XII век.* М., 1980; 3) *XIII век.* М., 1981; 4) *XIV-середина XV века.* М., 1981; 5) *Вторая половина XV века.* М., 1982; 6) *Конец XV-первая половина XVI века.* М., 1984; 7) *Середина XVI века.* М., 1985; 8) *Вторая половина XVI века.* М., 1986; 9) *Ко-*

нец XVI-начало XVII века. М., 1987 (to be completed); *Русская повесть XVII века*, М.-Л., 1954. *Русские повести XV-XVI веков*. М.-Л., 1958; *Художественная проза Киевской Руси XI-XIII веков*. Сост., перевод и примеч. И. П. Еремина и Д. С. Лихачева. М., 1957; *Повести Древней Руси XI-XII веков*. Вступит. статья Д. С. Лихачева. Л., 1983.

§ III. HISTORIES OF OLD RUSSIAN LITERATURE

Гудзий Н. К. *История древней русской литературы*. 7-е изд. М., 1966; Еремин И. П. *Лекции по древнерусской литературе*. 2-е изд. Л., 1987; *История русской литературы* в 10-ти тт., т. I-II, ч. 1-2, М.-Л., 1941; т. II. ч. 1. М.-Л., 1945; т. II, ч. 2, М.-Л., 1948; *История русской литературы* в 3-х тт., т. I, М.-Л., 1958; *История русской литературы* в 4-х тт., т. I, Л., 1980; *История русской литературы XI-XVII веков*. Под ред. Д. С. Лихачева. 2-е изд. М., 1985; Кусков В. В. 1) *История древнерусской литературы*. Курс лекций. 4-е изд. М., 1982; 2) *Хрестоматия исследований по древнерусской литературе*. М., 1987; *Словарь книжников и книжности Древней Руси*. Вып. I. XI-конец XIV в. Л., 1987.

§ IV. MAIN BIBLIOGRAPHICAL WORKS

Адрианова-Перетц В. П. и Покровская В. Ф. *Древнерусская повесть*. М.-Л., 1940; Будовниц И. У. *Словарь русской, украинской, белорусской письменности и литературы до XVIII века*. Отв. ред. Д. С. Лихачев. М., 1962; Дмитриева Р. П. *Библиография русского летописания*. М.-Л., 1962: Дробленкова Н. Ф. 1) *Библиография русских советских работ по литературе XI-XVII веков за 1917-1957 гг*. Под ред. и со вступит. статьей В. П. Адриановой-Перетц. М.-Л., 1961; 2) *Библиография работ по древнерусской литературе, опубликованных в СССР. 1958-1967 гг.*, ч. 1-2, Л., 1978-1979; Назаревский А. А. *Библиография древнерусской повести*. М.-Л., 1956.

§ V. TEXTOLOGY, PALAEOGRAPHY AND WATERMARKS

Карский Е. Ф. *Славянская кирилловская палеография*. Л., 1928; 2-е факсимильное изд., 1979; Лихачев Д. С. 1) *Текстология на материале русской литературы X-XVII вв*. 2-е изд. Л., 1983; 2) *Текстология. Краткий очерк*. М.-Л., 1964; Лихачев Н. П. *Палеографическое значение бумажных водяных знаков*, ч. I-III. СПб., 1899; Розов Н. Н. 1) *Русская рукописная книга. Этюды и характеристики*. Л., 1971; 2) *Книга Древней Руси XI-XIV вв*. М., 1977; 3) *Книга в России в XV веке*. Л., 1981; Тромонин К. Я. *Знаки писчей бумаги*. М., 1844; Черепнин Л. В. *Русская палеография*. М., 1956; Щепкин В. Н. *Русская палеография*. М., 1967; Янин В. Л. *Я послал тебе бересту*... 2-е изд., М., 1975.

§ VI. GENERAL STUDIES AND COLLECTIONS OF ARTICLES ON OLD RUSSIAN LITERATURE

Древнерусская литература: Источниковедение. Л., 1984; Еремин И. П. *Литература Древней Руси. Этюды и характеристики*. М.-Л., 1966; *Исследования по древней и новой литературе*. Л., 1987; *Истоки русской беллетристики. Возникновение жанров светского повествования в древнерусской литературе*. Л., 1970; Ключевский В. О. *Древнерусские жития святых как исторический источник*. М., 1871; Лихачев Д. С. 1) *Великий путь*. М., 1987; 2) *Великое наследие. Классические произведения литературы Древней Руси*. 2-е изд. М., 1980; 3) *Избранные работы* в 3-х томах. Л., 1987; 4) *Исследования по древнерусской литературе*. Л., 1986;

5) «Прогрессивные линии развития в истории русской литературы». See: *О прогрессе в литературе*. Л., 1977; 6) *Прошлое — будущему*. Статьи и очерки. Л., 1985; 7) *Развитие русской литературы X-XVII вв. Эпохи и стили*. Л., 1973; 8) *Русские летописи и их культурно-историческое значение*. М.-Л., 1947; 9) *Человек в литературе Древней Руси*. 2-е изд. М.-Л., 1970; Лихачева В. Д., Лихачев Д. С. *Художественное наследие Древней Руси и современность*. Л., 1971; Лурье Я. С. *Общерусские летописи XIV-XV вв.* Л., 1976; Моисеева Г. Н. *Древнерусская литература в художественном сознании и исторической мысли России XVIII века*. Л., 1980; Насонов А. Н. *История русского летописания XI-начала XVII века. Очерки и исследования*. М., 1969; Приселков М. Д. *История русского летописания XI-XV вв.* Л., 1940; Творогов О. В. *Древнерусские хронографы*. Л., 1975; *Чтения по древнерусской литературе*. Ереван, изд. Ереванского ун-та, 1980.

§ VII. THE ART AND CULTURE OF OLD RUSSIA

История культуры Древней Руси. Домонгольский период. Под ред. Н. Н. Воронина и М. К. Каргера. т. I., М.-Л., 1948; т. II., М.-Л., 1951; Лихачев Д. С. 1) *Культура русского народа X-XVII вв.* М.-Л., 1961; 2) *Культура Руси времени Андрея Рублева и Епифания Премудрого (конец XIV-начало XV века)*. М.-Л., 1962; *ТОДРЛ*, т. XXII, М.-Л., 1966; т. XXXVII, Л., 1983; *Памятники культуры. Новые открытия. Письменность, искусство, археология. Ежегодник*. М., 1985-1986; Панченко А. М. "Эстетические аспекты христианизации Руси". *Русская литература*, № I, 1988, с. 50-59.

§ VIII. FOLKLORE AND OLD RUSSIAN LITERATURE

Адрианова-Перетц В. П. *Древнерусская литература и фольклор*. Л., 1974; *Русская литература и фольклор (XI-XVII вв.)*. Л., 1970; Рыбаков Б. А., *Древняя Русь. Сказания. Былины. Летописи*. М., 1963.

§ IX. THE POETICS OF OLD RUSSIAN LITERATURE

Адрианова-Перетц В. П. *Очерки поэтического стиля Древней Руси*. М.-Л., 1947; Еремин И. П. (see § VI); Лихачев Д. С.: 1) *Литература. Реальность. Литература*. 2-е изд. Л., 1984; 2) *Поэтика древнерусской литературы*. 3-е изд., доп., Л., 1979; Лихачев Д. С., Панченко А. М. *"Смеховой мир" Древней Руси*. Л., 1976; 2-е изд. 1984; Лихачев Д. С., Панченко А. М., Понырко Н. В. *Смех в Древней Руси*. Л., 1984; Орлов А. С. *Об особенностях формы русских воинских повестей (кончая XVII в.)*. М., 1902; Творогов О. В. "Задачи изучения устойчивых литературных формул Древней Руси". *ТОДРЛ*, т. XX. М.-Л., 1964.

§ X. SERIAL PUBLICATIONS

1. **Publication of chronicles:** *Полное собрание русских летописей (ПСРЛ)*, тт. I-XXXVII (to be completed by the Archaeographical Commission of the USSR Academy of Sciences)

2. **Publication of translated and Slavic-Russian hagiographical works:** *Великие Минеи-Четьи*, СПб., 1868-1917 (Unfinished edition of the Archaeographical Commission of the USSR Academy of Sciences); see *ПЛДР* § II.

3. **Monuments of early literature and art:** *ПДП, ПДПИ*, вып. 1-90, СПб., 1878-1925 (издание ОЛДП); *Памятники старинной русской литературы*, изд.

Г. Кушелевым-Безбородко. *"Ложные" и "отреченные" книги русской старины*, собр. А. Н. Пыпиным. Вып. 1-4 СПб., 1860-1862.
4. **Collections of articles.** **Studies and materials on Old Russian literature:**
1) *Древнерусская литература и ее связи с новым временем.* М., 1967; 2) Сб. статей, М., 1961; 3) *Русская литература на рубеже двух эпох (XVII-начало XVIII века).* М., 1971; *ТОДРЛ*, тт. I-XLI. М.-Л., Л., 1934-1988.
5. **Dictionaries of Old Russian:** *Словарь русского языка XI-XVII вв.*, вып. 1-13, М., 1975-1987 (to be completed); Срезневский И. И. *Материалы для словаря древнерусского языка.* т. I-III, СПб., 1893-1902.

CHAPTER I

GENERAL WORKS

Адрианова-Перетц В. П. "Человек в учительной литературе Древней Руси". *ТОДРЛ*, т. XXVII, Л., 1972; *"Изборник" Святослава 1073 года.* Сб. статей. М., 1977; Истрин В. М. *Очерк истории древнерусской литературы домосковского периода (11-13 вв.).* Пг., 1922; Мещерский Н. А. 1) "Искусство перевода Киевской Руси". *ТОДРЛ*, т. XV. М.-Л., 1958; 2) "Проблемы изучения славяно-русской переводной литературы XI-XV вв." *ТОДРЛ*, т. XX. Л., 1964; 3) *Источники и состав древней славяно-русской переводной письменности X-XV веков.* Л., 1978; Робинсон А. Н. *Литература Древней Руси в литературном процессе средневековья XI-XIII вв. Очерки литературно-исторической типологии.* М., 1980; Романов Б. А. *Люди и нравы Древней Руси. Историко-бытовые очерки XI-XIII вв.* 2 изд., М.-Л., 1966; see bibliography for the Introduction: § V — Розов Н. Н. №№ 1, 2; § VI — Еремин И. П.; *Истоки русской беллетристики*, гл. 3-4; Лихачев Д. С. № 7, гл. 1, № 9, гл. 2-3.

TRANSLATED LITERATURE

a) **Apocryphal literature**
Лавров П. А. *Апокрифические тексты.* СПб., 1899; *Памятники отреченной русской литературы.* Собраны и изданы Н. С. Тихонравовым, т. I-II. СПб.-М., 1863; Порфирьев И. Я. 1) *Апокрифические сказания о ветхозаветных лицах и событиях по рукописям Соловецкой библиотеки.* СПб., 1877; 2) *Апокрифические сказания о новозаветных лицах и событиях по рукописям Соловецкой библиотеки.* СПб., 1890; see bibliography for the Introduction: § II — *ПЛДР*, № 2; § X, № 3; Пыпин А. Н. "Для объяснения статьи о 'ложных' книгах". *ЛЗАК*, вып. 1. СПб., 1862, с. 1-55; Тихонравов Н. С. "'Отреченные' книги древней России". See: Тихонравов Н. С. Соч., т. I. М., 1898, с. 127-255; Яцимирский А. И. *Библиографический обзор апокрифов в южнославянской и русской письменности. Апокрифы ветхозаветные*, вып. 1. Пг., 1921.

b) **Translated tales**
Григорьев А. Д. *"Повесть об Акире Премудром". Исследование и тексты.* М., 1913; Истрин В. И. *Александрия русских хронографов.* М., 1893 (texts and study); Кузьмина В. Д. *Девгениево деяние.* М., 1962 (texts and study); Мещерский Н. А. *"История иудейской войны" Иосифа Флавия в древнерусском переводе.* М., 1958 (texts and study); see bibliography for the Introduction: § II — *Изборник; ПЛДР* №№ 2, 3; *"Повесть о Варлааме и Иоасафе". Памятник древнерусской переводной литературы XI-XIII вв.* (Подг. текста, исслед. и комм. И. Н. Лебедевой.) Л., 1985.

c) **Collections of sayings, patericons**
"Изборник" великого князя Святослава Ярославича 1073 г. СПб., 1880 (see: *"Изборник" великого князя Святослава Ярославича 1073 года.* ЧОИДР, 1882,

кн. 4; *Синайский патерик*. Издание подготовили В. С. Голышенко, В. Ф. Дубровина. М., 1967; see bibliography for the Introduction: § II — *ПЛДР*, №№ 2-3; Еремин И. П. "К истории древнерусской переводной повести". *ТОДРЛ*, т. III, М.-Л., 1936; *"Изборник" Святослава 1073 г.* (Сборник статей). Отв. ред. Б. А. Рыбаков. М., 1977; Петров Н. И. *О происхождении и составе славяно-русского печатного Пролога*. Киев, 1875; Преображенский В. *Славяно-русский Скитский патерик*. Киев, 1909; Семенов В. А. 1) *"Мудрость Менандра" по русским спискам*. СПб., 1892; 2) *Изречения Исихии и Варнавы по русским спискам*. СПб., 1892; 3) *"Древняя русская Пчела по пергаменному списку"*. *СОРЯС*, т. LIV № 4. СПб., 1893.

d) **Chronicles**

Истрин В. М. *"Книги временныя и образныя Георгия Мниха". "Хроника Георгия Амартола" в древнем славяно-русском переводе*. Текст, исследование и словарь, тт. I-III. Пг.-Л., 1920-1980; Шусторович Э. М. *"Древнеславянский перевод хроники Иоанна Малалы. История изучения"*. *Византийский временник*, т. 30. М., 1969; See bibliography for the Introduction: § VI — Творогов О. В., гл. I.

e) **Literature on natural history**

Карнеев А. *"Материалы и заметки по литературной истории Физиолога"*. *ОЛДП*, т. XCII. СПб., 1891 (texts and study); *Книга, глаголемая Козьмы Индикоплова*. Изд. *ОЛДП*, т. LXXXVI, СПб., 1886; see bibliography for the Introduction: § II — *ПЛДР*, № 3.

THE TALE OF BYGONE YEARS

Повесть временных лет, ч. 1-2. М., 1950. (Сер. "Литературные памятники"; texts, article and commentaries by D. S. Likhachev); see bibliography for the Introduction: § II — *ПЛДР*, № 1; Творогов О. В. *"Повесть временных лет и Начальный свод. Текстологический комментарий"*. *ТОДРЛ*, т. XXX. Л., 1976; Шахматов А. А. 1) *"Повесть временных лет"*, т. I. Вводная часть. Текст. Примечания. *ЛЗАК*, вып. XXIX. Пг., 1916; 2) *"Разыскания о древнейших русских летописных сводах"*. *ЛЗАК*, вып. XX. СПб., 1908; see bibliography for the Introduction: § VI — Еремин И. П.; *Истоки русской беллетристики*, гл. 1; Лихачев Д. С., №№ 2, 8, 9; Приселков М. Д., с. 125.

ORATORICAL PROSE OF THE 11TH TO 13TH CENTURIES

Еремин И. П. 1) *"Литературное наследие Феодосия Печерского"*. *ТОДРЛ*, т. V. М.-Л., 1947 (texts of homilies and epistles); 2) *"Литературное наследие Кирилла Туровского"*. *ТОДРЛ*, т. XI. М.-Л., 1955 (study); *ТОДРЛ*, т. XII. М.-Л., 1956 (texts); *ТОДРЛ*, т. XIII. М.-Л., 1957 (texts); *ТОДРЛ*, т. XV. М.-Л., 1958 (texts); Молдован А. М. *"Слово о Законе и Благодати" Илариона*. Киев, 1984; Адрианова-Перетц В. П. *"Человек в учительной литературе Древней Руси"*. *ТОДРЛ*, т. XXVII. Л., 1972; Никольский Н. *О литературных трудах митрополита Климента Смолятича, писателя XII в.* СПб., 1892; see bibliography for the Introduction: § VI — Еремин И. П.; Лихачев Д. С., № 2.

THE INSTRUCTION OF VLADIMIR MONOMACHOS

Орлов А. С. *Владимир Мономах*. М.-Л., 1946 (study and texts); see bibliography for the Introduction: § II — *ПЛДР*, № 1; § VI — Лихачев Д. С., № 5.

OLD RUSSIAN *VITAE*

Жития св. Бориса и Глеба и службы им. Подготовил к печати Д. И. Абрамович. Пг., 1916 (ОРЯС); *Патерик Киево-Печерского монастыря.* Изд. Д. И. Абрамовича. СПб., 1911 (texts); *Успенский сборник XII-XIII вв.* Издание подготовили: О. А. Князевская, В. Г. Демьянов, М. В. Ляпон. М., 1971; see bibliography for the Introduction: § II—*ПЛДР*, № 1, 2; *Художественная проза Киевской Руси*; Адрианова-Перетц В. П.: 1) "Задачи изучения 'агиографического стиля' Древней Руси". *ТОДРЛ.* т. XX. М.-Л., 1964; 2) "К вопросу о круге чтения древнерусского писателя". *ТОДРЛ*, т. XXVIII. Л., 1974; Воронин Н. Н. "'Анонимное' сказание о Борисе и Глебе, его время, стиль и автор". *ТОДРЛ*, т. XIII. М.-Л., 1957; see bibliography for the Introduction: § VI—Еремин И. П.; *Истоки русской беллетристики*, гл. 2.

THE PILGRIMAGE OF ABBOT DANIEL

See bibliography for the Introduction: § II—*ПЛДР*, № 2; Данилов В. В. 1) "К характеристике *Хождения* Игумена *Даниила*". *ТОДРЛ*, т. X. М.-Л., 1954; 2) "О жанровых особенностях древнерусских хождений". *ТОДРЛ*, т. XVIII. М.-Л., 1962.

THE LAY OF IGOR'S HOST

Орлов А. С. *Слово о полку Игореве.* 2 изд., доп. М.-Л., 1946 (study and text); *Слово о полку Игореве.* Под ред. В. П. Адриановой-Перетц. М.-Л., 1950 (Сер. "Литературные памятники"; *Слово о полку Игореве.* 2 изд. "Библиотека поэта". Большая серия. Л., 1985; *Слово о полку Игореве.* Древнерусский текст. Переводы и переложения. Поэтические вариации. Вступит. статья Д. С. Лихачева. Статья, сост., и подг. текста Л. А. Дмитриева. Комм. Л. А. Дмитриева и О. В. Творогова. М., 1986; *Слово о полку Игореве.* Вступ. статьи, ред. текста, дословный и объяснительный перевод с древнерусского, примечания Д. С. Лихачева. М., 1980; *Слово о полку Игореве.* Вступ. статья Д. С. Лихачева. Ред. текста и прозаический перевод И. П. Еремина. Поэтический перевод В. А. Жуковского. М., 2 изд., 1967 (Сер. "Народная библиотека"); see bibliography for the Introduction: § II—*"Изборник"*; *ПЛДР*, № 2; Адрианова-Перетц В. П. *"Слово о полку Игореве" и памятники русской литературы XI-XIII веков.* Л., 1968; Демкова Н. С. *"Проблемы изучения Слова о полку Игореве".* See: *Чтения по древнерусской литературе.* Ереван, 1980; Дмитриев Л. А. 1) *История первого издания "Слова о полку Игореве". Материалы и исследования.* М.-Л., 1960; 2) "175-летие первого издания *Слова о полку Игореве.* Некоторые итоги и задачи изучения *Слова".* *ТОДРЛ*, т. XXXI, Л., 1976; Еремин И. П. "Жанровая природа *Слова о полку Игореве".* See: И. П. Еремин. *Литература Древней Руси,* гл., 1966; Лихачев Д. С. 1) "Взаимоотношение списков и редакций *Задонщины* (Исследование Анджело Данти)". *ТОДРЛ,* т. XXXI. Л., 1976, с. 165-175; 2) *"Слово о полку Игореве". Историко-литературный очерк.* М., 1976; 3) *"Слово о полку Игореве"—героический пролог русской литературы.* 2 изд. Л., 1967; 4) *"Слово о полку Игореве" и культура его времени.* Л., 1978; Моисеева Г. Н. *Спасо-Ярославский хронограф и "Слово о полку Игореве".* Л., 1977; Рыбаков Б. А. 1) *"Слово о полку Игореве" и его современники.* М., 1971; 2) *Русские летописцы и автор "Слова о полку Игореве".* М., 1972; *"Слово о полку Игореве".* Под ред. В. П. Адриановой-Перетц. Сб. статей. М., 1950; *"Слово о полку Игореве". Памятники литературы и искусства XI-XVII веков.* Сб. статей. М., 1978; *"Слово о полку Игореве" и памятники Куликовского цикла. К вопросу о времени написания "Слова"* М.-Л., 1966; *"Слово о полку Игореве"—памятник XII века.* Сб. статей, М.-Л., 1962.

General works: Робинсон А. Н., Соловьев А. В., Якобсон Р. О., *"Слово о полку Игореве" в переводах конца XVIII века.* Лейден, 1954.
Bibliography: Адрианова-Перетц В. П. (Сост.). *"Слово о полку Игореве". Библиография изданий, переводов и исследований.* М.-Л., 1940; Бегунов Ю. К. *"Слово о полку Игореве в зарубежном литературоведении".* (Краткий обзор.) See: *От "Слова о полку Игореве" до "Тихого Дона".* Л., 1969; Дмитриев Л. А. (Сост.) *"Слово о полку Игореве". Библиография изданий, переводов и исследований. 1938-1954.* М.-Л., 1955; see bibliography for the Introduction: § IV— Дробленкова Н. Ф., № 1-2; Попов П. Н. *"К библиографии Слова о полку Игореве".* ИОЛЯ, т. XV, вып. 3, М., 1956, с. 268-271; *"Слово о полку Игореве". Указатель литературы на русском языке 1968-1984 гг.* Ред. Ю. Г. Кондратьева. М., 1985 (ГБЛ); Творогов О. В. *"Слово о полку Игореве в советской филологической науке (1968-1977)".* Русская литература, Л., 1978; Якобсон Р. О. *"Изучение Слова о полку Игореве в Соединенных Штатах Америки".* ТОДРЛ, т. XIV. М.-Л., 1958 (Обзор за 1943-1956 гг.).
Dictionaries: *Словарь-справочник "Слова о полку Игореве".* Сост. В. Л. Виноградова. М.-Л., 1965-1984, вып. 1-6.

CHAPTER 2

CHRONICLE-WRITING

For texts of *The Galich-Volhynian Chronicle* see editions of *The Hypatian Chronicle:* ПСРЛ, т. II, СПб., 1908; М., 1962; see bibliography for the Introduction: § II—ПЛДР, № 3; *Новгородская летопись старшего и младшего изводов.* М., 1950; Лихачев Д. С. *"Летописные известия об Александре Поповиче"* ТОДРЛ, т. VII. М.-Л., 1949; Черепнин Л. В. *"Летописец Даниила Галицкого".* Исторические записки, № 12, 1941.

THE *SUPPLICATION* OF DANIEL THE EXILE

"Слово" Даниила Заточника по редакциям XII и XIII вв. и их переделкам. Подготовил к печати Н. Н. Зарубин. Л., 1932 (study and texts); see bibliography for the Introduction: § II—ПЛДР, № 2; Гудзий Н. К. *"К какой социальной среде принадлежал Даниил Заточник?"* Сб. статей к 40-летию уч. деят. А. С. Орлова. Л., 1934; Лихачев Д. С. *"Социальные основы стиля Моления Даниила Заточника".* ТОДРЛ, т. т. Х. Л., 1954; see bibliography for the Introduction: § VI—Лихачев Д. С., № 2.

TALES OF THE MONGOL INVASION OF RUSSIA

a) **For chronicle tales of the Mongol invasion** see the "Chronicle-writing" section
b) *The Lay of the Ruin of the Russian Land*
Бегунов Ю. К. *Памятник русской литературы XIII века. "Слово о погибели Русской земли".* М.-Л., 1965 (text and study); see bibliography for the Introduction: § II—ПЛДР, № 3; Гудзий Н. К. *"О Слове о погибели Рускыя земли".* ТОДРЛ, т. XII, М.-Л., 1956; Данилов В. В. *"Слово о погибели Рускыя земли как произведение художественное".* ТОДРЛ, т. XVI. М.-Л., 1960; Мещерский Н. А. *"К реконструкции текста Слова о погибели Рускыя земли".* Вестник Ленинградского ун-та. Серия языка и литературы, № 14, вып. 3, 1963; Соловьев А. В. *"Заметки к Слову о погибели Рускыя земли".* ТОДРЛ, т. XV, М.-Л., 1958; Тихомиров М. Н. *"Где и когда было написано Слово о погибели Русской земли".* ТОДРЛ, т. VIII, М.-Л., 1951.

c) **The Tale of Batu's Capture of Ryazan**
Лихачев Д. С. "Повести о Николе Заразском" (texts). *ТОДРЛ*, т. VII.
М.-Л., 1949; see bibliography for the Introduction: § II—*Воинские повести*;
ПЛДР, № 3; Лихачев Д. С. 1) *"Повесть о разорении Рязани Батыем"*. See:
Воинские повести Древней Руси. М.-Л., 1949; 2) See bibliography for the
Introduction: § VI—Лихачев Д. С., № 2; Путилов Б. Н. *"Песня о Евпатии
Коловрате"*. *ТОДРЛ*, т. XI. М.-Л., 1955.
d) **The Tale of Mercurius of Smolensk**
Белецкий Л. Т. *"Литературная история Повести о Меркурии Смоленском"*.
Исследование и тексты. *СОРЯС*, т. XCIX, № 8, Пг. 1922; see bibliography for
the Introduction: § II—*ПЛДР*, № 3.
e) **The writings of Serapion of Vladimir**
Петухов Е. *Серапион Владимирский, русский проповедник XIII века*. СПб.,
1888 (texts and study); see bibliography for the Introduction: § II—*ПЛДР*, № 3;
Гудзий Н. К. "Где и когда протекала литературная деятельность Серапиона
Владимирского?" *ИОЛЯ*, т. XI, вып. 5, М., 1952.

HAGIOGRAPHY

a) **The Life of Alexander Nevsky**
Бегунов Ю. К. *Памятник русской литературы XIII века "Слово о погибели
Русской земли"*. М.-Л., 1965; Мансикка В. *"Житие Александра Невского"*. Разбор
редакций и текст. СПб., 1913; see bibliography for the Introduction: § II—
ПЛДР, № 3; Лихачев Д. С. *"Галицкая литературная традиция в Житии
Александра Невского"*. *ТОДРЛ*, т. V. М.-Л., 1947.
b) **The Life of St Michael of Chernigov**
See bibliography for the Introduction: § II—ПЛДР, № 3.
c) **The Life of St Abraham of Smolensk**
Жития Авраамия Смоленского и службы ему. Подготовил к печати
С. П. Розанов. СПб., 1912; see bibliography for the Introduction: § II—*ПЛДР*,
№ 3; § VI—Ключевский В. О.

CHAPTER 3

CHRONICLE-WRITING

Псковские летописи, вып. 1. Приготовил к печати А. Н. Насонов. М.-Л.,
1941 (texts); *ПСРЛ*, т. XV; *Тверской сборник и Рогожский летописец*. М., 1965
(Тексты летописей и *Повести о Шевкале*); see bibliography for the Introduction:
§ II—*ПЛДР*, № 4; § VI—Лурье Я. С.; § VIII—Адрианова-Перетц В. П.

HAGIOGRAPHY

Псковские летописи, вып. 2. М., 1955, с. 82-87 (Текст *Повести о Довмонте*);
ПСРЛ, т. V. СПб. 1851, с. 207-215 (Текст *Повести о Михаиле Ярославиче
Тверском*); see bibliography for the Introduction: § II—*ПЛДР*, № 4; Кучкин В. А. 1) *"Сказание о смерти митрополита Петра"*. *ТОДРЛ*, т. XVIII. М.-Л.,
1962; 2) *Повести о Михаиле Тверском. Историко-текстологическое исследование*.
М., 1974; Охотникова В. И. 1) *"Повесть о Довмонте и княжеские жизнеописания XI-XIV вв."*. See: *Источниковедение литературы Древней Руси*. Л.,
1980, с. 115-128; 2) *Повесть о Довмонте. Исслед. и тексты*. Л., 1985;
Серебрянский Н. И. *Древнерусские княжеские жития*. М., 1915.

TRANSLATED TALES

a) **The Tale of the Indian Empire**
Сперанский М. Н. *"Сказание об Индийском царстве"*. *ИОРЯС*, т. III, 1930; see the bibliography for the Introduction: § II—*Изборник*; *ПЛДР*, № 3.
b) **The Lay of the Twelve Dreams of Emperor Shakhaishi**
Веселовский А. Н. *"Слово о двенадцати снах Шахаиши по рукописи XV в."*. *СОРЯС АН*, 1879, т. XX, № 2 (text); Кузнецов Б. И. *"Слово о двенадцати снах Шахаиши и его связи с памятниками литературы Востока"*. *ТОДРЛ*, т. XXX. Л., 1976; Рыстенко А. В. *Сказание о 12 снах царя Мамера в славяно-русской литературе.* Одесса. 1904.

EPISTLES

ПСРЛ, т. VI. СПб., 1853. Прибавления (Текст *Послания архиепископа новгородского Василия ко владыце тферскому Феодору о рае*); Тихонравов Н. С. *Памятники отреченной литературы*, вып. II, М., 1868, с. 59-77 (Текст *Повести о Макарии Римском*); see bibliography for the Introduction: § II—*ПЛДР*, № 4.

CHAPTER 4

GENERAL WORKS

Дмитриев Л. А. *"Нерешенные вопросы происхождения и истории экспрессивно-эмоционального стиля XV в."*. *ТОДРЛ*, т. XX. М.-Л., 1964; Лихачев Д. С. 1) *Культура Руси эпохи образования Русского национального государства (конец XIV-начало XVI в.).* Л., 1946; 2) "Некоторые задачи изучения второго южнославянского влияния в России". See: *Исследования по славянскому литературоведению и фольклористике. Доклады советских ученых на IV Международном съезде славистов.* М., 1960 (То же. Отдельным изд., М., 1958); 3) "Предвозрождение на Руси в конце XIV-первой половине XV в.". See: *Литература эпохи Возрождения и проблемы всемирной литературы.* М., 1967; see bibliography for the Introduction: § VI—Лихачев Д. С., № 9 гл. 4; § VII— Лихачев Д. С., № 2; Мошин В. "О периодизации русско-славянских литературных связей в X-XV вв." *ТОДРЛ*, т. XIX. М.-Л., 1963; Соболевский А. И. *Западное влияние на литературу Московской Руси XV-XVIII веков.* СПб., 1899.

CHRONICLE-WRITING

Приселков М. Д. *Троицкая летопись. Реконструкция текста.* М.-Л., 1950 (text); see bibliography for the Introduction: § VI—Лихачев Д. С., № 8, ч. IV; Лурье Я. С., гл. I; Творогов О. В., гл. I и V.

HAGIOGRAPHY AND PANEGYRICAL WORKS

Великие Минеи-Четьи (декабрь, дни 18-23), М., 1907 *(Житие митрополита Петра)*; *Житие Сергия Радонежского. ПДП.* СПб., 1888, вып. 70; *Житие святого Стефана, Епископа Пермского, написанное Епифанием Премудрым. Изд. Археографической комиссии.* СПб., 1897 (text); *ПСРЛ*, т. IV, вып. 2, ч. I. Л., 1925 *(Слово о житии и о преставлении великого князя Дмитрия Ивановича, царя Русьского)*; Прохоров Г. М. 1) *Памятники переводной и русской литературы XIV-XV веков.* Л., 1987; 2) *"Повесть о Митяе". Русь и Византия в эпоху Куликовской битвы.* Л., 1978 (Тексты сочинений Киприана); see bibliography for the Introduction: § II—*ПЛДР*, № 4.

Адрианова-Перетц В. П. *"Слово о житии и о преставлении великого князя Дмитрия Ивановича, царя русьскаго". ТОДРЛ.* т. V. М.-Л., 1947, Дмитриев Л. А. *"*Роль и значение митрополита Киприана в истории древнерусской литературы (к русско-болгарским литературным связям XIV-XV вв.)". *ТОДРЛ,* т. XIX, М.-Л., 1963; Салмина М. А. *"Слово о житии и о преставлении великого князя Дмитрия Ивановича, царя Русьскаго" памятник XVI в.* Проблемы изучения культурного наследия. М., 1985, с. 159-162; Яблонский В. *Пахомий Серб и его агиографические писания.* СПб., 1908; see bibliography for the Introduction: § VI—Дмитриев Л. А.; Ключевский В. О.

HISTORICAL LEGENDS

See bibliography for the Introduction: § II—*ПЛДР,* № 4.

MONUMENTS OF THE KULIKOVO CYCLE

На поле Куликовом. Рассказы русских летописей и воинские повести XIII-XV веков. М., 1980; *Повести о Куликовской битве.* Издание подготовили: М. Н. Тихомиров, В. Ф. Ржига, Л. А. Дмитриев. М.-Л., 1959; *ПСРЛ,* т. IV, ч. I. *Новгородская IV летопись,* вып. 1. Пг., 1915. (Текст *Летописной повести о Мамаевом побоище*); *Сказания и повести о Куликовской битве.* Изд. подг. Л. А. Дмитриев и О. П. Лихачева. Л., 1982 (Серия "Литературные памятники"); Шамбинаго С. К. *Повести о Мамаевом побоище.* СПб., 1906 (study and texts); see bibliography for the Introduction: § II—*Изборник;* *ПЛДР,* № 4; *Русские повести XV-XVI вв.;* Дмитриев Л. А. 1) "Публицистические идеи *Сказания о Мамаевом побоище". ТОДРЛ,* т. XI, 1955; 2) "Куликовская битва 1380 года в литературных памятниках Древней Руси". *Русская литература,* № 3, 1980, с. 3-29; Кирпичников А. Н. *Куликовская битва.* Л., 1980; *Куликовская битва.* Сб. статей. М., 1980; Лихачев Д. С. "Черты подражательности *Задонщины.* (К вопросу об отношении *Задонщины* к *Слову о полку Игореве.)" Русская литература",* 1964, № 3; see bibliography for the Introduction: § VI—Лихачев Д. С., № 2; *"Слово о полку Игореве" и памятники Куликовского цикла. К вопросу о времени написания "Слова".* М.-Л., 1966; *ТОДРЛ,* т. XXXIV. *Куликовская битва и подъем национального самосознания.* Л., 1979; Шахматов А. А. *Отзыв о сочинении С. К. Шамбинаго "Повести о Мамаевом побоище".* СПб., 1910.

TALES OF MONGOL RAIDS ON RUSSIA AFTER THE BATTLE OF KULIKOVO

ПСРЛ, т. IV, ч. I. *Новгородская IV летопись,* вып. 2. Л., 1925 *(Повесть о нашествии Тохтамыша на Москву); ПСРЛ,* т. XXIV. *Типографская летопись,* Пг., 1921 *(Повесть о Темир-Аксаке);* see bibliography for the Introduction: § II—*ПЛДР,* № 4.

CHAPTER 5

GENERAL WORKS

Дмитриева Р. П. "Четьи сборники XV века как жанр". *ТОДРЛ,* т. XXVII, Л., 1972; Казакова Н. А. *Западная Европа в русской письменности XV-XVI веков. Из истории международных культурных связей России.* Л., 1980; Казакова Н. А., Лурье Я. С. *Антифеодальные еретические движения XIV-начала XVI вв.* М.-Л., 1955; Лурье Я. С.: 1) *Идеологическая борьба в русской публицистике конца XV-начала XVI века.* М.-Л., 1960; 2) "Литературная и культурно-просветительная деятельность Ефросина в конце XV в.". *ТОДРЛ*, т. XVII. М.-Л., 1961; see bibliography for the Introduction: § VI—*Истоки русской беллетристики.*

HISTORICAL NARRATIVE. *THE TALE OF TSARGRAD*

Леонид (Кавелин). *"Повесть о Царьграде Нестора-Искандера XV века".* *ПДП*, изд. ОЛДП. СПб., 1886 (text); see bibliography for the Introduction: § II—*ПЛДР*, № 5; *Русские повести XV-XVI вв.*; Скрипиль М. О. "'История' о взятии Царьграда турками Нестора-Искандера". *ТОДРЛ*, т. X, М.-Л., 1954; Сперанский М. Н. "Повести и сказания о взятии Царьграда турками (1453 г.) в русской письменности XVI-XVII веков". *ТОДРЛ*, т. X, М.-Л., 1954; т. XII, М.-Л., 1956.

CHRONICLE-WRITING AND *THE RUSSIAN CHRONOGRAPH*

Творогов О. В. "К истории жанра хронографа". *ТОДРЛ*, т. XXVII, Л., 1972, с. 203-226; Шахматов А. А. *Обозрение общерусских летописных сводов XIV-XVI вв.* М.-Л., 1938; see bibliography for the Introduction: § VI—Лихачев Д. С., № 8; Лурье Я. С.; Творогов О. В.

HAGIOGRAPHY

a) **The Tale of the Life of St Michael of Klopsk**
Повести о житии Михаила Клопского. Подготовка текстов и статья Л. А. Дмитриева. М.-Л., 1958; see bibliography for the Introduction: § II—*Изборник; ПЛДР*, № 5.

b) **The Tale of Peter, Prince of the Horde**
See bibliography for the Introduction: § II—*Русские повести XV-XVI вв.*; § VI—Дмитриев Л. А., Ключевский В. О.

TRANSLATED TALES

a) **The Serbian Alexandreid**
Александрия. Роман об Александре Македонском по русской рукописи XV века. Изд. подготовили М. Н. Ботвинник, Я. С. Лурье и О. В. Творогов. М.-Л., 1965 (Сер. "Литературные памятники"); see bibliography for the Introduction: § II—*ПЛДР*, № 5; Ванеева Е. И. "К изучению истории текста сербской *Александрии* (На материале ленинградских списков XV-XVII вв.)". *ТОДРЛ*, т. XXX. Л., 1976.

b) **The Trojan tales**
Троянские сказания. Средневековые рыцарские романы о Троянской войне по русским рукописям XVI-XVII веков. Подг. текста и комм. М. Н. Ботвинника и О. В. Творогова. Л., 1972 (Сер. "Литературные памятники").

c) **Tales of Solomon**
Летопись русской литературы и древностей, изд. Н. С. Тихонравовым, т. IV, отд. 2, М., 1862, с. 112-121; *Памятники старинной русской литературы*, изд. Г. Кушелевым-Безбородко, вып. III; *"Ложные" и "отреченные" книги русской старины*, собр. А. Н. Пыпиным. СПб., 1862; see the bibliography for the Introduction: § II—*Изборник*; Веселовский А. Н. *Славянские сказания о Соломоне и Китоврасе и западные легенды о Морольфе и Мерлине.* СПб., 1872; see bibliography for the Introduction: § VI—*Истоки русской беллетристики*, гл. VIII.

d) **Stefanit and Ikhnilat**
"Стефанит и Ихнилат". Средневековая книга басен по русским рукописям XV-XVII вв. Изд. подг. О. П. Лихачева и Я. С. Лурье. Л., 1969 (Сер. "Литературные памятники").

ORIGINAL TALES

a) *The Tale of Babylon*
Скрипиль М. О. *"Сказание о Вавилоне". ТОДРЛ*, т. IX, Л., 1953 (с публикацией текста); see bibliography for the Introduction: § II — *ПЛДР*, № 5; *Русские повести XV-XVI вв.*; Дробленкова Н. Ф. "По поводу жанровой природы *Слова о Вавилоне". ТОДРЛ*, т. XXIV, Л., 1969.

b) *The Tale of Dracula* and *The Tale of Dmitry Basarga and His Son Borzosmysl*
Повесть о Дмитрии Басарге и о сыне его Борзосмысле. Исследование и подгот. текстов М. О. Скрипиля. Л., 1969; *Повесть о Дракуле*. Исследование и подготовка текста Я. С. Лурье. М.-Л., 1964; see bibliography for the Introduction: § II — *Изборник*; *ПЛДР*, № 5; *Русские повести XV-XVI вв.*; Лурье Я. С. "Еще раз о Дракуле и макиавеллизме". *Русская литература*, 1968, № 1.

c) *A Voyage Beyond Three Seas* by Afanasy Nikitin
"Хожение за три моря" Афанасия Никитина. 2 изд., доп. и перераб. Л., 1986 (Сер. "Литературные памятники"; Семенов Л. С. *Путешествие Афанасия Никитина*. М., 1980; see bibliography for the Introduction: § II — *ПЛДР*, № 5. § VI — Лихачев Д. С., № 5.

CHAPTER 6

GENERAL WORKS. MAIN IDEOLOGICAL PHENOMENA

Будовниц И. У. *Русская публицистика XVI в.* М.-Л., 1947; Дмитриева Р. П. *"Волоколамские четьи сборники XVI века". ТОДРЛ*, т. XXVIII. Л., 1974; Зернова А. С. *Начало книгопечатания.* М., 1947; Казакова Н. А. *Очерки по истории русской общественной мысли. Первая треть XVI века.*, Л., 1970; Малинин В. *Старец Елеазарова монастыря Филофей и его послания.* Киев, 1901; Масленникова Н. Н. "Идеологическая борьба в псковской литературе в период образования Русского централизованного государства". *ТОДРЛ*, т. VIII. М.-Л., 1951; Тихомиров М. Н. *Русская культура X-XVII вв.* М., 1968; see Chapter 5, "General works" section: Казакова Н. А.; Лурье Я. С.

THE TALE OF THE PRINCES OF VLADIMIR

Сказание о князьях Владимирских. Подг. текста и исследование Р. П. Дмитриевой. М.-Л., 1955.

HOUSEHOLD MANAGEMENT

"Домострой" по Коншинскому списку и подобным. К изданию приготовил А. С. Орлов. М., 1980; *"Домострой" по списку ОИДР.* М., 1882; Адрианова-Перетц В. П. "К вопросу о круге чтения древнерусского писателя". *ТОДРЛ*, т. XXVIII. Л., 1974.

HAGIOGRAPHY

See bibliography for the Introduction: § VI — Ключевский В. О.

THE TALE OF PETER AND FEBRONIA

Повесть о Петре и Февронии. Подг. текстов и исследование Р. П. Дмитриевой. Л., 1979; see bibliography for the Introduction: § II — *Изборник; Русские повести XV-XVI вв.;* § VI — Лихачев Д. С., № 2.

HISTORICAL NARRATIVE

a) **Chronicle-writing**
ПСРЛ, т. VII-VIII. *Воскресенская летопись.* СПб., 1856-1859; *Иоасафовская летопись* под ред. А. А. Зимина. М., 1957; *ПСРЛ,* т. IX-X. *Никоновская летопись.* СПб., 1862-1910, М., 1975; Клосс Б. М. *Никоновский свод и русские летописи XVI-XVII веков.* М., 1930; see bibliography for the Introduction: § VI — Лихачев Д. С., № 8.

b) **The Book of Degrees**
ПСРЛ, т. XXI, ч. I-II. *Книга Степенная царского родословия.* СПб., 1908-1913; Васенко П. Г. *"Книга Степенная царского родословия" и ее значение в древнерусской исторической письменности,* ч. I. СПб., 1904.

c) **The History of Kazan**
Волкова Т. Ф. "Работа автора *Казанской истории* над сюжетом повествования об осаде и взятии Казани". *ТОДРЛ,* т. XXXIX, Л., 1985, с. 308-322; *Казанская история.* Подг. текста, вступ. статья и прим. Г. Н. Моисеевой. М.-Л., 1954; Кунцевич Г. З. *История о Казанском царстве, или Казанский летописец.* СПб., 1905 (Исследование и тексты).

DISPUTE OF LIFE AND DEATH AND THE TALE OF THE CAMPAIGN OF STEPHEN BATHORY AGAINST PSKOV

Повести о споре Жизни и Смерти. Исследование и подг. текстов Р. П. Дмитриевой. М.-Л., 1964; *Повесть о прихожении Стефана Батория на град Псков.* Подг. текста и статьи В. И. Малышева. М., 1962; see bibliography for the Introduction: § II — *Изборник, Русские повести XV-XVI вв.*

THE TALE OF QUEEN DINARA

See bibliography for the Introduction: § II — *Русские повести XV-XVI вв.;* Сперанский М. Н. *"Повесть о Динаре* в русской письменности". *ИОРЯС,* т. XXXI. Л., 1926; Троицкая Т. С. "Ранние этапы литературной истории *Повести о Динаре* (XVI в.)". See: *Древнерусская рукописная книга и ее бытование в Сибири.* Новосибирск, 1982.

POLEMICAL WRITINGS

a) **Joseph of Volokolamsk**
Послания Иосифа Волоцкого. Подг. текста А. А. Зимина и Я. С. Лурье. Вступ. статья И. П. Еремина. М.-Л., 1959; *Просветитель, или обличение жидовствующих. Творение преподобного отца нашего Иосифа, игумена Волоцкого.* Казань, 1896; see bibliography for the Introduction § II — Еремин И. П.

b) **Metropolitan Daniel**
Жмакин В. *Митрополит Даниил.* М., 1881 (С публикацией сочинений).

c) **Vassian Patrikeyev and the Non-Possessors**
Казакова Н. А. *Вассиан Патрикеев и его сочинения.* М.-Л., 1960 (study and texts).

d) **Maxim the Greek**

Сочинения Максима Грека, ч. I-III. Казань, 1859-1861.
Буланин Д. М. *Переводы и послания Максима Грека. Неизданные тексты.* Л., 1984; Иванов А. И. *Литературное наследие Максима Грека. Характеристика, атрибуции, библиография.* Л., 1969; Синицына Н. В. *Максим Грек в России.* М., 1977.

e) **Ivan Peresvetov**

Сочинения И. Пересветова. Подг. текста А. А. Зимина. М.-Л., 1956; Зимин А. А. *И. С. Пересветов и его современники. Очерки по истории русской общественно-политической мысли середины XVI века.* М., 1958.

f) **The Correspondence of Ivan the Terrible with Kurbsky**

Переписка Ивана Грозного с Андреем Курбским. Подг. текста Я. С. Лурье и Ю. Д. Рыкова. Л., 1979; М., 1981 (Сер. "Литературные памятники"); *Послания Ивана Грозного.* Подг. текстов Д. С. Лихачева и Я. С. Лурье. М.-Л., 1951 (Сер. "Литературные памятники"); *Сочинения князя Курбского,* т. 1. Под ред. Г. З. Кунцевича. СПб., 1914. (*РИБ,* т. XXXI).
Лихачев Д. С. 1) *"Канон и молитва Ангелу Грозному Парфения Юродивого".* See: *Рукописное наследие Древней Руси. По материалам Пушкинского Дома,* Л., 1972; 2) *"Курбский и Грозный — были ли они писателями?" Русская литература,* № 4, 1972; see bibliography for the Introduction: § VI—Лихачев Д. С., № 2; Лурье Я. С. *"Был ли Иван IV писателем?" ТОДРЛ,* т. XV. Л., 1958; Скрынников Р. Г. 1) *"Мифы и действительность Московии XVI-XVII вв.". Русская литература,* № 3, 1974, с. 114-129; 2) *Переписка Грозного и Курбского. Парадоксы Эдварда Кинана.* Л., 1973.

CHAPTER 7

GENERAL WORKS

Адрианова-Перетц В. П. *"Исторические повести XVII в. и устное народное творчество". ТОДРЛ,* т. IX, М.-Л., 1958; Елеонская А. С., Орлов О. В., Сидорова Ю. Н., Терехов С. Ф., Федоров В. И. *История русской литературы XVII-XVIII вв.* М., 1969; Лихачев Д. С. 1) *"Семнадцатый век в русской литературе".* See: *XVII век в мировом литературном развитии.* М., 1969; 2) *"Система литературных жанров Древней Руси".* See: *Славянские литературы.* V Международный съезд славистов (София, сентябрь 1962). М., 1964; Назаревский А. А. *Очерки из области русской исторической повести начала XVII века.* Киев, 1958; Орлов А. С. *"О некоторых особенностях стиля великорусской исторической беллетристики XVI-XVIII вв.". ИОЛЯ,* т. XIII, 1908, кн. 4; Панченко А. М. *Русская стихотворная культура XVII века.* Л., 1973; Платонов С. Ф. *Древнерусские сказания и повести о Смутном времени XVII века как исторический источник.* 2-е изд. СПб., 1913; Робинсон А. Н. *Борьба идей в русской литературе XVII века.* М., 1974; Черепнин Л. В. *" 'Смута' и историография XVII века". Исторические записки,* 1945, т. XIV; see bibliography for the Introduction: § VI—Лихачев Д. С., № 7, 9; § IX—Лихачев Д. С., № 2; Орлов А. С.

POLEMICAL WRITINGS OF THE TIME OF TROUBLES AND HISTORICAL WORKS ON THE PERIOD

Памятники древней русской письменности, относящиеся к Смутному времени. Под ред. С. Ф. Платонова. 2-е изд., СПб., 1909, 3-е изд. Л., 1925, вып. I (*РИБ,* т. XIII); Кукушкина М. В. *"Семен Шаховской — автор Повести о Смуте".* See: *Памятники культуры. Новые открытия. Письменность. Искусство. Археология (Ежегодник 1974).* М., 1975. *Повесть о победах Московского государства.* Изд. подг. Г. П. Енин. Л., 1982 (Сер. "Литературные памятники").

a) **Ivan Timofeyev's** *Annals*
  "Временникъ" Ивана Тимофеева. Подготовка текста, перевод и комм.
О. А. Державиной. М.-Л., 1951.

b) ***The New Tale of the Most Glorious Russian Tsardom***
  *"Новая повѣстъ о преславномъ Россійскомъ царствѣ" и современная ей агитаціонная
патріотическая письменностъ.* Подг. текстов и исследование Н. Ф. Дробленко-
вой. М.-Л., 1960; see bibliography for the Introduction: § II — *Русская повѣстъ
XVII в.;* Солодкин Я. С. "К датировке и атрибуции *Новой повести о преславном
Россійском царствѣ". ТОДРЛ,* т. XXXVI, Л., 1981.

c) **The** *Tale* **of Abraham Palitsyn**
  Сказание Авраама Палицына. Подг. текста, комм. О. А. Державиной и
Е. В. Колосовой. М.-Л., 1955; see bibliography for the Introduction: § II —
Изборникъ.

HAGIOGRAPHICAL-BIOGRAPHICAL TALES

  Скрипиль М. О. *"Повѣстъ об Ульянии Осорьиной". ТОДРЛ,* т. VI, М.-Л., 1948
(texts and commentaries); see bibliography for the Introduction: § II — *Изборникъ;
Русская повѣстъ XVII в.;* § VI — *Истоки русской беллетристики,* с. 513-519.

VERSIFICATION

  Русская силлабическая поэзия XVII-XVIII в. Вступ. статья, подг. текстов и
прим. А. М. Панченко ("Библиотека поэта. Большая серия"). 2-е изд. Л., 1970.
  Панченко А. М. "Изучение поэзии Древней Руси". В кн.: *Пути изученія
древнерусской литературы и письменности.* Л., 1970.

NEW LITERARY AREAS (SIBERIA AND THE DON)

a) **Siberian chronicle-writing**
  Сибирскіе лѣтописи. Изд. Археографической комиссии. СПб., 1907; Дергачева-Скоп Е. И. *Из исторіи литературы Урала и Сибири XVII века.* Свердловск,
1965; Дергачева Е. И. *"Похвала Сибири* С. Е. Ремезова". *ТОДРЛ,* т. XXI,
М.-Л., 1965, с. 266-274; *Очерки русской литературы Сибири,* т. I (Дореволюцион-
ный период). Новосибирск. 1982 (Гл. I-III); Ромодановская Е. К. *Русская
литература в Сибири первой половины XVII в.* Новосибирск, 1973.

b) **Tales of Azov**
  Орлов А. С. *"Сказочные" повести об Азовѣ.* (Тексты и исследование).
Варшава, 1906; see bibliography for the Introduction: § II — *Воинскіе повести;
Изборникъ, Русская повѣстъ XVII в.;* Робинсон А. Н. "Поэтическая повесть об
Азове и политическая борьба донских казаков 1642 г.". *ТОДРЛ,* т. VI. М.-Л.,
1948.

CHAPTER 8

GENERAL WORKS

  Адрианова-Перетц В. П. *Очерки по истории русской сатирической литературы
XVII века.* М.-Л., 1937 (study and texts); *Демократическая поэзия XVII века.* Вступ.
статья В. П. Адриановой-Перетц и Д. С. Лихачева. Подг. текстов и прим.
В. П. Адриановой-Перетц. 2 изд. М.-Л., 1962 ("Библиотека поэта. Большая
серия"); Демин А. С. *Русская литература второй половины XVII-начала
XVIII века. Новые художественные представления о мире, природе, человеке.* М., 1977;
Лихачев Д. С. "Предпосылки возникновения жанра романа в русской литерату-
ре". See: *История русского романа.* В 2-х тт., т. I. М.-Л., 1962; Панченко А. М.

1) *Русская культура в канун петровских реформ.* Л., 1984; 2) *Чешско-русские литературные связи XVII века.* Л., 1969; *Русская демократическая сатира XVII века.* Подг. текстов, статья и комм. В. П. Адриановой-Перетц. 2-е изд., доп. М., 1977; see bibliography for the Introduction: § VI— *Истоки русской беллетристики,* гл. XI-XII; § IX—Лихачев Д. С., Панченко А. М.; *Литература первой половины XVII в.*; § I—Робинсон А. Н.

TRANSLATED TALES OF CHIVALRY AND ADVENTURE

Кузьмина В. Д. *Рыцарский роман на Руси. Бова, Петр Златых Ключей* М., 1964 (Исследования и текст); Петровский М. *"История о славном короле Брунцвике".* ПДП, т. LXXV. СПб., 1888 (text); see bibliography for the Introduction: § II— *Изборник.* Соболевский А. И. *Переводная литература Московской Руси XIV-XVII вв.* М., 1908.

RUSSIAN TALES OF THE SECOND HALF OF THE 17TH CENTURY

a) **The Tale of Sukhan**
Малышев В. И. *"Повесть о Сухане". Из истории русской повести XVII века.* М.-Л., 1956 (study and text).
b) **The Tale of Savva Grudtsyn**
Скрипиль М. О. *Повесть о Савве Грудцыне* (texts). ТОДРЛ, т. V, М.-Л., 1947; see bibliography for the Introduction: § II— *Изборник; Русские повести XVII в.*; Скрипиль М. О. 1) *Повесть о Савве Грудцыне* ТОДРЛ, т. II, М.-Л., 1935; 2) ТОДРЛ, т. III, М.-Л., 1936.
c) **The Tale of Woe-Misfortune**
Повесть о Горе-Злочастии. Изд. подгот. Д. С. Лихачев и Е. И. Ванеева. Л., 1984 (Сер. "Литературные памятники"). See bibliography for the Introduction: § II— *Изборник; Русские повести XVII в.,* § VI—Лихачев Д. С., № 5, 7 (гл. X).

THE TRANSLATED AND ORIGINAL *NOVELLA*

a) **Facetiae**
Державина О. А. *"Фацеции". Переводная новелла в русской литературе XVII века.* М., 1962 (study and texts).
b) **The Tale of the Drunkard, the Tale of Shemyaka's Trial, The Tale of Karp Sutulov, The Tale of Frol Skobeyev**
See bibliography for the Introduction: § II— *Изборник"; Русская повесть XVII в.; Литература второй половины XVII в. Русская демократическая сатира XVII в.*; Бакланова Н. А. *К вопросу о датировке "Повести о Фроле Скобееве".* ТОДРЛ, т. XIII, М.-Л., 1957; Фокина О. Н. *"Бытование Повести о бражнике в сборниках XVII века".* Русская книга в дореволюционной Сибири. Распространение и бытование. Новосибирск, 1986, с. 18-42.

HISTORICAL FICTION. TALES OF THE FOUNDING OF MOSCOW AND *THE TALE OF THE PAGE MONASTERY OF TVER*

Повести о начале Москвы. Исследование и подг. текстов М. А. Салминой. М.-Л., 1964; see bibliography for the Introduction: § II— *Изборник, Русская повесть XVII в.*; Дмитриева Р. П. *"Повесть о Тверском Отроче монастыре и исторические реалии".* ТОДРЛ, т. XXIV, Л., 1969, Шамбинаго С. К. *"Повести о начале Москвы".* ТОДРЛ, т. III, М.-Л., 1936; see bibliography for the Introduction: § VI—Лихачев Д. С., № 5.

DEMOCRATIC SATIRE

General works: Адрианова-Перетц В. П. *Демократическая поэзия XVII в.*; *Русская демократическая сатира XVII в.*; see bibliography for the Introduction: § II — *Изборник, Русская повесть XVII в.*; Лихачев Д. С. "Древнерусский смех". See: *Проблемы поэтики и истории литературы.* Сб. статей в честь 75-летия М. М. Бахтина. Саранск, 1973; see bibliography for the Introduction: § IX — Лихачев Д. С., Панченко А. М.

THE WRITINGS OF ARCHPRIEST AVVAKUM

"Житие протопопа Аввакума, им самим написанное", и другие его сочинения. Вступ. статья В. Е. Гусева. М., 1960; *"Житие протопопа Аввакума, им самим написанное", и другие его сочинения.* Иркутск, 1979; *Пустозерский сборник. Автографы сочинений Аввакума и Епифания* (text and study). Изд. подг. Н. С. Демкова, Н. Ф. Дробленкова, Л., 1975; Робинсон А. Н. *Жизнеописание Аввакума и Епифания.* Исследования и тексты. М., 1963; see bibliography for the Introduction: § II — *Изборник*; Виноградов В. В. "О задачах стилистики. Наблюдения над стилем *Жития* протопопа Аввакума". *Русская речь.* Сборник статей под ред. Л. В. Щербы, т. I, Пг., 1923; Демкова Н. С. *"Житие" протопопа Аввакума (Творческая история произведения).* Л., 1974; see bibliography for the Introduction; § VI — Лихачев Д. С., № 5; § IX — Лихачев Д. С., № 2; Лихачев Д. С., Панченко А. М.

BAROQUE IN 17TH-CENTURY RUSSIAN LITERATURE

Лихачев Д. С. "Была ли эпоха петровских реформ перерывом в развитии русской культуры?" See: *Славянские культуры в эпоху формирования и развития славянских наций XVIII-XIX вв.* М., 1978; Морозов А. А. "Проблема барокко XVII-начала XVIII в. (Состояние вопроса и задачи изучения)". *Русская литература*, № 3, 1962; see bibliography for the Introduction: № VI — Лихачев Д. С., № 7 (гл. 5).

SIMEON OF POLOTSK, SYLVESTER MEDVEDEV, KARION ISTOMIN

Вирши. Силлабическая поэзия XVII-XVIII веков. Ред. П. Н. Берков, вступ. статья И. Н. Розанова. Л., 1935 (texts and commentaries); Симеон Полоцкий. *Избранные сочинения.* Подг. текста, статья и комм. И. П. Еремина. М.-Л., 1953 (Сер. "Литературные памятники"); the "Versification" section; *Симеон Полоцкий и его книгоиздательская деятельность.* Сб. статей. М., 1962; see bibliography for the Introduction: § VI — Еремин И. П.

THE EMERGENCE OF THE RUSSIAN THEATRE

"Артаксерксово действо". Первая пьеса русского театра XVII в. Подгот. текста, статья и комм. И. М. Кудрявцева. М.-Л., 1957; *Ранняя русская драматургия (XVII-первая половина XVIII в.). Первые пьесы русского театра.* Изд. подг. О. А. Державина, А. С. Демин, Е. К. Ромодановская. Под ред. А. Н. Робинсона. М., 1972; *Русская драматургия последней четверти XVII и начала XVIII в.* Изд. подготовили О. А. Державина, А. С. Демин, В. П. Гребенюк. Под ред. О. А. Державиной. М., 1972; Софронова Л. А. *Поэтика славянского театра XVII-первой половины XVIII в. Польша, Украина, Россия.* М., 1981; see General Works: Демин А. С.; see bibliography for the Introduction: § IX — Лихачев Д. С., № 5 (с. 284-291).

INTRODUCTION

READERS AND ANTHOLOGIES

Translations: *A Treasury of Russian Spirituality.* Compiled and edited by G. P. Fedotov. London, 1952; Zenkovsky, S. A., *Medieval Russia's Epics, Chronicles and Tales.* New York, 1963 (2 ed., revised and enlarged, New York, 1974);

FOREIGN LITERATURE *

A Source Book for Russian History from Early Times to 1917. Ed. G. Vernadsky, Vol. 1, New Haven-London, 1972; Benz, E., *Russische Heiligenlegenden.* Zürich, 1953; *O Bojan, Du Nachtigall der alten Zeit. Sieben Jahrhunderte altrussischer Literatur.* Herausgeg. von H. Grasshoff, K. Müller, G. Sturm. Berlin, 1965; *Altrussische Dichtung aus dem 11.-18. Jahrhundert.* Aus dem Russischen herausgeg. von H. Grasshoff. Leipzig, 1971; Onasch, K., *Altrussische Heiligenleben.* Berlin, 1977; Leger, L., *La littérature russe.* Paris, 1892; *Literatura staroruska. Wiek XI-XVII. Antologia.* Opracowali W. Jakubowski, R. Łużny. Warszawa, 1971 (texts translated into English, French, German and Polish).

Texts: *Anthology of Old Russian Literature.* Ed. Ad. Stender-Petersen in collaboration with S. Congrat-Butlar. New York, 1954; *A Historical Russian Reader.* Ed. J. Fennell, D. Obolensky. Oxford, 1969; Sielicki, F., *Древнерусская литература.* Przewodnik tematyczny dla studentów filologii rosyjskiej. Wrocław, 1977.

---

* Works mentioned in the first section of the Bibliography ("Translations") are not included in the second and third sections ("Texts" and "Studies").

HISTORIES OF OLD RUSSIAN LITERATURE

Čiževskij, D., *History of Russian Literature. From the Eleventh Century to the End of the Baroque.* 'S-Gravenhage, 1960; Fennell, J., Stokes, A., *Early Russian Literature.* Berkeley-Los Angeles, 1974; *Literatura rosyjska. Podręcznik,* t. I. Układ i redakcja ogólna M. Jakóbca. Warszawa, 1970; Ljackij, E., *Historický přehled ruské literatury,* č. I. *Staré ruské písemnictví.* Praha, 1937; Михайлов, М. И., Старорусска литература *(X-XVII вв.).* Велико Търново, 1979; Picchio, R., *Storia della letteratura russa antica.* Milano, 1959 (2 ed., Firenze, 1968); Raab. H., *Geschichte der altrussischen Literatur.* Potsdam, 1957; Stender-Petersen, Ad., *Den russiske litteraturs historie,* t. I. København, 1952.

MAIN BIBLIOGRAPHICAL WORKS

A Bibliography of Works in English on Early Russian History to 1800. New York, 1969; Grimsted, P. K., *Archives and Manuscript Repositories in the USSR.* Princeton, 1972; Hille, A., *Bibliographische Einführung in das Studium der slawischen Philologie.* Halle, 1959; Kerner, R. J., *Slavic Europe. A Selected Bibliography in the Western European Languages.* Cambridge, Mass., 1918; Lencek, R. L., *A Bibliographical Guide to the Literature on Slavic Civilizations.* New York, 1966; *Mediaeval Slavic Manuscripts.* A bibliography of printed catalogues by D. Djaparidzé. Cambridge, Mass., 1957; Meyer, K., *Bibliographie zur osteuropäischen Geschichte. Verzeichnis der zwischen 1939 und 1964 veröffentlichten Literatur in westeuropäischen Sprachen zur osteuropäischen Geschichte bis 1945.* Berlin, 1972; Wytrzens, G., 1) *Bibliographische Einführung in das Studium der slavischen Literaturen.* Frankfurt am Main, 1972; 2) *Bibliographie der russischen Autoren und anonymen Werke.* Frankfurt am Main, 1975, S. 1-38; *Zeitschriften-Bestandsverzeichnisse. Bd. II. Slawistik. Stand vom I. Dezember 1967.* Ed. V. Krause. Berlin, 1968.

WORKS ON WATERMARKS

Briquet, C. M., *Les filigranes,* t. 1-4. Genève, 1907 (2 éd., t. 1-4, Amsterdam, 1968); Churchill, W. A., *Watermarks in Paper.* Amsterdam, 1935; *Monumenta Chartae Papyraceae historiam Illustrantia,* t. I-XIII. General Editors E. J. Labarre, J.S.G. Simmons. Hilversum, 1950-1973; Piccard, G., *Die Wasserzeichenkartei Piccard im Hauptstaatsarchiv Stuttgart,* Findbücher I-VIII. Stuttgart, 1961-1979.

GENERAL STUDIES AND COLLECTIONS OF ARTICLES
ON OLD RUSSIAN LITERATURE

Birnbaum, H., *On Medieval and Renaissance Slavic Writing.* The Hague-Paris, 1974; Brückner A. *O literaturze rosyjskiej i naszym do niej stosunku dziś i lat temu trzysta.* Lwów, 1906; Čiževskij, D., *Aus zwei Welten.* 'S-Gravenhage, 1956; Dujčev, I., 1) *Medioevo bizantino-slavo,* Vol. I-III. Roma, 1965-1971; 2) *Slavia Orthodoxa.* London, 1970; *Handbuch der Geschichte Russlands.* Herausgeg. von M. Hellmann et alii, Bd. 1-2. Stuttgart, 1976-1986; Matl. J., *Europa und die Slaven.* Wiesbaden, 1964; Obolensky, D., 1) *Byzantium and the Slavs. Collected Studies.* London, 1971; 2) *The Byzantine Inheritance of Eastern Europe.* London, 1982; Ostrogorsky, G., *Byzanz und die Welt der Slawen.* Darmstadt, 1974; Picchio, R., *Etudes littéraire slavo-romanes.* Firenze. 1978; Soloviev, A. V., *Byzance et la formation de l'Etat russe.* London, 1979; Trubetzkoy, N. S., *Vorlesungen über die altrussische Literatur. Mit einem Nachwort von R. O. Jakobson.* Firenze, 1973.

THE POETICS OF OLD RUSSIAN LITERATURE

Alissandratos, J., *Medieval Slavic and Patristic Eulogies.* Firenze, 1982; Čiževskij, D., 1) "On the Question of Genres in Old Russian Literature". *Harvard Slavic Studies,* Vol. II, 1954, pp. 105-115; 2) "Zur Stilistik der altrussischen Literatur. Topik". In: *Festschrift für M. Vasmer,* Wiesbaden, 1956, S. 105-112; 3) "Umkehrung der dichterischen Metaphern Topoi und andere Stilmittel". *Die Welt der Slaven,* Bd. VI, 1961, S. 337-354; Jagoditsch, R., "Zum Begriff der 'Gattungen' in der altrussischen Literatur". *Wiener slavistisches Jahrbuch,* Bd. 6. 1957/1958, S. 113-137; Lenhoff, G., "Toward a Theory of Protogenres in Medieval Russian Letters.". *The Russian Review,* Vol. 43, 1984, pp. 31-54; Picchio, R., 1) "Models and Patterns in the Literary Tradition of Medieval Orthodox Slavdom". In *American Contributions to the Seventh International Congress of Slavists,* Vol. II. *Literature and Folklore.* The Hague, 1977, pp. 439-467; 2) Върху изоколните структури в средневековна славянска проза. *Литературна мисъл,* № 3, 1980, с. 75-107; Schmidt. W.-H., *Gattungstheoretische Untersuchungen zur altrussischen Kriegserzählung.* Berlin, 1975.

MAIN JOURNALS ON THE HISTORY AND THEORY OF OLD RUSSIAN LITERATURE AND CULTURE

Archiv für slavische Philologie, Bd., 1-42, Berlin, 1876-1929; *Byzantinoslavica.* Praha, from 1929; *Cyrillomethodianum.* Thessalonique, 1971; *Harvard Slavic Studies.* Cambridge, Mass., from 1953; *Jahrbücher für Geschichte Osteuropas,* Bd. 1-6, Breslau, Wiesbaden, 1936-1941—first series; from 1953—new series; *Oxford Slavonic Papers.* Oxford, Vol. 1-13, 1950-1967—first series; from 1968—new series; *Полата кънигописьная.* Nijmegen, from 1978; *Revue des études slaves.* Paris, from 1921; *Ricerche Slavistiche.* Roma, Firenze, from 1952; *Russia Mediaevalis.* München, from 1973; *Slavia.* Praha, from 1922; *Slavia Orientalis.* Warszawa, from 1952; *The Slavonic and East European Review.* London, from 1922; *Die Welt der Slaven.* Wiesbaden, from 1956; *Wiener slavistisches Jahrbuch.* Wien, from 1950; *Zeitschrift für slavische Philologie.* Leipzig, Heidelberg, from 1924; *Zeitschrift für Slawistik.* Berlin, from 1956.

DICTIONARIES OF OLD SLAVONIC AND OLD RUSSIAN

Miklosich, F., *Lexicon palaeoslovenico-graeco-latinum.* Vindobonae, 1862-1865; Sadnik, L., Aitzetmüller, R., *Handwörterbuch zu den altkirchenslavischen Texten.* Heidelberg, 1955; *Slovník jazyka staroslověnského,* t. I-IV. Praha, 1958-1985 (to be completed).

CHAPTER I

GENERAL WORKS

Dvornik, F., "Byzantine Political Ideas in Kievan Russia". *Dumbarton Oaks Papers,* Vol. 9-10, 1955-1956, pp. 73-121; Fennell, J., Stokes, A., *Early Russian Literature.* Berkeley-Los Angeles, 1974, Chapter I, pp. 11-79; *Literatura rosyjska. Podręcznik,* t. I, Warszawa, 1970, cz. 1, rozdzial I, s. 31-72; Ljackij, E., *Historický přehled ruské literatury,* č. I. Praha, 1937, kapitola I-XIV, s. 20-126; Picchio, R., 1) *Storia della letteratura russa antica.* Milano, 1959. parte I, p. 11-90; 2) Мястото на старата българска литература в културата на средновековна Европа. *Литературна мисъл,* No. 8, 1981, с. 19-36; Podskalsky, G., *Christentum und theologische Literatur in der Kiever Rus' (988-1237).* München, 1982; Poppe, A., *Państwo ikościół na Rusi w XI wieku.* Warszawa, 1968; Raab, H., *Geschichte der altrussischen Literatur.* Potsdam, 1957, S. 17-50; Tschiževskij, D., 1) *Geschichte der altrussischen Literatur im 11., 12 und 13. Jahrhundert.* Frankfurt am Main, 1948; 2) *History of Russian Literature.* 'S-Gravenhage, 1960, Chapter 1-2, pp. 11-124.

TRANSLATED LITERATURE

a) **Vitae**
Translations: Onasch, K., *Altrussische Heiligenleben*. Berlin, 1977, S. 47-54 (German translation of extracts from *The Life of Alexis, the Man of God*).
b) **Collections of sayings, patericons**
Texts: *"Melissa"*. *Ein byzantinisches Florilegium, griechisch und altrussisch*. München, 1968 (*Slavische Propyläen*, Bd. 7); **patericons:** Wijk, N. van., *The Old Church Slavonic Translation of the* "'Ανδρων 'αγίων βίβλος". The Hague-Paris, 1975; Birkfellner, G., *Das Römische Paterikon*, Bd. 1-2. Wien, 1979; Николова С., *Патеричните разкази в българската средновековна литература*. София, 1980.
Studies: Marti, R., "Gattung Florilegien". In: *Gattungsprobleme der älteren slavischen Literaturen*. Berlin, 1984, S. 121-145.
c) **Apocryphal literature:**
Translations: *Стара българска литература*, т. I. *Апокрифи*. София. 1981 (a Bulgarian translation of apocryphal literature); Zenkovsky, S. A., *Medieval Russia's Epics, Chronicles and Tales*. 2 ed., New York, 1974; pp. 153-160; Onasch, K., *Altrussische Heiligenleben*. Berlin, 1977, S. 55-63; *Literatura staroruska*. Warszawa, 1971, s. 64-67 [translations of *The Descent of the Virgin to Purgatory* into English, German (extracts), Polish (extracts)].

Studies: Müller, L., "Die Offenbarung der Gottesmutter über die Höllenstrafen". *Die Welt der Slaven*, Bd. VI, 1961, S. 26-39; Naumov, A. E., *Apokryfy w systemie literatury cerkiewnosłowiańskiej*. Wrocław, 1976; Петканова, Д., *Апокрифна литература и фолклор*. София, 1978; Santos-Otero. A. de., *Die handschriftliche Überlieferung der altslavischen Apokryphen*, Bd. 1-2, Berlin-New York, 1978-1981.
d) **Translated tales**
Translations: Graham, H. F., "The Tale of Devgenij". *Byzantinoslavica*, t. 29, 1968, p. 51-91; Pascal, P., "Le Digénis slave ou la Geste de Devgenij". *Byzantion*, t. 10, 1935, p. 300-334. (translations of the *Deeds of Digenes* into English and French).

Studies: Entwistle, W. J., "Bride-snatching and the *Deeds of Digenis*". *Oxford Slavonic Papers*, Vol. 4, 1953, pp. 1-16, Grégoire, H., "Le Digénis russe". In: *Russian Epic Studies*. Ed. R. Jakobson, E. J. Simmons. Philadelphia, 1949, pp. 131-169; Soloviev, A., "La date de la version russe de Digénis Akritas". *Byzantion*, t. 22, 1952, p. 129-132.

e) **Chronicles and historical narrative**
Translations: Berendts, A., Grass, K., *Flavius Josephus vom Jüdischen Kriege*, t. 1-2, Dorpat, 1924-1927; Istrin, V. M., *La prise de Jérusalem par Josèphe le Juif*, t. I-II, Paris, 1934-1938 (translations of the *History of the Jewish War* by Josephus Flavius into German and French).
Texts: *Die Chronik des Georgios Hamartolos in altslavischer Übersetzung*. München, 1972 (*Slavische Propyläen*, Bd. 135, 1-2).
Studies: Hoecherl, A., *Zur Übersetzungstechnik des altrussischen "Jüdischen Krieges" des Josephus Flavius*. München, 1970; Weingart, M., *Byzantské kroniky v literatuře církevněslovanské*, č. 1-2, od. 1-2. Bratislava, 1922-1923.
f) **Literature on natural history.**
Translations: Aitzetmüller, R., *Das Hexaemeron des Exarchen Johannes*, Bd. 1-7. Graz, 1958-1975; *Йоан Екзарх Български. "Шестоднев"*. Превод от старобългарски на Н. Ц. Кочев. София, 1981 (translations of John the Exarch's *Hexaëmeron* into German and Bulgarian).
Studies: Jacobs, A., "Kosmas Indikopleustes, *Die Christliche Topographie*, in slavischer Übersetzung". *Byzantinoslavica*, t. 40, 1979, p. 183-198; Lägreid, A., *Der rhetorische Stil im Šestodnev des Exarchen Johannes*. Wiesbaden, 1965.

THE TALE OF BYGONE YEARS AND CHRONICLE-WRITING
OF THE 11TH AND 12TH CENTURIES

Translations: *The Russian Primary Chronicle.* By S. H. Cross. Cambridge. Mass., 1930 (2 ed., Cambridge, Mass., 1953); *Die altrussische Nestorchronik.* Herausgeg. von R. Trautmann. Leipzig, 1931; *Chronique dite de Nestor.* Traduite par L. Leger. Paris; 1884: *Nestorkrönikan översättning från fornryskan av A. Norrback.* Stockholm, 1919; *Cronica lui Nestor.* Traducere de Gh. Popa-Lisseanu. Bucuresti. 1935; *Powieść minionych lat.* Przekład F. Sielickiego. Wrocław, 1968; *Nestorův letopis ruský. Pověst dávných let.* Přeložil K. J. Erben. Praha, 1954 (translations of *The Tale of Bygone Years* into English, German, French, Swedish, Rumanian, Polish and Czech); Michell, R., Forbes, N., *The Chronicle of Novgorod.* London. 1914 (2 ed., New York, 1970); *Die Erste Novgoroder Chronik nach ihrer ältesten Redaktion.* Von J. Ditze. Leipzig, 1971 (translations of *The Novgorod First Chronicle* into English and German).
Studies: *Handbuch zur Nestorchronik.* Herausgeg. von L. Müller, Bd. I-III, 1-3 Lieferung. München, 1977-1984 (to be completed); Hurwitz, E. S., *Prince Andrej Bogoljubskij, The Man and the Myth.* Firenze. 1980; Müller, L., "Die 'dritte Redaktion' der sogennanten Nestorchronik". In: *Festschrift für M. Woltner zum 70.* Geburtstag. Heidelberg, 1967, S. 171-186; Stender-Petersen, Ad., *Varangica.* Aarhus, 1953.

ORATORICAL PROSE OF THE 11TH AND 12TH CENTURIES

Translations: Zenkovsky, S. A., *Medieval Russia's Epics, Chronicles and Tales.* 2 ed., New York, 1974, pp. 86-90; *Die Werke des Metropoliten Ilarion.* Übersetzt von L. Müller. München, 1971; Leger, L., *La littérature russe.* Paris, 1892, p. 2-4; *Literatura staroruska.* Warszawa, 1971. s. 42-43 [translations of Metropolitan Hilarion's *Sermon on Law and Grace* into English (extracts), German, French (extract), Polish (extracts)]; Zenkovsky, S. A., Op. cit., pp. 90-92 (translation of extracts from Cyril of Turov's *Sermon for Easter Sunday* into English).
Texts: Müller, L., *Des Metropoliten Ilarion Lobrede auf Vladimir den Heiligen und Glaubensbekenntnis.* Wiesbaden, 1962; Elbe, H., "Die Handschrift C der Werke des Metropoliten Ilarion". *Russia Mediaevalis,* t. II, 1975, S. 120-161; Kirill von Turov. *Zwei Erzählungen.* München, 1964 (*Slavische Propyläen,* Bd. 5); Kirill von Turov. *Gebete.* München, 1965 (*Slavische Propyläen,* Bd. 6).
Studies: Danti, A., "Sulla tradizione dello *Slovo o zakone i blagodati*". *Ricerche Slavistiche,* t. 17/19, 1970-1972, p. 109-117; Müller, L., "Neue Untersuchungen zum Text der Werke des Metropoliten Ilarion". *Russia Mediaevalis,* t. II, 1975, S. 3-91; Scholz, F., "Studien zu den Gebeten Kirills von Turov." In: *Sprache und Literatur Altrusslands.* Münster, 1987, S. 167-220; Vaillant, A., "Cyrille de Turov et Grégoire de Nazianze"; *Revue des études slaves,* t. 26, 1950, p. 34-50.

THE WRITINGS OF VLADIMIR MONOMACHOS

Translations: *The Russian Primary Chronicle.* By S. H. Cross. Cambridge, Mass., 1930, pp. 301-313 (2 ed., Cambridge, Mass., 1953); *O Bojan, Du Nachtigall der alten Zeit.* Berlin, 1965, S. 381-394; *Chronique dite de Nestor.* Traduite par L. Leger. Paris, 1884, p. 243-262; *Powieść minionych lat.* Przekład F. Sielickiego. Wrocław, 1968, s. 373-391; *Nestorův letopis ruský. Pověst dávných let.* Přeložil K. J. Erben, Praha, 1954, s. 201-215 (translations into English, German, French, Polish and Czech).
Studies: Čiževska, T., "Zu Vladimir Monomach und Kekaumenos". *Wiener slavistisches Jahrbuch,* Bd. 2, 1952, S. 157-160; Mathiesen, R., "A Textological Note

on the Works of Vladimir Monomach". *Ricerche Slavistiche,* t. 16, 1968-1969, p. 112-125; Müller, L., 1) "Die Exzerpte aus einer asketischen Rede Basilius des Grossen im *Poučenie* des Vladimir Monomach". *Russia Mediaevalis,* t. I, 1973, S. 30-48; 2) "Noch einmal zu Vladimir Monomachs Zitat aus einer asketischen Rede Basilius des Grossen". Ibid., t. IV. 1979, S. 16-24; Vaillant, A., "Une source grecque de Vladimir Monomaque". *Byzantinoslavica,* t. 10, 1949, p. 11-15.

THE EARLIEST RUSSIAN *VITAE*

Translations: *A Treasury of Russian Spirituality.* Compiled and edited by G. P. Fedotov. London, 1952, pp. 15-48; Benz. E., *Russische Heiligenlegenden.* Zürich, 1953, S. 82-156 (translations of the *Life of St. Theodosius of the Caves* into English and German); *O Bojan, Du Nachtigall der alten Zeit.* Berlin, 1965, S. 94-114 (translation of the *Tale of SS Boris and Gleb* into German); Revelli, G., *Boris e Cleb: due protagonisti del Medioevo Russo (le opere letterarie ad essi dedicate).* Abano Terme, 1987 (Italian translation of the literary cycle about SS Boris and Gleb).

Texts: *Die altrussischen hagiographischen Erzählungen und liturgischen Dichtungen über die Heiligen Boris und Gleb.* München, 1967 (*Slavische Propyläen,* Bd. 14).

Studies: Börtnes, J., "Frame Technique in Nestor's *Life of St. Theodosius*". *Scando-Slavica,* t. 13, 1967, p. 5-16; Müller, L., 1) "Studien zur altrussischen Legende der Heiligen Boris und Gleb". *Zeitschrift für slavische Philologie,* Bd. 23, 1954, S. 60-77; Bd. 25, 1956, S. 329-363; Bd. 27, 1959, S. 274-322; Bd. 30, 1962, S. 14-44; 2) "Neuere Forschungen über das Leben und die kultische Verehrung der Heiligen Boris und Gleb". *Opera Slavica,* Bd. 4, Göttingen, 1963, S. 295-317; Poppe, A., "Chronologia utworów Nestora hagiografa". *Slavia Orientalis,* rocz. 14, 1965, s. 287-305; Siefkes, F., *Zur Form des Žitije Feodosija.* Berlin-Zürich, 1970.

THE KIEV CRYPT PATERICON

Translations: Zenkovsky, S. A., *Medieval Russia's Epics, Chronicles and Tales.* 2 ed., New York, 1974, pp. 135-152; Benz, E., *Russische Heiligenlegenden.* Zürich, 1953, S. 175-243; *Literatura staroruska.* Warszawa, 1971, s. 71-72 (translations of extracts into English, German and Polish).

Texts: *Das Paterikon des Kiever Höhlenklosters.* München, 1964 (*Slavische Propyläen,* Bd. 2).

Studies: Bubner, F., *Das Kiever Paterikon.* Augsburg, 1969; Heppell, M., "The *Vita Antonii* a Lost Source of the *Paterikon* of the Monastery of Caves". *Byzantinoslavica,* t. 13, 1952, p. 46-58.

THE PILGRIMAGE OF ABBOT DANIEL

Translations: *The Pilgrimage of the Russian Abbot Daniel in the Holy Land. 1106-1107 A. D.* By C. W. Wilson, London, 1888; "Die Pilgerfahrt des russischen Abtes Daniel ins Heilige Land 1113-1115". Übersetzt von A. Leskien. *Zeitschrift des Deutschen Palästina-Vereins,* Bd. 7, 1884, S. 17-64; *Pèlerinage en Terre Sainte de l'igoumène russe Daniel, au commencement du XII-e siècle (1113-1115).* Traduit par A. de Noroff. St Petersburg, 1864; Khitrovo, B., *Itinéraire russes en Orient,* t. I, I. Genève, 1889, p. 1-83 (translations into English, German, and French).

Texts: *Abt Daniil. Wallfahrtsbericht.* München, 1970 (*Slavische Propyläen,* Bd. 36).

Studies: Seemann, K.-D., *Die altrussische Wallfahrtsliteratur.* München, 1976.

THE LAY OF IGOR'S HOST

For a list of translations of the *Lay* into foreign languages and foreign editions of the text see the books by V. P. Adrianova-Peretts (to 1938) and the work by H. R. Cooper (to 1976). **Studies:** Besharov, J., *Imagery of the Igor's Tale in the Light of Byzantino-Slavic Poetic Theory.* Leiden, 1956; *"La Geste du Prince Igor'"*. *Épopée russe du douzième siècle.* Ed. H. Grégoire, R. Jakobson, M. Szeftel. New York, 1948; Jakobson, R., *Selected Writings,* t. IV. *Slavic Epic Studies.* The Hague-Paris, 1966; Klein, J., *Zur Struktur des Igorlieds.* München, 1972; Menges, K. H., *The Oriental Elements in the Vocabulary of the Oldest Russian Epos, the "Igor' Tale".* New York, 1951; Picchio, R., "On the Prosodic Structure of the *Igor' Tale"*. *Slavic and East European Journal,* Vol. 16, 1972, pp. 147-162; *Russian Epic Studies.* Ed. R. Jakobson, E. J. Simmons. Philadelphia, 1949; Wollmann, S., *"Slovo o pluku Igorově" jako umělecké dílo.* Praha, 1958; Woltner, M., *Die Beziehungen des Igorliedes zur russischen Volkspoesie.* Leipzig, 1923.
Reference books: Čiževska, T., *Glossary of the "Igor' Tale".* London-The Hague-Paris, 1966; Cooper, H. R., *"The Igor Tale".* An Annotated Bibliography of 20th Century non-Soviet Scholarship on the *"Slovo o polku Igoreve".* London, 1978.

CHAPTER 2

GENERAL WORKS

Čiževskij, D., *History of Russian Literature.* 'S-Gravenhage, 1960, Chapter 2, pp. 124-144; Fennell, J., Stokes, A., *Early Russian Literature.* Berkeley-Los Angeles, 1974, Chapter 2, pp. 80-138; *Literatura rosyjska. Podręcznik,* t. I, Warszawa, 1970, cz. 1, rozdział 2, s. 73-83; Ljackij, E., *Historický přehled ruské literatury,* č. 1, Praha, 1937. kapitola XV-XVII, s. 127-152; Picchio, R., *Storia della letterature russa antica.* Milano, 1959, parte 2, p. 93-130; Raab, H., *Geschichte der altrussischen Literatur.* Potsdam, 1957, S. 51-55; Stender-Petersen, Ad., *Geschichte der russischen Literatur.* 2. Aufl. München, 1974, S. 131-156.

CHRONICLE-WRITING

Translations: Zenkovsky, S. A., *Medieval Russia's Epics, Chronicles and Tales.* 2 ed., New York, 1974, pp. 193-196 (English translation of the chronicle tale of the Battle on the Kalka); *A Source Book for Russian History from Early Times to 1917,* Vol. 1, New Haven-London, 1972, pp. 44-46 (English translation of extracts from the chronicle tales of the Mongol invasion); *The Galician-Volhynian Chronicle.* Translated by G. A. Perfecky, München, 1973. **Studies:** Čiževskij, D., "Zur Frage nach dem Stil der Hypatius-Chronik, I". *Südost-Forschungen,* Bd. 12, 1954, S. 79-109; Fennell, J. L. I., 1) "The Tale of Baty's Invasion of North-East Rus' and Its Reflexion in the Chronicles of the Thirteenth-Fifteenth Centuries". *Russia Mediaevalis,* t. III, 1977, p. 41-78; 2) "The Tale of the Death of Vasil'ko Konstantinovič". In: *Osteuropa in Geschichte und Gegenwart.* Festschrift für G. Stökl zum 60. Geburtstag. Köln-Wien, 1977, S. 34-46; 3) "The Tatar Invasion of 1223: Source Problems". *Forschungen zur osteuropäischen Geschichte,* Bd. 27, 1980, S. 18-31; 4) "Russia on the Eve of the Tatar Invasion". *Oxford Slavonic Papers,* Vol. 14, 1981, pp. 1-13; Lammich, M., *Fürstenbiographien des 13. Jahrhunderts in den russischen Chroniken.* Köln, 1973; Worth, D. S., "Linguistics and Historiography. A Problem of Dating in *The Galician-Volhynian Chronicle"*. In: Worth, D. S., *On the Structure and History of Russian.* München, 1977, pp. 221-235.

THE *SUPPLICATION* OF DANIEL THE EXILE

Translations: Zenkovsky, S. A., *Medieval Russia's Epics. Chronicles and Tales.*
2 ed., New York, 1974, pp. 250-255; Müller, K., "Sendschreiben Daniels des
Verbannten. Eine Übersetzung des altrussischen Denkmals ins Deutsche". *Zeitschrift
für Slawistik*, Bd. V, 1960, S. 432-445; Leger, L., *La littérature russe.* Paris, 1892,
p. 28-30; *Literatura staroruska.* Warszawa, 1971, s. 77-80 [translations into English,
German, French (extract) and Polish (extracts)].

Texts: *Das Gesuch Daniils.* München, 1972 (*Slavische Propyläen*, Bd. 123); *Daniil
Zatočnik. Slovo a Molenie.* Edizione critica a cura di M. Colucci e A. Danti. Firenze,
1977.

Studies: Colucci, M., "Le strutture prosodiche delle *Slovo Daniila Zatočnika*".
Ricerche Slavistiche, t. 20-21, 1973-1974, p. 83-123; Franklin, S., "Echoes of
Byzantine Elite Culture in Twelfth-Century Russia?". In: *Byzantium and Europe.
First International Byzantine Conference.* Athens, 1983, pp. 177-187.

TALES OF THE MONGOL INVASION OF RUSSIA

a) **For chronicle tales of the Mongol invasion see** the "Chronicle-writing" section.
b) **The Lay of the Ruin of the Russian Land.**
   Translations: Zenkovsky, S. A., *Medieval Russia's Epics, Chronicles and Tales.* 2
ed., New York, 1974, pp. 196-197; Soloviev, A. V., "Die Dichtung vom Untergang
Russlands". *Die Welt der Slaven*, Bd. IX, 1964, S. 225-245; *Literatura staroruska.*
Warszawa, 1971, s. 92-93 (translations into English, German and Polish).
   Texts: Gorlin, M., "Le Dit de la ruine de la terre Russe et de la mort du
grand-prince Iaroslav". *Revue des études slaves*, t. 23, 1947, p. 5-33.
   Studies: Philipp, W., "Über das Verhältnis des *Slovo o pogibeli Russkoj zemli*
zum *Žitie Aleksandra Nevskogo*". *Forschungen zur Osteuropäischen Geschichte*, Bd. 5,
1957, S. 7-37; Soloviev, A., 1) "Le Dit de la ruine de la terre Russe". *Byzantion*,
t. 22, 1952, p. 105-128, 2) "New Traces of the "Igor Tale" in Old Russian
Literature". *Harvard Slavic Studies*, Vol. I, 1953, pp. 73-81.
c) **The Tale of Batu's Capture of Ryazan**
   Translations: Zenkovsky, S. A., *Medieval Russia's Epics, Chronicles and Tales.* 2
ed., New York, 1974, pp. 199-207; *Altrussische Dichtung aus dem 11.-18. Jahrhundert.*
Leipzig, 1971, S. 100-113; *Literatura staroruska.* Warszawa, 1971, s. 85-89 [transla-
tions into English, German, and Polish (extracts)].
d) **The Tale of Mercurius of Smolensk**
   Translations: Zenkovsky, S. A., *Medieval Russia's Epics, Chronicles and Tales.* 2
ed., New York, 1974, pp. 208-211; Benz, E., *Russische Heiligenlegenden.* Zürich,
1953, S. 493-496 (translations into English and German).

THE WRITINGS OF SERAPION OF VLADIMIR

   Translations: Zenkovsky, S. A., *Medieval Russia's Epics, Chronicles and Tales.* 2
ed., New York, 1974, pp. 243-248.
   Studies: Bogert, R., "On the Rhetorical Style of Serapion Vladimirskij". In:
Medieval Russian Culture. Berkeley-Los Angeles-London, 1984, pp. 280-310; Gorlin,
M., "Sérapion de Vladimir, prédicateur de Kiev". *Revue des études slaves*, t. 24,
1948, p. 21-28.

HAGIOGRAPHY

a) **The Life of Alexander Nevsky**
   Translations: Zenkovsky, S. A., *Medieval Russia's Epics, Chronicles and Tales.* 2

ed., New York, 1974, pp. 225-236; *O Bojan, Du Nachtigall der alten Zeit.* Berlin, 1965, S. 116-125; *Literatura staroruska.* Warszawa, 1971, s. 96-98 [translations into English, German, and Polish (extracts)].
    Studies: Lammich, M., *Fürstenbiographien des 13. Jahrhunderts in den russischen Chroniken.* Köln, 1973; Philipp, W., "Heiligkeit und Herrschaft in der *Vita Alexander Nevskijs*". *Forschungen zur Osteuropäischen Geschichte.* Bd. 18, 1973, S. 55-72.
  b) **The Life of St. Michael of Chernigov**
    Studies: Dimnik, M., *Mikhail, Prince of Chernigov and Grand Prince of Kiev. 1224-1246.* Toronto, 1981.
  c) **Lives of zealots of the church**
    Translations: Benz, E., *Russische Heiligenlegenden.* Zürich, 1953, S. 267-283 (German translation from *The Life of St Barlaam of Khutyn*).
    Texts: *Die altrussischen hagiographischen Erzählungen und liturgischen Dichtungen über den Heiligen Avraamij von Smolensk.* München, 1970 (*Slavische Propyläen,* Bd. 15).

CHAPTER 3

GENERAL WORKS

Fennell, J. L. I., *The Emergence of Moscow 1304-1359.* Berkeley-Los Angeles, 1968; Picchio, R., *Storia della letteratura russa antica.* Milano, 1959, parte 2, p. 131-136.

CHRONICLE-WRITING

    Translations: *A Source Book for Russian History from Early Times to 1917,* Vol. 1, New Haven-London, 1972, pp. 52-53 (English translation of extracts from *The Tale of Shevkal*).
    Studies: Grabmüller, H.-J., *Die Pskover Chroniken,* Wiesbaden, 1975.

HAGIOGRAPHY

    Translations: Zenkovsky, S. A., *Medieval Russia's Epics, Chronicles and Tales,* 2 ed., New York, 1974, pp. 237-242 (English translation of *The Tale of Dovmont*); Onasch, K., *Altrussische Heiligenleben.* Berlin, 1977, S. 179-191 (German translation of extracts from *The Life of Metropolitan Peter*).

EPISTLES

    Translations: Onasch, K., *Altrussische Heiligenleben.* Berlin, 1977, S. 163-168 (German translation of extracts from Archbishop Basil of Novgorod's *Epistle* on paradise).

CHAPTER 4

GENERAL WORKS

Čiževskij, D., *History of Russian Literature.* 'S-Gravenhage, 1960, Chapter 5, p. 145-229; Fennell, J., Stokes, A., *Early Russian Literature.* Berkeley-Los Angeles, 1974, Chapter 2, pp. 80-138; *Literatura rosyjska. Podręcznik,* t. I. Warszawa, 1970, cz. 1, rozdział 3, s. 84-88; Ljackij, E., *Historický přehled ruské literatury,* č. 1. Praha, 1937, kapitola XVIII, s. 153-163; Picchio, R., *Storia della letteratura russa antica.* Milano, 1959, parte 2, p. 137-170; Raab, H., *Geschichte der altrussischen Literatur.* Potsdam, 1957, S. 56-58.

HAGIOGRAPHY AND PANEGYRICAL WORKS

Translations: Ignatiew, C., *Žitie Petra des Metropoliten Kiprian.* Wiesbaden, 1976 (German translation of *The Life of Metropolitan Peter*); *A Treasury of Russian Spirituality.* Compiled and edited by G. P. Fedotov. London, 1952, pp. 54-83; Benz, E., *Russische Heiligenlegenden.* Zürich, 1953, S. 295-362 (English and German translations of *The Life of St Sergius of Radonezh*); Zenkovsky, S. A., *Medieval Russia's Epics, Chronicles and Tales,* 2 ed., New York, 1974, p. 260-262 (English translation of an extract from *The Life of St Stephen of Perm*); Onasch, K., *Altrussische Heiligenleben.* Berlin, 1977, S. 239-264 (German translation of extracts from *The Life of St Cyril of the White Lake*); Zenkovsky, S. A., Op. cit., p. 316-322; *O Bojan, Du Nachtigall der alten Zeit.* Berlin, 1965, S. 126-139 (translations of *The Eulogy of the Life and Death of Grand Prince Dmitry, Son of Ivan, and Tsar of Russia* into English (extracts) and German).

Texts *Die Legenden des Heiligen Sergij von Radonež.* München, 1967 (*Slavische Propyläen,* Bd. 17); *Pachomij Logofet. Werke in Auswahl.* München, 1963 (*Slavische Propyläen,* Bd. 1).

Studies: Appel, O., *Die Vita des hl. Sergij von Radonež. Untersuchungen zur Textgeschichte.* München, 1972; Дончева-Понайотова, Н., *Киприан. Старобългарски и старорускu книжовник.* София, 1981; Kitch, F. M., *The Literary Style of Epifanij Premudryj.* München, 1976; Obolensky, D., "A Philorhomaios Anthropos. Metropolitan Cyprian of Kiev and All Russia (1375-1406)". *Dumbarton Oaks Papers,* Vol. 32, 1978, pp. 79-98; Орлов, Г., "Пахомије Србин и његова књижевна делатност у Великом Новгороду", *Прилози за књижевност, језик, историју и фолклор,* кн. 36, 1970, с. 214-239; Vodoff, W., "Quand a pu être composé le Panegyrique du Grand-prince Dmitrii Ivanovich, tsar' russe?" *Canadian-American Slavic Studies,* Vol. 13, 1979, pp. 82-101; Wigzell, F. C. M., "Convention and Originality in the *Life of Stefan of Perm.* A Stylistic Analysis". *The Slavonic and East European Review,* Vol. 49, 1971, pp. 339-354.

HISTORICAL LEGENDS

Translations: Zenkovsky, S. A., *Medieval Russia's Epics, Chronicles and Tales,* 2 ed., New York, 1974, pp. 311-314; Benz, E., *Russische Heiligenlegenden.* Zürich, 1953, S. 459-469 (English and German translation of tales about John of Novgorod).

Studies: Frolow, A., "Le *Znamenié* de Novgorod. Évolution de la légende". *Revue des études slaves,* t. 24, 1948, p. 67-81.

MONUMENTS OF THE KULIKOVO CYCLE

Translations: Jakobson, R., Worth, D.S., *Sofonija's Tale of the Russian-Tatar Battle on the Kulikovo Field.* The Hague, 1963; Sturm, G., "Übersetzung der *Zadonščina*". *Zeitschrift für Slawistik,* Bd. III, 1958, S. 700-710; Vaillant, A., *La Zadonščina.* Paris, 1967; *Literatura staroruska.* Warszawa, 1971, s. 105-109; Frček, J., *Zádonština.* Praha, 1948 [translations of *The Trans-Doniad* into English, German, French, Polish (extracts) and Czech]; *A Source Book for Russian History from Early Times to 1917,* Vol. 1, New Haven-London, 1972, pp. 55-56 (English translation of extracts from the chronicle tale of the Battle of Kulikovo).

Studies: Čiževska, T., "A comparative Lexicon of the *Igor' Tale* and the *Zadonščina*". In: *American Contributions to the Fifth International Congress of Slavists,* Vol. I. The Hague, 1963, pp. 49-57; Danti, A., "Criteri e metodi nella edizione della *Zadonščina*". *Annali della Facoltà di lettere e filosofia della Università degli studi di Perugia,* Vol. VI, 1968-1969, p. 187-220; Gaumnitz, H., "Wörterverzeichnis zur *Zadonščina*". *Russia Mediaevalis,* Bd. I, 1973, S. 64-107; Hill, E., *A British Museum Illuminated Manuscript of an Early Russian Literary Work "An Encomium to the Grand*

Prince Dimitri Ivanovich and to his Brother Prince Vladimir Andreyevich". Cambridge, 1958; Kralik, O., *Archetyp "Zádonštiny"*. Olomouc, 1972; Matejka, L., "Comparative Analysis of Syntactic Constructions in the *Zadonščina"*. In: *American Contributions to the Fifth International Congress of Slavists*, Vol. I. The Hague, 1963, pp. 383-403; Vaillant, A., "Les récits de Kulikovo: *Relation des chroniques et Skazanie de Mamaï"*. *Revue des études slaves*, t. 39, 1961, p. 59-89; Worth, D.S., "Lexico-Grammatical Parallelism as a Stylistic Feature of the *Zadonščina"*. In: Worth, D.S., *On the Structure and History of Russian*. München, 1977, pp. 221-235.

TALES OF MONGOL RAIDS ON RUSSIA AFTER THE BATTLE OF KULIKOVO

Translations: *A Source Book for Russian History from Early Times to 1917*, Vol. 1. New Haven-London, 1972, pp. 56-57 (English translation of extracts from *The Tale of Tokhtamysh's Campaign Against Moscow*).

CHAPTER 5

GENERAL WORKS

Čiževskij, D., *History of Russian Literature*. 'S-Gravenhage, 1960, Chapter 5, pp. 145-229; Fennell, J.L.I., *Ivan the Great of Moscow*. London, 1961; Freydank, D., "Der *Laodicenerbrief (Laodikiiskoe poslanie)"*. Ein Beitrag zur Interpretation eines altrussischen Textes. *Zeitschrift für Slawistik*, Bd. XI, 1966, S. 355-370; Haney, J.V., "*The Laodicean Epistle*. Some Possible Sources". *Slavic Review*, Vol. 30, 1971, pp. 832-842; Lilienfeld, F., "Die *Häresie* des Fedor Kuricyn". *Forschungen zur Osteuropäischen Geschichte*, Bd. 24, 1978, S. 39-64; *Literatura rosyjska. Podręcznik*, t. I. Warszawa, 1970, cz. 1, rozdział 3, s. 88-101; Ljackij, E., *Historický přehled ruské literatury*, č. 1, Praha, 1937, kapitola XIX, XX, XXII, s. 164-180, 191-199; Picchio, R., *Storia della letteratura russa antica*. Milano, 1959, parte 2, p. 170-229; Stökl, G., "Das Echo von Renaissance und Reformation im Moskauer Russland" *Jahrbücher für Geschichte Osteuropas*, Bd. VII, 1959, S. 413-430.

HISTORICAL NARRATIVE

Translations: *A Source Book for Russian History from Early Times to 1917*, Vol. 1. New Haven-London, 1972, pp. 78-80 (English translation of extracts from chronicle tales of the victory over Novgorod); *Bericht über die Eroberung Konstantinopels*. Übersetzt von M. Braun, A. M. Schneider. Leipzig, 1943 (German translation of Nestor-Iskander's *Tale of Tsargrad*).
Studies: Dujčev, I., "La conquête turque et la prise de Constantinople dans la littérature slave contemporaine". *Byzantinoslavica*, t. 14, 1953, p. 14-54; t. 16, 1955, p. 318-329; t. 17, 1956, p. 276-340; Unbegaun, B., "Les relations vieux-russes de la prise de Constantinople". *Revue des études slaves*, t. 9, 1929, p. 13-38.

HAGIOGRAPHY

Translations: Zenkovsky, S.A., *Medieval Russia's Epics, Chronicles and Tales*, 2 ed., New York, 1974, pp. 301-310 (English translation of *The Life of St Michael of Klopsk*); *Die Erzählung über Petr Ordynskij*. Berlin, 1979 (German translation of *The Tale of Peter of the Horde*).

TALES

Texts: *Život Aleksandra Velikoga*. Izdao V. Jagič. Zagreb, 1871; *Приповетка о Александру Великом у старој српској књижевности*. Критички текст и расправа од

С. Новаковића. У Београду, 1878; Berk, Ch.A., van den, *Der "serbische" Alexanderroman*, 1. Halbbd. München, 1970 (*Slavische Propyläen*, Bd. 13, 1). **Studies:** Giraudo, G., *Drakula.* Venezia, 1972; Маринковић, Р., *Српска Александрија.* Београд, 1969; Mazon, A., 1) "Le nom du chamir dans la légende vieux-russe de Salomon et Kitovras". In: *Mélanges, publiés en l'honneur de P. Boyer.* Paris, 1925, p. 107-114; 2) "Le centaure de la légende vieux-russe de Salomon et Kitovras". *Revue des études slaves,* t. 7, 1927, p. 42-62; Striedter, I., "Die Erzählung vom walachischen Vojevoden Dracula in der russischen und deutschen Überlieferung". *Zeitschrift für slawische Philologie,* Bd. 29, 1961, S. 398-427.

VOYAGE BEYOND THREE SEAS
BY AFANASY NIKITIN

Translations: Maior, R.H., *India in the Fifteenth Century Being a Collection of Narratives of Voyages to India.* London, 1857; Meyer, K. H., *Die Fahrt des Athanasius Nikitin über die drei Meere.* Leipzig, 1920; Atanazy Nikitin. *Wędrówka za trzy morza.* Przełożyła H. Willman-Grabowska. Wrocław, 1952; *Putování ruského kupce Afanasije Nikitine přes tři moře.* Připravil V. Lesný. Praha, 1951 (English, German, Polish and Czech translations).
Studies: Lenhoff, G., "Beyond Three Seas. Afanasij Nikitin's Journey from Orthodoxy to Apostasy". *East European Quarterly,* Vol. XIII, 1979, pp. 431-447.

CHAPTER 6

GENERAL WORKS

Andreyev, N., *Studies in Muscovy.* London, 1970; Čiževskij, D., *History of Russian Literature.* 'S-Gravenhage, 1960, Chapter 6, pp. 230-310; *The Council of 1503. Source Studies and Question of Ecclesiastical Landowning in Sixteenth-Century Muscovy.* Cambridge, Mass., 1977; Donnert, E., *Russland an der Schwelle der Neuzeit,* Berlin, 1972; Fennell, J., Stokes, A., *Early Russian Literature.* Berkeley-Los Angeles, 1974, Chapter 3, pp. 139-190; Grobovsky, A.N., *The "Chosen Council" of Ivan IV. A Reinterpretation.* New York, 1969; *Literatura rosyjska. Podręcznik,* t. I, Warszawa, 1970, cz. I, rozdział 4, s. 102-122; Ljackij, E., *Historický přehled ruské literatury,* č. 1, Praha, 1937, kapitola XXI, XXIII-XXX, s. 181-190, 200-269; Nørretranders, B., *The Shaping of Czardom under Ivan Groznyj.* Copenhagen, 1964; Picchio, R., *Storia della letteratura russa antica.* Milano, 1959, parte 3, p. 233-283; Raab, H., *Geschichte der altrussischen Literatur.* Potsdam, 1957, S. 59-63.

MAIN IDEOLOGICAL AND CULTURAL
PHENOMENA OF THE 16TH CENTURY.

Translations: Haney, J.A.V., "Moscow—Second Constantinople, Third Rome or Second Kiev?" *Canadian Slavic Studies,* Vol. 3, 1968, pp. 354-367; *O Bojan, Du Nachtigall der alten Zeit.* Berlin, 1965, S. 230-236 (English and German translations of *The Legend of the Princes of Vladimir*); Zenkovsky, S.A., *Medieval Russia's Epics, Chronicles and Tales,* 2 ed., New York, 1974, pp. 324-332; *O Bojan...,* S. 238-260 [translations of *The Tale of the White Klobuk* into English (extract) and German]; Duchesne, E., *Le Stoglav ou les cent chapitres.* Paris, 1920 (French translation of the *Hundred Chapters*); *A Source Book for Russian History from Early Times to 1917,* Vol. 1, New Haven-London, 1972, pp. 164-165; *O Bojan...,* S. 396-408; *Altrussische Dichtung aus dem 11.-18. Jahrhundert.* Leipzig, 1971, S. 127-138; Duchesne, E., *Le Domostroi, Ménagier russe du XVIᵉ siècle.* Paris, 1910; *Literatura staroruska.* Warszawa, 1971, s. 123-125 [translations of the *Household Management* into English (extracts), German (extracts), French and Polish (extract)].

Studies: Florovskij, A.V., "Die Anfänge des Buchdruckes bei den Ostslaven". *Slavische Rundschau,* 1940, Heft 1-2, S. 66-90; Jagoditsch, R., "Zu den Quellen des altrussischen *Domostroj*". In: *Österreichische Beiträge zum V. Internationalen Slavistenkongress.* Sofia, September 1963. Graz-Köln, 1963, S. 40-48, Kämpfer, F., "Beobachtungen zu den Sendschreiben Filofejs". *Jahrbücher für Geschichte Osteuropas,* Bd. XVIII, 1970, S. 1-46; Niess, H. P., "Der *Domostroj* oder *Wie man als rechtgläubiger Christ leben soll*". *Kirche im Osten,* Bd. 14, 1971, S. 26-67; Ostrogorskij, G., "Les décisions du *Stoglav,* concernant la peinture d'images et les principes de l'iconographie byzantine". In: *L'Art byzantin chez les Slaves,* t. I, Paris, 1930, p. 393-411; Stremooukhoff, D., "La tiare de saint Sylvestre et le Klobuk blanc". *Revue des études slaves,* t. 34, 1957, p. 123-128.

THE TALE OF PETER AND FEBRONIA

Translations: Zenkovsky, S.A., *Medieval Russia's Epics, Chronicles and Tales,* 2 ed., New York, 1974, pp. 291-300; *O Bojan, Du Nachtigall der alten Zeit.* Berlin, 1965, S. 140-153; *Literatura staroruska.* Warszawa, 1971, s. 116-119 [translations into English. German and Polish (extracts)].
Studies: Conrad, B., "Die Erzählung von Petr und Fevronija". In: *Gattungsprobleme* der älterer slavischen Literaturen. Berlin, 1984, S. 35-60; Haney, J.V., "On the *Tale of Peter and Fevroniia,* Wonderworkers of Murom". *Canadian-American Slavic Studies,* Vol. 13, 1979, pp. 139-162.

HISTORICAL NARRATIVE

a) **Chronicle-writing**
Translations: *A Source Book for Russian History from Early Times to 1917,* Vol. 1, New Haven-London, 1972, pp. 84-85, 132-134, 141-145 (English translations of extracts from the chronicle stories of the capture of Pskov and the events of 1539-1565).
b) **History of Kazan**
Translations: *Historie vom Zartum Kasan (Kasaner Chronist).* Übersetzt von F. Kämpfer. Graz-Wien-Köln, 1969.
Studies: Kämpfer, F., "Die Eroberung von Kasan 1552 als Gegenstand der zeitgenössischen russischen Historiographie". *Forschungen zur Osteuropäischen Geschichte,* Bd. 14, 1969, S. 7-161; Pelenski, J., *Russia and Kazan. Conquest and Imperial Ideology (1438-1560s).* The Hague-Paris, 1974.

TALES

Translations: Zenkovsky, S.A., *Medieval Russia's Epics, Chronicles and Tales,* 2 ed., New York, 1974, pp. 355-365 (English translation of extracts from *The Tale of the Campaign of Stephen Bathory Against Pskov*).
Studies: Lewandowski, Th., *Das mittelniederdeutsche Zwiegespräch zwischen dem Leben und dem Tode und seine altrussische Übersetzung.* Köln, 1972; Stricker, G., *Stilistische und verbalsyntaktische Untersuchungen zum Moskovitischen Prunkstil des 16. Jahrhunderts.* München, 1979.

POLEMICAL WRITINGS

a) **Joseph of Volokolamsk**
Studies: Špidlik, T., *Joseph de Volokolamsk.* Roma, 1956; Szeftel, M., "Joseph Volotsky's Political Ideas in a New Historical Perspective". *Jahrbücher für Geschichte Osteuropas,* Bd. XIII, 1965, S. 19-29.

b) **Vassian Patrikeyev**
　　Studies: Dewey, H., Matejic, M., "The Literary Arsenal of Vassian Patrikeew".
The Slavonic and East European Journal, Vol. 10, 1966, pp. 440-452.
c) **Maxim the Greek**
　　Translations: Denissoff, E., *Maxime le Grec et l'Occident.* Paris-Louvain, 1943;
Langeler, A. J., *Maksim Grek, byzantijn en humanist in Rusland.* Amsterdam, 1986
(French and Dutch translations of extracts).
　　Studies: Baracchi, M., "La lingua di Maksim Grek". *Istituto Lombardo.*
Rendiconti. Classe di lettere e sciênze morale e storiche, Vol. 105, 1971, p. 253-280;
Vol. 106, 1972, p. 243-267; Haney, J. V., *From Italy to Muscovy. The Life and Works*
of Maksim the Greek. München, 1973; Schultze, B., *Maksim Grek als Theologe.* Roma,
1963.
d) **Ivan Peresvetov**
　　Translations: *Scritti politici di Ivan Semënovic Peresvetov.* A cura di G. M. Basile.
Milano, 1976.
　　Studies: Danti, A., "Ivan Peresvetov. Osservazioni e proposte". *Ricerche*
Slavistiche, t. 12, 1964, p. 3-64; Philipp, W., *Ivan Peresvetov und seine Schriften zur*
Erneuerung des Moskauer Reiches. Königsberg-Berlin, 1935.
e) **Ivan the Terrible and Prince A. M. Kurbsky**
　　Translations: *The Correspondence Between Prince A. M. Kurbsky and Tsar*
Ivan IV of Russia. Ed. by J. L. I. Fennell. Cambridge, 1955; Stählin, K., *Der*
Briefwechsel Iwans des Schrecklichen mit dem Fürsten Kurbskij. Leipzig. 1921; *Ivan le*
Terrible. Épîtres avec le prince Kourbski. Traduction de D. Olivier. Paris, 1959; *Lettere*
e testamento di Ivan il Terribile. Traduzione di M. Olsùfieva. Firenze, 1958 (2 ed.,
Milano, 1972); *Ivan den Skraekkelige. Brevveksling med Fyrst Kurbskij 1564-1579.*
Oversat af B. N. Nørretranders. Munksgaard, 1959; *Literatura staroruska.* Warszawa,
1971, s. 129-131; *Listy Ivana Hrozného.* Přeložil K. J. Erben. Praha, 1957 [transla-
tions of the epistles of Ivan the Terrible to A. M. Kurbsky into English, German,
French, Italian, Danish, Polish (extracts) and Czech]; *Prince A. M. Kurbsky's History*
of Ivan IV. Ed. by J. L. I. Fennell. Cambridge, 1965; *Prince André Kurbski. Histoire*
du règne de Jean IV (Ivan le Terrible). Traduction de M. Forstetter. Genève, 1965
(English and French translations of Kurbsky's *History*).
　　Texts: *Der Briefwechsel zwischen Andrej Kurbskij und Ivan dem Schrecklichen.*
Herausgeg. von H. Neubauer, J. Schütz. Wiesbaden, 1961; Tumins, V. A., *Tsar*
Ivan IV's Reply to Jan Rokyta. The Hague-Paris, 1971; *Kurbskijs "Novyj Margarit".*
Untersucht und in Auswahl ediert von F. Liewehr. Prag, 1928; *Andrej Michajlovič*
Kurbskij. "Novyj Margarit". Herausgeg. von I. Auerbach, Lfg. 1-4. Giessen,
1976-1978.
　　Studies: Auerbach, I., 1) "Die politischen Vorstellungen des Fürsten Andrej
Kurbskij". *Jahrbücher für Geschichte Osteuropas,* Bd. XVII, 1969, S. 170-186; 2) *Andrej*
Michajlovič Kurbskij: Leben in osteuropäischen Adelgesellschaften des XVI. Jahrhunderts.
München, 1985; Freydank, D., 1) "A. M. Kurbskij und die Theorie der antiken
Historiographie". In: *Orbis mediaevalis.* Festgabe für A. Blaschka zum 75.
Geburtstag. Weimar, 1970, S. 57-77; 2) "A. M. Kurbskij und die Epistolographie
seiner Zeit". *Zeitschrift für Slawistik,* Bd. XXI, 1976, S. 319-333; Rossing, N., Rønne,
B., *Apocryphal—Not Apocryphal? A Critical Analysis of the Discussion Concerning the*
Correspondence Between Tsar Ivan IV Groznyj and Prince Andrej Kurbskij.
Copenhagen, 1980.

CHAPTER 7

GENERAL WORKS

　　Čiževskij, D., *History of Russian Literature.* 'S-Gravenhage, 1960, Chapter 6,
pp. 310-319; Fennell, J., Stokes, A., *Early Russian Literature.* Berkeley-Los Angeles,

1974, Chapter 5, pp. 207-268; *Literatura rosyjska. Podręcznik*, t. I, Warszawa, 1970, cz. 1, rozdział 4, s. 122-127; Ljackij, E., *Historický přehled ruské literatury*, č. 1, Praha, 1937, kapitola XXXI, s. 270-279; Picchio, R., *Storia della letteratura russa antica*. Milano, 1959, parte 3, p. 285-309; Raab, H., *Geschichte der altrussischen Literatur*. Potsdam, 1957, S. 64-71.

POLEMICAL WRITINGS OF THE TIME OF TROUBLES AND HISTORICAL WORKS ON THE PERIOD

Translations: *A Source Book for Russian History from Early Times to 1917*, Vol. 1, New Haven-London, 1972, pp. 189-192; Zenkovsky, S. A., *Medieval Russia's Epics, Chronicles and Tales*, 2 ed., New York, 1974, pp. 380-386 (English translation of extracts from the *Tale* of Abraham Palitsyn); *A Source Book...*, Vol. 1, pp. 145-146, 188 (English translation of extracts from Ivan Timofeyev's *Annals*); Zenkovsky, S. A., Op. cit., pp. 388-390; *O Bojan, Du Nachtigall der alten Zeit*. Berlin, 1965, S. 273-319 [translations of *The Tale of the Book of Former Years* into English (extracts) and German].
Studies: Keipert, H., *Beiträge zur Textgeschichte und Nominalmorphologie des "Vremennik Ivana Timofeeva"*. Bonn, 1968; Rehder, P., "Zum *Vremennik* des D'jaken Ivan Timofeev". *Die Welt der Slaven*, Bd. X, 1965, S. 123-143; Sbriziolo, I. P., *Struttura, lingua e stile dei viděnija del seicento russo*. Roma, 1981.

HAGIOGRAPHICAL-BIOGRAPHICAL TALES

Translations: Zenkovsky, S. A., *Medieval Russia's Epics, Chronicles and Tales*, 2 ed., New York, 1974, pp. 391-399; Benz, E., *Russische Heiligenlegenden*. Zürich, 1953, S. 435-440 (English and German translations of *The Tale of Juliana Osorgina*).

VERSIFICATION

Translations: Zenkovsky, S. A., *Medieval Russia's Epics, Chronicles and Tales*. 2 ed. New York, 1974, pp. 487-489, 512-514 (English translations of extracts from *The Epistle of One Nobleman to Another* and Ivan Khvorostinin's *Discourse Against Heretics and Vilifiers*).
Texts: *Die älteste ostslawische Kunstdichtung. 1575-1647*. Herausgeg. von H. Rothe, 1-2. Halbbd. Giessen, 1976-1977.

NEW LITERARY AREAS
a) **Siberian chronicle-writing**
Translations: *Yermak's Campaign in Siberia. A Selection of Documents.* Translated by T. Minorsky, D. Wileman. London, 1975, p. 62-86 (English translation of the *Esipov Chronicle*).
b) **Tales of Azov**
Translations: *O Bojan, Du Nachtigall der alten Zeit*. Berlin, 1965, S. 321-346 (German translation of the "poetic" tale of Azov).

CHAPTER 8

GENERAL WORKS

Čiževskij, D., *History of Russian Literature*. 'S-Gravenhage, 1960, Chapter 7, pp. 320-382. *Literatura rosyjska. Podręcznik*, t. I, Warszawa, 1970, cz. 1, rozdział 5, s. 128-170; Ljackij, E., *Historický přehled ruské literatury*, č. 1, Praha, 1937, kapitola XXXVIII-XLI, s. 348-379; Picchio, R., *Storia della letteratura russa antica*. Milano, 1959, parte 3, p. 311-355.

TRANSLATED TALES OF CHIVALRY AND ADVENTURE

Translations: Zenkovsky, S. A., *Medieval Russia's Epics, Chronicles and Tales*, 2 ed., New York, 1974, pp. 506-510 (English translation of *The Tale of Sukhan*); *O Vasiliji Zlatovlasém, kralevici České země.* Přeložila S. Mathauserová. Praha, 1982 (Czech translation of *The Tale of Vasily the Golden-Haired*).
Texts: Polívka, J., *Kronika o Bruncvíkovi v ruské literatuře.* V Praze, 1892.
Studies: Baumann, W., *Der Sage von Heinrich dem Löwen bei den Slaven.* München, 1975; Mayer, G., "*Bova-Studien*". *Die Welt der Slaven*, Bd. VIII, 1963, S. 275-298, 348-375.

THE TALE OF SAVVA GRUDTSYN

Translations: Zenkovsky, S. A., *Medieval Russia's Epics, Chronicles and Tales*, 2 ed., New York, 1974, pp. 453-474; *Die Geschichte vom reichen und angesehenen Kaufmann Karp Sutulow und seiner überaus klugen Frau, die ihr eheliches Lager nicht entehrte.* Herausgeg. von H. Grasshoff. Leipzig, 1977, S. 38-63 (English and German translations).

THE TALE OF WOE-MISFORTUNE

Translations: Zenkovsky, S. A., *Medieval Russia's Epics, Chronicles and Tales*, 2 ed., New York, 1974, pp. 490-501; *Altrussische Dichtung aus dem 11.-18. Jahrhundert.* Leipzig, 1971, S. 154-167 (English and German translations).
Studies: Harkins, W. E., 1) "Russian Folk Ballads and the *Tale of Misery and Ill Fortune*". *American Slavic and East European Review*, Vol. 13, 1954, p. 402-413; 2) "The Mystic Element in the *Tale of Gore-Zločastie*". In: *For R. Jakobson. Essays on the Occasion of his Sixtieth Birthday.* The Hague, 1956, pp. 201-206; 3) "The Symbol of the River in the *Tale of Gore-Zločastie.* In: *Studies in Slavic Linguistics and Poetics in Honor of B. O. Unbegaun.* New York-London, 1968, pp. 55-62; Mazon, A., "*Malheur-Mauvais Destin*". *Revue des études slaves*, t. 28, 1951, p. 17-42.

THE TRANSLATED AND ORIGINAL *NOVELLA*

Translations: Zenkovsky, S. A., *Medieval Russia's Epics, Chronicles and Tales*, 2 ed., New York, 1974, pp. 449-452, 475-486; *Die Geschichte vom reichen und angesehenen Kaufmann Karp Sutulow und seiner überaus klugen Frau, die ihr eheliches Lager nicht entehrte.* Herausgeg. von H. Grasshoff. Leipzig, 1977 (English translations of *The Tale of Shemyaka's Trial* and *The Tale of Frol Skobeyev*, and German translations of *The Tale of the Drunkard, The Tale of the Peasant's Son, The Tale of Shemyaka's Trial, The Tale of Karp Sutulov* and *The Tale of Frol Skobeyev*).
Studies: Murko, M., *Die Geschichte von den sieben Weisen bei den Slaven*, Wien, 1890.

HISTORICAL FICTION. TALES OF THE FOUNDING OF MOSCOW

Studies: Dewey, H. W., "Tales of Moscow's Founding". *Canadian-American Slavic Studies*, Vol. 6, 1972, pp. 595-605.

DEMOCRATIC SATIRE

Translations: *Die Geschichte vom reichen und angesehenen Kaufmann Karp Sutulow und seiner überaus klugen Frau, die ihr eheliches Lager nicht entehrte.* Herausgeg. von H. Grasshoff, Leipzig, 1977 (German translation of satirical texts). **Texts:** Lunden, S. S., "Список XVII века азбуки о голом и небогатом человеке". *Scando-Slavica,* t. 9, 1963, p. 169-185.

THE WRITINGS OF ARCHPRIEST AVVAKUM

Translations: *The Life of the Archpriest Avvakum written by himself.* Translated by J. Harrison, H. Mirrlees. London, 1924 (2 ed., London, 1963); *Das Leben des Protopopen Avvakum.* Übersetzt von G. Hildebrandt. Göttingen, 1965; *La vie de l'archiprêtre Avvakum, écrite par lui-même.* Traduite par P. Pascal. Paris, 1938 (2 éd., Paris, 1960); *Vita dell' arcipretre Avvakum.* Traduzione di L. Radoyce. Torino, 1962; *Żywot protopopa Awwakuma przez niego samego nakreślony i wybór innych pism.* Przełożył W. Jakubowski. Wrocław, 1972; *Život protopopa Avvakuma.* Přeložil B. Ilek. Praha, 1975; *Život protopopa Avvakuma.* Přeložil J. Komorovský. Bratislava, 1976; *Avvakum protopópa önéletírása, Jepifanyij szerzetes önéletírása.* Fordította és a jegyzeteket írta Juhász József. Budapest, 1971 (translations of the *Life* of Avvakum into English, German, French, Italian, Polish, Czech, Slovakian, and Hungarian). **Studies:** Hauptmann, P., *Altrussischer Glaube. Der Kampf des Protopopen Avvakum gegen die Kirchenreformen des 17. Jahrhunderts.* Göttingen, 1963; Ilek, B., *Život protopopa Avvakuma. Studie o stylu.* Praha, 1967; Pascal, P., *Avvakum et les debuts du raskol.* Paris, 1938 (2 éd., Paris-La Hage, 1963); Zenkovsky, S. A., "The Old Believer Avvakum, His Role in Russian Literature". *Indiana Slavic Studies,* Vol. 1, 1956, pp. 1-51.

BAROQUE IN 17TH-CENTURY RUSSIAN LITERATURE

Texts: Nilsson, N. Å., *Russian Heraldic Virši from the 17th Century.* Stockholm, 1964. **Studies:** Dębski, J., 1) "Z obserwacji nad spuścizną poetycką Kariona Istomina". *Zeszyty naukowe Uniwersytetu Jagiellońskiego. Prace historycznoliterackie,* zesz. 37, 1979, s. 35-48; 2) "Antyk na warsztacie poetyckim rosyjskich sylabistów". Ibid., zesz. 43, 1982, s. 177-193; Łużny, R., *Pisarze kręgu Akademii Kijowsko-Mohylańskiej a literatura polska.* Kraków, 1966; Suchanek, L., 1) "Thanatos i eschatologia. Z obserwacji nad poezją baroku rosyjskiego". *Rocznik Komisji historycznoliterackiej,* t. 12, 1974, s. 3-21; 2) "Poezja żałobna baroku rosyjskiego". *Zeszyty naukowe Uniwersytetu Jagiellońskiego. Prace historycznoliterackie,* zesz. 33, 1975, s. 33-45; 3) "Rosyjski poemat eschatologiczny epoki baroku". *Slavia Orientalis,* rocz. 24, 1975, s. 39-44.

SIMEON OF POLOTSK

Translations: Zenkovsky, S. A., *Medieval Russia's Epics, Chronicles and Tales,* 2 ed., New York, 1974, pp. 518-519; *Altrussische Dichtung aus dem 11.-18. Jahrhundert.* Leipzig, 1971, S. 201-205 (English and German translations of selected verse). **Studies:** Hippisley, A., 1) "Cryptography in Simeon Polockij's Poetry". *Russian Literature,* Vol. 15, 1977, pp. 389-402; 2) *The Poetic Style of Simeon Polotsky.* Birmingham, 1985; Łużny, R., *Psałterz Rymowany Symeona Połockiego a Psałterz Dawidów Jana Kochanowskiego". *Slavia Orientalis,* rocz. 15, 1966, s. 3-27.

THE EMERGENCE OF THE RUSSIAN THEATRE

Translations: Günther, K., *"Das Moskauer Judithdrama von Johann Gottfried Gregorii"*. In: *Studien zur Geschichte der russischen Literatur des 18. Jahrhunderts,* Bd. IV, Berlin, 1970, S. 41-207 (German translation of the play *Judith*). **Texts:** *La Comédie d'Artaxerxès.* Textes publiés par A. Mazon et F. Cocron. Paris, 1954; Günther, K., "Das Weimarer Bruchstück des ersten russischen Dramas *Artaxerxovo Dejstvo* (1672)". In: *Studien zur Geschichte der russischen Literatur des 18. Jahrhunderts,* Bd. III, Berlin, 1968, S. 120-178. **Studies:** Günther, K., "Neue deutsche Quellen zum ersten russischen Theater". *Zeitschrift für Slawistik,* Bd. VIII, 1963, S. 664-675; Unbegaun, B. O., "Les débuts de la versification russe et *La Comédie d'Artaxerxès"*. *Revue des études slaves,* t. 32, 1955, p. 32-41.

INDEX

A

B

C

R REQUEST TO READERS

aduga Publishers would be glad to have your opinion of this book, its translation and design and any suggestions you may have for future publications.

Please send all your comments to 17, Zubovsky Boulevard, Moscow, USSR.

ИБ № 1440

Редактор русского текста Ю. Козловский
Контрольный редактор А. Буяновская
Художник Э. Зарянский
Художественный редактор С. Барабаш
Технический редактор А. Агафошина